Midwest Studies in Philosophy
Volume IV

MIDWEST STUDIES IN PHILOSOPHY

EDITED BY PETER A. FRENCH, THEODORE E. UEHLING, JR., HOWARD K. WETTSTEIN

Virtually all papers in MIDWEST STUDIES IN PHOLOSOPHY are invited and previously unpublished. The editors will, however, consider unsolicited manuscripts that are received by January of the year preceding the appearance of a volume. All manuscripts must be pertinent to the topic area of the volume for which they are submitted. Address manuscripts to The Editors, MIDWEST STUDIES IN PHILOSOPHY, University of Minnesota, Morris; Morris, MN 56267.

The articles in MIDWEST STUDIES IN PHILOSOPHY are indexed in THE PHILOSOPHER'S INDEX.

Forthcoming Volumes:

Volume V   February 1980 Studies in Epistemology
Volume VI February 1981 Studies in the Foundations of Analytic Philosophy

Previously Published Volumes:

Volume I   February 1976 Studies in the History of Philosophy
Volume II   February 1977 Studies in the Philosophy of Language
Volume III February 1978 Studies in Ethical Theory

Midwest Studies
in
Philosophy
Volume
IV
Studies in Metaphysics

Editors

PETER A. FRENCH
THEODORE E. UEHLING, JR.
HOWARD K. WETTSTEIN

University of Minnesota Press ● Minneapolis

Published by the University of Minnesota Press,
2037 University Avenue Southeast,
Minneapolis, Minnestoa 55455
Printed in the United States of America

Library of Congress Cataloging in Publication Data

Main entry under title:

Studies in Metaphysics.

      (Midwest studies in philosophy; v. 4)
       1. Metaphysics—Addresses, essays, lectures.
I. French, Peter A.   II. Uehling, Theodore Edward.
III. Wettstein, Howard K.   IV. Series.
BD111.S79   110   79-10221
ISBN 0-8166-0887-3
ISBN 0-8166-0888-1 pbk.

Midwest Studies in Philosophy
Volume IV
Studies in Metaphysics

Midwest Studies in Philosophy
Volume IV

Universals

PETER STRAWSON

Huizinga, noting the vogue that the problem of universals enjoyed throughout the Middle Ages and the fact that the controversy was still unresolved in his day, was disposed to find, in its persistence, confirmation of his view of philosophy as a form of agonistic play. It is certainly true that there has always been, and is still, a rough division between those who "countenance," or take a welcoming attitude to, universals and those who would prefer to admit the existence of nothing but particular objects and events. But it may be possible to find, for this continuing division, some further explanation to supplement, at least, that which appeals to love of competition on the part of men in general and philosophers in particular.

Hostility to universals usually goes with complacency about particulars. Those philosophers who are suspicious of general properties, sorts, relations, and types usually have no doubts about the reality of people, physical objects, datable events, and tokens. This partiality of theirs has sometimes seemed paradoxical. For it has seemed unclear how they, or anyone else, could distinguish and identify the particular individuals they so readily accept unless they could distinguish and identify some, at least, of the general sorts or kinds to which those individuals belong and some, at least, of the general features that characterize them. If practical recognition of particular things entails practical recognition of general things, why should theoretical recognition, so readily accorded to the former, be given so grudgingly, if at all, to the latter?

Part of the answer lies in a certain anxiety or fear: the fear of the making of myths, objectionable in themselves and productive of absurdity. The fear has a more specific character. Let it be granted that spatio-temporal particulars — or spatio-temporal particulars of certain sorts — are model cases of what really exists or occurs. The fear is that a theoretical commitment to the existence of universals amounts to a confused half-assimilation of the general to the particular, accompanied, perhaps, by a confused analogical picture of the relations of these spurious quasi-particulars, the universals, to the actual objects to be found in space and time. Plato is represented as the prime example of this confusion; and who is to say he is free from it? The Forms are altogether too like quasi-prototypes. That the fear has, or sometimes has, this character is also suggested by the unpleasant image of a "bloated" or "overpopulated" universe so frequently used by those who would eschew theoretical commitment to abstract entities.

Should we not, in our sophisticated days, have progressed beyond these myths and hence beyond these fears of myth? Surely no one denies that different particular things may share identical properties, may belong to the same kinds; that different pairs or trios of particular things may stand in the same relations. And if so, what can be wrong with, what myth need attend, the admission that there *are* properties, kinds, relations that different particular things or pairs or trios of them may share? Indeed, the admission is implicit in the use, as just made, of the phrases, 'identical property', 'same kind', 'same relation'.

To this there is a stubborn, familiar reply. There is nothing wrong with saying that there *are* properties, kinds, etc., if the remark is construed as merely an idiomatically permissible way of saying that different particular things may alike, for example, be red or white or dogs or trees; that different particular pairs may alike, for example, be such that one member loves, or is larger than, the other. But the suspicion lingers that the remark is taken, by those who think it worth making, to carry some further and disputable commitment. As for the point about practical recognition, it is again harmless to say that the ability to distinguish and identify particular individuals depends upon the ability to distinguish and identify general kinds and properties, if the remark is properly construed. We may admit that the ability to recognize a particular individual as the particular individual it is depends, in general, upon the ability to recognize it *as* a tree, say, or *as* a dog. If this is all that recognition of the general kind comes to, it may safely be acknowledged. But the ability to recognize something as a dog does not require that we have to recognize, in any sense, a further thing, the universal, *dog*.

To these replies there is an equally stubborn rejoinder. Why the reductive tone? Grant that the practical ability to recognize the universal amounts to no more than the ability to recognize its instances as being such. But note that to make the point thus generally is already to recognize, in another sense, the universal itself. Grant that the existence of universals is no more than the fact, or the possibility, that particular things do, or might, exemplify them. But acknowledge that the fact or possibility of their being exemplified is no less than the fact of their existence.

I shall suggest that the fears and tensions here recalled are likely to continue for as long as philosophical discussion of the topic continues.

Such a suggestion may appear profoundly unsatisfactory. It may be objected that we now have a clear-cut way of resolving the issue or at least of construing it as an issue that can be resolved in a clear-cut way. For the elegant and perspicuous notation of standard logic has suggested a test whereby we can determine just what ranges of items are such that we are inescapably committed to belief in their existence. The suggestion is most prominent in the work of Professor Quine, to whom it is primarily due. Quine summed up the test in a celebrated epigram: "To be is to be the value of a variable." It can be expressed in slightly more traditional terminology as follows: the only things we are bound to acknowledge as entities, as existing, are those that we find it indispensable, for the expression of our beliefs, to reckon among the subjects of our predications or—which comes to the same thing—among the objects of reference. To apply the test, we must submit the referential extravagance of natural language to a discipline of regimenting paraphrase that aims at maximum ontological economy. And to help us weed out the bogus pretenders to the status of entities, we have a second test: nothing is to count as an entity unless there is a clear general principle of identity for all things of its kind. Quine summed up the second test, too, in an epigram: "No entity without identity." To see the connection between the two tests, it is enough to recall the notation of logic. The subjects of predication are just the objects that the variables of quantification range over. Those variables are essentially   such as to be able to stand on either side of the identity-predicate. If the variables purport to range over items for which a principle of identity is lacking, then the sentences containing such variables have no determinate sense.

Unfortunately the hope, which these tests might seem to offer, of clear-cut decision on our question turns out to be an illusory hope. It is true that the substantial particular individuals of the world—Aristotle's primary substances—pass both tests with impressive ease and success. And this is a satisfactory result insofar as scarcely any rational man would, even in his philosophical moments, wish to question the existence of such objects. These objects pass the first test, one might say, ahead of all competitors. They are the primary subjects of predication. As I have written elsewhere, "we tell the day-to-day story of the world, we describe the changing postures of its states of affairs, essentially by means of predications of which such objects are the subjects; and we cannot seriously envisage any alternative way of doing so."[1] They pass the second test too; for the common concepts under which such particular individuals are identified yield of themselves general principles of identity for their particular instances. If, for example, one has mastered the common concept "horse," one has thereby mastered a general principle for counting, distinguishing, and identifying particular things, namely horses.

However, when one turns to consider the case of universals or of purported abstract entities generally, disillusion sets in. One is led to question the relevance of the second test and the utility of the first. I do not mean that one is led to question the slogan "No entity without identity"—in its strict and literal meaning; for certainly there exists nothing that is not identical with itself. But if the slogan is construed as meaning "No entity without a *common* principle of identity for all things of a kind to which the purported entity belongs," then its relevance to the case of universals or purported abstract entities generally must come into question. For universals and abstract entities generally—if such exist—are distinguished from spatio-temporal particulars in general precisely by the fact that each has an *individual* essence which constitutes its *individual* identity. So there is no need of a common principle of identity for all universals of some kind to which the given universal belongs. To insist on this requirement would be arbitrarily to fix the rules of the game so that only spatio-temporal particulars and some favored types of abstract object, like sets and numbers, could win it.

To expand a little on this point. Suppose 'F' is a predicate and 'Ø' the corresponding name of the universal—if such exists. Then we have

$$x \text{ is } F \text{ (say, "witty" or "red" or "triangular")}$$

and

$$x \left\{ \begin{array}{l} \text{is an instance of} \\ \text{exemplifies} \end{array} \right\} \emptyset \text{ (say "wit" or "red" or "triangularity").}$$

To grasp the sense of F *is* to grasp the principle of identity for Ø. It is not *eo ipso* to grasp a general, common principle of identity for things of the kind to which Ø belongs. There may or may not be such a principle. In the case of intellectual qualities (the general kind to which wit belongs) or in the case of colors (the general kind to which red belongs) there is no such principle. In the case of geometrical shapes it is perhaps arguable that there is. But the point is that we do not need such a principle. For in the sense of the predicate, and hence in the sense of the associated name for the universal, we already have the essence, the individual principle of identity, of the universal thing—if there exists such a thing. The case is quite different with particular things: their names—their proper names—contain in their sense, insofar as they can be said to have a sense, no *individual* principles of identity for the individuals that bear them. When we seek a principle of identity for them, we do indeed have to have recourse to the general sort or kind to which they belong; to a sortal concept that covers them; to a general principle of identity for all things of that sort. Hence, if we amend the slogan, as just now rejected, to read "No *particular* entity without a common principle of identity for all things of a kind to which the purported particular entity belongs," then the slogan is plausible enough. Unamended, it simply begs the general question against general things. (As already indicated, this is not to say that no abstract entities pass the test. Some do; but there is no reason why all should; and many do not.)

The first test—that of indispensability as subjects of predication—may seem at first sight a little more promising. For it is easy to think of simple cases of successful reductive paraphrase, cases in which, for example, without loss of intended sense, we can eliminate reference by name to abstract qualities in favor of general reference to particulars that characteristically have or lack those qualities, coupled with predicates corresponding to the quality-names. But to infer from such trivial successes that we could, without a crippling effect on discourse, bring about any significant reduction in the range of abstract reference by such means, is to make a wholly unjustified leap; as the study of almost any page of theoretical writing would show. And to cripple discourse is to cripple thought.

Moreover, even if the paraphrasability claim could be made good, the fact would not, by itself, serve the intended purpose. For it might be that the availability of the sentence to be paraphrased was a necessary condition of our thinking the thought to which we then try to approximate in the substitute sentence or sentences. Committed in thought to what we shun in speech, we should then seem like people seeking euphemisms in order to avoid explicit mention of distasteful realities.

The main point, however, is not that the suggested tests fail, through irrelevance in the case of the second and ineffectiveness in the case of the first, to yield any significant reduction in what adherents of the tests would call our ontological commitment to abstract entities. The point is, rather, that they fail in the more general aim *true* of providing a clear-cut means of resolving, in any way at all, the issue that has formed the matter of perennial debate. For if it would be a mistake to think that the tests supply a clear means of limiting our ontological commitment, it would be no less a mistake to conclude that their failure to do so provides of itself a clear and final demonstration of the existence — or of our commitment to belief in the existence — of qualities, properties, types, and abstract entities generally, besides the particular events, objects, and processes that take up space or occur in time in the natural world and that *exemplify* qualities, *belong to* kinds, and are *of* types. It is not, indeed, a mistake that disappointed adherents of the tests are likely to make; they are more likely to give up their adherence. But in asking why these things are so, one may uncover the real source of the poignancy of the perennial debate.

The source lies, I suggest, in a certain inevitable tension in our thought. To *TENSION* locate that tension, we must first recall those considerations that underlie the whole problem, considerations of the utmost generality, relating to features characteristic of any stage of human thought and experience which deserve the names — indeed to any stage of the thought and experience of any being endowed, as Kant would say, with sensibility and understanding. At the most elementary level they amount to this: that we cannot think of, or, in a full sense, perceive, any natural thing, whether object or event, without thinking of it, or perceiving it, under *some* general aspect; as being so-and-so or a such-and-such; as having some general character or as being of some general kind. Generality and particularity are alike necessary features, and mutually dependent features, of our experience; as of our speech. This being so, it is natural that we should at least be under the impression that we can distinguish in thought between particular objects and events in nature and the general characters *BET.* and types that those objects and events exemplify; and indeed that we can extend *REALITY OF* our thought to embrace types and characters perhaps not exemplified at all by any *UNIVERSAL* particular things, or complexes of things, in nature. Should we not, then, recognize that qualities, properties, types, hence universals (*exist,*) as abstract objects of thought, distinct from particular objects in nature? *bad enough without italics*

But here we already meet the source of tension. For when, and if, we are disposed to acquiesce in an affirmative answer to this question, we encounter the full and fierce pressure of a different disposition: a strong, natural disposition to under- *AND* stand by the notion of existence the same thing as existence in nature; to think that *ROBUST* whatever exists at all exists in nature and that whatever relations hold between things *ONTOL.* are relations that are exemplified in nature. No reconciliation of the two dispositions is possible. For universals, if they exist at all, do not exist in nature. They are *incorrigibly* abstract; objects, if objects at all, of thought alone, even if indispensable objects of developed thought.

But if universals, if they exist, are outside nature, how are they related to the natural objects that exemplify or instantiate them? To repeat the professional terms,

Does 'encounter' refer to 'intuit' or 'be given'? If so, universals are *not encountered, and nothing else is.

'exemplification' or 'instantiation', seems to be to give no reply at all to this question. But it is the only reply that the believer in universals can safely give. For the question, the demand for an account of the relation, really incorporates the naturalist prejudice—if I may call it so *without* prejudice. So Plato, though right to place universals outside nature, was wrong to seek even a suggestive analogy in nature—for example, copy and original, production-line model and prototype—for the relation of exemplification. The relation of exemplification is not a natural relation and can have no natural analogues. Aristotle was right to reject the analogy, but wrong to try, if he did try, to locate universals in nature. But it is not clear that he did try; for to say that universals are *in* particulars may not be an attempt to identify any natural relation, even by way of natural analogy; it may simply be to say that universals exist in nature only insofar as, and in the sense that, their instances exist in nature; and that they do not exist at all in any other sense.

The believer in universals, then, must be prepared to say that though instances of (some) universals are encounterable, and recognizable, in nature, the universal itself, the abstract thing, is not. The abstract thing is an object of thought alone. (The natural thing is an object of thought too, but not of thought alone.) But thinking takes place in nature. So the believer must also say that we can, in nature, think of the abstract thing which is not in nature as well as recognizing, in nature, its natural instances. (He may say that implicit in our recognition of the instance, the thing in nature, as what it is, is a capacity, even if an undeveloped capacity, to think of the abstract thing, the universal it is an instance of.)

TIME   Here he is exposed to another challenge from our native naturalism, that challenge which perhaps has more force than any other, since it covertly appeals to what seems the most fundamental dimension of natural existence, namely, time. It runs: If these supposed entities are objects of thought, and objects of thought alone, are we not obliged to say one of two things: either that they come into existence when first conceived of and enjoy, while they exist, only a mind-dependent existence; or that they pre-exist their conception, waiting, in some non-natural sphere of their own, to be discovered by minds? And does not either answer seem singularly unattractive? Indeed both are unattractive, and both must be rejected by the believer; not in favor of a third temporal alternative, but on the ground that temporal predicates have no application to abstract objects, that they neither come into existence at a certain time nor exist sempiternally; that they are not in time. And here the believer has to resist the pressure of the naturalist prejudice at its strongest, the sense that whatever exists at all exists in time.

If he has stomach for this, he faces a third challenge. For it often seems that when we appear to be talking about universals, naming them and quantifying over them in such ways that we can find no plausible paraphrase, that both captures our thought and dispenses with such reference, yet we may have no further intention than to speak of what is found in nature. Should we not then conclude that even in our apparently ineliminable reference to universals we have nothing more than a feature of idiom, a *façon de parler*, an especially and perhaps inimitably vivid or economical way of suggesting, or alluding to, a more or less determinate, more or less compendious, array of natural facts — offering, perhaps, at the same time, a picture, not to be taken literally, like the personifications of eighteenth-century poetry — so that our thought has really no object other than natural things?

This is a point at which the believer can make a concession without surrendering his belief. If aggressively disposed, he may say that the occurrence of such apparent reference to universals is dependent upon the possibility of genuine reference to them; or, more bluntly, that it is only because they exist, as objects of thought, outside nature, that we can thus appear to refer to them even when we are speaking only of what is in nature. Because they exist, as objects of thought only, we can use their names to speak, picturesquely and indirectly, not of them at all, but of merely natural things that are not only objects of thought.

But the believer may not make quite so strong a claim. He may remark simply that the way just discussed is not the only way in which we use the names of universals or quantify over them. For sometimes we speak of the non-natural relations that hold between universals, or abstract entities, themselves. This we do whenever we speak of conceptual (or logical or analytic or semantic) necessities; for these are outside nature too. It is not, for example, a natural fact that scarlet things are necessarily red. When we assert, or think of, these necessities, the objects of our thought, whether they are directly named or represented by predicates, are the abstract entities themselves. It is not claimed that the existence of conceptual necessities is *explained* by a further fact, namely the existence of non-natural relations between universals or abstract entities generally. Rather, they are the same thing, neither more nor less than each other. And it is admitted that when we speak explicitly of non-natural relations between universals, the words we use are often borrowed from the vocabulary of relations exemplified in nature: for example 'includes', 'excludes', 'is incompatible with'. So we seem to picture these relations on analogy with, for example, spatial relations. Here again we see how natural is the fear that theoretical recognition of universals involves myth and confusion. The pictures seem to haunt us, however hard we try to neutralize them; and, of course, there is a quite blatant irony in the attempt to neutralize them by saying that universals are *outside* nature. But if we are to say that necessary truths are truths at all, then we must say that they are truths about objects of thought alone (concepts, universals, abstract entities); and this is why some who think that every truth must be a truth about the natural world are found to declare that all of what are called necessary truths say the same thing, namely nothing. *or careless, perhaps* NATUR. REDUCTION

The more careful of committed naturalists, of course, will avoid this rather baffling epigram. He has more considered things to say. He will attempt what might be called a naturalistic reduction of our intuitions of conceptual necessity. For thinking, after all, is something that occurs in nature. So he will seek an account of these intuitions in terms of what is naturally found — in terms of this or that natural mental content or in terms of this or that natural, and socially reinforced, disposition to behavior, especially linguistic behavior. Talk of grasping or perceiving necessary relations between abstract objects or concepts he will see as at best an attempt to do justice to some aspects of the phenomenology of thought, but as a misguided attempt insofar as it appears to invoke objects that have no place in this, the natural, and the only, world. His opponent, on the other hand, will continue to insist that the fact that thinking is a natural phenomenon does not require that all its objects be so too; and that recognition of the full powers of thought is *eo ipso* recognition of its abstract objects.

As I have already suggested, I do not think that the dispute is finally resolvable. In saying this I do not mean that there is a right answer which will remain forever hidden from us because we lack the power to reach that impartial vantage point from which the truth can be discerned and the final judgment delivered. I mean, rather, that there is no such vantage point; neither in the natural world nor out of it; for any location of our judgment seat would be a prejudgment of the issue. If I am right in this, then the picture of a profound metaphysical disagreement should ideally be replaced by that of a choice: between the adoption of a naturalist stance, with a consequential restriction of the notion of existence to what is found in nature; and a contrary willingness to extend the notion to thought-objects, exemplifiable, but not locatable, in nature. Ideally still, it should not matter greatly which choice is made; for any pair of philosophers of opposed persuasions (or, in this matter, perhaps, of temperaments) should be able to appreciate, across their difference in idiom, the force of each other's attempts on the less general and more substantial problems that confront them both. But this *is* ideal; and it seems more likely that the old debate will continue, in variant guises and variant forms, as long as our civilization lasts. May that be long indeed!

Note

1. See "Entity and Identity," in *Contemporary British Philosophy*, Fourth Series, ed. H. D. Lewis (London, 1976).

Naturalist prejudices: - P8- whatever exists, exists in time.

Universals or Family Resemblances?

RICHARD E. GRANDY

The concept of sameness has challenged philosophical speculation for millennia, but some philosophers believe that we have recently made progress in resolving issues between nominalists and realists through the introduction of the idea of family resemblances. Renford Bambrough's "Universals and Family Resemblances"[1] is a particularly good starting point for any discussion of this topic inasmuch as he claims that Wittgenstein's analysis of family resemblance should be applied to all terms of a language, not simply to some limited subset that contrasts with other types of terms.[2] Although I share Bambrough's conviction that the family resemblance concept is a significant one, I shall show that the victory that Bambrough's Wittgenstein wins over both realists and nominalists is a temporary one and that more sophisticated forms of realism and nominalism require a correspondingly more sophisticated formulation of the Wittgensteinian doctrine, probably more sophisticated than one can find in the Wittgensteinian corpus.

Bambrough's first brief characterization of the three positions is:

> The nominalist says that games have nothing in common except that they are called games.

> The realist says that games must have something in common, and he means by this that they must have something in common other than that they are games.

> Wittgenstein says that games have nothing in common except that they are games.[3]

The difficulty with these positional slogans is that we must determine what the phrases 'nothing (something) in common' are intended to refer to. We could, for example, take the dispute between nominalist and realist to be a matter of whether necessary and sufficient conditions can be given for the application of each word in a language. Clearly more is meant by 'in common' than is explicitly expressed, for games all have in common that they are activities, 'chairs' that they are furniture and so on. No, what is meant by 'something in common' must be something that the objects referred to by a name have in common with each other and that no other object has. This is a point that is obvious when mentioned, but is often neglected. For example, presentations of the family resemblance concept often give abstract examples by imagining that there are a set of relevant properties say A, B, C, D, and E and illustrating a family by supposing that the members of the family have respectively the properties

$$\begin{array}{ccccc} a_1 & a_2 & a_3 & a_4 & a_5 \\ A\ B\ C\ D & A\ B\ C\ E & A\ B\ D\ E & A\ C\ D\ E & B\ C\ D\ E.^4 \end{array}$$

But in this case the evident, if superficial, anti-Wittgensteinian reply is that these objects do indeed have something in common, namely

$$(A\&B\&C\&D)v(A\&B\&C\&E)v(A\&B\&D\&E)v(A\&C\&D\&E)v(B\&C\&D\&E),$$
or even $(A\&B)v(A\&C)v(B\&C)$.

But a more fully fleshed example would include the fact that in contrasting categories there might be objects with A&B, or perhaps even A&B&C.

We should note that it is not an open option on Bambrough's interpretation of Wittgenstein to suggest that the above expressions do not truly represent something in common because they are complex. Bambrough claims that all terms are family resemblance terms, hence no distinction between complex and simple terms seems appropriate here. Furthermore, it would be peculiar for the argument between nominalists and realists to turn upon whether certain linguistic expressions were or were not complex. If a realist claimed vindication with regard to Fs because they all and only had G, then surely a nominalist would reply that this shows only that they have in common that they are all also called "G."

Traditionally, of course, the dispute was not over whether all instances of a general term had *something* in common but over whether they had in common that they were instances of a universal. Realists were realists about universals, and nominalists denied that anything nonlinguistic and nonparticular bound together those items of which a term is true. Wittgenstein's arguments are not directly relevant to this issue, for there is no argument derivable from the fact that games bear a family resemblance to each other that shows that they cannot all instantiate a universal. The only theory that would possibly be jeopardized would be one that asserted that instances of a term resembled each other because they all *resembled* the universal. But unless one holds a resemblance theory of instantiation, the family resemblance argument is beside this point.

We are forced now to reconsider the question "What sense can be attached to the critical phrase 'something in common' that will produce an intelligible realist-nominalist disagreement that a Wittgensteinian can resolve?" One possibility is the following: According to one possible view of language, let us call it the Naive Linguistic Realist position, human language arises because human beings perceive that there are various kinds of objects in the world and adopt (in some suitably loose sense of adopt) conventions that enable them to refer to these kinds of objects by various general terms. According to another possible view, which we shall call the Naive Linguistic Nominalist, there are certain sets of objects that people find it convenient to group together because of their interests and beliefs, and people adopt conventions that enable them to refer to the members of these sets by various general terms. The Naive Linguistic Realist and Naive Linguistic Nominalist agree that there is an isomorphism between thought and kinds of objects in the world, but they disagree about whether this is because thought mirrors the structure of the world or because thought imposes structure on the world. This issue would likely be a fundamental one for any philosopher who held such an isomorphism view of thought and the world, or who had at one time held such a view.[5]

What both views share is the assumption that language is a merely conventional matter that exists for the purpose of expressing the antecedent facts or thoughts. "In a proposition a thought finds an expression that can be perceived by the senses."[6] One possibility for interpreting the family resemblance view as an alternative to both nominalist and realist would be to take it as arguing that language plays some more significant role than either the Naive Linguistic Realist or Naive Linguistic Nominalist allows. Certainly one could hardly argue that it plays less of a role than they think.

In order to evaluate this suggestion as to the intended import of the family resemblance conception, we must first refine further the alternative positions. *Prima facie,* the realist has a serious objection to the nominalist position, for it would appear miraculous that different persons agreed in their independent application of a general term G if these objects had nothing in common. That is, if we imagine the not unusual circumstances in which two competent English speakers are each separately confronted by an object they have never before seen and both agree that it is a dog, how is the nominalist to explain this fact if not by appeal to the similarity between this dog and others (plus, of course, the linguistic training of the speakers)?

A second query that a realist could raise about the nominalist position as briefly described by Bambrough would concern the difference between something being called G and its being G or being properly called G. If Gs have nothing in common other than being called "G," then it would appear that being called "G" is sufficient for being G. But this does not do justice to any of the normative notions associated with language use, the contrast between truth and falsity, the possibility of misdescribing and so on.

Both of these queries are directed at the Naive Linguistic Nominalist and the underlying assumption that language consists of the conventional imposition of a mentally determined structure on the world. The first point is that this picture of language cannot account for the social facts of language, that different speakers can agree on the application of terms to previously unencountered objects. Thus they are responding to some degree to a structure that is dependent at least partly on the world. The second objection points out that at least to some extent the structure imposed on the world is not totally arbitrary, that we ourselves distinguish between correctness and incorrectness.

Does the Naive Linguistic Realist have a satisfactory explanation for these phenomena? The simplest explanation would be that objects are called G because they all and only share some property G; that an application of the term G to an object is correct if and only if that object has the property G. The social character of language is derivative from the realist assumption, for the explanation of why speakers agree in the application of some terms is that the property P is perceptible to speakers.

The difficult question that must be raised about these explanations is how the connection between a general term in the language and a property is established. Any given object has many properties and even a fairly large finite collection will share many properties, so it does not suffice to establish that P is the property characteristic of Gs for speakers to pick out some samples of objects that they call G. Two possible answers would appear to be (1) that the property P is picked out from others by the intentions of the speakers, (2) the property P that is characteristic of Gs is the most salient property possessed by the exemplars and not possessed by negative exemplars.

Are these actually two distinct replies? It is difficult to see how one can intend to convey to another person that P rather than P' or P'' is the characteristic property of Gs unless one has some expectation that the listener will grasp what is intended. One cannot (usually) intend what one believes to be very improbable. But one can only believe it probable that a listener or learner will understand which property is intended if that property is salient. Of course, one need not rely on untrained, unguided, or untutored salience; pointing, verbal qualifications, suitable settings, and other means can be used to influence the person and the salience of P for them.

This argument appears to show that the realist must make reference to speakers in the characterization of which properties are associated with general terms of a language. Returning to Bambrough's final summation of his view, we can paraphrase one of his conclusions along somewhat different lines.

> The realist talks of properties and qualities until, when properties and qualities have been explained in terms of other properties and other qualities, he can at last do nothing but point to the *resemblances* between the objects that are said to be characterized by such and such a property or quality.[7]

Our interpretation of the debate makes it less a matter of ultimate metaphysical explanations and more a matter of providing explanations of various aspects of language. But we have seen that the realist appears to be forced into the position where he must make reference either to resemblances or to the behavior of speakers of the language.

We should consider next whether Bambrough is correct about the other complementary half of his conclusion:

> The nominalist talks of resemblances until he is pressed into a corner where he must acknowledge that resemblance is unintelligible except as resemblance

in a respect, and to indicate the respect in which objects resemble one another is to indicate a *quality* or *property.*[8]

It is true, of course, that resemblance always carries with it some relativization, perhaps tacit or contextual, a respect. One recent experimental confirmation of this intuitively plausible assertion is Labov's work showing that a single object is classified by subjects as a vase, a bowl, or a cup depending on contextual elements.[9] Another rich source of examples is to consider the various respects in which two countries, for example, the U.S.A. and the U.S.S.R., resemble one another, and those in which they do not.

Bambrough's argument requires not only the fact that resemblance is resemblance in some respect, however, for he claims that indicating the respect in which objects resemble each other is to indicate a quality or property. It would be possible to defend this claim by definition, by stipulating that any specification of a respect of resemblance *ipso facto* counts as the specification of a property. But let us see if we can find a more interesting defense of this claim. In many cases the claim is true — to explain what a dachshund and German Shepherd have in common that they do not share with poodles is to pick out some property such as that of originating in Germany. The obvious place to look for counterexamples, however, is the case of family resemblance concepts.

As remarked earlier, for any finite set of examples of a family resemblance concept one will be able to find Boolean combinations of properties that differentiate the instances from non-instances. However, it would be a mistake to infer from this that the complex condition adequately expresses the concept, for there is no guarantee that further instances will fit the pattern. So the respect in which the instances resemble each other may not be specifiable in any interestingly non-circular way. They will resemble each other in that they will all be instances of this concept, the concept that will be generalized from these instances.

To return to our original starting point, we have seen that the simple-minded realism characterized by Bambrough cannot be defended, for reference to the linguistic communities' members is required for specification of the property that is associated with a general term. But Bambrough's nominalist has not been the victor either, for it is not simply a matter of being called an F that makes an object an F, and thus it is not simply being called Fs that all Fs have in common. And, finally, the Wittgensteinian position that "games have nothing in common except that they are games" has been seen to be much too simple-minded. A characterization of what games have in common will require reference to the linguistic community and to their dispositions to classify objects and activities. And it may be that there is no noncircular way to characterize the common features of games, the degree of overlap required, the importance of contrast with other categories, and so on. But this does not imply that there is not an objective reality to which the linguistic community is responding.

The demise of the simple realism discussed leaves us with a deep problem as to the significance to be attached to calling a classification "objective"; we are unwilling to acquiesce in the casual attitude of the nominalist who assures us that there is no significance to be attached to the term, but we are far from understanding it. A philosophically insightful characterization of the extension of a general term must, as we have seen, make reference to a linguistic community and to its past, future, and possible behavior. That speakers agree that an object is an F does not make it an F. Their verdict can be overthrown by themselves if they discover that some of their assumptions, presuppositions, contextual influences, perceptions, and many other factors were in some way inaccurate or inappropriate. And we can, even if hesitantly, overthrow their verdict as outside observers if we have good grounds for believing that *if* they had certain further information of the kinds above that they *would* (or would have) changed their verdict.

It might be objected that we could provide a slightly neater theory by making reference not to a linguistic community and its possible behavior, but to a single idealized speaker of the language and her or his possible behavior. After all, if one idealized speaker would, in ideal circumstances, classify something as an F, then any other idealized speaker in the same circumstances would agree. I believe we should resist this elegance, for the assumption that we can project from the linguistic community a single idealized speaker is a major assumption and one that leads to a significant oversimplification of the nature of language. It is quite possible that in the actual development of a language speakers will disagree over a matter of categorization. If we assume an ideal speaker view of the language, then one of the disputants must be correct and another incorrect, whereas in fact the language may simply not be sufficiently precise and well-determined to render a verdict in the case in question.

Utilizing an idealized speaker characterization of linguistic correctness underplays the role of agreement in judgments among the speakers of the language. This is not to say that in all cases where speakers disagree there is no fact of the matter, but rather to emphasize that we have not yet been able to draw any clear, sharp principled line between disagreements over matters of fact and disagreements about linguistic usage, whether past or proposed. It is no accident that the discussion of family resemblances is followed in the *Philosophical Investigations* by the treatment of following a rule and the private language argument. But these matters are the topic of another paper.

Notes

1. Renford Bambrough, "Universals and Family Resemblances," *Proceedings of the Aristotelian Society*, 1960-61, 61, pp. 207-22; references in this paper are to the reprinting in *Wittgenstein: The Philosophical Investigations*, ed. George Pitcher (Englewood Cliffs, 1966).

2. *Ibid.*, pp. 192-95.

3. *Ibid.*, pp. 198-99.

4. *Ibid.*, p. 189.

5. For example, *Tractatus Logico-Philosophicus*, 2.2 "A picture has logico-pictorial form in common with what it depicts" and 3 "A logical picture of facts is a thought" suggest strongly that Wittgenstein had himself in mind, if my interpretation of the significance of the family resemblance issues is correct.

6. *Ibid.*, 3.1.

7. Bambrough, "Universals and Family Resemblances," p. 204.

8. *Ibid.*, p. 204.

9. "The Boundaries of Words and Their Meanings," eds. C. J. N. Bailey and R. W. Shuy, *New Ways of Analyzing Variation in English,* (Washington, 1973), pp. 340-73.

Mind, Brain, and Causation

J. L. MACKIE

Although minds are not distinct things from brains, mental properties are distinct from physical properties, and mental facts are different from neurophysiological facts. But what, then, is the causal role of mental facts and properties? When desire and belief (or knowledge) together lead to a decision and an action that involves bodily movement, do the relevant mental facts and properties help causally to bring about that movement and that action? Or do the physical (including neurophysiological) facts and properties constitute a sufficient cause of that movement and that action, so that the related mental elements are causally idle and redundant? Is epiphenomenalism right in treating the mental elements as only effects of physical factors, and not also causes? At first sight, neither answer seems acceptable. The epiphenomenalist view that the mental aspect of our desires, beliefs, and decisions is causally idle is strongly at variance with our ordinary understanding of these matters. It is also hard to reconcile with an evolutionary theory: if consciousness evolved through natural selection, it must have contributed causally to the survival of the species in which it was developing. On the other hand it seems plausible to suppose that it is one neurophysiological occurrence that causes another, so that what brings about the bodily movements that constitute the action (or else are part of it, and in conjunction with external circumstances causally determine the other parts of it) is not the agent's desires and beliefs as such, but their neurophysiological basis. The continuity of the causal process is on the physical side, and there is no room for mental elements to intervene and make a difference.

These problems arise only if mental elements such as desires, beliefs, and conscious experiences are distinguished from the physical features of brain states and processes. Defenders of the mind-brain identity theory have argued from such difficulties to the denial of the distinction. It would indeed be awkward to recognize mental features but leave them causally idle. We should need one-way causal laws to connect them with their neurophysiological basis, and these laws would be loose ends in the network of scientific laws, "nomological danglers." But we cannot deny that there are conscious experiences, and (as I shall show) there is no way in which they can be reduced without remainder to their physical basis.

We are faced, then, with what looks like an inconsistent triad of propositions, each of which is highly plausible on its own. Mental facts and properties are distinct from physical ones. Mental facts and properties are causally operative in human action, not idle or redundant. Yet physical (including neurophysiological) elements constitute sufficient causes of the bodily movements that determine actions.

I want to treat this as an ontological problem, not a linguistic one. It is sometimes argued that language could change so that talk about brain processes and the like would replace talk about experiences. Well, suppose that it could, and did: this would not settle our problem. Part of this problem is whether this reformed language would be adequate, whether it would cover the world, not merely in the sense of reporting and predicting all concrete occurrences under some description, but also in the sense of not leaving undescribed some perfectly real and (to us at least) interesting features. It is argued more plausibly on the other side that whatever discoveries science comes up with, and whatever arguments physicalist philosophers deploy, we shall always go on speaking in terms of experiences and intentional thought, and that talk about actions belongs firmly within this branch of ordinary language. But, even if this is so, it does not settle the issue in the opposite sense: the question remains whether this persistent way of speaking expresses a truth or a systematic error. To take an analogous case, it might well be that we shall always go on speaking of colored objects in a way that implicitly treats colors-as-seen as objective. But the doctrine of secondary qualities may nonetheless be correct; this way of speaking may embody an error. The practical indispensability of the language of consciousness might indeed result from and be indirect evidence for the presence of irreducible mental properties, but it does not settle the issue directly or in itself. Our problem is about what properties actually are there, and their causal relations; it is not about our present language and conceptual scheme, nor is it about how these could or could not be altered.

I should briefly sum up the case for the distinctness of mental properties. There are several sorts of feature that are, *prima facie* at least, distinctively mental. First, there are the "raw feels" or phenomenal qualities: almost all of us know what it is to feel pain, to see something red, to hear a high note, to feel cold, and so on. Second, we have perceptions that are as of independently existing things in an objective spatio-temporal order. Third, we have propositional attitudes, beliefs, desires, and so on, that concern various things other than those mental states themselves in such a way that they cannot be adequately described except by including a description of whatever it is they are about. The desire that it should be fine tomorrow is just that: no way of describing it will do justice to it unless it somehow captures and encapsulates the possible state of affairs, its being fine tomorrow. Features of both the second and the third sort have been put under the heading of intentionality, and we need not discuss whether they are really different from one another, or whether the second is analyzable in terms of the third. The important point is that no features of these three sorts seem to be exhaustively analyzable into or reducible to any system of features of sorts other than these three, that is, uncompromisingly physical features.

This becomes plain if we examine what are offered as analogous cases of reductive identification: the table is nothing but a cloud of particles, lightning is nothing but an electrical discharge, heat is nothing but the kinetic energy of molecules, and the gene is nothing but the DNA (or RNA) molecule. Granted that where the table is there is no persisting continuous solid, though to sight and touch there appears to be one. We can explain away the continuous solidity as an appearance: that is just how what is there looks and feels to us. We replace some of the supposed qualities of the table with parts of the content of our conscious experiences. Similarly, where we see the lightning there is nothing but an electrical discharge and photons being sent out from it; but we see it as a bright flash. Again the brightness is shifted from the external object to become part of the content of consciousness. And the same with heat as we feel it. But it is obvious that this method of explaining things away will not do for experiences themselves and their contents. Its looking thus and so to us is one of the features that is embarrassing for the physicalist, and the explanation that it only looks to us as if it looks thus and so is not only absurd but useless: it would leave us with an unexplained item of the same sort on our hands. The gene is in a different position. It is initially introduced only as a hypothetical entity, as that which plays a certain causal role, interacting in regular ways with other genes, in determining the inheritance of characteristics. To start with, it is simply that, whatever it may be that does such and such. It is therefore freely up for identification with whatever may later be discovered to do this job. There is no appearance here to be explained away. If mental features were analogous to genes, if they were introduced simply as otherwise unknown causes of behavior, as the grounds, whatever they may be, of dispositions, there would be no obstacle to reductive identification. If my desire to do X were merely something or other in me which brings it about that in favorable circumstances I (tend to) do X, then indeed it could be exhaustively identified with some neurophysiological condition that has only impeccably physical properties. Similarly, if, as in Smart's notorious example, my having a certain after-image was known to me simply as something going on in me which is like what goes on in me when my eyes are open (etc.) and there is a yellowish orange patch on the wall, then my having of this experience could be exhaustively identified with a brain process. Identity theorists have therefore been tempted to give accounts of these sorts. But implausibly. I know what an orange after-image looks like, and I know at least the central cases of my desiring to do X as involving fully conscious thought about doing X. The phenomenal and intentional features cannot plausibly be denied, and once they are recognized even as merely apparent they cannot be explained away. The only available method of explaining apparent features away fails here through circularity.

Our problem is that once we have accepted an irreducible distinction between mental and physical facts and properties, and have allowed that physical facts and properties constitute sufficient causes of actions, we seem to be forced to admit that mental facts and properties are epiphenomenal, causally idle; yet this conclusion is itself implausible. This problem, however, involves two important items of causal theory. First, it arises, on our assumptions, only if we take facts and properties as causes. If a cause were always a concrete thing or a concrete event, we could say that what was causally responsible for an action was a neurophysiological structure or event: this structure or event could have mental features as well as purely physical ones, but, given this approach, there would be no sense in asking which features were operative and which were idle: what was causally operative was the concrete whole. But though this sort of report is allowable, it is not the only sort that is allowable, and it cannot cover on its own everything that is important about causation. We can and frequently do distinguish, within concrete things and events, those features that are relevant to a certain outcome. Although it was the one concrete event, Tommy's eating of a number of apples, that caused both his immediate stomach ache and his later poisoning, it was the fact that the apples were unripe that caused the stomach ache and the fact that they had been sprayed with paraquat that caused the poisoning. We have to recognize fact- and property-causes as well as concrete-event and thing-causes. So once the mental features have been distinguished even as features of a physical thing, we can ask intelligibly whether they are causally relevant to actions or not. Second, our problem involves the direction of causation. It is only on the assumption that any particular causal relationship is asymmetrical that we can formulate epiphenomenalism and suggest that there is only a one-way causal path from the neurophysiological to the mental, and hence that even if certain mental facts are necessary and sufficient (in the circumstances) as temporal antecedents of actions, they are nonetheless causally idle and redundant. Also, it is natural to suppose that each mental item occurs at the same time, or has the same temporal duration, as its neurophysiological basis, so that if there is causal asymmetry here it must consist of something other than succession in time. It may be, then, that the key to our problem lies in the understanding of causal asymmetry. I have tried more than once to analyze it, but with less than complete success[1]; I shall try again, from a different starting point.

Here, as elsewhere, there are three sorts of questions, conceptual, epistemological, and ontological, that are liable to be mixed up with one another. We can ask what concept we have of causal asymmetry; again, what knowledge we have of it and how we acquire that knowledge; and third what constitutes causal asymmetry in the objects, what directedness there is in the objective relation between a cause and its effect. The answers to questions of these three sorts may be related to one another, but they could diverge radically. Let us start with conceptual analysis, and then, if we can elucidate the concept of causal direction, consider what knowledge we have that applies this concept and what observations could have generated it, and whether we can claim objective validity for it or for anything related to it.

We often think of the direction of causation as a direction of conditionality: the effect is conditional upon, depends upon, the cause in some sense in which the cause is not conditional upon the effect. Now some conditional relationships are nonsymmetrical: if A is a necessary condition of B, B need not be a necessary condition of A, and equally if A is a sufficient condition of B, B need not be a sufficient condition of A. (Though on some analyses if A is necessary for B, B is sufficient for A, and *vice versa,* so that if A is necessary and sufficient for B, B must also be necessary and sufficient for A.) But these nonsymmetries are not what we want. A cause, or a causally relevant factor, may be sufficient (in the circumstances) for its effect; again, it may be necessary; the causal asymmetry is different from and cuts across the contrast between necessity and sufficiency. Causal priority can combine equally well with necessity or with sufficiency. In fact, on the most natural interpretation something must have causal priority to count as a necessary condition, or as a sufficient one, or both. On this interpretation it will not follow that if A is a necessary condition of B, B is a sufficient condition of A, and so on. If A and B are single (token) events, such converse relationships cannot hold, and even if they are event types there is no reason to expect them to hold.

It seems, then, that we cannot derive a direction of conditionality from necessity and sufficiency, whether or not we add "in the circumstances." We have either to add the conditional and causal priority as a further factor, or to follow the natural interpretation which takes it to be included, but as something not yet analyzed or explained, in the relation of necessity, or sufficiency, or their conjunction. I have previously, on this account, despaired of finding an analyzable direction of conditionality. But an article by David Sanford has persuaded me that it is possible, though the analysis I shall offer is rather different from his.[2]

Let us work with examples of what are, so far as we can tell at the start, simultaneous causes and effects. One such example is von Wright's of a box with two buttons on top, so connected inside that if you press either button both go down together; let us call the buttons A and B. In the circumstances A's going down is necessary and sufficient for the simultaneous going down of B, and *vice versa:* but on some one occasion when I press A, A's going down is causally prior to B's. We can believe this even if we think there is strict simultaneity — B starts to go down at exactly the same instant as A. Our concept of causal priority is not that of being earlier in time. I have argued elsewhere that in such cases as this we rely on the continuity of causation: since it is A that my finger presses, I am confident that A's movement is causally prior to B's because I believe that the movement of my finger is causally prior to both, and A's movement comes between that of my finger and that of B in a physically continuous causal line. But this is pretty clearly not what we mean when we say that A's movement is on this occasion causally prior to B's, and it is unhelpful because it merely refers us to the still-to-be-analyzed causal priority of my finger movement, or perhaps of my decision to press A. What we mean is rather this. Although in these circumstances the movement of either button is necessary and sufficient for that of the other, it is not so in other possible circumstances. We could open the box and cut or disconnect whatever it is that links A with B, and then the movement of neither button would be necessary or sufficient for that of the other. If the connection between them had been broken, A would still have gone down when I pressed A, but (other things being equal) B would not. It is, I suggest, in this sense that in the actual case, where the connection is not broken, B's movement is conditional upon A's: it wouldn't be occurring but for the connection with A. The conditionally dependent (and therefore, in our concept, causally posterior) item is the one which would or might have been absent if the connection between them had not been there, but things had been otherwise as far as possible the same.

This is offered as a conceptual analysis, but it also indicates how observations and especially experiments could suggest and confirm such directed conditionality. By making various changes and then pressing either button again I could check what it was that linked them, and I could note which moved and which failed to move when I pressed each with the connection broken. Of course, our general experience tells us to expect that it will be the one we press that moves in these circumstances, but that is only because our experience includes plenty of roughly analogous experiments. A priori it is conceivable that, when I press A with the connection broken, only B should go down. If it did, I should conclude that when they were connected and I pressed A and both went down, it was B's movement that was conditionally and causally prior to A's. So the detection of conditonal and causal priority is independent of the physical continuity of the causal line, and it is a synthetic truth that we can in general rely on such continuity as an indicator of causal priority, a truth for which we need, and have, empirical evidence.

Another example (used by Sanford) takes as the two causally related items the rotation of the drive shaft (propeller shaft) and the rotation of the rear wheels of a car. When the engine is moving the car along a level road, the rotation of the wheels depends on that of the drive shaft. On our conceptual analysis, this means that if the connection between the two rotations had not been there — say, if the differential had failed or had been missing — but things had otherwise been as far as possible the same, the drive shaft would have been rotating but not the wheels. In fact it is a bit more complicated: the drive shaft would have been rotating faster. That is, there are both conditional and causal priorities running in both directions. The drive shaft's rotation is maintaining that of the wheels, while that of the wheels is holding back that of the shaft. That the wheels are rotating at all is conditional upon the rotation of the shaft, but that the shaft is rotating no faster than it is is conditional upon the frictionally limited rotation of the wheels. And, of course, all this is reversed when the car is being pushed.

Generalizing, then, if on a particular occasion A's doing X is causally related to B's doing Y, and if they had not been so related but things had otherwise been as far as possible as they were, A would still have been doing X but B would (or might) not have been doing Y, then A's doing X is conditionally and causally prior to B's doing Y. And this holds whether A's doing X is necessary for B's doing Y, or sufficient, or both.

We can thus formulate directed conditionality in terms of appropriate counterfactual conditionals, of which the key one is "If the connection had not been there . . ." These, like other counterfactuals, can be supported, though not conclusively established, by observation of closely analogous but slightly changed situations. An assumption about the uniformity of the course of nature in the relevant respects allows us to take what happens there and apply it, counterfactually conditionally, to the present case. And this direction of conditionality seems to be the core of our concept of the direction of causation. The experiments and observed regularities that support these counterfactuals are the source of our knowledge of causal asymmetry.

I have treated the button and car examples as ones in which cause and effect are contemporaneous. In reality, there will be a small time lag (for example, between the instant at which the rotation of the shaft reaches a certain speed and that at which the rotation of the wheels reaches the corresponding speed) owing to the elasticity of the connecting materials. But the temporal order thus set up between cause and effect is something quite different both from the direction of conditionality as it figures in our concept of causal order and from the observed contrasts and regularities that give rise to and justify that concept. We could make these observations and assert the conditional dependence in complete ignorance of the time lags. Their coincidence is a synthetic and empirical truth, like the agreement, noted above, between physical continuity and causal priority.

This account can be extended to examples where there is not even an appearance of simultaneity, where the effect plainly follows the cause in time. What here corresponds to breaking the connection will be making a small change in the circumstances such that the causal relation no longer holds. For example, the near end of a fuse is lit, the flame burns along it and a heap of gunpowder which the far end of the fuse is touching explodes. We repeat the experiment with the end of the fuse not touching the gunpowder and there is no explosion. So we say, about the original case, that if the far end of the fuse had not been touching the gunpowder, the near end would still have burned but there would have been no explosion. This is the analysis of the claim that the burning of the near end of the fuse is the cause and the explosion the effect.

It might be objected that we are begging the question by taking as the most nearly analogous case without the connection one in which the near end is lit: why not take one where, though the fuse is not lit and its far end is not touching the gunpowder, there still is an explosion? Would not this suggest that if the connection had been absent, the explosion would have occurred in the original case but not the burning of the near end of the fuse, thus reversing, on our analysis, the direction of conditionality? Yes, this would follow if we found a lot of cases, all otherwise very similar, divided into a class where there was contact between fuse and gunpowder, an explosion, and an earlier fuse-burning, and a class in which there was no contact, an explosion, and no earlier fuse-burning. This would constitute *prima facie* evidence for time-reversed conditional dependence of the earlier burning on the later explosion. But, of course, we do not get this pattern of evidence. Consider a case in which the explosion occurs but there is no contact with the fuse.

In cases most like this, except that there is contact, there is no strong tendency for there to have been an earlier burning of the near end of the fuse. We do not need to make a question-begging estimate of similarity to conclude that the counter-factual supported by the actual pattern of resemblances and differences is "If the connection had not been there, the near end of the fuse would have burned but there would have been no explosion," not "If the connection had not been there, there would have been an explosion but the near end of the fuse would not have burned." The observed evidence, in the light of our analysis, supports a synthetic, empirical, judgment that the conditional and causal order here coincides with the temporal order.

What I have sketched here is a conceptual analysis of causal asymmetry based on the direction of conditionality, and a related epistemic analysis. Since I deny that counterfactual conditionals with unfulfilled antecedents (other than those whose antecedents entail their consequents) can be simply and straightforwardly true, I cannot offer it also as a factual analysis, as an answer to the ontological question about causal asymmetry. But such asymmetry in the objects will consist at least in those contrasting regularities, those patterns of resemblances and differences, the detection of which gives rise to and supports those counterfactual judgments. It is a further question whether this account can be developed so as to accommodate my earlier suggestion that the direction of causation is linked with the contrast between fixity and nonfixity, and that an effect is fixed only by way of its cause. Leaving this aside, the account so far given may be enough to throw some light on the causal relations between mental and physical features and on the suggestion that mental features may be causally redundant.

If we apply our conceptual analysis here, the suggestion that the mental features are epiphenomenal amounts to this: if the connection between the neurophysiological basis and the mental features had been missing, but things had been otherwise as unchanged as possible, that basis would have been as it is but the mental features would not have been there. Similarly, the suggestion that these features are causally idle or redundant amounts to this: if the connection between the neurophysiological basis and the mental features had been missing, but things had been otherwise as unchanged as possible, then although the mental features would have been lacking, the actions to which we ordinarily take those mental features to be causally contributing would still have occurred. (Of course, if we take these mental features to be constitutive elements in those actions, to be contributing to them logically, we cannot say that *those actions* would still have occurred: the suggestion must then be that something just like those actions except for the absence of these mental features would still have occurred; it does not matter whether we should call this an action or not.) It is a confirmation of our analysis that this is just what we would ordinarily take these suggestions to imply.

But, then, what if the connection between the neurophysiological basis and the mental features could not have been missing? On this supposition, neither of the above-stated possibilities could arise. If the connection between two items could not have been lacking, then on our analysis there can be no direction of conditionality between them, and neither can be causally prior to the other. (Also, as I suggested earlier, the mental features and their basis may be strictly contemporaneous, so that neither is temporally prior to the other.) Nor will it make sense to say that the mental features are idle: the actions could not have occurred without them. Two items neither of which could have occurred without the other do not compete for a causal role: even if one is a sufficient as well as a necessary cause of some outcome, the other will be a necessary and sufficient cause of it too.

However, this suggestion that the connection *could not* have been lacking, that neither item *could* have occurred without the other, needs to be made more precise. Let us distinguish the derived biological laws that govern the behavior of various living things, but which themselves depend partly on structures developed by evolution, from basic physico-chemical laws that constitute the framework within which evolution takes place.[3] The suggestion that matters for our purposes is that our "neither item could have occurred without the other" should be a consequence of those basic laws, not conditional upon any particular evolved structure. For this suggestion would at once solve one part of our original problem. "If consciousness evolved through natural selection, it must have contributed causally to the survival of the species in which it was developing." If mental features had been causally idle, how could they have been naturally selected? The reply is that if these features were linked to their neurophysiological basis by laws of the framework within which evolution occurred, and this basis gave rise to actions that were useful for survival, these features would automatically be selected along with their basis: evolution simply could not have developed the basis without the consciousness.

But this seems to solve only one part of the problem, leaving another part unsolved. Would what I have offered validate our ordinary conviction that mental features play a real part in bringing actions about? Or is it somehow cheating? Have I really left the mental features idle and redundant after all, and merely blocked the simplest way of formulating that redundancy? Would the present suggestion make consciousness merely an unavoidable accompaniment of something causally operative and useful, but not causally operative and useful itself?

However, it is not easy to pin down any sense in which the mental features would, on this account, be idle. Perhaps it is, as I have said, that the continuity of causation would lie on the physical side. Some continuous processes would connect the neurophysiological basis, rather than the mental features, with the movements that determine or constitute an action. Before that, other continuous processes would connect whatever the causally relevant antecedents were with this basis rather than with the mental features. Putting these two together, we have a picture in which continuous causal lines go through the basis but by-pass consciousness. But this picture does not really justify the inference that consciousness is idle or redundant if, given only the fundamental laws of the natural world, that particular basis could not have occurred without it.

Moreover, there are other connections that link antecedents and consequents more particularly with the mental side. Suppose that I visually perceive, fairly accurately, some three-dimensional scene. This achievement will be partly the result of very complicated learned methods of processing sensory input, but these methods are by now built into me and work automatically. No doubt the neurophysiological states and occurrences that are the basis of my now seeing things roughly as they are must somehow represent the way these things are: the scene must be somehow neurally encoded. But the content of my visual experience represents the things as they are far more directly: how the things look *resembles* how they are much more than does their neural encoding. And this resemblance is invariant through widely different sensory inputs: I keep on seeing the scene as it is from different positions and under different lighting conditions. The inbuilt methods of processing sensory input have been selected and reinforced primarily by their success in achieving this. Much the same holds also on the output side: in innumerable ordinary successful performances there is, in an obvious sense, a resemblance between what I intend to do and what I actually achieve, and this resemblance is invariant through changes in the conditions and the details of such performances. Economical and explanatorily simple accounts of both perception and intentional action turn upon these resemblances, and could not be replaced by purely physical accounts without loss of this simplicity. This is one reason among others why talk about experiences and intentions is most unlikely ever to be replaced by any physicalist substitutes. The possible substitutes would be not only unfamiliar to us but also more complex and so less explanatory. Donald Davidson is, I think, wrong in saying that there cannot be psycho-physical laws, but what is true is that there will be only complex, not simple, psycho-physical laws, and therefore that the physical accounts to which psychical accounts will be correlated by those laws will be far less simple and straightforward. This applies not only to accounts of single processes of perception and action, but also to any evolutionary account of how our powers of perception and action have come into existence. The utility or survival value of seeing things roughly as they are and of being able to bring about states of affairs that we desire is more obvious, and more open to general description, than the value of their purely physical bases. The most economical general causal accounts will often be ones that use not-simply-replaceable mentalistic terms. This can be set against the admitted fact that the related causal continuities in each individual sequence of events will lie on the physical side.

However, the main point is that the members of a pair of causally inseparable items cannot compete with one another for a causal role. Whatever one item causes, its inseparable companion causes too, despite the fact that the items in question may enter into different relations of continuity and resemblance. While in general we can, and in formulating explanatory causal statements we do, discriminate between the features or aspects of a concrete event, picking out some rather than others as causally relevant to some outcome, we cannot do this with the members of a causally inseparable cluster of features. To this extent and in this special sort of case we cannot improve upon a concrete event as a cause.

I have not, of course, shown that mental features and their neurophysiological bases are in fact causally inseparable in the required strong sense.[4] I merely offer it as a suggestion that is made plausible just by the fact that it could solve the otherwise very puzzling problem set out at the beginning of this paper. I offer it particularly to those who feel the force of the arguments for the mind-brain identity theory, but who are (rightly) skeptical of the assertion that mental features are identical with physical ones, who find a property-identity thesis (as opposed to a thing-identity or concrete-event-identity thesis) untenable or even incomprehensible. Perhaps what is or should really be meant is not strictly the identity of mental and neurophysiological features, but rather their causal inseparability in a strong sense, related to the fundamental laws of working of the natural world.

Notes

1. Especially in Chapter 7 of *The Cement of the Universe* (Oxford, 1974).

2. David H. Sanford, "The Direction of Causation and the Direction of Conditionship," *Journal of Philosophy*, 73 (1976):193-207.

3. The former would have been different if evaluation had happened to get off to a different start, or if conditions had been different along the road, and if there are highly evolved life forms in other planets somewhere, the derived biological laws that govern their behavior may well be different from those that hold on earth. But the basic laws, whatever they are, will be the same everywhere, and would still have been the same here even if evolution had taken some quite different turn.

4. It is, indeed, likely that the relation is a bit more complicated, that while there could not be just this basis without this mental feature, it is only that there could not be this mental feature without *some* member of a disjunction of alternative physical bases. But this complication is irrelevant to the present problem.

Causality, Identity, and Supervenience
in the Mind-Body Problem

JAEGWON KIM

I

It has seemed obvious to many philosophers that certain bodily events cause mental events and that certain mental events in turn cause bodily events. Nothing is more obvious than the observation that our desires and beliefs cause our actions, and that pains cause groans and winces. It is part of our common-sense knowledge that dehydration causes the sensation of thirst or that pains are caused by tissue damages. In fact, that total denial of psychophysical causal relations has been thought to have the consequence that we never perform actions and that we never perceive anything.[1] For it has been argued that the concept of an action is the concept of some bodily motion caused by desire and belief, and that it is part of the concept of perceiving an object that the object perceived is a causal factor in the production of an appropriate perceptual experience. The fact of psychophysical causal relations has been thought to constitute part of the data that must be explained, or at least explained away, by any satisfactory theory of mind. Few philosophers have called this datum itself into question.

The problem of giving an account of how psychophysical causation is possible, however, has not been an easy one. Not only has this problem played a pivotal role in shaping doctrines concerning the mind-body problem, but also it has often been the rock on which many mind-body theories have foundered. Initially, the Cartesians faced the puzzle of how a nonspatial, immaterial soul could exert an influence upon inert matter. Their problem was made even more perplexing by the theory of dynamics some of them accepted, namely the doctrine that motion of matter can be initiated or altered only by a direct and contiguous impact of another bit of matter. Descartes tried to make things easier for the soul by having it influence motions of very fine and light "animal spirits" rather than have it directly move heavy lumps of matter such as muscles and limbs. But it should be obvious that this is no real help; however light and volatile animal spirits may be, the ques-

31

tion remains how an immaterial soul lacking in spatial dimension and mass, something that could not properly be said to be anywhere in physical space, can initiate or control the motion of material particles with mass and inertia. It is interesting to note that a very recent account of psychoneural interaction given by Sir John C. Eccles[2] bears a striking resemblance to this Cartesian strategy. According to Eccles, an immaterial act of volition needs to cause only a single neutron to fire in order to initiate the fairly massive neural discharge needed for the movement of a limb. The activation of this single "trigger neuron" could initiate, Eccles reasons, the activation of a massive group of neurons which are "poised" for action. How much easier it is for the soul to bring about the discharge of a single neuron than, say, that of five thousand. Easier it may be, but more intelligible it is not. To someone who demands an account of the conceivability of psychoneural causation, the soul's acting on a single neuron is conceptually as unintelligible as its acting on five thousand. For the difficulty is essentially that any psychoneural causal action appears to involve a form of psychokinesis, and what is being demanded, rightly or wrongly, is an explanation of what goes on at this psychoneural interface.

I am not sure that this demand for a psychophysical causal mechanism is justified, but it is clear that as long as we stay within the kind of dualistic framework defended by Descartes there is no visible way to satisfy it. Demands for causal mechanism must come to an end at some point, and the psychoneural interface may be as good a point as any as a stopping place. Ultimately, how or why a fundamental physical event causes another physical event may be as much of a mystery as how or why raw feels and perceptual images emerge from the electrochemical activities going on within the gray matter in our skulls.

II

Recent concerns with psychophysical causation do not stem from the Cartesian problem of devising a psychoneural causal mechanism, but rather from considerations concerning certain general requirements of the causal relation and the question whether psychophysical causation, within a dualistic framework, can meet these requirements. One such consideration, forcefully advanced by Donald Davidson,[3] derives from the Humean requirement that causal relations must instantiate exceptionless, deterministic laws. In view of this nomic condition on causal relations it would seem that psychophysical causal relations must instantiate psychophysical laws, laws connecting types of psychological events with types of physical events. Somewhat crudely speaking, if this pain causes me to wince, or this pinprick causes a pain sensation, then there must be laws connecting pains and winces, and pinpricks and pains, perhaps with the addition of appropriate standing conditions. According to Davidson, however, there are no psychophysical laws, and, given the nature of mental and physical concepts, there cannot be any. The system of mental concepts and the system of physical concepts are "nomologically incommensurable" (this is not Davidson's expression) with each other, and we can no more expect laws connecting mental terms with physical ones than laws connecting "emeralds" with "grue." In brief, therefore, Davidson's problem is *how psychophysical causation is possible in the absence of psychophysical laws.*

Davidson's own solution to this problem is to embrace the physicalist thesis that mental events are after all physical events, presumably neural events in the brain, and that, as a result, psychophysical causation turns out to be nothing but physical-physical causation subsumed under purely physical laws. This argument for the identification of the mental with the neural is novel; however, viewed in the broad context of providing an account of psychophysical causation, Davidson's solution is an instance of the classic physicalist solution to this problem. Psychophysical causation is no problem because psychophysical causation is really physical-physical causation. It is just that in case of a psychophysical causal relation, one term of the causal relation is describable in mentalistic concepts; but it is under its physical description that its causal role is properly authenticated.

Obviously, the crucial premise in Davidson's argument for the identity thesis is what Davidson calls "the anomalism of the mental," namely the thesis that there are no psychophysical laws. In fact, as Davidson recognizes, he needs a stronger premise to the effect that there are no psychological laws at all, whether psychophysical or purely psychological. For if there are purely psychological laws connecting types of psychological events, then Davidson would need further arguments to rule out the possibility that a given cause-effect pair in a psychophysical causal relation may be subsumed under such a law, the physical event in this pair receiving a psychological description. Davidson's arguments for the impossibility of psychophysical laws are intriguing but difficult to interpret, and I do not propose to discuss them here.[4] But we need to say a few things about the question of psychophysical laws itself.

According to Davidson, a mental event, say, pain, that enters into a causal relation, must receive a physical description in order to be subsumed by a physical law, physical laws being the only kind of laws that there are. But how are we to decide whether any given physical description of this pain is a *correct* description? When we speak of a micro-description of some macro-process such as thermal expansion of metals, it surely makes sense to speak of *correct* or *incorrect, adequate* or *inadequate,* micro-descriptions of the phenomena. Presumably, a description in terms of such things as increase in molecular energy and its effects on molecular bondings, etc., would be more nearly correct than a description in terms of, say, flow of caloric fluids. Now, when we speak of physical descriptions of mental events, we presumably have in mind some neurophysiological descriptions of certain central processes specific to types of mental states. Thus, pains might receive a description in terms of the excitation of certain "nociceptive neurons" in the cortex and higher brain stem; and a tingling sensation may receive a description in terms of the excitation pattern of a group of neurons in the sensory-motor cortex, and so on. *It is difficult to see how such neurophysiological descriptions can be chosen apart from our discovery of psychoneural correlations between phenomenal mental events, such as pains and tinglings, on the one hand, and certain underlying neural processes on the other.* Moreover, it is difficult to see why such correlations should fail to be "lawlike" in any relevant and appropriate sense of this expression. For they seem to be just the sort of empirical correlations that are subject to confirmation by observation of favorable instances, and that can support counterfactuals.

Thus, it appears that Davidson's solution to his problem of psychophysical causation undercuts one of the very assumptions needed to generate the problem, namely the assumption of the impossibility of psychophysical laws. In fact, I find Davidson's blanket denial of the possibility of psychological laws a bit fantastic. Davidson's arguments for mental anomalism are geared specifically to *intentional mental attitudes,* such as beliefs, desires, hopes, and regrets, and appear to ignore altogether those mental events often called "phenomenal" or "phenomenological," namely raw feels, visual images, and the like. It seems to me that it is an important working assumption of those engaged in neurophysiological and neuropsychological research that there are lawlike correlations between sensory events and neural processes, and that the uncovering of these correlations is an extremely important goal of their research. Indeed, it is difficult to think of some aspects of the research done by, say, Wilder Penfield and his associates, as anything but an attempt to map neural processes with sensory responses.[5] It will be tedious to go over even a sample of the passages one can easily collect in the recent literature in neuropsychology to illustrate this point, but let me cite just one passage in which the assumption is clearly made that some neural process or mechanism must underlie an observed sensory process:

> A lost limb may be replaced by a phantom limb, often with pain to which the patient exhibits exaggerated emotional reactions. Similarly exaggerated painful emotional reactions occur following a lesion of primary sensory pathways in the thalamus, the well-known *thalamic syndrome.* Loss of normal sensation from the hand due to a lesion of its nerve supply may be replaced by a hand which is excruciatingly painful to the slightest touch, *causalgic pain.* When of long standing, this condition is particularly resistant to surgical treatment. Section of the nerves supplying the painful hand may not bring relief. *Such observations suggest that central brain mechanisms upon which conscious sensory experience depends must have the capability of being activated independently of the information arriving over normal sensory input channels* [emphasis added]. Electrophysiological studies have abundantly confirmed this conclusion by the recording of 'spontaneous' neuronal discharge in many cells of all sensory pathways, including the retinae, providing they have not been silenced with anesthesia. . . . Certainly many central neurons, even in specific sensory systems, show much continuous activity in the absence of deliberate stimulation, and many respond to a stimulus by an arrest or inhibition of their discharge. Such evidence demands a re-evaluation of the nature of the dependency of the brain upon activation from incoming sensory impulses for perceptual awareness.[6]

III

Davidson's version of the problem of psychophysical causation can be dissipated if, as we have argued, there are psychophysical laws after all. But it turns out

that there is little solace to be gained from the existence of such laws. Far from resolving the problem of psychophysical causation, the existence of psychophysical
correlation laws can be seen to generate the problem of psychophysical causation in
a new form.

Let M be a mental event (type), and let P be its neural correlate. This means,
of course, that M occurs to an organism at a time just in case the organism instantiates P at the same time. Thus, M and P are "simultaneous nomic equivalents"[7] of
each other. Assume further that M is a cause of a physical event P^* (this is the posited psychophysical causal relation), and in accordance with the Humean conception
of causation, we further assume that there is a law linking M with P^*. It follows
that, in virtue of the nomic equivalence between M and P, a law exists that links P
and P^*; namely, there is a law to the effect that P-events are regularly followed by
P^*-events. This is a simple consequence of our assumptions. Now we can see three
related puzzles arise.

The problem of pre-emption. Given that M and P are nomic equivalents and
given that there is a law linking P with P^*, as well as one linking M with P^*, P appears to have at least as strong a claim as M to be the cause of P^*. As an example,
suppose that pain has a nomic equivalent in neural processes, say, the activation of
nociceptive neurons in the cortex and higher brain stem. The original assumption of
psychoneural causation might be that pains cause withdrawals of the affected limb.
Now, given that pain occurs if and only if nociceptive neurons fire, what reason is
there for *not* saying that it is the latter event, the activation of these neurons, that
caused the limbs to withdraw? In fact, the temptation to say this would become irresistible if, as is likely, a reasonably complete causal chain can be discovered that
leads from this neural event to the contraction of appropriate muscles responsible
for the limb movement. Suppose further that there is no separate causal chain of
events leading from the pain to the limb movement — that is, no causal path from
the pain to the limb motion that does not coincide with the causal chain from the
excitation of nociceptive neurons to the limb motion. It seems likely that there is
no *independent* causal path available by which the pain can reach the bodily effect.
If this is the case, as indeed is likely, then we will say not only that the neural event
is the cause of the limb motion, but also that the causal status of the pain is in
danger of being pre-empted by its neural correlate. It would seem that under these
circumstances pain's claim to be a cause of the bodily movement must depend on
its relationship to the excitation of these neurons, and that the independent causal
status of pains is substantially diminished. If, of course, pain can be regarded as the
cause of its neural correlate, it could retain its full-fledged causal role; however, the
relation of a psychological event with its neural correlate is not happily regarded as
one of cause and effect. The two events are absolutely simultaneous,[8] and, moreover, there is as much reason to regard the neural correlate to be the cause of pain
as there is for regarding the pain as the cause of its neural correlate.

The problem of spurious overdetermination. Some philosophers, like Goldman
and Horgan,[9] maintain that both pain and neuronal excitation are *each individually*
a sufficient cause of the limb movement, in virtue of the two laws, one connecting

M with P^* and the other P and P^*, and under a simple Humean conception of causation each would count as a sufficient cause of the occurrence of P^*. This solution is called "dual causation": pain and neuronal excitation are *dual causes* of the limb movement. As its advocates are well aware, an immediate difficulty this approach faces is this: if pain and neuronal excitation are each a sufficient cause of the movement of the limb, then why is not this a case of causal *overdetermination?* Standardly, an event is causally overdetermined if there are two distinct events each of which is a sufficient cause of it, and the present case seems to fit this description. It seems to be plainly wrong, however, to think of cases like this as cases of overdetermination. The motion of the limb is not overdetermined by pain *and* the neural event underlying the pain.

The problem of spurious partial cause. If pain and the excitation of nociceptive neurons always co-occur as a matter of law, a crucial experiment in which one of them, but not the other, is made to occur is not nomologically possible. There can be no simple and direct experimental evidence to show that either pain or the firing of nociceptive neurons alone is a sufficient cause of the limb movement. If this is the case, how do we rule out the hypothesis, which seems plainly absurd, that pain and excitation of these neurons *jointly* form a single sufficient set of causal factors of the limb movement, neither being a sufficient cause by itself? Thus, given that M and P are simultaneous nomic equivalents, we need an explanation of why it is wrong to think of them as only necessary causes of the motion of the limb, rather than individually sufficient causes of it.

The three problems we have just enumerated are mutually related and find expression in the writings of various philosophers. For example, Norman Malcolm[10] is one philosopher who is worried that if a complete and comprehensive neurophysiological system of explanation is possible for all our bodily motions, then this would preempt the causal and explanatory efficacy of our common-sense psychological explanation of bodily motions in terms of beliefs, desires, intentions, reasons, and so on.

Much was made by the initial advocates of the Identity Theory, such as Herbert Feigl and J. J. C. Smart, of the so-called problem of "nomological danglers."[11] Briefly, the problem was supposed to be that unless psychoneural identities are accepted, psychoneural correlations will forever remain unexplained and unexplainable danglers. The problems we have formulated can be called, collectively, "the problem of causal danglers." If a mental event M has a simultaneous physiological equivalent, it becomes a dangling cause, dangling from its physical correlate, and its causal role is threatened. Given what we know of the essentially discontinuous nature of our mental life, there is an irresistible push toward accepting the physical correlate as the *real substantive cause* of whatever the mental event is initially thought to cause. The causal potency of the mental is in need of vindication.

IV

The problems we have formulated can be generalized in two significant ways: first, it can be shown that these difficulties have nothing intrinsically to do with the psychophysical problem but rather are general problems arising also for cases involving only physical properties and events. Second, it can be seen that these problems arise even if we waive the existence of a pervasive system of psychophysical biconditional laws, or in the case of particular types of mental events, we waive the existence of simultaneous nomic equivalents.

Consider the identity "water = H_2O." Here we are identifying the stuff water with an aggregate of H_2O molecules, and such an identity is thought to be essential in the reductive explanation of the gross, macro-properties of water in terms of its micro-structures. But what would be wrong with saying, not that water *is* H_2O, but rather that water and H_2O are always co-present, that as a matter of law, wherever and whenever there is water, at that precise place and time there is H_2O, and that these two are distinct substances? This would be absurd, but why is it? It is evident that refusal to identify water with H_2O will give rise to some strange questions: if this cupful of water has the mass of one kilogram, how much of this mass should be attributed to the water and how much to the H_2O molecules that are in the cup? If the entire content of the cup is one kilogram, surely not both the water and the H_2O could each be one kilogram. Water is wet; is H_2O also wet? Water dissolves lumps of sugar; does H_2O also have this power? It is clear that all of these questions are either dissipated or given trivial answers once we identify water with H_2O; there is here one substance, not two occupying the same volume of space and time.

But when *properties* and *events* rather than *stuff* are considered, the situation seems somewhat different: the temptation to identify macro-properties of water, such as its transparency and thermal behavior, with its micro-molecular properties is not, at first blush, as compelling. Take the temperature of a given body of water, and its micro-counterpart, the mean kinetic energy of the H_2O molecules comprising the body of water. Are these one property, or two related but distinct properties? Is the state or event of this water's temperature being such-and-such the same event or state as the water's mean molecular kinetic energy being such-and-such? Answers to these questions are less obvious because considerations that are so compelling in the case of water-H_2O identification do not seem to apply here. An exact spatio-temporal coincidence of events does not imply identity of these events: two distinct events can occupy the same spatio-temporal volume (consider a falling body whose temperature is rising at the same time: the fall and the rise in temperature are two distinct events occurring in the same place at the same time). Nor do events and states have such properties as mass, transparency, ductility, freezing point, etc.

However, there *is* one kind of consideration applying to events and states, or properties, which seems to incline us in favor of identifying macro-properties with their micro-counterparts. It concerns the causal powers of events and properties, and this is no surprise since one primary function of events, states, and properties is to serve as terms of causal relations, that is, as causes and effects. Consider again this body of water having such-and-such temperature and its having such-and-such mean molecular kinetic energy. A lump of wax is dropped into the boiling water and it melts. What is the cause of the melting of the wax? We would ordinarily say, of course, that the water's high temperature is the cause of the melting. But what of the causal role of the water's high mean molecular kinetic energy? It is easily seen that the three problems we formulated with regard to psychophysical causation emerge here as well. To begin with, the high mean molecular energy threatens to pre-empt the causal role of the temperature, especially if a detailed causal story can be told of how the violent motion of H_2O molecules leads to the melting of the wax. Second, the dualistic position that refuses to identify temperature with average molecular kinetic energy faces the problem of spurious overdetermination: how can we avoid saying that the melting of the wax is overdetermined by two distinct causes, the high temperature of the water and its high mean molecular kinetic energy? Third, if temperature is distinct from mean kinetic energy of molecules, how do we know that the high temperature and high mean kinetic energy of molecules do not *together* form a sufficient cause of the wax melting, each being only a necessary but not a sufficient cause of it?

Just as in the case of substance or stuff identity the problem of dividing and apportioning various properties (such as mass) is a powerful reason to adopt identity rather than mere lawlike correlation, so in the case of event and property identity the problem of dividing and properly apportioning causal roles may be one irresistible argument for identifying macro-states and properties with their micro-counterparts. In any case, it is clear that the three puzzles we formulated earlier for psychophysical causation emerge as *general* problems where two properties or states of an object or structure are nomologically coextensive, as in the case of macro-properties and their micro-correlates. The problem, in brief, is that of apportioning causal powers between the two nomically coextensive properties or events.

As noted above, however, it is possible to generalize these problems a step further. Again, let us begin with a psychological case. Take the mental event we might characterize as "thinking of Vienna."[12] Many of us have thought of Vienna at various times, and now that I have mentioned it I daresay many of us are engaging in this mental activity at this moment. When I think of Vienna I may think of the famous composers associated with that city; at other times I may have a vivid image of bombed out city blocks; when you think of Vienna, you may be recollecting a particularly pleasant hotel you stayed in last summer, and so forth. What I am trying to point out is that there seems to be no uniform *mental content* to the event-type "thinking of Vienna," and that, perhaps because of this, *it is highly unlikely that some uniform neural state will correlate, in a one-to-one fashion, with the occurrence of this psychological event.* It just is not the sort of psychological event for which anyone will look for a neural correlate. The same point can be made with a large number of what intuitively would pass as types of mental events, especially those having to do with thinking, believing, wanting, hoping, etc., mental acts which take objects or propositions as their grammatical objects. Take, for example, remembering. For one thing we do not expect that there will be any subjectively perceived difference between one who truly remembers and one who only seems to remember but does not; the two persons may have identical internal representations, and both believe that these are representations of some past events which they witnessed. But it is possible that only one of them was an actual witness of the event, and it is this person who remembers. Clearly it would be absurd to look for a "simultaneous nomic equivalent" in neural processes of remembering, say, your first day in the kindergarten. Or take wanting: if two persons both want to spend the summer on Cape Cod, is there any reason to expect that they will exemplify some identical neural process? Is there some uniform neural process that occurs to all and only those who want to spend the summer on the Cape? A similar point could be made with regard to beliefs, and a host of other mental events and states that enter into our common-sense everyday psychological explanations of our actions and inactions. We may call these mental events "nomologically incommensurable" with respect to neural states and processes.

This sort of nomological incommensurability with respect to microphysical processes is nothing unique to mental processes. It seems to me that most of the properties that we ordinarily attribute to middle-sized things and events around us are nomologically incommensurable with micro-properties and structures. We do not expect to discover some uniform microphysical state underlying, say, tables, rocks, trees, automobile accidents, collapsing bridges, bendings, breakings, meltings, and so forth. Some tables are large, some small; some made of wood, some plastic, some steel, some marble; some are square and tall, some round and low.

The problem is how we find a proper causal role for these nomologically incommensurable properties. We often take a desire-belief complex as an explanation of an action (action in this context being taken as "bodily movement," such as the flexing of a finger). If there is a neural correlate of a given belief-desire complex, then at the least some causal role could be assigned to it (although we have seen earlier that the existence of such a neural correlate generates its own puzzles); it could ride, piggyback, on its neural correlate which is the crucial link in the physical chain of events leading to the flexing motion of the finger. But if there is no neural correlate for the belief-desire complex, how would we trace a causal chain from it to the bodily motion? Notice that in the absence of neural correlates for beliefs and desires, the identity solution is not even available as an alternative: it is normally supposed that the identity of the mental with the physical requires, as a necessary condition, a pervasive type-to-type correspondence between the mental and the neural.

It seems, therefore, that we are caught in a dilemma: if psychological events have neural correlates, then their causal roles are threatened by these neural processes; and if they do not, they cannot claim, or so it seems, any causal role at all, to begin with. In either case the causal and explanatory potency of psychological events vis-à-vis bodily events is in doubt.

V

It is by now clear that the identity solution is extremely appealing — in fact, all but compelling — as a response to these problems. If we could say that pain is identical with its neural correlate, there would be no problem of accounting for the causal role of pain independently of that of the correlated neural process. For pain and the neural correlate would be one and the same; they share their causal properties as well as other properties. Similarly, the identification of temperature with mean molecular kinetic energy, water-solubility of sugar with its molecular structure, thermal and electrical conductivity of metals with their microstructure permitting electron-flow, heat with molecular motion, etc., will neatly solve the problems of pre-emption, spurious overdetermination, and spurious partial cause. Appealing though the identity solution may be, I want to explore an alternative solution in the balance of this paper. There are two reasons for this. First, in the psychophysical case, there are some weighty arguments against identification. Among them are the essentialist arguments deriving from Descartes and refined recently by Kripke, and the argument from the phenomenal properties of certain psychological events.[13] It is not my aim here to argue against psychophysical identification; my aim is simply to explore and develop an alternative solution in case we choose, for whatever reason, not to go for the identity solution. Second, we have seen reason to think that a large number of psychological events lack neural correlates, and if this is the case, a type-to-type psychoneural identification would have to be ruled out. Some philosophers have talked of the possibility of token-to-token psychoneural identity in the absence of type-to-type psychophysical correlations;[14] however, it has not been made clear how this is possible — it is not clear what could be a workable criterion of such an identity. In fact, it is not obvious that a precise sense can be attached to this notion of token-to-token identity of events (except such unhelpful suggestions as that events are the same just in case they have all properties in common, or that events are the same if they have the same causes and same effects). The alternative to the identity solution that I shall develop could, in fact, be viewed as giving a useful sense to this idea of token-to-token identity of events.

Let us return to microphysically incommensurable properties, such as being a table and automobile accidents. There may be no uniform microphysical structure that is had by all and only tables in this world, and there almost certainly is no uniform micro-process underlying all and only automobile accidents. And yet we seem to share the conviction that all that happens in this world is fixed once what happens at the micro-level is completely fixed, and that if God were to create a world, all he needs to do is to create the basic particles, their configurations, and the laws that are to govern the behavior of these basic entities.[15] He need not *also* create tables and trees and refrigerators; once the micro-world is fixed, the rest will take care of itself. In other words, we seem to have the belief that these microphysically incommensurable properties and events are nonetheless microphysically determinate in the following sense: *if two organisms are microphysically indistinguishable from each other, then they will share the same psychological life; and if two physical objects are microphysically indistinguishable from each other, then they will share the same macro-properties.* Even if, as the so-called functional-state theory of mind alleges, pain can be multiply realized in diverse physical structures so that it is highly unlikely, from an empirical standpoint, that some unique physicochemical state correlates with pain, still if a person feels pain, then any other person who is in the same neural state will also experience pain. Even if there is no microphysical state correlating with being a table, any two objects sharing the same microphysical states (the same atoms structured in the same manner) will both be tables or fail to be tables.[16] In this sense these microphysically incommensurable properties are still microphysically determinate. As we shall say, they are "supervenient upon" or "consequential to" microphysical states and properties. Once the microphysical properties are fixed, these macro-properties are also fixed.

The concept of "supervenience" or "consequential property" is one that has been primarily used in value theory. G. E. Moore, R. M. Hare, and others have suggested that, while the property of moral goodness and other evaluative properties are not naturalistically definable, they are "supervenient" upon naturalistic properties; that is to say, two things cannot differ in moral or other evaluative properties unless they also differed in some naturalistic characteristic.[17] In a similar vein, Donald Davidson has recently maintained that although there are no psychophysical laws, and a fortiori no neural correlates for the mental, still the mental is dependent on the physical in the sense that two things cannot differ in a psychological respect unless they differ in some physical respect;[18] that is to say, once the physical properties of a structure are completely fixed, then what, if any, psychological life will emerge in that structure is thereby completely determined.

A formal characterization of supervenience is best carried out in terms of a relationship between two sets of properties.[19] We shall say:

A family of properties M is supervenient upon a family of properties N with respect to a domain D just in case for any two objects in the domain D if they diverge in the family M then necessarily they diverge in the family N; that is to say, for any x and y in D if x and y are indiscernible with respect to the properties in the family N, then necessarily x and y are indiscernible with respect to the properties in M.

(In this definition the sets of properties M and N are assumed to be closed under complementation, conjunction, disjunction, and any other permissible property-forming operations.) This captures the idea of supervenient or consequential property as used in value theory in a straightforward way: according to this definition, the set of evaluative properties will be consequential upon the set of naturalistic or descriptive properties; at least, this is the intended result of those who spoke of ethical properties as supervenient or consequential properties. The exact force of the modal term 'necessarily' used in the definition remains to be specified. Moral theorists like Moore and Hare, I believe, had a very strong sense of 'necessity' here, something like logical or metaphysical necessity; I think they would have said that there is no logically or metaphysically possible world in which two things sharing all factual characteristics could differ in moral or other evaluative properties. In what follows we shall generally treat the modal force of the concept of supervenience as an unspecified parameter, to be fixed to suit the particular occasion of its use. But two interpretations of 'necessity' will be of predominant importance: one is that of logical or metaphysical necessity and the other that of nomological or physical necessity (where 'physical', of course, does not contrast with 'psychological').

Given the supervenience of M on N, what property-to-property correlations obtain between them? Should we expect there to be specific correlations between properties in the two families? If psychological properties supervene on neural properties, does this imply that there are psychoneural correlations? I have shown elsewhere that the answer to this is a qualified but important yes.[20] To summarize these results: it can be shown that for each property P in the supervenient family M which is instantiated in the domain D there exists in the base set N a property Q which is a sufficient condition for it. That is to say, for each instantiated property P in the supervenient set there exists an M-N correlation of the form "$Q \rightarrow P$," where Q is an N-property. It follows, therefore, that if psychological properties supervene on physical properties, then each instantiated psychological property will have a sufficient condition in physical properties: for each such psychological property P, there will be a psychophysical correlation of the form "$Q \rightarrow P$," where Q is a physical property. This correlation affirms that any organism or structure exemplifying the physical property Q will also exemplify the psychological property P. The existence of this general property-to-property correlation is a straightforward logical consequence of the supervenience of the mental upon the physical.

The above consequence is actually somewhat stronger than it appears. If a property P in the supervenient set M is not instantiated, then its complement, not-P, is, and according to the above result, not-P has a sufficient condition C in the base set N. It follows that the property P has a necessary condition in the set N, namely not-C. This follows from the closure of M and N under complementation. Thus, most properties in the supervenient set will have both necessary conditions and sufficient conditions in the base set; whether any will have a condition in the base set that is both necessary and sufficient is another question. (It can be shown that under certain further conditions that indeed is the case; under certain nontrivial conditions each property in the supervenient set can be shown to be *biconditional*-correlated with a property in the base set — that is, each property in the supervening family has a "nomic equivalent" in the base family.[21])

What we have just said about the property-to-property connections between a supervenient family of properties and its supervenience base family becomes clear when we see that the concept of supervenience can be given an equivalent alternative definition as follows:

A family M of properties is *supervenient upon* a family N of properties with respect to a domain D *just in case* necessarily, for each property P in M and each object x in D such that x has P, there exists a property Q in N such that x has Q and any object y in D which has Q also has P.

This definition more directly states that each (instantiated) property in the supervenient set has a sufficient condition in the supervenient base set.

An interesting aspect of this conception of supervenience, which is apparent from our second definition, is this: *two instances of the same property may not have the same supervenience base property.* Consider x's being in pain and y's being in pain. If the psychological supervenes on the neurological, there is some neurological condition C such that x is in C and any other thing which is in C also is in pain. Again, our definition implies that there is some neurological condition C^* such that y is in C^*, and anything in C^* also feels pain. But it is an open question whether C is the same as C^*. In fact, we would expect them to be distinct: the neurological basis of pains in humans is likely to be different from that in, say, reptiles or crustaceans, a point often emphasized by the functional-state theorists. The same goes for, say, tables. Tables supervene on basic physical properties in the sense that, for any table, there is a set of basic physical properties (dimensions, rigidity, etc.) such that the given table has them and anything else that has them is also a table. It is clear that different tables are going to have different supervenience base properties.

I have used the expression 'supervenience base property' without a formal explanation, but its intuitive meaning should be obvious. Suppose that being a good man supervenes on various character and personality traits and dispositions, such as being generous, being kind, being wise, truthful, courageous, sympathetic, and so on. Now suppose that St. Francis is a good man in virtue of being generous, sympathetic, and honest; then these three properties would be the *supervenience base of St. Francis's being a good man.* Notice that if Socrates is a good man in virtue of, say, being wise, courageous, and truthful, then these properties would be the *supervenience base* of Socrates' being a good man. So, although here we have one property, being a good man, its particular instances could have different supervenience bases. More generally, we may define the concept of supervenience base as follows:

> Let M supervene on N, and let P be any property in M such that an object x has P. Then a subset B of N is a *supervenience base property* ("supervenience base," for short) of the event x's having P just in case B is a minimal set such that x has the properties in B and anything else having these properties has P.

The condition of *minimality* is imposed for obvious reasons, namely to eliminate irrelevant properties from supervenience bases; for if minimality is not included, any superset of a supervenience base of a given event will also be a supervenience base for it. Two things should be noted: first, an event, x's having P, may have more than one supervenience base (namely, there can be supervenient overdetermination), and second, as we just saw, x's having P and y's having P, where x is not the same thing as y, may have, and are likely to have, different supervenience bases.

Let us further note that if every property P in the family of properties M has a nomological equivalent in the family N, that is, there is a biconditional correlation (with a suitable modal force) relating each property in M with some property in N, then M is supervenient upon N. Thus, the existence of a comprehensive set of psychophysical *biconditional laws* would entail the supervenience of the psychological upon the physical. Theory reduction is standardly thought to be based on such biconditionals, and therefore psychophysical reducibility entails the supervenience of the psychological on the physical. The interest of the concept of supervenience lies chiefly in that it can be thought of as a natural generalization of these concepts, reducibility and determination of one family of properties by another via biconditional nomic equivalents. It gives us a broader conception of determination of one family of properties by another where there is no simple reducibility via a pervasive system of biconditional correlations. And I believe the concept of supervenience as we have developed it here gives a precise expression to what seems to be a very intuitive idea underlying such beliefs as that the micro-processes determine macro-phenomena, that the physical determines the mental, and that the factual and the descriptive determine the evaluative.

VI

Our approach to the problem of psychophysical causation is based on the idea that the causal role of an event, especially that of a nomologically incommensurable event, can be explained via the causal role of the event on which it supervenes. What was the cause of St. Francis's being a good man? If the supervenience base of his being a good man is his being generous, sympathetic, and truthful, then whatever caused St. Francis to have these properties is the cause of his being a good man. His being a good man is the causal result of those genetic and environmental conditions that are causally responsible for his acquiring these virtues. Similarly, the causal effects of his being a good man, e.g., his helping of the poor and the sick, are the causal effects of his being generous, sympathetic, and honest. There is a sense in which his being a good man *consists in, amounts to,* and *is nothing over and beyond* his being generous, sympathetic, and truthful. The idea of a supervenience base of an event gives a precise meaning to these expressions often used in a reductive context. On the other hand, Socrates' being a good man, being supervenient upon a different base, say being wise and courageous, may have causes and effects quite dissimilar from those of St. Francis's being a good man. It is not just that being a good man, in conjunction with dissimilar conditions, leads to different effects; it is, rather, that being a good man represents, or consists in, different properties in different instances, and even when combined with similar conditions, can lead to different causal consequences. This, of course, does not mean that they cannot share some of the causal consequences; they undoubtedly do, and in fact their supervenience bases may have a significant overlap. In any case, I think the concept of supervenience base gives us one precise sense in which we can speak of "token identities" for events and states. St. Francis's being a good man is "token-identical" with his being generous, sympathetic, and honest, and Socrates' being a good man is "token-identical" with his being wise and courageous. This in spite of the failure of the type-identity between being a good man and being wise and courageous, or between being a good man and being generous, sympathetic, and honest. I do not believe that talk of "token-identity" is necessarily helpful; generally speaking, talk of "kinds" of identity is often misleading, and it is best, I believe, to speak of supervenience bases rather than token-identity. We shall consider below the question whether a concrete event should indeed be identified *tout court* with its supervenience base.

I find a similar approach plausible and illuminating in the case of micro-macro examples. The macro-property of water-solubility may be exemplified in diverse molecular structures, there being no single uniform molecular structure possessed by all and only water-soluble substances. Certain gases may be water-soluble in virtue of their molecular structure M, and certain solids may be water-soluble in virtue of having a different molecular structure M^*. Thus M will be the supervenience base of these gases' solubility in water, and M^* will be that of these solids' solubility in water, and they will ground the causal role of the solubility of these substances in the sense that a detailed description of the causal process whereby they dissolve in water will make essential reference to their respective molecular structures M or M^*.

The relationship between a property or an event and its supervenience base itself is not happily considered as a causal relation, although it is an important variety of what may broadly be termed a "determinative relation," and there is no causal path from the supervenient event to an effect that is independent of the causal path from the supervenience base to that effect. It is because of this second fact that the supervenient event is not a cause comparable in status to its supervenience base; in effect, it has no causal status apart from its supervenience on a base event that has a more direct causal role.

Let us now turn to the problem of psychophysical causation. Suppose that an occurrence of pain causes a limb withdrawal. Within the framework thus far developed this situation will be represented in the following way: this particular pain has a supervenience base, say, the excitation of certain neural fibers, although, as the functionalists argue, there may be no biconditional law correlating pains and this sort of neural base. (Thus, the notion of supervenience base corresponds roughly to the notion of "physical realization" often used by the functionalists). The limb withdrawal, too, is supervenient upon certain specific bodily motions. At the level of generality at which psychological theory is formulated, the notion of a limb itself is not a purely physicochemical, or even anatomical, notion; just as tables and chairs supervene on physicochemical structures, limbs similarly supervene on anatomical-structural states (think of the limbs of different actual and possible biological species, perhaps even mechanical structures to which psychological theory is applicable). What counts as a *withdrawal* of a limb, again, is not definable in terms of mere physical motion; it is a "functionally characterized" concept which may find diverse "physical realizations" in different organisms. Our thesis is that in any given concrete instance in which a limb withdrawal takes place, there is a supervenience base characterizable at the more basic level of anatomy and physiology, and that there is a causal path from the supervenience base of the particular instance of pain to this supervenience base of this particular instance of limb withdrawal. It is also part of our account that the causal role of the pain vis-à-vis the limb withdrawal is explained in terms of this more basic underlying causal chain between the two physical or physiological states upon which they respectively supervene.

Schematically, the situation can be represented as follows: let P and Q have as their supervenience bases P* and Q* respectively. *Ex hypothesi*, P causes Q. This is explained by the following items: P is supervenient on P^*, P^* causes Q^* in accordance with the standard nomological and other requirements of causation, and Q is supervenient on Q^*. The causal relation between P and Q, the two supervenient events, holds by courtesy of the underlying causal relation between P^* and Q^*, their respective supervenience bases.

Let us now see how the three problems of psychophysical causation are resolved or dissipated under our account.

The problem of pre-emption. There is a sense in which the causal role of the supervenience base P^* is more direct and more important, for there is no independent causal path from the supervenient event P to the effect Q or Q^*. Thus, in this sense, the causal role of P is in part pre-empted. However, our account gives a precise picture of how the pre-emption occurs, and explains its nature and extent. The account does not deprive the supervening event of a causal role; it explains its causal role via its relationship to a more fundamental causal process.

The problem of spurious overdetermination. Fundamental to the idea of causal overdetermination is the idea of *two separate causal paths* leading to the overdetermined effect. I do not believe that any sort of "counterfactual dependency" between the two paths will destroy the fact of overdetermination. That is, even if there are causal and other connections between the two causal chains so that if one had not occurred the other would not have, there would still be causal overdetermination as long as there are two distinct causal paths leading to the effect. According to our account, there is only one causal path, from P^* to Q^*; there is no causal path starting from P and terminating at Q that does not contain the path from P^* to Q^* as an integral and essential segment. So there is no overdetermination according to the proposed account.

The problem of spurious partial cause. Here the problem was this. If P has a simultaneous nomic equivalent Q, then for any event R normally considered as an effect of P, or of Q, on what basis can we rule out the hypothesis that P and Q jointly make up a sufficient cause of R, each of them being only a necessary factor in this sufficient set. It seems wrong to say that, for example, pain and its neural correlate jointly make up a single sufficient cause of the groan. Now, according to the account developed here, the pain is only a supervenient cause of the groan, and its causal role is dependent on that of its neural correlate which has a direct causal role with respect to the groan. Thus, the pain is not fully comparable to its neural correlate with regard to the causal role vis-à-vis the groan; in an important sense the pain has no independent causal power, and therefore the question of spurious partial cause does not arise. Both the pain and the groan are determined by the brain activity that forms the supervenience base of the pain: the relation of this brain activity to the pain is that of supervenient determination, and the relation of the brain activity to the groan is that of causation.

Before closing I shall consider two possible objections to our account. First, it may be said if an event supervenes on another, then according to the proposed account their causal roles coincide completely, and given this there is no reasonable motivation to distinguish between the two events. This consideration could be based on the so-called causal criterion of event identity favored by some philosophers:[22] events are the same which have the same causes and same effects. Thus, it might be said, the account proposed here does not differ from the identity solution in a substantive manner.

My reply to this is as follows. There are some reasons for saying that the supervenience relation of the sort we have in mind must be distinguished from that of identity. In the mind-body case there are some persuasive arguments to show that mental (especially phenomenal) properties must be distinguished from physical or neurological properties. A detailed discussion of this controversial issue, however, lies beyond the scope of the present paper. Second, on my view of the nature of events and their identity condition, elaborated elsewhere,[23] events are the same which share the same "constitutive object," the same "constitutive property," and the same "constitutive time." More simply, the event of x's having property P at time t is the same event as y's having property Q at t' just in case $x = y$, $P = Q$, and $t = t'$. Thus, event identity implies identity of the properties involved. Now if some psychological events lack "simultaneous nomic equivalents" in neural processes, the identity solution to the mind-body problem is not available. Absence of such biconditional psychophysical laws, of course, is perfectly compatible with the supervenience of psychological properties and events on the neural properties and processes. Finally, should we decide to go for the identity solution, our account gives us a criterion of how particular psychophysical identities are to be formulated and confirmed. A given concrete psychological event would, under the identity approach, be identified with its neurological supervenience base; as we noted, the account gives a sense to the so-called token identity between the psychological and the neural.

The second point I would like to consider is the following possible objection: the account we have developed relegates the mental to the status of epiphenomena, for they do not have causal powers that are independent of the causal powers of their supervenience base. Their causal status is not unlike that classically assigned to "mere epiphenomena," events that are caused by others but that have no causal powers of their own, events that dangle from the causal network of full-fledged events and processes. So the proposed account is nothing but a form of epiphenomenalism.

My response is that if this be epiphenomenalism let us make the most of it. It seems to me that unless we give up the guiding idea that in some important sense the mental is dependent on the physical, Cartesian dualism must be ruled out. In fact, if there is something like supervenience of the mental on the physical in the sense explicated in this paper, Cartesian dualism cannot be entertained as a possible solution. I have not specifically argued against the identity solution. But if we believe there are problems with the identity approach, then it seems to me that the sort of account we have given, which we might call "supervenient dualism," is the most plausible one. To be sure, it bears a family resemblance with epiphenomenalism, but I believe that is not to the discredit of the theory. For macro-phenomena in general, I believe, are supervenient on micro-processes, and their causal roles must

48   JAEGWON KIM

be explicated in terms of the fundamental micro-causal processes. Equally important is the fact that our account does not deprive the mental of its causal powers;
it holds only that their causal powers are dependent on the causal powers of underlying physical processes.[24]

Notes

1. Norman Malcolm makes this point in "The Conceivability of Mechanism," *Philosophical Review* 77 (1968):45-72.

2. See, for example, *The Understanding of the Brain* (New York, 1973).

3. In "Mental Events" in Lawrence Foster and J. W. Swanson (eds.), *Experience and Theory* (Amherst, Mass., 1970).

4. But see G. William Lycan's detailed and informative discussion of Davidson's arguments, in "Functionalism and Psychological Laws," forthcoming. See also Lycan's "On the Possibility of Psychological Laws," forthcoming.

5. See, for example, Wilder Penfield and Theodore Rasmussen, *The Cerebral Cortex of Man* (New York, 1957).

6. H. H. Jasper, "Brain Mechanism and States of Consciousness" in *Brain and Conscious Experience,* ed. John C. Eccles (New York, 1966), pp. 260-61.

7. This term is borrowed from Alvin I. Goldman, "The Compatibility of Mechanism and Purpose," *Philosophical Review* 78 (1969):468-82.

8. This is mentioned by Goldman to make a similar point. Whether there can be genuine simultaneous causal relations, however, is a point of some controversy.

9. Goldman, "The Compatibility of Mechanism"; Terence Horgan, "Reduction, Causation, and the Mind-Body Problem" (unpublished). Horgan is concerned in this paper with much the same problem as our problem of "pre-emption"; however, he formulates the problem exclusively under the assumption of complete reducibility of psychological theory to physical theory. As will become clearer, I do not. See also Horgan's "Supervenient Bridge Laws" (forthcoming).

10. Malcolm, "The Conceivability of Mechanism," Keith Campbell, too, is concerned with this problem in his *Body and Mind* (New York, 1970), pp. 51-52. He uses it as an argument to reject classic interactionist dualism.

11. H. Feigl, *The Mental and the Physical* (Minneapolis, 1967). J. J. C. Smart, "Sensations and Brain Processes," *Philosophical Review* 68 (1959):141-56.

12. I discussed this and similar examples in "Phenomenal Properties, Psycho-physical Laws, and the Identity Theory," *The Monist* 56 (1972):177-92.

13. Saul Kripke, "Naming and Necessity" in *Semantics of Natural Language,* eds. Donald Davidson and Gilbert Harman (Dordrecht, 1972). Kim, "Phenomenal Properties, Psycho-physical Laws, and the Identity Theory."

14. Donald Davidson, "Mental Events"; Jerry Fodor, *The Language of Thought* (New York, 1975); Thomas Nagel, "Physicalism," *Philosophical Review* 74 (1965): 339-56. On the possibility or impossibility of type-to-type psychophysical correspondence, see also Charles Taylor, "Mind-Body Identity, a Side Issue?", *Philosophical Review* 76 (1967):201-13; Bruce Goldberg, "The Correspondence Hypothesis" 77 (1968):438-54; William C. Wimsatt, "Reductionism, Levels of Organization, and the Mind-Body Problem" in *Consciousness and the Brain*, eds. G. G. Globus, G. Maxwell, and I. Savodnik (New York, 1976).

15. This corresponds to what Horgan calls "the supervenience principle" in his "The Supervenience of the Mental" presented at the annual meetings of the American Philosophical Association, Eastern Division, 1976. See also his "Supervenient Bridge Laws" and Stephen P. Stich, "Autonomous Psychology and the Belief-Desire Thesis," forthcoming.

16. The *concept* of being a table contains, arguably, a mental component having to do with purposes and functions, in which case another example could be used. This, however, does not mean that being a table does not supervene on microphysical states; all that needs to be done is

CAUSALITY, IDENTITY, AND SUPERVENIENCE   49

to choose a wider supervenience base, assuming, of course, that the mental, as a whole, supervenes on the physical. As some philosophers have pointed out to me (David Sanford, John Perry, and others), similar points can be made about certain psychological examples, such as thinking of Vienna. Whether a person who is in a certain *current* psychological state is thinking of Vienna is likely to depend on the person's *past* associations with that city. All this means, of course, is that thinking of Vienna does not depend on a person's *current* physiological state; we need to take a wider (temporally stretched) supervenience base.

17. Moore, *Philosophical Studies* (London, 1922); Hare, *The Language of Morals* (London, 1952).

18. Davidson, "Mental Events."

19. The formal details of "supervenience" are worked out in somewhat greater detail in my "Supervenience and Nomological Incommensurables," *American Philosophical Quarterly* 15 (1978):149-56.

20. "Supervenience and Nomological Incommensurables."

21. *Ibid.* Because of the additional assumptions needed and the complexity of these biconditionals, whether or not these correlations are "lawlike" could be debated.

22. For example, Davidson in "The Individuation of Events" in *Essays in Honor of Carl G. Hempel,* ed. Nicholas Rescher (Dordrecht, 1969).

23. See, for example, "Events as Property Exemplifications" in *Action Theory,* eds. Myles Brand and Douglas Walton (Dordrecht, 1976).

24. My research was supported by the National Science Foundation. I have benefited from discussions with Peter Achinstein, Terence Horgan, John Perry, David Sanford, Dale Gottlieb, and George Wilson.

Cheap Materialism

GEORGE WILSON

1

Many, if not most, formulations of the theory that sensations are identical with neural processes (IT) have operated within a rather surprising ontological framework. The following well-known passage from Smart adumbrates the assumptions that define the framework in question.

> I am not arguing that the after-image is a brain-process, but that the experience of having an after-image is a brain-process. It is the *experience* which is reported in the introspective report. Similarly, if it is objected that the after-image is yellowy-orange, my reply is that it is the experience of seeing yellowy-orange that is being described, and this experience is not a yellowy-orange something. So to say that a brain-process cannot be yellowy-orange is not to say that a brain-process cannot in fact be the experience of having a yellowy-orange after-image. There is, in a sense, no such thing as an after-image or sense-datum, though there is such a thing as the experience of having an image,. . .[1]

This passage is, no doubt, gnomic, but three leading contentions emerge.

A) There exist experiences (experiencings, havings) of sensations. These are conceived of as *events* or *processes* that persons and other sentient organisms undergo.

B) Sensations, *qua* objects of experience, do not (in some sense) exist.

Finally, the "proper" formulation of IT is given by

IT$_1$) It is the experiences of sensations that are identical with neural processes. Even before Smart made them, these claims were suggested in Place's original paper[2], and they underlie many later defenses of IT. For instance, they have been adopted by both Nagel and Kim.

Instead of identifying thoughts, sensations, afterimages, and so forth with brain processes, I propose to identify a person's having the sensation with his body's being in a physical state or undergoing a physical process. Notice that both terms of this identity are of the same logical type, namely (to put it in neutral terminology) a subject's possessing a certain attribute. The subjects are the person and his body (not his brain), and the attributes are psychological conditions, happenings, and so forth, and physical ones. The psychological term of the identity must be the person's having a pain in his shin rather than the pain itself, because although it is undeniable that pains exist and people have them, it is also clear that this describes a condition of one entity, the person, rather than a relation between two entities, a person and a pain. For pains to exist is for people to have them. This seems to me perfectly obvious, despite the innocent suggestions of our language to the contrary.[3]

Sensations as mental objects, such as after-images, sense data, and pains, are eliminated, but unlike Rorty we retain sensations as mental events . . .
. . .a person's having a pain at t is of course not throbbing; and that of course is the whole point of this approach. . . . The event we have is a person's having a throbbing pain (it may be useful to express this event as "a person's having-a-throbbing-pain" to emphasize the fact that on the present approach "throbbing pain" is not a nominal term). It is this event, a person's having a throbbing pain, that is to be identified with a brain event. Similarly, there is no object, a visual image, that has the property of being dim; rather, the event which the identity theory is anxious to identify with a brain event is a person's sensing a dim visual image at a time, where sensing a dim visual image is the mental property the person exemplifies at that time.[4]

In light of these and a host of similar passages by other writers on the subject,[5] each of A), B) and IT$_1$) deserves to be reckoned as a standard component of the contemporary identity theory.

This "standard" position, as B) and IT$_1$) suggest, holds that the "naive" version of IT

IT$_2$) Sensations are identical with neural processes.

is to be rejected. In the passage quoted above, Smart is pointing out that IT$_1$) is immune from the so-called phenomenal properties objection. Kim goes so far as to speak of this putative fact as constituting "the whole point" of this formulation of IT. In its most familiar form, this objection contends that sensations could not be neural processes because there are phenomenal property predicates, for example, 'appears red', 'feels painful', 'looks dim', etc., which are true of sensations but could not be true of any neural process. In a variant form, it would be argued that phenomenal properties are *essential* properties of the sensations that they qualify while these same properties could be, at best, only contingent properties of a neural process.[6] Presumably, however, these properties, if properties of anything, are properties of the sensations and not properties of experiencings of sensations. For this reason, Smart and others maintain that such objections are irrelevant to IT$_1$).

Despite the fact that the ontological framework of A), B), and IT_1) is so commonly invoked, as a whole it has received very little serious critical attention. Theses A) and B), particularly, are asserted with little or no defense. To evaluate these last two tenets of the standard framework adequately would be a complex and difficult task. The usual statement of these proposals—and *my* statements of A) and B) exemplify this—are, in many important ways, obscure. Moreover, a reasonably full evaluation of clarified versions would require consideration of a wide range of conceptual and/or theoretical issues. Quine has shown us that there is generally no short *a priori* way of deciding comprehensive ontological claims. Nevertheless, I will argue, in the following section, that there is a *prima facie* case in favor of A) and a *prima facie* case against B). These results, of course, disrupt the standard ontological framework of IT and raise the question of the prospects of IT_1) within the altered scheme. In the third and fourth sections of the paper, I will try to show that even if we repudiated B) and even if some version of the phenomenal properties objection forced us to reject the "naive" IT_2), it still would not follow that IT_1) is incorrect. In short, we could have a kind of mixed position which endorses a dualism of sensations but holds that experiences of sensations are simply neural processes. This package, I will maintain, is in no way incoherent, and, in fact, has various attractions as a type of theory in the area. In the final section, I will briefly consider the question of whether this mixed position could be, in any sense, a variety of materialism. I conclude that it may provide the foundations for all of the materialism we either need or deserve. Therefore, I call it "Cheap Materialism."

II

Thesis A), the proposal that experiences of sensations exist, is crucial to IT_1) in that its truth is presupposed if IT_1) is to be nonvacuous. Surprisingly, I know of no argument in favor of A) presented in the literature. It is possible to suspect that the standard identity theorist, having eliminated sensations by way of B), requires A) to provide IT with a subject matter. Nevertheless, a more charitable view is available.

Intuitively, it seems that if I have experienced a sensation at a certain time, then it thereby follows that there is something which I experienced at that time—namely, a sensation. Of course, the standard identity theorist seems to deny this apparent tautology, but we will return to that issue in a moment. In any case, it seems equally and in the same way true that if I have experienced a sensation at a time, then it thereby follows that something has *happened to me* at that time. But now if we ask what it was that happened to me, the natural answer, the grammatically felicitous answer, is not that it was the sensation experienced but the having or the experiencing of the sensations that happened then. I suspect that the case for A) is based largely on taking these last intuitions seriously and literally.

The considerations involved can be spelled out more meticulously.[7] From the statement, for example,

1) A experienced an after-image at the Savoy Ballroom in the presence of 500 people.

it follows that

2) Something happened to A at the Savoy Ballroom in the presence of 500 people.

2) apparently contains an initial existential quantifier which presumably ranges over events. Thus, the simplest and most straightforward rendering of its logical form would be

2′) ($\exists$e) (e happened to A & e happened at the Savoy Ballroom & e happened in the presence of 500 people).

But if 2) is to be parsed as 2′), we will want to know what event it is that makes them true. As suggested above, it does not seem quite right to suppose that it was the after-image which A experienced that happened to him. It is not the after-image itself which happened in the Savoy Ballroom in the presence of 500 people. A visually experienced the after-image or he "saw" the after-image, but the after-image did not happen to him. What happened to A, what took place in the ballroom, was the having of the after-image. To this extent, at least, an act-object analysis of sensation-experiences seems correct. We speak as though there were both sensations and experiencings of sensations and as if the two classes were mutually exclusive. We seem to distinguish between, for example, *the experience, pain,* meaning by this just the pain experienced, and *the experience of pain,* meaning by this the having or experiencing of that pain.

If all of this is correct, then 1) should exemplify the form

1′) ($\exists$e) (e is an experiencing of an after-image & e happened to A & e happened at the Savoy Ballroom & etc.)

This provides an easy account of why 1) entails 2), but, at the same time, it commits us to experiences or experiencings of sensations as proposed in A).

This putative distinction betwen sensations and experiences of sensations may easily be slighted if there is indeed an act-object or event-object ambiguity in the term 'experience'. The tendency to overlook such a distinction would be reinforced by the fact that the having of a sensation and the sensation itself can both be said to "occur" and they both necessarily occur at and during the same time. However, we have to be careful that the sense of "occur" is the same in both instances. Notice how the same issue arises in a totally different case.

Suppose that a patch of colored light is projected (or an ink mark appears) on a certain surface for 5 seconds. We can say both that

The patch of light occurs (appears, is exhibited) for 5 seconds.

and that

The projection (projecting) of the patch of light occurs (happens, takes place) for 5 seconds.

Yet surely we have clear grounds for distinguishing between the patch of light projected and the process of projecting that patch of light. Indeed, it is not even clear that we can say of the patch of light that it happens or takes place and of the projection process that it appears or is exhibited. If we are willing to draw such a distinction here, there is no reason why we should find the intuitive distinction between sensations and experiences of sensations to be more mysterious or problematic. Of course, the most that we have in these considerations is reason to think that our ordinary discourse about the having of sensations does commit us to experiences of sensations in something like the way envisaged by thesis A); but in the course of this paper, we will see that there are important theoretical grounds for wishing to respect and maintain this intuitive commitment.

These last remarks suggest a distinction which the standard framework of IT does not accept. That framework requires the existence of experiences, but, in thesis B), seems not to countenance sensations. Smart tells us that sensations, in some important sense, do not exist, but he fails entirely to specify that sense. The quotation from Nagel seems to indicate that the sense in question is the literal sense. If I understand him correctly, the statement

3) Sensations exist

is true only if it is understood as a kind of abbreviation for

4) People experience sensations.

But 3) is false or, more likely, it is ill-formed if it is construed literally as

5) $(\exists x)$ (x is a sensation).

This means, as Nagel affirms, that 4) does not have the form of

6) $(\exists x)$ (x is a person & $(\exists y)$ (y is a sensation & x experiences y),

but rather

7) $(\exists x)$ (x is a person & x experiences - a - sensation),

where the hyphens preclude the existence of additional logical structure. Here again, I know of no argument for this position except for the point that if we were to accept it, the phenomenal properties objection would not arise.

This sort of eliminative view of sensations faces a problem which the standard proponent of IT will find difficult to resolve. Consider

8) A is experiencing a dim, blurred after-image which was yellow but now is orange and is in the center of his visual field . . .

The triple dots are meant to indicate that there is no definite limit to the length to which such a description would be filled out. 8), however, seems to entail such sim-statements as these:

A is experiencing a dim after-image in the center of his visual field;
A is experiencing a blurred, orange after-image;
A is experiencing an after-image;

and so on. How are we to explain the basis of our intuitive recognition of these entailments? The simplest supposition, once more, is that 8) has the form

8') ($\exists$x) (A is experiencing x & x is an after-image & x is dim & x is blurred & etc.),[8]

and that corresponding forms are assigned to each of 8)'s intuitive consequences. The usual theory of first-order consequence validates the relevant logical connections. The difficulty for thesis B) lies in the fact that this treatment will also validate the inference from 8) to

($\exists$x) (x is an after-image).

Yet this is exactly the kind of statement that the eliminative view of sensations will not allow.

The standard identity theorist is here in a very delicate situation. If I am right about the kind of case that can be made in support of A), a defender of this position cannot deny the force and relevance of these considerations *against* B) since the argumentation in both cases seems to involve similar considerations. As far as the purely logical problem goes, the standard theorist might propose to render 8) as

8'') ($\exists$e) (e is an experiencing of an after-image & e happens to A & e is dim & e is blurred & etc.).

This would equally account for the range of entailments in question, but it ought to be unsatisfactory to him for at least two related reasons. First, it is intuitively incorrect since it is not the having of the after-image which appears dim and orange and, second, the standard theorist wants to insist on exactly this point to show that IT_1) is not directly subject to the phenomenal properties objection at all. If he were to try to bypass 8') in favor of 8''), this supposed advantage of IT_1) would be immediately and completely undone.

The only genuine option open to an advocate of B) is to come up with a workable alternative account of the entailments at issue. Such an account would have to share many of the merits of relative simplicity, naturalness, and completeness possessed by the standard first-order account. This means, at a minimum, that such an alternative should have application in other regions of the language, that is, it should be more than just an *ad hoc* device for shoring up B). The difficulties of carrying out this program in a manner coherent with the whole standard framework constitutes a strenuous challenge to any eliminative view of sensations that stops short of denying that people experience sensations.

Nevertheless, it is possible to feel that this is merely delaying doom — that once we have accepted sensations, the "proper" identity thesis IT_1) must fail. The reasoning is roughly as follows. Since sensations *do* exemplify phenomenal properties, they cannot be successfully identified with any physical item, event, or state. But this means that an experience of a sensation *essentially involves* a nonphysical constituent (the sensation). A sensation is *the object of* a sensation–experience in a way in which it cannot sensibly be an *object of* a neural process. Therefore, experiences of sensations cannot be purely physical events or processes either. I suspect that something like these considerations explains the relatively constant conjunction of B) with IT_1). At any rate, Kim explicitly endorses the relevant conclusion.

The important point to notice in the quotation from Smart [the quotation given at the beginning of this paper], however, is this: he denies that there are such things as after-images and sense data. And this seems both sound and inevitable. If the basis of the objection from phenomenal properties is correct, the identity theory cannot tolerate *mental objects* like sense data and pains as legitimate entities in one's world. If they exist and have the phenomenal properties they are assumed to have, the identity theory is false.[9]

It is clear from the context of the article that the identity thesis that Kim refers to is IT_1).

There are two major steps in this reasoning. i) The phenomenal properties objection defeats the "naive" identity thesis IT_2) and ii) if IT_2) is false, then IT_1) is false as well. About the truth of (i) I am unsure and I have nothing new to add on this most debated of all topics connected with IT. The issues that it raises are both complex and obscure. There is, after all, a kind of *prima facie* absurdity in supposing that, for example, the predicate 'appears red', as applied to after-images, applies literally and correctly to any neural process. This apparent absurdity might be explained away if we were to succeed in making philosophical sense of the notion that predicates somehow "signify" the same properties as those signified by certain predicates of neurophysiology. But making sense of this idea involves making sense of the concept of a property in general, the concept of property identity in particular, and the relevant semantical concept of "signification." We still seem to be pretty much in the dark as to whether these projects can be carried out successfully. Also, even if they can, we need to know whether the results would tend to support an identity thesis like IT_2). Here, I believe, the prospects are dubious.

Hilary Putnam[10] has stressed the point that this strategy is in danger of postulating implausibly comprehensive mind-body correlation laws. Presumably, if a property P is identical with a property Q, then P and Q are at least extensionally equivalent. Suppose that ⌜is a ψ⌝ is a predicate of the neurophysiology believed to signify the same property as that signified by some phenomenal properties predicate, for example, 'feels painful'. Since every organism that experiences pain experiences something (the pain) which has this phenomenal property, then the putative property identification entails that an organism experiences pain at a given time if and only if it is undergoing a neural process that exemplifies ψ at that time. Given the enormous neurophysiological diversity among the various actual and physically possible species whose members may experience pain, this commitment to strong species-independent correlation laws seems to be a tenuous matter indeed. The strategy envisaged in the previous paragraph is liable to rest IT on empirical foundations it cannot sustain. It is therefore a matter of considerable interest to see if there is a defense of IT_1) and a corresponding form of materialism that would allow us to look upon this whole issue of the phenomenal properties objection as a matter of relative indifference.

The key to such a possibility lies in evaluating step ii) above—the claim that if $\sim IT_2$) then $\sim IT_1$). In the next two sections, I will try to show that this claim is mistaken. There is no simple connection between these two versions of the identity theory. If this is correct, then we may obtain the surprising but desirable results just described.

<h1 style="text-align:center">III</h1>

In this section, I assume, as a working hypothesis, that a dualistic view of sensations is true. That is, I assume that there are sensations and that some form of the phenomenal properties objection shows them to be nonphysical. I will try to establish quite directly that all of this is compatible with IT_1) by describing one amplified version of IT_1) that explicitly countenances nonphysical sensations. I will argue, as far as possible in a limited space, that this particular amplification is consistent, coherent, and, in a number of respects, theoretically attractive. In this section, I will describe this amplified version of IT_1) in some detail and explain, while clearing away some confusion, the kind of theory it purports to be. In particular, I will indicate the kinds of evidence upon which it does and does not rest. In the following section, I try to show that the view is not just internally coherent while being conceptually unsatisfactory from a broader perspective. Clearly, it is impossible to deal with every possible objection that might be raised, but I do try to show that two general and powerful objections will not work.

The central claim I make is that rejection of IT_2) does not require rejection of IT_1) and the amplified "model" of IT_1) that I describe is presented at some length solely to establish this point. In fact, as we will see later, there are probably alternative "models" of IT_1) which would serve the same purposes. One central advantage of working with a fairly definite conception of the way in which IT_2) might be false and IT_1) true is that it will enable us to see how the notion that this cannot be always involves the importation of some controversial alternative theory of the nature of experiences which it is just the business of IT_1) to oppose. The "intuitions" that may seem to rule out IT_1) simply beg the question in favor of a competing dualistic theory of experiences.

To begin a description of this extended version of IT_1), we review the basic features of a version of classical epiphenomenalism. According to this position, sensations are not identical with physical events, states, etc. Sensations, so conceived, belong to a distinct realm of the mental. Sensations and neural processes are held to be related, in one direction only, by causation. That is, on this view, certain neural processes are causes of sensations but sensations themselves are causally ineffacacious. Sensations are neither causes nor causal factors of neural processes or of the peripheral behavior of sentient organisms. It is especially this last claim which has made classical epiphenomenalism so counterintuitive relative to our common-sense beliefs. Surely we know, for example, that pain causes pain behavior and epiphenomenalism seems to deny this. On the other hand, epiphenomenalism maintains, not only that neural processes cause sensations, but that some neural processes *directly cause* sensations. Given a sensation s, there is a unique neural process n such that n causes s *and* there is no event x such that n causes s *by* causing x which, in turn, causes s. Some neural processes may indirectly cause sensations by causing other neural processes which lead in a causal chain to the occurrence of a sensation. However, at some point, the sensation and a specific neural process are linked together directly in the chain.

So far this position considers only sensations and *their* relations to neural processes, but in the previous section we saw that a case could be made for recognizing experiences of sensations as distinct from the sensations they involve. The question arises as to how classical epiphenomenalism might be embedded within this more generous ontological scheme. The obvious possibility, given present concerns, is to suggest that experiences of sensations are identical with those neural processes that directly cause sensations. In short, we extend the version of epiphenomenalism just described within the broader scheme by incorporating the "proper" identity thesis IT_1).

This kind of quasi-epiphenomenalism stands to lose much of the paradoxical character of its classical counterpart. Distinguishing between sensations and experiences of sensations, it is possible to hold that although the experienced pain or after-image is never a cause of behavior, the experiencing of that pain or after-image may be. In the previous section, it was proposed that what thereby happens to someone experiencing a sensation *is* the experiencing of that sensation, and we can go on to propose that it is *this* happening, this event, which, strictly speaking, has the causal properties we ordinarily ascribe to sensations. In this way, quasi-epiphenomenalism seems not so much to conflict with as to refine upon our common-sense beliefs about sensations and the causation of behavior.

Having ascribed these causal properties to the experiences of sensations, it also becomes possible to broach familiar grounds for identifying these experiences with appropriate neural processes. Most important, we expect to discover neural processes that share these causal properties with what we call "experiencings of sensations." We expect it will turn out that there are neural processes which are produced by the same range of external and internal stimuli that cause, for example, experiences of pain. And these same neural processes should turn out to play the same causal role in eliciting behavior that experiences of pain are thought to play. If these expectations are realized, then the fact that these causal properties are shared provides a strong initial reason for accepting IT_1). Accepting this identification allows us to avoid what otherwise seems a curious and systematic causal overdetermination of sensation-induced behavior. In the context of quasi-epiphenomenalism, IT_1) makes it possible to reconcile the common-sense belief that sensation-experiences cause behavior with the general methodological conviction that all behavior can be explained in purely physical terms. We can also explain our somewhat vague but compelling notion that experiences are, in some sense, "inner" events. These and related grounds would render IT_1) both reasonable and attractive.

As noted before, these considerations are familiar from the literature as the evidential foundation of IT_1). What is more, it seems to me that they represent the kind of characteristic mix of empirical and methodological argument that typically constitute the grounds for theoretical identification in any science. IT_1) is a theoretical hypothesis that deserves to be taken seriously. However, if we are to forestall certain objections to IT_1) as developed in the present context, it is equally important to see that and to see why certain other considerations, common in the recent literature, should *not* be employed in its defense.

Too often the evidential basis for IT_1) that I have outlined has been combined with an analysis of sensation terms where this analysis is meant to fortify the identity thesis. It is claimed that a term of the form ⌜experience of a sensation of type ϕ⌝ is to be analyzed in a certain "topic-neutral" fashion. The most popular analysandum has the form ⌜event of the kind which is characteristically caused by stimuli of type ψ and/or which characteristically causes behavior of type ϕ⌝. If some such proposal were acceptable, then the truth of IT_1) might be partly established as a matter of the *meaning* of these sensation terms. Moreover, in virtue of these topic-neutral paraphrases, there would be a case to be made for the eliminative view of sensations in B). Many others have pointed out that all such paraphrases seem hopelessly implausible and this, I believe, is correct. But there is a deeper reason why it was a mistake from the beginning to tie the theoretical identification to questions of meaning or sense in this way.

A different example illustrates the danger. Imagine a people who are speakers of English and speak, as we do, of "shadows" and "the casting of shadows." We suppose that their scientific beliefs about light phenomena are quite primitive so that they believe that shadows are intangible, dark, gossamer-like entities which are usually enfolded within a physical object. In certain circumstances, they believe, light falling on an object can cause the object to "cast" its shadow—to throw it out quite literally upon an appropriately adjacent surface. Finally, imagine that scientists among these people come to develop a very basic optics in which it is proposed that this old idea of what it is to cast a shadow is wrong. Rather, they announce, the casting of a shadow *is* the interception of light rays by a physical object situated between a light source and a surface illuminated by that source. In this case, it is perfectly clear that there are two distinct matters here. On the one hand, there is the proposed theoretical identification of shadow casting with light interception and this proposal is correct. But a proposal to the effect that this identification is, even partially, an explication of what these people *mean* by the phrase 'casting a shadow' would be completely wrong. The two proposals ought to be kept quite distinct.

Similarly, the quasi-epiphenomenalist extension of IT_1) is not to be construed as asserting that ⌜experience of a sensation of type ϕ⌝ means something like ⌜process of a kind that directly causes sensations of type ϕ⌝. Not only would this suggestion be utterly implausible, but, by bringing in intuitions about meaning, we open the way to those "intuitions" that suggest that $-IT_2$) must lead to $-IT_1$). If we compare a phrase like 'experiences a pain' with phrases like 'experiences a warm fire' and 'experiences a fine wine', we are liable to suppose that, as a matter of meaning, experiencing is, in each case, a kind of *perception*. Of course, having adopted this idea, we may reach the conclusion that experiencing a sensation is a very special kind of perception—a kind of "inner," "direct" perception—but a perception of the sensation nonetheless. Finally, it becomes extremely difficult to resist the idea that this inner act of perception must surely be more than just a process in the nervous system.

Whether 'experiencing' has the same "perceptual" sense in these different instances I neither know nor care. The point is that this question is no more relevant to IT_1) than the same kind of question about the sense of 'cast' in 'cast a shadow' is relevant to the theoretical identification in that case. I remarked in the second section that in distinguishing between sensations and experiences of sensations we were accepting a part of the traditional act-object analysis of experiencing. But the other part of this analysis is the thesis that an experience of a sensation is an act of inner perception of the sensation. Acceptance of the first part does not make acceptance of the second inevitable. It is not necessary to rehearse the familiar difficulties that attend this central component of the "mental eye" picture of the mind. What we have in this conception is simply one theoretical alternative to the quasi-epiphenomenalism sketched in this section. The "inner perception" view of experiences is a rival, strongly dualistic in tendency, to the thesis that experiences are neural processes that directly cause sensations. Our ultimate decision between these and any other theoretical possibilities rests, as usual, on broad issues of empirical fact combined with concerns about overall theoretical utility. Again, there is no short *a priori* road to this decision.

IT_1) can seem threatened by the possible falsity of IT_2) if, as noted before, we are disturbed by the following reflection. If sensations are nonphysical, then experiences of sensations essentially involve a nonphysical item and so cannot be purely physical processes themselves. We are now in a position to diagnose the problem. If there are nonphysical poltergeists that produce unearthly wails in the night, then I suppose that there is a sense in which the poltergeists are "involved," perhaps essentially, in the sounds they make. From this it hardly follows that the sound of a poltergeist is not a physical process identifiable with waves of the usual type in the air. How the poltergeists produce these physical effects is a different question. The concept of an item being "involved" in an event is extremely broad and vague, and there are many ways in which such an involvement can take place. All that is initially clear is that the rival theories in the sensation case provide different accounts of the nature of that involvement here. If we hold an inner perception view of sensation experiences, we will suppose that sensations are involved as the entities perceived, the objects of the acts of perception. On the quasi-epiphenomenalist view of experiencings, sensations are involved as the direct nonphysical effects of these occurrences. It, therefore, seems impossible to construct a non-question-begging argument against IT_1) along these lines. A theory of the way in which sensations are essentially involved in sensation-experiences stands or falls with the theory of the nature of these experiences that incorporates it. What makes the inference from $-IT_2$) to $-IT_1$) so "intuitive" is the temptation to suppose, based on vague impressions of meaning, that experiences of sensations must be conceived of as perceptions of sensations. But this temptation and the impressions of meaning that go with it are red herrings that throw the proper theoretical perspective seriously askew.

The quasi-epiphenomenalism of this section illustrates the possibility of joining IT_1) with a dualistic view of sensations. Having attempted to clarify some points concerning the epistemic status of this theory, we have so far seen no reason for judging it to be either inconsistent or incoherent in some more subtle way. However, we can substantially strengthen this claim by considering two important sources of possible residual discomfort. We turn to these in the next section.

IV

One familiar type of dissatisfaction with any form of epiphenomenalism is expressed in the following passage by Feigl.

> It accepts two fundamentally different sorts of laws—the usual causal laws and laws of psychophysiological correspondence. The physical (causal) laws connect the events in the physical world in the manner of a complex network, while the correspondence laws involve relations of physical events with purely mental "danglers." These correspondence laws are peculiar in that they may be said to postulate "effects" (mental states as dependent variables) which by themselves do not function, or at least do not seem to be needed, as "causes" (independent variables) for any observable behavior.[11]

According to the quasi-epiphenomenalism of the previous section, experiences of sensations would not be "nomological danglers" in Feigl's sense, but sensations would be. They are conceived of as items with a determinate causal ancestry but no causal progeny. The objection that Feigl raises, as I understand it, is not just that nomological danglers are peculiar or queer—that objection is too diffuse to discuss—but that it is strikingly incongruent that only sensations or, at least, that only mental items should dangle in this manner. No doubt the realm of the mental is unique in various ways, but it is suspiciously *ad hoc* and inexplicable that it should be *uniquely* in this realm that we should find entities lacking all causal efficacy.

If this last claim were correct, then it would have some persuasive force against any type of epiphenomenalism. The problem with this objection, however, lies in the fact that it is far from clear that the claim is, in fact, correct. It is, I think, an open question as to whether nomological danglers are restricted to the mental realm or whether an analogue of epiphenomenalism is a *characteristic* conceptual strategy by means of which we accommodate the existence of a range of sensible objects, both private and public, within the scientific picture of the world. There is serious reason to suppose that for example,

rainbows and other optical atmospheric phenomena,
shadows and holograms,

and

certain types of public auditory phenomena like musical overtones

are standardly treated as nomological danglers in the required sense.

The rainbow example illustrates the general case. Physicists describe the underlying physical processes that are said to "produce," "give rise to," or "cause" rainbows, atmospheric halos, coronas, and afterglows.[12] Notice that the quoted terms more or less explicitly relate the physical processes to the optical items as causes to effects. Rainbows, we are told, are produced by the diffraction of light rays passing through collocations of water molecules suspended in the atmosphere. In fact, since no intervening causal process is postulated, we can suppose that the diffraction directly causes the occurrence of the rainbow. The rainbow itself, on the other hand, is not treated as a cause or causal factor of further events.

It might be replied that however scientists themselves tend to describe these matters, we might as well identify the rainbows, halos, etc., with the corresponding physical processes. Nevertheless, the idea that we could maintain such an identification faces a very familiar obstacle. What would we take to be strictly identical with the rainbow? The process of diffraction? The suspended water particles? The diffracted light rays? None of the various possibilities seem satisfactory. One has only to think of the whole range of predicates that a particular rainbow might satisfy. We have, for example,

'having an arch-like shape',
'growing dimmer',
'being colored (in a certain characteristic way)',

and so on. Nothing in the physicists's austere vocabulary is likely to denote an entity of which all such predicates are true. Does the diffraction process have an arch-like shape? Do the suspended water particles contain a band of bright yellow? It is hard to see how such claims could be defended.

I need not claim that no such defense could possibly be given. Obviously, we are concerned here with a close analogue to the phenomenal properties objection. Just as I did not try to decide whether that objection was fatal to IT_2), I will not try to decide whether its analogue here is fatal to any deep theoretical identification of rainbows and similar phenomena. The crucial point is that the problems in both cases seem essentially the same and so the mental and nonmental cases should stand or fall together. *If* the phenomenal properties objection shows sensations to be nonphysical—and this has been a working hypothesis—then rainbows, etc., are not likely to be theoretically reducible to purely physical processes either. Finally, if this is so, then there are public, nonmental entities that will have to count also as "nomological danglers" within our widest conceptual scheme. Indeed, as I suggested before, the usual scientific discussions of such phenomena already present them, in effect, in just these terms. Thus, the charge that epiphenomenalism ascribes to sensations a unique and unprecedented metaphysical status is, at best, a charge "not proven." There is nothing *a priori* absurd about the idea that the fundamental physical processes give rise to special kinds of ephemeral entities that play no further role in the causal history of the world. Once again, it *may* be our *characteristic* way of allowing for certain kinds of purely sensible items to grant that this is so.

These considerations will aid us in evaluating one further objection, an objection directed more specifically at IT_1) within the framework of quasi-epiphenomenalism. We remarked, in the second section, that sensations and experiences of sensations exhibit a special kind of ontological dependence. That is, it seems to be some kind of necessary truth that a sensation s exists at t iff the experience of s is taking place at t.[13] This special ontological dependence becomes the basis of an objection that suggests that the discussion up to this point has overlooked the force of the "essentially" in the intuition we expressed by saying that nonphysical sensations are *essentially involved* in experiences of sensations. The argument may be formulated as follows. We have just granted that

9) It is necessary that if s had not existed at t, then the experience of s would not have occurred at t.

Now, let n be any neural process that we might want to identify with the experience of s. It seems as though n fails to share with the experience of s the complex counterfactual property specified in 9). In other words,

10) It is not necessary that if s had not existed at t, then n would not have occurred at t.

Surely, we think, there are conceivable circumstances in which n would have taken place but in which s would have failed to occur. For instance, it seems as though n might have occurred without s if the nervous system in which n actually has occurred had been removed from the organism in which it is normally embedded and were activated at t in a laboratory set up. Or, n might occur without s in a world in which the psychophysical laws were very different. There might have been a world without sentience in which no neural process in living organisms produced sensations. We might, the argument continues, have had grounds for rejecting 10) if we could claim that sensation s was identical with some physical constituent or intrinsic feature of n. But if a dualistic theory of sensations is assumed, then the possibility of this response has been foreclosed. Therefore, experiences of sensations cannot be neural processes.[14]

Let us, however, examine these intuitions from the point of view of the epiphenomenalist. An exponent of this view should reject 10) as either false or indeterminate in truth value. In the first place, he will want to hold that there is certainly a kind of impossibility about n's taking place, at least in normal conditions, without s. He maintains, after all, that n directly causes s and this thesis will imply two others. He will believe that there is a *type* of neural process ψ and a *type* of sensation ϕ such that n belongs to ψ and s belongs to ϕ and such that there is a law-like connection between occurrences of ψ's *in living organisms* and occurrences of ϕ's in these same organisms. Moreover, this will be a strong law-like connection because he believes that ψ's *directly* cause ϕ's so that there is no possibility of intervening circumstances which abort a "normal" causal chain linking ψ's with ϕ's. Thus, he will have the result that it was *physically* or *nomologically* necessary that if s had not existed in this particular organism at t, then n would not have occurred in that organism at t either.

Nevertheless, it appears that we still have a variety of non-normal circumstances in which n occurs but s does not, and this is all that premise 10) requires. But now the exact nature of the possibilities these circumstances represent ought to be reconsidered. For example, it is possible to allow, in the case of the disembodied neural system, that a neural process exactly like n in its intrinsic features might occur without the existence of s or any other sensation. This can be granted while denying that any such process, occurring in such a way in such a radically different context, could actually be *this* particular neural process n. Take any complex neural process that is taking place within me now. Would any process that might happen in my disembodied nervous system, no matter how much it physically resembled this present event, actually be one and the same as this event now? The same question can be raised about any possible neural process that happens in a possible world with radically different psychophysical laws. To answer these questions, if they can be answered at all, a decision would have to be reached as to how actual and possible particular events are to be individuated. I do not know how that decision is to be reached, but I believe that there is a tentative "intuition" that the answer to the more specific questions should be "No!"

Compare these questions with the question: "Is it possible for this rainbow now occurring to exist if this particular diffraction process had not taken place? I think we are just as puzzled by this question as we are by the one in the sensation-neural process case. But, here again, if we are referring to that rainbow which this diffraction process is now producing, then there is some inclination to answer "No!" The basis of this intuition, in both cases, may be the idea that it is a necessary condition for an event e to be identical with an event e' that, at least, the direct causes and effects of e and e' must be the same.[15]

If this last notion were accepted, then the quasi-epiphenomenalist could deny 10) on the grounds that it is physically impossible, under any conceivable circumstances, for s to exist at t without n's happening at the same time.

My own feeling is that the truth value of 10) is indeterminate in that none of our "intuitions" about identity and difference among concrete events are sufficient to force a clear-cut decision in the relevant problem cases. Even this is enough to undercut the objection with which we began, since it requires that 10) be known to be true.

It may still seem as if there is something to the objection, however, for it is puzzling that, whatever the subtle issues connected with 10), 9) appears to be clearly true even when 'necessity' is understood in a very strong sense. But this apparent clarity dissipates when it is noticed that 9) can be read in two different ways:

9') It is necessary that if s had not existed at t, then nothing would have been the experience of s at t,

and

9'') It is necessary that if s had not existed at t, then that event which is the experience of s would not have happened at all.

However, if we try to interpret 9) as 9'), the would-be objection cannot get started at all. To see this, consider the fact that the statement

i) It is necessary that if the United States had never been founded, then the first president of the United States would never have existed,

is ambiguous between

ii) It is necessary that if the United States had never been founded, then no one would ever have been the first president of the United States,

and

iii) It is necessary that if the United States had never been founded, then that person who was the first president of the United States would never have existed.

Notice that we cannot treat the occurrence of 'the first president of the United States' in ii) as a genuine singular term in referential position. It is false—in any sense of 'necessity'—that it is necessary that if the United States had not been founded, no one would have been George Washington. And yet, this hardly shows that George Washington was not the first president of the United States. ii) says correctly that it is a matter of *analytical* necessity that if the United States had not been founded, then no one would have had the *property* of being a United States president elected before any other. Similarly, 9') tells us that it is *analytically* necessary that if s had not existed at t, then nothing would have had the *property* of being (uniquely) an experience of s at t. But just as we cannot validly substitute for 'the first president of the United States' in ii), concluding that Washington was not the first president, we cannot validly substitute for 'the experience of s at t' in 9'), concluding that n was not that experience. Since the objection under consideration requires the possibility of such substitution, it had better interpret 9) as 9'').

This hardly helps. The truth value of 9'') seems no easier to evaluate than the truth value of 10). It is difficult to see how we can pronounce on 9'') independently of our theory about the nature of sensation-experiences and about the relations between these occurrences and the sensations they involve. Someone who accepts IT_1) will think that 9'') is true if and only if 10) is false no matter how he assigns a truth value to 10). However, even if it were allowed that we know, independently of any such specific theory, that 9'') is true—that that which is the experience of s is *essentially* accompanied by the occurrence of s—then we are simply back where we were before. For we saw, in our discussion of 10), that the quasi-epiphenomenalist may very well grant that it is nomologically essential that n is accompanied by s. The burden shifts back to the proponent of the objection. He must show that there is a kind of necessity—call it "metaphysical necessity"—that is clearly distinct from what the quasi-epiphenomenalist recognizes as nomological or physical necessity and, in terms of which, both 9'') and 10) are known to be true. There may be some way of showing this, but I doubt it.

Cheap Materialism is the conjunction of the following four theses. There are experiences of sensations (A)) and they are identical with neural processes (IT_1)).

There are also sensations ($\sim$B)) and they are nonphysical entities ($\sim$IT$_2$)). What I have been calling "quasi-epiphenomenalism" has been designed to demonstrate that this conjunction is perfectly consistent and suffers from no obvious conceptual incoherence. I am also inclined to believe that there are alternative ways of extending IT$_1$) that would also constitute "models" of Cheap Materialism. On a kind of *double-aspect* version of IT$_1$) certain neural processes are thought to be *experienced as* sensations of various types. Experiences of sensations are identified with those neural processes that are experienced as sensations. "Being experienced as" is treated as a genuine relation holding between neural processes and sensations conceived as genuine existents. This relation plays the same role in such a double-aspect view as direct causation plays in quasi-epiphenomenalism. I will not try to defend the overall coherence of this alternative, but, if it is coherent, then Cheap Materialism need not be tied to all the specific aspects of quasi-epiphenomenalism. In any case, I conclude that the major thesis of this and the preceding section is established. A dualistic theory of sensations does not entail the falsity of the "proper" identity thesis IT$_1$).

V

It might be argued that Cheap Materialism is, in sundry ways, cheap enough, but it may not be so easily agreed that it is materialism at all. How can a position that includes a dualistic theory of sensations constitute a form of materialism?

The answer is likely to be that it is and it is not, and the reason for this unsatisfactory answer lies in the fact that we currently do not know what the doctrine of materialism or physicalism is supposed to be. In the literature it is possible to find at least a half dozen accounts of what materialism is, no pair of which is equivalent and all of which are desperately obscure. It is obviously impossible, in these last few pages, to sort out even a small part of the confusion this situation engenders. What I would like to do is simply this. I will suggest that there are at least two traditions of—two types of—doctrine that have been commonly dubbed "materialism." Given these two traditions, it is probably true that Cheap Materialism is not a materialism according to the first and it probably is a materialism according to the second. The "probably" here is a consequence of the fact that in neither case will we have formulated a completely clear and determinate issue. Nevertheless, even the tentative results should considerably clarify the nature of certain major issues in the area.

One materialist tradition represents that position as being a kind of strong *ontological* hypothesis. We are all familiar with various very loose formulations of such a thesis. We are told that sentient organisms are *nothing more than* very complex purely physical entities or that it is possible to give a *complete description* of sentient organisms in purely physical terms. Perhaps, a slight improvement in the same vein would be

C) Every predicate true of a sentient organism signifies either a physical or a topic-neutral property of that organism.[16]

Whether something like C) is even intelligible is a matter that would require us to decide two enormous issues. First, we would have to deal with those problems with this sort of talk about properties and property identity that I mentioned in the second section. Second, we would have to advance some reasonable criterion of what is to count as a *physical* property. I am happy to sidestep these matters altogether and to admit that if there is a version of C) with a definite sense, then almost certainly Cheap Materialism is not materialism in that sense.

There is also an important kind of methodological doctrine that is standardly associated with materialism. David Lewis presents the idea in this way: "There is some unified body of [physicalistic] scientific theories, of the sort we now accept, which together provide a true and exhaustive account of all physical phenomena (that is, all phenomena describable in physical terms)."[17] Lewis says that this is "a vital part" but not the whole of a "full-blooded" materialism. "Full-blooded" materialism, presumably would be an ontological doctrine like C). Lewis stresses the methodological importance of the quoted hypothesis and his remarks are underscored by the appearance of a similar conception in a basic text on neuropsychology. Charles Butter, a well-known practitioner of the discipline, claims: "A basic working assumption of behavioral science is that the behavior of organisms is like all other material events in that it is determined by physical events and can be predicted when all relevant conditions are known."[18] Butter's name for this view is 'mechanism'. Despite the differences between these passages, they both converge toward the thesis that

D) It is possible to provide a *complete explanation* of the behavior of sentient organisms in purely physical terms.

This at least will serve as a first approximation to the proposal in question. In a moment, we will look at a possible refinement of D).

Whether D) deserves to be called a version of materialism I will not attempt to decide. Certainly, hypotheses of this type are very often spoken of as materialist in conception and, as a central "working assumption" (Butter's phrase) of neuropsychology, it constitutes "a vital part" (Lewis's phrase) of the traditional materialist picture of the world. I am inclined to say that it constitutes *the* vital part of that picture. The main threat of Cartesian dualism to the research program of a systematic neuropsychology is constituted by its assertion that much sentient behavior cannot be completely explained in terms of the types of physical processes and physical principles that have proved successful in other domains. This assertion is a consequence of the Cartesian's view that, for example, sensation-experiences are nonphysical events together with his acceptance of the idea that these experiences play a genuine causal role in eliciting behavior. The working neuropsychologist may be unsure which of these propositions he rejects, but he will definitely refuse to postulate the occurrence of nonphysical processes in the explanations he offers of human and animal behavior. D) is a rough statement of the fundamental conviction that underlies this refusal.

So, is Cheap Materialism compatible with a reasonable version of D)? Let us begin by noting that since this paper has been concerned merely with theories that purport to identify sensation-experiences with neural processes and not with those similar theories concerning the propositional attitudes, it is appropriate and helpful to restrict the present question within the limited domain. That is, we want to consider only those instances of behavior that are a) caused by sensation-experiences and b) not caused by these experiences *via* the intervention of beliefs, desires, intentions, etc. I mean to include here relatively simple, more or less automatic behavior such as wincing, scratching, blinking, and involuntary acts of crying out or drawing away a part of the body. I mean to exclude cases such as the one in which my experiencing pain causes me to go to the doctor but only because I believe that he may be able to alleviate the pain. I will call this loosely characterized class of behavior "S-behavior."

By observing this simplifying restriction, it is possible to restate D), the thesis of methodological materialism, in a somewhat more perspicuous form. Actually, the thesis can be divided into two parts the first of which is

D_1) If e is an item of S-behavior, then every event, process, or state e' that is a cause or causal factor of e is a physical event, process, or state.

D_1) is fairly close to Butter's formulation of mechanism. Probably, however, most philosophers believe that if one event is causally relevant to a second, then there must be some causal law that this pair of events appropriately instantiates. A full and explicit explanation of why the first event occurred in terms of the second cited as a causal factor would include a statement of this law. The passage from Lewis calls attention to the fact that the materialist expects these laws to be laws of a *physical* science. Therefore, the second part of D) becomes

D_2) If e' plays a causal role in producing the S-behavior e, then there is a causal law L, linking e' and e, which is formulatable in purely physical terms.

I will take the conjunction of D_1) and D_2) to define methodological materialism.

Since I complained before about the obscurity of ontological theses like C), I should acknowledge that D_1) and D_2) are far from problem-free. Among other things, we need a criterion of what it is to be a physical event, process, and state, and the concepts of "cause" and "causal factors" are surrounded by well-known difficulties. Nevertheless, D_1) and D_2) seem clear enough to show that Cheap Materialism is compatible with both.

The materialistic heart of Cheap Materialism is its acceptance of IT_1), and this seems sufficient to guarantee the truth of D_1). It is assumed that sensation-experiences are causal factors of S-behavior, and IT_1) tells us that they are simply neural processes. Beyond this, all that is needed for the truth of D_1) is the assumption that every other condition that is causally relevant to S-behavior—for example, the occurrence of receptor stimuli, stimuli-induced processes in the organs, muscles, and nervous system—is a physical condition. But this assumption seems relatively trivial.

The situation connected with D_2) is somewhat more complicated. Although Cheap Materialism is surely consistent with D_2), it does not ensure its truth. The following possibility is left open. It could happen that e' is an experience of some sensation and such that

11) e' is identical with some neural process n,

and

12) e' is causally relevant to an item of S-behavior e,

even though

13) the only laws linking e' with e' are laws that subsume e' under a description of the form $\ulcorner$ is an experience of type ϕ $\urcorner$.

In other words, e' would belong to no physical type ψ such that there is a behavior type ϕ which e exemplifies where the connection between ψ-instances and ϕ-instances is law-like. Since e' is assumed in 11) to be a neural process, there would be physical types to which it belonged but none of these would connect nomically with any behavior type subsuming e. Thus, it is logically possible for Cheap Materialism to be true and D_2) false.

Nevertheless, Cheap Materialism may require that this is no more than a *mere* logical possibility. If we really believed that there was no causal law linking n and e where n is described in physical terms, then this would give us strong reason to believe that

14) n is not causally relevant to e

and hence that 11) is false. It would seem to us that there was a property, that is, being causally relevant to e, which e' and n did not share. The grounds for proposing this particular identity would be absent in the first place. After all, the evidential foundation of IT_1) lies largely in our expectation that for any sensation-experience it is in principle possible to identify independently a neural process that shares its causal properties. For this reason, Cheap Materialism may be more than just consistent with D_2); it may carry a kind of epistemic commitment to its truth.

We are left, I believe, with the following situation confronting us. It is a key task of further research, not only to find acceptable formulations of both ontological and methodological materialism, but also to examine with greater care the kinds of theoretical interest and importance that *do and do not* attach to each. In this last section, I have briefly indicated why the interest and importance of D_1) and D_2) to the research program of neuropsychology seems fairly clear. At the same time, I have voiced tentative skepticism about both the coherence and the importance of a "full-blooded" ontological position. The present argument seems to secure us this much. One is liable to believe that methodological materialism can be defended as a viable position only if *either* we can first defend a form of ontological materialism *or* we can accept some classical form of epiphenomenalism that denies that behavior is caused by experiences of sensations. But this belief is incorrect. A version of

Cheap Materialism such as the quasi-epiphenomenalism of sections III and IV provides a foundation for methodological materialism without either the rabid reductionism of the former or the counterintuitive consequences of the second. Since the classical varieties of epiphenomenalism have never found much favor, ontological and methodological materialism have appeared essentially linked together as part of the general strategy directed against Cartesian dualism. But, if, as I have been suggesting, it is principally methodological materialism that we are most concerned to defend *and* this can be done without deciding whether after-images and bodily sensations are "really" identical with events in the nervous system, then the debates over this and connected issues may continue to rage, but we will have reason to await the results, if any are forthcoming, with less than bated breath. Perhaps, these questions will be leading questions in some discipline of "pure ontology," but, if so, I am inclined to say, so much the worse for pure ontology. Cheapness is not all, but there is no point in continuing to pay a price much greater than our genuine philosophical perplexities exact.[19]

Notes

1. J. J. C. Smart, "Sensations and Brain Processes," *Philosophical Review* 68 (1959):150-51.
2. U. T. Place, "Is Consciousness a Brain Process?", *British Journal of Psychology* 48 (1956): 40-50.
3. Thomas Nagel, "Physicalism," *Philosophical Review* 74 (1965):341-42.
4. Jaegwon Kim, "Phenomenal Properties, Psychophysical Laws, and the Identity Theory," *The Monist* 56 (1972):182-83.
5. To cite just two other well-known sources where this ontological framework is accepted, there is David Armstrong, *A Materialist Theory of Mind* (London, 1968); James Cornman, *Materialism and Sensations* (New Haven, 1971).
6. Although it clearly is not the main argument, this type of consideration seems to be suggested by some of Saul Kripke's remarks in "Naming and Necessity" in *Semantics for Natural Languages,* eds. G. Harman and D. Davidson (Dordrecht, 1972), especially pp. 335-42.
7. Donald Davidson has indicated the relevance of this type of consideration, although with reference to actions, in "The Logical Form of Action Sentences," in *The Logic of Decision and Action,* ed. Nicholas Rescher (Pittsburgh, 1967), pp. 81-95.
8. Of course, if the discussion a few paragraphs back is correct, then 8') actually has the still more articulated form of

($\exists$e) ($\exists$x) (e is an experiencing of x & e happened to A & x is an after-image & x is dim & etc.)

For brevity, I ignore the richer structure here.
9. Kim, "Phenomenal Properties, Psychophysical Laws, and the Identity Theory," p. 182.
10. Hilary Putnam, "Psychological Predicates," in *Art, Mind, and Religion,* eds. W. H. Capitan and D. D. Merrill (Pittsburgh, 1967), pp. 44-55.
11. Herbert Feigl, "Mind-Body, *Not* a Pseudo-Problem," in *Dimensions of the Mind,* ed. Sidney Hook (New York, 1961), p. 37. Also Feigl's remarks on p. 70 of *The "Mental" and the "Physical"* (Minneapolis, 1958) make it clear that his objection is to the presumed uniqueness of nomological danglers in the range of the mental.
12. A good, typical example of the use of "causal" locations in this connection is given in Peter E. Kraght, "Atmospheric Optical Phenomena," in *Van Nostrand's Scientific Encyclopedia,* Fifth Edition, ed. Douglas M. Considine (New York, 1976), pp. 228-30.

13. It is worth noting, in light of earlier examples, that this kind of ontological dependence is not unique to the sensation case. For example, it is necessary that a shadow exists at t iff something is casting that shadow at t.

14. The possibility of this kind of consideration was suggested to me by Kripke's argumentation in "Naming and Necessity," but this does not represent an argument he presents there. He does not consider the type of position now under discussion. However, I believe that *some* of my remarks on the present argument are relevant to *some* of the points he suggests.

15. This condition is, in effect, accepted by others. It is entailed by but does not entail the "criterion" of event identity espoused by Donald Davidson in "The Individuation of Events" in *Essays in Honor of Carl Hempel,* eds. Nicholas Rescher, et. al. (New York, 1970), pp. 178-98, and suggested in Nagel, "Physicalism."

16. For a useful and careful attempt to formulate a version of ontological materialism, see Cornman, *Materialism and Sensations.* I believe that the attempt, for all its merits, fails.

17. David Lewis, "An Argument for the Identity Theory, with Addena," in *Materialism and the Mind-Body Problem,* ed. David M. Rosenthal (Englewood Cliffs, N.J., 1971), p. 169.

18. Charles Butter, *Neuropsychology: The Study of Brain and Behavior* (Belmont, CA, 1968), p. 2.

19. Thanks for helpful advice to David Sachs, Mark Wilson, and a reader for *Midwest Studies in Philosophy.*

Individualism and the Mental

TYLER BURGE

Since Hegel's *Phenomenology of Spirit*, a broad, inarticulate division of emphasis between the individual and his social environment has marked philosophical discussions of mind. On one hand, there is the traditional concern with the individual subject of mental states and events. In the elderly Cartesian tradition, the
spotlight is on what exists or transpires "in" the individual—his secret cogitations,
his innate cognitive structures, his private perceptions and introspections, his grasping of ideas, concepts, or forms. More evidentially oriented movements, such as behaviorism and its liberalized progeny, have highlighted the individual's publicly observable behavior—his input-output relations and the dispositions, states, or events
that mediate them. But both Cartesian and behaviorist viewpoints tend to feature
the individual subject. On the other hand, there is the Hegelian preoccupation with
the role of social institutions in shaping the individual and the content of his
thought. This tradition has dominated the continent since Hegel. But it has found
echoes in English-speaking philosophy during this century in the form of a concentration on language. Much philosophical work on language and mind has been in the
interests of Cartesian or behaviorist viewpoints that I shall term "individualistic."
But many of Wittgenstein's remarks about mental representation point up a social
orientation that is discernible from his flirtations with behaviorism. And more recent work on the theory of reference has provided glimpses of the role of social
cooperation in determining what an individual thinks.

In many respects, of course, these emphases within philosophy—individualistic and social—are compatible. To an extent, they may be regarded simply as different currents in the turbulent stream of ideas that has washed the intellectual
landscape during the last hundred and some odd years. But the role of the social
environment has received considerably less clear-headed philosophical attention
(though perhaps not less philosophical attention) than the role of the states, occurrences, or acts in, on, or by the individual. Philosophical discussions of social factors

have tended to be obscure, evocative, metaphorical, or platitudinous, or to be bent on establishing some large thesis about the course of history and the destiny of man. There remains much room for sharp delineation. I shall offer some considerations that stress social factors in descriptions of an individual's mental phenomena. These considerations call into question individualistic presuppositions of several traditional and modern treatments of mind. I shall conclude with some remarks about mental models.

I. TERMINOLOGICAL MATTERS

Our ordinary mentalistic discourse divides broadly into two sorts of idiom. One typically makes reference to mental states or events in terms of sentential expressions. The other does not. A clear case of the first kind of idiom is 'Alfred thinks that his friends' sofa is ugly'. A clear case of the second sort is 'Alfred is in pain'. Thoughts, beliefs, intentions, and so forth are typically specified in terms of subordinate sentential clauses, that-clauses, which may be judged as true or false. Pains, feels, tickles, and so forth have no special semantical relation to sentences or to truth or falsity. There are intentional idioms that fall in the second category on this characterization, but that share important semantical features with expressions in the first—idioms like 'Al worships Buicks'. But I shall not sort these out here. I shall discuss only the former kind of mentalistic idiom. The extension of the discussion to other intentional idioms will not be difficult.

In an ordinary sense, the noun phrases that embed sentential expressions in mentalistic idioms provide the *content* of the mental state or event. We shall call that-clauses and their grammatical variants "*content clauses.*" Thus the expression 'that sofas are more comfortable than pews' provides the content of Alfred's belief that sofas are more comfortable than pews. My phrase 'provides the content' represents an attempt at remaining neutral, at least for present purposes, among various semantical and metaphysical accounts of precisely how that-clauses function and precisely what, if anything, contents are.

Although the notion of content is, for present purposes, ontologically neutral, I do think of it as holding a place in a systematic *theory* of mentalistic language. The question of when to count contents different, and when the same, is answerable to theoretical restrictions. It is often remarked that in a given context we may ascribe to a person two that-clauses that are only loosely equivalent and count them as attributions of the "same attitude." We may say that Al's intention to climb Mt. McKinley and his intention to climb the highest mountain in the United States are the "same intention." (I intend the terms for the mountain to occur obliquely here. See later discussion.) This sort of point extends even to content clauses with extensionally non-equivalent counterpart notions. For contextually relevant purposes, we might count a thought that the glass contains some water as "the same thought" as a thought that the glass contains some thirst-quenching liquid, particularly if we have no reason to attribute either content as opposed to the other, and distinctions between them are contextually irrelevant. Nevertheless, in both these examples, every systematic theory I know of would want to represent the semantical contribution of the content-clauses in distinguishable ways—as "providing different contents."

One reason for doing so is that the person himself is capable of having different attitudes described by the different content-clauses, even if these differences are irrelevant in a particular context. (Al might have developed the intention to climb the highest mountain before developing the intention to climb Mt. McKinley—regardless of whether he, in fact, did so.) A second reason is that the counterpart components of the that-clauses allude to distinguishable elements in people's cognitive lives. 'Mt. McKinley' and 'the highest mountain in the U.S.' serve, or might serve, to indicate cognitively different notions. This is a vague, informal way of generalizing Frege's point: the thought that Mt. McKinley is the highest mountain in the U.S. is potentially interesting or informative. The thought that Mt. McKinley is Mt. McKinley is not. Thus when we say in a given context that attribution of different contents is attribution of the "same attitude," we use 'same attitude' in a way similar to the way we use 'same car' when we say that people who drive Fords (or green 1970 Ford Mavericks) drive the "same car." For contextual purposes different cars are counted as "amounting to the same."

Although this use of 'content' is theoretical, it is not I think theoretically controversial. In cases where we shall be counting contents different, the cases will be uncontentious: On any systematic theory, differences in the *extension*—the actual denotation, referent, or application—of counterpart expressions in that-clauses will be semantically represented, and will, in our terms, make for differences in content. I shall be avoiding the more controversial, but interesting, questions about the general conditions under which sentences in that-clauses can be expected to provide the same content.

I should also warn of some subsidiary terms. I shall be (and have been) using the term *'notion'* to apply to components or elements of contents. Just as whole that-clauses provide the content of a person's attitude, semantically relevant components of that-clauses will be taken to indicate notions that enter into the attitude (or the attitude's content). This term is supposed to be just as ontologically neutral as its fellow. When I talk of understanding or mastering the notion of contract, I am not relying on any special epistemic or ontological theory, except insofar as the earlier-mentioned theoretical restrictions on the notion of content are inherited by the notion of notion. The expression, *'understanding (mastering) a notion'* is to be construed more or less intuitively. Understanding the notion of contract comes roughly to knowing what a contract is. One can master the notion of contract without mastering the term 'contract'—at the very least if one speaks some language other than English that has a term roughly synonymous with 'contract'. (An analogous point holds for my use of 'mastering a content'.) Talk of notions is roughly similar to talk of concepts in an informal sense. 'Notion' has the advantage of being easier to separate from traditional theoretical commitments.

I speak of *attributing* an attitude, content, or notion, and of *ascribing* a that-clause or other piece of language. Ascriptions are the linguistic analogs of attributions. This use of 'ascribe' is nonstandard, but convenient and easily assimilated.

There are semantical complexities involving the behavior of expressions in content clauses, most of which we can skirt. But some must be touched on. Basic to the subject is the observation that expressions in content clauses are often not inter-substitutable with extensionally equivalent expressions in such a way as to maintain the truth value of the containing sentence. Thus from the facts that water is H_2O and that Bertrand thought that water is not fit to drink, it does not follow that Bertrand thought that H_2O is not fit to drink. When an expression like 'water' functions in a content clause so that it is not freely exchangeable with all extensionally equivalent expressions, we shall say that it has *oblique occurrence*. Roughly speaking, the reason why 'water' and 'H_2O' are not interchangeable in our report of Bertrand's thought is that 'water' plays a role in characterizing a different mental act or state from that which 'H_2O' would play a role in characterizing. In this context at least, thinking that water is not fit to drink is different from thinking that H_2O is not fit to drink.

By contrast, there are non-oblique occurrences of expressions in content clauses. One might say that some water—say, the water in the glass over there—is thought by Bertrand to be impure; or that Bertrand thought that *that* water is impure. And one might intend to make no distinction that would be lost by replacing 'water' with 'H_2O'—or 'that water' with 'that H_2O' or 'that common liquid', or any other expression extensionally equivalent with 'that water'. We might allow these exchanges even though Bertrand had never heard of, say, H_2O. In such purely non-oblique occurrences, 'water' plays *no role* in providing the *content* of Bertrand's thought, *on our use of 'content'*, or (in any narrow sense) in characterizing Bertrand or his mental state. Nor is the water part of Bertrand's thought content. We speak of Bertrand *thinking his content of* the water. At its nonoblique occurrence, the term 'that water' simply isolates, in one of many equally good ways, a portion of wet stuff to which Bertrand or his thought is related or applied. In certain cases, it may also mark a context in which Bertrand's thought is applied. But it is expressions at oblique occurrences within content clauses that primarily do the job of providing the content of mental states or events, and in characterizing the person.

Mentalistic discourse containing obliquely occurring expressions has traditionally been called *intentional discourse*. The historical reasons for this nomenclature are complex and partly confused. But roughly speaking, grammatical contexts involving oblique occurrences have been fixed upon as specially relevant to the representational character (sometimes called "intentionality") of mental states and events. Clearly oblique occurrences in mentalistic discourse have something to do with characterizing a person's epistemic perspective—how things seem to him, or in an informal sense, how they are represented to him. So without endorsing all the commitments of this tradition, I shall take over its terminology.

The crucial point in the preceding discussion is the assumption that obliquely occurring expressions in content clauses are a primary means of identifying a person's intentional mental states or events. A further point is worth remarking here. It is normal to suppose that those content clauses correctly ascribable to a person that are not in general intersubstitutable *salva veritate*—and certainly those that involve extensionally non-equivalent counterpart expressions—identify different mental states or events.

I have cited contextual exceptions to this normal supposition, at least in a manner of speaking. We sometimes count distinctions in content irrelevant for purposes of a given attribution, particularly where our evidence for the precise content of a person or animal's attitude is skimpy. Different contents may contextually identify (what amount to) the "same attitude." I have indicated that even in these contexts, I think it best, strictly speaking, to construe distinct contents as describing different mental states or events that are merely equivalent for the purposes at hand. I believe that this view is widely accepted. But nothing I say will depend on it. For any distinct contents, there will be imaginable contexts of attribution in which, even in the loosest, most informal ways of speaking, those contents would be said to describe different mental states or events. This is virtually a consequence of the theoretical role of contents, discussed earlier. Since our discussion will have an "in principle" character, I shall take these contexts to be the relevant ones. Most of the cases we discuss will involve *extensional* differences between obliquely occurring counterpart expressions in that-clauses. In such cases, it is particularly natural and normal to take different contents as identifying different mental states or events.

II. A THOUGHT EXPERIMENT

IIa. First Case

We now turn to a three-step thought experiment. Suppose first that:

A given person has a large number of attitudes commonly attributed with content clauses containing 'arthritis' in oblique occurrence. For example, he thinks (correctly) that he has had arthritis for years, that his arthritis in his wrists and fingers is more painful than his arthritis in his ankles, that it is better to have arthritis than cancer of the liver, that stiffening joints is a symptom of arthritis, that certain sorts of aches are characteristic of arthritis, that there are various kinds of arthritis, and so forth. In short, he has a wide range of such attitudes. In addition to these unsurprising attitudes, he thinks falsely that he has developed arthritis in the thigh.

Generally competent in English, rational and intelligent, the patient reports to his doctor his fear that his arthritis has now lodged in his thigh. The doctor replies by telling him that this cannot be so, since arthritis is specifically an inflammation of joints. Any dictionary could have told him the same. The patient is surprised, but relinquishes his view and goes on to ask what might be wrong with his thigh.

The second step of the thought experiment consists of a counterfactual supposition. We are to conceive of a situation in which the patient proceeds from birth through the same course of physical events that he actually does, right to and including the time at which he first reports his fear to his doctor. Precisely the same things (non-intentionally described) happen to him. He has the same physiological history, the same diseases, the same internal physical occurrences. He goes through the same motions, engages in the same behavior, has the same sensory intake (physiologically described). His dispositions to respond to stimuli are explained in physical theory as the effects of the same proximate causes. All of this extends to his interaction with linguistic expressions. He says and hears the same words (word forms) at the same times he actually does. He develops the disposition to assent to 'Arthritis can occur in the thigh' and 'I have arthritis in the thigh' as a result of the same physically described proximate causes. Such dispositions might have arisen in a number of ways. But we can suppose that in both actual and counterfactual situations, he acquires the word 'arthritis' from casual conversation or reading, and never hearing anything to prejudice him for or against applying it in the way that he does, he applies the word to an ailment in his thigh (or to ailments in the limbs of others) which seems to produce pains or other symptoms roughly similar to the disease in his hands and ankles. In both actual and counterfactual cases, the disposition is never reinforced or extinguished up until the time when he expresses himself to his doctor. We further imagine that the patient's non-intentional, phenomenal experience is the same. He has the same pains, visual fields, images, and internal verbal rehearsals. The *counterfactuality* in the supposition touches only the patient's social environment. In actual fact, 'arthritis', as used in his community, does not apply to ailments outside joints. Indeed, it fails to do so by a standard, non-technical dictionary definition. But in our imagined case, physicians, lexicographers, and informed laymen apply 'arthritis' not only to arthritis but to various other rheumatoid ailments. The standard use of the term is to be conceived to encompass the patient's actual misuse. We could imagine either that arthritis had not been singled out as a family of diseases, or that some other term besides 'arthritis' were applied, though not commonly by laymen, specifically to arthritis. We may also suppose that this difference and those necessarily associated with it are the only differences between the counterfactual situation and the actual one. (Other people besides the patient will, of course, behave differently.) To summarize the second step:

> The person might have had the same physical history and non-intentional mental phenomena while the word 'arthritis' was conventionally applied, and defined to apply, to various rheumatoid ailments, including the one in the person's thigh, as well as to arthritis.

The final step is an interpretation of the counterfactual case, or an addition to it as so far described. It is reasonable to suppose that:

> In the counterfactual situation, the patient lacks some—probably *all*—of the attitudes commonly attributed with content clauses containing 'arthritis' in oblique occurrence. He lacks the occurrent thoughts or beliefs that he has arthritis in the thigh, that he has had arthritis for years, that stiffening joints and various sorts of aches are symptoms of arthritis, that his father had arthritis, and so on.

We suppose that in the counterfactual case we cannot correctly ascribe any content clause containing an oblique occurrence of the term 'arthritis'. It is hard to see how the patient could have picked up the notion of arthritis. The word 'arthritis' in the counterfactual community does not mean *arthritis*. It does not apply only to inflammations of joints. We suppose that no other word in the patient's repertoire means *arthritis*. 'Arthritis', in the counterfactual situation, differs both in dictionary definition and in extension from 'arthritis' as we use it. Our ascriptions of content clauses to the patient (and ascriptions within his community) would not constitute attributions of the same contents we actually attribute. For counterpart expressions in the content clauses that are actually and counterfactually ascribable are not even extensionally equivalent. However we describe the patient's attitudes in the counterfactual situation, it will not be with a term or phrase extensionally equivalent with 'arthritis'. So the patient's counterfactual attitude contents differ from his actual ones.

The upshot of these reflections is that the patient's mental contents differ while his entire physical and non-intentional mental histories, considered in isolation from their social context, remain the same. (We could have supposed that he dropped dead at the time he first expressed his fear to the doctor.) The differences seem to stem from differences "outside" the patient considered as an isolated physical organism, causal mechanism, or seat of consciousness. The difference in his mental contents is attributable to differences in his social environment. In sum, the patient's internal qualitative experiences, his physiological states and events, his behaviorally described stimuli and responses, his dispositions to behave, and whatever sequences of states (non-intentionally described) mediated his input and output—all these remain constant, while his attitude contents differ, even in the extensions of counterpart notions. As we observed at the outset, such differences are ordinarily taken to spell differences in mental states and events.

IIb. Further Exemplifications

The argument has an extremely wide application. It does not depend, for example, on the kind of word 'arthritis' is. We could have used an artifact term, an ordinary natural kind word, a color adjective, a social role term, a term for a historical style, an abstract noun, an action verb, a physical movement verb, or any of various other sorts of words. I prefer to leave open precisely how far one can generalize the argument. But I think it has a very wide scope. The argument can get under way in any case where it is intuitively possible to attribute a mental state or event whose content involves a notion that the subject incompletely understands. As will become clear, this possibility is the key to the thought experiment. I want to give a more concrete sense of the possibility before going further.

It is useful to reflect on the number and variety of intuitively clear cases in which it is normal to attribute a content that the subject incompletely understands. One need only thumb through a dictionary for an hour or so to develop a sense of the extent to which one's beliefs are infected by incomplete understanding.[1] The phenomenon is rampant in our pluralistic age.

a. Most cases of incomplete understanding that support the thought experiment will be fairly idiosyncratic. There is a reason for this. Common linguistic errors, if entrenched, tend to become common usage. But a generally competent speaker is bound to have numerous words in his repertoire, possibly even common words, that he somewhat misconstrues. Many of these misconstruals will not be such as to deflect ordinary ascriptions of *that*-clauses involving the incompletely mastered term in oblique occurrence. For example, one can imagine a generally competent, rational adult having a large number of attitudes involving the notion of sofa—including beliefs that *those* (some sofas) are sofas, that some sofas are beige, that his neighbors have a new sofa, that he would rather sit in a sofa for an hour than on a church pew. In addition, he might think that sufficiently broad (but single-seat) overstuffed armchairs are sofas. With care, one can develop a thought experiment parallel to the one in section IIa, in which at least some of the person's attitude contents (particularly, in this case, contents of occurrent mental events) differ, while his physical history, dispositions to behavior, and phenomenal experience—non-intentionally and asocially described—remain the same.

b. Although most relevant misconstruals are fairly idiosyncratic, there do seem to be certain types of error which are relatively common—but not so common and uniform as to suggest that the relevant terms take on new sense. Much of our vocabulary is taken over from others who, being specialists, understand our terms better than we do.[2] The use of scientific terms by laymen is a rich source of cases. As the arthritis example illustrates, the thought experiment does not depend on specially technical terms. I shall leave it to the imagination of the reader to spin out further examples of this sort.

c. One need not look to the laymen's acquisitions from science for examples. People used to buying beef brisket in stores or ordering it in restaurants (and conversant with it in a general way) probably often develop mistaken beliefs (or uncertainties) about just what brisket is. For example, one might think that brisket is a cut from the flank or rump, or that it includes not only the lower part of the chest but also the upper part, or that it is specifically a cut of beef and not of, say, pork. No one hesitates to ascribe to such people content-clauses with 'brisket' in oblique occurrence. For example, a person may believe that he is eating brisket under these circumstances (where 'brisket' occurs in oblique position); or he may think that brisket tends to be tougher than loin. Some of these attitudes may be false; many will be true. We can imagine a counterfactual case in which the person's physical history, his dispositions, and his non-intentional mental life, are all the same, but in which 'brisket' is commonly applied in a different way—perhaps in precisely the way the person thinks it applies. For example, it might apply only to beef and to the upper and lower parts of the chest. In such a case, as in the sofa and arthritis cases, it would seem that the person would (or might) lack some or all of the propositional attitudes that are actually attributed with content clauses involving 'brisket' in oblique position.

d. Someone only generally versed in music history, or superficially acquainted with a few drawings of musical instruments, might naturally but mistakenly come to think that clavichords included harpsichords without legs. He may have many other beliefs involving the notion of clavichord, and many of these may be true. Again, with some care, a relevant thought experiment can be generated.

e. A fairly common mistake among lawyers' clients is to think that one cannot have a contract with someone unless there has been a written agreement. The client might be clear in intending 'contract' (in the relevant sense) to apply to agreements, not to pieces of paper. Yet he may take it as part of the meaning of the word, or the essence of law, that a piece of formal writing is a necessary condition for establishing a contract. His only experiences with contracts might have involved formal documents, and he undergeneralizes. It is not terribly important here whether one says that the client misunderstands the term's meaning, or alternatively that the client makes a mistake about the essence of contracts. In either case, he misconceives what a contract is; yet ascriptions involving the term in oblique position are made anyway.

It is worth emphasizing here that I intend the misconception to involve the subject's attaching counterfactual consequences to his mistaken belief about contracts. Let me elaborate this a bit. A common dictionary definition of 'contract' is 'legally binding agreement'. As I am imagining the case, the client does not explicitly define 'contract' to himself in this way (though he might use this phrase in explicating the term). And he is not merely making a mistake about what the law happens to enforce. If asked why unwritten agreements are not contracts, he is likely to say something like, 'They just aren't' or 'It is part of the nature of the law and legal practice that they have no force'. He is not disposed without prodding to answer, 'It would be possible but impractical to give unwritten agreements legal force'. He might concede this. But he would add that such agreements would not be contracts. He regards a document as inseparable from contractual obligation, regardless of whether he takes this to be a matter of meaning or a metaphysical essentialist truth about contracts.

Needless to say, these niceties are philosopher's distinctions. They are not something an ordinary man is likely to have strong opinions about. My point is that the thought experiment is independent of these distinctions. It does not depend on misunderstandings of dictionary meaning. One might say that the client understood the term's dictionary meaning, but misunderstood its essential application in the law—misconceived the nature of contracts. The thought experiment still flies. In a counterfactual case in which the law enforces both written and unwritten agreements and in which the subject's behavior and so forth are the same, but in which 'contract' *means* 'legally binding agreement based on written document', we would not attribute to him a mistaken belief that a contract requires written agreement, although the lawyer might have to point out that there are other legally binding agreements that do not require documents. Similarly, the client's other propositional attitudes would no longer involve the notion of contract, but another more restricted notion.

f. People sometimes make mistakes about color ranges. They may correctly apply a color term to a certain color, but also mistakenly apply it to shades of a neighboring color. When asked to explain the color term, they cite the standard cases (for 'red', the color of blood, fire engines, and so forth). But they apply the term somewhat beyond its conventionally established range—beyond the reach of its vague borders. They think that fire engines, including *that* one, are red. They observe that red roses are covering the trellis. But they also think that *those* things are a shade of red (whereas they are not). Second looks do not change their opinion. But they give in when other speakers confidently correct them in unison.

This case extends the point of the contract example. The error is linguistic or conceptual in something like the way that the shopper's mistake involving the notion of brisket is. It is not an ordinary empirical error. But one may reasonably doubt that the subjects misunderstand the dictionary meaning of the color term. Holding their non-intentional phenomenal experience, physical history, and behavioral dispositions constant, we can imagine that 'red' were applied as they mistakenly apply it. In such cases, we would no longer ascribe content-clauses involving the term 'red' in oblique position. The attribution of the correct beliefs about fire engines and roses would be no less affected than the attribution of the beliefs that, in the actual case, display the misapplication. Cases bearing out the latter point are common in anthropological reports on communities whose color terms do not match ours. Attributions of content typically allow for the differences in conventionally established color ranges.

Here is not the place to refine our rough distinctions among the various kinds of misconceptions that serve the thought experiment. Our philosophical purposes do not depend on how these distinctions are drawn. Still, it is important to see what an array of conceptual errors is common among us. And it is important to note that such errors do not always or automatically prevent attribution of mental content provided by the very terms that are incompletely understood or misapplied. The thought experiment is nourished by this aspect of common practice.

IIc. Expansion and Delineation of the Thought Experiment

As I have tried to suggest in the preceding examples, the relevant attributions in the first step of the thought experiment need not display the subject's error. They may be attributions of a true content. We can begin with a propositional attitude that involved the misconceived notion, but in a true, unproblematic application of it: for example, the patient's belief that he, like his father, developed arthritis in the ankles and wrists at age 58 (where 'arthritis' occurs obliquely).

One need not even rely on an underlying *mis*conception in the thought experiment. One may pick a case in which the subject only partially understands an expression. He may apply it firmly and correctly in a range of cases, but be unclear or agnostic about certain of its applications or implications which, in fact, are fully established in common practice. Most of the examples we gave previously can be reinterpreted in this way. To take a new one, imagine that our protagonist is unsure whether his father has mortgages on the car and house, or just one on the house. He is a little uncertain about exactly how the loan and collateral must be arranged in order for there to be a mortgage, and he is not clear about whether one may have mortgages on anything other than houses. He is sure, however, that Uncle Harry paid off his mortgage. Imagine our man constant in the ways previously indicated and that 'mortgage' commonly applied only to mortgages on houses. But imagine banking practices themselves to be the same. Then the subject's uncertainty would plausibly not involve the notion of mortgage. Nor would his other propositional attitudes be correctly attributed with the term 'mortgage' in oblique position. Partial understanding is as good as misunderstanding for our purposes.

On the other hand, the thought experiment does appear to depend on the possibility of someone's having a propositional attitude despite an incomplete mastery of some notion in its content. To see why this appears to be so, let us try to run through a thought experiment, attempting to avoid any imputation of incomplete understanding. Suppose the subject thinks falsely that all swans are white. One can certainly hold the features of swans and the subject's non-intentional phenomenal experience, physical history, and non-intentional dispositions constant, and imagine that 'swan' meant 'white swan' (and perhaps some other term, unfamiliar to the subject, meant what 'swan' means). Could one reasonably interpret the subject as having different attitude contents without at some point invoking a misconception? The questions to be asked here are about the subject's dispositions. For example, in the actual case, if he were shown a black swan and told that he was wrong, would he fairly naturally concede his mistake? Or would he respond, "I'm doubtful that that's a swan," until we brought in dictionaries, encyclopedias, and other native speakers to correct his usage? In the latter case, his understanding of 'swan' would be deviant. Suppose then that in the actual situation he would respond normally to the counterexample. Then there is reason to say that he understands the notion of swan correctly; and his error is not conceptual or linguistic, but empirical in an ordinary and narrow sense. (Of course, the line we are drawing here is pretty fuzzy.) When one comes to the counterfactual stage of the thought experiment, the subject has the same dispositions to respond pliably to the presentation of a black specimen. But such a response would suggest a misunderstanding of the term 'swan' as counterfactually used. For in the counterfactual community, what they call "swans" could not fail to be white. The mere presentation of a black swan would be irrelevant to the definitional truth 'All swans are white'. I have not set this case up as an example of the thought experiment's going through. Rather I have used it to support the conjecture that *if* the thought experiment is to work, one must at some stage find the subject believing (or having some attitude characterized by) a content, despite an incomplete understanding or misapplication. An ordinary empirical error appears not to be sufficient.

It would be a mistake, however, to think that incomplete understanding, in the sense that the argument requires, is in general an unusual or even deviant phenomenon. *What I have called "partial understanding" is common or even normal in the case of a large number of expressions in our vocabularies.* 'Arthritis' is a case in point. Even if by the grace of circumstance a person does not fall into views that run counter to the term's meaning or application, it would not be in the least deviant or "socially unacceptable" to have no clear attitude that would block such views. 'Brisket', 'contract', 'recession', 'sonata', 'deer', 'elm' (to borrow a well-known example), 'pre-amplifier', 'carburetor', 'gothic', 'fermentation', probably provide analogous cases. Continuing the list is largely a matter of patience. The sort of "incomplete understanding" required by the thought experiment includes quite ordinary, nondeviant phenomena.

It is worth remarking that the thought experiment as originally presented might be run in reverse. The idea would be to start with an ordinary belief or thought involving no incomplete understanding. Then we find the incomplete understanding in the second step. For example, properly understanding 'arthritis', a patient may think (correctly) that he has arthritis. He happens to have heard of arthritis only occurring in joints, and he correctly believes that that is where arthritis always occurs. Holding his physical history, dispositions, and pain constant, we imagine that 'arthritis' commonly applies to rheumatoid ailments of all sorts. Arthritis has not been singled out for special mention. If the patient were told by a doctor 'You also have arthritis in the thigh', the patient would be disposed (as he is in the actual case) to respond, 'Really? I didn't know that one could have arthritis except in joints'. The doctor would answer, 'No, arthritis occurs in muscles, tendons, bursas, and elsewhere'. The patient would stand corrected. The notion that the doctor and patient would be operating with in such a case would not be that of arthritis.

My reasons for not having originally set out the thought experiment in this way are largely heuristic. As will be seen, discussion of the thought experiment will tend to center on the step involving incomplete understanding. And I wanted to encourage you, dear reader, to imagine actual cases of incomplete understanding in your own linguistic community. Ordinary intuitions in the domestic case are perhaps less subject to premature warping in the interests of theory. Cases involving not only mental content attribution, but also translation of a foreign tongue are more vulnerable to intrusion of side issues.

A secondary reason for not beginning with this "reversed" version of the thought experiment is that I find it doubtful whether the thought experiment always works in symmetric fashion. There may be special intuitive problems in certain cases—perhaps, for example, cases involving perceptual natural kinds. We may give special interpretations to individuals' misconceptions in imagined foreign communities, when those misconceptions seem to match our conceptions. In other words, there may be some systematic intuitive bias in favor of at least certain of our notions for purposes of interpreting the misconceptions of imagined foreigners. I do not want to explore the point here. I think that any such bias is not always crucial, and that the thought experiment frequently works "symmetrically." We have to take account of a person's community in interpreting his words and describing his attitudes—and this holds in the foreign case as well as in the domestic case.

The reversal of the thought experiment brings home the important point that *even those propositional attitudes not infected by incomplete understanding* depend for their content on social factors that are independent of the individual, asocially and non-intentionally described. For if the social environment had been appropriately different, the contents of those attitudes would have been different.

Even *apart* from reversals of the thought experiment, it is plausible (in the light of its original versions) that our well-understood propositional attitudes depend partly for their content on social factors independent of the individual, asocially and non-intentionally construed. For each of us can reason as follows. Take a set of attitudes that involve a given notion and whose contents are well-understood by me. It is only contingent that I understand that notion as well as I do. Now holding my community's practices constant, imagine that I understand the given notion incompletely, but that the deficient understanding is such that it does not prevent my having attitude contents involving that notion. In fact, imagine that I am in the situation envisaged in the first step of one of the original thought experiments. In such a case, a proper subset of the original set of my actual attitude contents would, or might, remain the same—intuitively, at least those of my actual attitudes whose justification or point is untouched by my imagined deficient understanding. (In the arthritis case, an example would be a true belief that many old people have arthritis.) These attitude contents remain constant despite the fact that my understanding, inference patterns, behavior, dispositions, and so on would in important ways be different and partly inappropriate to applications of the given notion. What is it that enables these unaffected contents to remain applications of the relevant notion? It is not *just* that my understanding, inference patterns, behavior, and so forth are enough like my actual understanding, inference patterns, behavior, and so forth. For if communal practice had *also* varied so as to apply the relevant notion as I am imagining I misapply it, then my attitude contents would not involve the relevant notion at all. This argument suggests that communal practice is a factor (in addition to my understanding, inference patterns, and perhaps behavior, physical activity, and other features) in fixing the contents of my attitudes, even in cases where I fully understand the content.

IId. Independence from Factive-Verb and Indexical-Reference Paradigms

The thought experiment does not play on psychological "success" verbs or "factive" verbs—verbs like 'know', 'regret', 'realize', 'remember', 'foresee', 'perceive'. This point is important for our purposes because such verbs suggest an easy and clearcut distinction between the contribution of the individual subject and the objective, "veridical" contribution of the environment to making the verbs applicable. (Actually the matter becomes more complicated on reflection, but we shall stay with the simplest cases.) When a person knows that snow is common in Greenland, his knowledge obviously depends on more than the way the person is. It depends on there actually being a lot of snow in Greenland. His mental state (belief that snow is common in Greenland) must be successful in a certain way (true). By changing the environment, one could change the truth value of the content, so that the subject could no longer be said to know the content. It is part of the burden of our argument that even intentional mental states of the individual like beliefs, which carry no implication of veridicality or success, cannot be understood by focusing purely on the individual's acts, dispositions, and "inner" goings on.

The thought experiment also does not rest on the phenomenon of indexicality, or on *de re* attitudes, in any direct way. When Alfred refers to an apple, saying to himself "That is wholesome," what he refers to depends not just on the content of what he says or thinks, but on what apple is before him. Without altering the meaning of Alfred's utterance, the nature of his perceptual experiences, or his physical acts or dispositions, we could conceive an exchange of the actual apple for another one that is indistinguishable to Alfred. We would thereby conceive him as referring to something different and even as saying something with a different truth value.

This rather obvious point about indexicality has come to be seen as providing a model for understanding a certain range of mental states or events—*de re* attitudes. The precise characterization of this range is no simple philosophical task. But the clearest cases involve non-obliquely occurring terms in content clauses. When we say that Bertrand thinks of some water that it would not slake his thirst (where 'water' occurs in purely non-oblique position), we attribute a *de re* belief to Bertrand. We assume that Bertrand has something like an indexical relation to the water. The fact that Bertrand believes something of some water, rather than of a portion of some other liquid that is indistinguishable to him, depends partly on the fact that it is water to which Bertrand is contextually, "indexically" related. For intuitively we could have exchanged the liquids without changing Bertrand and thereby changed what Bertrand believed his belief content *of*—and even whether his belief was true of it.[3] It is easy to interpret such cases by holding that the subject's mental states and contents (with allowances for brute differences in the contexts in which he applies those contents) remain the same. The differences in the situations do not pertain in any fundamental way to the subject's mind or the nature of his mental content, but to how his mind or content is related to the world.

I think this interpretation of standard indexical and *de re* cases is broadly correct, although it involves oversimplifications and demands refinements. But what I want to emphasize here is that it is inapplicable to the cases our thought experiment fixes upon.

It seems to me clear that the thought experiment need not rely on *de re* attitudes at all. The subject need not have entered into special *en rapport* or quasi-indexical relations with objects that the misunderstood term applies to in order for the argument to work. We can appeal to attitudes that would usually be regarded as paradigmatic cases of *de dicto,* non-indexical, *non-de-re,* mental attitudes or events. The primary mistake in the contract example is one such, but we could choose others to suit the reader's taste. To insist that such attitudes must all be indexically infected or *de re* would, I think, be to trivialize and emasculate these notions, making nearly all attitudes *de re*. All *de dicto* attitudes presuppose *de re* attitudes. But it does not follow that indexical or *de re* elements survive in every attitude. (Cf. notes 2 and 3.)

I shall not, however, argue this point here. The claim that is crucial is not that our argument does not fix on *de re* attitudes. It is, rather, that the social differences between the actual and counterfactual situations affect the *content* of the subject's attitudes. That is, the difference affects standard cases of obliquely occurring, cognitive-content-conveying expressions in content clauses. For example, still with his misunderstanding, the subject might think that this (referring to his disease in his hands) is arthritis. Or he might think *de re* of the disease in his ankle (or of the disease in his thigh) that his arthritis is painful. It does not really matter whether the relevant attitude is *de re* or purely *de dicto*. What is crucial to our argument is that the occurrence of 'arthritis' is oblique and contributes to a characterization of the subject's mental content. One might even hold, implausibly I think, that all the subject's attitudes involving the notion of arthritis are *de re,* that 'arthritis' in that-clauses *indexically* picks out the property of being arthritis, or something like that. The fact remains that the term occurs obliquely in the relevant cases and serves in characterizing the *dicta* or contents of the subject's attitudes. The thought experiment exploits this fact.

Approaches to the mental that I shall later criticize as excessively individualistic tend to assimilate environmental aspects of mental phenomena to either the factive-verb or indexical-reference paradigm. (Cf. note 2.) This sort of assimilation suggests that one might maintain a relatively clearcut distinction between extramental and mental aspects of mentalistic attributions. And it may encourage the idea that the distinctively mental aspects can be understood fundamentally in terms of the individual's abilities, dispositions, states, and so forth, considered in isolation from his social surroundings. Our argument undermines this latter suggestion. Social context infects even the distinctively mental features of mentalistic attributions. No man's intentional mental phenomena are insular. Every man is a piece of the social continent, a part of the social main.

III. REINTERPRETATIONS

IIIa. Methodology

I find that most people unspoiled by conventional philosophical training regard the three steps of the thought experiment as painfully obvious. Such folk tend to chafe over my filling in details or elaborating on strategy. I think this naivete appropriate. But for sophisticates the three steps require defense.

Before launching a defense, I want to make a few remarks about its methodology. My objective is to better understand our common mentalistic notions. Although such notions are subject to revision and refinement, I take it as evident that there is philosophical interest in theorizing about them as they now are. I assume that a primary way of achieving theoretical understanding is to concentrate on our *discourse* about mentalistic notions. Now it is, of course, never obvious at the outset how much idealization, regimentation, or special interpretation is necessary in order to adequately understand ordinary discourse. Phenomena such as ambiguity, ellipsis, indexicality, idioms, and a host of others certainly demand some regimentation or special interpretation for purposes of linguistic theory. Moreover, more global considerations — such as simplicity in accounting for structural relations — often have effects on the cast of one's theory. For all that, there is a methodological bias in favor of taking natural discourse literally, other things being equal. For example, unless there are clear reasons for construing discourse as ambiguous, elliptical or involving special idioms, we should not so construe it. Literal interpretation is *ceteris paribus* preferred. My defense of the thought experiment, as I have interpreted it, partly rests on this principle.

This relatively non-theoretical interpretation of the thought experiment should be extended to the gloss on it that I provided in Section IIc. The notions of misconception, incomplete understanding, conceptual or linguistic error, and ordinary empirical error are to be taken as carrying little theoretical weight. I assume that these notions mark defensible, common-sense distinctions. But I need not take a position on available philosophical interpretations of these distinctions. In fact, I do not believe that understanding, in our examples, can be explicated as independent of empirical knowledge, or that the conceptual errors of our subjects are best seen as "purely" mistakes about concepts and as involving no "admixture" of error about "the world." With Quine, I find such talk about purity and mixture devoid of illumination or explanatory power. But my views on this matter neither entail nor are entailed by the premises of the arguments I give (cf. e.g., IIId). Those arguments seem to me to remain plausible under any of the relevant philosophical interpretations of the conceptual-ordinary-empirical distinction.

I have presented the experiment as appealing to ordinary intuition. I believe that common practice in the attribution of propositional attitudes is fairly represented by the various steps. This point is not really open to dispute. Usage may be divided in a few of the cases in which I have seen it as united. But broadly speaking, it seems to me undeniable that the individual steps of the thought experiment are acceptable to ordinary speakers in a wide varity of examples. The issue open to possible dispute is whether the steps should be taken in the literal way in which I have taken them, and thus whether the conclusion I have drawn from those steps is justified. In the remainder of Section III, I shall try to vindicate the literal interpretation of our examples. I do this by criticizing, in order of increasing generality or abstractness, a series of attempts to reinterpret the thought experiment's first step. Ultimately, I suggest (IIId and IV) that these attempts derive from characteristically philosophical models that have little or no independent justification. A thoroughgoing review of these models would be out of bounds, but the present paper is intended to show that they are deficient as accounts of our actual practice of mentalistic attribution.

I shall have little further to say in defense of the second and third steps of the thought experiment. Both rest on their intuitive plausibility, not on some particular theory. The third step, for example, certainly does not depend on a view that contents are merely sentences the subject is disposed to utter, interpreted as his community interprets them. It is compatible with several philosophical accounts of mental contents, including those that appeal to more abstract entities such as Fregean thoughts or Russellian propositions, and those that seek to deny that content-clauses indicate any *thing* that might be called a content. I also do not claim that the fact that our subject lacks the relevant beliefs in the third step follows from the facts I have described. The point is that it is plausible, and certainly possible, that he would lack those beliefs.

The exact interpretation of the second step is relevant to a number of causal or functional theories of mental phenomena that I shall discuss in Section IV. The intuitive idea of the step is that none of the different physical, non-intentionally described causal chains set going by the differences in communal practice need affect our subjects in any way that would be relevant to an account of their mental contents. Differences in the behavior of other members of the community will, to be sure, affect the gravitational forces exerted on the subject. But I assume that these differences are irrelevant to macro-explanations of our subjects' physical movements and inner processes. They do not relevantly affect ordinary non-intentional physical explanations of how the subject acquires or is disposed to use the symbols in his repertoire. Of course, the social origins of a person's symbols do differ between actual and counterfactual cases. I shall return to this point in Sections IV and V. The remainder of Section III will be devoted to the first step of the thought experiment.

IIIb. Incomplete Understanding and Standard Cases of Reinterpretation

The first step, as I have interpreted it, is the most likely to encounter opposition. In fact, there is a line of resistance that is second nature to linguistically oriented philosophers. According to this line, we should deny that, say, the patient really believed or thought that arthritis can occur outside of joints because he misunderstood the word 'arthritis'. More generally, we should deny that a subject could have any attitudes whose contents he incompletely understands.

What a person understands is indeed one of the chief factors that bear on what thoughts he can express in using words. If there were not deep and important connections between propositional attitudes and understanding, one could hardly expect one's attributions of mental content to facilitate reliable predictions of what a person will do, say, or think. But our examples provide reason to believe that these connections are not simple entailments to the effect that having a propositional attitude strictly implies full understanding of its content.

There are, of course, numerous situations in which we normally reinterpret or discount a person's words in deciding what he thinks. Philosophers often invoke such cases to bolster their animus against such attributions as the ones we made to our subjects: "If a foreigner were to mouth the words 'arthritis may occur in the thigh' or 'my father had arthritis', not understanding what he uttered in the slightest, we would not say that he believed that arthritis may occur in the thigh, or that his father had arthritis. So why should we impute the belief to the patient?" Why, indeed? Or rather, why do we?

The question is a good one. We do want a general account of these cases. But the implied argument against our attribution is anemic. We tacitly and routinely distinguish between the cases I described and those in which a foreigner (or anyone) utters something without any comprehension. The best way to understand mentalistic notions is to recognize such differences in standard practice and try to account for them. One can hardly justify the assumption that full understanding of a content is in general a necessary condition for believing the content by appealing to some cases that tend to support the assumption in order to reject others that conflict with it.

It is a good method of discovery, I think, to note the sorts of cases philosophers tend to gravitate toward when they defend the view that the first step in the thought experiment should receive special interpretation. By reflecting on the differences between these cases and the cases we have cited, one should learn something about principles controlling mentalistic attribution.

I have already mentioned foreigners without command of the language. A child's imitation of our words and early attempts to use them provide similar examples. In these cases, mastery of the language and responsibility to its precepts have not been developed; and mental content attribution based on the meaning of words uttered tends to be precluded.

There are cases involving regional dialects. A person's deviance or ignorance judged by the standards of the larger community may count as normality or full mastery when evaluated from the regional perspective. Clearly, the regional standards tend to be the relevant ones for attributing content when the speaker's training or intentions are regionally oriented. The conditions for such orientation are complex, and I shall touch on them again in Section V. But there is no warrant in actual practice for treating each person's idiolect as always analogous to dialects whose words we automatically reinterpret—for purposes of mental content attribution—when usage is different. People are frequently held, and hold themselves, to the standards of their community when misuse or misunderstanding are at issue. One should distinguish these cases, which seem to depend on a certain *responsibility* to communal practice, from cases of automatic reinterpretation.

Tongue slips and Spoonerisms form another class of example where reinterpretation of a person's words is common and appropriate in arriving at an attribution of mental content. In these cases, we tend to exempt the speaker even from commitment to a homophonically formulated assertion content, as well as to the relevant mental content. The speaker's own behavior usually follows this line, often correcting himself when what he uttered is repeated back to him.

Malapropisms form a more complex class of examples. I shall not try to map it in detail. But in a fairly broad range of cases, we reinterpret a person's words at least in attributing mental content. If Archie says, 'Lead the way and we will precede', we routinely reinterpret the words in describing his expectations. Many of these cases seem to depend on the presumption that there are simple, superficial (for example, phonological) interference or exchange mechanisms that account for the linguistic deviance.

There are also examples of quite radical misunderstandings that sometimes generate reinterpretation. If a generally competent and reasonable speaker thinks that 'orangutan' applies to a fruit drink, we would be reluctant, and it would unquestionably be misleading, to take his words as revealing that he thinks he has been drinking orangutans for breakfast for the last few weeks. Such total misunderstanding often *seems* to block literalistic mental content attribution, at least in cases where we are not directly characterizing his mistake. (Contrary to philosophical lore, I am not convinced that such a man cannot correctly and literally be attributed a belief that an orangutan is a kind of fruit drink. But I shall not deal with the point here.)

There are also some cases that do not seem generally to prevent mental content attribution on the basis of literal interpretation of the subject's words in quite the same way as the others, but which deserve some mention. For almost any content except for those that directly display the subject's incomplete understanding, there will be many contexts in which it would be misleading to attribute that content to the subject without further comment. Suppose I am advising you about your legal liabilities in a situation where you have entered into what may be an unwritten contract. You ask me what Al would think. It would be misleading for me to reply that Al would think that you do not have a contract (or even do not have any legal problems), if I know that Al thinks a contract must be based on a formal document. Your evaluation of Al's thought would be crucially affected by his inadequate understanding. In such cases, it is incumbent on us to cite the subject's eccentricity: "(He would think that you do not have a contract, but then) he thinks that there is no such thing as a verbally based contract."

Incidentally, the same sort of example can be constructed using attitudes that are abnormal, but that do not hinge on misunderstanding of any one notion. If Al had thought that only traffic laws and laws against violent crimes are ever prosecuted, it would be misleading for me to tell you that Al would think that you have no legal problems.

Both sorts of cases illustrate that in reporting a single attitude content, we typically suggest (implicate, perhaps) that the subject has a range of other attitudes that are normally associated with it. Some of these may provide reasons for it. In both sorts of cases, it is usually important to keep track of, and often to make explicit, the nature and extent of the subject's deviance. Otherwise, predictions and evaluations of his thought and action, based on normal background assumptions, will go awry. When the deviance is huge, attributions demand reinterpretation of the subject's words. Radical misunderstanding and mental instability are cases in point. But frequently, common practice seems to allow us to cancel the misleading suggestions by making explicit the subject's deviance, retaining literal interpretation of his words in our mentalistic attributions all the while.

All of the foregoing phenomena are relevant to accounting for standard practice. But they are no more salient than cases of straightforward belief attribution where the subject incompletely understands some notion in the attributed belief content. I think any impulse to say that common practice is *simply* inconsistent should be resisted (indeed, scorned). We cannot expect such practice to follow general principles rigorously. But even our brief discussion of the matter should have suggested the beginnings of generalizations about differences between cases where reinterpretation is standard and cases where it is not. A person's overall linguistic competence, his allegiance and responsibility to communal standards, the degree, source, and type of misunderstanding, the purposes of the report—all affect the issue. From a theoretical point of view, it would be a mistake to try to assimilate the cases in one direction or another. We do not want to credit a two-year-old who memorizes 'e = mc^2' with belief in relativity theory. But the patient's attitudes involving the notion of arthritis should not be assimilated to the foreigner's uncomprehending pronunciations.

For purposes of defending the thought experiment and the arguments I draw from it, I can afford to be flexible about exactly how to generalize about these various phenomena. The thought experiment depends only on there being some cases in which a person's incomplete understanding does not force reinterpretation of his expressions in describing his mental contents. Such cases appear to be legion.

IIIc.   Four Methods of Reinterpreting the Thought Experiment

I now want to criticize attempts to argue that even in cases where we ordinarily do ascribe content clauses despite the subject's incomplete understanding of expressions in those clauses, such ascriptions should not be taken literally. In order to overturn our interpretation of the thought experiment's first step, one must argue that none of the cases I have cited is appropriately taken in the literal manner. One must handle (apparent) attributions of unproblematically true contents involving incompletely mastered notions, as well as attributions of contents that display the misconceptions or partial understandings. I do not doubt that one can erect logically coherent and metaphysically traditional reinterpretations of all these cases. What I doubt is that such reinterpretations taken *in toto* can present a plausible view, and that taken individually they have any claim to superiority over the literal interpretations—either as accounts of the language of ordinary mentalistic ascription, or as accounts of the evidence on which mental attributions are commonly based.

Four types of reinterpretation have some currency. I shall be rather short with the first two, the first of which I have already warned against in Section IId. Sometimes relevant mentalistic ascriptions are reinterpreted as attributions of *de re* attitudes *of* entities not denoted by the misconstrued expressions. For example, the subject's belief that he has arthritis in the thigh might be interpreted as a belief *of* the non-arthritic rheumatoid ailment that it is in the thigh. The subject will probably have such a belief in this case. But it hardly accounts for the relevant attributions. In particular, it ignores the oblique occurrence of 'arthritis' in the original ascription. Such occurrences bear on a characterization of the subject's viewpoint. The subject thinks of the disease in his thigh (and of his arthritis) in a certain way. He thinks of each disease that it is arthritis. Other terms for arthritis (or for the actual trouble in his thigh) may not enable us to describe his attitude content nearly as well. The appeal to *de re* attitudes in this way is not adequate to the task of reinterpreting these ascriptions so as to explain away the difference between actual and counterfactual situations. It simply overlooks what needs explication.

A second method of reinterpretation, which Descartes proposed (cf. Section IV) and which crops up occasionally, is to claim that in cases of incomplete understanding, the subject's attitude or content is indefinite. It is surely true that in cases where a person is extremely confused, we are sometimes at a loss in describing his attitudes. Perhaps in such cases, the subject's mental content *is* indefinite. But in the cases I have cited, common practice lends virtually no support to the contention that the subject's mental contents are indefinite. The subject and his fellows typically know and agree on precisely *how to confirm or infirm* his beliefs—both in the cases where they are unproblematically true (or just empirically false) and in the cases where they display the misconception. Ordinary attributions typically specify the mental content without qualifications or hesitations.

In cases of partial understanding—say, in the mortgage example—it may indeed be unclear, short of extensive questioning, just how much mastery the subject has. But even this sort of unclarity does not appear to prevent, under ordinary circumstances, straightforward attributions utilizing 'mortgage' in oblique position. The subject is uncertain whether his father has two mortgages; he knows that his uncle has paid off the mortgage on his house. The contents are unhesitatingly attributed and admit of unproblematic testing for truth value, despite the subject's partial understanding. There is thus little *prima facie* ground for the appeal to indefiniteness. The appeal appears to derive from a prior assumption that attribution of a content entails attribution of full understanding. Lacking an easy means of attributing something other than the misunderstood content, one is tempted to say that there *is* no definite content. But this is unnecessarily mysterious. It reflects on the prior assumption, which so far has no independent support.

The other two methods of reinterpretation are often invoked in tandem. One is to attribute a notion that just captures the misconception, thus replacing contents that are apparently false on account of the misconception, by true contents. For example, the subject's belief (true or false) that that is a sofa would be replaced by, or reinterpreted as, a (true) belief that that is a *chofa,* where 'chofa' is introduced to apply not only to sofas, but also to the armchairs the subject thinks are sofas. The other method is to count the error of the subject as purely metalinguistic. Thus the patient's apparent belief that he had arthritis in the thigh would be reinterpreted as a belief that 'arthritis' applied to something (or some disease) in his thigh. The two methods can be applied simultaneously, attempting to account for an ordinary content attribution in terms of a reinterpreted object-level content together with a metalinguistic error. It is important to remember that in order to overturn the thought experiment, these methods must not only establish that the subject held the particular attitudes that they advocate attributing; they must also justify a *denial* of the ordinary attributions literally interpreted.

The method of invoking object-level notions that precisely capture (and that replace) the subject's apparent misconception has little to be said for it as a natural and generally applicable account of the language of mentalistic ascriptions. We do not ordinarily seek out true object-level attitude contents to attribute to victims of errors based on incomplete understanding. For example, when we find that a person has been involved in a misconception in examples like ours, we do not regularly reinterpret those ascriptions that involved the misunderstood term, but were untuitively unaffected by the error. An attribution to someone of a true belief that he is eating brisket, or that he has just signed a contract, or that Uncle Harry has paid off his mortgage, is not typically reformulated when it is learned that the subject had not fully understood what brisket (or a contract, or a mortgage) is. A similar point applies when we know about the error at the time of the attribution—at least if we avoid misleading the audience in cases where the error is crucial to the issue at hand. Moreover, we shall frequently see the subject as sharing beliefs with others who understand the relevant notions better. In counting beliefs as shared, we do not require, in every case, that the subjects "fully understand" the notions in those belief contents, or understand them in just the same way. Differences in understanding are frequently located as differences over other belief contents. We agree that you have signed a contract, but disagree over whether someone else could have made a contract by means of a verbal agreement.

There are reasons why ordinary practice does not follow the method of object-level reinterpretation. In many cases, particularly those involving partial understanding, finding a reinterpretation in accord with the method would be entirely nontrivial. It is not even clear that we have agreed upon means of pursuing such inquiries in all cases. Consider the arthritic patient. Suppose we are to reinterpret the attribution of his erroneous belief that he has arthritis in the thigh. We make up a term 'tharthritis' that covers arthritis and whatever it is he has in his thigh. The appropriate restrictions on the application of this term and of the patient's supposed notion are unclear. Is just any problem in the thigh that the patient wants to call 'arthritis' to count as tharthritis? Are other ailments covered? What would decide? The problem is that there are no recognized standards governing the application of the new term. In such cases, the method is patently *ad hoc.*

The method's willingness to invoke new terminology whenever conceptual error or partial understanding occurs is *ad hoc* in another sense. It proliferates terminology without evident theoretical reward. We do not engender better understanding of the patient by inventing a new word and saying that he thought (correctly) that tharthritis can occur outside joints. It is simpler and equally informative to construe him as thinking that arthritis may occur outside joints. When we are making other attributions that do not directly display the error, we must simply bear the deviant belief in mind, so as not to assume that all of the patient's inferences involving the notion would be normal.

The method of object-level reinterpretation often fails to give a plausible account of the evidence on which we base mental attributions. When caught in the sorts of errors we have been discussing, the subject does not normally respond by saying that his views had been misunderstood. The patient does not say (or think) that he had thought he had some-category-of-disease-like-arthritis-and-including-arthritis-but-also-capable-of-occurring-outside-of-joints in the thigh *instead* of the error commonly attributed. This sort of response would be disingenuous. Whatever other beliefs he had, the subject thought that he had arthritis in the thigh. In such cases, the subject will ordinarily give no evidence of having maintained a true object-level belief. In examples like ours, he typically admits his mistake, changes his views, and leaves it at that. Thus the subject's own behavioral dispositions and inferences often fail to support the method.

The method may be seen to be implausible as an account of the relevant evidence in another way. The patient knows that he has had arthritis in the ankle and wrists for some time. Now with his new pains in the thigh, he fears and believes that he has got arthritis in the thigh, that his arthritis is spreading. Suppose we reinterpret all of these attitude attributions in accord with the method. We use our recently coined term 'tharthritis' to cover (somehow) arthritis and whatever it is he has in the thigh. On this new interpretation, the patient is right in thinking that he has tharthritis in the ankle and wrists. His belief that it has lodged in the thigh is true. His fear is realized. But these attributions are out of keeping with the way we do and should view his actual beliefs and fears. His belief is not true, and his fear is not realized. He will be relieved when he is told that one cannot have arthritis in the thigh. His relief is bound up with a network of assumptions that he makes about his arthritis: that it is a kind of disease, that there are debilitating consequences of its occurring in multiple locations, and so on. When told that arthritis cannot occur in the thigh, the patient does not decide that his fears were realized, but that perhaps he should not have had those fears. He does not think: Well, my tharthritis *has* lodged in the thigh; but judging from the fact that what the doctor called "arthritis" cannot occur in the thigh, tharthritis may not be a single kind of disease; and I suppose I need not worry about the effects of its occurring in various locations, since evidently the tharthritis in my thigh is physiologically unrelated to the tharthritis in my joints. There will rarely if ever be an empirical basis for such a description of the subject's inferences. The patient's behavior (including his reports, or thinkings-out-loud) in this sort of case will normally not indicate any such pattern of inferences at all. But this is the description that the object-level reinterpretation method appears to recommend.

On the standard attributions, the patient retains his assumptions about the relation between arthritis, kinds of disease, spreading, and so on. And he concludes that his arthritis is not appearing in new locations—at any rate, not in his thigh. These attributions will typically be supported by the subject's behavior. The object-level reinterpretation method postulates inferences that are more complicated and different in focus from the inferences that the evidence supports. The method's presentation in such a case would seem to be an *ad hoc* fiction, not a description with objective validity.

None of the foregoing is meant to deny that frequently when a person incompletely understands an attitude content he has some other attitude content that more or less captures his understanding. For example, in the contract example, the client will probably have the belief that if one breaks *a legally binding agreement based on formal documents,* then one may get into trouble. There are also cases in which it is reasonable to say that, at least in a sense, a person has a notion that is expressed by his dispositions to classify things in a certain way—even if there is no conventional term in the person's repertoire that neatly corresponds to that "way." The sofa case may be one such. Certain animals as well as people may have non-verbal notions of this sort. On the other hand, the fact that such attributions are justifiable *per se* yields no reason to deny that the subject (also) has object-level attitudes whose contents involve the relevant incompletely understood notion.

Whereas the third method purports to account for the subject's thinking at the object level, the fourth aims at accounting for his error. The error is construed as purely a metalinguistic mistake. The relevant false content is seen to involve notions that denote or apply to linguistic expressions. In examples relevant to our thought experiment, we ordinarily attribute a metalinguistic as well as an object-level attitude to the subject, at least in the case of non-occurrent propositional attitudes. For example, the patient probably believes that 'arthritis' applies in English to the ailment in his thigh. He believes that his father had a disease called "arthritis." And so on. Accepting these metalinguistic attributions, of course, does nothing *per se* toward making plausible a denial that the subjects in our examples have the counterpart object-level attitudes.

Like the third method, the metalinguistic reinterpretation method has no *prima facie* support as an account of the language of mentalistic ascriptions. When we encounter the subject's incomplete understanding in examples like ours, we do not decide that all the mental contents which we had been attributing to him with the misunderstood notion must have been purely metalinguistic in form. We also count people who incompletely understand terms in ascribed content clauses as sharing true and unproblematic object-level attitudes with others who understand the relevant terms better. For example, the lawyer and his client may share a wish that the client had not signed the contract to buy the house without reading the small print. A claim that these people share *only* attitudes with metalinguistic contents would have no support in linguistic practice.

The point about shared attitudes goes further. If the metalinguistic reinterpretation account is to be believed, we cannot say that a relevant English speaker shares a view (for example) that many old people have arthritis, with *anyone* who does not use the English word 'arthritis'. For the foreigner does not have the word 'arthritis' to hold beliefs about, though he does have attitudes involving the notion arthritis. And the attribution to the English speaker is to be interpreted metalinguistically, making reference to the word, so as not to involve attribution of the notion arthritis. This result is highly implausible. Ascriptions of such that-clauses as the above, regardless of the subject's language, serve to provide single descriptions and explanations of similar patterns of behavior, inference, and communication. To hold that we cannot accurately ascribe single content-clauses to English speakers and foreigners in such cases would not only accord badly with linguistic practice. It would substantially weaken the descriptive and explanatory power of our common attributions. In countless cases, unifying accounts of linguistically disparate but cognitively and behaviorally similar phenomena would be sacrificed.

The method is implausible in other cases as an account of standard evidence on which mental attributions are based. Take the patient who fears that his arthritis is spreading. According to the metalinguistic reinterpretation method, the patient's reasoning should be described as follows. He thinks that the word 'arthritis' applies to a single disease in him, that the disease in him called "arthritis" is debilitating if it spreads, that 'arthritis' applies to the disease in his wrists and ankles. He fears that the disease called "arthritis" has lodged in his thigh, and so on. Of course, it is often difficult to find evidential grounds for attributing an object-level attitude *as opposed* to its metalinguistic counterpart. As I noted, when a person holds one attitude, he often holds the other. But there are types of evidence, in certain contexts, for making such discriminations, particularly contexts in which *occurrent* mental events are at issue. The subject may maintain that his reasoning did not fix upon words. He may be brought up short by a metalinguistic formulation of his just-completed ruminations, and may insist that he was not interested in labels. In such cases, especially if the reasoning is not concerned with linguistic issues in any informal or antecedently plausible sense, attribution of an object-level thought content is supported by the relevant evidence, and metalinguistic attribution is not. To insist that the occurrent mental event really involved a metalinguistic content would be a piece of *ad hoc* special pleading, undermined by the evidence we actually use for deciding whether a thought was metalinguistic.

In fact, there appears to be a general presumption that a person is reasoning at the object level, other things being equal. The basis for this presumption is that metalinguistic reasoning requires a certain self-consciousness about one's words and social institutions. This sort of sophistication emerged rather late in human history. (Cf. any history of linguistics.) Semantical notions were a product of this sophistication.

Occurrent propositional attitudes prevent the overall reinterpretation strategy from providing a plausible total account which would block our thought experiment. For such occurrent mental events as the patient's thought that his arthritis is especially painful in the knee this morning are, or can be imagined to be, clear cases of object-level attitudes. And such thoughts may enter into or connect up with pieces of reasoning—say the reasoning leading to relief that the arthritis had not lodged in the thigh—which cannot be plausibly accounted for in terms of object-level reinterpretation. The other reinterpretation methods (those that appeal to *de re* contents and to indefiniteness) are non-starters. In such examples, the literally interpreted ascriptions appear to be straightforwardly superior accounts of the evidence that is normally construed to be relevant. Here one need not appeal to the principle that literal interpretation is, other things equal, preferable to reinterpretation. Other things are not equal.

At this point, certain philosophers may be disposed to point out that what a person says and how he behaves do not infallibly determine what his attitude contents are. Despite the apparent evidence, the subject's attitude contents may in all cases I cited be metalinguistic, and may fail to involve the incompletely understood notion. It is certainly true that how a person acts and what he says, even sincerely, do not determine his mental contents. I myself have mentioned a number of cases that support the point. (Cf. IIIb.) But the point is often used in a sloppy and irresponsible manner. It is incumbent on someone making it (and applying it to cases like ours) to indicate considerations that override the linguistic and behavioral evidence. In Section IIId, I shall consider intuitive or *a priori* philosophical arguments to this end. But first I wish to complete our evaluation of the metalinguistic reinterpretation method as an account of the language of mentalistic ascription in our examples.

In this century philosophers have developed the habit of insisting on metalinguistic reinterpretation for any content attribution that directly *displays* the subject's incomplete understanding. These cases constitute but a small number of the attributions that serve the thought experiment. One could grant these reinterpretations and still maintain our overall viewpoint. But even as applied to these cases, the method seems dubious. I doubt that any evidentially supported account of the language of these attributions will show them in general to be attributions of metalinguistic contents—contents that involve denotative reference to linguistic expressions.

The ascription 'He believes that broad overstuffed armchairs are sofas', as ordinarily used, does not in general *mean* "He believes that broad, overstuffed armchairs are covered by the expression 'sofas'" (or something like that). There are clear grammatical and semantical differences between

(i) broad, overstuffed armchairs are covered by the expression 'sofas'

and

(ii) broad, overstuffed armchairs are sofas.

When the two are embedded in belief contexts, they produce grammatically and semantically distinct sentences.

As noted, ordinary usage approves ascriptions like

(iii) He believes that broad, overstuffed armchairs are sofas.

It would be wildly *ad hoc* and incredible from the point of view of linguistic theory to claim that there is *no* reading of (iii) that embeds (ii). But there is no evidence from speaker behavior that *true* ascriptions of (iii) always (or perhaps even *ever*) derive from embedding (i) rather than (ii). In fact, I know of no clear evidence that (iii) is ambiguous between embedding (i) and (ii), or that (ii) is ambiguous, with one reading identical to that of (i). People do not in general seem to regard ascriptions like (iii) as elliptical. More important, in most cases no amount of nonphilosophical badgering will lead them to withdraw (iii), under some interpretation, *in favor of* an ascription that clearly embeds (i). At least in the cases of *non-occurrent* propositional attitudes, they will tend to agree to a clearly metalinguistic ascription—a belief sentence explicitly embedding something like (i)—in cases where they make an ascription like (iii). But this is evidence that they regard ascriptions that embed (i) and (ii) as both true. It hardly tells against counting belief ascriptions that embed

(ii) as true, or against taking (iii) in the obvious, literal manner. In sum, there appears to be no ordinary empirical pressure on a theory of natural language to represent true ascriptions like (iii) as *not* embedding sentences like (ii). And other things being equal, literal readings are correct readings. Thus it is strongly plausible to assume that ordinary usage routinely accepts as true and justified even ascriptions like (iii), literally interpreted as embedding sentences like (ii).

There are various contexts in which we may be indifferent over whether to attribute a metalinguistic attitude or the corresponding object-level attitude. I have emphasized that frequently, though not always, we may attribute both. Or we might count the different contents as describing what contextually "amount to the same attitude." (Cf. Section I.) Even this latter locution remains compatible with the thought experiment, as long as both contents are *equally attributable* in describing "the attitude." In the counterfactual step of the thought experiment, the metalinguistic content (say, that broad, overstuffed armchairs are called "sofas") will still be attributable. But in these circumstances it contextually "amounts to the same attitude" as an object-level attitude whose content is in no sense equivalent to, or "the same as," the original object-level content. For they have different truth values. Thus, assuming that the object-level and metalinguistic contents are equally attributable, it remains informally plausible that the person's attitudes are different between actual and counterfactual steps in the thought experiment. This contextual conflation of object-level and metalinguistic contents is not, however, generally acceptable even in describing non-occurrent attitudes, much less occurrent ones. There are contexts in which the subject himself may give evidence of making the distinction.

IIId. Philosophical Arguments for Reinterpretation

I have so far argued that the reinterpretation strategies that I have cited do not provide a plausible account of evidence relevant to a theory of the language of mentalistic ascriptions or to descriptions of mental phenomena themselves. I now want to consider characteristically philosophical arguments for revising ordinary discourse or for giving it a nonliteral reading, arguments that rely purely on intuitive or *a priori* considerations. I have encountered three such arguments, or argument sketches.[4]

One holds that the content clauses we ascribed must be reinterpreted so as to make reference to words because they clearly concern linguistic matters—or are about language. Even if this argument were sound, it would not affect the thought experiment decisively. For most of the mental contents that vary between actual and counterfactual situations are not in any intuitive sense "linguistic." The belief that certain armchairs are sofas is intuitively linguistic. But beliefs that some sofas are beige, that Kirkpatrick is playing a clavichord, and that Milton had severe arthritis in his hands are not.

But the argument is unpersuasive even as applied to the contents that, in an intuitive sense, do concern linguistic matters. A belief that broad, overstuffed armchairs are sofas is linguistic (or "about" language) in the same senses as an "analytically" true belief that no armchairs are sofas. But the linguistic nature of the latter belief does not make its logical form metalinguistic. So citing the linguistic nature of the former belief does not suffice to show it metalinguistic. No semantically relevant component of either content applies to or denotes linguistic expressions.

Both the "analytically" true and the "analytically" false attitudes are linguistic in the sense that they are tested by consulting a dictionary or native linguistic intuitions, rather than by ordinary empirical investigation. We do not scrutinize pieces of furniture to test these beliefs. The pragmatic focus of expressions of these attitudes will be on usage, concepts, or meaning. But it is simply a mistake to think that these facts entail, or even suggest, that the relevant contents are metalinguistic in form. Many contents with object-level logical forms have primarily linguistic or conceptual implications.

A second argument holds that charitable interpretation requires that we not attribute to rational people beliefs like the belief that one may have arthritis in the thigh. Here again, the argument obviously does not touch most of the attitudes that may launch the thought experiment; for many are straightforwardly true, or false on ordinary empirical grounds. Even so, it is not a good argument. There is nothing irrational or stupid about the linguistic or conceptual errors we attribute to our subjects. The errors are perfectly understandable as results of linguistic misinformation.

In fact, the argument makes sense only against the background of the very assumption that I have been questioning. A belief that arthritis may occur in the thigh appears to be inexplicable or uncharitably attributed only if it is assumed that the subject must fully understand the notions in his attitude contents.

A third intuitive or *a priori* argument is perhaps the most interesting. Sometimes it is insisted that we should not attribute contents involving incompletely understood notions because *the individual must mean something different by the misunderstood word than what we non-deviant speakers mean by it.* Note again that it would not be enough to use this argument from deviant speaker meaning to show that the subject has notions that are not properly expressed in the way he thinks they are. In some sense of 'expressed', this is surely often the case. To be relevant, the argument must arrive at a negative conclusion: that the subject cannot have the attitudes that seem commonly to be attributed.

The expression 'the individual meant something different by his words' can be interpreted in more than one way. On one group of interpretations, the expression says little more than that the speaker incompletely understood his words: The patient thought 'arthritis' meant something that included diseases that occur outside of joints. The client would have misexplained the meaning, use, or application of 'contract'. The subject applied 'sofa' to things that, unknown to him, are not sofas. A second group of interpretations emphasizes that not only does the speaker misconstrue or misapply his words, but he had *in mind* something that the words do not denote or express. The subject sometimes had in mind certain armchairs when he used 'sofa.' The client regarded the notion of legal agreement based on written documents as approximately interchangeable with what is expressed by 'contract', and thus had such a notion in mind when he used 'contract'. A person with a problem about the range of red might sometimes have in mind a mental image of a non-red color when he used 'red'.

The italicized premise of the argument is, of course, always true in our examples under the first group of interpretations, and often true under the second. But interpreted in these ways, the argument is a *non sequitur.* It does not follow from the assumption that the subject thought that a word means something that it does not (or misapplies the word, or is disposed to misexplain its meaning) that the word cannot be used in literally describing his mental contents. It does not follow from the assumption that a person has in mind something that a word does not denote or express that the word cannot occur obliquely (and be interpreted literally) in that-clauses that provide some of his mental contents. As I have pointed out in Section IIIb, there is a range of cases in which we commonly reinterpret a person's incompletely understood words for purposes of mental-content attribution. But the present argument needs to show that deviant speaker-meaning always forces such reinterpretation.

In many of our examples, the idea that the subject has some deviant notion *in mind* has no intuitively clear application. (Consider the arthritis and mortgage examples). But even where this expression does seem to apply, the argument does not support the relevant conclusion. At best it shows that a notion deviantly associated with a word plays a role in the subject's attitudes. For example, someone who has in mind the notion of an agreement based on written documents when he says, "I have just entered into a contract," may be correctly said to believe that he has just entered into an agreement based on written documents. It does not follow from this that he *lacks* a belief or thought that he has just entered into a contract. In fact, in our view, the client's having the deviant notion in mind is a *likely consequence* of the fact that he believes that contracts are impossible without a written document.

Of course, given the first, more liberal set of interpretations of 'means something different', the fact that in our examples the subject means something different by his words (or at least applies them differently) is *implied* by certain of his beliefs. It is implied by a belief that he has arthritis in the thigh. A qualified version of the converse implication also holds. Given appropriate background assumptions, the fact that the subject has certain deviant (object-level) beliefs is implied by his meaning something different by his words. So far, no argument has shown that we cannot accept these implications and retain the literal interpretation of common mentalistic ascriptions.

The argument from deviant speaker-meaning downplays an intuitive feature that can be expected to be present in many of our examples. The subject's willingness to submit his statement and belief to the arbitration of an authority suggests a willingness to have his words taken in the normal way—regardless of mistaken associations with the word. Typically, the subject will regard recourse to a dictionary, and to the rest of us, as at once a check on his usage and his belief. When the verdict goes against him, he will not usually plead that we have simply misunderstood his views. This sort of behavior suggests that (given the sorts of background assumptions that common practice uses to distinguish our examples from those of foreigners, radical misunderstandings, and so forth) we can say that in a sense our man meant by 'arthritis' *arthritis*—where *'arthritis'* occurs, of course, obliquely. We can say this despite the fact that his incomplete understanding leads us, in one of the senses explicated earlier, to say that he meant something different by 'arthritis'.

If one tries to turn the argument from deviant speaker-meaning into a valid argument, one arrives at an assumption that seems to guide all three of the philosophical arguments I have discussed. The assumption is that what a person thinks his words mean, how he takes them, fully determines what attitudes he can express in using them: the contents of his mental states and events are strictly limited to notions, however idiosyncratic, that he understands; a person cannot think with notions he incompletely understands. But supplemented with this assumption, the argument begs the question at issue.

The least controversial justification of the assumption would be an appeal to standard practice in mentalistic attributions. But standard practice is what brought the assumption into question in the first place. Of course, usage is not sacred if good reasons for revising it can be given. But none have been.

The assumption is loosely derived, I think, from the old model according to which a person must be directly acquainted with, or must immediately apprehend, the contents of his thoughts. None of the objections explicitly invoke this model—and many of their proponents would reject it. But I think that all the objections derive some of their appeal from philosophical habits that have been molded by it. I shall discuss this model further in Section IV.

One may, of course, quite self-consciously neglect certain aspects of common mentalistic notions in the interests of a revised or idealized version of them. One such idealization could limit itself to just those attitudes involving "full understanding" (for some suitably specified notion of understanding). This limitation is less clearcut than one might suppose, since the notion of understanding itself tends to be used according to misleading stereotypes. Still, oversimplified models, idealizations, of mentalistic notions are defensible, as long as the character and purpose of the oversimplifications are clear. In my opinion, limiting oneself to "fully understood" attitudes provides no significant advantage in finding elegant and illuminating formal semantical theories of natural language. Such a strategy has perhaps a better claim in psychology, though even there its propriety is controversial. (Cf. Section IV.) More to the point, I think that models that neglect the relevant social factors in mentalistic attributions are not likely to provide long-run philosophical illumination of our actual mentalistic notions. But this view hardly admits of detailed support here and now.

Our argument in the preceding pages may, at a minimum, be seen as inveighing against a long-standing philosophical habit of denying that it *is* an oversimplification to make "full understanding" of a content a necessary condition for having a propositional attitude with that content. The oversimplification does not constitute neglect of some quirk of ordinary usage. Misunderstanding and partial understanding are pervasive and inevitable phenomena, and attributions of content despite them are an integral part of common practice.

I shall not here elaborate a philosophical theory of the social aspects of mentalistic phenomena, though in Section V I shall suggest lines such a theory might take. One of the most surprising and exciting aspects of the thought experiment is that its most literal interpretation provides a perspective on the mental that has received little serious development in the philosophical tradition. The perspective surely invites exploration.

IV. APPLICATIONS

I want to turn now to a discussion of how our argument bears on philosophical approaches to the mental that may be termed *individualistic*. I mean this term to be somewhat vague. But roughly, I intend to apply it to philosophical treatments that seek to see a person's intentional mental phenomena ultimately and purely in terms of what happens to the person, what occurs within him, and how he responds to his physical environment, without any essential reference to the social context in which he or the interpreter of his mental phenomena are situated. How I apply the term 'individualistic' will perhaps become clearer by reference to the particular cases that I shall discuss.

a.   As I have already intimated, the argument of the preceding sections affects the traditional intro- (or extro-) spectionist treatments of the mind, those of Plato, Descartes, Russell, and numerous others. These treatments are based on a model that likens the relation between a person and the contents of his thought to seeing, where seeing is taken to be a kind of direct, immediate experience. On the most radical and unqualified versions of the model, a person's inspection of the contents of his thought is infallible: the notion of incompletely understanding them has no application at all.

The model tends tǒ encourage individualistic treatments of the mental. For it suggests that what a person thinks depends on what occurs or "appears" within his mind. Demythologized, what a person thinks depends on the power and extent of his comprehension and on his internal dispositions toward the comprehended contents. The model is expressed in perhaps its crudest and least qualified form in a well-known passage by Russell:

> Whenever a relation of supposing or judging occurs, the terms to which the supposing or judging mind is related by the relation of supposing or judging must be terms with which the mind in question is acquainted. . . . It seems to me that the truth of this principle is evident as soon as the principle is understood.[5]

Acquaintance is (for Russell) direct, infallible, non-propositional, non-perspectival knowledge. "Terms" like concepts, ideas, attributes, forms, meanings, or senses are entities that occur in judgments more or less immediately before the mind on a close analogy to the way sensations are supposed to.

The model is more qualified and complicated in the writings of Descartes. In particular, he emphasizes the possibility that one might perceive the contents of one's mind unclearly or indistinctly. He is even high-handed enough to write, "Some people throughout their lives perceive nothing so correctly as to be capable of judging it properly."[6] This sort of remark appears to be a concession to the points made in Sections I and II about the possibility of a subject's badly understanding his mental contents. But the concession is distorted by the underlying introspection model. On Descartes' view, the person's faculty of understanding, properly so-called, makes no errors. Failure to grasp one's mental contents results from either blind prejudice or interference by "mere" bodily sensations and corporeal imagery. The implication is that with sufficiently careful reflection on the part of the individual subject, these obstacles to perfect understanding can be cleared. That is, one need only be careful or properly guided in one's introspections to achieve full understanding of the content of one's intentional mental phenomena. Much that Descartes says suggests that where the subject fails to achieve such understanding, no definite content can be attributed to him. In such cases, his "thinking" consists of unspecifiable or indeterminate imagery; attribution of definite conceptual content is precluded. These implications are reinforced in Descartes' appeal to self-evident, indubitable truths:

> There are some so evident and at the same time so simple that we cannot think of them without believing them to be true.... For we cannot doubt them unless we think of them; and we cannot think of them without at the same time believing them to be true, i.e. we can never doubt them.[7]

The self-evidence derives from the mere understanding of the truths, and fully understanding them is a precondition for thinking them at all. It is this last requirement that we have been questioning.

In the Empiricist tradition Descartes' qualifications on the direct experience model—particularly those involving the interfering effects of sensations and imagery—tend to fall away. What one thinks comes to be taken as a sort of impression (whether more imagistic or more intellectual) on or directly grasped by the individual's mind. The tendency to make full comprehension on the part of the subject a necessary condition for attributing a mental content to him appears both in philosophers who take the content to be a Platonic abstraction and in those who place it, in some sense, inside the individual's mind. This is certainly the direction in which the model pulls, with its picture of immediate accessibility to the individual. Thus Descartes' original concessions to cases of incomplete understanding became lost as his model became entrenched. What Wölfflin said of painters is true of philosophers: they learn more from studying each other than from reflecting on anything else.

The history of the model makes an intricate subject. My remarks are meant merely to provide a suggestive caricature of it. It should be clear, however, that in broad outline the model mixes poorly with the thought experiment of Section II, particularly its first step. The thought experiment indicates that certain "linguistic truths" that have often been held to be indubitable can be thought yet doubted. And it shows that a person's thought *content* is not fixed by what goes on in him, or by what is accessible to him simply by careful reflection. The reason for this last point about "accessibility" need not be that the content lies too deep in the unconscious recesses of the subject's psyche. Contents are sometimes "inaccessible" to introspection simply because much mentalistic attribution does not presuppose that the subject has fully mastered the content of his thought.

In a certain sense, the metaphysical model has fixed on some features of our use of mentalistic notions to the exclusion of others. For example, the model fastens on the facts that we are pretty good at identifying our own beliefs and thoughts, and we have at least a *prima facie* authority in reporting a wide range of them. It also underlines the point that for certain contents we tend to count understanding as a sufficient condition for acknowledging their truth. (It is debatable, of course, how well it explains or illumines these observations.) The model also highlights the truism that a certain measure of understanding is required of a subject if we are to attribute intentional phenomena on the basis of what he utters. As we have noted, chance or purely rote utterances provide no ground for mental content attributions; certain verbal pathologies are discounted. The model extrapolates from these observations to the claim that a person can never fail to understand the content of his beliefs or thoughts, or that the remedy for such failure lies within his own resources of reflection (whether autonomous and conscious, or unconscious and guided). It is this extrapolation that requires one to pass over the equally patent practice of attributing attitudes where the subject incompletely understands expressions that provide the content of those attitudes. Insistence on metalinguistic reinterpretation and talk about the indefiniteness of attitude contents in cases of incomplete understanding seem to be rearguard defenses of a vastly overextended model.

The Cartesian-Russellian model has few strict adherents among prominent linguistic philosophers. But although it has been widely rejected or politely talked around, claims that it bore and nurtured are commonplace, even among its opponents. As we have seen in the objections to the first step of the argument of Section II, these claims purport to restrict the contents we can attribute to a person on the basis of his use of language. The restrictions simply mimic those of Descartes. Freed of the picturesque but vulnerable model that formed them, the claims have assumed the power of dogma. Their strictures, however, misrepresent ordinary mentalistic notions.

b.   This century's most conspicuous attempt to replace the traditional Cartesian model has been the behaviorist movement and its heirs. I take it as obvious that the argument of Section II provides yet another reason to reject the most radical version of behaviorism—"philosophical," "logical" or "analytical" behaviorism. This is the view that mentalistic attributions can be "analytically" defined, or given strict meaning equivalences, purely in non-mental, behavioral terms. No analysis resting purely on the individual's dispositions to behavior can give an "analytic" definition of a mental content attribution because we can conceive of the behavioral definiens applying while the mentalistic definiendum does not. But a new argument for this conclusion is hardly needed since "philosophical" behaviorists are, in effect, extinct.

There is, however, an heir of behaviorism that I want to discuss at somewhat greater length. The approach sometimes goes by the name "functionalism," although that term is applied to numerous slogans and projects, often vaguely formulated. Even views that seem to me to be affected by our argument are frequently stated so sketchily that one may be in considerable doubt about what is being proposed. So my remarks should be taken less as an attempt to refute the theses of particular authors than as an attack on a way of thinking that seems to inform a cluster of viewpoints. The quotations I give in footnotes are meant to be suggestive, if not always definitive, of the way of thinking the argument tells against.[8]

The views affected by the argument of Section II attempts to give something like a philosophical "account" of the mental. The details and strategy—even the notion of "account"—vary from author to author. But a recurrent theme is that mental notions are to be seen ultimately in terms of the individual subject's input, output, and inner dispositions and states, where these latter are characterized purely in terms of how they lead to or from output, input, or other inner states similarly characterized. Mental notions are to be explicated or identified in functional, non-mentalistic, non-intentional terminology. Proponents of this sort of idea are rarely very specific about what terms may be used in describing input and output, or even what sorts of terms count as "functional" expressions. But the impression usually given is that input and output are to be specified in terms (acceptable to a behaviorist) of irritations of the subject's surfaces and movements of his body. On some versions, neurophysiological terms are allowed. More recently, there have been liberalized appeals to causal input and output relations with particular, specified physical objects, stuffs, or magnitudes. Functional terms include terms like 'causes', 'leads to with probability n', and the like. For our purposes, the details do not matter much, as long as an approach allows no mentalistic or other intentional terms (such as 'means' or that-clauses) into its vocabulary, and as long as it applies to individuals taken one by one.

A difference between this approach and that of philosophical behaviorism is that a whole array of dispositional or functional states—causally or probabilistically interrelated—may enter into the "account" of a single mental attribution. The array must be ultimately secured to input and output, but the internal states need not be so secured one by one. The view is thus not immediately vulnerable to claims against simplistic behaviorisms, that a *given* stimulus-response pattern may have different contents in different social contexts. Such claims, which hardly need a defender, have been tranquilly accepted on this view. The view's hope is that differences in content depend on functional differences in the individual's larger functional structure. From this viewpoint, analytical behaviorism erred primarily in its failure to recognize the interlocking or wholistic character of mental attributions and in its oversimplification of theoretical explanation.

As I said, the notion of an account of the mental varies from author to author. Some authors take over the old-fashioned ideal of an "analysis" from philosophical behaviorism and aim at a definition of the meaning of mentalistic vocabulary, or a definitional elimination of it. Others see their account as indicating a series of scientific hypotheses that identify mental states with causal or functional states, or roles, in the individual. These authors reject behaviorism's goal of providing meaning equivalences, as well as its restrictive methods. The hypotheses are supposed to be type or property identities and are nowadays often thought to hold necessarily, even if they do not give meaning relations. Moreover, these hypotheses are offered not merely as speculation about the future of psychology, but as providing a philosophically illuminating account of our ordinary notion of the mental. Thus if the view systematically failed to make plausible type identities between functional states and mental states, ordinarily construed, then by its own lights it would have failed to give a philosophical "account" of the mental. I have crudely over-schematized the methodological differences among the authors in this tradition. But the differences fall roughly within the polar notions of *account* that I have described. I think our discussion will survive the oversimplifications.[9]

Any attempt to give an account of specific beliefs and thoughts along the lines I have indicated will come up short. For we may fix the input, output, and total array of dispositional or functional states of our subject, as long as these are non-intentionally described and are limited to what is relevant to accounting for his activity taken in isolation from that of his fellows. But we can still conceive of his mental contents as varying. Functionally equivalent people—on any plausible notion of functional equivalence that has been sketched—may have non-equivalent mental-state and event contents, indicated by obliquely non-equivalent content clauses. Our argument indicates a systematic inadequacy in attempts of the sort I described.

Proponents of functionalist accounts have seen them as revealing the true nature of characteristic marks of the mental and as resolving traditional philosophical issues about such marks. In the case of beliefs, desires, and thoughts, the most salient mark is intentionality—the ill-specified information-bearing, representational feature that seems to invest these mental states and events.[10] In our terminology, accounting for intentionality largely amounts to accounting for the content of mental states and events. (There is also, of course, the application of content in *de re* cases. But we put this aside here.) Such content is clearly part of what the functional roles of our subjects' states fail to determine.

It is worth re-emphasizing here that the problem is unaffected by suggestions that we specify input and output in terms of causal relations to particular objects or stuffs in the subject's physical environment. Such specifications may be thought to help with some examples based on indexicality or psychological success verbs, and perhaps in certain arguments concerning natural kind terms (though even in these cases I think that one will be forced to appeal to intentional language). (Cf. note 2.) But this sort of suggestion has no easy application to our argument. For the relevant causal relations between the subject and the physical environment to which his terms apply—where such relations are non-intentionally specified—were among the elements held constant while the subject's beliefs and thoughts varied.

The functionalist approaches I have cited seem to provide yet another case in which mental contents are not plausibly accounted for in non-intentional terms. They are certainly not explicable in terms of causally or functionally specified states and events of the *individual* subject. The intentional or semantical role of mental states and events is not a function merely of their functionally specified roles in the individual. The failure of these accounts of intentional mental states and events derives from an underestimation of socially dependent features of cognitive phenomena.

Before extending the application of our argument, I want to briefly canvass some ways of being influenced by it, ways that might appeal to someone fixed on the functionalist ideal. One response might be to draw a strict distinction between mental states, ordinarily so-called, and psychological states. One could then claim that the latter are the true subject matter of the science of psychology and may be identified with functional states functionally specified, after all. Thus one might claim that the subject was in the same psychological (functional) states in both the actual and the imagined situations, although he had different beliefs and thoughts ordinarily so-called.

There are two observations that need to be entered about this position. The first is that it frankly jettisons much of the philosophical interest of functionalist accounts. The failure to cope with mental contents is a case in point. The second observation is that it is far from clear that such a distinction between the psychological and the mental is or will be sanctioned by psychology itself. Functionalist accounts arose as philosophical interpretations of developments in psychology influenced by computer theory. The interpretations have been guided by philosophical interests, such as throwing light on the mind-body problem and accounting for mentalistic features in non-mentalistic terms. But the theories of cognitive psychologists, including those who place great weight on the computer analogy, are not ordinarily purified of mentalistic or intentional terminology. Indeed, intentional terminology plays a central role in much contemporary theorizing. (This is also true of theories that appeal to "sub-personal" states or processes. The "sub-personal" states themselves are often characterized intentionally.) Purifying a theory of mentalistic and intentional features in favor of functional or causal features is more clearly demanded by the goals of philosophers than by the needs of psychology. Thus it is at least an open question whether functional approaches of the sort we have discussed give a satisfactory account of *psychological* states and events. It is not evident that psychology will ever be methodologically "pure" (or theoretically purifiable by some definitional device) in the way these approaches demand. *This* goal of functionalists may be simply a meta-psychological mistake.

To put the point another way, it is not clear that functional states, characterized purely in functional, non-intentional terms (and non-intentional descriptions of input and output) are the natural subject matter of psychology. Psychology would, I think, be an unusual theory if it restricted itself (or could be definitionally restricted) to specifying abstract causal or functional structures in purely causal or functional terms, together with vocabulary from other disciplines. Of course, it *may* be that functional states, functionally specified, form a psychological natural kind. And it is certainly not to be assumed that psychology will respect ordinary terminology in its individuation of types of psychological states and events. Psychology must run its own course. But the assumption that psychological terminology will be ultimately non-intentional and purely functional seems without strong support.

More important from our viewpoint, if psychology did take the individualistic route suggested by the approaches we have cited, then its power to illumine the everyday phenomena alluded to in mentalistic discourse would be correspondingly limited.

These remarks suggest a second sort of functionalist response to the argument of Section II, one that attempts to take the community rather than the individual as the object of functional analysis. One might, for example, seek to explain an individual's responsibility to communal standards in terms of his having the right kind of interaction with other individuals who collectively had functional structures appropriate to those standards. Spelling out the relevant notions of interaction and appropriateness is, of course, anything but trivial. (Cf. Section V.) Doing so in purely functional, non-intentional terms would be yet a further step. Until such a treatment is developed and illustrated in some detail, there is little point in discussing it. I shall only conjecture that, if it is to remain non-intentional, such a treatment is likely to be so abstract—at least in our present state of psychological and sociological ignorance—that it will be unilluminating from a philosophical point of view. Some of the approaches we have been discussing already more than flirt with this difficulty.

c.   Individualistic assumptions about the mental have infected theorizing about the relation between mind and meaning. An example is the Gricean project of accounting for conventional or linguistic meaning in terms of certain complex intentions and beliefs of individuals.[11] The Gricean program analyzes conventional meaning in terms of subtle "mutual knowledge," or beliefs and intentions about each others' beliefs and intentions, on the part of most or all members of a community. Seen as a quasi-definitional enterprise, the program presupposes that the notion of an individual's believing or intending something is always "conceptually" independent of the conventional meaning of symbols used to express that something. Insofar as 'conceptually' has any intuitive content, this seems not to be the case. Our subject's belief or intention contents can be conceived to vary simply by varying conventions in the community around him. The content of individuals' beliefs seems sometimes to depend partly on social conventions in their environment. It is true that our subjects are actually rather abnormal members of their community, at least with respect to their use and understanding of a given word. But normality here is judged against the standards set by communal conventions. So stipulating that the individuals whose mental states are used in defining conventional meaning be relevantly normal will not avoid the circularity that I have indicated. I see no way to do so. This charge of circularity has frequently been raised on intuitive grounds. Our argument gives the intuitions substance. Explicating convention in terms of belief and intention may provide various sorts of insight. But it is not defining a communal notion in terms of individualistic notions. Nor is it reducing, in any deep sense, the semantical, or the intentional generally, to the psychological.

d.   Individualistic assumptions have also set the tone for much discussion of the ontology of the mental. This subject is too large to receive detailed consideration here. It is complicated by a variety of crosscurrents among different projects, methodologies, and theses. I shall only explore how our argument affects a certain line of thinking closely allied to the functionalist approaches already discussed. These approaches have frequently been seen as resuscitating an old argument for the materialist identity theory. The argument is three-staged. First, one gives a philosophical "account" of each mentalistic locution, an account that is *prima facie* neutral as regards ontology. For example, a belief or a thought that sofas are comfortable is supposed to be accounted for as one functionally specified state or event within an array of others—all of which are secured to input and output. Second, the relevant functionally specified states or events are expected to be empirically correlated or correlatable with physiological states or events in a person (states or events that have those functions). The empirical basis for believing in these correlations is claimed to be provided by present or future physical science. The nature of the supposed correlations is differently described in different theories. But the most prevalent views expect only that the correlations will hold for each organism and person (perhaps at a given time) taken one by one. For example, the functionally specified event type that is identified with a thought that sofas are comfortable may be realized in one person by an instance (or "token") of one physiological event type, and in another person by an instance of another physiological event type. Third, the ("token") mental state or event in the person is held to be identical with the relevant ("token") physiological state or event, on general grounds of explanatory simplicity and scientific method. Sometimes, this third stage is submerged by building uniqueness of occupancy of functional role into the first stage.[12]

I am skeptical about this sort of argument at every stage. But I shall doubt only the first stage here. The argument we gave in Section II directly undermines the attempt to carry out the first stage by recourse to the sort of functionalist approaches that we discussed earlier. Sameness of functional role, individualistically specified, is compatible with difference of content. I know of no better non-intentional account of mentalistic locutions. If a materialist argument of this genre is to arrive, it will require a longer first step.

I shall not try to say whether there is a philosophically interesting sense in which intentional mental phenomena are physical or material. But I do want to note some considerations against materialist *identity* theories.

State-like phenomena (say, beliefs) raise different problems from event-like phenomena (say, occurrent thoughts). Even among identity theorists, it is sometimes questioned whether an identity theory is the appropriate goal for materialism in the case of states. Since I shall confine myself to identity theories, I shall concentrate on event-like phenomena. But our considerations will also bear on views that hope to establish some sort of token identity theory for mental states like beliefs.

One other preliminary. I want to remain neutral about how best to describe the relation between the apparent event-like feature of occurrent thoughts and the apparent relational feature (their relation to a content). One might think of there being an event, the token thought event, that is in a certain relation to a content (indicated by the that-clause). One might think of the event as consisting—as not being anything "over and above"—the relevant relation's holding at a certain time between a person and a content. Or one might prefer some other account. From the viewpoint of an identity theory, the first way of seeing the matter is most advantageous. So I shall fit my expositon to that point of view.

Our ordinary method of identifying occurrent thought events and differentiating between them is to make reference to the person or organism to whom the thought occurs, the time of its occurrence, and the content of the thought. If person, time, and content are the same, we would normally count the thought event the same. If any one of these parameters differs in descriptions of thought events (subject to qualifications about duration), then the events or occurrences described are different. Of course, we can differentiate between events using descriptions that do not home in on these particular parameters. But these parameters are dominant. (It is worth noting that differentiations in terms of causes and effects usually tend to rely on the content of mental events or states at some point, since mental states or events are often among the causes or effects of a given mental event, and these causes or effects will usually be identified partly in terms of their content.) The important point for our purposes is that in ordinary practice, sameness of thought content (or at least some sort of strong equivalence of content) is taken as a necessary condition for sameness of thought occurrence.

Now one might codify and generalize this point by holding that no occurrence of a thought (that is, no token thought event) could have a different (or extensionally non-equivalent) content and be the very same token event. If this premise is accepted, then our argument of Section II can be deployed to show that a person's thought event is not *identical* with any event in him that is described by physiology, biology, chemistry, or physics. For let *b* be any given event described in terms of one of the physical sciences that occurs in the subject while he thinks the relevant thought. Let '*b*' be such that it denotes the same physical event occurring in the subject in our counterfactual situation. (If you want, let '*b*' be rigid in Kripke's sense, though so strong a stipulation is not needed.) The second step of our argument in Section II makes it plausible that *b* need not be affected by counterfactual differences in the communal use of the word 'arthritis'. Actually, the subject thinks that his ankles are stiff from arthritis, while *b* occurs. But we can conceive of the subject's *lacking* a thought event that his ankles are stiff from arthritis, while *b* occurs. Thus in view of our initial premise, *b* is not identical with the subject's occurrent thought.[13]

Identity theorists will want to reject the first premise the premise that no event with a different content could be identical with a given thought event. On such a view, the given thought event that his ankles are stiff from arthritis might well have been a thought that his ankles are stiff from tharthritis, yet be precisely the same token thought event. Such a view is intuitively very implausible. I know of only one reasonably spelled-out basis of support for this view. Such a basis would be provided by showing that mentalistic phenomena are causal or functional states, in one of the strong senses discussed earlier, and that mental events are physical tokens or realizations of those states. If 'that thought that his ankles are stiff from arthritis' could be accounted for in terms like 'that event with such and such a causal or functional role' (where 'such and such' does not itself involve intentional terminology), and if independently identified physical events systematically filled these roles (or realized these states), we could perhaps see a given thought event as having a different role—and hence content—in different possible situations. Given such a view, the functional specification could perhaps be seen as revealing the contingency of the intentional specification as applied to mental event tokens. Just as we can imagine a given physiological event that actually plays the role of causing the little finger to move two inches, as playing the role of causing the little finger to move three inches (assuming compensatory differences in its physiological environment), so we could perhaps imagine a given thought as having a different functional role from its actual one—and hence, assuming the functionalist account, as having a different content. But the relevant sort of functionalist account of intentional phenomena has not been made good.[14]

The recent prosperity of materialist-functionalist ways of thinking has been so great that it is often taken for granted that a given thought event might have been a thought with a different, obliquely non-equivalent content. Any old event, on this view, could have a different content, a different significance, if its surrounding context were changed. But in the case of occurrent thoughts—and intentional mental events generally—it is hardly obvious, or even initially plausible, that anything is more essential to the identity of the event than the content itself. Materialist identity theories have schooled the imagination to picture the content of a mental event as varying while the event remains fixed. But whether such imaginings are possible fact or just philosophical fancy is a separate question.[15]

At any rate, functionalist accounts have not provided adequate specification of what it is to be a thought that ____, for particular fillings of the blank. So a specification of a given thought event in functionalist terms does not reveal the contingency of the usual, undisputed intentional specifications.

Well, *is* it possible for a thought event to have had a different content from the one it has and be the very same event? It seems to me natural and certainly traditional to assume that this is not possible. Rarely, however, have materialists seen the identity theory as natural or intuitive. Materialists are generally revisionist about intuitions. What is clear is that we currently do identify and distinguish thought events primarily in terms of the person who has them, the rough times of their occurrence, and their contents. And we do assume that a thought event with a different content is a different thought event (insofar as we distinguish at all between the thinking event and the person's being related to a thought content at a time). I think these facts give the premise *prima facie* support and the argument against the identity theory some interest. I do not claim that we have *"a priori"* certainty that no account of intentional phenomena will reveal intentional language to be only contingently applicable to belief states or thought events. I am only dubious.

One might nurture faith or hope that some more socially oriented functionalist specification could be found. But no such specification is ready to hand. And I see no good reason to think that one must be found. Even if such a specification were found, it is far from clear that it would deflect the argument against the identity theory just considered. The "functional" states envisaged would depend not merely on what the individual does and what inner causal states lead to his activity—non-intentionally specified—but also on what his fellows do. The analogy between functional states and physiological states in causing the individual's internal and external activity was the chief support for the view that a given token mental event might have been a token of a different content. But the envisaged socially defined "functional states" bear no intuitive analogy to physiological states or other physical causal states within the individual's body. Their function is not simply that of responding to environmental influences and causing the individual's activity. It is therefore not clear (short of *assuming* an identity theory) that any event that is a token of one of the envisaged socially defined "functional states" could have been a token of a different one. The event might be essentially identified in terms of its social role. There is as yet no reason to identify it in terms of physically described events in the individual's body. Thus it is not clear that such a socially oriented functional account of thought contents would yield grounds to believe that the usual intentional specifications of mental events are merely contingent. It is, I think, even less clear that an appropriate socially oriented functional account is viable.

Identity theories, of course, do not exhaust the resources of materialism. To take one example, our argument does not speak directly to a materialism based on composition rather than identity. On such a view, the same physical material might compose different thoughts in different circumstances. I shall say nothing evaluative about this sort of view. I have also been silent about other arguments for a token identity theory—such as those based on philosophical accounts of the notions of causality or explanation. Indeed, my primary interest has not been ontology at all. It has been to identify and question individualistic assumptions in materialist as well as Cartesian approaches to the mental.

V. MODELS OF THE MENTAL

Traditional philosophical accounts of mind have offered metaphors that produce doctrine and carry conviction where argument and unaided intuition flag. Of course, any such broad reconstructions can be accused of missing the pied beauties of the natural article. But the problem with traditional philosophy of mind is more serious. The two overwhelmingly dominant metaphors of the mental—the infallible eye and the automatic mechanism—have encouraged systematic neglect of prominent features of a wide range of mental phenomena, broadly speaking, social features. Each metaphor has its attractions. Either can be elaborated or doctored to fit the facts that I have emphasized. But neither illumines those facts. And both have played some part in inducing philosophers to ignore them.

I think it optimistic indeed to hope that any one picture, comparable to the traditional ones, will provide insight into all major aspects of mental phenomena. Even so, a function of philosophy is to sketch such pictures. The question arises whether one can make good the social debts of earlier accounts while retaining at least some of their conceptual integrity and pictorial charm. This is no place to start sketching. But some summary remarks may convey a sense of the direction in which our discussion has been tending.

The key feature of the examples of Section II was the fact that we attribute beliefs and thoughts to people even where they incompletely understand contents of those very beliefs and thoughts. This point about intentional mental phenomena is not everywhere applicable: non-linguistic animals do not seem to be candidates for misunderstanding the contents of their beliefs. But the point is certainly salient and must be encompassed in any picture of intentional mental phenomena. Crudely put, wherever the subject has attained a certain competence in large relevant parts of his language and has (implicitly) assumed a certain general commitment or responsibility to the communal conventions governing the language's symbols, the expressions the subject uses take on a certain inertia in determining attributions of mental content to him. In particular, the expressions the subject uses sometimes provide the content of his mental states or events even though he only partially understands, or even misunderstands, some of them. Global coherence and responsibility seem sometimes to override localized incompetence.

The detailed conditions under which this "inertial force" is exerted are complicated and doubtless more than a little vague. Clearly, the subject must maintain a minimal internal linguistic and rational coherence and a broad similarity to others' use of the language. But meeting this condition is hardly sufficient to establish the relevant responsibility. For the condition is met in the case of a person who speaks a regional dialect (where the same words are sometimes given different applications). The person's aberrations relative to the larger community may be normalities relative to the regional one. In such cases, of course, the regional conventions are dominant in determining what contents should be attributed. At this point, it is natural to appeal to etiological considerations. The speaker of the dialect developed his linguistic habits from interaction with others who were a party to distinctively regional conventions. The person is committed to using the words according to the conventions maintained by those from whom he learned the words. But the situation is more complicated than this observation suggests. A person born and bred in the parent community might simply decide (unilaterally) to follow the usage of the regional dialect or even to fashion his own usage with regard to particular words, self-consciously opting out of the parent community's conventions in these particulars. In such a case, members of the parent community would not, and should not, attribute mental contents to him on the basis of homophonic construal of his words. Here the individual's intentions or attitudes toward communal conventions and communal conceptions seem more important than the causal antecedents of his transactions with a word—unless those intentions are simply included in the etiological story.

I shall not pursue these issues here. The problem of specifying the conditions under which a person has the relevant general competence in a language and a responsibility to its conventions is obviously complicated. The mixture of "causal" and intentional considerations relevant to dealing with it has obvious near analogs in other philosophical domains (etiological accounts of perception, knowledge, reference). I have no confidence that all of the details of the story would be philosophically interesting. What I want to stress is that to a fair degree, mentalistic attribution rests not on the subject's having mastered the contents of the attribution, and not on his having behavioral dispositions peculiarly relevant to those contents, but on his having a certain responsibility to communal conventions governing, and conceptions associated with, symbols that he is disposed to use. It is this feature that must be incorporated into an improved model of the mental.

I think it profitable to see the language of content attribution as constituting a complex *standard* by reference to which the subject's mental states and events are estimated, or an abstract grid on which they are plotted. Different people may vary widely in the degree to which they master the elements and relations within the standard, even as it applies to them all. This metaphor may be developed in several directions and with different models: applied geometry, measurement of magnitudes, evaluation by a monetary standard, and so forth. A model I shall illustrate briefly here borrows from musical analysis.

Given that a composer has fulfilled certain general conditions for establishing a musical key, his chordal structures are plotted by reference to the harmonic system of relations appropriate to the tonic key. There is vast scope for variation and novelty within the harmonic framework. The chords may depart widely from traditional "rules" or practices governing what count as interesting or "reasonable" chordal structures and progressions. And the composer may or may not grasp the harmonic implications and departures present in his composition. The composer may sometimes exhibit harmonic incompetence (and occasionally harmonic genius) by radically departing from those traditional rules. But the harmonic system of relations applies to the composition in any case. Once established, the tonic key and its associated harmonic framework are applied unless the composer takes pains to set up another tonic key or some atonal arrangement (thereby intentionally opting out of the original tonal framework), or writes down notes by something like a slip of the pen (suffering mechanical interference in his compositional intentions), or unintentionally breaks the harmonic rules in a massive and unprincipled manner (thereby indicating chaos or complete incompetence). The tonic key provides a standard for describing the composition. The application of the standard depends on the composer's maintaining a certain overall coherence and minimal competence in conforming to the standard's conventions. And there are conditions under which the standard would be replaced by another. But once applied, the harmonic framework—its formal interrelations, its applicability even to deviant, pointless progressions—is partly independent of the composer's degree of harmonic mastery.

One attractive aspect of the metaphor is that it has some application to the case of animals. In making sounds, animals do sometimes behave in such a way that a harmonic standard can be roughly applied to them, even though the standard, at least in any detail, is no part of what they have mastered. Since they do not master the standard (though they may master some of its elements), they are not candidates for partial understanding or misunderstanding. (Of course, this may be said of many people as regards the musical standard.) The standard applies to both animals and people. But the conditions for its application are sensitive in various ways to whether the subject himself has mastered it. Where the subject does use the standard (whether the language, or a system of key relationships), his uses take on special weight in applications of the standard to him.

One of the metaphor's chief virtues is that it encourages one to seek social explications for this special weight. The key to our attribution of mental contents in the face of incomplete mastery or misunderstanding lies largely in social functions associated with maintaining and applying the standard. In broad outline, the social advantages of the "special weight" are apparent. Symbolic expressions are the overwhelmingly dominant source of detailed information about what people think, intend, and so forth. Such detail is essential not only to much explanation and prediction, but also to fulfilling many of our cooperative enterprises and to relying on one another for second-hand information. Words interpreted in conventionally established ways are familiar, palpable, and public. They are common coin, a relatively stable currency. These features are crucial to achieving the ends of mentalistic attribution just cited. They are also critical in maximizing interpersonal comparability. And they yield a bias toward taking others at their word and avoiding *ad hoc* reinterpretation, once overall agreement in usage and commitment to communal standards can be assumed.

This bias issues in the practice of expressing even many differences in understanding without reinterpreting the subject's words. Rather than reinterpret the subject's word 'arthritis' and give him a trivially true object-level belief and merely a false metalinguistic belief about how 'arthritis' is used by others, it is common practice, and correct, simply to take him at his word.

I hardly need re-emphasize that the situation is vastly more complicated than I have suggested in the foregoing paragraphs. Insincerity, tongue slips, certain malapropisms, subconscious blocks, mental instability all make the picture more complex. There are differences in our handling of different sorts of expressions, depending, for example, on how clear and fixed social conventions regarding the expressions are. There are differences in our practices with different subject matters. There are differences in our handling of different degrees of linguistic error. There are differences in the way meaning-, assertion-, and mental-contents are attributed. (Cf. note 4.) I do not propose ignoring these points. They are all parameters affecting the inertial force of "face value" construal. But I want to keep steadily in mind the philosophically neglected fact about social practice: Our attributions do not require that the subject always correctly or fully understand the content of his attitudes.

The point suggests fundamental misorientations in the two traditional pictures of the mental. The authority of a person's reports about his thoughts and beliefs (*modulo* sincerity, lack of subconscious interference, and so forth) does not issue from a special intellectual vision of the contents of those thoughts and beliefs. It extends even to some cases in which the subject incompletely understands those contents. And it depends partly on the social advantages of maintaining communally established standards of communication and mentalistic attribution. Likewise, the descriptive and explanatory role of mental discourse is not adequately modeled by complex non-intentional mechanisms or programs for the production of an individual's physical movement and behavior. Attributing intentional mentalistic phenomena to individuals serves not only to explain their behavior viewed in isolation but also to chart their activity (intentional, verbal, behavioral, physical) by complex comparison to others—and against socially established standards.[16] Both traditional metaphors make the mistake, among others, of treating intentional mental phenomena individualistically. New approaches must do better. The sense in which man is a social animal runs deeper than much mainstream philosophy of mind has acknowledged.[17]

Notes

1. Our examples suggest points about learning that need exploration. It would seem naive to think that we first attain a mastery of expressions or notions we use and then tackle the subject matters we speak and think about in using those expressions or notions. In most cases, the processes overlap. But while the subject's understanding is still partial, we sometimes attribute mental contents in the very terms the subject has yet to master. Traditional views take mastering a word to consist in matching it with an already mastered (or innate) concept. But it would seem, rather, that many concepts (or mental content components) are like words in that they may be employed before they are mastered. In both cases, employment appears to be an integral part of the process of mastery.

2. A development of a similar theme may be found in Hilary Putnam's notion of a division of linguistic labour. Cf. "The Meaning of 'Meaning'," *Philosophical Papers* 2 (London, 1975) pp. 227 ff. Putnam's imaginative work is in other ways congenial with points I have developed. Some of his examples can be adapted in fairly obvious ways so as to give an argument with different premises, but a conclusion complementary to the one I arrive at in Section IIa:

Consider Alfred's belief contents involving the notion of water. Without changing Alfred's (or his fellows') non-intentional phenomenal experiences, internal physical occurrences, or dispositions to respond to stimuli on sensory surfaces, we can imagine that not water (H_2O), but a different liquid with different structure but similar macro-properties (and identical phenomenal properties) played the role in his environment that water does in ours. In such a case, we could ascribe no content clauses to Alfred with 'water' in oblique position. His belief contents would differ. The conclusion (with which I am in sympathy) is that mental contents are affected not only by the physical and qualitatively mental way the person is, but by the nature of his *physical environment*.

Putnam himself does not give quite this argument. He nowhere states the first and third steps, though he gives analogs of them for the meaning of 'water'. This is partly just a result of his concentration on meaning instead of propositional attitudes. But some of what he says even seems to oppose the argument's conclusion. He remarks in effect that the subject's *thoughts* remain constant between his actual and counterfactual cases (p. 224). In his own argument he explicates the difference between actual and counterfactual cases in terms of a difference in the extension of terms, not a difference in those aspects of their meaning that play a role in the cognitive life of the subject. And he tries to explicate his examples in terms of indexicality—a mistake, I think, and one that tends to divert attention from major implications of the examples he gives. (Cf. Section IId.) In my view, the examples do illustrate the fact that all attitudes involving natural kind notions, including *de dicto* attitudes, presuppose *de re* attitudes. But the examples do not show that natural kind linguistic expressions are in any ordinary sense indexical. Nor do they show that beliefs involving natural kind notions are always *de re*. Even if they did, the change from actual to counterfactual cases would affect oblique occurrences of natural kind terms in that-clauses—occurrences that are the key to attributions of cognitive content.

(Cf. above and note 3.) In the cited paper and earlier ones, much of what Putnam says about psychological states (and implies about mental states) has a distinctly individualistic ring. Below in Section IV, I criticize viewpoints about mental phenomena influenced by and at least strongly suggested in his earlier work on functionalism. (Cf. note 9.)

On the other hand, Putnam's articulation of social and environmental aspects of the meaning of natural kind terms complements and supplements our viewpoint. For me, it has been a rich rewarder of reflection. More recent work of his seems to involve shifts in his viewpoint on psychological states. It may have somewhat more in common with our approach than the earlier work, but there is much that I do not understand about it.

The argument regarding the notion of water that I extracted from Putnam's paper is narrower in scope than our argument. The Putnam-derived argument seems to work only for natural kind terms and close relatives. And it may seem not to provide as direct a threat to certain versions of functionalism that I discuss in Section IV: At least a few philosophers would claim that one could accommodate the Putnamian argument in terms of *non*-intentional formulations of input-output relations (formulations that make reference to the specific nature of the physical environment). Our argument does not submit to this maneuver. In our thought experiment, the physical environment (sofas, arthritis, and so forth in our examples) and the subject's causal relations with it (at least as these are usually conceived) were held constant. The Putnamian argument, however, has fascinatingly different implications from our argument. I have not developed these comparisons and contrasts here because doing justice to Putnam's viewpoint would demand a distracting amount of space, as the ample girth of this footnote may suggest.

3. I have discussed *de re* mental phenomena in "Belief *De Re*," *The Journal of Philosophy* 74 (1977):338-62. There I argue that all attitudes with content presuppose *de re* attitudes. Our discussion here may be seen as bearing on the details of this presupposition. But for reasons I merely sketch in the next paragraph, I think it would be a superficial viewpoint that tried to utilize our present argument to support the view that nearly all intentional mental phenomena are covertly indexical or *de re*.

4. Cf. my "Belief and Synonymy," *The Journal of Philosophy* 75 (1978):119-38, Section III, where I concentrate on attribution of belief contents containing "one criterion" terms like 'vixen' or 'fortnight' which the subject misunderstands. The next several pages interweave some of the points in that paper. I think that a parallel thought experiment involving even these words is constructible, at least for a narrowly restricted set of beliefs. We can imagine that the subject believes that some female foxes—say, those that are virgins—are not vixens. Or he could believe that a fortnight is a period of ten days. (I believed this for many years.) Holding his physical history, qualitative experience, and dispositions constant, we can conceive of his linguistic community defining these terms as he actually misunderstands them. In such a case, his belief contents would differ from his actual ones.

5. Bertrand Russell, *Mysticism and Logic* (London, 1959), p. 221. Although Russell's statement is unusually unqualified, its kinship to Descartes' and Plato's model is unmistakable. Cf. Plato, *Phaedrus*, 249b-c, *Phaedo*, 47b6-c4; Descartes, *Philosophical Works*, eds. Haldane and Ross 2 vols. (New York, 1955), *Rules for the Direction of the Mind*, section XII, Vol. I, pp. 41-42, 45; *Principles of Philosophy*, Part I, XXXII-XXXV. Vol. I, pp. 232-33; *Replies*, Vol. II, 52; Hume, *A Treatise of Human Nature*, I, 3,5; II, 2,6; Kant, *A Critique of Pure Reason*, A7-B11; Frege, *The Foundations of Arithmetic*, section 105; G. E. Moore, *Principia Ethica*, 86.

6. Descartes, *Principles of Philosophy*, XLV-XLI.

7. Descartes, *Philosophical Works*, Vol. II., *Replies*, p. 42.

8. Certain movements sometimes called "functionalist" are definitely not my present concern. Nothing I say is meant to oppose the claim that hypotheses in psychology do and should make reference to "sub-personal" states and processes in explaining human action and ordinary mental states and processes. My remarks may bear on precisely how such hypotheses are construed philosophically. But the hypotheses themselves must be judged primarily by their fruits. Similarly, I am not concerned with the claim that computers provide an illuminating perspec-

tive for viewing the mind. Again, our view may bear on the interpretation of the computer analogy, but I have no intention of questioning its general fruitfulness. On the other hand, insofar as functionalism is merely a slogan to the effect that "once you see how computers might be made to work, you realize such and such about the mind," I am inclined to let the cloud condense a little before weighing its contents.

9. A representative of the more nearly "analytical" form of functionalism is David Lewis, "Psychophysical and Theoretical Identifications," *Australasian Journal of Philosophy* 50 (1972):249-58: "Applied to common-sense psychology—folk science rather than professional science, but a theory nonetheless—we get the hypothesis . . . that a mental state M . . . is definable as the occupant of a certain causal role R—that is, as the state, of whatever sort, that is causally connected in specified ways to sensory stimuli, motor responses, and other mental states" (249-50). Actually, it should be noted that the argument of Section I applies to Lewis's position less directly than one might suppose. For reasons unconnected with matters at hand, Lewis intends his *definition* to apply to relational mentalistic predicates like 'thinks' but not to complex predicates that identify actual mental states or events, like 'thinks that snow is white'. Cf. *Ibid.*, p. 256, n13. This seems to me a puzzling halfway house for some of Lewis's philosophical purposes. But our argument appears to apply anyway, since Lewis is explicit in holding that physical facts about a person taken in isolation from his fellows "determine" all his specific intentional events and states. Cf. 'Radical Interpretation', *Synthese* 27 (1974):331ff. I cite Lewis's definitional approach because it has been the most influential recent piece of its genre, and many of those influenced by it have not excluded its application to specific intentional mental states and events. Other representatives of the definitional approach are J. J. C. Smart, "Further Thoughts on the Identity Theory," *Monist* 56 (1972):149-62; D. W. Armstrong, *A Materialist Theory of Mind* (London, 1968), pp. 90-91 and *passim;* Sidney Shoemaker, "Functionalism and Qualia," *Philosophical Studies* 27 (1975):306-7. A representative of the more frequently held "hypothesis" version of functionalism is Hilary Putnam, "The Mental Life of Some Machines," *Philosophical Papers* 2 (Cambridge, 1975), and "The Nature of Mental States," *Ibid.*, cf. p. 437: ". . . if the program of finding psychological laws that are not species specific . . . ever succeeds, then it will bring in its wake a delineation of the kind of functional organization that is necessary and sufficient for a given psychological state, as well as a precise definition of the notion 'psychological state'." In more recent work, Putnam's views on the relation between functional organization and psychological (and also mental) states and events have become more complicated. I make no claims about how the argument of Section II bears on them. Other representatives of the "hypothesis" approach are Gilbert Harman, "Three Levels of Meaning," *The Journal of Philosophy* 65 (1968); "An Introduction to 'Translation and Meaning'," *Words and Objections,* eds. D. Davidson and J. Hintikka (Reidel, 1969), p. 21; and *Thought* (Princeton, 1973), pp. 43-46, 56-65, for example, p. 45: ". . . mental states and processes are to be functionally defined (by a psychological theory). They are constituted by their function or role in the relevant programme"; Jerry Fodor, *The Language of Thought* (New York, 1975), Chapter I; Armstrong, *A Materialist Theory of Mind*, p. 84. An attempt to articulate the common core of the different types of functionalist "account" occurs in Ned Block and Jerry Fodor's "What Psychological States are Not," *Philosophical Review* 81 (1972), p. 173: ". . . functionalism in the broad sense of that doctrine which holds that type identity conditions for psychological states refer only to their relations to inputs, outputs and one another."

10. Often functionalists give mental contents only cursory discussion, if any at all. But claims that a functional account explains intentionality by accounting for all specific intentional states and events in non-intentional, functional language occur in the following: Daniel Dennett, *Content and Consciousness* (London, 1969), Chapter II and *passim;* Harman, *Thought,* for example, p. 60: "To specify the meaning of a sentence used in communication is partly to specify the belief or other mental state expressed; and the representative character of that state is determined by its functional role"; Fodor, *The Language of Thought,* Chapters I and II, for

120   TYLER BURGE

example, p. 75: "The way that information is stored, computed . . . or otherwise processed by the organism explains its cognitive states and in particular, its propositional attitudes"; Smart, "Further Thoughts on the Identity Theory"; Hartry Field, "Mental Representation," *Erkennt-nis* 13 (1978): 9-61. I shall confine discussion to the issue of intentionality. But it seems to me that the individualistic cast of functionalist accounts renders them inadequate in their handling of another major traditional issue about intentional mental states and events—first-person authority.

11. H. P. Grice, "Meaning," *Philosophical Review* 66 (1957):377-88; "Utterer's Meaning, Sentence-Meaning, and Word-Meaning," *Foundations of Language* 4 (1968):225-42; Stephen Schiffer, *Meaning* (Oxford, 1972), cf. especially pp. 13, 50, 63ff; Jonathan Bennett, "The Meaning-Nominalist Strategy," *Foundations of Language* 10 (1974):141-68. Another example of an individualistic theory of meaning is the claim to explicate all kinds of meaning ultimately in psychological terms, and these latter in functionalist terms. See, for example Harman, "Three Levels of Meaning," note 9. This project seems to rest on the functionalist approaches just criticized.

12. Perhaps the first reasonably clear modern statement of the strategy occurs in J. J. C. Smart, "Sensations and Brain Processes," *Philosophical Review* 68 (1959):141-56. This article treats qualitative experiences; but Smart is explicit in applying it to specific intentional states and events in "Further Thoughts on the Identity Theory." Cf. also David Lewis, "An Argument for the Identity Theory," *The Journal of Philosophy* 63 (1966):17-25; "Psychophysical and Theoretical Identifications"; Armstrong, *A Materialist Theory of Mind, passim;* Harman, *Thought*, pp. 42-43; Fodor, *The Language of Thought*, Introduction.

13. The argument is basically Cartesian in style, (cf. *Meditations* II), though the criticism of functionalism, which is essential to its success, is not in any obvious sense Cartesian. (Cf. note 14.) Also the conclusion gives no special support to Cartesian ontology. The terminology of rigidity is derived from Saul Kripke, "Naming and Necessity," *Semantics of Natural Language*, eds., Davidson and Harman (Dordrecht, 1972), though as mentioned above, a notion of rigidity is not essential for the argument. Kripke has done much to clarify the force of the Cartesian sort of argument. He gives such an argument aimed at showing the non-identity of sensations with brain processes. The argument as presented seems to suffer from a failure to criticize materialistic accounts of sensation language and from not indicating clearly how token physical events and token sensation events that are *prima facie* candidates for identification could have occurred independently. For criticism of Kripke's argument, see Fred Feldman, "Kripke on the Identity Theory," *The Journal of Philosophy* 71 (1974):665-76; William G. Lycan, "Kripke and the Materialists," *Ibid.,* pp. 677-89; Richard Boyd, "What Physicalism Does Not Entail," *Readings in the Philosophy of Psychology*, ed. N. Block (forthcoming); Colin McGinn, "Anomalous Monism and Kripke's Cartesian Intuitions," *Analysis* 37 (1977):78-80. It seems to me, however, that these issues are not closed.

14. It is important to note that our argument against functionalist specifications of mentalistic phenomena did not depend on the assumption that no occurrent thought could have a different content from the one it has and be the very same occurrence or event. If it did, the subsequent argument against the identity theory would, in effect, beg the question. The strategy of the latter argument is rather to presuppose an independent argument that undermines non-intentional functionalist specifications of what it is to be *a* thought that (say) sofas are comfortable; then to take as plausible and undefeated the assumption that no occurrent thought could have a different (obliquely non-equivalent) content and be the same occurrence or event; and, finally, to use this assumption with the modal considerations appealed to earlier, to arrive at the non-identity of an occurrent thought event with any event specified by physical theory (the natural sciences) that occurs within the individual.

Perhaps it is worth saying that the metaphorical claim that mental events are identified by their *role* in some "inference-action language game" (to use a phrase of Sellars's) does not provide a plausible ground for rejecting the initial premise of the argument against the identity theory. For even if one did not reject the "role-game" idea as unsupported metaphor, one could agree with the claim on the understanding that the roles are largely the intentional contents themselves and the same event in *this* sort of "game" could not have a different role. A possible view in the philosophy of mathematics is that numbers are identified by their role in a progression and such roles are essential to their identity. The point of this comparison is just that appeal to the role metaphor, even if accepted, does not settle the question of whether an intentional mental event or state could have had a different content.

15. There are *prima facie* viable philosophical accounts that take sentences (whether tokens or types) as truth bearers. One might hope to extend such accounts to mental contents. On such treatments, contents are not things over and above sentences. They simply *are* sentences interpreted in a certain context, treated in a certain way. Given a different context of linguistic interpretation, the content of the same sentence might be different. One could imagine mental events to be analogous to the sentences on this account. Indeed, some philosophers have thought of intentional mental events as being inner, physical sentence (or symbol) tokens—a sort of brain writing. Here again, there is a picture according to which the same thought event might have had a different content. But here again the question is whether there is any reason to think it is a true picture. There is the prior question of whether sentences can reasonably be treated as contents. (I think sentence types probably can be; but the view has hardly been established, and defending it against sophisticated objections is treacherous.) Even if this question is answered affirmatively, it is far from obvious that the analogy between sentences and contents, on the one hand, and thought events and contents, on the other, is a good one. Sentences (types or tokens) are commonly identified independently of their associated contents (as evidenced by inter- and intra-linguistic ambiguity). It is *relatively* uncontroversial that sentences can be identified by syntactical, morphemic, or perceptual criteria that are in principle specifiable independently of what particular content the sentence has. The philosophical question about sentences and contents is whether discourse about contents can be reasonably interpreted as having an ontology of nothing more than sentences (and intentional agents). The philosophical question about mental events and contents is "What is the nature of the events?" "Regardless of what contents are, could the very same thought event have a different content?" The analogous question for sentences—instead of thought events—has an uncontroversial affirmative answer. Of course, we know that when and where non-intentionally identifiable physical events have contents, the same physical event could have had a different content. But it can hardly be *assumed* for purposes of arguing a position on the mind-body problem that mental events are non-intentionally identifiable physical events.

16. In emphasizing social and pragmatic features in mentalistic attributions, I do not intend to suggest that mental attributions are any the less objective, descriptive, or on the ontological up and up. There are substantial arguments in the literature that might lead one to make such inferences. But my present remarks are free of such implications. Someone might want to insist that from a "purely objective viewpoint" one can describe "the phenomena" equally well in accord with common practice, literally interpreted, or in accord with various reinterpretation strategies. Then our arguments would, perhaps, show only that it is "objectively indeterminate" whether functionalism and the identity theory are true. I would be inclined to question the application of the expressions that are scare-quoted.

17. I am grateful to participants at a pair of talks given at the University of London in the spring of 1978, and to Richard Rorty for discussions earlier. I am also indebted to Robert Adams and Rogers Albritton whose criticisms forced numerous improvements. I appreciatively acknowledge support of the John Simon Guggenheim Foundation.

Deviant Causal Chains

CHRISTOPHER PEACOCKE

I shall discuss the basis of the distinction between deviant and nondeviant causal chains in action and perception. An example of a deviant causal chain in action is an example in which an agent has desires and beliefs that make it reasonable for him to ϕ, and that cause him to ϕ, but in which he does not ϕ intentionally. A crude case is provided by a bank clerk who wants more money and knows that he could without detection write some accounts financially favorable to himself, and who is so distracted by these beliefs and desires that he absent-mindedly writes his own rather than another's name on a line that will result in a large payment of money to himself. In the case of the perception of objects in space, a deviant chain is present in examples in which although a man's experience as of its being ϕ is caused by its being ϕ, this experience does not count as perception; consider for instance the case of a man who with his eyes open but under the influence of a hallucinogen is surrounded by redwood trees that produce a scent that causes him to have a vivid visual image of redwood trees which happens precisely to match his surroundings.

Some writers—Kenny is an example[1]—have taken the existence of deviant causal chains in the case of action to be a decisive objection to causal theories of rational action. So part of the interest in giving an account of the basis of nondeviance lies in supplying an essential component of any defense of the view that explanation of an agent's actions in terms of his beliefs, desires, and intentions is *some* species of causal explanation. Analogous remarks apply to causal theories of perception. But there is another reason for interest in the basis of the distinction. Elsewhere I argue that a common structure of explanation, appropriately labeled "holistic," is exemplified both by the explanation of a rational agent's actions in terms of his beliefs and desires, and by the explanation of the course of a person's experience in terms of the joint factors of his particular location in a spatio-temporal frame and the features and qualities displayed at the place at which he is

123

located.[2] These two explanatory schemes are definitive of the provinces of the intentional and the perceptual respectively. If these views are correct, then we should expect the basis of the distinction between deviant and nondeviant chains in both the action and the perception cases to be the same, or at least both instances of a uniform formula applicable in any area of holistic explanation. But having acknowledged this as one source of interest in the issue, I will not in fact appeal in this paper to consideration drawn from a theory of holistic explanation: the arguments and examples I offer can stand (or fall) independently of the acceptance of any such theory.

1. SOME INADEQUATE SUGGESTIONS

Plainly what separates the deviant from the nondeviant chains cannot be the falsity in the deviant cases of such counterfactuals as "If the belief and desire had been absent, the bodily movement would not have been as it actually was, or would not have existed at all," since such counterfactuals are in general *true* in the deviant cases. Nor can we always say that the description under which an event is explained in the deviant examples is different from that one would expect from the beliefs and desires. No doubt the bank clerk did not have the intention to inscribe his name there and then, but in other cases the intention is present and there is such a match with it. If Chopin on some occasion had intended and decided to play the piano as if nervous, and his possession of this plan to play less than perfectly itself so upset him that he played nervously, he would have done exactly what he intended.[3] Perhaps then it may be said that there can never be a *perfect* match with a given intention to ϕ in these deviant cases, because the intention to ϕ is the intention that one should ϕ as a result of one's possession of this very intention *via* a nondeviant chain. Now even if such a view did not wrongly involve ascribing to anyone with intentions use of a distinction between deviant and nondeviant chains of which he may never have dreamed, it could not help us here: in these examples the reason that the token actions do not match such intentions is simply that they are produced by a deviant chain. The suggestion gives no clue about what it *is* for a chain to be deviant.[4]

A much more hopeful suggestion is that intentional behavior is in some way characteristically sensitive to certain facts. One must be very careful in how one tries to sharpen this vague thought. Adam Morton has considered the example of a man, Leo, who thinks that the only way to fulfil his desire to injure a certain other man is to point his pistol north-northeast and pull the trigger;[5] as Leo is preparing to do this, his hand trembles with excitement, the trigger is squeezed, and the pistol happens to be pointing in the right direction. Morton says this is not a case of intentional action because the action was in a certain way not responsive to information:

> For if Leo's information (true or false) about the location of his supposed insulter had changed at the last moment, his time and direction of firing would still have been as they were (p. 14).

What is the "last moment" here? Does Morton mean (a) the last moment before (or better: a moment arbitrarily close to) the moment at which the agent decides to fire, or does he mean (b) the last moment before (a moment arbitrarily close to) the moment at which the agent squeezes the trigger? With this question in mind, consider the following example. In any case whatever of human action, an efferent nerve impulse is sent from the central nervous system to the relevant limb. There will be some small, finite time interval between the transmission and the start of movement of the agent's body, within which, of course, the agent can do nothing intentionally to prevent the initiation of the movement. Now consider an example in which this transmitted message is blocked, drowned out, or destroyed halfway along its path by some neural state that is a result of the agent's nervousness that itself results from the agent's possession of the belief and desire; and we can suppose too that this blocking neural state itself produces by transmission at some later stage of the route a movement of the very type originally intended. (It does not matter whether this is neurophysiologically possible for humans: it is sufficient that it is conceivable in some being to the actions of which we would apply to the belief/desire scheme of explanation.) Now let us return to the ambiguity in Morton's question. If Morton meant (a), the last moment before the decision, then the condition he suggests is not sufficient for intentional action, because in our case, though the movement is not intentional under any description, new information received just before the decision may still affect which type of bodily movement is such that a token of that type is produced. If however Morton meant (b), the last moment before the movement itself is executed, then the condition is not necessary for intentional action, for in clearly nondeviant cases of action new information at *that* stage is too late to affect which type of movement is performed.

Nor will it help to appeal to the idea of the belief and desire "controlling" the remainder of the subsequent movement. No such continuation need be intended, as for instance in the case of the man mistakenly taken for dead after some disaster who may intend just to make his hand discernibly move as a sign of life; and anyway the explanation of what it is to "control" something seems simply to raise our original questions.

All these examples have direct analogues for the case of the perception of things in space that for fear of tedium I shall not trace out.

It is extremely natural, and it seems to me ultimately correct, to say that the nondeviant causal chains are those in which the truth of the sentence that forms the consequent of the *a priori* principle for the scheme of H. E. in question—that someone ϕ's or has an experience as of its being ϕ—is explained in a favored, sensitive way by (in the respective schemes) the agent's attitudes or the world being a certain way. The remainder of this section I shall devote to an attempt to make more explicit and to sharpen the formulation of this idea of sensitivity. First, I shall reject several inadequate explanations of the idea; then I shall give a different criterion for the case of action and go on to apply it to the perception of things in space.

A first suggestion for explaining that notion of sensitivity might be to say that the mechanism exhibited in a causal chain from certain attitudes to a corresponding movement does not exhibit the required sensitivity if any stage of the chain it produces could have been produced by entirely different attitudes. The "could have" here is, superficially at least, non-epistemic. The motivation of this particular initial suggestion is clear enough: the thought behind it is that, for instance, nervousness may be produced by many different beliefs and desires. Thus, even though a belief and a desire, or even an intention, may cause nervousness that in turn causes an instance of the intended action-type, the chain is counted as deviant because one of its stages, that of nervousness, could have been produced by many other beliefs and desires (or even by states other than propositional attitudes).

But this suggestion does not work. Consider the later stages of a perfectly normal nondeviant chain. It seems plain that such later stages could have been produced by a sophisticated neurophysiologist with technical apparatus intervening in a man's nervous system at some earlier point (be it centrally or peripherally). The neurophysiologist might even, perversely, produce the later stages of a chain that lead to a movement the neurophysiologist knew his subject had reason not to perform. Of course such a movement would not ordinarily be intentional; the present point is just that the fact that such a case is possible shows that it is not necessary for a chain to be nondeviant that its stages subsequent to the first could not have been produced in any other way, nor by other states of the agent. The requirement is much too strong.

The defender of this first suggestion might appeal to a certain kind of essentialism to meet that objection. He might say there is one—not the only, but one— notion of a state such that if certain facts or events cause an object to be in a certain state S, nothing other than those events and facts could cause that object to be in just that state S. The defender may go on to say that if he uses *this* notion of a state in the formulation of his "could have" criterion, the objection just raised will no longer go through. This is true. We do not, however, need to stop to assess the plausibility of the implied essentialism about these states in order to see that such essentialism will not help the defender. For if the essentialism about states implies that the stages of a nondeviant chain could not have had other causes, it equally implies that the state of nervousness and its successors in a *deviant* chain equally could not, on that notion of state, have had different causes. The weakening that the appeal to essentialism produces is too great: the criterion it yields fails to characterize obviously deviant chains as deviant.

There are other replies that may be given on behalf of the first suggestion: as, for instance, a requirement that in assessing other possible causes of the stages of a chain we exclude routes that go *via* the will of another person. I shall consider such views later. There are other criticisms that might be made: how would this first suggestion accommodate the case of a man who becomes nervous in only one kind of circumstance, a Siegfried? For then the "could have" test wrongly yields, on one reading, the verdict that movements produced by such nervousness are intentional.

Let us turn now to a second suggestion. This second suggestion is that what makes a chain deviant is a certain *independence* of some of its stages from certain truths. Consider the case of the bodily movement produced by nervousness that is caused by the intention to ϕ and that produces a movement that is a ϕ-ing (or a movement of a kind would be ϕ-ing if the chain were nondeviant). In this case we may say that the nervousness leads to a bodily movement that is a ϕ-ing quite independent of the fact that a movement of the kind it is is in those circumstances believed to be a ϕ-ing. That is, the fact that certain bodily movements are believed to be ϕ-ings has no causal influence on the fact that the earlier stages of the chain, in particular the stage of nervousness, are as they are. Again this suggestion may reasonably claim to express one sense of "sensitivity."

The suggestion as it stands is too crude: for it does not pronounce the following case to be deviant, which it is. A man, in contemplating an action, may come to realize that only bodily movements of one particular kind will be instances of his intended action. Because of past associations in his history, the belief that he has to make this kind of movement may make him nervous: and a deviant causal chain from the belief and desire through the intention and the nervousness to an action of the intended kind may be the result. But in this kind of example it is not true that the intermediate stages of the chain are uninfluenced by which bodily movements are believed to be ϕ-ings[6] for such truths or beliefs do have an influence—they produce the nervousness.

A third suggestion is that the second suggestion was correct to appeal to a concept of independence, but failed to elucidate that concept correctly. It is this suggestion that I shall develop and tentatively endorse. Of the nervous state in a deviant chain, we may say the following: it has no intrinsic feature F that is both produced by the intention to ϕ and that causally *explains* in the circumstances the production of a bodily movement of just the kind in question, one that is believed to be a ϕ-ing.

There is much here that calls for qualification and elucidation; and, above all, we shall want to see a rationale for the requirement. The initial, crude thought behind the suggestion is that even if the nervousness is produced in the way it is in the example given in response to the second suggestion, it is still not true in that case that some specific feature F of that nervous state, where F results from the intention to ϕ, determines that the resulting bodily movement is one of a type believed to be a ϕ-ing—as opposed to its determination by other features of the state and by the circumstances that surround the later stages in which the nervousness is transformed into other (in the human case, neural) states. It seems intuitively attractive to say the chain involving nervousness is deviant because the nervous state produces the bodily movement it does only because the circumstances surrounding the later stages of the chain are as they are. But it is obvious that this cannot be by itself entirely the correct reason: for it is equally true that good earlier stages of standard chains in quite central cases of intentional action produce the bodily movement they do only because the circumstances surrounding the later stages of the *nondeviant* chain are as *they* are. More needs to be said. We have, in effect, a dilemma to avoid. Even if we restrict the notion of "circumstances" to those specified by truths other than those stating that a certain bodily movement physically specified is believed to be a ϕ-ing there and then, we can still state the following dilemma: if we fail to make reference to the role of later circumstances in the production of the bodily movement, we wrongly exclude some (indeed quite plausibly all) standard chains; while if we bring them in, we wrongly include some deviant ones. We need a somewhat more satisfactory formulation of the intuitive dividing line here.

We may truly say of the nervousness examples that when the state of nervousness does not have features specifically reflecting the intention to ϕ, the circumstances surrounding the chain by virtue of which the nervousness results in a movement of a kind believed to be a ϕ-ing hold independently of, are not produced by, the intention to ϕ. Although the bodily movement that results may well be causally determined, it can remain true that it is in a sense accidental that a movement that is believed to be a ϕ-ing results, an accident in the sense that the later stages of the chain from certain attitudes to the bodily movement are determined in their causally relevant features independently of the possession by the agent of these attitudes. A parallel with a certain conceivable kind of camera may help here. Consider a camera containing black and white film. In the causal chain leading to the production of a picture, between the stage of the pattern of light falling on the film and the reaction on the film, there is a loss of sensitivity to the color of the original scene: the state of the film after exposure does not specifically reflect those colors. Now suppose the camera to include a device that reintroduces color solely from the shades of grey fixed by the state of the film, a device that produces only one color for any given shade of grey even though many distinct colors may have produced that shade of grey. In some cases the device may produce colors that match those of the original scene. It is then accidental that the final picture matches the scene in the same sense that it is accidental that a bodily movement that is believed to be a ϕ-ing results from the intention to ϕ in the nervousness examples. It may be causally determined that the scene is colored as it actually is, but even though a statement of matching follows from these two causally determined truths, that is not sufficient for the matching to be nonaccidental in our present sense: for that one must cause the other (or they must have a common cause) via the right kind of causal route. We still have not said what that is.

2. DIFFERENTIAL EXPLANATION

I plan now to proceed as follows. In the cases of deviant causal chains, we have a failure of what I shall label "differential explanation" to hold between certain truths and certain other truths. I shall give two examples of failure of differential explanation in areas distinct from action and perception, and then go on to give a brief account of what is involved in differential explanation.

First, consider that camera with the color reinsertion device. Let us take it as it is, and add yet another device to it. We add a second light- and color-sensitive device, which operates a second shutter; this shutter opens only if a certain definite total pattern of colors in the surrounding scene is picked up by this light- and color-sensitive device: the pattern might be that determined by a foursquare view of the Doge's Palace at noon in May. Let us call this camera "the second camera": this is now a camera that has two shutters, one linked to the new device, and also contains the color reinsertion mechanism. Then it is true that the particular pattern of colors, and nothing weaker, enters the explanation of the distribution of colors in the picture produced: in this respect, it, of course, differs from the first camera, in which citing the distribution of colors involves some redundancy—the explanation there need cite only the distribution of light classified according to the shade of grey it produces. Nevertheless, in the way I am using the term, the distribution of colors does not differentially explain the pattern of colors in the picture produced by the second camera (unless we suppose, as we are not, some mechanism linking the scene and the grey-to-color conversion device).

Some may be tempted to remark of this example that they do not agree that the distribution of colors explains the distribution of colors in the picture taken by the second camera: the distribution of colors in the external scene explains the opening of the second shutter, and thus in the circumstances explains why some picture was taken; for, in the case of a camera like this, the external distribution of colors does not explain the details of the particular picture produced. It is not to be denied that we sometimes use 'explains' this way. But it is also clear that when we do so, 'explains' means more than 'nonredundant part of the total explanation': what more is involved is the object of our search, and the correct remark about the use of 'explains' does not by itself bring us nearer that goal.

Other examples of the failure of differential explanation to hold as a relation between certain truths can be constructed by taking the second camera's additional shutter as a model. In normal surroundings, the pattern of nucleotides in the DNA molecules that constitute genes differentially explains a vast range of the characteristics of the human being that develop in accordance with the instructions they encode. But it is not inconceivable that in the future a biochemist should be able, as it were, to place a gate across the route of development from the genes to the final product so that only genes that were tokens of a fully determinate type would find their instructions implemented, for only tokens of this type would pass through the gate. If such a gate were in operation, but owing to unfortunate (or fortunate) later conditions, not all aspects of the encoded plan were chemically implemented, then the following could be true: in the explanation of why the organism is as it is, the fact that its genes are tokens of the given type plays a nonredundant part—for if it had not had genes of this type, there would have been no organism at all. Nevertheless, the complete specification of this type does not differentially explain in such circumstances the characteristics of the organism. (Note that the organism might by a fluke, in fact be of exactly the same kind that it would have been if all the components of its genetic program had been implemented under standard conditions, the conditions genes of that kind had evolved to cope with.)

It is evident that what is involved in differential explanation needs for its statement finer distinctions than a simple use of necessary and sufficient conditions can supply. For, in cases where we do have differential explanation, what differentially explains is not by itself sufficient for what is so explained (the distribution of colors in the external scene differentially explains the colors of the picture in an adequately working ordinary camera, but the film needs to be working); while equally a condition that fails to differentially explain may be necessary in the circumstances for that condition.

The simplest case in which we can draw the finer distinction that is relevant for us is one in which we have a law (or a derived law, or more generally any acceptable explanatory principle) of this form, where '*t*' ranges over times and '*n*' over numbers and '*k*( )' is some numerical functor:

$$\forall x \ \forall t \ \forall n(Fxt \ \& \ Gxnt. \supset Hxk(n)(t+\delta t)).$$

Suppose we have as *explanans* that *Fxt* and *Gxnt* for some particular *x, t* and *n*. These conditions are jointly sufficient and severally necessary for the *explanandum Hxk(n)(t+δt)*: in these respects the two conditions are symmetrically related to the *explanandum*. Nevertheless, we may say that the differential explanation of *x*'s being *H* to degree *k(n)* at the time *t+δt* is that it was at *t G* to degree *n*, just because according to the principle of the explanation invoked there is a functional connection expressed by *k* between the two.

More generally, we may offer this rough definition. For any object *x*, *x*'s being *φ* differentially explains *y*'s being *ψ* iff *x*'s being *φ* is a nonredundant part of the explanation of *y*'s being *ψ*, and according to the principles of explanation (laws) invoked in this explanation, there are functions (such as *k* in the above example) specified in these laws such that *y*'s being *ψ* is fixed by these functions from *x*'s being *φ*. There are at least two possible sources of misunderstanding to be noted here. The first is that the gerund '*x*'s being *φ*' is not to be taken as referring to some entity in the world (relative to an assignment to '*x*'). "Differentially explains" is of the same category as "explains" itself: it is an operator that takes a pair of sentences (closed or open) to yield a sentence that is open if at least one of the sentences on which it operates is open. '*x*'s being *φ*' is just a convenient form in which to indicate the sentence on which 'differentially explains' is operating. Any adequate extension of Davidson's paratactic account of the logical form of sentences of indirect discourse to include relational indirect discourse will be applicable to 'differentially explains' too. A second possible misunderstanding should be ruled out if we note explicitly that 'fixed' adverts only to the uniqueness of determination by the function (as a matter of mathematics in numerical cases): it does not imply that the laws are not statistical.

The functions specified in the laws invoked in an explanation may be defined not only over numbers but also over colors, chemical elements, compounds, shapes, and so forth. It should be clear how this is relevant to our more recent examples. In the case of the picture produced by the second camera, a sentence stating the distribution of colors in the external scene is a nonredundant part of the *explanandum* consisting of a sentence that stated, using presumably elementary mathematical apparatus, the distribution of colors in the picture produced: but it is not the case that any operative principle of explanation makes that second distribution a function of the first—it is determined, rather, by the function obtained by the operation of the color conversion device applied to the distribution of light classified by the shades of grey it produces on the film before the color conversion device operates. Analogous remarks apply in the genetic example.[7]

In all the examples given so far, the condition that differentially explains has been an element of a set of conditions such that the principle of explanation employed in the particular case in question implies that if similar conditions had been met by other objects at other times, a corresponding *explanandum* sentence would be true: the set of antecedent conditions is strongly sufficient. There are important kinds of empirical explanation where such strong sufficiency is absent, but the kind of functional connection involved in other cases of differential explanation remains present, and we shall still apply the latter concept in such cases. John Mackie considers the example of a chocolate machine he labels "*L*" that will "not in normal circumstances produce a bar of chocolate unless a shilling is inserted, but it may fail to produce a bar even when this is done."[8] Of a similar machine we may be in a position to say that its production of a bar of a specified size is differentially explained by the value of the coin inserted, there being a listable functional relation between coin value and size of bar produced, without any implication that the differentially explaining condition is an element of a set of conditions strongly sufficient for the production by that machine of a bar of that size. (Admission of this case will be important in the application of this distinction.)

"Differentially explains" is a transitive relation: that follows simply from the fact that if x's being F differentially explains y's being G and y's being G differentially explains z's being H, then, in effect, by taking the composition of the two functions that verify these two relations, we obtain a function that verifies that x's being F differentially explains z's being H. More important for us is the fact that under simplifying assumptions, the converse is also true. Suppose, what is not true generally, but may hold locally of particular systems of objects, that we can divide time into intervals such that at each interval, any state of the world that is causally produced at all is causally produced by the state of the world at the previous time interval. Now suppose that x's being F at interval t differentially explains z's being H at interval $t+2$. Under this assumption, we must have that for some object y and for some property G, x's being F at t differentially explains y's being G at $t+1$ and that in turn differentially explains z's being H at $t+2$. For if that were not so, then under this assumption, z's being H at $t+2$, whatever it is a function of according to the operative principles of explanation, it will not be a function by those principles of x's being F at interval t. This has the following implication for any system that fulfills the assumption about intervals: if the state of one object at one time is to differentially explain the state of another object at a later time, then at every intervening time interval there must be some object in some state G such that its being in state G is differentially explained by, or as we may conveniently say for the converse of this relation, *specifically reflects* the fact that x was F at t, and its being in state G also differentially explains the final object in question being in the specified state. There must be such a chain of such features or states G of the intermediate stages for a claim of differential explanation to be true. This is not to say that to *know* such claims to be true we have to know what these intermediate features are: at most, we need for that to know that there *are* such features. When there are such features, we may say that the chain is *sensitive,* relative to an initial object's being in a certain state.

It will no doubt have been evident for some pages that I am going to claim that for a chain from the intention to ϕ to a bodily movement believed to be a ϕ-ing to be nondeviant, the agent's possession of the intention to ϕ must differentially explain his bodily movement of a kind believed by him to be a ϕ-ing (and differentially explain it under that description, of course).[9] The sense of this claim is not immediately clear, since it is not obvious what it might mean to talk of something's being a function of an intention, according to the operative principles of explanation. I shall take for granted in this section a principle the content of and evidence for which must be given elsewhere, namely the principle that every psychological state in which a given person is at some given time is realized for that person at that time by some physical state.[10] Now the requirement on differential explanation in nondeviant action chains is that the fact that a bodily movement of a kind believed to be a ϕ-ing occurs be differentially explained (under its bodily movement description) by the neurophysiological state that for the given agent at the given time realizes his psychological state of intending to make a bodily movement of a kind he takes to be a ϕ-ing in the circumstances (for a specific substitution for 'ϕ'). (Many refinements are possible here but this gives the general plan.) In the case of someone "acting" out of nervousness, his bodily movement is differentially explained not by the physiological realization of his intention, but by the physiological states with which the nervousness interacts to produce a bodily movement that may just happen to match his original intention, but which is no function of the intention (its neurophysiological realization) according to the principles of explanation involved.[11] Note that since realization is relative to an agent and a time, and since agents vary in their beliefs about how to ϕ, for a given ϕ it will not always be the *same* law that covers the explanation of the bodily movement when the chain is nondeviant. The law can vary from person to person, and will often be a law stated at the electrochemical level.

A rational agent might be such that his internal physiology has the property that there is a probabilistic element in the chain from certain intentions to action; perhaps in 50 percent of cases the intention is realized, and in 50 percent chaotic bodily movement results. Here one's intuition is that this fact need not prevent the appropriate bodily movements from being intentional when they do result (in roughly half of the cases). The earlier admission that what differentially explains need not be strongly sufficient for what it differentially explains means that this intuition is not incompatible with the account in terms of differential explanation. In the nonchaotic chains, sensitivity as defined above may be preserved.

When we drop simplifying assumptions, the converse of transitivity need no longer hold for differential explanation. We might have an example like this: there are two causal routes from the intention that the agent has at time t. One of them produces a state in the agent that starts to hold from $t+1$ onward, the other producing at $t+5$ a triggering event which may be an event of the same kind for many different intentions, but which together with the other persisting state also caused by the intention leads to a bodily movement of the kind the agents intended. In such a case, even though the triggering is not specific to the particular intention in question, provided the state on which it acts is so, then the condition of differential explanation of the action under the relevant description by the intention is fulfilled.

I do not claim that this account of differential explanation and its application here will not need a great deal of refinement and qualification (I am sure it will): I want here only to claim that its materials will function as the core of any better revision. We shall later find some confirmation for this in its analogue for the case of the perception of things in space; but before I turn to that, I shall make a few more comments on the distinction and its application.

Differential explanation may be preserved by all kinds of unusual re-routings of the causal chains involved in action, and when it is so preserved, intentional action will be produced.[12] This holds not only of such traditional prosthetic devices as artificial limbs but also of more recherché cases. If a man after some brain injury were unable to realize his intentions because of some blockage in his central nervous system, it is not absolutely inconceivable that a surgeon should re-route standard chains in a way that involved a device in one part of the brain transmitting radio signals, and another part receiving and transforming these signals; the states of these objects could be differentially explained in the right way, and if they did, it seems wrong to deny that this man acts intentionally when such mechanisms are operative. It seems clear that he could be in other respects like any other human being. I am not, therefore, in agreement with those who would require for a bodily movement to be intentional under some description that the route from intention to movement not pass outside the agent's body. It seems obvious too that a variation of the example shows it to be too strong to require that no physical object outside the agent's body may play a role in the causal chain: perhaps an external and separate "boosting" device increases the radio signal before it is picked up by another part of the brain. Perhaps those who maintain the bodily requirement would say that in this case the external device is really part of the agent's body. But if that is so, it is clear that what is to be counted as part of his body is being determined by the route that already identified nondeviant causal chains follow, rather than conversely.

Is the criterion rather much too strong and not really necessary for intentional action? One reason that might be offered for that view is this: a man may realise that the only hope he has of performing a certain "act" is to make himself so nervous that he then, in the circumstances, acts wholly as a result of nervousness. So he takes a drug that makes him nervous, and then acts in the desired way, and achieves his ends in the way planned by him. Do we not have here intentional action without fulfillment of differential explanation? Here one's first intuition, which may not be incorrect, is to say roughly this:

The token event that is his bodily movement is not intentional under any description: this is, of course, not to say that *(ceteris paribus)* he cannot be held responsible for it, since he may have chosen, as he did in our example, to place himself in that state knowing its likely consequences. It is also not to deny that the movement was intentional in some weaker, second-level sense, namely that it was the planned consequence of something that was intentional in the primary sense (swallowing the drug); but that is not enough to make it intentional in the primary sense.

But there is perhaps a better treatment of cases in which account was taken by the agent in his plan of the likelihood of nervousness, a treatment I shall mention but leave for further consideration rather than endorse here. Consider the following case. As Freud's servant I form on Monday the intention to break the master's vase on Wednesday when I pick it up. Call this intention i. But I also know that I, and everyone else like me in such circumstances, shall become extremely nervous once the vase has actually been picked up. I know too, we are to suppose, that an inevitable consequence of such nervousness is a loosening of the grip and a smashing of the vase. So I know that intervening and operative nervousness will not prevent attainment of my goal. On Monday I decide also, since I am bad at remembering how my more devious plans are meant to work, that I must continue to have an ordinary intention to break my master's vase throughout Tuesday and Wednesday until it is the appropriate moment on Wednesday for it to become operative. (I also lose the knowledge about the intervening nervousness and its effects.) I am successful in continuing to have the intention of breaking the vase in the normal way and have the latter intention (i') at the relevant time on Wednesday, when I pick up the vase and then drop it out of nervousness. Now was the event e of my releasing my grip intentional or not? When we reflect both upon what actually happened and upon my quite reliable plan of Monday, we can no more give a nonrelative answer to this question than we can to the question "Is New York north?" when there is no tacit fixing in some way or other of some place relative to which the question is being asked. We ought to say that e is intentional with respect of intention i but not with respect to intention i'.[13] Here intentions are "individuated" not only by their content, but also by when they are possessed (and perhaps by more too). (Again, I do not take the apparent quantification over intentions to be ineliminable.) The view that 'is intentional' is a relational predicate (expression) dovetails neatly with the account of the deviant/nondeviant distinction in terms of sensitivity and differential explanation. On that account nondeviancy is, roughly, a matter of the nature of the causal chain from intention to event, and it is clear that a chain from one intention can have the features and a chain from another intention not possess them. There is no deviancy of chain from the original intention i of Monday because from the point of view of that intention the anticipated nervousness plays a role in the agent's practical reasoning analogous to that played by an anticipated crosswind in a helmsman's practical reasoning about the angle at which to hold the tiller. We tend to overlook, the suggestion would go, the fact that 'is intentional' in the sense in which it abbreviates 'is intentional under some description' is further relative to an intention just because normally only one intention is in question.[14]

Let us turn now to perception. The criterion I have given for nondeviancy of chain in the action case has a natural and attractive analogue in the perceptual case. It is simply that for an experience as of its being ϕ to be really of its being ϕ, its being ϕ must differentially explain the occurrence of the experience event under the description "experience as of its being ϕ." The attractions of such a suggestion are straightforward. The case of the scent-producing redwoods does not yield an experience that is really a perception of its being ϕ because what differentially explains the experience of the specific kind actually produced is some past memory, some half-remembered dream or picture, in any case something other than the redwood trees being arranged in such a corresponding configuration around the experiencer.[15] The requirement of differential explanation also properly excludes an example suggested by Strawson: that of a hallucinating man who hallucinates a brain that matches his own brain which is, of course, (in a broader sense than that required by my criterion) causally involved in the generation of the hallucination. In such a case there are no features F of the intermediate brain state stages or of the final experience that specifically reflect, are differentially explained by, the fact that the brain is thus-and-so, grey and damp, say Strawson himself has a different explanation of the failure of the hallucinating brain to yield perception of the brain that is hallucinating; I shall return shortly to discuss his account.

Some may be tempted to offer a different reason for denying the title of perception to the experience that it is ϕ in these examples, namely, the absence of a rather different kind of sensitivity. For example, if one of the trees in the clump of redwoods were to move, there would be no corresponding change in the experience (or no nonaccidental change); if the hallucinating brain changed color or shape, there need be no causally induced change in the would-be experience; and so forth. Such counterfactuals are indeed often relevant to the question of whether an experience is perception. But they are so because they are generally good evidence that the stages of the chain exhibit the sort of sensitivity we have already identified. Moreover, there are cases in which the criterion provided by such counterfactuals and that of differential explanation diverge, and in which differential explanation seems to match our intuitive judgements. Suppose a man perceives a group of objects in a television studio thtat is insulated from all outdoor light. Now these objects are arranged in such a way that if any one of them moved or visually altered, all the lights in the studio would go out and nothing would be visually perceived. The truth of this counterfactual casts, of course, no doubt whatsoever upon the perceiver's claim to see that the objects are arranged as they in fact are. Now consider a refinement of our redwood example. We can imagine it to be the case that the man receives the scent of redwoods only because of a peculiar air current set up by the exact pattern of the clump of trees in the wind, and that if any part of them moved, the scent and so also the man's experience would vanish.[16] Yet this refinement does not incline us to say that then he perceives the redwood trees, or perceives that they are in such-and-such a configuration. The difference between the studio and the redwood examples lies in the *actual* differential explanation of the relevant property of the experience by the objects in the studio being thus-and-so, and the corresponding actual sensitivity of the intermediate stage of the chain in the studio example. Appeal to the counterfactuals themselves is not capable of explaining all the examples for which we have to account: their truth is at best empirically and in a practically reliable way a sign of the existence of an actual chain with the required sensitivity. But the philosophically significant point is that such a chain can be present without a difference in the counterfactuals.[17]

It may be said that I have simply not considered sufficiently complex counterfactuals to give the counterfactual theory a fair trial; perhaps in the last example we should have considered the counterfactual "If any of the objects in the studio were to alter visually, then either there would be no experience at all, or else there would be a correspondingly changed experience." Yet obviously this counterfactual could be false if the turning out of the lights produced a hallucination; and it could be also only "accidentally" true from the point of view of perception if we think of devious enough examples. I conjecture that for any appropriate noncircular counterfactual, however complex, we can always find some imaginary example in which the holding of that counterfactual is either not necessary or not sufficient for perception: and this is true, if it is, because whether someone's experience is a perception or not is a matter of how things are actually related to him, not a matter of how they might be. (Of course if explanation—and hence differential explanation—is definable in terms of counterfactuals, this conjecture must be qualified to exclude those conditions that analyze the notion of differential explanation itself.)

I have so far offered some considerations in favor of the view that fulfillment of the differential explanation condition is necessary for nondeviance of causal chain. I want now in both the action and perception cases to consider whether more needs to be added to differential explanation to obtain a sufficient condition of nondeviancy; in doing so, I shall also consider some rival theories of deviance, notably those of Strawson in the case of perception and Pears in the case of action.[18] Let us take action first.

One reason it may be thought that differential explanation ("DE") is not in general sufficient for nondeviancy of chain is a feeling that one cannot simply "walk into" an action aid, something that is in no way excluded by the requirement of DE. The thought seems to be that only after a certain amount of use of a mechanism can the bodily movements produced through it be intentional of the agent (it can be the practice with the mechanism that matters to this objector, and not the absence of knowledge of how the mechanism works—this may still be absent after some practice). But the principle that one cannot "walk into" an action aid and start acting intentionally immediately does not seem to me to be acceptable. A doctor might help someone who suffers a deficiency preventing his neurons from transmitting messages by giving him tablets to consume that permit him to realize his intentions; the patient may start acting intentionally immediately. But a man with the same illness might happen to eat something containing the same substance, and then in realizing his intentions be acting intentionally. It is no answer to such

an example to say that we can include this possibility just because the ingested substance restores a normal mechanism of working: for it need not—the substance con-
sumed might be one not naturally found in the body, and its operation might involve by-passing (while fulfilling the DE condition) some of the usual steps. Indeed
in one famous actual example, the former condition was fulfilled.[19]

A second objection to the sufficiency of DE for nondeviancy is provided by
the thought that the DE requirement does not exclude the possibility that the chain
from intention to bodily movement passes through the intentions of a second person. This second person might, for instance, be a knowledgeable neurophysiologist
who decides on a particular occasion to produce in me exactly the motor impulses
needed to realize what he knows, from my neurophysiological states, to be my intentions. Is my bodily movement really intentional when my arm moves exactly as
I intended it to? It is not plausible to say that it is so without qualification. Why is
this so?

It may be said that it is so because it is not true in such an example that it is
reliably the case that if there is a bodily movement of the (putative) agent, then it is
one that matches his intention: the intervening neurophysiologist might not have
chosen to produce the corresponding movement. But the absence of this kind of
reliability, "conditional reliability" as it is naturally called, cannot be the explanation of the deviancy. Conditional reliability in the absence of DE is not sufficient
for nondeviancy, as the Chopin example shows, and in the presence of DE it is
much too strong to require it for nondeviancy of chain. There could be a substance
in the brain that is, for a given person, only fortuitously present, and which stops
neural messages becoming scrambled: if this substance were absent, it could be reliably the case that some bodily movement were made, though there would in general then be no matching with the intention. So if the substance were not reliably
present, a conditional reliability requirement is not fulfilled. This would not prevent intentionality of the putative agent's bodily movements under appropriate
descriptions when the substance did happen to be present.

A better reason is provided by David Pears in his treatment of a somewhat
similar example.[20] Of the concept of the originator of an action, he writes that "the
description of [such examples] naturally puts a great strain on such a conservative
concept." When we say that an event is, under a given description, intentional of a
person, we normally imply that that person was the originator of that event. It is
not clear whether there is such a person as *the* originator of the bodily movement in
our example; but if there is, it is certainly not the person whose brain the neurophysiologist is inspecting. If the implication about origination is to be retained,
then the requirement of DE must be filled out to one that also requires that the
chain from intention to bodily movement not run through the intentions of another
person.[21]

One consideration that might make someone reluctant to accept such a modified DE account as sufficient for nondeviancy is this. If a man fortuitously comes
to be equipped with an action aid, then from his point of view it may well be a matter of luck that his psychological states produce matching actions: but this is hardly

our normal picture of intentional action. It is hard to state this objection without supplying an answer to it. A plausible case may be made that the intention to ϕ implies the belief that one will ϕ;[22] if the appropriate belief is absent, so will the intention be. But there is also another point to be made about such cases. It is not obvious that an event of ϕ-ing can be said to be intentional under that description only if the agent intended to ϕ. If a man acts in the hope of success, while believing his chances are infinitesimal, but thinking he has nothing to lose by trying, then we may be reluctant to make so strong a statement as that he intends to bring about the event under the given description (we can say only that he is aiming at it); but it would be wrong, apparently, to say in a case in which he succeeds that the event produced was not intentional of him. In such examples, one may even be quite ignorant of how the desired consequence will come about if indeed it does come about.[23]

3. COMPARISONS WITH RIVAL THEORIES

I fear that the view I have so far defended about the conditions for nondeviancy in the action case makes me in the terminology of David Pears a "psychological feudalist": "although [psychological feudalism] allows that some physiological infrastructure is needed, it treats the nature and work of the actual serfs as wholly irrelevant to life at the top."[24] Pears himself has a different theory of deviance, and toward the end of a fascinating paper, he himself gives this summary of the restrictions he would suggest in order to exclude the deviant chains from intention to bodily movement:

> First, the agent must intend to bring about the bodily movement through the essential initiating event. Second, he must intend that the sequence of intermediate stages that follow that event should belong to a reliable type. Third, the reliable type of sequence must be specified in his intention as either the normal type for human agents or else a variation produced by a prosthetic device which is, in some sense, part of himself and operated by himself alone. (p. 68)[25]

The "essential initiating event" takes place in the cortex; nevertheless, according to Pears the first condition above does not require all (or even any) human agents to have knowledge of events under neurophysiological descriptions. For my given intention to produce a bodily movement, the corresponding event (if such exists) has a psychological description: "it is the act of will to make that particular movement" (p. 65).

These initiating events are the causal basis of the agent's noninferential (fallible) knowledge that he is making what he takes to be the appropriate movement. Now perhaps a clever neurophysiologist might succeed in severing the causal route from such initiating events back to the agent's beliefs. But even if that did prove to be possible, it would not clearly be any objection to Pears's view: even if such initiating events might not then be properly described as "acts of will," they are still of the same physiological kind in important respects as those that were, and this could be said to be part of what is distinctive of nondeviant chains. Nor is it obviously an objection that the account works only for humans, and not for all conceivable rational agents: for an act of will may with a degree of plausibility be identified with an event of trying, and a case may perhaps be made[26] that such events are required conceptually for intentional action, that is in nondeviant chains in this field.

The difficulty for Pears's suggestion lies, rather, in the possibility of deviance in the chain after an appropriate initiating event: the kind of case that would arise if, for instance, a neurophysiologist connected up certain parts of a man's central nervous system in such a way that after occurrences of a given kind of initiating event, the resulting impulse travels along the artificially produced path and causes nervousness. Pears holds that nervousness imports deviance because "nervousness is not a reliable type of link in the sequence of stages leading to [action of the intended type]" (p. 68). I shall consider reliability later. But we can note now that it cannot be the complete story, because there are cases where the chain is completely reliable after an appropriate initiating event, but in which the bodily movement is not intentional under the appropriate description—for instance it might well be that Chopin and anyone with a similar history simply could not intend to play the piano as if nervous, attempt to act on this intention, and also succeed in producing a bodily movement intentional under not only the description "playing the piano" but also under the description "as if nervous." (Of course, the nervousness could be accommodated in Chopin's plan; but this would be like the imagined servant of Freud we considered earlier and is not a feature of the case now in question.) We still need the requirement of differential explanation to exclude this kind of example: reliability is not sufficient.

David Pears's first two conditions start "the agent intends that . . .". This seems to require that any human agent have particular propositional attitudes with respect to acts of will or events of trying if he is to act intentionally; and this does not seem to be necessary: however necessary such events may be for intentional action, it does not seem to be necessary that the agent have any particular attitudes with respect to those events. A defender of Pears on this point might try to appeal to "the" causal theory of perception: it is still true, he may say, that a man's experience is a perception of a given object only if a certain kind of causal connection links the object with the man, whether he believes the causal theory of perception or not. This is, of course, quite true, but it does not parallel Pears's claim on intentional action because in the perceptual case we require only connections of a certain kind (partly given in the differential explanation condition) and not belief in or other attitudes about those connections.

What of reliability? We saw that Pears required that the sequence of intermediate stages from the initiating event "belong to a reliable type." We need to be very careful here. On the one hand, as we saw, some kinds of reliability seem not to be sufficient: there might be some kinds of action or even kinds of bodily movement such that it is a nomologically true generalization for creatures of the species in question that anyone intending to perform an action or movement of that kind under certain conditions will act out of nervousness.[27] On the other hand, some kinds of reliability appear not to be necessary. For instance, a quite nondeviant ordinary chain meeting the differential explanation condition may have a stage that produces the next stage with a probability of only 10 percent: this seems to me not to cast doubt on the intentionality of the resulting movement in cases where all the stages are so produced. Here to speak of a reliable *type* does not by itself save the requirement, for the type is not reliable.

These observations would still be compatible with the different requirement for nondeviancy of chain: that the circumstances that produce the sensitivity of the stages of an actual chain, when one is produced, be reliably present. So should we impose that? There are several considerations against doing so. First, the condition seems intuitively too strong. For instance, a man might be like the rest of us except that his brain cells do not reliably produce one of the substances required for the transmission of neural impulses: this fact seems to cast no doubt on the status of causal chains from intention to action when the substance is adequately produced upon a particular occasion. Similar observations apply if atmospheric conditions affect the operation of the prosthetic radio device we imagined earlier. Second, the condition is more clearly wrong in the perceptual case—for otherwise we would not be able to say that on a moonless night one could see an unlit farmhouse suddenly in a flash of lightning. Third, 'is nondeviant' is an absolute predicate of particular chains and not at all relative to some further description or predicate; whereas 'reliably' is quite plausibly so relative. (Given that a child has spots of a certain kind, it is reliably measles; given he or she was born at c_1 or . . . or c_k, where the c_i are the birthplace coordinates of all those who get measles, it is not reliable.) Are the circumstances to be counted as reliably present absolutely if reliably present under *some* description? Then it seems they will almost always count as reliably present (with the approximate truth of physical determinism on the macroscale). But the circumstances will never count as reliably present if required to be so relative to *every* description of those circumstances.[28]

It is, of course, not enough simply to argue against the reliability condition: we must also treat the examples others have invoked the reliability condition to explain. One vivid case is given by Pears[29], who discusses a gunman who intends to fire his gun and whose cortex sends out the initiating event: unknown to the gunman, the nerve to his index finger has been severed, but the intended movement still takes place because the impulse produced by the initiating event attracts some lightning which itself generates the required impulse in the severed section of the nerve. Pears says there is a strong case against calling the firing of the gun intentional because the performance lacks primary reliability, that is, the goal was not "achieved by dependable stages."[30] However, the probability case suggests that dependability is not required, and the example of the prosthetic radio device can easily be modified so that it is something external that is not dependably present and produces a nondeviant chain.

Does this mean the criterion of differential explanation commits us to saying Pears's gunman acts intentionally? No: on that criterion, the judgment has to turn on further details of the case. If the mechanism by which the impulse attracts the lightning is (roughly) such that, in the actual circumstances, it could easily have attracted lightning that would have produced impulses with quite different effects, the condition on specific reflection will fail and the movement will not be intentional—the differential explanation of the movement under the description "movement of a kind believed in the circumstances to be a squeezing of a trigger" will relate not to the properties of the impulse but to the properties of the lightning present (where these are not, in turn, differentially explained by properties of the impulse). On the other hand, if there is specific reflection, the lightning is no different from a rather unreliable external action-aid, of a kind a patient might think at least better than nothing.[31]

There is a version of the reliability requirement that is not touched by these criticisms. A nondeviant chain, it may be said, need not be such that it is reliably the case that: if a chain of its kind is given an input (the intention to ϕ/it's being ϕ at a certain place), it delivers a matching output (an action believed to be a ϕ-ing/an experience as of its being ϕ). Rather, what is required is: it is reliably the case that *if* a chain of that kind is given an input *and* it in fact delivers an output, the output will match the input in the sense required for the given scheme of holistic explanation. But this is precisely the requirement of "conditional reliability" we considered and rejected several pages ago. We may also note the following point in addition to the arguments that were given then. There is a sense in which, subsequent to the initial "accident," a perceptual system with a triggering device that delivered the contents of some memory store on to the retina of the system (analogous to the triggering device that opened the second shutter in our second camera example), may meet a requirement of conditional (or even stronger) reliability. We do seem to need the refinement that differential explanation supplies, or at least the features this idea attempts to capture.[32]

Now let us consider another rival theory, that of Strawson,[33] which it may be claimed offers a better account of the examples we have already cited in the case of perception.

Strawson agrees with Grice that for an experience to be the perception, it seems to be a certain causal connection is required between what it seems to be of and the experience itself; and he agrees also that this condition is not sufficient. But the extra that is required for a sufficient condition is not, according to him, to be gained by placing further restrictions upon the mode of causal dependence: rather, the counterexamples such as the brain case and Kinglake's hallucination are to be excluded by certain restrictions implicit in the naive concept of perception. These restrictions flow from and are unified by the idea of a spatiotemporal location of an observer and his perspective or point of view at that location with that orientation. Thus, one can see only what is not masked or obstructed from one; one can see only what is in a certain spatial range, one's arc of vision, and so forth. The hallucinating man does not count as perceiving his own brain because that is masked from him by his cranium; Kinglake did not really hear the bells because of the remoteness of that event from him in time at the time of his experience. Strawson holds that as knowledge of perceptual mechanisms increases, it is natural to introduce superior, refined concepts of perception, and these will very likely make reference to *kinds* of causal dependence; but, he holds, we should recognize these developments as just that, refinements of the naive concept, rather than as verdicts of a pre-theoretical concept on newly discovered actual examples. It should be clear that the criterion of differential explanation I have proposed places me in disagreement with Strawson's position, and I should in fairness note before developing the point further that Strawson himself is extremely tentative in stating his own view: "*perhaps* the point is a fine one, *perhaps* not ultimately settleable" (81), he writes.

We may note in passing that Strawson's account of the perceptual case is *prima facie* not generalizable to the action case, with which we have seen so many parallels: for his solution makes reference to the idea of a spatiotemporal point of view which (apparently) has no analogue in the explanation of intentional action. But, of course, this remark should not prevent consideration of Strawson's theory in its own right. (Perhaps this hope of a unified account is merely a chimera produced by an overambitious theory.)

A second preliminary observation to be made before we consider the details of Strawson's account is that there is one important respect in which an account employing differential explanation sides with him and against some more extreme conceivable views. Strawson holds (in his own words, my italics) "it does not seem that there is any concealed, implicit reference, *however unspecific,* to modes or mechanisms of causal dependence" in the naive concept of perception (p. 81). The DE account differs from this in placing restrictions on the kind of dependence. But, on the other hand, the DE condition sides *with* Strawson in that the restrictions it imposes on the causal chain are not stated in concepts drawn from the special sciences, concepts unavailable to the everyday master of the naive concept of perception. So the view I am defending is less extreme than one according to which the results of scientific investigation are relevant to a correct specification of the *concept* of a perceptual experience (or an intentional action).[34]

The point of the three main remarks I shall now make is to try to establish the following case: that where Strawson's restrictions diverge from the account I have suggested, the verdicts given by the (or at least my) naive concept of perception are predicted by the account appealing to DE; that where Strawson's principles are correct, an essential element in their correctness is the application of some concept in conformity with the DE account; and that where the Strawsonian restrictions are read without any limitation on the mode of causal dependence, there is a serious threat of circularity. These claims may be illustrated as follows. (i) Strawson's explanation of the hallucinating brain example is that this is no case of perception because the brain is masked from the putative perceiver by the (opaque) cranium. But this explanation does not cover all the cases on which the naive concept confidentially pronounces: for if our crania were transparent, and our heads of such a shape that one could normally see a corner of one's brain through it, and a hallucinating man had an experience as of such a corner of his brain, it seems clear (and on the basis of the naive concept) that this would not *ipso facto* make the case into one of perception. Strawson defends the claim that *some* causal requirement is implicit in the naive concept of perception on the ground that Lady Macbeth's nurse will realize that she cannot cure her lady's hallucination by spreading some actual blood on her hands; and equally we may say that when someone is hallucinating as a result of taking a drug, an experience as of some corner of his brain, we have no refinement of the concept of perception in order to understand the idea that his hallucination is not removed or turned into a perception by replacing part of his cranium with a newly shaped and transparent component. It seems to me that this point, if taken, shows that restrictions on the external positioning of the perceiver together with general requirements on causation and matching will never be sufficient to capture the naive concept of perception: be they ever so difficult to state within the acceptable constraints of a philosophical analysis, the naive concept still does impose restrictions upon the internal stage of the causal chain.

It may be said that Strawson could meet the case of the hallucinating transparent cranium by naturally extending his theory thus. Once we have a set of conditions, such as his "restrictions," the obtaining of any one of which blocks perception, they may be naturally extended to a wider set by the following principle: if a person has an experience, and none of the restriction conditions is violated, the experience may, nevertheless, fail to count as perception if it is true that if one of them *were* to be violated in the circumstances, the experience would still be present. This would then exclude the case of the transparent cranium because if an opaque object obstructed the relevant (part of the) cranium from the experiencer, there would still be an experience of the given kind there actually is.[35] However, my point (ii) is that Strawson cannot legitimately use the obstruction restrictions, and I turn immediately to this.

(ii) Strawson appealed to facts about obstruction to block some putative counterexamples to his account. But of course spatial obstruction does not hinder sight if the obstructing object is transparent (otherwise glasses could never aid vision and one could never see someone through a window). Now what are transparent objects? They are ones that are not merely translucent, they are ones you can *see* through. So to limit Strawson's restriction to non transparent objects would be circular. Appeal might in principle be made to relative nondistortion of the light pattern as a definition of transparency: but to do so would reintroduce reference to modes of causal dependence which Strawson seemed to wish to avoid.[36] Strawson's view that there is no such restriction "however unspecific" seems to block even attempts to explain transparency in terms that appeal to the normal mode of transmission and not the concept of light as such.

(iii) My third comment is on the implicit use of DE and other considerations in the application of some of the concepts used in the restrictive principles to which Strawson appeals and which he says flow from the idea of a spatiotemporal point of view. Consider the notion of the "arc of vision" (p. 79). An arc of vision for a perceiver with a given orientation at a given point (with a given location for other objects) is a volume of space, for it is that within which an object must lie to be visible by that perceiver then. But it is clear that regions of space that correspond with the perceiver's "blind spot" must be excluded, even though neither masked nor obstructed: for objects in that region are not counted as visible by that perceiver then, even if (by techniques now familiar from the previous examples) these objects play a causal role in the production of an experience. (More spectacular cases may be constructed if we imagine the perceiver to be suffering from *scotoma*.) Another example concerns the *range* of a given sense, a concept also employed by Strawson. It seems plain that the range of a sense not only varies with the occasion and (in the case of human sight) say the conditions of illumination, but also on a given occasion with the conditions of illumination in various regions of a volume of space. A man on board a yacht sailing parallel to the resorts on the Côte d'Azur at night may be able to see what happens on the waterfront at Cannes and not what is happening on the surface of the water between him and the town. What unifies the visible regions on an occasion and from occasion to occasion? My claim is that it is in part the sensitivity of the stages of chains from the objects within these regions to the experiences, which is in these examples the ground of differential explanation. Of course the *a posteriori* ground of such sensitivity is the reflection of light from these regions (or objects in these regions); but it is not necessary for the position developed here to maintain that the concept of light, that physical phenomenon, enters the naive concept of perception; what matters is the resulting differential explanation itself, which has been defined without reference to any particular physical phenomenon.

4. REFINEMENTS

What is the role of examples in fixing the extension of 'perceives'? There can be no objection of general principle to the view that the extension is fixed in part by citing particular sequences of objects that stand in the relation. Such a procedure need not be circular if the examples are not specified, as they need not be, using 'perceives' or expressions to be defined in terms of it. Just such a general picture of the fixing of the extension of natural kind terms has rightly come to seem plausible from the work of Kripke and Putnam, and the arguments used in defense of that picture might be applied too in the case of perception. It is of no avail to argue that the examples used in fixing the extension either have some common property in virtue of which they are all instances of perception or do not and the extension has not properly been unified. For such an alleged dilemma ignores the now familiar possibility that the unifying principle supplied by the examples can both classify together the objects in the extension and yet be discovered *a posteriori* from the examples: again, compare gold and its atomic structure.

Nevertheless, this said there seem to be strong reasons for not applying the natural kind model to the determination of the extension of 'perceives'. In the case of gold, we are confident that a few samples (indeed one) will fix the extension of "gold" (given that it is a substance-word), because we are confident that there are scientifically fundamental characteristics from which the other relevant properties of the samples flow. But in the case of perception, even if we could give, as we could well hope to, an account of what scientifically identified relations underlie and explain some identified actual examples of the relation of perception, that would not properly fix the extension of 'perceives'. To mention a few reasons: we wish to apply the concept of perception to conceivable creatures with different physico-chemical realizations from our own; we wish to allow prosthetic devices and re-routings in at the very least internal stages of the chain; and so forth. The concept of perception, unlike that of a substance, is not one that determines a notion of kind such that any example of perception falls under a unique kind, and such that what is quite generally necessary and sufficient for perception can be discovered by empirical investigation of examples of that kind. Thus, we cannot wholly avoid the traditional hard work of the method of imagined examples and the testing of the appropriate intuitions of the masters of the concept of perception against them.[37]

Does this show that examples do not have any role to play in fixing the extension of 'perceives'? I do not think so, for there is a different role that it is plausible to say has to be played by them. This is the identification of *which* stage of a nondeviant, sensitive chain is the one such that objects at that stage are said to be the objects perceived. In an adequately sensitive chain, a full analysis would need to filter out perfectly differentially explanatory stages both earlier and later than the desired ones. Sensitive later stages to be excluded include electro-chemical cross-sections of the optic nerve, the pattern of light in the lens of the eye, and so forth. We have an earlier stage that needs to be excluded if the perceptible state of a perceived object specifically reflects its state five minutes ago; or again a man might make an object whose perceptible qualities are geared by radio transmission to the perceptible qualities of some qualitatively identical object outside the range of any of a perceiver's senses, to the extent that the condition of differential explanation of the man's experiences under suitable conditions by the wrong object is met. It is plausible that the appropriate *stage* of a sensitive chain is fixed by examples.[38] In the case of human vision, it is an *a posteriori* fact that the objects thus fixed (in a further elaboration of the condition) are roughly those such that the specific pattern of light reaching the perceiver is caused by reflection of light off those objects' surfaces in the case of ambient light, or by emission from them in the case of radiant light.

A competing suggestion about the means of determination of the stage of the causal chain such that objects at that stage may be said to be perceived is this. We were eager to allow much earlier that the substituends for 'ϕ' in 'experience as of its being ϕ' may include physical object vocabulary: an experience may be as of a girl walking across Hyde Park at a certain time of year, as viewed from a particular angle. Why should not the fixing of the appropriate stage of the causal chain be done by the content of these descriptions? For they certainly speak of objects of a kind found at only a certain stage of the causal chain; and it need in no way be required for such a suggestion that all the objects of the kinds mentioned in the "as of" description of an experience that is a perception count as perceived. The suggestion might be an initial restriction upon which further supplementary conditions are imposed. Yet even with these points noted, there seem to be severe difficulties in developing the proposal. Even when the description of what the experience is as of includes physical object vocabulary, and is the one it is entirely natural for the perceiver to offer, and the experience *is* a perception, this proposal can pick out the wrong stage. For a man may from time to time have opaque bodies floating in the fluid of his eye or chemical patches on his retina and know from an oculist that this is the usual cause of experiences of a certain kind that he has: the description of his experience "as of the opaque bodies in the fluid of my eyes floating around again" (or "as of the chemical patterns on my retina again") may be the one he naturally offers. If on a particular occasion this is a fair description of his experience, and yet this once there *are* opaque bodies suspended in the air, but not in the fluid of his eye, then he does on our normal concept of perception count as perceiving the bodies in the air: but on a simple version of the suggestion being considered, he would not count as perceiving them, for they are not at the stage of the eye in the causal chain. There would too, of course, be problems about experiences that we want to count as perceptions of an object and for which the experiencer can offer only phenomenal descriptions. Presumably the defender of this competing position will have to move to the view that the appropriate stage of the chain is fixed by the requirement that it is the stage such that the (great?) majority of descriptions of what experiences are "as of " and that are cast in physical object vocabulary are of objects of a kind found at that stage. But this statement of the view has the consequence that it is impossible, as a matter of the nature of the concept of perception, that there should be a community of people who use the concept of perception, fix the same stage such that objects at that stage are the candidates for perception as we ourselves do, but be such that their perceptual systems being very much more clogged than are ours, the great majority of their "as of" descriptions in physical object vocabulary that are applied to their experiences relate to malfunctionings in or properties of their perceptual systems. Although such a situation would be strange and unusual, and would have to meet other conditions in order for the members of such a community to be able to impose the structure needed if the minority of their experiences that are of objects at the right stage is to be regardable as produced by tracing a route in a spatiotemporal world, it seems quite implausible to say that all such cases are conceptually excluded by the notion of perception. (For instance, the experiences produced when there is misfunctioning or some blocking might still within the terms of a legitimate example in fact, though of course not as an *a priori* necessity, have distinctive phenomenal characteristics.) In any case, I am not clear that the general suggestion being proposed is not circular: for do we not say that our experiences are *as of* those states of affairs that involve objects that we ordinarily *perceive*?

If there is indeed an element in the concept of perception that can be fixed only by giving examples of the perception relation, why is there such a role for examples in the perception case and not, apparently, in the action case? The reason seems to be this. In the action case, the other states in the causal chain from intention to action that equally differentially explain the bodily movement in the required way are not themselves in general states that are the physical realizations of an agent's intentions. A crucial point of difference between the action and the perception schemes is that in the action but not in the perception case, the state that is the cause is specified with an intensional embedding (the substituends for 'ϕ' in 'intention to ϕ'); in the perception case, the corresponding intensionally specified state, 'experience as of its being ϕ', is at the effect end of the chain. We correspondingly have no difficulty, and there is no need for an ostensive fixing of the effect end of the causal chain in perception, for in general at only one of these stages is there an experience.[39]

There remain many examples that meet the requirements both of differential explanation and the stage condition fixed by examples of the perception relation, and the status of which as instances of perception may reasonably be questioned. They include cases of light from an object that is reflected off the surface by a mirror, hearing a voice over a telephone, or a gramophone record, watching television and, a rather different kind of case, that in which an intervening brain surgeon produces in me what is necessary for the occurrence in me of a visual experience that matches exactly what he himself is seeing. Even if we temporarily ignore that last kind of case, it would not be correct to say of the remaining cases that linguistic practice unambiguously delivers the verdict that they are cases of perception. One is said to see the car to the rear "in the mirror," to have heard Schnabel "on record," or the prime minister "on the phone." The fact that in answer to the question "Which car did you see?", asked when one has seen one in the mirror, one cites a particular car as an appropriate answer is not decisive in answering the question of whether there is unqualified perception in these examples. For the answer that specifies a particular car may be more appropriate not because perception here is unconditional, but because to say "None at all" as one's answer is more misleading in that it might be taken to imply that one had not even seen a car in the mirror.

The case of the experience-producing surgeon is rather different from these examples, because in these latter examples it is not plausible to attribute their failure as unconditional examples of perception to a link between perception and knowledge: the qualifications "in the mirror," "on the phone," and so forth, are appropriate even when there is no question but that the would-be perceiver is in a position by being in such contact with the object to gain knowledge of the object. This is not in general so with the experience-producing surgeon: here it seems more attractive to explain the failure of unconditional perception by the failure of such a chain to be (in the relevant cases) a method of gaining knowledge of the objects that the surgeon himself perceives.

It would be too strong to state such a connection between perception and knowledge like this: an experience is a perception of an object only if it is produced by a means that actually yields knowledge of that object. There are clear counter-examples to a link that tight. A man may know he is taking part in a series of experiments on perception and cortical stimulation; and he may have no idea whether his current visual experience as of a machine with dials on it is a perception or not; but if this *is* an experience caused in the usual way by light reflected off the object reaching his eye, followed by the usual steps of the causal chain, the experiencer is seeing that machine with dials even though he is not thereby in a position actually to know that any such machine exists.[40] But, of course, this obvious kind of example in no way discredits a view according to which there is perception in these examples because the experience is produced by a means which in ordinary circumstances does yield knowledge of the putatively perceived object.

If there is such a link between perception and knowledge, then an additional requirement that naturally covers our most recently introduced batch of examples is that the experience to be a perception must be produced by the usual causal means of transmission from the relevant objects in examples of the perception relation, which example of the usual means (say a pattern of light) is then processed by a sequence of objects whose operation is sufficient in normal circumstances to yield, for the person whose experience it is, knowledge of those objects. The brain of the experience-producing surgeon will not in general be such an object.

For anyone pursuing as such the philosophy of perception and knowledge there are a number of questions to be investigated at this point, notably whether these restrictions in terms of knowledge are too strong, whether they themselves are sufficient to exclude all the examples that we want to in which the causal chain goes through the will of another, and whether an independent requirement needs to be tacked on, and so forth. I shall not pursue these questions here because it is clear that any satisfactory consideration of them would involve a much more extensive inquiry into the theory of knowledge than is appropriate when our main concern is holistic explanation and its structure. But it should be explicitly noted that an introduction of a link with knowledge in no way makes the role of differential explanation redundant. For, first, it may well be argued that not only the concept of explanation but also that of differential explanation needs to be employed in a satisfactory account of knowledge. Second, the notion of what is and what is not a means of gaining knowledge seems irrelevant to the deviant/nondeviant distinction in the action case. Even if the knowledge requirement were in a way to swallow up (by including) the differential explanation requirement, the common part of the distinction in each scheme can still be the requirement of differential explanation.[41]

It will have been clear when I have been discussing perception that I have been sliding between various locutions and hiding a cluster of important smaller issues. I have written about the question of what makes an experience as of its being ϕ into a perception that it is ϕ. But plainly "perceives that it is ϕ" is not a locution that will do just the work required of it, since it seems to imply that the perceiver believes that it is ϕ; whereas the question of belief should be left open by that of perception. The idea of the experience as of its being ϕ being a perception *tout court* is, conversely, too weak; this would be the case if I had an experience as of a green book on the table in front of me and yet the book was not green, or some stage in the relevant causal chain was not sensitive in the right way to its being green. There is no objection, however, to introducing a notion of an experience (a token event) e being perceptual under description D, somewhat analogously to the concept of a bodily movement (a token event) e being intentional under a description D. There are differences, of course: for instance, on one way of using the phrase 'intentional under description D,' an event can be intentional under a description only if the event itself satisfies the description, while there is clearly no way of using "perceptual under a description" in this way, for the descriptions in the perceptual case are what the experience is "as of."

Why is it that we do not, in fact, employ a notion of an experience being perceptual under a description? Well, what we *do* employ is the concept of perceiving an object; and presumably the empirical reason we normally find this sufficient to our purposes is that human beings' perceptual systems are so similar that in normal circumstances when we know roughly the environment in which x is placed and know what y is like, we know roughly the kind of experience the perceiver x will have given just the further information that x is perceiving y. Clearly, no corresponding *a posteriori* truth holds with respect to the concept that we might introduce, namely that of having an intention with respect to an object: "An intention to do *what* with it?" is a reasonable question about an agent and an object even in normal circumstances.

I have not yet suggested a definition of the relation of perceiving an object, but there is a natural starting point of some plausibility in the framework I have been offering. It is this:

an experience (token event) e is a perception of object x iff
there is some property ψ such that

(i) $\psi(x)$
(ii) $\psi(x)$ is the differential explanation of e being an experience as of an object being ψ (at the time, for the possessor of the experience)
(iii) $\psi(x)$ is a condition at the right stage of the causal chain as determined by the examples of "perceives" used in fixing the concept.[42]

Thus suppose I have an experience as of a black speck of a certain shape on my spectacles. I may, in fact, be really seeing a ship just coming over the horizon, and, if I am, this definition will count me as seeing the ship because the differential explanation at the appropriate stage of the chain of my having an experience of just this kind is that the ship on the horizon is of a certain shape and made of an opaque substance. But I do not perceive the door of the bridge of the ship according to this definition, because there is nothing in an "as of" clause describing the experience that is differentially explained by the door of the bridge of the ship being thus-and-so. I offer this definition as a first step in need of further elaboration.

The notions of perception and of intentional action are everyday ones and as such it is reasonable to require that any elucidation of them have an adequate answer to the question "What is the *point* of the distinction?", in particular here the distinction between deviant and nondeviant chains. Further, an adequate answer to this question should appeal to and not go beyond everyday, nontechnical interests of those employing the concept. The differential explanation account has a clear way of meeting this point about point: on this account, in nondeviant chains the relevant properties of the experience or action are specifically explained by the world being as it is or the propositional attitudes being as they are. When a description of an action or an experience is explained nondeviantly, the applicability of those descriptions genuinely mirrors, in a nonreductive way, the obtaining of truths that employ the distinctive concepts of the objective world or the agent's propositional attitudes. The end products of the nondeviant chains give us a glimpse of these realms as they really are.[43]

Notes

1. *Will, Freedom and Power* (Oxford, 1975), p. 121.

2. Some arguments for this claim are summarized in "Holistic Explanation: Outline of a Theory" in the second volume of papers drawn from the U.K. Thyssen Conferences, edited by Ross Harrison (Cambridge, forthcoming).

3. In this example, Chopin's playing is intentional under the description 'playing the piano' but not under the description 'as if nervous'. It is not always true that if an event is intentional under one of the descriptions specified by the agent's intention, it is intentional under all of the descriptions specified by the agent's intention. A man may intend to raise his hand and intend to trace out a certain curve in doing so. A nervous state itself caused by his intention may cause horizontal movements of his hand that, in fact, match his intention: in such an example, it could be true that the agent intentionally raises his hand, but the horizontal movements of his hand are not intentional under description.

4. The dialectical irrelevance of such a suggestion may be compared with the remark that in some form a description theory of singular genuine reference must be true because if R is the relation that must hold between an utterance token a and object x for the former so to refer to the latter, the description 'the object to which a bears R' will be a reference fixing description: this vacuous remark tells us nothing about the nature of R.

It should be clear that it is even more immediately circular to say that the examples so far considered provide no objection to a theory according to which for intentionality of an event under a description, the "desire to perform an action of type x should result in an *action* of type x" (thus I. Thalberg, *Perception, Emotion and Action* (Oxford, 1977), p. 59). If those events are actions that are intentional under description, then such a theory simply helps itself to the notion to be explained, that of an event's being intentional under some description, in employing the concept of an action.

5. "Because He Thought He Had Insulted Him," *Journal of Philosophy* 72 (1975):5-15.

6. I distinguish where it matters between the agent's intention to ϕ and what he believes to be a ϕ-ing in the circumstances not because I am not concerned with the final stage of the agent's practical reasoning (on the contrary, I am concerned with that stage): I distinguish the two because even at that final stage, there is still a distinction to be drawn. In the example given in an earlier section of an agent whose visual field is (unbeknownst to him) distorted, we can make sense of the idea that the bodily movement he believes to be a stretching out of his arm that culminates in reaching the glass will not, in fact, be a reaching of the glass, even though he the agent may not have the concepts to describe noncircularly the bodily movement of which he does believe that it will be a reaching toward the glass in the circumstances.

7. In the treatment of these examples, we are, of course, relying heavily on an an "explains" relation that takes a pair of sentences to form a sentence, rather than on a causation relation between token events (thing in the world). To this extent, I regard the terminology of "deviant causal *chains*" as unfortunate: for it is not properties of the events themselves but, rather, more complex conditions relating to the principles of explanation that I am claiming to be the basis of the distinction.

8. J. L. Mackie, *The Cement of the Universe* (Oxford, 1974), p. 41.

9. Note that if this is correct for schemes of holistic explanation generally, then we have a "transcendental" derivation of the principle that a scheme of holistic explanation can be applied to a field of phenomena only if certain parts of it are governed by laws, possibly of a statistical kind: without such laws, there can be no differential explanation.

10. Given the use made of this assumption in the next sentence of the text, it should be clear that a principle about realization and not supervenience is what we need. Even if the state upon which a psychological predicate supervenes is finitely specificable, it can still be that (a) there is no finite or r.e. specification of all the circumstances upon which the given predicate will supervene; and more to the present point (b) other psychological predicates—perhaps certain beliefs—may also supervene on the given physical description upon which the intention supervenes. In that case to require as we do specific reflection of *that* physical state would be much too strong; while, on the other hand, given only supervenience, there may be no more restrictive physical state upon which the intention supervenes but nothing else does.

11. Note also, then, that according to the conditions proposed here, we do not have intentional action if the kind of nervousness that results in any given circumstances specifically reflects the agent's intention to ϕ but no feature so reflecting the agent's intention is causally influential on later stages of the chain.

12. "unusual": A. Goldman, *A Theory of Human Action* (New York, 1970), p. 61.

13. Strictly, we should say that the suggestion is that the two "place" '*e* is intentional under description ϕ' is to be replaced with the three "place" '*e* is intentional under description ϕ with respect to intention *i*'. One difference between this suggestion and that of the previous paragraph is that under the latter, my dropping of the vase as Freud's servant is not literally intentional under any description at all.

14. Care in specifying the description under which an event is intentional sometimes simply dissolves some alleged problems. *Analysis* "Problem" number 16 (March 1977) set by R. J. Butler was this:

> If Brown in an ordinary game of dice hopes to throw a six and does so, we do not say that he threw the six intentionally. On the other hand if Brown puts one live cartridge into a six-chambered revolver, spins the chamber as he aims it at Smith and pulls the trigger hoping to kill Smith, we would say if he succeeded, that he killed Smith intentionally. How can this be so, since in both cases the probability of the desired result is the same?

The alleged problem simply arises from not comparing like with like. The shooter has control over the conditional that if the gun fires, then it fires in one direction rather than another. But he does not have control over whether the gun fires at all. So we say that he intentionally shot Smith, but not that it was intentional of him that a full rather than an empty chamber was engaged. Now in the dice case, the agent has control over whether, for instance, the die falls on one side of the table with the six uppermost *if* it falls with the six uppermost at all, but he does not have control over the antecedent of this conditional. We say in this case exactly what we would expect to say by analogy with the gun example: it may be intentional of the agent that the die falls on the left-hand side of the table, but not that it falls with a six uppermost. Butler's problem arises only when we compare a condition over which the agent does have control in the gun case with a corresponding condition in the dice case over which he does not have control.

15. The criterion also covers the case of Kinglake's hallucination cited by Strawson ("Causation in Perception" in *Freedom and Resentment and Other Essays* (London, 1974), pp. 77-78) in a specially pleasing way if Kinglake's diagnosis (p. 78, footnote) was correct: Kinglake wrote that the heat, dryness, and stillness had rendered his hearing organs "liable to tingle under the passing touch of some mere memory."

16. Imagine, too, if you like, for a strict parallel that the experiencer has an experience as of a black and white silhouette of these redwood trees.

17. Note that while the studio example shows that the truth of counterfactuals of the kind "If the scene were different in certain respects, the experience would be different" are not *necessary* for nondeviance of the chain, the refined redwood example shows that the truth of counterfactuals of the kind "If the scene were different in certain respects, there would be no experience of the kind there actually is" are not *sufficient* for nondeviance of the chain.

The studio example also shows the sensitivity condition to be different from H. H. Price's well-known distinction between "standing" and "differential" conditions (*Perception* 2nd ed. (London, 1950), p. 70). In the course of his formulation of the causal theory, which he unfortunately never separates from the false claim that perceptual knowledge of external objects is essentially inferential, Price says that standing conditions are those "necessary to all the visual sense-data alike." This condition is underspecified: is what is in question all the visual data of a given occasion, or all the visual data ever of a given perceiver? Grice reads Price the former way and objects that Price's use of the distinction is not sufficient to cover all cases ("The Causal Theory of Perception', P.A.S.s.v. 1962); and it is also not necessary because the whole of my visual field may be taken up by a uniformly colored wall without it being false that I see *it*. On the particular-occasion construal of Price, the inside studio scene being as it is, is a *standing* condition in Price's sense, and so he would wrongly fail to count this as a case of perception.

The nonparticular occasion construal of Price yields an even more implausible theory; since the operation of the generator in another room is not a causal precondition of *all* my visual sense-data, the standing/differential condition would not exclude that the generator was perceived.

18. P. F. Strawson, "Causation"; D. F. Pears "The Appropriate Causation of Intentional Basic Actions," *Critica* 7 (1975).

19. The case of L-DOPA: see Oliver Sacks's engrossing descriptions and history in his book *Awakenings* (London, 1976). The substance in the relevant part of the brain is not L-DOPA, but dopamine: dopamine, however, cannot be absorbed by the brain (Sacks, p. 54), and so L-DOPA was fed to the patients.

Note that such examples can be adapted to show that it is incorrect to require for the intentionality of a ϕ-ing under that description that the agent's belief that he *can* ϕ in the circumstances be knowledge: this would not be true in a drug example in which the agent has inferred from false premises that the drugs he is taking will restore a certain mechanism which they in fact by-pass.

20. "Intentional Basic Actions," p. 66.

21. Clearly, some obvious refinements are appropriate here. For instance, if I suffer from akinesia, and I get another person to move my arm for me, and this movement is a signaling to a third person outside the window, it may not be wrong to say that the movement of my arm (*not* my moving it—no such thing occurred) is intentional under a description relating to signaling. If we decide it is, then the additional requirement of the text must be restricted to descriptions that are "basic" in the agent's plan.

22. For answers to some possible objections to this claim, see Paul Grice's "Intention and Uncertainty" (British Academy Lecture, 1971) pp. 4-5; and also Harman, op. cit.

23. Nevertheless, all this said, I have much less confidence in the efficiency of the DE account than in its necessity.

24. "Intentional Basic Actions," p. 56. I should perhaps say explicitly that I do not hold the findings of the physiological sciences to be irrelevant to the *extension* of the psychological concepts in question, but only to the concepts themselves.

25. I should in fairness note that David Pears has told me that he no longer places any weight on reliability in excluding deviant chains.

26. For a colorful defense of such a view, a defense that contains additional material that need not be adopted by someone who holds the view in question, see Brian O'Shaghnessy, "Trying (as the Mental 'Pineal Gland')," *Journal of Philosophy* 70 (1973):365-86.

27. There is a puzzling passage about reliability in Pears's paper (p. 67): I will quote five consecutive sentences from it: "If the motor nerves to my left hand were almost gone, I would seldom succeed in clenching it. But when I did clench it, I would be doing so intentionally, Such examples could be multiplied. They show that it is too much to require that the prior stages of a basic action should be reliable. All that we ought to require is that they should belong to a reliable type of sequence." Why does the clenching example meet this last requirement? This is to ask what the verifying reliable type of sequence might be in the example. It cannot be that specified by "chain beginning with an initiating event (act of will) continuing with an impulse through the remaining nerves," for that is not reliable. Is the case one of intentional action because if such a chain operated and the other nerves were functional, then there would reliably be the effect of the required kind? But to allow that would trivialize the requirement, because any chain at all could be embedded in some circumstance or other that acts as a failsafe mechanism. (We could not make use of the fact that in the clenching example, the additional circumstances are more of the same kind as those already present—more nerves—because we do not want to exclude the possibility of diverse kinds of efferent pathways in intentional action for some conceivable creatures.)

28. A fourth problem might be that a definition employing reliability might wrongly make the intentionality of a particular action intrinsically a matter of degree.

29. "Intentional Basic Actions," p. 59.

30. *Ibid.*, p. 52.

31. I should emphasize that I am not here committing myself either way about the need for a reliability requirement outside what Pears characteristically calls the "vestibule" of action, that is in the stages of the chain later than those from the intention to the bodily movement.

32. It should be noted too that the "reliably *matching*" interpretation of the reliability condition would count as nondeviant the causal chain in the gunman and lightning case in the version in which there *is* "specific reflection."

33. "Causation." Page references are to that volume.

34. "But you yourself use technical concepts from the philosophy of explanation in elucidating differential explanation." But there are expressions in ordinary use whose mastery requires some tacit grasp of the concept of DE, a concept that, of course, does not need to be introduced via any particular *a posteriori* science. For example, we have already noted that "explains" is undoubtedly sometimes used in the sense of "differentially explains" (as when someone insists that in the second camera example, what explains the distribution of colors in the

picture is not the distribution of colors in the external scene). An example of a concept that perhaps embeds the notion of DE is that of a *fossil*.

35. Note, though, that this extension of Strawson's theory would have to be modified to accommodate the possibility that if a condition that violated one of the restrictions were to obtain, it might be one that itself caused a previously perceptual experience to be hallucinatory.

36. I am thus not in agreement with Pears who writes it is "only Strawson's treatment of the internal stage" of the causal chain that is vulnerable to objections ("The Causal Conditions of Perception," *Synthese* 33 (1976):36.

In fact, it is not at all obvious that Strawson's obstruction restrictions are true even when applied only to opaque objects. Light rays are bent by large objects like the sun in a way that may allow an observer on earth to see a star that is in (*some*) spatial sense obstructed from him by another heavenly body.

37. In "The Causal Conditions of Perception" Pears writes of Strawson's objection to Grice that it is circular to say that the appropriate causal chains for perception are those of the kind(s) operative in normal cases of perception, and says that it

> goes too far. For Grice's account of the causal line appropriate to seeing implies that it is a single line, or, at least, a limited disjunction of lines, and this is certainly not something that guarantees its own truth in a circular way. It is a contingent fact . . . the general causal connection between objects and the visual experiences that match them might have followed a largely different line on each occasion. Although this is extremely improbable, it is not inconceivable (p. 30).

Presumably Strawson could reply to one of the points Pears is making here by noting that a definition can be circular without it being true that anything not falling under it necessarily fails to fall under it. But there is also a threat to a simple Gricean position in Pears's further observations here, because even if there are only a few causal routes followed in actual cases of perception, the view that there could have been many imposes an obligation on those elucidating the concept of perception to state the condition in virtue of which those hypothetical routes would in the hypothetical circumstances be sufficient for perception. Pears's own later appeal (p. 33) to the reliable delivery of matching visual experiences suggests that the smallness of the number of actual routes is not playing an essential part in his defense of his views.

38. If the relevant stage is so fixed, we would expect it to be indeterminate whether a person could in principle see by means of sound waves. But it does seem to be thus indeterminate. More generally, from the arguments I have already given we ought to expect a range of indeterminacy. I argued against applying the natural kind model to "perceives" on the ground that there was no scientifically fundamental characteristic for examples to fix: and similar considerations apply to the right stage of the causal chain.

39. "Then why on your view is there not a corresponding need for an ostensive fixing of which events are intentional in the action case?" it will be asked. The answer is that an intention is always an intention to do such-and-such in the world, so in this case the content of the intentionally specified state *does* help fix the relevant stage. In the perception case, although the relevant ϕ may contain physical object vocabulary, we use the notion of perceiving an *object* that we do not in the action case that is part of the source of this difference (see later discussion).

40. For an outline of theory of knowledge that handles the absence of knowledge in this example very satisfactorily, see Alvin Goldman, "Discrimination and Perceptual Knowledge," *Journal of Philosophy* 73 (1976):771-91.

41. Why is there not (if there is not) a concept related to the intentional as knowledge is to the perceptual? One answer might be this. In the perceptual case, the causal chain culminates in a mental event, and so it is reasonable to ask about the relation of such events to a state of the person whose mental event it is; in the action case, the event in which the causal chain culminates is not mental, so there is no question of there being a person whose mental event it is, and to whose knowledge states we might try and relate the event.

42. Two comments on this definition: (a) The quantification into the "differentially explains" context here is done consciously. I cannot answer the alleged objections to this here, except to say that "explains" and "differentially explains" are not transparent in the extremely strong sense (with respect to descriptions having narrower scope than the operators in question) required for the conditions of application for the Frege argument to be fulfilled. (b) The use of "as of" does not produce circularity. e is an experience as of its being ϕ for person y at time t iff e is of the same phenomenal kind as an experience of y's that would be differentially explained by its being ϕ given y's physiological constitution at t and the environmental conditions at t. This explanation does not employ the concept of perception.

43. I am grateful for advice and comments to Michael Barger, Gareth Evans, Jennifer Hornsby, David Pears, and Stephen Schiffer.

Mind and Change of Mind

ANNETTE BAIER

To possess the right to stand securely for oneself . . . the right to affirm one-self, this . . . is a ripe fruit but also a late fruit: how long must this fruit have hung on the tree unripe and sour! And for how much longer a time nothing whatever was to be seen of any such fruit. (Nietzsche, *Genealogy of Morals*)

I shall take up Nietzsche's investigation into the many things presupposed in the existence of a person with the right to make a promise. He emphasized the selective memory that must be "burned in," the selective ignoring, the regulation, foresight, premeditation that must precede the right to ordain the future in a promise. A promise is not merely a fixing of the future—any intention is that—it is a renunciation of the liberty to change one's mind, to revise that fixing. Where Nietzsche saw the "real problem regarding man" as the emergence of an animal with the right to make a promise, I want to shift the problem back and consider what sort of thing a person must be, what capacities and training one must have, to possess the liberty voluntarily restricted in a promise. It is the "short willed unreliable creatures," who are the forerunners of Nietzsche's sovereign free men of their word, whom I shall take as my problem. I shall investigate the abilities that even Nietzsche's proud paragons must possess before they can selectively inhibit them in their rare reluctant promises.

My concern with change of mind is a concern with *mind* more than with morals or supra-morals, with the capacity rather than the liberty to change one's mind. At a certain point in exploring that capacity, however, the line between abilities and acknowledged liberties will become blurred. Change of mind is a topic worth exploring at this point in the debate in philosophy of mind for a variety of reasons. Some of these reasons will emerge at the end of this paper, after the investigation itself, but one can be mentioned at the start.

One general reason for attention to this phenomenon is methodological. Change of mind occupies an intermediate status, among mental phenomena as we know them, and this very intermediate status promises insight into the *continuity* of human thinking with its animal origins. Change of mind displays less advanced capacities than promising, or scientific theorizing, or examining one's conscience; but it involves a step beyond the purposive monotony of animal intelligence and the seemingly random veering of, say, birds to flight. It is intermediate between intelligent animal goal pursuit and the highest human or "angelic" (and "demonic") understanding, so holds out promise of displaying intelligibly the transitions from one to the other. Its suitability for this continuity-preserving role is increased by its being intermediate along another dimension also, the cognitive-practical one. Change of mind is a change in neither of the philosophers' two favorite states: belief and desire. Like intention, it straddles theoretical and practical reason, and also like it, is concerned neither with the true, *simpliciter,* nor with the good, *simpliciter,* but with a fusion of the two, or perhaps with something more primitive and more fundamental than either, out of which both those two sacred idols of our philosophical tribe are self-conscious and intellectualized abstractions or distillates. To return to Nietzsche's metaphor, they are *"late* fruits," and the flower from which they grow lacks the differentiation to be found in the variety of its final fruits. Or so I shall eventually argue. For the moment I wish merely to recommend the investigation of change of mind because we do not need to speak of either the true or the good in analyzing it. If to believe is to believe true, then by focusing on belief as the paradigmatic mental state we will likely end, like Davidson, concluding that without the concept of truth there can be no believing, so only interpreters of language can be believers. To choose belief as the central mental state is to start on a road that soon forks into the Davidsonian route, of restricting mental states to language users, and the Dennett-[1] de Sousa route, which splits belief into two problematically related sorts—belief in *truths,* or human belief, where degree of belief is inadmissible, and reliance on facts or high probabilities, where there can be degrees, and which can be attributed wherever such attribution helps in the prediction of an "intentional system's" behavior. Unlike Dennett and like Davidson, I prefer to keep the term "belief" for what can be self-consciously assented to and professed by language users; but in what follows I shall be making room for its more primitive ancestors and explaining how their logic can be so different from the logic of belief in truth.

The methodological advantage of attention to intention and to change of mind, rather than to belief, is that, because we can delay the discussion of *truth*-seeking, we can avoid both of these paths which threaten to cut off our mental capacities from anything from which they conceivably might have developed. If one takes the Davidsonian path, then the emergence of a thinking species becomes a real mystery, so different is it from any other species. Those who take the other path, the bifurcation of belief path, need not deny continuity between Bayesian animal belief and Fregean human assent to truth, but making that continuity plain becomes unnecessarily difficult. Since, like Descartes in the first and third *Meditations,* I believe we cannot rest content with any version of *res cogitans* which does not hold out hope that the answer we give to the question "What is it?" can be made to fit with the answer given to "How, and from what, did it come to be?" I prefer to work first on the mental states that seem, while interestingly mental, to be close enough to their plausibly postulated animal antecedents to promise the required harmony between the accepted analysis, or systematic account, of mind, and its eventual phylogenetic explanation. In the end, of course, the story would have to be continued to show how, out of a hunter and food gatherer, there developed not merely a creature capable of intention and of change of mind, but also a promiser and a truth collector. Hume noted, "There cannot be two passions more nearly resembling each other than those of hunting and philosophy." (*Treatise*, 451) The love of truth which he likens to hunting is not that pragmatic belief formation he had described in Book One, but the "love of knowledge which displays itself in the sciences," and in philosophy, that is with self-conscious truth-collecting, a human habit he treats as on a par with hunting plover, or troutfishing, where the catch is the better the bigger it is and where there is an odd need in the huntsman to pretend that the catch is *useful*, intended for someone's consumption.[2] My concern will be not with truth collecting or with the animal beliefs underlying other hunts, but with what mediates between them, with appropriate action and warranted assertion rather than with either purposive action and its implicit belief, or with self-conscious pursuit of the good and the true. It will help my exposition of that often neglected intermediate area to invent a species who develop just that far and do not go on to become truthseekers. We could call these mythical creatures, who have eaten the fruit of the tree of the appropriate and the inappropriate, the correct and the incorrect, but not yet the fruit of the tree of knowledge, and of good or evil, the "half-innocent," or, following Frankfurt,[3] the "half-wanton." Once they and their changes of mind have been described, we can go on to complicate the story by seeing what happens to them and their changes of mind when the promising and the truth-collecting mania get a hold, when their innocence is fully lost.

One recent attempt to reconstruct our path out of the garden of animal innocence is that provided by Jonathan Bennett, in *Linguistic Behavior*.[4] Bennett defends a concept of animal belief and develops from that an account of how such belief might come to be expressed and communicated, first by iconic signs, later by non-iconic language. His half-wantons indulge in iconic meanings, make snake signs to one another, and so are set on a slippery, sloping path of tempting communication opportunities which lands them eventually in a speech community. I shall be offering a different account of the half-wanton stage, but in presenting my half-wantons as animals with the ability, not to make icons, but to change their minds, I shall be developing and narrowing a useful concept Bennett provides, that of a "revised registration." If Bennett is right, the capacity for *revision* of a cognitive state, or "registration," is essential to a believer. To have belief states is also to have changes in such states. I think that Bennett is onto something of great importance here, that we can see what a mental state is by attending to its mode of changing. I shall, in what follows, be using the strategy his account suggests, trying to under-

stand mind by understanding alterations in a mind, and in particular those alterations we dignify with the label "changes of mind." My half-wantons are to have the
capacity for such changes, and what I shall be investigating is just how much, and
how little, that capacity involves. We can, I hope, see more clearly what does and
does not count as a mind by seeing what does and does not count as a change of
mind. We can understand thought by understanding second thoughts.

I shall at times be using as data our ordinary linguistic usage, but I shall be
assembling that because it points us toward a concept of mind that is suggestive and
illuminating in its own right, independent of its support from ordinary usage. I shall
not be assuming that the only changes in what is really mind are those changes we
call changes of mind. Rather, I proceed in the hope that by looking at that narrow
class we can get ourselves properly centered, so that we can the better find our way
about in the larger field of human mental events and discern true relationships
there.

Not every alteration of "cognitive state" or "registration," or "Bayesian belief" is a change of mind. Acquiring new information which pushes back the fron-
tiers of one's ignorance is not, for us or for our half-wanton ancestors, a change of
mind, nor is the mere updating of old information, letting one's mind reflect the
changes in the observed world around one. A change of mind *is* a correction, but
not all cases of mistake-correction, and no cases or ignorance-remedying, count as
such changes. If the mistake is corrected by the bitter experience of acting on the
mistaken belief, and acting unsuccessfully, then there will probably be what, to use
Bennett's language, is a revision of a "registration," but not a change of mind. If I
thought the ice was strong enough to support me, skate on it, and sink, I end up
knowing better but not having changed my mind. Learning from sweet and bitter
experience is what, within limits, all intelligent animals do, but the prerogative of
change of mind rests on a different sort of learning. Bitter though it always is to be
found to be in the wrong, the bitterness of being corrected *before* one puts a belief to the test of experience, being corrected by *someone* rather than by "experience," is like the bitterness of pills we cultivate a taste for, because of what they
save us from, and also because of the sweets such "lessons" make available to us,
including that sweet which Hume called "the pleasure of the game alone." (*Treatise, 452*)

But not every case of correcting a belief *before* bitter experience counts as a
change of mind. Simply accepting a correction from a teacher or authority is not
changing one's mind. If I have misread an atlas, and have a mistaken belief about
the distance between two cities, which you correct for me, I do not change my
mind about the distance. Why? Is it because of the passive role I played in both the
revision and the original belief acquisition? Is it that I never "had a mind" on the
matter, if all I did was consult an atlas? If I had estimated the distance, say from
the time taken to fly or drive between them, then revised that estimate after considering the fact that the plane's flight was not as the crow flies, that would be a
change of mind. What are the relevant differences? Is estimation of distance a *mental* activity while consulting an atlas is not? Or is atlas-consulting an activity beyond

the capacity of a half-wanton, excluded because it is too sophisticated rather than insufficiently mental? If the half-wantons are to be given all and only those capacities needed for change of mind, then at this point I must simply set aside, as a problem to be addressed later, the question of whether acceptance of a corrected atlas-reading displays less or more than what is needed for change of mind. For the moment I shall simply point out that although estimation of distance is uncontroversially an activity we share with half-wantons and with other animals, it is not so evident that revision of such estimates can be attributed to mere animals and it is the revisions that are our focus of attention. We want to know which revisions are changes of mind. What, then, is special about such changes, and about the way we form those beliefs, the correction of which counts as change of mind?

One clue here is that we do not need to *make up our mind* what the atlas says, indeed only in exceptional cases would anything count as making up one's mind on this matter. I am not saying that change of mind can occur only after decisions, after datable happenings called "making up one's mind," but I do think that where the latter notion gets no grip at all, then changes of mind are also excluded. We can speak of making up one's mind in judgment of distance, in evaluation of evidence, and in all non-algorithmic cognitive tasks, including, perhaps, the *making* of maps and atlases, and in some cases, reading them; but the primary cases of this phenomenon are practical ones, where we make up our mind what to *do* rather than what to say or what to think; so it may be best, at this point, to look at cases of change of mind on practical matters, cases of changing intentions.

The clearest cases of change of mind, as of making up one's mind, are practical. One changes one's mind when one changes one's plans. But, as there were cases of belief-alteration that were not changes of mind, so there are cases of change in one's intentions that are excluded, and the exclusions highlight what remains. Two extremes seem to be not changes of mind. On the one hand, variations in how one implements one's intentions—switching a heavy bag one is carrying from the left to the right hand, when the left arm tires, is not a change of mind, even if the switch makes a significant difference, for the agent, to the outcome of the intentional activity—say if it permanently injures an already weak right elbow. Such alterations in what one is doing, substitutions of one bit of one's "work force" for another, are normal semi-automatic happenings in any intentional activity. They indicate no change of mind or plan, if whatever "plan" there was was not specific about such details. What one intended was to carry the bag, with either arm, with whatever switches one felt like at the time, and that was what was done, without any change of mind. A change of mind that is a change of intention is the replacement of one action plan by another. Where there was no action plan, or where it was nonspecific on details, no change of mind can occur. I do not change my mind when, walking along a path, I move aside, off the path, to get out of the way of an oncoming cyclist. Most intentions include, implicitly or explicitly, contingency plans for a range of possible circumstances. Varying one's intentional activity to fit varying circumstances, like updating one's version of current circumstances, requires no change of mind.

At the other extreme from such changes in the disjunctively planned or unplanned if sometimes important details of plan execution are some big changes in one's whole goal structure, which are also not what we mean by changes of mind. A radical conversion is different, and not merely in degree, from a change of mind. It would be an insult to the person who renounces his worldly position and turns to a life of poverty and religious devotion to say that he had undergone a change of mind. To call Saul's conversion on the Damascus road a change of mind suggests ulterior motives—it suggests that he made the change for the sake of power, or for publicity, or for money, or even for treasures in heaven—that the conversion was phoney. Paul did change his mind when, for example, after a dream he went to Macedonia, instead of staying in Troas, as originally planned. A change of mind is a change in one's goals short or long term, not in that for the sake of which those goals were adopted.

Such radical changes in ultimate values are not helpfully seen merely as changes in long range rather than short range goals. It is not that changes of mind occur only when there are changes in short-range objectives, within a stable context of long-term ones. Changes of mind may concern my longest term goals and are still distinguishable from radical alteration in values. If, in my twenties, I buy a piece of land intended as the site for a retirement home (or, if you insist on longest range, as a burial plot) then later sell it and buy land, for the same purpose, in another country, then I have changed my mind about where I wish to live the end of my life. It would invite confusion to insist that, since my concern to live agreeably in retirement remains unaltered, the change of mind concerned less than ultimate goals. Comfortable old age is no farther away from the young investor than living in the selected retirement home. If we say that the young person saved in order to invest in order to buy a retirement home, in order to live in it in old age, in order to have an agreeable old age, the last member of this ordered series gives, not a further goal, but rather the reason why the last-mentioned goal, living in the retirement home, is adopted. Living there is not a means to a good old age, it is a component of that. It is the good for the sake of which the goals were adopted.[5]

This contrast between change of goals and change in that for the sake of which the goals are adopted is important for distinguishing us from half-wantons. We *are* capable of conversion, and even of rational conversion, and this possibility reverberates, as it were, throughout our lower-level decisions. We can call everything in question. The specter of ultimate doubt haunts our, but not the half-wantons', lives. We need not rule out the possibility that they too might undergo changes in ultimate values, perhaps even to know that they do, and wait for the next "switch of sakes." But if they do undergo such changes, they, unlike us, will be really passive, in relation to such changes, will be slaves of their values if not of their passions. In even our own case we typically see such radical changes as forced upon us. Something *happened* to Saul on the Damascus road. But we take and impute responsibility for such conversions, and it is important that they can be reason-governed. The possibility of such ultimate change being "our own" is what Sartre, and Charles Taylor,[6] call freedom. Such higher reflection on that for the sake of which goals are adopted can lead to risky "bets on the good," acts of commitment, which are beyond the capacity of the half-wantons. When such bets seem safe or irresistible bets, we speak, as Descartes did, of a compulsion that is the highest freedom. Religious converts speak this language:

> Take me to you, imprison me, for I
> Except you enthrall me, never shall be free,
> Nor ever chaste, except you ravish me.

(John Donne, Holy Sonnet, XIV).

The half-wantons will have the thralldom without the freedom.

When a radical change, free or unfree, brings in its train more humdrum changes, will the latter count as changes of mind? Can a change of mind be dictated from "above," as it were? I think this depends on whether the higher change is one we feel *we* brought about, one for which we accept responsibility, or whether we feel we had no choice. Since the half-wantons never have such choices, none of their changes of mind will be dictated from above, nor will ours insofar as we exercise only the capacities we share with them. If I cancel my concert subscription because I am retiring to a convent, after a Saul-like irresistible conversion to a life of contemplation, it would be misleading to say I had changed my mind about the concert series. That occurs when I cancel it, say, so that I can be more flexible about *when* I listen to music, or because I find I enjoy recorded music as much as live music, or even because I wish to devote all my evenings to philosophy. Of course, it is conceivable that all along I had planned to switch at this point in life, from occasional concert-going to monomanic philosophic endeavors, so the change in life-style would not then indicate any conversion or change of mind. A change of mind must be distinguished from a change of activity that is not counter to previous plan, and also from changes of activity in that for the sake of which we plan whatever we do plan, do what we do. The passively undergone radical change is like a change in the situation. The world of the convert is a different world from that of the sinner. No situation transformations, internal or external, are grounds for change of mind. If, on my way to the bank to deposit some cash I am robbed of it, my not proceeding on to the bank signifies no change of mind. Changes of mind come about after a review, or refocusing, on features in the old, unchanged situation and its options. Saul on the Damascus road was, as it were, robbed of the ability to go on persecuting the Christians. The blinding light and reproachful voice were, like the robber on the way to the bank, not merely unforeseen, they restructured the situation so totally that the agent found himself in a whole new arena.

The border between new light on an old situation and a new situation is no clear border*line.* Suppose I had decided to take a cab to work rather than the bus, but outside my house, before finding a cab, am offered a lift by a neighbor. Do I, in accepting that lift, change my mind about the cab? An unforeseen option is provided, which decides me. It is not clear whether this is a change of mind, whether the neighbor's offer changes my mind for me. I am inclined to say that the appearance of new attractive options, added to the old ones, is a reason for a change of mind, but the elimination of old favored options takes matters out of one's hands, so presents one with a new matter to have a mind on, not reason to change one's mind. What are clearly ruled out as changes of mind, whatever we say on these more difficult cases, are both those alterations of intentional activity made necessary by circumstance, and such alterations as follow, not from the mere addition of a new attractive option, but from some blinding light (but *not* the "natural light" of reason), which transfigures and restructures all the options. Exactly what an option is, and how we divide up the future action-manifold into distinguishable options, is not easy to say. Here I am relying on an unanalyzed concept of an action plan, and its alternatives, which, to be precise, would need to be spelled out as a connected sequence of exercises of distinguishable competences, on occasions specified as opportunities for such exercises.[7]

So far I have claimed that changes of mind, in the practical area, are not changes necessitated by circumstance, nor are they changes in, or normally subsequent upon, changes in fundamental values. It is now time to look and see what does make us, and the half-wantons, change our minds. What does change one's mind? Such things as previously unnoticed relationships, causal and non-causal, ill-appreciated sequences and consequences, overlooked or unrealized meanings, known but forgotten facts. If someone gets me to change my mind, it will be more a case of "You are right. I was forgetting that (or I overlooked that, or I hadn't seen it that way)—you've changed my mind for me," than of "That's news to me—and it changes my mind." If the news is of a new attractive option, or if it is news that makes the existing options look different in order of attractiveness, then it could be the ground for change of mind. But news that merely selects between contingency plans within an option will do just that, not precipitate a change of mind. Suppose a president has decided on a makework program of a certain definite scope to cope with unemployment. News that the unemployment level has dropped may lead to change of mind concerning the scope of the program, or, if the drop is dramatic, to the scrapping of the program. But normally the adopted plan will have been flexible, embedding many contingency plans for changing levels of unemployment, so that news about the current level, as long as it is a change within the range for which the program was designed, will merely select among according-to-plan subplans, not bring about a change of mind. A change of mind is based upon a reviewing of the options facing one, possibly in the light of updated information, including information about new options, but not in the light of news that destroys the originally chosen option, or that totally transforms the situation, so that a new problem faces one. The new light on the old problem can come from new information, but also from remembering previously forgotten relevant facts, or from coming to realize how a rule applies, or from seeing the irrelevance or lesser relevance of what one had previously given weight to. One's previous stupidity need not have lain in ignorance or mistake, but in forgetfulness, a squinting soul, or blindness to what was there to see, or obsession with one thing there to see, in failure to ignore what should be ignored, and to notice what is there within one's cognitive reach, to put it together, realize[8] what it means, to consider it properly. Consider—the original sense is astrological. Change of mind comes after reconsidering, restudying the stars, the entrails, the "costs and benefits" or other auguries. But a radical shift in the method of considering—switching from astrology to rational decision theory—is, like radical change in values, more than a change of mind, transforming as it would the very activity of considering and, with it, what counts as things to consider. Change of mind occurs against a stable background of procedures and in the calm between revolutionary transvaluations of values.

An important member of the list of things that can be grounds for change of mind is a realization that some rule applies, or of the inapplicability of a rule one had tried to bring to bear on the matter. The half-wantons, must, like us, be capable of rule observation. They, unlike animals, have conventions, and these generate reasons for change of mind, as well as providing, when their application is unclear, matters on which to make up and change one's mind. The guest who goes toward his host with hand outstretched ready for a handshake may change his mind when, from his hosts's stance, he realizes that protocol demands a bow, or a formal kiss. The half-wanton mind that is changed in a change of mind is equipped not merely with purposes and unquestioned ultimate values but with customs and conventions whose bearing on the current situation may leave room for difference of opinion, and for change of mind. Recognition of when and how a law or convention applies exercises one's mind, but need exercise neither reasoning power nor purposive intelligence. The believer, or even exbeliever, who takes off his hat, perhaps also crosses himself, on entering a church, exhibits neither animal cunning nor critical reason, merely a sense of occasion, but, if his companion fails to observe the convention, may appropriately admonish him, *"Think where you are!."* Thinking shows itself and reveals qualities of mind, as much in recognition of occasion as in working out means to ends, or proofs of theorems, as much in observance as in observation. The customs in which we were trained provide us with reasons that complicate, enrich, sometimes override, those which animal purpose provides, and they prepare the way for those *self*-critical conventions, appeal to which we call reason. The half-wantons have customs, but not the custom of custom-criticism. They are pious dogmatists with respect to both conventions and values.

What exactly have we bestowed on the half-wantons in giving them rules and conventions? We have given them an order in their behavior which mere goal-pursuit would not provide. We have given them the capacity for game-playing, and for transferring to their serious life, out of games, some of the structure that obtains in the game. The new order is deontological rather than teleological. Not all play imitates serious pursuit of goals, and it would confuse matters to construe game-playing as teleological, as like an animal's search for food. (Perhaps the term "goal-directed" should be left for activity in those highly structured and usually competitive games where there *are* goals, and where there is winning and losing.) Some play mimics the teleological order of serious animal life, but all play mimics, or exemplifies, the difference convention makes to human life, the constraints and opportunities it provides. Take a simple skipping game, in which a piece of rope is used to provide both the means and the obstacle to success at that game. If a player, frustrated at his companions' greater skills at skipping, uses the rope to beat them or tie them up, he has displayed that versatile instrumental reason Descartes spoke of, but such purposive action puts him out of skipping bounds. Within the bounds, the conventions, of the skipping game, the rope is only for skipping with, just as within the nongame of normal speech, the sounds made are for communication, not for noise or music. Conventions in and out of games provide reasons for conformity to them and a change of mind may often concern, or be due to, a realization of what such conformity demands.

It seems reasonable to suppose that this recognition of the rope's restricted role, in the game, and of the significance of the hat-removal in a religious context, could come about only in a community that trains its members. Our half-wantons, then, are social animals, and their ability to conform to mutual expectations goes along with their ability to train and be trained, to allow "the actions of each of us to have a reference to those of the other, and to be performed upon the supposition that something is to be performed on the other part." (Hume, *Treatise*, 490) Must we give them language? It seems artificial to deny them it, since language-learning is so clear and important an example of initiation into conventions, as Hume noted in the passage cited. Unlikely though it is that the half-wantons will fail to add language-invention to their other inventions and conventions, what seems strictly necessary for their capacity to change their minds on the sort of grounds discussed is not language itself, but any of its cousin conventions. Let us suppose, then, that the half-wantons have conventions but not yet linguistic conventions. They train their initiates in their procedures and can indicate approval and disapproval, encouragement and discouragement. One ground for change of mind will be one's peers' disapproval of actions one is preparing to undertake. The half-wantons care about conformity and attempt to do the accepted thing, to reach approved goals in approved ways. The expression of approval and disapproval, assent and dissent, must, for the half-wantons, take a nonverbal form—head movements, laughter, frowns, raised eyebrows, encouraging smiles. But since even for us language users, the training in our own language must at least begin this way, there is no particular problem in supposing that the half-wantons can train one another without a language to help them do so. And as, in language learning, the pupil learns from the linguistic response as well as from the nonlinguistic response of the trainer, so in any convention-governed activity, the learner will advance by being included in the activity, by being treated as if he understands before he fully understands.

The denial of language to the half-wantons will limit their ability to represent their conclusions concerning matters of fact. They may have maps, like ours a mixture of the iconic and the conventional, astronomical charts, and perhaps pictures of hunted animals. A change of mind about geographical or astronomical fact will show in an alteration of their maps. A corrected map reading, by contrast, will be a correction in the map-guided intentional activity, and it will be difficult to separate out the map-based belief from the intention relying on it. Where the only things read are maps and charts, misreadings will not be easily distinguishable from other sorts of mis-moves in the map-guided activity. But as long as the half-wantons can, not merely communicate their agreement and disagreement with one another's moves, but indicate a variety of grounds for such responses—pointing, say, to the map, not the storm clouds, when trying to dissuade a fellow from proceeding on the longer path to the destination, we can allow them some discrimination of the fact-reliance component in their intentions, and of the fact-representing role of their maps.

We have, then, a community of half-wantons who, while incapable of conversion, of discerning the possible error of their ways, are capable not merely of animal learning from experience, of trial and error, but of discerning and correcting that error which consists in straying from the way laid down by rules and conventions. They can discern the incorrect as well as the unsuccessful. Is it this, the presence of convention, which makes the difference between having and not having the capacity for change of mind? The thesis I want to defend is that change of mind involves but is not the same as revision of rule application. Only because the half-wantons are rule-observers, mutual regulators, have they the liberty of change of mind. But this change is a revision of a decision more involved than simple rule application. It includes deciding whether the rules apply at all, how to combine correctness with success, how to blend one's second nature, as a trained rule-respecter, with one's original nature as an intelligent animal. Because the half-wantons have both intelligence and a sense of what is required, what is proper, but have no inflexible instinct to tell them when the deontological should prevail, and when the teleological, they must somehow make up their own minds about this.[9] They must exercise *judgment*. What is revised in a change of mind is neither simply a means-end calculation, nor simply the application of a rule to a case, but a judgment that such calculation is appropriate, that the rule is applicable, that it should or should not impose constraints on the means-end calculation. Change of mind is revision of judgment, following on a reviewing of the considerations. Considering, forming an opinion, and judging are the thinkings whose rethinking is change of mind. Neither the adoption of necessary means to one's ends nor the observance of categorical imperatives (of morals or manners or mathematics) gives one's mind any room to operate. Where matters are cut and dried, where there is no choice of what to do, we can "use our brains," exhibit intelligence, even conscientiousness, but not wisdom or even prudence. These show only in matters where there is room for difference of opinion, where no problem-solver gives *the* correct answer, where thoughts tend to be followed by second thoughts.

In the special human case where what is judged is a person's status in the eyes of the law, the specialization of function typical of a legal system makes the task of judging the business of an expert, the judge, but the general features of judgment still obtain. The judge is an expert on the law, but the law does not make his decisions for him. A judge, making up his mind on a case, has, to guide him, a stable background of valid statute, accepted precedent, agreement about the spirit as well as the letter of the law; but these give him room for judgment. A judge in a court of appeal may reverse that original decision, change the Law's mind on a case, but not by rejecting that background.

Both in the law and in ordinary life, judgment, like virtue, is not itself taught, but it is intimately connected with what must be taught, if it determines the way in which what we have been taught gets combined with what we knew or learned without teaching. Only if we have acquired a second nature do we have the job of combining that with our first nature (turning eating into dining, and all the other transformations Gass[10] has so brilliantly analyzed), forming a whole person and shaping a life appropriate to persons with such a nature. We are not, and cannot be, instructed in how to make such judgments well, as we are instructed on how to genuflect and how to count. Perennial attempts are made to reduce such thinking to rule—but it resists the attempt. The higher order activity of criticizing, rather than that of teaching, is what we depend on for acquiring standards of judgment. It is because others once rethought our thinking, reconsidered what we considered, reviewed what we had in view in making up our minds, that we now can recognize reasons for change of mind. Others seconded, or opposed, our judgment, and so we learned when second thoughts were needed. The critic is different from the detector of mistakes, and different also from the efficiency expert. Criticism may be directed at inefficiency, at sloppy procedure, but it goes beyond that and may challenge ends as well as means, the appropriateness and timeliness of procedures as well as their time-saving success. The hard questions requiring judgment rather than know-how concern the appropriate use of conventions and procedures. Here criticism outruns instruction. We can recognize bad judgment without being able to give a recipe for avoiding it. We all expect more of our pupils than we have imparted by instruction. Example, encouragement, criticism, take over where instruction leaves off. Although not instructed in how to make up one's mind judiciously, we are criticized for doing so injudiciously, and we depend on others for the recognition of good judgment, as well as for one precondition of it, initiation into those conventional procedures for which judgment finds a proper place, as it puts animal purpose in its place. The thoughtless person, the fool, fails not in reasoning nor necessarily in goal pursuit, but in proper judgment, of when to calculate, when not, when to genuflect and when to be still, when to speak and when to keep silent.

A machine that simulated even half-wanton thought would need a similar richness of "imputs" into and constraints upon its "thinking." It would need an analogue to animal appetite, to communicated convention, and to communicated criticism of its actions, its way of spending its time. It would need to know, not merely how to calculate and count, but what to take into account, *what* to count, for how much, and when. For thinking beings, for us and the half-wantons, there is a time for all things under the sun; but no clock, and no clockwork calculation or routine, tells that time.

Change of mind, then, is a matter of having second thoughts which are revised judgments, revised to correct faults of judgment which others helped us learn to discern by their response to our unrevised judgments. We revise judgment to avoid anticipated criticism, expecting the revised judgment to be affirmed by our potential critics. What *we* judge *two* times is sound.

For the half-wantons, now revealed as our real Rylean ancestors,[11] criticism will take the form of withholding reassurance or affirmation, and perhaps of indicating the ground for an alternative judgment. Without language they will not have a way of recognizing the general faults of judgment, and what leads to it, faults which we can recognize, like forgetfulness, thoughtlessness, rashness, lack of a sense of proportion, myopia, obsession with one aspect of a matter, inability to ignore distracting irrelevancies. The half-wantons may be able to discern and correct what are, in fact, specific instances of these, but scarcely to discern them as instances of specific sorts of fault, if they have no language in which to articulate either the grounds of their agreement or disagreement, or their detailed assessment of their fellows' judgments. The point of withholding language from them was to discover just how much they might do without it and where its absence would limit them. Without language they can not merely have other convention-guided activities, but they can make up their minds and change their minds, and help one another do so. They can, without language, represent and indicate some facts relevant to judgment; but the sort of representation that would discriminate the thoughtless person from the forgetful person seems necessarily non-iconic, and any conventions used to make such distinctions would *be* linguistic conventions. What language can do, which the resources we have given the half-wantons cannot do, is to discriminate and represent norm-governed activities as such, the moves and the reasons for them, the faults and the virtues of the players. Such ability to represent themselves as thinkers could transform the half-wantons into us, since once their own procedures, including their critical responses to one another's judgments, can be articulated and described, the activity of criticism can be directed upon itself.

There is no automatic transfer of the activity of criticism from its usual target, individual performance, including judgment in making up and changing one's mind, to the practice of criticism itself. The thoughtful person applies critical standards to his judgment, so is prone to second thoughts and changes of mind; but more than thoughtfulness is needed to be critical about the standards of criticism themselves, to be critical through and through. Such meta-criticism, criticism directed at itself, is reason's province. The thoughtful person may examine his life, without having examined his method of examination. It remains an open question whether reason pays, by its own coin or any other, whether a life examined by examined standards is better than a less reflectively examined life, whether we lead a better life than the half-wantons. The half-wantons engage in critical judgment of one anothers' judgment, but criticism of criticism requires a language, a way of representing the critical enterprise and articulating its standards, positioning them for critical survey. What we call *rational* norms are standards of criticism that we take to bear, or to have borne, critical inspection. What we say *three* times is *true*? Once we have rational as well as thinking beings, the balance of nature and convention, nature and second nature, established by less critical thinking, can be upset, and then we are apt to get attempts to deny or banish mere less-than-rational convention, definitions of rationality as mere efficient goal pursuit. (Sometimes what we say the third time is simplistic.)

The liberty to change one's mind, then, rests upon membership in a community where there is mutual recognition, which trains its members in some conventions, but not necessarily linguistic ones, and which has the practice of affirmation, of second-thinking an individual's judgment about how to use the training received. Where there is the possibility of such interpersonal affirmation, such heteropersonal second thinking, there will soon also be auto-personal second thoughts, attempts to improve one's judgment so that it can be reaffirmed by one's potential critics. Second thoughts follow on interpersonal second-thinking. An individual can change his own mind because others once have tried to change it for him, have responded to his judgments with their assent or dissent. The mental events that are changes of mind reveal the interdependence of thinkers, and the limits of the dependence of thought on language. A half-wanton has enough of a mind to be able to change it. The half-wanton mind, and ours insofar as we are capable of just such second thoughts, is mind as Wittgenstein and Ryle presented it, the precariously maintained possession, of some moderately sociable and moderately intelligent animals, of a capacity for minding how their moves measure up to shared critical, but not necessarily *thoroughly* critical, standards.

The view of mind I have endorsed is, then, different from that widely held view that takes language to be essential to thinking. I have suggested that it is essential for fully reflective thinking, for the search for the final truth and the ultimate good, but not for its more modest basis, the attempt to avoid the incorrect and the inappropriate. I shall conclude by making a schematic comparison of the view I have endorsed with that of Bennett and Davidson, and with that of Dennett, using the Cartesian view as the background for the comparison. One can find in Descartes' writings about finite mind a variety of emphases and claims. These can be labeled and expressed thus:

(a) *Reflexiveness:* A thinker is aware of itself as a thinker.
(b) *Heteronomy:* A thinker is aware of a better thinker, in comparison with which its own thinking may be imperfect, and whose reassurance it needs to combat self-doubt.
(c) *Representation:* A thinking thing has ideas with "objective reality."
(d) *Intellect:* A thinking thing discerns truths, can see clearly and distinctly the relations between its ideas.
(e) *Will:* A thinking thing accepts or rejects truth-candidates, or postpones decision.
(f) *Versatile Expressive Speech:* A thinking thing can express its thoughts in speech.
(g) *Response:* A thinking thing can respond appropriately to what is said to it.
(h) *Convention and Custom:* A thinking thing has learned a language, its ability for (f) depends upon "the customs in which we were trained." (*Passions of the Soul*, Part First, XLIV)
(i) *Versatile Intelligent Problem Solving:* A thinking thing can use its reason in all sorts of situations.

These nine capacities of Cartesian mind are not an unordered list, but they are only partially ordered by Descartes himself. The last four are clearly thought by him to be less basic than the first five; but beyond that little can be said, despite his claim to have isolated the essence of mind. If we take (b) seriously, and consider Descartes' views about the nature of truth for that super-thinker, then we would need to make (c), (d), and (e) dependent on a special case of (h), namely on what God decrees to be truth. Truth is correspondence, success in representation, for Descartes but not for his authoritative thinker. Perhaps the best summary formula to extract from Descartes' account would be this:

"I am a thinker. Anyone whom a thinker repeats or reaffirms, or who can reaffirm what a thinker proposes, is itself a thinker."

This would cover the Divine Thinker, but at the cost of narrowing the test for admitting finite fellow-thinkers from appropriate speech response to appropriate assent. Descartes rightly expresses real doubt about which thinker does the second-thinking. "In some way I have the idea of the infinite earlier than the finite, to wit, the idea of God before that of myself." (*Third Meditation*)

Bennett's emphasis on iconic meaning as intermediary between animal belief and full linguistic meaning gives this ordering of the Cartesian features:[12] (i), with modified (d) and (e), then (c) and (g), then (f), then (h) and perhaps (b). Self-consciousness, (a), enters very early, with (g). The early place given to representation makes his view different from both mine and Dennett's, while my view differs from both Dennett's and Bennett's in its emphasis on (b) and on (h).

A view like Davidson's[13] picks up Descartes' emphasis (f) and (g), and makes thinking essentially a matter of the ability to use and interpret speech. His account gives a crucial role to one custom-dependent custom, that of "interpretation," that is to a version of (g) and of (h). He argues for the primacy, among thoughts, of beliefs, and the dependence of belief on "interpretation." To believe is to believe true, and truth enters the picture when the believer is an interpreter of the beliefs of others, expressed in language. Thus "a creature must be a member of a speech community to have the concept of belief" and to have a belief is to have the contrast between true and false belief, and so to have the *concept* of belief.

I find Davidson's account to exemplify what Ryle called the intellectualist legend, the tendency to "suppose that the primary exercise of minds consists in finding the answers to questions, and that their other occupations are merely applications of considered truths, or even regrettable distractions from their considerations."[14] Davidson, I think, confuses understanding with interpretation and unduly emphasizes understanding language, which is merely *one* convention our thought presupposes, essential though it may be for some thinking.

Davidson's account highlights language, one of the external criteria Descartes gave for detecting the presence of inner thought. Dennett's[15] account, like Bennett's, gives priority to the other external criterion, (i), intelligence in behavior. It is taken as basic because the other features presuppose its presence. On the story Dennett gives, they emerge in the following order: from intelligent pursuit of goals, from the sort of rationality possessed by any "intentional system," anything we have reason to treat as possessing beliefs and desires, we move to the special case of the system that *reciprocates* such treatment—that has beliefs about our beliefs, second-order beliefs. Any creature capable of manipulating our beliefs, would have this reciprocity, a special version of (g), appropriate response to other thinkers. From that Dennett moves to the special case of such reciprocity that is involved in linguistic response, where the intentions are Gricean,[16] that is, are not only higher order, but include a reference back to one's own lower-order intentions. Once we have that, we have the seed from which self-consciousness grows. We have persuasion, mutual persuasion, ascription of responsibility, and the attitudes to others taken in such activities can be turned on oneself. "Acting on a second order desire, doing something to bring it about that one acquires a first order desire, is acting on oneself just as one would act on another person: one schools oneself, one offers persuasions, arguments, threats, bribes, in the hope of inducing oneself to acquire the first order desire."[17] Dennett, then, has a Rylean account of Cartesian self-consciousness, (a), which links it intimately with (g), response to others, and with (f), language.

What is not clear to me is exactly how Dennett sees (c), representation, coming into the picture, nor where he places (h), convention, in the developmental story. For Gricean intentions to have a reasonable chance of success, that is for them to be *intentions* rather than wild hopes, there must already be a public language, a set of accepted speech conventions, some version of (h). We cannot get "the meaning" out of "utterer's meaning," if the utterer must depend on common knowledge of *the* meaning, in his intention to produce a specific uptake in the hearer by the hearer's recognition of his intention to get just that uptake. Gricean intentions depend on conventions and do not generate them. So I think that to get individual linguistic intentions one must have some account of convention, of the shared intentions of the group.[18]

About representation Dennett says "we should be particularly suspicious of the argument I was tempted to use, viz., that *representations* of second order intentions would depend on language. For it is far from clear that all or even any of the beliefs and other intentions of an intentional system need to be *represented* 'within' the system for us to get a purchase on predicting its behavior by ascribing such states to it."[19] He says this when discussing reciprocity. I think he would agree that by the time one has persuasion there must be some representation of belief, and, for unspoken self-persuasion, there must be representation "within the system."

Dennett has given us an illuminating way to order some of the Cartesian mental factors. One begins with intelligent behavior, using a crude version of intellect and will as postulates to explain that. The crucial next step is the presence of reciprocal response, leading to linguistic response, enabling mutual persuasion and so self-consciousness. The story I have told is not very different, but it gives more weight to convention and to nonlinguistic conventions and also to a secular version of Descartes' awareness of a superior more authoritative thinker. These differences between my account and Dennett's make my story more heavily indebted to Ryle than is his, though his is certainly not unRylean, given the central place in it of the concept of a higher-order act. Dennett's preference for propositions, and for treating all mental attitudes as propositional attitudes, gives his account the pervasive intellectualist bias against which Ryle warned us, and which my account was designed to avoid. Perhaps if propositions were treated as no more than the formal objects of acts of proposing, with only such structure as such objects need have, then addiction to propositions would be harmless and we could get progressively richer structures as the act of proposing becomes more sophisticated, when language is present. With these reservations about propositions, and about the adequacy of Gricean intentions to generate any conventional meaning, and with my added emphasis on an initially authoritarian training for the eventual thinkers, so that they are forever haunted or reassured by a superior thinker looking over their shoulder, checking up on or endorsing their thinking, my account of what it is to be a thinker is not so different from Dennett's account of what it is to be almost a person.

I have, by inventing the half-wantons, artificially introduced a fairly sharp break between thinking and fully rational and reflective thinking, claiming that it is not necessary for thought as such, for mind and change of mind, to have full self-consciousness, or representation, or language. The half-wanton thinkers have other-consciousness, the desire to think acceptably, that is they have the capacity for appropriate response to fellow thinkers. They have a nonlinguistic version of (h), convention, and they have the special cases of (g), which are responses to training and to criticism, which therefore involve (b) their acceptance of an authority external to their individual thinking, that is, they are heteronomous. Given these three features in addition to their animal base of purposive intelligence, they are thinkers. When they add language, representation, and full critical self-consciousness, particularly consciousness of their own already existent critical procedures, then they will have stepped into the harsh light of reason and can acquire Descartes' version of intellect and will, become seekers of the truth, lovers of the good, and aspirants to autonomy. But this late fruit, reason, ripens from the green fruit of mutual criticism of judgment, and from the flower of animal intelligence only when that is pollinated with conformity to convention. Realization that the conventions and resulting practices are *ours,* and can be changed, that criticism can be turned on articulated practices as well as individual participants in a practice, is the sometimes indigestible late fruit, sour even when ripe. And if the ripeness of that late fruit lies in full self-consciousness, reflexiveness, as the whole modern philosophical tradition from Descartes through Leibniz, Kant, Hegel, to Nietzsche, affirms and reaffirms, then in part that ripeness will show in recognition of one's origins and one's relatives.

To be a thinker at all is to be responsive to criticism, a participant in a practice of mutual criticism and affirmation. A rational self-conscious thinker will turn a critical eye on purported armchair reconstructions of one's ancestry, one's own revisions of them included. Once one has eaten the sour apple of reason, even change of mind becomes reflexive, directed on its own analysis.[20]

Notes

1. Dennett, in his reply (forthcoming in *Brainstorms*) to the original version of this paper (given at the Chapel Hill Colloquium in Philosophy, October 16, 1977), endorsed a distinction introduced by Ronald de Sousa, in "How to Give a Piece of Your Mind; or, a Logic of Belief and Assent," *Review of Metaphysics* 25 (1971):52-79. The distinction is between Bayesian animal belief and human assent to linguistically formulated truth-candidates, which must be either assented to or rejected—a version of the Cartesian will that affirms or denies the ideas which the intellect has already scrutinized. Such assent is seen to involve an act of commitment, a bet on truth. Some such bets are uninteresting because sure bets. (Again, compare Descartes in the *Fourth Meditation:* "If I always understood clearly what is true and what is good I would never need to deliberate about what choice and judgment I ought to make, and so I would be entirely free without ever being indifferent." Descartes was no gambler and insisted that any bet on truth be a sure bet, but he did separate out the act of assent of the will from the prior understanding which made it a *safe* bet.) The bets that are risky are the ones we are likely to revoke in a change of mind, according to Dennett. As will become clear, my account of change of mind makes it a second bet, not on truth but on appropriateness; that is to say, I want to delineate a level intermediate between animal Bayesian belief and language-requiring assent to truths.

2. Dennett, following de Sousa, suggests that the distinction between animal belief and linguistically articulate assent gives us the right basis for an account of both self-deception and *akrasia*. The former, presumably, will be the sin of assenting to what one does not believe, the latter the sin of believing and acting on what one would not assent to. Hume clearly thinks the need to try to *connect* intellectual truth-seeking (assent) to pragmatic belief and action is merely itself a bit of self-deception, and that the higher wisdom would lie in recognizing it as no more than a pleasurable game that need connect with the beliefs we rely on no more closely than does backgammon. If we insist on putting something we value at risk in our gaming or our intellectual assent, that is merely to make the game exciting. "Human life is so tiresome a scene, and men generally are of such indolent dispositions, that whatever amuses them, tho' by a passion mixed with pain, does in the main give them a sensible pleasure." (*Treatise,* 452) I have discussed Hume's account of the relation of intellect to passion and action in "Helping Hume to Compleat the Union," forthcoming in *Philosophy and Phenomenological Research.*

3. Harry Frankfurt, "Freedom of the Will and the Concept of a Person," *Journal of Philosophy* 68 (1971):5-20. Frankfurt's "wantons" are distinguished by their absence of higher-order mental attitudes of a specific sort, namely desires to desire, higher order "volitions." My half-wantons have higher-order attitudes, since they want others to echo their own attitudes. Among higher-order attitudes we need to distinguish not merely relative height (second, third, fourth level), but also homogeneous from heterogeneous attitudes, and also self-confined from other-involving higher-order attitudes. Frankfurt is interested in a particular self-confined homogeneous case, the desire to desire. My half-wantons have other-involving homogeneous and heterogeneous higher-order desires, and some of these are indirectly reflexive or self-directed. The hope that others will affirm one's judgment, will judge as one judged, is self-directed without being self-confined.

4. Jonathan Bennett, *Linguistic Behaviour* (Cambridge University, 1976).

5. The difference between doing something *as a means to* attaining something else, and doing it *for the sake of* some good it contains, recognizes, or celebrates, has been explored and developed, in a perhaps controversial way, by Heidegger, and by Hannah Arendt in *The Human Condition.* She restricts the proper applicability of "for the sake of" to actions in the public arena, in what she calls the space between persons, who have a common conception of a good life. Means-end reasoning, by contrast, is available to the perhaps solitary *homo faber,* whose "work" is goal-directed, guided by the conception of what it is he is making, rather than, like public "action," done for some goodness' sake. More recently, Alan Donagan has spoken up for the irreducibility of sakes, in a section of his *The Theory of Morality* (Chicago, 1977) entitled

"The Limits of Purpose." He distinguishes what he calls purposive teleology from the teleology of ultimate and "non-producible" ends.

6. "Responsibility for Self," in *The Identities of Persons*, ed. A. Rorty (University of California, 1976).

7. I have tried to say something about this in "Intentionality of Intentions," *Review of Metaphysics* 30 (1977):389-414; and in "Ways and Means," *Canadian Journal of Philosophy*, March, 1972. Harman's account of intention formation, in "Practical Reasoning," *Review of Metaphysics* 29 (1976):431-63, is helpful here.

8. Elsewhere, in "Realizing What's What," *Philosophical Quarterly*, (Oct. 1976), I have tried to say how realizing is related to knowing.

9. A fascinating alternative account of how our ancestors coped with such situations is to be found in Julian Jaynes, *The Origin of Consciousness in the Breakdown of Bicameral Mind* (Boston, 1976.) Unfortunately, I did not discover Jaynes's book until after this paper was completed. Jaynes's hypothesis is that before the development of conscious independent judgment (in my sense) humans heard voices or saw visions instructing them what to do. These were objectifications of the products of their own brain's right hemisphere, not yet in full communication with the left problem-solving hemisphere. Jaynes's account takes for granted that persons, or proto-persons, with bicameral minds had language, so that, like Saul, they heard *voices* instructing them what to do. My half-wantons are more advanced than Jaynes's bicameral men in that half-wantons can judge for themselves (in a qualified sense) in novel or difficult situations; but they are less advanced in having been, for my special purposes, artificially denied language. But I am in agreement with Jaynes that language is a precondition of full self-consciousness, or what I later call reflexiveness, and I certainly agree that any of our *actual* ancestors who were capable of judgment and revised judgment probably *did* have language.

10. William Gass, "The Stylisation of Desire," in *Fiction and the Figures of Life* (New York, 1972).

11. I refer here to Wilfrid Sellars's influential paper "Empiricism and the Philosophy of Mind" in *Science, Perception and Reality* (New York, 1963). Sellars takes the Ryleans to have language but no recognition of unspoken thoughts, nor privileged access to them. My Ryleans depend less on language, more on other conventions and the mutual recognitions they involve. I call the half-wantons our "ancestors," but they might also be taken to be ourselves as children, on the verge of language acquisition. I present them as our forebears rather than as ourselves when children, since children are members of a community containing rational adults, who educate them; so a child's half-wanton mind is, right from the start, affected by the pressure to become a truth-speaking rational adult.

12. Jonathan Bennett, *Linguistic Behaviour*, p. 112.

13. "Thought and Talk," in *Mind and Language*, ed. Guttenplan (Oxford, 1975).

14. Gilbert Ryle, *Concept of Mind* (London, 1949), p. 26.

15. "Conditions of Personhood," in A. Rorty, *Identities of Persons*.

16. H. P. Grice, "Utterers' Meaning and Intention," *Philosophical Review* 78 (1969):147-77.

17. Dennett, "Conditions of Personhood," p. 193.

18. I do not think Lewis, in *Convention* (Cambridge, 1969), gives us what we need, but Shwayder provides a richer concept, in *Stratification of Behavior* (New York, 1965), p. 303. I have begun to discuss shared intentions in "Mixing Memory and Desire," *American Philosophical Quarterly* 13 (1976):213-20, and in "Intention, Practical Knowledge and Representation" in *Philosophy of Action*, ed. Brandt and Walton (Reidel, 1976).

19. "Conditions of Personhood," p. 185. Dennett refers here to his earlier paper, "Brain Writing and Mind Reading," in *Language, Mind and Knowledge* (Minneapolis, 1975). Dennett's quoted recognition that inner representation is not of the essence of intentions, including Gricean intentions, does not itself settle the question of whether he sees language as primarily a means of outer representation. I interpret his account to be giving language a "manipulative"

role before it is used for representation, and on that interpretation his position is significantly different from Bennett's.

20. The revisions this reconstruction has undergone owe much to many constructive critics looking over my shoulder—to Daniel Dennett, John Haugeland, John Cooper, Kurt Baier. Obvious, I hope, will have been the influence on this essay in sociometaphysics of the writings of Ryle, Sellars, Davidson, Dennett, Bennett, and also Norman Malcolm's Presidential Address, "Thoughtless Brutes."

Why There Are No People

PETER UNGER

Imagine, if you will, a somewhat uncommonly shaped object, one whose shape is not very irregular or bizarre, perhaps, but which is at least sufficiently so that we have no common name or expression for an object with a shape of that sort. Following this instruction, then, you have not imagined a pyramid, or cylindrical object, for those are readily spoken of in available terms. I shall call your imagined object a *nacknick*, which term you are to apply also to such various other objects as you deem suitably similar in shape to the first. In this way, we have invented a new word together: I have given you the form of the inscription, 'nacknick', and some instructions which help to delimit the meaning. But only you have enough of an idea of the word to put it to much use. That is because, according to this little story, you have not revealed your imagined shape to me, or done much else to give me a useful idea of it.

Let us change the story a bit. In this version, you do not first imagine any object. Rather, I now actually place before you an object of the sort which, we have supposed, you imagined in the first version. Pointing to this uncommonly shaped thing, I then say to you, "This object is a nacknick, as are various others that are suitably similar in shape to it." To be emphatic and explicit, in both versions I may go on to add these following words to my instructions: "Don't think that an object must be *exactly* the same as this one in shape to be a nacknick. Rather, while such exact sameness is amply sufficient, any object that differs in shape from a nacknick only minutely will also be a nacknick. There is, then, no particular limit on shapes for nacknicks. At the same time, however, many objects will differ from nacknicks, as regards their shape, substantially and significantly, and these will not be nacknicks. These remarks apply, of course, not only to actual objects, which might be found in reality, but also to such merely possible objects as might be only imagined." I do not think that, in adding these explicit instructions, I would be changing the learning situation in any substantial way. Rather, I would only be making explicit what would otherwise be learned implicitly. Except for this rather minor matter, and the fact that we set out intentionally to invent a new expression, the word you have just come to understand is of a piece with much that you learned at your mother's knee. The newness and the explicit character of this experience with 'nacknick', however, let us reflect productively on what logical features are common to both the invented terms and the expressions learned in childhood.

1. THE ARGUMENT FROM INVENTED EXPRESSIONS

What reflection reveals, I suggest, is that a common feature of 'nacknick' and so many other terms is that they are all logically inconsistent expressions. On a par with 'perfectly square triangle', the supposition that anything satisfies 'nacknick' implies a logical contradiction. The instructions that served explicitly to introduce 'nacknick', and that now serve to govern the term, were so devised as to ensure this surprising result. Because of this, we can bring out the inconsistency in the term by reflecting on those instructions, with no need for us to enter into lengthy, complex argumentation as to what the word really means.

Our instructions endowed 'nacknick' with such a meaning that it is now governed by at least these two conditions:[1]

(1n) If some (actual or only possible) entity satisfies 'nacknick', then any (actual or only possible) entity that differs *minutely*, in shape, from that putative satisfier *also satisfies* the expression.

(2n) If some (actual or only possible) entity satisfies 'nacknick', then there are some (actual or only possible) entities each of which differs *substantially*, in shape, from that putative satisfier and each of which does *not* satisfy the expression.

As stepwise reasoning shows, because it is governed by these two conditions, 'nacknick' is an inconsistent term.

We may begin by considering some shaped object, if only a possible one, that is *not* a nacknick; for, according to my instructions, and (2n), if there are nacknicks, there must be some such. Having done this, we want now to reason that, according to these same instructions, the considered object *also is* a nacknick. Well, let us now think about an alleged nacknick, perhaps even the object from which, presumably, I taught you the expression. If this is a nacknick, then, according to my instructions, and to (1n), so too is an object only minutely different in shape from it, in particular, one that is minutely more alike in shape to the object that we have agreed is not a nacknick. Now, as this *new*, minutely differing object is also a nacknick, as my instructions have indicated, *so too is another* object that differs from *it*, in the same direction, by at least roughly that same minute amount. It is not hard to see, then, that a sequence of reasoning takes us to the step where an object, only minutely more alike in shape to our "paradigm" nacknick than is our considered non-nacknick, will be declared a nacknick. Then, finally, the object that, we agreed, was not a nacknick will also be a nacknick. According to my instructions, then, there are objects that both are nacknicks and are not. The word 'nacknick', the relevant aspects of which these instructions determine, is an inconsistent expression.

It might be objected against this reasoning that there are sequences of minute differences that will not take us to our agreed non-nacknick, but rather will approach a limit that is safely within the range where proper nacknicks may be recognized. If this is so, the objection continues, then we cannot draw the conclusion that, as the instructions have it, there are objects that both are and are not nacknicks. But unfortunately for this objection, the existence of such limited sequences will not prevent the inconsistent conclusion from being drawn. For our instructions explicitly stated that there is no particular limit on shape for nacknicks, and so they ensured troublesome sequences to be available for our stepwise reasoning. For example, one available sequence is presented when we consider one billion roughly equal steps of difference spanning the range from our paradigm to our considered non-nacknick. This sequence means a long argument for us, if things are spelled out in detail, but the inconsistent conclusion is forced upon us all the same. It is pretty clear, I suggest, that because of our devised instructions, our invented expression 'nacknick', despite its utility and natural appearance, is indeed a logically inconsistent expression.

I shall employ this observation of inconsistency as a premise in an argument, the Argument from Invented Expressions:[2]

(I)   The invented expression 'nacknick' is logically inconsistent.

The conclusion of our argument is to be the proposition that there are no people. To get it from our premise about 'nacknick', we need a good deal more. Most of this remainder will be contained in this second premise:

(II) The expression 'person' is logically on a par with 'nacknick'; if the latter is inconsistent, then so is the former.

A great deal of this essay will be spent in supplying support for this crucial second premise. There will be great resistance, of course, toward its acceptance. For it is quickly quite obvious that, in conjunction with the eminently attractive first premise, it logically yields the startling conclusion:

(A) The expression 'person' is logically inconsistent.

Before a lengthy discussion of the claimed logical parity is entered into, a few brief remarks are in order to motivate (II), so that the lengthier, more analytical discussion may appear worth the effort.

Now, as I have set things up here, the only thing important to an object's being a nacknick is the shape it has, though even this matter, of course, evaporates in inconsistency. So, in this regard, our invented word parallels certain ordinary expressions: for example, 'cubical object', in contrast to 'perfect cube'. Further, while

I have specified only shape as important for nacknicks, I could have easily specified *additional* requirements for our putative objects, for example, that a nacknick be a certain sort of nicknack. Any such additional requirement could not, of course, have rendered the word consistent: given the determinative instructions regarding shape, nothing could have done that. With only shape in the picture, our example has a certain purity and simplicity. But as regards the basic question, that of inconsistency, our invented word might be the same as expressions that cannot be so neatly described.

Again, our learning situation involved just one paradigm nacknick, imagined or presented, and this artifice also gives our examples a certain simplicity and purity, perhaps one not often found in the more ordinary course of things. But we could have made things more ordinary without importantly altering our examples: For example, originally, I could have asked you to imagine several shaped objects, each to have a quite similar unfamiliar shape. In the second story, I could have presented you with several similarly shaped objects. And, then, when things were to be made explicit, I could have altered my instructions, slightly, to suit. So, whether we have a single paradigm or a multiplicity is not crucial to the logic of the expression learned.

At this point, our second premise will have a certain plausibility at least. As our first premise, (I), is so hard to deny, our conclusion from it and (II), that is, the startling (A), will now also be at least plausible. But however surprising it may be, (A) does not directly concern the existence, or nonexistence, of persons. It is, after all, about an expression, 'person', and is not directly about any putative people. To get a conclusion directly to concern our desired subject matter, however, is now quite easy. We need only add to what we have, this final premise:

(III)   If the expression 'person' is logically inconsistent, then there are no people.

In conjunction with (III), our other premises validly yield our intended final conclusion:

(B)   There are no people.

And, this final premise, (III), really is a logically unobjectionable proposition.

To deny the idea that an inconsistent expression does not apply to anything, one must be involved in a confusion. For what is inconsistent expression? It is an expression for which the supposition that it does apply leads to a contradiction. But, then, that supposition cannot be true. Thus the expression does not apply. But what confusion might be responsible for such an absurd denial?

The chief culprit, I suppose, will be a failure to distinguish between, first, our using an expression to refer to certain objects and, on the other hand, an expression actually applying to, or being true of, those objects. You and I, for example, may agree to use the expression 'perfectly square triangle', even given what it now means, to refer to such tomatoes as are both yellow and sweet. With normal suppositions in force, including the existence of people, there may well be such tomatoes and we may well usefully refer to them with that expression. But we may be confident that those tomatoes are not perfectly square triangles, even though we refer to them as such, and that there are no such triangles anywhere. We may be just as confident, then, that whatever use we are putting it to, our chosen expression, being inconsistent, is true of no existing entities at all. So much, then, for denials of our final premise.[3]

We have much to discuss, however, as regards our other two premises, in particular, premise (II), where logical parity is claimed for 'person' and 'nacknick'. My support for this idea, which will afford some support to our first premise as well, will come largely in terms of an account of 'person' as a *vague discriminative expression*. On this account, all such expressions, including the invented 'nacknick', are logically inconsistent. Briefly and roughly, we may provide some idea of these expressions: First, in that they are *vague,* these terms contrast with, say, 'inch', which, we may allow, precisely purports to discriminate the inch from all other lengths. Second, in that they are *discriminative,* these terms contrast with the vague expression 'entity', which does not purport to discriminate anything from anything else, supposing that we may allow that anything at all is an entity. And, finally, the vagueness of these terms is essentially *involved in* their purported discriminations. So, they will contrast with 'entity which is less than two', supposing that this expression is about as vague as 'entity', but that this vagueness does not enter into its purported discrimination (of some numbers from others).

I am about to exhibit my account, which, while it is incomplete, should be detailed enough to indicate that its main lines are adequate. Before I do so, let me remark that I am well aware of a flaw that my account of these expressions is bound to have: If the account is right, then, as 'person' is inconsistent, there are none of us, and so no statements, accounts, or arguments that we produce or understand. The account implies a paradoxical situation. But this paradox, I shall argue, does not nullify the account. Rather, it bespeaks its comprehensiveness and that of "an intellectual need to begin anew."

2. AN ACCOUNT OF SOME COMMON VAGUE EXPRESSIONS

The inconsistency of 'nacknick' may be crudely characterized as stemming from the following two rough conditional statements:

> If something differs from a nacknick *minutely,* then it *also* is a nacknick (no matter in what *way* it thus differs).
> If something is a nacknick, then there are things that differ from it in *certain ways* by a *lot,* so much so that they are *not* nacknicks.

If someone, not a philosopher, were asked to express that inconsistency without any specific reference to shape, I think he would express it, well enough for his purpose, in these terms or terms similar to them. Now, if we want, as philosophers, to give a general characterization of the inconsistency, we too shall avoid any reference to any specific property. But we shall try to be a bit clearer about the offending differences than the obscure reference to a *way.* Accordingly, the conditions we should exhibit will not be the sort a typical learner would be likely to articulate. Still, in learning the expression in question, he may learn such underlying conditions.

I shall endeavor, then, to present two conditional statements that characterize 'nacknick', as well as many ordinary vague expressions. The terms I mean to characterize may be regarded as forming an important, but not exhaustive, group among the vague discriminative ones: those that are (purely) qualitative expressions. To indicate these expressions, we may distinguish, well enough for the purpose, between the qualitative or internal properties of an entity and, in contrast, its external properties, or relations. Thus, we shall say that two blue rectangular solids may be the same as regards all their qualitative properties but different as regards certain of their relations, for example, as regards their spatial relations to other objects. Whether an expression is vague or not, we shall say that it is (purely) qualitative just in case it is governed by this following condition: If an entity satisfies the expression, then so too does any entity which shares that satisfier's qualitative properties, that is, which is qualitatively identical with the satisfier. Thus, the expression 'perfect cube', while not vague, is qualitative, as are also the vague expressions 'cubical object' and 'nacknick'.

Among vague discriminative terms, the qualitative ones satisfy this stronger condition: If an entity satisfies the expression, then so does any entity that either (a) is qualitatively identical to that satisfier or else (b) is minutely different from it. It is to be understood, as is most natural, that the minute differences alluded to in (b) are in respect of qualitative properties, rather than relations. As is evident from our previous reasoning, the important problems with these expressions derive from (b); thus, in our subsequent discussion we may in general safely ignore (a), and focus on this problematic aspect.

Focusing on (b), we may present our characteristic conditions as follows, with the help of some terms to be clarified later, namely, *dimensions of difference* and *directions* along them, which are here to concern only the internal properties of the entities involved, as opposed to their external relations:[4]

(1) With respect to any qualitative vague discriminative expression, there are dimensions of difference, with directions along them, such that if some (actual or only possible) entity satisfies the expression, then all *minute* differences from the entity with respect to any one of these dimensions will find *other* (actual or only possible) entities that satisfy, and will find no (such) entity that does not satisfy the expression, providing that such a found entity does not differ more than minutely in any other such regard.

(2) With respect to any qualitative vague discriminative expression, if some (actual or only possible) entity satisfies it, then among the dimensions and directions that suffice for satisfaction under (1), there is at least one dimension of difference and at least one direction along it such that, with respect to these, there are (actual or only possible) entities each of which differs *substantially* from that putative satisfier and each of which does *not* satisfy the expression.

The conditions given in these two statements, along with such discussion as clarifies and supports them, form the heart of my account of vague discriminative expressions. Now this account would, of course, be uninteresting should there be many expressions, but none which are qualitative vague discriminative ones. But this is not so. On the contrary, providing that there are any expressions at all, there are a significant number of this sort, including 'bumpy', 'tall man', 'stone', and 'person'.

The second of these conditions, in (2), is to the purported effect that these expressions are to *discriminate* their satisfiers *from* other entities. This condition, which indicates some objects as *falling outside* an expression's range, we shall call the *discriminative* condition. The first condition is to the effect that, supposing any entity does, various ones together are to satisfy the expression, but no definite bound is to be placed on those to be included. Thus, we shall call this condition the *vagueness* condition for the expression in question.

While both of these two conditions are required to generate our noted inconsistency, it is the vagueness condition over which most discussion is likely to arise. Accordingly, let us first try to get an idea of its import. To do so, we may contrast 'bumpy', a qualitative vague discriminative term, with 'flat' (or with 'absolutely flat') and 'not flat', which are relevantly precise. If a surface is bumpy, that is, satisfies 'bumpy', and is not just not flat, then, just as our condition directs, so too is any surface that is no more than minutely different from it, even as regards shape. If a surface is (absolutely) flat, however, there will be minutely differing surfaces, in shape, that will not be (absolutely) flat. They will have only a few tiny bumps on them, in some cases, but not so much as to be bumpy. Likewise, if a surface is not (absolutely) flat, it will not follow that all minutely differing surfaces are also not flat. Consider a nearly flat surface. There will be a (possible) surface whose shape, while minutely different from it, is different in just such a way that it will be flat. Intuitively, I suggest, of these expressions, only 'bumpy' would be regarded as a vague term. The fact that only it is governed by our first condition, then, helps show the intuitive point of that requirement.[5]

To understand both of our conditions, we should explicate our talk of *dimensions of difference*, for that is a somewhat technical expression whose connection with our ordinary vague thinking cannot be evident. We may begin our explication by noting that things do not just differ as such, but always *differ in* one or more *ways* or *respects*. For example, a heavy red stone differs from things that are not red in respect of *color*, and from things that are not heavy in respect of *weight*. Now, with many such respects, we may, to a certain extent at least, speak comparatively of how much things differ. In respect of color, for example, we say that our red stone differs *more* from things that are blue *than* from those that are purple. In respect of weight, it differs more from things, or at least stones, that are very light than from those of a moderate or intermediate weight. Thus, we think of a *dimension* of color, and also a *dimension* of weight, as a *dimension of difference*. All of this is quite ordinary to think. What is less common, but I think still quite available, is the idea that many things vary, too, with regard to stoniness, that is, with respect to how close they are to being a stone, in the case of a certain stretch, or with respect to how good an example of a stone, in the case of another one. Thus, we may recognize such a more complex, less easily described dimension, according to which a very light, blue pebble differs *more* from a similarly light, similarly colored twig, or piece of cloth, *than* it does from a heavy red stone. And, with regard to this same dimension, of *stoniness*, if you will allow that expression, the pebble may differ less from the stone than it does from a boulder, even if the pebble and boulder are in most other respects quite like each other and quite different from the stone. Accordingly, we may say that along *at least one* dimension of difference a red stone differs more from a blue stone than it does from a red pebble, while along *at least one other* dimension, the differences run differently.

What we count as a dimension may include other dimensions, but perhaps in no orderly way. Color, which we have taken as a dimension, is often said to include hue, saturation, and brightness. Perhaps where we spoke of our red stone differing from a blue stone as regards the dimension of color, we might have more specifically said that they differ as regards the dimension of hue. But there is no competition here, nor any need for us to think that there are any ultimate dimensions of difference. Our ordinary thinking does not suggest that, but neither do our two conditions of typical vagueness. For our second condition says, not that there is *one* dimension of difference along which a vague expression will not (any longer) be satisfied, but that there is *at least one* such dimension. Now, my talk of dimensions may harbor a whole host of problems. But that is no fault of it here. For we are trying to reflect the features of our common vague expressions, including whatever problems they may harbor.

Our conditions speak, not only of dimensions of difference, but also of *directions* along these dimensions. What are these directions? In regards to any dimension, say, that of color, we can think of small differences *accumulating* until large ones are reached. This thought of accumulation implies a direction in which the accumulation takes place. Without any direction, such as that *from* red *through* purple *to* blue, there would not be the order among colored things which we suppose there to be. Similarly, a stone differs from a boulder in one direction, while it differs from a pebble or grain in another. We do not always have convenient expressions to label these directions, just as with the dimensions along which they are directions. But it must be admitted, I think, that they do have a place in our thinking with vague terms.

We want our expressed conditions to explain the force of arguments that are forceful.[6] To do this, we must notice that certain of our vague terms are meant to discriminate those entities purportedly falling under them from others that lie only in certain directions, and not in others. For example, the expression 'tall man' purports discrimination of its satisfiers from men who lie, with respect to the satisfiers, only in the downward direction of height, and not in the upward direction. How this means inconsistency for the expression is indicated by considering sorites arguments against the existence of tall men.[7]

In respect of height, here the relevant dimension, two men may differ by a foot and we deem the one a tall man and the other not. For example, one may be six feet six, plus or minus a thousandth of an inch, and the other five feet six, plus or minus that. In the *downward direction,* this difference of a foot would be relevantly substantial; in line with our second condition, the man of five feet six would, thus, *not* be a tall man. In the other, upward direction, no discrimination of the satisfier from anything is purported, and so no problems arise. Just as a man of six feet six is tall, so any man of greater height is a tall man, or so we commonly believe. The substantial difference of a foot, then, means nothing in the upward direction: unlike a man of five feet six, a man of seven feet six is (supposed to be) a tall man.

This purported discrimination in the downward direction is enough to provide an argument that turns on the inconsistency of 'tall man'. We choose a man somewhere down there in height, for example, a man of five feet six, who is supposed not to be a tall man. And, we can show, by the condition of (1), that he also *is* a tall man (if any man is). For if the man of six-six is tall, then so is a man minutely less in height, say, a thousandth of an inch less, plus or minus a small fraction of that. And if he too, then also another, whose height is about a thousandth of an inch less. And, so, by steps, if there is any tall man, then our man of five-six is one of these. But, as we have supposed, he is not. And, while we might seek to avoid the contradiction by saying that, contrary to what we supposed, the man of five-six is after all only a tall one, this is no avoidance but only a futile postponement. For according to our second condition, there must be *some* (actual or only possible) man down there who is *not* tall. But, whomever we choose, our first condition then forces us to draw the opposite conclusion about him as well. Thus, the purported discrimination cannot be made; the expression is an inconsistent one.

There is a potential source of ambiguity which, while I do not think I have invited it, can be placed beyond serious question rather quickly. It might be thought that, according to our second condition, so long as the dimension and direction are appropriate, *any* substantial difference from a satisfier will take us to objects, actual or only possible, that do not satisfy. This would be an unfortunate interpretation, as the following example makes clear: If the difference between a six-six man and a five-six one is substantial, then so is that between a man of eight feet and a six-six man. But, while the latter is, then, a substantial difference, and can be taken in the right direction, it does not take us to a man who, by common judgment, is not tall. But our condition does not say that *just any* entity that thus differs from a satisfier will not satisfy the expression in question; rather, it implies only that there must be *at least some* such. In the present case, there is indeed a plenitude of relevant possible cases. For example, all the possible men with heights less than five feet six will differ sufficiently from the eight foot man. Thus, these men, who are not tall, will allow us to derive a contradiction from the assumption that the eight-footer is a tall man.

In disarming a potential source of ambiguity, we have entered upon the finer points of our account. In this vein, we may notice the final, or 'providing', clause of our vagueness condition. Now, that clause may seem to make matters complex, but it is only a way of providing for what would usually be understood anyway. For we are to understand that such a minute difference, by itself, will not make the difference between satisfier and nonsatisfier, not that the presence of one such small difference will ensure a second satisfier, no matter how different from the original that second entity might otherwise be. By the same token, even with this "providing" clause, our vagueness condition can be applied, in stepwise fashion, any number of times. For while various other differences may add up so that they are eventually more than minute ones, even by common-sense reckoning, in any one step no such large difference will ever be encountered.[8]

Because our conditions do not specify or mention any particular dimensions of difference, or directions along them, but only require, for satisfaction, the existence of some, we cannot state our conditions in a mutually independent form. Thus our reference in (2) to what is required in (1). We need this to make sure that the differences added up by repeated applications of (1) are comparable to those for which (2) indicates an opposite claim, so that a contradiction will arise, supposing there is any satisfier. With 'nacknick', shape was specified as relevant; by specifying it once in each, independently specified conditions could be given for the term. A similar situation occurs with the ordinary vague expression 'tall man', where we may mention *height* as the dimension, and specify the *downward* direction along it. But oftentimes, we shall be in no position to provide such specific, independently specifiable conditions.

Our conditions make reference to possible entities that may not be actual. By this device, we may explain, for example, our ready judgment that six-inch men would not be tall men, even supposing there are no actual men of that height. For we are very ready to withhold 'tall man' from such an imaginary case. Now, if such an explanatory reference to possible entities is avoidable, then we may just consider it a convenience here, for brevity. If, on the other hand, an implication of such dubious objects is required, that should mean trouble for these vague expressions. But even if such a problem means, all over again, the worst for these terms, I shall not dwell on the matter now. For the same difficulty, if there is one, would appear quite as damaging to various expressions that are not vague: if something satisfies "is not a perfect cube," then there are objects, actual or only possible, that differ from that satisfier in shape, and that, thus, do *not* satisfy the expression. In other words, such problems are not peculiar to our topic.

Let us turn now to discuss some of the limits of our offered conditions, for they are not meant to cover every conceivable topic. We may begin by noting a vague expression that is not governed by our second, or discriminative, condition, namely, the expression 'part of physical reality'. Now, this term is, of course, a qualitative one; if an entity is part of physical reality, then so too is any other qualitatively just like it. And, second, this expression is a vague one; if anything, it is even *more* vague than 'stone'. At the same time, it is governed by our first, or vagueness, condition: If an entity is a part of physical reality, then so too is any other that, with respect to any dimension of difference, is minutely different from it. And, third, the expression is, quite obviously, a discriminative one: it is not to apply to such a putative abstract entity as the number three. But, the discriminations it makes do not appear to *involve* its vagueness, at least not in the ordinary way we have been noticing. For it does not seem that there is any dimension, or spectrum, of graded differences, where parts of physical reality are somewhere to leave off and other entities are to be newly encountered. So, our expression 'part of physical reality' does not seem to be of the sort we have called *vague discriminative*. At the same time, it is not governed by our second condition.

Finally, let us look at some limits of our vagueness condition, and try to see what they may, or may not, mean for us. Toward this end, we notice the contrast between two kinds of vague discriminative expression: those that are (purely) qualitative and those that are not. Only the first of these will be governed by our vagueness condition, in (1), for the notion of *dimension of difference* there employed concerned only differences as regards qualities, or internal properties. Thus, for an easy example, two men may be qualitatively the same, but only one may bear the relation to a woman of being married. Thus, only the other of them is a bachelor. The word 'bachelor', then, is not a qualitative term. As such, it is not governed by our vagueness condition: Scratch the married man alone, so that now he is minutely different from the bachelor as regards his internal properties. But though he is minutely different from an entity that satisfies 'bachelor', this married man does not satisfy the word.

A less obvious example is provided by John Tienson.[9] He points to certain expressions for artifacts, for example, 'table top' and 'door'. Consider two qualitatively identical objects, each crafted in different areas by different people, quite independently. The first is meant to serve just as a door, and does so. The second is meant to serve just as a table top, as it does. It seems clear that, supposing there are table tops, only one of these is that. Scratching one, which means a minute difference between them now, as regards internal properties, will, of course, not alter the situation. Upon reflection, then, it appears that there will be many vague discriminative terms that are not qualitative ones, and that do not satisfy the vagueness condition for our qualitative expressions. Consequently, to have a general account of discriminative vagueness, we need a vagueness condition for these terms as well, along with a matching discriminative condition. But, what does this mean for our main topic?

Even without much thought on the matter, it is quite clear that 'person', unlike 'bachelor' and 'door', is indeed a purely qualitative term. Perhaps some creature qualitatively identical to me, but very far away, might not be a human being should he lack certain relations, causal or otherwise, to all (earthly) humans.[10] But he would still be a person for all that. Consequently, as our chief interest here is in 'person', and in putative persons, it is not much to present purposes to provide such more general conditions for discriminative vagueness as we now, admittedly, do desire.

Still, a suggestion or two seems to be in order, to give some idea of how our account of vague terms might be extended from the purely qualitative ones to cover vague discriminative expressions generally. For a start, we may alter our vagueness condition so that the dimensions of difference involved, and so the minute differences with regard to them, will now concern external relations as well as internal properties. With this alteration we may declare an entity obtained from an alleged door to be a door, should the change be a suitably small one, such as will, in fact, be produced by the net removal of a peripheral atom. For this obtained object's relations to other things will differ only minutely from those of the original satisfier, all things considered, whether or not we regard it as the very same object as that original. But while we thus achieve some added explanatory power, this alteration provides only a rather weak, or unambitious, vagueness condition: Another door, far away from the original, and with internal properties only minutely different, may well not be declared a door. For, all things considered, the external relations of this distant object may be so different from the first, it seems, that no declaration concerning it will be available to us. To group these two doors together, a stronger vagueness condition is needed. A suitable one might be obtained, I suggest, if we do not speak of external relations generally, but limit our reference to those relations the bearing of which, by an object, are relevant to whether or not the object is (supposed to be) a satisfier, for example, a door. If these relevant relations are just the same or minutely different for the two objects, and their internal properties are also the same or minutely different, then they shall be grouped together as well. With these provisos, we may now have a suitable vagueness condition for all discriminative vague terms, as we have been understanding this category of expressions.

For such an extension of our account, I am inclined to think that our original discriminative condition will prove adequate, with its reference to the dimensions in the paired vagueness condition matching things up appropriately. But, if that is not quite right, a suitable matching condition should not be far to seek. These are my suggestions, then, for extending my account from its present exclusive concern with purely qualitative terms to cover vague discriminative expressions generally. Having made them, I shall not pursue the matter here, but will only note that most of the remarks to be made about the qualitative ones will apply as well to the others. Hence, in what follows, I often shall speak indiscriminately of vague discriminative terms, in general, and those of them that are qualitative vague expressions.

3. THE IDEA OF INCOMPLETE EXPRESSIONS

The main lines of our account are now before us. On this account, vague discriminative expressions are inconsistent terms. Against our account, others may be proposed. Perhaps the most common and appealing alternative will be the idea that these vague terms are *incomplete expressions.* Typically, at least, this idea will derive from the thought that each of our vague expressions has *borderline cases,* that is, cases that neither *definitely* satisfy the term nor *definitely* do not. The reason for these cases, the idea will then go, is that the vague expression says nothing about them one way or the other. This lack of content or commitment is owing to the term's being incomplete, that is, incompletely defined.[11] Now, even if there were something in the idea of an incomplete term, its application to our typical vague expressions would now seem to be quite dubious. For these expressions seem logically on a par with 'nacknick', and that invented expression is (completely) inconsistent, and so is not an incomplete one. But matters are worse than that for our alleged alternative account. For, as I shall argue, this idea of incompleteness is incoherent, as is even the thought of borderline cases, on which it depends.

Let us begin our discussion by seeing that our own account implies the result I seek to establish. Now, on our account, typical vague expressions apply to no cases whatsoever, for they are each logically inconsistent. Hence, we may say all cases are decided negatively by each such term. Thus, no cases are borderline cases, and no expression is incomplete. Here is another way of seeing that, on our account, there are no borderline cases: Any borderline case for an expression requires positive cases, which satisfy the expression. For a case that is (on the) borderline is, on some relevant dimension, *between positive cases* and negative ones. On our account, there are no positive cases; thus, no borderline ones either. So it is amply clear that as our account has it, there are no vague discriminative expressions that are incomplete. In that I shall be arguing for this same conclusion, I shall be reasoning that this result is a virtue of our account.

Let us focus on the notion of borderline cases. These are supposed to be cases to which the expression in question does not *definitely* apply and does not *definitely* not apply. But what can be the proper force of this 'definitely' here? Imagine a typical vague expression and an object. Consider the statement that (1) the expression neither definitely applies to the object nor definitely does not. And consider as well the apparently simpler statement that (2) the expression either applies to the object or does not apply to it. Now, the former statement either is consistent with the latter, simpler one or else it is not. Suppose it *is* consistent with the simpler statement. What the simpler statement says is that each case is one where the expression applies or else is one where it does not apply, and so it leaves no room for any borderline cases. So, for all the statement with 'definitely' then says, there will be no borderline cases. Thus, if our two statements are mutually consistent, the one with 'definitely' cannot coherently indicate any borderline case. Well, then, let us suppose the alternative, that the first statement is *not* consistent with the second. Now, we shall want to notice the logical status of that second statement: it is necessarily true. For this statement is but a special consequence of a quite general necessary truth: with regard to any given object, any relation, and any entity, that object either bears that relation to that entity or does not bear the relation to the entity.[12] Now, if the object is an expression, that cannot change matters; nor can things be altered when the relation is that of application, whatever the entity in question might be. The truth of our simpler statement, (2), then, cannot be seriously challenged. But, if (1), our 'definitely' statement, is not then consistent with (2), (1) will not itself be true, and so it will not correctly indicate any borderline cases. Thus, in either case, that is, in any case, there are no borderline cases.

Our statement with 'definitely', it is true, at first appears to suggest coherently some cases of a third logical kind, though this appearance cannot be borne out. I should try to explain the illusory appearance here. The explanation, I think, falls into two parts: first, talk with 'definite' can be used, coherently, we may allow, to describe certain behavioral situations. And, once that is managed, the description can lead to the incoherent idea that, underlying the described behavior, there are logically borderline cases. Let us discuss the first part, for that is where the trouble starts.

With regard to a typical vague expression, a normal person will sometimes be in a state of hesitancy, uncertainty, and, perhaps, even confusion. With regard to certain (real or only imagined) objects, which he may call "borderline cases," he will have no definite disposition or tendency to apply the term nor any definite tendency to withhold it. These objects will contrast with others, for which the person has such a tendency to apply the term, as well as with still others, for which he has a definite disposition to withhold the expression. And, these behavioral contrasts can hold, not just for a single individual at a moment, but for a society during a long period of time. Where such a broadly based pattern of dispositions exists, we may give a certain currency to talk of "borderline cases." But that talk, to remain coherent, must confine itself to reporting upon the behaviors in question; it cannot properly entail, to explain the behavior, situations where an expression does not apply to an object and also does not not apply to it.

The behavioral contrasts just remarked, it may be appreciated, will hold just as well for invented inconsistent expressions, like 'nacknick'. A given individual will be ready to apply "nacknick" to certain objects, and to withhold it from others, but will be uncertain about still a third group. And, should the term gain currency, a more general behavioral pattern to the same effect would doubtless ensue. Objects in the third group might well be regarded, quite generally, as borderline cases. So long as nothing of much logical import is thus implied, such parlance may be allowed. But, clearly, nothing much more than reportage upon these dispositions could be coherently conveyed by such talk of borderlines. For, clearly, 'nacknick' is an inconsistent expression, and actually applies to no cases whatsoever. So it is with all vague discriminative expressions, both invented and inherited.

Except in the irrelevant behavioral sense of the expression, then, there can be no borderline cases. Thus, there are none to threaten our account; there is no competition for us from the idea of vague expressions as incomplete. For any incompleteness will arise only over logically borderline cases, and so the suggestion of incomplete expressions is not a coherent idea. Though we have just made short work of the idea of incomplete expressions, there will be some, no doubt, who will be loathe to part with it. The reason for their reluctance is simple: the idea can be made to appear very attractive. For our reasonings to have maximum effect here, we must consider the motivation from which such an appearance can derive.

The motivation underlying the idea of incomplete expressions is due primarily, I think, to a misplaced analogy between linguistic expressions and mathematical functions. For a mathematical function to yield a value for an object, that function must be defined for, or with respect to, that object. Typically, it will be so defined only if someone, a mathematician, does something, only if he defines it for the object. If nothing is done, then the function is undefined for the object, and it yields no particular value in the case. If one thinks of a linguistic expression as yielding a positive value for those objects it applies to, and a negative one for those it does not, one is well on his way toward applying this analogy.

Like the functions of mathematics, it may then be thought, an expression will yield a value only in the case of those objects for which it is defined. And, it will be defined for an object only if some people *have defined* the expression for the object. Now, this thinking continues, the people may have defined it positively with regard to a certain object: in that case, the value there will be positive, and the expression will apply to the object. Or, they may have defined it negatively: then, the value there will be negative, and the expression will not apply. Or, as in mathematics, they may not have defined it with regard to the object. In this last case, the expression will be *undefined* with respect to the object, it will yield no value there, neither positive nor negative; and, so, it will neither apply to the object nor not apply to it. Rather, it will find a borderline case in the object, thus being an incomplete expression.

According to one way of viewing the matter, a mathematical function that is defined for certain objects but not for others may be completed, so that it is then defined for those others as well. Analogously, the idea of incomplete expressions may be further developed: A vague discriminative expression may be made more precise by completing its definition. So long as the previously positive cases remain as such, and so with the previously negative ones, a completion will be admissible. Thus, for a typical vague expression, there will be a great, perhaps an infinite, variety of admissible completions, none of which violates the meaning with which the expression had been endowed. Any such completion will decide, whether positively or negatively, each of the expression's borderline cases. And, what can determine which completion we fix upon, if ever we desire to make precise a certain vague expression, will be the purposes we then wish it to serve. So, the acceptable completion we choose need not be an arbitrary choice.

The idea of incomplete expressions is thus a very attractive idea. According to it, our expressions are each consistent and more: through their already defined cases, they provide us with stable contrasts, with an intellectual anchor. At the same time, through their borderline cases, they provide us with the opportunity for creative conceptual choice. But, in addition to resting on an incoherent notion of borderline cases, this appealing picture rests upon a weak or misplaced analogy between mathematical functions and the expressions of our language.

What is it, in the special sense intended, for an expression to be defined? Of course, it is not for it to be defined in the usual sense, where a statement is made that elucidates the term's meaning. For, many precise terms, completely defined in our special sense, have never had their meaning thus elucidated and, on the other side, certain vague words have had their meaning made tolerably plain. On the contrary, what is here alluded to is simply this: the expression has been endowed with such meaning that, with respect to some objects at least, that meaning determines whether or not the term applies to those objects. Once we realize that this is what this talk of definition comes to, we can see that the idea of incomplete definition amounts to nothing. For, with respect to any expression, and any object, unless we define that expression with respect to that object, that is, unless society has endowed it with such meaning as determines whether or not it applies to the object, the expression will *not* apply to the object. If we insist that the term's not applying to an object means that it yields a (negative) value for that object, then a (negative) value will be yielded even if nothing has been done to produce such a result. Consider the expression 'ouch'. It has not been defined with respect to the Empire State Building. Yet, it does *not apply* to that entity. If we insist that this means 'ouch' yields a negative value for the Building, then so be it. Of course, one might not insist that 'ouch' yields a value here. But, still, it does not apply to the Building. So, however we describe matters, we cannot coherently apply the offered analogy.

A function, then, if not suitably defined, may yield no value with regard to a certain object, neither positive nor negative. But, whether owing to what is dictated by its meaning or not, an expression will apply to a given object or else it will not do so. Unlike the function, with its values, there is no further course for the expression to take.

The idea of incomplete expressions is itself inconsistent. It can offer no genuine alternative to our account of vague expressions as inconsistent terms. Let us inquire somewhat more deeply now as to the nature of their inconsistency.[13]

4. VAGUENESS AND GROUNDLESS INCONSISTENCY

It is easy to assume that any inconsistent expression results from a clash between ideas each of which is itself quite consistent. Our by now familiar expression 'perfectly square triangle' may be reckoned an example of this. As such, that expression may be regarded as governed by two quite precise conditions, which may be expressed as follows:

(1t) If some (actual or only possible) entity satisfies the expression 'perfectly square triangle', then (since that putative satisfier is a perfectly square object) the satisfier has exactly four interior angles.

(2t) If some (actual or only possible) entity satisfies the expression 'perfectly square triangle', then (since that putative satisfier is a triangle) the satisfier has exactly three interior angles.

The clash here is between the idea of having exactly four such angles, which implies having more than three, and that of having exactly three, which implies not having more than three. We might say that the inconsistency in 'perfectly square triangle' is *grounded* in the clash between these two consistent conceptions. It is easy to assume, then, that every inconsistent expression must be grounded in at least one such clash as that. On the contrary, however, it is a feature of vague discriminative terms that their inconsistency is *not* thus grounded, but is relevantly *groundless*.

And, it is a virtue of our two conditions for such expressions that they serve to bring out this groundlessness.

The differences that figure in our vagueness condition are referred to as *minute* ones, and those of our discriminative condition as *substantial* in amount or size. Whatever the meaning of 'minute' and 'substantial', we may take it that nothing satisfies both of these at once, whether the thing in question be a slice of meat, a number, or a difference. The terms 'minute' and 'substantial', then, purport to be mutually exclusive in their application; if they have any application, it must respect this condition. It is in virtue of this exclusivity that these terms might appear to underlie successful discriminations purported by our vague discriminative expressions. But 'minute' and 'substantial' are themselves discriminative vague terms. So, both of them are inconsistent expressions; neither has any real application at all, thus none which is exclusive of the other's. Even so, the inconsistency of other discriminative vague terms may be understood in terms of the inconsistency of each of these two expressions. At the same time, their own inconsistency may also be understood in terms of themselves. While these two terms are thus rather deeply placed, they provide no clash between consistent conceptions. Accordingly, the inconsistencies they serve to explain are relevantly groundless.

What is it, after all, for one object to differ minutely from another, in a certain respect, for that difference between them to be a minute one? If that difference is minute, then so is a difference, along the same dimension, which is only minutely greater than it. This leads to the conclusion that a certain difference, deemed substantial, and so *not* minute, must be deemed as well a minute one. Thus, there is no minute difference in the first place.

Let us reconsider our paradigm nacknick and the object we agreed to be so different from it as to be not a nacknick. The difference between these two, we supposed, was a substantial one, and so not a minute difference. But an object that was about a billionth of the way from the paradigm to the non-nacknick differed minutely from the paradigm. If it did, then so did the next object in the considered sequence, for the extra billionth of the way thus added will not mean the difference between a minute difference here and one that is not. But, then, the difference between the paradigm and the still next object will also be a minute one, on the same principle. By stepwise reasoning, we shall thus conclude that the difference between the paradigm and the considered non-nack is a minute difference. This lets us, in turn, conclude two things: first, we may conclude that the supposed non nacknick is also a nacknick, which helps show how the quantitative term 'minute' underlies 'nacknick'. And, second, we deduce the related contradiction: that the supposed substantial difference, between the paradigm and the agreed non-nacknick, is also a minute one.

In general, we may say that when adding a minute difference to another, the result is a larger difference that is still a minute one. Suppose someone took exception to this generality, thinking that there might be two *big* differences *for* minute ones, so that when *they* were added the result failed to be a minute difference. Let us consider one of these: it is supposed to be large for a minute difference. Let us consider as well a difference, the same in dimension and direction, that is only one *millionth* of *its* magnitude. This latter difference will not be a large one, even for a minute difference; it will be minute for a minute difference. But if it is minute for a minute difference, then so is one that is only two millionths the magnitude of the large minute difference, for the extra millionth cannot mean that we have gotten to a minute difference of some other sort. By stepwise reasoning, we may eventually conclude that our original minute difference, supposedly large for such a difference, is also minute for a minute difference. And, we may do as much for the large minute difference to which it might be added. Adding two such differences, each of which may thus be reckoned minute even for minute differences, cannot, then, yield a difference that is not minute.[14]

The idea of a substantial difference is relevantly on a par with that of a minute one. If a given difference is substantial, then so is one that is only minutely less. But however small we require a difference to be so that it fail to be substantial, we may eventually reach it. Thus, any such difference will be declared substantial, as well as not substantial.

The points we have made about 'minute' and 'substantial' can also be made about other pairs of similar terms, about 'small' and 'large', for example. Each member of such a pair will be a *quantitative* vague discriminative expression; one of them will purport to denote things whose magnitude is *less than* any to which the other can properly apply, the other to denote to opposite effect. Of course, a term may be quantitative in this sense and also be a purely qualitative expression in the sense we previously defined. In every case, I hypothesize, the inconsistency of vague discriminative expressions may be understood in terms of some such quantitative pair or pairs. When a pair is suitable for such understanding, we may call it an *underlying pair* for the expression in question. So, each typical vague expression has at least one such underlying pair.

In giving my conditions, in (1) and (2), for qualitative vague terms, I employed the term 'minute'. This was a measure in the direction of caution. For while a more common word like "small" appears suitable to underlie many such expressions, for which of course "minute" will also serve, there may be some for which only the latter term will prove adequate. It is worth noting, I think, that with many vague terms the sorites arguments that spell trouble can be quite short. For example, I think we regard a man of six-two as tall, but one of five-eleven as not a tall man. But half an inch will not mean the difference between a tall man and not. So, an explicit but quite short argument will yield no tall men at all. I suggest that this helpful shortness is due largely to the fact that 'small' is enough to underlie the first condition for 'tall man'. Consequently, 'minute' here gives us, with a longer argument, a luxury of caution.

This groundless inconsistency, characteristic of vague discriminative terms, is not to be conflated with the fact that the noted stepwise reasoning exposes the inconsistency of the expressions in question. To clarify this point, we may invent expressions whose inconsistency is exposed in that stepwise manner, but that do not have the feature of groundless inconsistency. In one respect, that of having their inconsistency grounded in precise, consistent concepts, such expressions will be like 'perfectly square triangle'. In another, that associated with the stepwise reasoning, they will be unlike such an obviously inconsistent expression, and will be like our typical vague terms. Because of this latter likeness, such an invented term would, under suitable circumstances, prove useful to many normal people. Let me proceed to invent such a useful expression.

A *tinkergrid,* we might say, is something that one might endeavor to build out of the most typical items found in a tinkertoy set. These items are of two kinds: sticks and wheels. Now, the term 'stick', as well as 'wheel', is a vague discriminative one, and so it has groundless inconsistency. Thus, we do not want our invented 'tinkergrid' to be defined in terms of sticks and wheels, for then the invented term would also have groundless inconsistency. Let us better say, then, that what one would endeavor to build with a tinkertoy set would be, not a tinkergrid itself, but a physical realization of a tinkergrid. The tinkergrid itself would be a mathematical entity, composed of other mathematical entities, which are its *basic parts:* line segments of unit length, which one might use sticks to endeavor to realize, and nodes, where line segments can connect at right angles, for which a wheel might be used. The idea of a tinkergrid, then, is that of a certain mathematical structure. But, of course, there might be no more possibility of such a structure than of a structure that is a perfectly square triangle.

Now, to define the general conception of a tinkergrid, we begin with the more particular idea of a *paradigm tinkergrid.* A paradigm tinkergrid, we shall say, is in the form of a cube, with ten-unit line segments to each of its twelve edges; each edge, then, contains eleven nodes, two at its ends and nine internally. This tinkergrid is composed of a thousand unit cells, each in the form of a cube composed of twelve segments and eight nodes. The cells are arranged in such a way that they do not overlap, but are suitably adjacent, so that the whole tinkergrid is perfectly constituted of them: ten layers each with ten columns and ten rows of unit cells. It should appear clear how, using the standard tinkertoy items, one would try to realize a paradigm tinkergrid. So much for paradigm tinkergrids; what of those that are not paradigms?

As our definition is to have it, a paradigm tinkergrid is but one sort of tinkergrid; related to it are other sorts, which are all suitably related to each other. We shall not put this by means of any quantitive vague discriminative expression for that would involve 'tinkergrid' in groundless inconsistency, which we are to avoid. Thus, we do *not* have as a second clause of our definition any such conditional as this one: If something is a tinkergrid, then anything that differs from it by *a little bit* is also a tinkergrid. Rather, we shall put our second clause more suitably in some such terms as these: If something is a tinkergrid, then anything that differs from it by *the removal or addition of one or two basic parts* is also a tinkergrid.

While we thus move to avoid groundless inconsistency, we have not yet ensured any inconsistency at all for our invented term, but only a certain bizarreness. For without any further clause in our definition, our term allows a tinkergrid to have no basic parts at all. Such a "null tinkergrid" would be a most peculiar entity, of course; still, according to the definition's progress so far, there they will be. But insofar as null tinkergrids are claimed by our invented expression, and no claim is made in the opposite direction, 'tinkergrid' will be quite unlike most ordinary terms. To make it more like them, we add this last clause to our definition: Any tinkergrid is composed of a finite positive number of basic parts. Now, our invented expression will have it that there are no "null tinkergrids," and it will indeed be much more like our ordinary terms. For, with this last clause, we have ensured that our invented expression will be an inconsistent one.

The inconsistency of 'tinkergrid' may be exhibited as follows: First, a paradigm tinkergrid is a tinkergrid, indeed, one having a certain finite positive number of basic parts, say, N of them. But, then, so will be an entity that, may be obtained from it by the removal of one part, which will have N-1 basic parts. By stepwise reasoning, we must conclude that there will be a tinkergrid with N-N basic parts, that is, with none at all. But our expression also requires that any tinkergrid have some positive number of such parts. Thus, this last item, with no basic parts, both is a tinkergrid and also is not one.

While this invented term is thus inconsistent, I have little doubt that it could be easily learned and put to use by many normal people, in various suitable circumstances. In the first place, few would notice that there was any inconsistency here. Indeed, few would notice that, without the final clause, there would be null tinkergrids. Despite the term's having grounded inconsistency, most people would get the idea that a tinkergrid was available only at levels "well above" that where no basic parts remain. So little, then, will these ideas be related to our expression's meaning. And, perhaps more important, even once the inconsistency is pointed out, as we did here, the problem is shunted aside.

Insofar as I have been successful, 'tinkergrid', while inconsistent, has not been defined by using any discriminative vague term in an essential role. Accordingly, the inconsistency thus generated is not relevantly groundless; it is not like that observed with typical vague expressions. Like the inconsistency in 'square triangle', the inconsistency in 'tinkergrid' involves a clash between ideas that are each precise, consistent ones. But of the two, only 'tinkergrid' has grounded inconsistency of a sort that allows for a quite useful expression, potentially, as useful as typical vague ones.

5. PARADIGMS IN PERSPECTIVE

We began with a putative paradigm of a nacknick, imagined or real, with something that was to satisfy the expression. But as further imposed conditions determined matters, the beginning object could not possibly satisfy the invented term. For, as that expression was thus determined to be logically inconsistent, no object at all could satisfy it. By parity of reasoning, we have suggested that a logically similar situation holds for our ordinary vague discriminative expressions. Against this suggestion, one might try to strengthen the role of paradigms in the learning situations, not only as regards our ordinary expressions, but also as concerns such explicitly invented ones as 'nacknick'. The objection to our reasoning would then proceed

along some such lines as these: When I instructed you that any object minutely differing from a nacknick (as regards shape) would also be a nacknick, what you really
accepted, and had as a determinant of your new useful expression, was not quite
what I instructed you. Instead, it was this rather similar sounding, but logically
quite different, condition: If something is (not just any old nacknick, but) a *paradigm* nacknick, then any object differing from it minutely (in shape) is a nacknick.
But, the objection continues, this "paradigmatic" condition, even in conjunction
with other learned conditions for the term, causes no troublesome inconsistency.
As this was the true situation even with 'nacknick', we may be quite confident that
this sort of thing occurs with our typical vague inherited expressions. Consequently, the objection concludes, they may be satisfied by their paradigm cases, as well
as by various other objects.[15]

A good deal later on, in Section 9, I shall discuss the question of "what you
really got out of my instructions." And I shall there argue that whatever else you
may have gotten, one thing you got was the vagueness condition, with no reference
to paradigms, that I actually offered to you. And, so, I shall argue, that troublesome condition helped to determine 'nacknick' for you, whatever else may also
have played such a determining role. If this is so, then your 'nacknick' will be an
inconsistent expression, since you were given our other, discriminative condition
for it. For once those two conditions govern a term, that term will be an inconsistent one, however many further conditions may also govern it. But for now, realizing that our recent objection may possibly be deficient in some such other respects
as we have just indicated, let us focus only on the condition that it claims is so readily learned. Is this paradigmatic condition quite free from difficulties, and suitable
for an objection to our account? I shall argue that, for at least three reasons, it is
not: first, it is unlikely that we learn it (unlikelier still that we learn it without
learning the simpler offered condition); second, it would involve us in inconsistency anyway, and, third, should the first two reasons be discounted, the condition
would have our apparently vague terms be precise and not vague at all.

The first argument proceeds from the recognition that 'paradigm nacknick'
will be just as much a vague discriminative term as 'nacknick' itself. Suppose that
we have an alleged paradigm nacknick before us. After a while, even less than a
second, the object loses some atoms, generally more than any it might have then
gained. This will have various effects upon the object. As regards various dimensions, generally including that of shape, the object will be minutely different from
the way it was. But despite these minute differences, we regard the object now before us as being a paradigm nacknick. Now, as relevant expressions with the word
'paradigm' will thus also be vague discriminative ones, the sort of condition that is
to govern 'nacknick' must govern them as well. To deny this is to impose an entirely
ad hoc restriction on the situation, and one which, we have just seen, runs counter
even to common-sense judgments. So, we must now have this condition as well: if
something is a paradigm *paradigm nacknick,* then any object that differs from it minutely (in shape) is a *paradigm nacknick.* But, of course, matters do not rest here,
for the expression 'paradigm paradigm nacknick' is also a vague discriminative one.

Thus, an infinite chain is established. Do we learn, with 'nacknick', such an infinity of governing conditions? I find the suggestion quite incredible.

On the view I am advocating, each of these infinite conditions does hold true. Indeed, in each case, a stronger condition holds true, from which one of these former may be deduced. For example, I advocate that this condition holds: If an object is a paradigm nacknick, then any object that differs from it minutely (in shape) is also a paradigm nacknick (and so, of course, it is a nacknick). But, on my view, a person, a small child, for example, can learn and understand one of the conditions without having to learn an infinity of them. On the objector's view, infinitely more learning must be done by such a person.

As an addendum to this first argument, we may note that, from an intuitive perspective, this objection gets things backward. The objection would have it that our understanding of 'nacknick', or 'stone', is dependent on that of 'paradigm nacknick', or 'paradigm stone'. But, intuitively, in ordinary situations, the contrary seems to hold. We first learn 'stone' and only then understand longer expressions of which it is a part, like 'expensive stone', 'poor example of a stone', or 'paradigm case of a stone'. Returning to our small child, we can believe that he might understand 'stone' without yet understanding any of these longer expressions. But he could not attach much significance to any of them without first understanding 'stone'.

A second argument is readily at hand should it be needed. Now, for the sake of argument, let us suppose that, for all we have just said, "paradigm nacknick" and its associated infinity may all be learned quite easily even by tiny tots. But even supposing this, we now have to confront the problem of groundless inconsistency. For it seems that if something is minutely different from a paradigm nacknick (in shape), then something which is, in that same direction, only a tiny, minute bit more different, will also be minutely different from the paradigm nacknick. But, by reasoning familiar from the previous section, we shall then have to conclude of any shaped object that it is minutely different from a paradigm nacknick. So, on our new paradigmatic condition, it must be a nacknick. But by our discriminative condition for 'nacknick', some such objects will not be nacknicks. So, our paradigmatic condition will not provide us with a consistent expression.

In reply to this, the objection might have it that a similar paradigmatic condition applies to our underlying quantitative vague expressions, for example, to 'minute'. But is there any plausibility to the idea that we have a paradigm of something minute? What would this putative paradigm be? But, perhaps, then, we should expand the quantitative expression that now is to have a paradigm. What is it to be: 'minutely different', 'minutely different from something as regards shape', 'minutely different from a paradigm nacknick as regards shape', or what? The choice seems hopeless. For there seems no paradigm that we have for *any* of these expressions. Moreover, the expressions that have 'nacknick' as a component seem to get ordinary learning the wrong way round, as before, while those that lack such a component seem too general to have much bearing on the case at hand.

Even if both of the previous two arguments are discounted, and we presume that our paradigmatic condition is both easily learned and also results in no inconsistency, that condition would not seem to serve the purposes for which it was introduced. For, as a third argument shows, the condition would then have it that our apparently vague expressions were actually precise ones, and so not vague at all: We begin by remembering, from Section 3, our truism that a given expression either applies to a certain object or does not apply. This will hold true for 'paradigm nacknick'. Thus, this expression will apply to just those cases in a perfectly definite range, and to any others it will not apply. So, 'paradigm nacknick' will be a precise expression. By the same reason, 'minutely different in shape from a paradigm nacknick' will also be a precise expression. So, both indirectly and also quite directly, we may reason that precisely the same will hold for the simpler 'nacknick' itself: it will be a precise expression and, as such, not a vague one. So, contrary to all appearances, 'nacknick', as well as 'stone', will be absolutely precise, and thus will not be vague at all. This final failure of our paradigmatic condition suggests a thought whose importance goes beyond our interest in rebutting objections to our account. The only way for our apparently vague terms to be vague is for them to be inconsistent. Were they not inconsistent, they should have to be precise, which they are not.

6. SORITES ARGUMENTS, COUNTERFACTUAL REASONING, AND OBSCURE DIMENSIONS

The stepwise reasoning we have recently gone through, to exhibit the inconsistency in our invented expressions, 'nacknick' and 'tinkergrid', is hardly new to philosophical discussion. Such reasoning is characteristic of *sorites arguments,* which, following the classical case of the alleged heap, or *soros,* seek to show that certain entities, ordinarily alleged to exist, in fact do not. In Section 2, we encountered one such argument, against the existence of tall men. That argument, following tradition, was exhibited in a highly realistic form. With normal suppositions in force, the instances in the sequence over which reasoning ranged were all to be found in the actual world. The realism was available for us, we might say, because of the *relevantly gradual* nature of the actual world. This gradualness, and the attendant realism, is in one way all to the good: It makes sorites arguments hard to dismiss, if not to ignore, by serious thinkers who encounter them. But in another way, I think, a concentration on realistic examples can be unfortunate: it can blind us to the conceptual basis of the arguments. So, to help illuminate this basis, let us engage in some suitably counterfactual reasoning.[16] The appropriate reasoning, as will shortly appear, is more thoroughly counterfactual, or hypothetical, than that usually encountered in philosophy, as well as in everyday thinking. It requires us to imagine people living in a world different from ours who are themselves imagining a world different from theirs, in particular, a world just like ours. In a way, then, we might think of this reasoning as doubly counterfactual. But I cannot see that the extra imagination involved causes any serious difficulties.

Suppose, then, that according to some law of nature, all of the men who ever lived, and who ever will, were either exactly ten feet in height or else nine feet, and that they were aware of their heights. Now, let us suppose as well that, even with this knowledge, these men had the same expression 'tall man' as we now do, complete with the same meaning; they might even speak English, or an exact counterpart. Supposing this, it would be common for them to judge that all men were tall men. And, supposing them to be aware of the law governing their heights, they would judge further that all men would always be tall men, as indeed, in a sense, they must. These men could *imagine* a man of five feet six, of course, just as we can imagine one of six inches. But for them, such men would be only imaginary.

Could a philosopher among them, who wanted to construct a sorites against the existence of tall men, develop an effective sorites? It seems clear to me that he could do as well as we now can. It is just that his arguments, by our previous suppositions, would be conducted in a counterfactual manner. The philosopher would bid his fellows to consider a world just like ours in fact is, where the distribution of actual heights would thus be greatly increased in number and also shifted downward. They would agree that a man of six feet six *would still be* tall, but a man of five feet six *would not be*. Our philosopher would then have available a principle, in counterfactual form, corresponding to our first condition for qualitative vagueness: If a man of a certain height *would be* a tall man, then so too *would be* a man whose height *would be* no more than a thousandth of an inch less. Thus, our philosopher could conclude that *if* there *are* any tall men, then a man of five feet six *would be* a tall man *and also would not be* one. Since he now could reason that there really are not any tall men in the first place, our philosopher would have constructed an effective sorites against tall men, though he employed counterfactual reasoning in the process. Thus, we have supported the idea that a sorites argument against tall men is essentially a conceptual argument, which fits in so well with our account of vague discriminative expressions.

Just as our account of vague expressions has it, our counterfactual sorites against tall men served to indicate that 'tall man' is inconsistent. Its inconsistency is generated by our two conditions for qualitative vague terms. The second condition says that an expression of that sort will purport to distinguish, with respect to *at least one* relevant dimension of difference, those entities that satisfy it from those that do not. This condition, being quite general, does not specify or characterize the dimensions to be involved. It is up to us in any particular case to pick out a relevant dimension, as a basis for our stepwise reasoning, or else to conduct that reasoning in such a way that, we can be confident, it will cover at least one such dimension. In the case of 'tall man', our understanding of the expression allows us to be confident that height is relevant. With 'stone', as already indicated, no such relevant dimension is ready to be so clearly specified: Size itself is not crucial. If you pour an Alice-in-Wonderland potion on a stone, it will get much smaller, but will still be a stone (if one before). Perhaps, 'size in relation to structure' is more like it, but I cannot say exactly what that means, much less how it is to be treated as a dimension of difference. But we may build confidence, nevertheless, that 'stone' is a logically inconsistent expression.

Toward this end, we may look for a variation or gradation in things that will have associated with it a relevant gradation in at least one dimension that plays a discriminative role with 'stone'. Our actual world, with its considerable divisibility of "material complexes" suggests to us a suitable procedure. By removing a single peripheral atom gently from an alleged stone, and then tossing it randomly away, one will progressively produce a sequence of entities, going down to a single atom, whose properties, with regard to a relevant dimension, will vary quite gradually. With this procedure, we remain quite in the dark as to *what* dimensions of difference (are supposed to) form the basis of our term's discriminations. But whatever ones they may be, we can be confident that at least one is covered by a sequence of entities, many millions in number, obtained in this systematic manner. Let us construct, then, a suitable *sorites of decomposition by minute removals.*

By having relevant properties vary gradually with our minute removals, nature conspires to suggest to us an effective sorites against stones, in a rather realistic form. For it is easy to find acceptable each of these two conditional propositions, at least as true in fact:

(i) For anything there may be, if it is a stone, then the net removal from it of a single atom, in a way most preservative of there being a stone in the situation, will not mean the difference as to whether or not there is at least one stone in the situation.

(ii) For anything there may be, if it is a stone, then it consists of more than a hundred atoms but of a finite number of them.

These two premises, we may notice, will yield us a contradiction from the rather common-sensical assertion

There is at least one stone.

For, consider any plausible candidate for stonehood: That entity will consist of a finite number of atoms, say N, where N is greater than one hundred. That is assured us by our second premise. But, by our first premise we are told that by taking away an atom, we shall still have a stone, now one with N-1 atoms. According to that same premise, then, by stepwise reasoning, we shall have a stone even when what is before us is only an object consisting of ten atoms, or, indeed, even when we have no atoms at all. But this contradicts what (ii) tells us: as there are not more than a hundred atoms there, there is no stone in the situation.

Now, it is, of course, not part of the meaning of 'stone' that any stone should consist of atoms, let alone more than a hundred but some finite number of them. Indeed, so far as I can discern, it is not even required by our term that any portion of a stone should be physically removable from the remainder. Further, providing that some is thus removable, and even removed, there's nothing in 'stone' which says that the rest will not suddenly vanish, or suddenly serve to constitute something utterly different, for example, an exotic plant. That none of these things happen, and that our argument proceed in way of a gradual sequence of suitable entities is, we might say, wholly a matter of worldly, contingent fact. But as presented, our sorites against stones might seem to depend on these suppositions. This appearance is easily dispelled, however. For we may combine the idea of counterfactual reasoning, previously discussed, with the systematic procedure used for obscure dimensions just developed. Without going into much detail, we may imagine a philosopher, with our same language, living in a very different world from ours, where his alleged stones cannot be decomposed. But, if he were imaginative enough, he could contemplate a world just like ours, where stones can be appropriately picked apart. If his world contained stones, then so too would ours, he could reason. Then he could show himself that ours would not and, thus, none anywhere.

We are next to pass to a direct discussion of 'person', and of putative people. Pursuing the ideas so far developed, we shall argue that the expression cannot be satisfied, and that there really are no such entities as people. Before we do so, I should note briefly that many objections have been raised against sorites arguments, even against what might be regarded as the most realistic sort. While I think there is little merit in any of these objections, it is not a main purpose of mine here to meet them. To the extent that my present account is well argued, of course, that provides some support for sorites arguments. Thus, indirectly, the account gives a reply to all objections to these reasonings. But I leave to other places the matter of detailed responses to particular objections.[17]

To give you an idea, however, of what one must accept if one is to reject sorites arguments, I shall just mention two points that I discuss elsewhere.[18] First, to reject our sorites against stones, we must accept this: there will be certain stones, composed of many billions of atoms, whose continued existence, with no atoms replaced, requires every single one of these billions! Can you believe that there are ever any stones whose essence is as refined and tenuous as that? A second thought, on the side of language, mirrors the first: Consider the sentence, "There is a stone before me now," and discount all problems of vagueness except those most directly concerned with 'stone'. With a promising candidate for stonehood before you, imagine peripheral atoms extracted in the style of our sorites. We are to evaluate the sentence after each net removal. We suppose the sentence at first to express a genuine statement that is true. But can a single atomic removal alter the proper evaluation? To suppose it can requires us to suppose an enormous sensitivity on the part of our word 'stone'. This, I suggest, is quite incredible.

7. THE INCONSISTENCY OF 'PERSON'

It is now time to extend the results so far obtained to the key expression 'person'. I shall argue that this term is a qualitative vague discriminative term and, as such, it is inconsistent. Accordingly, as nothing then satisfies the expression, anymore than anything satisfies 'perfectly square triangle', there are no people. Like perfectly square triangles, people are logically impossible entities.

Should we arrive at such a negative result for people, a paradoxical situation will arise. Briefly, if there is not anybody, then there is no one to understand these alleged accounts, arguments, and conclusions to that effect. So, perhaps, these last may themselves be negated or dismissed as "self-defeating." But, if our account is otherwise unobjectionable, we may then employ it again, to complete a paradoxical circle and begin a new one. Now, in the section directly to follow this one, I shall argue that this admitted paradox cannot seriously nullify our nihilistic account. But, first, in this present section, I shall argue that the paradoxical situation cannot be avoided. I shall argue, that is, that our account of vague expressions cannot be brought to rest at some relatively unproblematic stopping point.

The expression 'person' is a vague discriminative term and, as such, an inconsistent expression. To support this thought, suitable sorites arguments shall be sought. Now, as with 'stone', I have no very good idea how to specify adequately those dimensions of difference with respect to which 'person' purports to make discriminations. It is not that I have nothing at all to say on the matter: Perhaps, power of thought, or intelligence, provides one such dimension; perhaps capacity for varied feelings and experiences provides one. But I should prefer to regard these proposals as primarily illustrative, and to construct our sorites arguments on the basis of ideas in which I have more confidence. Toward this end, we recall our experience with 'stone', for we had success there by adopting a procedure that required no specification of dimensions. So, let us look for a sorites of decomposition by minute removals that will work well for 'person'. We may best begin in a moderately realistic vein. Then we can move to the utterly fantastic, so that the conceptual nature of the arguments may be more clearly perceived.

In our common thinking on the matter, though this was not always so, it is supposed that there are some people, if not all, who are composed of many cells, though of a finite number. We distinguish, of course, between a person and his body. But, then, while we think the body to be of a certain weight, and to be composed of such cells, we *also* think the person himself to be. Now, some people, I suppose, do not go along with this idea and think that, whatever might be true of the body, the person himself never consists of any cells, or of any other spatially extended things. But even these people, I imagine, will agree that, in the case of many people, each of whom has a body, there is a certain *close association,* or *intimate relation,* whatever its specific character, between each of these people and his or her respective body. (That intimate relation, for all I am saying, *might* be that of identity.) And, no doubt, they will also agree that there is a close relation, perhaps another one, between each of these people and those cells serving to compose his or her body. So, all of us may agree that if there are any people at all, then some of them, at least, are in a close association with certain cells, or with certain groups or complexes of cells, and that each such suitable group, while containing more than ten cells, has only a finite number of cells in it.

Now, I think that another thing we agree on is this: that if there is a person in a situation, and that person is in some such aforesaid close relation with a certain group of cells, then, if only one cell is removed from the group, and this is done in a

way most conducive to there being a person in such a close relation with the remaining cells, then there will be a person in the situation after the removal. In certain instances, of course, this *way* will have to include the importation into the situation of certain life-support apparatus, and of certain items for supporting consciousness. For matters with people seem more complex than with stones, however
unreal all of these may eventually prove to be. We may say, then, that whatever
substances or properties are *supported by* some cells, so that a person is there in
close association, they will also be supported, and in sufficient degree, with only
one cell less, providing, of course, that the lesser complex is so chosen, and so allowed to function, that it can do as good a job at such supporting as is possible for
a group obtained by such a slight removal. Of course, in the cases to be considered,
the imported material does *not* replace cells; rather like a kidney machine, it just
helps cells, and what they serve to constitute, to function.

These shared suppositions yield a sorites argument to the effect that there are
no people at all. For, if any person is closely associated with a certain group of
cells, say, N in number, so will one be there with a group of N-1 cells. I suppose
that, as matters progress, we shall get down to a brain, in a vat, then half a brain,
then a third, and then a sixteenth. In each case, we must say, there is a person in
the situation, one who is in a special close association with the remaining cells.
Eventually, there are but three living cells in some sort of combination, and it must
be said that there is a person there. But we have also agreed that, with no more than
ten cells, there will be no such associated person. Thus, supposing there to be a person at the start, there both is and is not a person in close association with our three
cells. Of course, this argues that there never are any people in close association with
any groups of cells. So, finally, we may conclude, there really are not any people
at all.

With an appropriately realistic argument before us, it is now time to reason
counterfactually, so as to see the conceptual basis of the idea that there are no
people. Let us imagine a world in which there are entities that we should consider
persons, and that consider themselves as such. We shall suppose that these putative
people have a language just like ours. They are a bit more intelligent than we, but
their powers of imagination far exceed our own. Their greatest differences from us,
however, are these: unlike us, these people have no physical existence; they have no
bodies nor are they in any very close relation with any physical phenomena. Further, as a matter of imagined fact, they are neither divisible, diminishable, nor even
susceptible of any major change. Each of them has always existed and always will
exist, and always is at or near the peak of his sensibilities and powers. So, these beings are, I suppose, quite as some philosophers have supposed ourselves really to be.
Finally, let us suppose that there are no other sentient beings in this world.

Consider a critical philosopher among them. How might he convince himself
that his term 'person', which is the same as our expression, is a logically inconsistent term? Now, he has no relevant gradations in reality to help him base a sorites
argument. And, we suppose, it is not clear to him either how to specify the dimensions of difference with respect to which 'person' purports to discriminate. Now,

what this reasoner should do is try to supply himself with a sequence of imagined entities that differed gradually with regards to at least one such relevant dimension. While by our poor standards it would take a great feat of imagination, how better for him to do this than to imagine a world just like ours is (supposed to be) in fact? In this world, thus imagined by him, whatever features were relevant would be supported by brains, each of which was composed of billions of cells.

Our philosopher, in particular, might imagine someone exactly like you yourself; living, kicking, breathing, and thinking, if anyone ever does, in just such a world as you now find yourself to be. He would think to himself, we may suppose, first, that if *anyone is* a person, then this being like you *would be* a person, for that is our same word, 'person', that is figuring in his premising. What more would that free spirit endeavor to think? Well, we might imagine, he could say to himself that, under the total circumstances imagined, if there is indeed a person just like you, then so too will there by a person when a single cell is removed, most conducively for the continued support of a person, from those that may have supported the original candidate. Far better than we can do, he could imagine in detail the importation of those life-support and consciousness-support systems involved in a most conducive way, so as to establish a suitable sequence of entities. Of course, he can imagine this while starting, not only with an imagined counterpart of you, but with that of any of a great variety of the putative people we suppose to populate our world. For our world, in general, he could then premise that a single cell removed, in such a circumstance and manner, will never mean the difference between at least one person being in the situation and there being none. For he could reason that, in such a world, no one cell will mean a difference, on the dimensions in question, to which 'person' is sensitive. Further, our thinker could say that, in this world, when there were no more than ten cells in a relevant group or complex, then there *would be* no person in the situation. From these premises, by familiar stepwise reasoning, our philsopher would now conclude that if a being like yourself would be a person, then, with ten cells supporting at their best and utmost, there *both would be a person in close association and also would not be.* Thus, he should conclude that the being first imagined, the one just like you yourself, was never any person in the first place. And, finally, by his very first premise, he could now reason that there were not, or are not, any people at all. Thus, without any reality to help him, our imagined philosopher could see for himself that there could never be any people, even while having no clear idea how to specify what dimensions of difference served to determine the impossibility thus perceived.

I have made my imagined philosopher a most pristine soul, a being whose "nature in itself" would seem immune to sorites arguments. Moreover, if he appreciated his nature, that awareness would do nothing to suggest our word 'person'. But so long as this being does share our expression, he may reason to expose its inconsistency and, thus, its lack of application. To make these points, I made my imagined philosopher as described.

There is another reason, too, for my giving this being such a logically unobjectionable nature. For philosophers have sometimes suggested that our own natures are much as I have stipulated his to be and, what is perhaps more interesting here, even that our term 'person' analytically requires such a nature for its application. Now, let us suppose that any being with such a nature as that cannot be dimensionally compared with, or related to, any other being. With these suppositions in force, we may advance, for 'person', a condition of *incomparability:*

> (3p) If an entity satisfies 'person', then there is no dimension of difference such that with regard to it there are entities which differ from that putative satisfier.

According to this condition, there will be no entities that thus differ minutely, or substantially, from a satisfier. So, one might well think that were such a condition to hold for 'person', but perhaps not for 'stone', then, unlike 'stone', 'person' might be a perfectly consistent term after all.[19]

But this supposition of consistency for 'person' would be much mistaken. For as our sorites arguments indicate, 'person' is a vague discriminative expression and, whatever else may be true of it, the term is governed by (1) and (2), our dimensional conditions of vagueness and of discriminativeness. So long as these conditions do govern it, which we have seen no good reason to deny, the expression will be inconsistent. Whatever further conditions may govern it as well cannot erase the two for which we have argued or, then, the contradictions that they serve to generate. This incomparability condition, if there be one governing 'person', will not make matters better for the term. On the contrary, it will serve only to compound the term's troubles. For taken together with either of our prior two conditions for 'person', the incomparability condition, (3p), yields a contradiction from the supposition that any entity satisfies the term. For, by either of the prior two, if there is a person, then there *are* entities that differ *dimensionally* from any satisfier. And, by our new condition, if there is a person, then there are *no* such entities. Hence, if there is a person, then there both are and also are not such dimensionally differing entities, which is absurd. Hence, by (1) and (3p), and also by (2) and (3p), there are no people. Supposing an incomparability condition for 'person', we should say, not that it is a consistent term, but, on the contrary, that "person" is *inconsistent from multiple sources.*

The inconsistency of 'person' means that no people exist; they can exist no more than can perfectly square triangles. Do I exist, then, but am no person after all? Things would seem otherwise: If I exist, then there is at least one person. So, as there are none, there is no me. This result, paradoxical to say the least, can be obtained as well by sorites arguments where there is a purported direct reference to myself, by means, for example, of such terms as 'I', 'Peter Unger', and so on. The most imaginative of our counterfactual sorites arguments might be out of place with these terms, or at least might have a rather different bearing on the issues. Our more realistic versions, however, will have obviously close parallel arguments. Take away one peripheral cell from Peter Unger, with suitable life-support systems in place, and that will not mean the difference between Unger and no Unger. But, with ten cells there is no Unger. So, there never was that Unger.

The analysis of, or the account of, even the most realistic arguments with such singular terms will require, of course, the presentation of conditions that logically govern the key singular expressions. No doubt, these conditions will be importantly analogous to those given here for qualitative vague terms; perhaps our suggestions for such terms as 'door' will be of some help. But these analytical questions take us beyond our topic.

More to the present point, 'person' is hardly the only qualitative vague expression whose inconsistency means much difficulty for us here. For example, the expression 'entity with a capacity for thought' means similar troubles for us, however that expression may relate to 'person'. For the arguments that point up the inconsistency in 'person' will do as much for this longer expression. Moreover, as this expression is of the purely qualitative sort, even the supporting account of the arguments will be along the same familiar lines. Thus, for quite familiar reasons, it may be concluded that there are no entities with a capacity for thought. As with thought, no capacity for experience could be ours, nor for feeling, nor for anything of importance. As regards each of these negative matters, we have, paradoxically enough, not only adequate arguments, but accounts of how those arguments work adequately. For the key expressions involved are, in each case, vague discriminative terms of the purely qualitative sort.

8. THE INABILITY OF PARADOX TO NULLIFY THIS ACCOUNT

Paradox, already indicated, can easily be made manifest: if there are no beings with any capacity for thought, then no argument or statement can be understood, or accepted at all, and so none to the effect that there are no such beings. So it seems that we are driven back logically to the assertion of our existence, of the existence of beings that can think. Thus, there is next the implication that our expressions 'person' and 'thinking being' do indeed apply. And so, finally, we have the implication that these terms are logically consistent ones. But things do not really stop here, either. For, along lines that are by now familiar, we may in turn reduce these assertions to absurdity. Thus, their negations obtain, including the proposition that there are no beings with any capacity for thought. The reasoning goes around and around. What are we to make of this paradoxical situation? Should we hold onto common sense robustly and say that the only genuine errors are in our account of vagueness and in its connecting sorites arguments? Following this course, we might better try to be comfortable. For then thoughts of absurdity will be harder to keep in mind. But perhaps, "so to try to say," paradox does little to nullify the basic point and value of our radical account and arguments.

In available terms, for want of any better, I have argued that many of our common expressions are logically inconsistent terms, including such key expressions as 'person' and 'entity with a capacity for thought'. Much of my argument began with the invention of a term, 'nacknick', for which inconsistent instructions were given in its very introduction. Then, as our sorites arguments progressively indicated, there appeared no logically relevant difference between 'nacknick' and such common expressions as 'stone' and even 'person'. To be sure, the latter terms are not learned from any explicit instructions at all. But there is still a parity of inconsistency, or at least a very strong suggestion of it, that supports my account of the ordinary terms as logically inconsistent. Despite whatever paradoxes our account may engender, then, how can this apparent parity be rationally denied?

To deny the shared inconsistency, one cannot rationally rely on pointing to paradox. For, let us consider the implications of our lessons with 'nacknick'. Now, as this term concerns only the shape of objects, it is idle to suppose that it might yield the sort of paradox that an expression like 'thinking being' was recently observed to do. What is less idle, however, is to imagine that inconsistent instructions were, at a suitable point, *imposed upon* the learning of such terms as 'person' and 'thinking being'. Let us imagine, then, a society much like ours, with this exception: *After normal early learning had occurred,* explicit inconsistent instructions were given to the moderately young. Thus, children would hear words like these: "Typical vague words that you have learned, like 'stone' and 'person', will now be more clearly revealed to you. To begin with, each of you should know that each of these words serves to discriminate, or distinguish, different sorts of things. So, the word 'stone' distinguishes between the stones and everything else, which differ so from stones that they do not fit the meaning of the word. Of course, this word is a vague one, and you should know this about it too: if something is a stone, and so fits the word 'stone' properly, then anything that differs from it only a little bit will also fit the word, that is, will also be a stone. To be sure, there is no definite limit as to how much something may differ from a stone and for it yet to be a stone. All of this, you are to understand, is part of what it is for the word 'stone' to be a vague word while still allowing us to make useful discriminations with it. And, of course, these points apply just as well to other typical vague words, for example, to such words as 'house', 'person', 'red', 'soft', 'tall', 'running', 'thinking', and so on. Now, none of this should come as a surprise to any of you; in fact, in a way, you have known it already. But it is just as well for us to be explicit about these things, for us to have them out in the open."

What results would such instructions have if they were often involved in teaching routines? As the people in this society are to be much like ourselves, it must be supposed that they will master what they are thus taught, should much training be imposed. Later in life, even, should someone manage to claim some such word to be precise, the people will appeal to the teachings, which they could recite with little distortion. Thus, if someone said that a stone could not be less than one inch in diameter, but that it could be less than one and one millionths inches, he would be accused of violating the meaning of 'stone' just as we should accuse him. Unlike us, however, the people in this other society, to support the charge that such a claim of precision is in way of being an arbitrary stipulation, would appeal to the explicit, repeated teaching routines. They would appear to be in a quite obviously good position, then, to claim that there is indeed a stipulation here and, moreover, one which conflicts with the learned, accepted meaning of the word.

Now, let us suppose that, just as I am doing for our own words, a philosopher in this society puts forward the idea that typical vague terms are inconsistent. This is hardly an arbitrary supposition now, given what we have already imagined. For if I have supposed as much with no such explicit teaching to suggest the thought to me, how much easier it will be for a thinker who is amidst so much apparent inconsistency. Focusing on the teaching, he would point out the inconsistency in the instructions. Now, in that society, since the people are assumed to be much like us, there would be thinkers of a rather conservative bent, who would wish to cleave to the accepted thinking of their culture. How should these conservatives defend that thinking; how should they rationally reply to the nihilistic critic?

Whatever replies may be open to them, it seems to me that *among the least effective* of these would be an appeal to comprehensive paradox. True enough, if such expressions as their 'person' and 'thinking being' are logically inconsistent, as the explicit instructions for them indicate, then they would have to conclude that no one could accept, or even understand, the critic's arguments. But if the matter were allowed to rest there, or even if the burden of argument were thought to be substantially shifted, those conservative thinkers would display terribly little philosophical sense, and virtually no depth of thought or understanding. Generally, we may note that any thoroughgoing radical critique of a language, or a system of thought, conducted in the terms or concepts of what is criticized, must, of course, have this paradoxical quality. But this does not mean that such a criticism cannot be, so to try to say, appropriate to its object. In the society now under consideration, whatever most of its members may think on the matter, such a criticism will be quite appropriate indeed.

Now, it seems clear to me that the situation is not relevantly different in our own case. It is, of course, true that things are not exactly the same with us, for we have had no explicit instructions for our typical vague terms, much less have we any that are inconsistent. But, as our arguments have indicated, what our imagined society's members will have learned explicitly we seem to have learned implicitly. The logic of our expressions is not at variance with theirs. So, it is most unlikely, I submit, that pointing to paradox will be futile against their radical critic but rational against a critic in our less explicit society. As it will not be rational there, so it is not rational here. Pointing to paradox, then, does little or nothing to nullify these present efforts.

The point that paradox cannot nullify our account will stand just as well should we agree that, in addition to the paradoxical situation already noted, various other, perhaps deeper, paradoxes are consequences of our account. For example, it might be held that if there are no entities with any capacity to think, or to use language, then there will be no sentences, or any other expressions. And, it might be held that if there are none of these latter, then there are no statements or propositions, no arguments or accounts of any sort, and not just none that are ever understood or accepted. If this may be maintained, then fuller, or more direct, paradoxes can be added to our account's consequences. But, as our discussion has already indicated amply, this will do little to worsen matters for us. For, *whatever* paradoxes our account should engender will all be rationally treated alike. They all will best be taken, it seems clear, as showing the comprehensiveness of our radical account, rather than its futility.

9. A REEXAMINATION OF OUR ARGUMENT FROM INVENTED EXPRESSIONS

Our account of vague expressions has been provided. It has given support to our Argument from Invented Expressions, support which will not be nullified by any charges of paradox. If we are to maintain common sense still, and hold that there really are people, we must object to one of the premises of that Argument, though few courses for such an objection appear still to be available. To take last things first, there is little to be said against the Argument's final premise:

> (III) If the expression 'person' is logically inconsistent, then there are no people.

For a denial of it, as I have argued in Section 1, will rest only upon a confusion. So, objections must come against its first two premises, for the Argument's form is not faulty. At the outset of our reexamination of them, we note that at this point these premises look well supported. So, now, I suggest, the burden of argument is on any attempted objection. Can this burden be shouldered effectively?

Let us reexamine our second premise, in an attempt to review matters back to our beginning:

> (II)   The expression 'person' is logically on a par with 'nacknick'; if the latter is inconsistent, then so is the former.

So far as we have been able to discern, from our early experiments onward, there is indeed this logical parity. If the matter is just an empirical, or contingent, or causal one, to be decided primarily by experiment and observation, then parity seems surely right. For only the most tortuous and forced interpretation of our recent experiments and observations would have things be otherwise. For an objection to (II) to be at all plausible, then, it must be maintained that it is for some conceptual or logical reasons that there is a disparity between our invented expression and our ordinary one. Now, we have already argued that, whatever else may be true of it, 'person' is a qualitative vague discriminative term. As such, it is logically on a par with such other, less central common expressions as 'stone', 'tall man,' and 'cubical object'. So, in effect, what the objection must claim is that there is a logical barrier to a parallel between 'nacknick' and 'cubical object', and even 'object whose shape is quite similar to that of a cube'. But how might the claim of such a logical barrier be rationally supported?

The support required would have to come in the form of 'logical' truths, which would logically yield the statement of no logical parity. But anything that might be even plausibly considered a logical truth appears quite inadequate to provide the needed deduction. Here is an example of the problem, with a candidate for relevant logical truth that is much better than most I have examined: One must understand an invented expression, if one understands it at all, in terms of a set of expressions (each of which is not invented and) each of which is consistent. While it might later be doubted, let us now grant that, in a relevant sense, this is indeed a logical truth. But, even so, of what use will it be in deriving logical disparity between invented and ordinary vague expressions?

We have already encountered an invented expression which, if any ordinary term satisfies this offered condition, quite nicely meets the alleged requirement. That expression is 'tinkergrid', which I introduced and discussed in Section 4. Discounting any minor lapse, I showed there that, unlike both ordinary vague terms and also the invented 'nacknick', the invented 'tinkergrid', while it was indeed inconsistent, had inconsistency which was relevantly grounded. What seemed to hold only between 'nacknick' and the ordinary terms, none of which appear to satisfy our offered requirement, was the *further* parallel of having *groundless* inconsistency. So, even if we grant the offered requirement, the most it could logically yield, it should be clear, is that ordinary vague expressions will differ from 'nacknick' as regards the source or nature of whatever inconsistency they might have. The parity we are concerned with, however, concerns whether, like both 'nacknick' and also 'tinkergrid', typical vague expressions are, in any way, and from whatever source, logically inconsistent. As regards the required disparity, then, the offered requirement, even if logically true, is powerless to yield any result.

While our reconsideration of 'tinkergrid' has shown the offered requirement to be irrelevant, it suggests as well great doubt as to its truth. It seems incredible to suppose that we might have invented a term like 'tinkergrid' to parallel our ordinary vague terms but failed with 'nacknick'. For of the two useful, inconsistent inventions, it is the latter that seems to provide the closer parallel here. So, our problems compound: to have a (logical) truth presented in the first place, we are constrained to weaken our alleged requirement. Perhaps the following has a decent chance for truth: One must understand an invented expression, if at all, in terms of a set of expressions (each of which is not invented and) at least some of which are consistent terms. But, now, we have available to yield contradiction, in addition to the clashes between consistent ideas that 'tinkergrid' displayed, the inconsistency in various vague expressions (which are not invented).

The experience we have just suffered is typical of what I have encountered in my examination of objections to (II), the second premise of our Argument. The more an offered proposition looks like it might be a logical truth, and so suitable for a counterargument in that respect, the less it looks relevant to yielding the required deduction of disparity. No candidate, then, of which I am aware, looks very promising, and no suitable counterargument appears forthcoming. While these matters must, perhaps, always be somewhat inconclusive, it thus seems to me that there is no good objection to the apparent logical parity between the invented and ordinary expressions.

There is only one place left for an objection to be effective against our Argument, namely, in the place of our first premise:

(I)   The invented expression 'nacknick' is logically inconsistent.

This question brings us back to the beginning of our essay. Could we have misinterpreted our little learning experiments, so that the apparently obvious and rational interpretation was really out of place all along? As with (II), if the matter is essentially an empirical, or contingent one, there would be little chance indeed that we have been misinterpreting things, and that some ingenious complicated hypothesis must be preferred. Thus, the objection must be that there is some logical barrier to the truth of our first premise. But how might it be argued that we have been laboring under such an intellectual illusion?

The occurrence of a definite description at the head of our premise, "the invented expression 'nacknick'," may trigger the response that there may in fact never have been any such invented expression. If so, then this premise will fail of truth, whatever other status should then be accorded it. Now, it is clearly no good to deny the thought that if there is any expression 'nacknick', then it is an invented term. But it will also do no good to challenge the premise on the ground that there is no expression 'nacknick' at all. For anything which will serve to argue that much, it appears, will undermine as well the idea that there are ordinary vague expressions, including 'cubical object' and 'person'. The paradoxical consequences of our own account, for example, can be used to this effect against the premise; but they will undermine as well any typical vague expression, including 'person'. So, this is no good way to challenge our premise, as it gets rid of the baby along with the bath water. Similar maneuvers will prove to no better critical effect. For example, it is no good to find 'nacknick' an expression but a meaningless one, for how should 'cubical object' and 'person' then prove meaningful? The only plausible manner of objection, then, will allow 'nacknick' as an expression that either is consistent or else inconsistent.

It remains to object, of course, that this invented expression cannot possibly be, in any sense that it might have, an inconsistent expression. It appears that the teacher, at least, has an understanding of such an inconsistent term, but this appearance, the objection continues, must be an intellectual illusion. How might this be cogently maintained? I suspect that an idea which might motivate this objection is the by now old one that meaning is use, or is a function of use, though perhaps in one of that idea's newer guises or forms. But, in whatever form, this idea looks quite unrealistic. Even when we consider terms that are not vague, and which may be allowed as consistent, there seems little value in this approach. Consider a surface. With certain purposes in mind, someone may say "This is flat," his idea being that the surface is suitable for those purposes. Weeks later, he may return with other purposes, and say of the same surface "This is not flat," and then turning to another surface may say of it "That one is flat." But, we may suppose, the original surface did not become any less flat, and even may have been somewhat improved in that respect. Weeks later still, with a third set of purposes, the same individual may declare the second surface to be not flat, now declaring a third surface to be a flat one. And, so it may go, half a dozen times or more. How is this most plausibly to be accounted? Surely, the meaning of the words did not relevantly change. And, just as surely, the meaning of 'flat' does not concern anyone's purposes. The realistic explanation, I suggest, involves supposing that *none* of the surfaces here *ever are flat,* and that while actually speaking falsely, the man is informally implying in each case something like this: The currently indicated surface is sufficiently close to being (absolutely) flat so as to be suitable for the purposes the speaker and hearer now have in mind.[20]

If even apparently consistent terms are best accounted by thus distinguishing meaning and semantic application from the uses to which the words are put, at least as much should be expected where the terms appear to be inconsistent expressions. I think we may do well now to consider once again our invented term 'tinkergrid'. This is a term that is to apply only to certain abstract, mathematical objects. To say of a wooden structure that it is a tinkergrid, just for this reason, a plain failure to speak the truth. If use is to match with truth and meaning here, it will have to come from quarters much further removed from directly observable behaviors and stimuli. Perhaps we might ask various people to try to imagine tinkergrids. Various people, perhaps unaware of any inconsistency, will frequently allege success. They are using the term to describe what they imagine. But, I think we may agree that they can be imagining no such thing, and that a literally accurate description of what they imagine can be given only in some other terms. To go on multiplying examples and considerations would be inappropriate for us now. To be sure, it is most unlikely that anything can be said on these matters that will prove absolutely conclusive. But, lacking such certainty, perhaps we may still agree that I have invented some inconsistent expressions, even if those terms are well suited for our use.

At this point, a subtler, and somewhat more plausible, objection may be attempted. The idea here is to grant that 'nacknick' is an inconsistent expression, but to deny it much of a place in our experimental learning situations. It is not obvious, however, precisely how this will serve to challenge our Argument. So, let us discuss the matter.

The attempted objection may take any of several forms, but they are all more or less equivalent to this: our 'nacknick' is a term with two (or more?) meanings. In one sense, which it does seem forced to deny it, the term is indeed an inconsistent one. In this sense, however, the objection continues, the term is not a useful expression. The sense in which the term is useful is another sense, in which the term is consistent. And, what has happened in the learning situation? The teacher has intended by his instructions, to inculcate in his hearers (or readers) the expression 'nacknick' in its inconsistent sense. But what his instructions actually have done is to *suggest* to the hearers *another* sense for the term, a consistent useful one. The hearers then learn 'nacknick' only in this latter sense; the former never gets further than the teacher's sounds or marks.[21]

This objection, we may see, attempts to force an equivocation upon our Argument. Interestingly, the term upon which the equivocation focuses is not a common, accepted one, but is our invented 'nacknick' itself. For the Argument to seem to work, 'nacknick' must have one meaning in the first premise, on which the term is inconsistent, and another meaning in the second premise, on which the term is consistent. As the Argument thus equivocates, it is not a cogent piece of reasoning.

This objection has some plausibility, but it will not bear scrutiny. For it to work, we must suppose that the only way for 'nacknick' to be logically on a par with ordinary vague terms, in particular, with 'person', is for the new expression to be taken in a consistent sense. But, might not there be a deep parallel here between the two, so that 'person' as well as 'nacknick' has an inconsistent meaning? If so, then our Argument will not equivocate, but will concern both terms, as regards their inconsistent meanings. As such, it will be a cogent piece of reasoning, though perhaps a bit limited in its scope.

My suggestion of this deep parallel implies that the inconsistent sense for 'nacknick' did get further than my marks or sounds, that it was inculcated in you. What might support this suggestion? We remember our instructive society, where inconsistent instructions for learned ordinary terms became a matter of widespread, repeated scholastic drill. Now, we need only extend our experiments with 'nacknick' to match their drills with 'stone', 'cubical object', and 'person'. So, let us imagine that after I taught you 'nacknick', we went over the instructions so much that you had them down pat. In such a case, there is no plausibility at all in supposing the inconsistent sense got no further than my marks or sounds, and never entered your learning. For, now, you would be confident that the aforesaid instructions governed your 'nacknick', which you had learned from me. Indeed, after you perceive the inconsistency in your term, you will be able to say of other expressions, which are *not* thus inconsistent, that they are thus different from the expression you just learned. Thus, you will say that 'perfect cube' is logically quite different from the term you learned from me. But, of course, you will be ready to use 'nacknick' for many objects anyway and to withhold it of many others. It appears quite easy to tell how our extended experiments will turn out, and what those results show. For what occurs there explicitly also occurs, implicitly, in our original experiments.

Now, none of this is to deny that my instructions may have inculcated in you, in *addition* to 'nacknick' in the inconsistent sense, a consistent sense for the expression. And, it is not to deny that this consistent sense may have been important, even essential, for the term's being a useful one for you. I think these last possibilities to be, in fact, quite unlikely. But there is still some plausibility in the idea of them. What is important for us to notice now is, first, how much less plausible it is to think that with 'nacknick', as well as with 'person', no inconsistent sense ever got to you at all, no matter what else may have gotten to you, and, second, that it is this much less plausible idea that is required for the charge of equivocation to work against our Argument.

To appreciate fully the failure of this charge, we should understand that whatever we may say of 'nacknick' in these regards, we may say with just as much reason, or just as little, in regards to 'stone' and 'person'. Thus, even if it concerns terms only in one, conscious meaning, our Argument will have a second premise suitable to match its first. For example, we may grant that there is an unconscious, consistent sense for 'nacknick' which, in our experiments, you learned and then employed. Then we might say, of course, that you *also* used the term in its inconsistent sense, perhaps doing so in (the process of) using it in its consistent one. But then we might just as well say the same for 'person', or 'stone': We learn two senses and, when we use 'stone' in its inconsistent sense, we do so in (the process of) using it in its unconscious, consistent sense. For another example, we might say that the consciously learned sense is never useful, and that there appears to be a use for 'nacknick' only in this inconsistent sense. But, then, of course, we might just as well say that 'stone' is perfectly idle in its conscious, inconsistent sense, and is used only in that unconscious sense in which it is a consistent expression. Whatever we may say for 'nacknick', we should understand, we may just as well say for 'stone' and for 'person'. So, to repeat, our Argument does not rely upon equivocation, but is an adequate piece of reasoning.

This final objection has failed. But it suggests some ideas, recently considered, that, while they do not constitute an objection to our Argument, may serve to place limits on its application. For, if there may be two senses of 'nacknick', and thus of 'person' also, it might be said that our Argument concerns these expressions in only one of those senses, the inconsistent one. Thus, for all that piece of reasoning says, there may be a consistent sense for 'person', as well as for 'nacknick', and, in *that* sense, there may well be plenty of people. If our Argument is thus limited, then the interest of our conclusion, it might be said, will be equally limited, though perhaps still of some significance. What are we to make of this?

In the first place, we should remind ourselves that the postulation of these additional meanings appears to be quite gratuitous and, if it actually is so, then nothing further need be said. Indeed, can't we leave it at that? For these alleged meanings are not only wholly unconscious ones, but we are to have no clue as to how anyone might ever become aware of them. Of course, someone might take a stab at articulating his putative unconscious meaning of 'person', but how should he ever judge his success, let alone the propriety of extending his suggestion to my own putative unconscious meaning for the term? To my mind, the postulation of these alleged meanings looks to be a desperate pretense.

But suppose we grant that there really are such shared consistent unconscious meanings. So far as I can tell, we still cannot say anything much as to what they are. Unlike the conscious inconsistent meanings, for which we can give at least such conditions as in (1) and (2), these postulated entities are utterly obscure and mysterious. But if we do not have any idea as to these obscure meanings, then we have none either as to what it is for an entity to be a person, or even to be a nacknick. Thus, with respect to any entity whatever, even an alleged shoelace, we have no idea either as to whether it is a person or a nacknick, or both, or neither. In *this* sense of person—and how many others like it—perhaps there may be ever so many people. But now the matter has become utterly mysterious and obscure. If this is all there is to our Argument's being limited, that reasoning seems not to have any serious limitations.

10. SOME OUTSTANDING PROBLEMS POSED BY THIS ACCOUNT AND ITS RELATION TO THEM

Largely by providing and employing an account of typical vague expressions as logically inconsistent, I have argued that there are no people. We have discussed the chief objections to the account, including the charge of paradox, and we have supported the account by answering or disarming them. Thus, paradoxically enough, I suggest that at this point my account is to be accepted, at least as a working hypothesis for certain problems. I should now like briefly to discuss three of these.

A. The Problem of Explanation

If 'person' is an inconsistent term, then *how* are *any* entities able, so to say, to use it as successfully as it appears gets done quite regularly? Indeed, how does this happen with any inconsistent expression? If such an expression is tied to consistent terms, so that it functions in place of them, then the matter is not very problematic. We saw this before, in Section 1, where we discussed a working agreement to use 'perfectly square triangle' in place of 'tomato which is both yellow and sweet', supposing the latter expression to be consistent. But, without any such supposition as that, which is our present problem situation, there is considerable explanatory difficulty.

If our account is right, then any explanation given in available terms must eventually, like the terms themselves, prove logically incoherent. So, we should not expect too much here in the way of valuable results. Nevertheless, it is unhelpful to say nothing more than that there is nothing for us to do. For, even if they are incoherent, the questions that introduced this problem for us appear to point up some puzzling phenomena. So, I shall stick my neck out now and offer the beginnings of an explanatory suggestion.

Perhaps we might understand the role of putative paradigms on the model of an animal's learning to respond to a stimulus. A rat can be taught to press a nearby bar just when a certain sort of stimulus is present, for example, a triangular object. After learning with this stimulus, what happens with rats when, on the next trial, a somewhat different stimulus is for the first time presented, perhaps a more or less rounded triangular object? We may plot measures of response against difference from the original shape, those measures being frequency of any response, quickness of response when one is made, strength of response, such as pressure on the bar, and so on. With such suitable measures, a gradient, or curve, will be established for a rat population and, by extrapolation, for a typical rat member. For almost any rat, the peak of the gradient will center quite precisely on the original shape, the slope away from that varying somewhat from rat to rat. We might say, then, that each rat has his own idea of a *triangular object*, though there is important commonality to their ideas.

I suggest that our conception of a triangular object, and of a nacknick, is similarly based. Much as a rat can be trained to respond to an alleged paradigm nacknick, so I can more quickly learn to respond more flexibly with regard to such putative objects, and with respect to my invented term for them. And, of course, so can you. While our centers will not differ much, though with different people and different individual paradigms *some* difference is to be expected, our slopes may be expected to differ significantly, especially for cases far away from center. Thus, various behavioral borderline cases will arise where you and I are inclined toward disparate judgments. Now, suppose my interior decorator tells me to use a nacknick in a certain place, though any shaped nacknick will be suitable. In a store, I come upon a "borderline case" while shopping in your company. I am inclined to judge it a nacknick, you to judge it not one. Who is right? It would be silly for us, even if we thought there were some nacknicks, to force the issue and to declare that there must be a fact of the matter. Behaving typically, we would not do that. Rather, I suggest, we should treat the matter as a social problem, with each person having a chance to influence the other. Now, to move you to my side, to apply, I will rely on the vagueness condition: Look, this is so like those others, in shape, which you agree are nacknicks; so why should we stop just there, and not here? To move me, not to apply, you will rely on the discriminative condition: But, see here, we have to stop *somewhere,* or just any old thing will do; so why not stop there, which is a perfectly good place to do so? In the logic of the situation itself, there is nothing to settle matters. So, things get settled by further considerations. For example, if you are an architect, and I have no strong interest in conventional shape description, I may well yield to you, expecting like treatment from you in areas where my classificatory interests are the stronger. Of course, if you are a king and I am a peasant, then I may expect to do a good deal more yielding on matters generally. The discriminative vagueness of 'nacknick', as established in our conditions, allows these accommodations to take place with no one getting the idea that he is giving up any truth, or being hypocritical.

Even in one's own case, the matter is similar. If my decorator told me to use a nacknick, and I happen to have a putative borderline case free to hand, while most nacknicks would be quite expensive for me, I might rely on the vagueness condition to allow me to judge it a nacknick, even should I otherwise not be much inclined to do so. I want to follow my decorator's advice, and I also want to use what is free if possible, so as to keep my expenses down. By appealing to the vagueness condition, I can happily satisfy both of my desires.

Now, I do not mean to place much stock in this bare explanatory suggestion. It points up a virtue, though, in our account, and a corresponding problem with other ways of thinking about vague expressions. For people do differ as to how to handle many such behavioral borderline cases, and a given person often differs from himself over time. These do not appear to be matters of losing truth, where thoughts of self-deception should enter, or thoughts of losing one's faculties owing to social pressure. On the idea that 'nacknick' is consistent, and that it actually applies to a whole bunch of things, which are exactly the nacknicks, these bizarre thoughts move to take over. For, as we saw in Section 3, in every case, 'nacknick' either applies or else it does not, so that there are no logical borderline cases. Thus, on this more usual idea, in accommodating, someone will often give up truth (for falsity). But on our account, there are no such strange losses to be further accounted.

In a way, though, the main point for us now is to see how we have succeeded in *avoiding* the complex problem of explanation. We have done so by introducing 'nacknick', and by then formulating our Argument from Invented Expressions. For, just as with ordinary vague terms, with 'nacknick' also we have no good detailed *explanation of how* it might be useful to us even while it is inconsistent. But, we may *accept the idea that* 'nacknick' is both useful and inconsistent, and also that it is relevantly similar to 'cubical object' and to other typical vague expressions. So, even in the absence of a worked out explanation for them, we may accept the idea that our common vague expressions are useful even while they are inconsistent.

Of course, were I able to offer a good explanation of how they were useful, that would offer *more* support for our account of common vague discriminative terms. Similarly, were I able to offer a detailed explanation for 'nacknick', that would further my support for my thoughts about it. In each case, the better the explanation, the more the support we add. But, then, all of this is in the area of adding support to an account which, by other means, is already supported. On the other hand, should no good explanation be forthcoming for any of these terms, that would not, I suggest, detract much from the credibility of my account. For the problem of explanation might just be too difficult for anybody.

B. *The Problem of Scope and Comparison*

On my account, our language is inconsistent in a certain respect: it is inconsistent in (the fact that it has) its qualitative vague discriminative expressions, including 'being with a capacity for using language'.[22] Already we have found a fair number and variety of expressions to be of this sort. Our success suggests that we inquire as to which other terms can also be thus categorized. This is an inquiry into the problem of the *scope* of our account.

One of the first things we shall wish to examine, as regards the scope of our account, are those expressions that are the negatives of expressions we have already accounted. Thus, we look at such expressions as 'not a nacknick' and 'not a person'. While syntax thus often suffices to spot such terms, we may semantically define a negative of an expression *e* quite simply: *n* is a negative of *e* just in case, with respect to any entity, *n* applies to the entity if and only if *e* does not apply to it. Thus, 'person' is a negative of 'not a person' just as the latter is a negative of the former. We should inquire, then, whether a negative of a qualitative vague discriminative expression is also an expression of that sort. The issues here are, I think, exceptionally difficult and complex. Partly for this reason, I have not broached them in our previous discussions. For now, I think it will be enough to say this: If our negatives are also terms of our key category, that will mean a further source of contradictions and paradoxes.

For consider 'not a stone' and suppose it applies to a certain group of twenty atoms, or to something they constitute. Now, if our first condition governs this expression, we may keep adding suitable atoms, one at a time, and it will apply to the result in each case. But, if our second condition also governs it, we must reach an entity that does *not* satisfy 'not a stone', if not by *that* additive process then by *some* such procedure. But, then, as 'not a stone' does *not* apply to this entity, any *negative* of it *will* apply to it, including 'stone'. Thus, this entity, which by our vagueness condition is not a stone, also is a stone. Thus, 'not a stone' does not apply to our original complex of twenty atoms. So, any negative of 'not a stone' applies to that complex. Thus, as 'stone' is such a negative, those twenty atoms constitute a stone! But, then, our familiar arguments show, as well, that those few atoms do not compose a stone.[23]

What we say about our negative expressions, then, will determine whether or not such new sources of paradox and contradiction are upon us. But, even if we eventually say that these negatives are indeed of our typical vague variety, and so have these paradoxes upon us, that will do nothing to discredit seriously our account of them, or of any other terms. For the points we made about paradox before, in Section 8, apply in full generality. Thus, in particular, they will fully cover these present matters.

On a slightly more positive note, another thing we shall want to examine, in connection with the scope of our account, is the logic of vague discriminative terms that are not purely qualitative. For powerful sorites arguments are available to refute the existence of those entities that putatively satisfy 'bachelor', 'door', and many other terms, including arguments of a relevantly counterfactual form. To explain these arguments, we want to exhibit conditions that govern the key terms, according to which those terms are inconsistent. I believe that many proper names will find their logic exposed in this manner, as will various expressions that have been supposed interestingly similar to names. In Section 2, I made some brief suggestions for extending our account to cover discriminative expressions generally. But, we want to go far deeper into the matter.

While there is no real line separating them, we may conveniently move from discussing this problem of scope to examining the related problem of *comparison*. What we want to do here is show that the sort of source of inconsistency so far discussed, which has much to do with vagueness, is not an isolated phenomenon of our language, but is only one of several linguistic sources of inconsistency. As a possible example of another type of source, we may consider the putative expression 'expression that does not apply to itself'. It seems that there really cannot be any such expression, for if there is one, then it applies to itself if and only if it does not, which is absurd. This might be just a surprising case of reason cutting through illusory appearance. But, it may not stop there. For if this alleged expression is really not anything genuine, then, it seems, there will not really be any expression 'expression that applies to itself'. But, if not that, then not either 'expression that applies to something other than itself' nor, then, 'expression that applies to something'. But, if not this last, then it seems there is no real expression 'expression'. And, with this last gone, it seems we must conclude, in fact, that there are no expressions, and so no languages, at all. So, comparative matters merit further examination.[24]

Now, we should notice that the putative expression 'expression that does not apply to itself', supposing it does exist, might well be a vague discriminative expression. If so, then it will yield inconsistency from at least two sorts of source. And, if that is so, then so much the better for our present account.

C. The Problem of Replacement

What I regard as the most difficult problem posed by my account, but also the most important, is that of devising consistent expressions to replace the inconsistent ones that have been prevalent to date. Part of the problem is that it is unclear even in what sense or way the new terms will *replace* the old. But the most dizzying part is that the devising seems to require an indefinite number of choices for us to make, and while these choices look like extremely important ones, they must be entirely arbitrary. While these two parts may not exhaust this problem, it will be enough for us now, in an attempt to understand the problem's difficulty, to focus our discussion upon them exclusively.

In what sense or way is a newly devised term to *replace* an existing ordinary one, for example, to replace 'stone'? Normally, we should think of replacing one term by another where we think of two consistent terms involved. Thus, an old expression may apply to certain cases that we want to capture as well with a new term, but it may include other cases that we want newly to exclude. So, the new term will be defined accordingly. If we then give up the old term, and no other available expression comes near to applying and excluding along these lines, we shall naturally think of having replaced the old term by the new. But, in the present case, each old term is inconsistent, applying to no cases at all. So, what does any do that a new term may do with a difference?

A "pragmatic" answer seems the only one relevant. While our inconsistent terms are all logically on a par, different ones serve us differently. Roughly, this difference in service is due to different response repertoires associated with the different terms. Each term has, for any speaker at any time, associated with it a certain pattern of responses to different possible situations. While there is some variation here, there will be, even across many speakers over a substantial period of time, a considerable amount of agreement in response for a term. So, for each inconsistent term, we might devise a consistent one that is to have a rather similar response repertoire. Still, as conflicting responses each has no claim to be (more) in accord with the old term itself, a ruling in favor of some, and against others, will have no basis in the meaning of the common term. But someone's repertoire will suffer should any decision be made. Thus, it is not easy to tell what can possibly count as a successful outcome for such a project.

Let us pretend that, for many vague expressions, this difficulty has been resolved. We are now to replace our term 'person'. For this particular task, we should reflect back on situations we have imaginatively encountered already. For example, when we remove peripheral neurons, one at a time, from an alleged person, there really seems nothing to choose, despite our generous reference to a "way most conducive to there still being a person." Thus, at (virtually) any point, the removal of (almost) any particular neuron does not leave an entity that is, in any acceptable sense, any *less of a person* than would be left instead with the removal of (almost) any other. With nothing for a guide, how are "we" to choose an expression that, unlike 'person', will select certain removals as preferable to others.

To highlight the problem, consider two rather different sequences of removal, each disposing of the same number of neurons, millions of them, where the net result, in terms of eventually supported capacities, is quite dissimilar. Now, in certain cases of this sort, our associated response repertoire may indicate one resulting entity to be preferred as a person over the other. For example, the capacities supported at the end of one sequence may be much greater as regards feelings, while the main advantage resulting from another sequence may lie in the less personal area of physical dexterity. But, in many other such cases, while the net results from the sequences are apparently different in important ways, there seems nothing to choose between them as far as being a person is concerned: suppose one entity is more intelligent and is better able to experience pleasure, while the other is more sympathetic and is more sensitive to varieties of pain. Now, what we are to do, in devising a new term, is to make a choice anyway for even such arbitrary cases, which choice will then be reflected in how the term itself "decides things."

These dizzying matters get far more difficult when the underlying circle of our thought is exposed and appreciated. For, we want our key terms, like 'person', to reflect certain interests, which will favor those entities included under the term over those not so included. But whose interests will these be? They cannot be the interests of any people, since there are not any such things. But, even supposing any of our descriptions to be coherent, should the interests of entities less brilliant than Einstein be accorded in devising a most suitable replacement for 'person'? Should any weight be given to having eyes whose color lies within a certain precise range (of bright blue)? Should entities with a very low degree of musical aptitude be excluded altogether? We have firm ideas and strong feelings on these matters, but who are we to have feelings and ideas that matter? There appears to be an impossible bootstrap operation required of any attempt at replacement to achieve any priority or even significance. Indeed, I cannot see how there could be, in any area of intellectual endeavor, a harder problem than this one.[25]

Notes

1. In formulating these conditions, I have been helped by correspondence with John Tienson.

2. I use the plural term 'Expressions' in naming this Argument because, while I, in fact, chose to begin with 'nacknick', and with certain matters of shape, I could have begun as well with other matters and invented expressions.

3. My discussion of this matter emerged from conversation with Samuel Wheeler.

4. I am indebted to several people for help in formulating these complex statements, especially to Terence Leichti. But there have been so many problems with previous versions that I despair that some must still remain. I trust, however, that the reader will not judge my philosophy primarily in terms of formulational details.

5. For an extended discussion of the semantics of 'flat', and of other such *absolute terms*, see chapter II of my book *Ignorance* (Oxford, 1975).

6. For an alternative interpretation of why sorites arguments are sound, see two papers by Samuel Wheeler: "Reference and Vagueness," *Synthese*, Vol. 30, No. 3/4 (April/May, 1975) and "On That Which Is Not," *Synthese* (forthcoming).

7. In the case of (almost) all the sorites arguments presented in this paper, in regards to matters of formulation, I am indebted to Terence Leichti.

8. On the need for such a "providing" clause, I am indebted to James Van Cleve.

9. In John Tienson, "Can Things of Different Natural Kinds Be Exactly Alike?", *Analysis* 37 (1977):190-97.

10. This is suggested by the main point of Tienson's paper, "Can Things of Different Natural Kinds Be Exactly Alike?"

11. Perhaps the most prominent recent exponent of this idea of incompleteness, or of an idea much like it, is Michael Dummett in his unfortunately named "Wang's Paradox," *Synthese* 30 (1975), especially as on pages 309-12.

12. As I hope is indicated by the language, this general proposition is not intended to concern future situations. As regards the future, I think there are genuine problems, as made famous by Aristotle and his argument of the sea battle.

13. Various remarks in the section just ended are in response to conversations with Terence Leichti and with David Lewis.

14. This argument, adapted, shows that there is no genuine dyadic relation of *similarity*. For we can now show that if there is such a relation, then it must be transitive. But, also, quite clearly, if there is such a relation, then it is not transitive. Thus, despite intellectual appearances to the contrary, there is no real similarity relation. (The question of *respects*, and of *degrees*, of similarity changes nothing here.) This point first emerged for me in discussion with Vincent Tomas.

15. This objection, or one much like it, was offered to me in conversation by Terence Leichti and also by David Lewis. What I go on to say about the matter is indebted to these helpful conversations.

16. For impressing upon me the importance of counterfactual reasoning in relation to sorites arguments, I am indebted to discussion with David Lewis.

17. See three recent papers of mine: "I Do Not Exist," in *Epistemology in Perspective*, ed. Graham Macdonald (London, forthcoming), which is the festschrift for Professor Sir A. J. Ayer; "There Are No Ordinary Things," *Synthese*, forthcoming: "Skepticism and Nihilism," *Nous*, forthcoming.

18. See the three papers cited in the just previous note.

19. For discussion regarding an incomparability condition for 'person', I am indebted to James Van Cleve.

20. The points just made were suggested to me by an unpublished paper of John Tienson's, "An Argument Concerning Quantification and Propositional Attitudes." I make some related points in *Ignorance*.

21. This objection, or one much like it, was offered in conversation by David Lewis.

22. Saying that a language is inconsistent is admittedly somewhat unnatural. But if one specifies appropriate respects in which it might be inconsistent, that unnaturalness will be harmless.

23. If 'not a stone' is indeed a vague discriminative expression, the foregoing argument will go against a good deal of what I said in Section 4 of "There Are No Ordinary Things." But most of what I said there is directed against certain arguments from common sense and, as such, still will stand.

24. The paradox just sketched derives from the Grelling, which in turn derives from the Liar. The Liar is attributed by scholars to the great Megarian thinker Eubulides, who is also credited with inventing the sorites, as well as other important arguments. For some recent research on Eubulides, see Jon Moline, "Aristotle, Eubulides and the Sorites," *Mind* 78 (1969): 343-407. To my mind, it is puzzling how much this great philosopher has been neglected.

25. In writing this paper, I have been fortunate in having been helped by many people, too many to thank each individually. However, I should like to express thanks now to three who were especially helpful: Terence Leichti, David Lewis, and Samuel Wheeler.

On the Logic of Purpose

RODERICK CHISHOLM

1. I will first make certain general points about intentional contexts, referring in particular to believing and to purposive or intentional activity. Then I will try to sketch the sense in which the concept of purposive or intentional activity is basic to the philosophical theory of action.

The points about intentional contexts are worth making, I think, for philosophers are very often led astray by failure to take account of them. Thus the fact that people do believe things, think about things, and have certain goals or purposes has its ontological implications. It means that we stand in certain relations to states of affairs or propositions and also that we stand in certain relations to attributes or properties. But there is a very important sense, which I will try to make clear, in which these *ontological objects* of our intentional attitudes may yet be such as not to enter into the *contents* of these attitudes. And there is a sense in which the objects that do seem to be a part of the *contents* of these attitudes may yet not be the *ontological objects* of these attitudes. But philosophers often confuse object with content and they often confuse content with object.

In discussing these points, I will consider the following attitudes in order: belief *de dicto*; belief *de re*; purposive activity, or endeavor, *de dicto*; and purposive activity, or endeavor, *de re*. Then I will try to develop further the concept of endeavor.

2. So that I may make the points I have in mind with as little circumlocution as possible, I propose we restrict the locution

S believes that *p*

(where '*p*' may be replaced by any English sentence) to what we may call its ordinary *de dicto* sense.

This will mean, for one thing, that we cannot existentially generalize over any term within the sentence in the place of '*p*'. Thus if our *de dicto* belief sentence is

Jones believes that the tallest man is wise

we cannot take it to entail

There is an x such that Jones believes that x is wise.

Nor can we replace any term within the sentence occupying the place of 'p' by any other term having the same extension. Hence, even if we know both that (1) the tallest man is the fastest runner and (2) Jones believes that the tallest man is wise, we cannot, on the basis of this information, draw the inference to

Jones believes that the fastest runner is wise.

Another way of characterizing this *de dicto* use of "Jones believes that the tallest man is wise" is to say this: If we know that the sentence is true, in this *de dicto* use, then we may say of Jones that, if he is asked "Is the tallest man wise?", if he understands the question, and if he intends to reply honestly and correctly, then he will endeavor to reply in the affirmative.

In suggesting that we restrict the locution "S believes that p" to this *de dicto* sense, I am *not* suggesting that the locution is, in fact, so restricted in ordinary English. (Sometimes it would seem to be so restricted but at other times it is not.)

If we are sensitive to the ontological implications of belief, the ontological implications of the fact that people believe things, we will realize that

(1)   Jones believes that the tallest man is wise

implies that

(2)   There is something that Jones believes.

If we do not see this at once, perhaps it will help us if we consider such facts as the following. If we know, not only that (1) is true, but also that Smith believes that the tallest man is wise, then we may infer that there is something that both Jones and Smith believe. We may obviously infer (2) from this last fact; but the truth of (2) is hardly dependent upon the fact that Smith happens to believe the same thing Jones does.

Given, then, that (1) does imply (2), it is useful for philosophical purposes to make (1) more explicit. The logical structure of (1) is somewhat more adequately exposed if we rewrite it as

(3)   Jones accepts the proposition that the tallest man is wise.

Statement (3) expresses a straightforward dyadic relation between Jones and a certain proposition, enabling us to infer "There exists an x and a y such that x accepts y."

Thus our sentence (3) is an instance of this general schema:

S accepts the proposition that p.

I propose we take this locution as the paradigmatic expression of belief *de dicto* and introduce the more ordinary locution, instanced by (1), as an abbreviation. Thus we will have

D1   S believes that p = Df S accepts the proposition that p.

The definition is schematic; we may replace 'p' by any English sentence.

Referring now to our general schema, 'S accepts the proposition that p, I will say that the part after the word 'accepts' (namely, 'the proposition that p') *designates the ontological object* of the belief, and that the part after the word 'that' (namely, the sentence occupying the place of 'p') *express the content* of the belief. Instead of thus using the word 'content', we could also say that the part after the word 'that' tells us *what* it is that the man believes.

To understand the point of the expression '*what* it is that the man believes', let us suppose that the following statement is true:

(4)   The proposition that the tallest man is wise is identical with the proposition that is expressed on the top of page 17 of B.

(We may imagine that 'B' is a definite description of a certain book.) Statement (4) illustrates different ways of designating one and the same proposition. The first description—'the proposition that the tallest man is wise'—could be said to give us the *essence* of the proposition in question: for that proposition, and only that proposition, is such that it *necessarily* has whatever property is implied by saying that it is the proposition that the tallest man is wise. But the second description in statement (4)—'the proposition that is expressed on the top of page 17 of B'—does not, in the same sense, tell us *what* the proposition in question is. It does pick out the proposition from among all other objects, but it does so only by citing certain accidental features of that proposition, certain things that happen to be true of it in the world but that are not true of it in every possible world.

Let us say that the first expression ('the proposition that the tallest man is wise') gives us an *essential description* of a certain proposition and that, given our assumption that (4) is true, the second expression ('the proposition expressed on the top of page 17 of B') gives us an *accidental description* of that same proposition.

The distinction is important for it enables us to put clearly what we might put somewhat more obscurely as follows: "A proposition may be the *object* of a man's belief even though the man does not thereby believe anything about that proposition. And a man may believe something *about* a certain proposition even though that proposition is not the *object* of his belief."

To put this more clearly, I will attempt to illustrate and describe two fallacies that one readily commits when one considers philosophical questions about believing.

I will call the first fallacy "the fallacy of inferring the content of belief from an accidental description of the object of belief." (An alternative label, perhaps somewhat less misleading, would be: "the fallacy of taking an accidental description of the content of belief.") To illustrate the fallacy, let us continue to suppose that (1), (2), (3), and (4) are true. From (3) and (4) we may deduce

(5)   Jones accepts the proposition that is expressed on the top of page 17 of B.

We commit "the fallacy of inferring the content of belief from an accidental description of the object of belief," if we take (4) and (5) to imply

> (6)   Jones believes that the proposition that is expressed on the top of page 17 of *B* is true.

If one understands our undefined expression '*x* accepts *y*' in the sense that is here intended, then one can readily imagine conditions in which (1) and (4) and therefore also (5) are true and in which (6) is false. Suppose, for example, that (1), (4), and (5) are true and that Jones does not have the concepts requisite for understanding what is meant by the English sentence "the proposition expressed on the top of page 17 of *B* is true"; possibly he lacks the concept of *page*, or of *truth*, or of a *proposition*. In such a situation (6) will be false.

How, then, shall we characterize "the fallacy of inferring the content of belief from an accidental description of the object of belief"? One commits this fallacy if one argues in the following way:

The premises of the argument tell us that there is a certain proposition *x* that is the ontological object of a man's belief and they characterize *x* by means of an accidental definite description but not by means of an essential definite description. And the conclusion of the argument contains an essential description of the object of belief and thus tells us *what* the proposition is that the man believes.

(And so, as we have noted, to describe the fallacy we do not really need to introduce the term 'the content of the man's belief'. This is just as well, for we can readily imagine a philosopher reacting this way: "You say the man's belief has an ontological object and that it *also* has a content? What does he believe, then—the object, or the content, or something made up of both?")

I have said that there is also a second fallacy that one readily commits when one considers philosophical questions about believing. This fallacy is, in a certain sense, the converse of "the fallacy of inferring the content of belief from an accidental description of the object of belief." I shall call it "the fallacy of inferring the object of belief from a partial description of the content of belief." (An alternative label would be: "the fallacy of inferring the object of belief from a partial description of *what* is believed.")

To illustrate "the fallacy of inferring the object of belief from a partial description of the content of belief," we have only to revise the assumption of our former example. For one commits this fallacy if one takes (6) and (4) to imply (1). Let us imagine, then, that (6) and (4) are true. As before, the proposition on the top of page 17 *B* is the proposition that the tallest man is wise. And now we picture a situation in which (6) is ture—a situation in which Jones can be said to believe, *de dicto*, that the proposition on the top of page 17 of *B* is true. Perhaps Jones has been persuaded that *B* is composed of holy scriptures or that it is the work of some other completely reliable authority, and he has been persuaded further that there is one and only one sentence on the top of page 17 and that this sentence expresses a proposition. But Jones has not seen the book and does not know *what* this proposition is; hence he has no idea that (4) is true. In this case (6) will be true; Jones will believe that the proposition expressed on page 17 of *B* is true. But this situation is quite compatible with the negation of (1); that is to say, it is quite compatible with saying that Jones does not believe that the tallest man is wise. Perhaps Jones does not think that there *is* a tallest man, or perhaps he thinks that being tall is incompatible with being wise.

How, then, will we characterize "the fallacy of inferring the object of belief from a partial description of the content of belief"? I suggest that one commits this fallacy if one argues in the following way:

The premise of the argument tells us *what* it is that a man believes and a proper part of this characterization is a reference to a certain proposition. But the premise does not tell us that *x* is *what* the man believes. (That is to say, the premise could be put in this form: "S accepts the proposition that *p*." In the sentence occupying the place of '*p*' there occurs an accidental description of a proposition *x*, but *x* is not implied by the proposition designated by the sentence in the place of '*p*'.) And the conclusion of the argument tells us that the man accepts *x*.

3. I will now make analogous points about *de re* belief.

If we remain sensitive to the ontological implications of belief, we will realize that

(1.1)   The tallest man is believed by Jones to be wise

implies

(2.1)   There is something that Jones attributes to the tallest man.

(In the place of 'attributes to the tallest man', we might say 'believes of the tallest man'.) If one does not see immediately that (1.1) implies (2.1), one has only to note that, if (2.1) is true, and if the tallest man is also believed by Smith to be wise, then we could say that there is something that both Jones and Smith attribute to the tallest man. The logical structure of (1.1), then, is somewhat more adequately expressed if we rewrite it as

(3.1)   Jones attributes the property of being wise to the tallest man.

Our sentence is thus an instance of this general schema

S attributes to *x* the property of being *F*

where the letter '*F*' is replaceable by any predicate-expression (for example, 'wise' or 'such that he is wise' or 'such that he is wise and all men are mortal').

I propose we take this locution as the paradigmatic expression of belief *de re* and introduce the more ordinary locution, instanced by (1.1), as an abbreviation. Thus we will have

   D2   *x* is believed by S to be *F* = Df S attributes the property of being
          F to *x*.

Let us say, of any sentence fulfilling the schema 'S attributes the property of being *F* to *x*', that the expression in the place of 'the property of being *F*' designates the *property attributed*. (Presumably we should say that the *object* of any such *de re* belief is the thing designated by the expression in the place of '*x*'.) Thus, in the case of (3.1), the *property attributed* is the property of being wise (and the *object* to which it is attributed is the tallest man). And let us say that the predicative expression in the place of '*F*' expresses the *content of the property attributed*. Thus, in (3.1), the word 'wise' expresses the content of the property attributed.

We will now distinguish two fallacies and illustrate them by supposing that the following is true:

(4.1)   The property most frequently attributed to Solomon is the property of being wise.

Given our use of 'attributes' and D2 above, we may note that (1.1) and (4.1) together imply

(5.1)   The property most frequently attributed to Solomon is attributed by Jones to the tallest man.

I will call the first fallacy "the fallacy of inferring the content of the property attributed from an accidental description of the property attributed." One commits this fallacy if one supposes that (4.1) and (5.1) together imply

(6.1)   The tallest man is such that Jones believes that he has the property most frequently attributed to Solomon.

Suppose that (1.1) and (4.1) and therefore also (5.1) are true, but that Jones does not have the concepts requisite for understanding what is meant by 'the property most attributed to Solomon'; perhaps he does not know what attribution is or he does not know what a property is. Then (6.1) will be false.

In thus committing "the fallacy of inferring the content of the property attributed from an accidental description of the property attributed," one argues in the following way. The premises of the argument tell us that there is a certain property *x* which a man attributes to something, but they characterize *x* by means of an accidental definite description and not by means of an essential definite description. And the conclusion of the argument contains an essential description of the property *x* and thus tells us *what* the property is that the man has attributed. (The point of 'accidental description' will be clear if we look back to (4.1). 'The property most frequently attributed to Solomon' is an accidental description of a certain property; it does not tell us *what* the property is. But 'the property of being wise' is nonaccidental; it *does* tell us *what* the property in question is.)

I will call the second fallacy "the fallacy of inferring the property attributed from a partial description of its content." One commits this fallacy if one takes (6.1) and (4.1) to imply (1.1). Let us imagine that (6.1) and (4.1) are true. Jones mistakenly thinks that the property most frequently attributed to Solomon is that of being honest; the tallest man is thought by Jones to be honest; and, reflecting on these two facts, Jones concludes, with respect to the tallest man, that he has the property most frequently attributed to Solomon. But these assumptions are quite consistent with our supposing also that the tallest man is thought by Jones to be stupid and not to be wise at all.

In thus committing "the fallacy of inferring the property attributed from a partial description of its content," one argues in the following way. The premise tells us *what* property a man has attributed and thus gives us the content of that property. In describing this property, the premise makes use of an accidental description of a certain *other* property x. And the conclusion tells us that x is the property that the man has attributed.

4. The following summary may throw light on what has been said about the two ways of believing. The letters 'F' and 'G' occupy the places of predicative expressions and 'the F' is short for 'the thing which is F'.

(a) S believes that the F is G
(b) The F is believed by S to be G
(c) S believes that the proposition that the F is G is true
(d) The proposition that F is G is believed by S to be true
(e) The proposition that the F is G is accepted by S
(f) S believes that the F has the property of being G
(g) The F is believed by S to be such that it has the property of being G
(h) S attributes the property of being G to the F

These eight locutions are easily confused with each other and such confusion sometimes infects what has been written about the philosophy of belief. But the foregoing considerations should help us to distinguish them.

Let us ask, with respect to each of these locutions, which ones of the others it entails. (I here use 'entail' in such a way that a proposition p may be said to *entail* a proposition q, if and only if, p is necessarily such that, whoever accepts it, accepts q.)

If 'accepts' and 'attributes' are restricted in the ways in which I have proposed, and if definitions D1 and D2 are accepted, then we may assert that the following entailment relations hold:

a entails e
b entails h
c entails a, d, and e
e entails a
f entails a and e
g entails b and h
h entails b

But no additional entailment relations hold between any two of these eight locutions.

5. I now make analogous points, somewhat more briefly, about purpose—or, more exactly, about that concept which I believe to be fundamental to and characteristic of the theory of purpose and hence also of the theory of action. This concept may

be expressed in English by means of the locution 'acting with a certain intention'. The concept is, in essential respects, like that of believing. It is intentional. It has a *de dicto*, or propositional, interpretation and also a *de re* interpretation. And it is subject to fallacies analogous to those we have distinguished in the case of believing. But unlike believing, it is also essentially *causal*.

We may begin, then, with what is expressed by the locution

S acts with the intention of bringing it about that *p*

(where "*p*" may be expressed by any English sentence). In ordinary English this locution may have both a *de dicto* and a *de re* interpretation. But in what follows, let us restrict the locution to a *de dicto* interpretation and then find another way of expressing *de re* propositions about intention and purposive activity.

The *de dicto* interpretation of the above locution, then, may be characterized, *mutatis mutandis*, in the way in which we characterized the *de dicto* interpretation of 'S believes that *p*'.

If we know that

(1.2)   Jones acts with the intention of bringing it about that the Vice President is elected President

then we may infer

(2.2)   There is something that Jones is endeavoring to bring about.

(If the word 'endeavor' suggests an *effort* not suggested by (1.2), then (2.2) might be reworded as: "There is something which is such that Jones is acting with the intention of bringing it about." But the briefer locution is somewhat more convenient.) We may make the logical structure of (1.2) somewhat more explicit by reformulating it as

(3.2)   Jones undertakes to bring about that state of affairs which is its obtaining (being the case) that the Vice President is elected President.

In the general schema

S undertakes to bring about that state of affairs which is its obtaining that *p*

we may say that that part of the expression that follows the verb 'bring about' expresses the *ontological object* of the endeavor and that the sentence occupying the place of '*p*' expresses the *content* of the endeavor (or the content of the object of endeavor).

We will take our general schema as undefined and introduce our original 'acts with the intention' expression as a reformulation:

D3   S acts with the intention of bring it about that *p* = Df S undertakes to bring about that state of affairs which is its obtaining that *p*

The analogues of the fallacies we discussed in connection with belief *de dicto* may now be illustrated by reference to the following:

(4.2)   That state of affairs which had long been Agnew's favorite is that state of affairs which is its obtaining that the Vice President is elected President.

(5.2)   That state of affairs which had long been Agnew's favorite is one that Jones undertakes to bring about.

(6.2)   Jones acts with the intention of bringing it about that that state of affairs which had long been Agnew's favorite obtains.

Given D3 and our use of 'undertakes' in the undefined schema, we may note that (1.2) and (4.2) together entail (5.2).

We may now say that "the fallacy of inferring the content of endeavor from an accidental description of the object of endeavor" is illustrated by the inference, from (1.2) and (4.2), to (6.2). The fallacy, then, is exhibited by an argument of this form: the premises tell us that a certain proposition or state of affairs *x* is the ontological object of a man's endeavor and then characterize *x* by means of an accidental definite description but not by means of an essential definite description. And the conclusion of the argument contains an essential description of the object of endeavor and thus tells us *what* it is that the man is endeavoring to bring about.

"The fallacy of inferring the object of endeavor from a partial description of the content of endeavor" is illustrated by the inference, from (6.2) and (4.2), to (1.2). The fallacy is exhibited by an argument of this sort. The premise tells us *what* it is that a man is endeavoring to bring about and a proper part of this characterization is a reference to a certain state of affairs *x*, but the premise does not tell us that *x* is *what* the man is endeavoring to bring about. (The premise could be put in the form 'S endeavors to bring about that state of affairs which is *p*'. In the sentence occupying the place of '*p*' there occurs an accidental description of the state of affairs *x*, but *x* is not implied by the state of affairs designated by the sentence in the place of '*p*.') And the conclusion of the argument tells us that the man is endeavoring to bring about *x*.

6. Analogous considerations hold of *de re* purposive activity.

If we know that

(1.3)   The Vice President is such that Ford acts with the intention of bringing it about that he is elected President

we may infer

(2.3)   There is a property such that Ford acts with the intention of causing the Vice President to have that property.

To make the logical structure of (1.3) more explicit, we may reword it as

(3.3)   The property of being elected President is one such that Ford undertakes to cause the Vice President to have it.

Our sentence is thus an instance of the general schema

The property of being F is such that S undertakes to cause x to have it

where 'F' is replaceable by any predicate expression. We will take this locution as undefined and introduce *de re* locution of (1.3) as a reformulation:

D4 x is such that S acts with the intention of bringing it about that it
       is F = Df The property of being F is one such that S undertakes to
       cause x to have it.

The analogues of our two fallacies may be illustrated by reference to the following:

(4.3)   The property of being elected President is the property Senator
         Jackson wants most to have.

(5.3)   The property that Senator Jackson wants most to have is one
         such that Ford undertakes to cause the Vice President to have it.

(6.3)   The Vice President is such that Ford acts with the intention of
         bringing it about that he has the property Senator Jackson wants
         most to have.

Given our use of 'undertakes' and D4, we may say that (1.3) and (4.3) together imply (5.3). But if we think that (1.3) and (4.3) also imply (6.3), we commit "the fallacy of inferring the content of the property endeavored from an accidental description of the property endeavored." And if we think that (6.3) and (4.3) together imply (1.3), we commit "the fallacy of inferring the property endeavored from a partial description of its content."

In committing "the fallacy of inferring the content of the property endeavored from an accidental description of the property endeavored," one argues as follows. The premises of the argument tell us that there is a certain property x which is such that someone undertakes to cause a certain thing to have it. But the premises characterize x by means of an accidental definite description and not by means of an essential definite description. And the conclusion of the argument contains an essential description of the property x and thus tells us *what* the property is that the man undertakes to cause the thing to have.

And in committing "the fallacy of inferring the property endeavored from an accidental description of its content," one argues as follows. The premise tells us *what* property a man is undertaking to cause a thing to have and thus gives us the content of that property. In describing this property, the premise makes use of an accidental description of a certain *other* property x. And the conclusion tells us that x is the property that the man is undertaking to cause the thing to have.

7. We introduced a table earlier to throw light on what had been said about the ways of believing. We now introduce a corresponding table for endeavor. We compare, then, eight schemata:

(a)   S acts with the intention of bringing it about that F is G.

(b)   The F is such that S acts with the intention of bringing it about that it is G.

(c)   S acts with the intention of bringing it about that that state of affairs, which is its obtaining that the F is G, obtains.

(d)   The state of affairs which is its obtaining that the F is G is one such that S acts with the intention of bringing it about that it obtains.

(e)   The state of affairs which is its obtaining that the F is G is undertaken by S.

(f)   S acts with the intention of bringing it about that the F has the property of being G.

(g)   The property of being G is one such that S undertakes to cause the F to have it.

These locutions, like the eight we singled out in the case of belief, are readily confused with each other. But it is essential to the philosophical theory of purpose to see what the relations are that hold among them.

If 'undertakes' is interpreted in the way I have proposed, and if we make use of definitions D3 and D1, then we may say, as before, that the following entailment relations hold:

a entails e
b entails h
c entails a, d, and e
e entails a
f entails a and e
g entails b and h
h entails b

And no further entailment relations hold between any two of these eight locutions.

The locutions for endeavor, then, are analogous to those we distinguished in the case of belief.

8. Let us now consider in more detail the concept of *agency*.

I have suggested that the undefined *de dicto* and *de re* concepts, made use of in D3 and D4, are fundamental to the theory of agency. In what follows I will restrict myself to the *de dicto* concept ('S undertakes to bring about that state of affairs which is its obtaining that p' or, more briefly, 'S undertakes p'), but much of what I will have to say may also be carried over into analysis of purposive activity *de re*.

I have said that intention or purposive activity, unlike believing, is essentially causal. Let us import into our analysis, then, the concept of *causal contribution*, where this is thought of as pertaining to a relation that holds between events or states of affairs. For this concept of event causation, along with our concept of undertaking, gives us most of what we need for the theory of agency.

The concept of event causation may be expressed in the locution 'x contributes causally to y' — or, if one prefers, 'the occurrence of x contributes causally to the occurrence of y'. (The latter locution has the advantage of enabling us to say 'the occurrence of x at t' contributes causally to the occurrence of y at t'''; but for simplicity we will ignore such temporal references in much of what follows.)

In terms of event causation, so considered, and our undefined concept of undertaking, we may now define agent causation.

We will say first that, if a man's undertakings contribute causally to something, then he *does* something which contributes causally to that something:

D5   S does something at t that contributes causally to x = Df   There is a y such that S's undertaking y at t contributes causally to x.

We will also say that, if a man thus does something that contributes to x, then *he* contributes causally to x. And we will say further that a man contributes causally to his own undertakings (even though he may not be said, in the sense of D5, to do anything that contributes causally to his undertakings). And so we define agent causation as follows:

D6   S contributes causally at t to p = Df   Either (a) S does something at t that contributes causally to p, or (b) there is a q such that S undertakes q at t and S-undertaking-q is p, or (c) there is an r such that S does something at t that contributes causally to r, and p is that state of affairs which is S doing something that contributes causally to r.

Just as we have introduced 'S undertakes x' as short for 'S undertakes to bring about x', let us introduce 'S brings about x' (and 'S makes x happen') as short for the longer and more cautious 'S contributes causally to the occurrence of x'. Similarly, the schema 'S undertakes p' will be short for 'S undertakes to bring about that state of affairs which is its occurring that p'; and 'S brings about p' will be short for 'S contributes causally to that state of affairs which is its occurring that p'.

We may now abbreviate certain theorems about agency. These theorems are consequences of: the ontology of events and states of affairs we have presupposed; and the interpretation we have given to the undefined concept of undertaking.

T1   If S contributes causally to p, then p.

T2   If S does something that contributes causally to p, then S contributes causally to his doing something that contributes causally to p.

T3   If S contributes causally to p, there exists a q such that S undertakes q.

T4   If S undertakes p, then S contributes causally to S undertaking p.

But the following principles, it should be noted, are *not* consequences of what we have said:

If S undertakes p, then p.

If S brings about p, then S undertakes p.

If S undertakes p, then S undertakes S's undertaking p.

9. Finally, let us see how certain other concepts, central to the theory of agency may be explicated in the terms that we have introduced.[1]

The five definitions that follow pertain to the distinction between means and ends and, generally, to the things we may say using the expression 'for the purpose of'. We first introduce the latter expression:

> D7   S undertakes x and does so for the purpose of bringing about y =
> Df S undertakes to bring about that state of affairs which is:
> (i) x and (ii) his-undertaking-x contributing causally to y.

Suppose a man is trying to blow up the palace and his purpose in so doing is to bring about the death of the King. He has two intentional objects, one of them subordinate to the other. In such a case he is undertaking to blow up the palace and doing so (that is, undertaking this) *for the purpose of* bringing about the death of the King. To say that he does this is not to say that he succeeds — either in blowing up the palace or in bringing about the death of the King.

An alternative concept would be obtained if the definiens of D7 were revised to read:

> S undertakes to bring about that state of affairs which is: (i) x and
> (ii) x contributing causally to y.

The expression we defined in D7 — 'S undertakes x and does so for the purpose of bringing about y' is intentional with respect to both variables; it does not imply that either of the states of affairs, x or y, obtains. But the following expression is intentional only with respect to the second variable:

> D8   S contributes causally to x for the purpose of bringing about y =
> Df There is a z such that: (1) S undertakes z for the purpose of
> bringing about that state of affairs which is (i) z and (ii) his-
> undertaking-z contributing causally to y; and (2) his undertaking
> z contributes causally to x.

If the agent of our example succeeded in blowing up the palace, we may say he did so for the purpose of bringing about the death of the King. Or if he did not succeed in either of these ends, but blew himself up instead, we may say he contributed causally to his own death and did so for the purpose of blowing up the palace and also for the purpose of bringing about the death of the King.

As in the case of D7, we may contrast the concept here defined with what we would have if we replaced '(i) z and (ii) his-undertaking-z contributing causally to y' by

> (i) z and (ii) z contributing causally to y.

The state of affairs referred to by the 'x' in the expression defined by D8, unlike that referred to by the 'x' in D7, need not be one that the agent undertakes.

We next suggest how to explicate such terms as 'means' and 'ends'. Thus, if a man undertakes x and does so for the purpose of bringing about y (D7), we may say that he undertakes x *as a means* to y.

> D9 x is for S at t a *means* to y = Df S undertakes x at t and does so for the purpose of bringing about y.

Some things are undertaken *merely as means*. Will we say that the expression 'x is for S a mere means to something else' may be defined in this way: "There is a y such that x is for S a means to y"? This is not quite right, for it may be that, of the various possible means to y, S has picked out x as being one that is worth pursuing on its own account. Of the various ways of preserving his health, a man may choose walking on the ground that it is worth doing for its own sake, whereas taking an unpleasant medicine would not be worth doing for its own sake. Where the means is thus something that is also chosen for its own sake, the agent undertakes a certain causal chain, not only in order that the final member of that chain be realized, but *also* in order that one of the earlier members be realized. Let us say, then:

> D10 x is for S a *mere means* to something else = Df (i) There is a y such that x is for S a means to y and (ii) for every z, if x is for S a means to z, then it is false that S undertakes z for the purpose of bringing about x.

The ultimate goal or end of a man's activity at any time, then, is something that he undertakes but not as a mere means.

> D11 x is an *ultimate end* for S = Df (i) S undertakes x and (ii) it is false that x is for S a mere means to something else.

Thus, if walking is undertaken, not only as a means to health but as an end in itself, then the man undertakes a certain chain of events, not only in order that he may be healthy, but also in order that he may walk.

In considering the morality of intention, we may wish to distinguish between the preliminary steps that a man makes toward a certain goal (the assassin loads his gun) from what he takes to be the final step (he pulls the trigger). Thus, we may have

> D12 S intends x as a *preliminary step* toward bringing about y = Df S undertakes x and does so for the purpose of bringing it about that someone brings about y.

In the definiens of D12, we appeal to the concepts defined in D5 and D8. A man who is thus taking preliminary steps is acting with the intention of contributing causally to his own subsequent endeavors.

When the agent undertakes what he takes to be the final step, then we may say that he has *made an attempt*:

> D13 S *makes an attempt* to bring about x = Df S undertakes x and and S does not undertake anything as a preliminary step toward bringing about x.

When the assassin buys his gun or when he loads it, he has not yet made an attempt to kill his victim; but, in the normal case, he does make such an attempt when he pulls the trigger.

It is also useful to single out those endeavors that are completely successful — where everything goes as planned and where the goal is not achieved merely by fluke or despite the agent's endeavors.

> D14 S is *completely successful* in his endeavor at t to bring about x =
> Df (i) makes an attempt at t to bring about x and (ii) everything
> he then undertakes for the purpose of bringing about x
> contributes causally to x.

Let us note, finally, how one's *basic actions* would be characterized within our present scheme of concepts. These actions can be defined, in a straightforward way, as those things we bring about without undertaking any *other* things for the purpose of bringing them about. Or, more accurately

> D15 S brings about x as a *basic act* at t = Df (i) S undertaking x
> contributes causally at t to x and (ii) there is no y such that S
> undertakes y at t for the purpose of bringing about x.

We should distinguish the concept of basic act from the following concept of direct causation:

> D16 S brings about x *directly* at t = Df (i) S contributes causally at t
> to the occurrence of x and (ii) there is no y such that (a) S
> contributes causally at t to y and (b) y contribures causally to x.

If a man brings about anything at all, then, presumably, he brings about some things as *basic acts* and he also brings about some things *directly*. But we must distinguish the things he brings about as basic acts and the things he brings about directly. Thus the man's own undertakings will be things he brings about directly. But his undertakings are not basic acts, for basic acts are undertaken and undertakings are not. The mark of a basic act is that, although it is undertaken, nothing is undertaken as a *means* to bringing it about. And the mark of what one brings about directly is that, although it is brought about, it is not brought about by some *other* thing the agent brings about.[2]

Notes

1. I have discussed some of these concepts in greater detail in a number of earlier writings: "On the Logic of Intentional Action," in *Agent, Action, and Reason*, ed. Robert Binkley (Toronto, 1971), pp. 36-39; and "The Structure of Intention," *Journal of Philosophy* 67 (1970): 633-47.

2. A more detailed defense of this system of concepts may be found in my Carus Lectures, *Person and Object: A Metaphysical Study* (La Salle, 1977).

Substance: The Constitution of Reality

P. M. S. HACKER

1. INTRODUCTION

Substances, understood as material particulars, are the constituents of the world, the furniture of reality. Substance, in a different use of the term, is the stuff of which concrete individual things consist. Substances are made of, constituted of, some stuff or other, some substance or kinds of substance. It is in this sense of the term that we talk of chemical substances, or that we say of a thing that it is coated with a sticky substance. The interplay between the conceptual structures that are concerned with things and those that are concerned with the matter of which they are made is complex, subtle, and of great philosophical interest. The way in which the two kinds of structure interlock to generate the possibility of thought about form and matter, of reference to objects and their constitution, gives rise to a multitude of philosophical questions which have preoccupied philosophers from Aristotle to the present.

We are concerned with two of the most general categories of empirical thought, so, not surprisingly, many of the paramount issues revolve around the general relation between things (concrete particulars) and that of which they are constituted. Is everything made of something (matter or "stuff") or other, or are there things not made of anything? Are there things made of something other than material stuff? Conversely, if we wonder whether form can free itself from matter, can matter free itself from form? Is the being of matter to constitute things, or can formless matter exist?

A variety of questions concerning priorities can be raised. Is matter ontologically prior to things? When the world, the totality of things, emerged from the primeval chaos, was form imposed upon formless matter? It is indifferent whether this is taken in the Biblical mode whereby God's word created the heavens and earth and all things in them out of chaos, or whether it is taken in the scientific mode whereby the universe emerged from the explosion of some inconceivably dense primeval plasma. If everything is made of something, then it might seem that matter is ontologically prior to objects. But then if matter can only exist in the form of the constitution of material things, then the categories are coordinate.

There is little reason to think that things are logically reducible to matter — that statements about things can be replaced without change of sense by statements about matter — but there may be a temptation to reduce matter to things. On the one hand, one might think that words such as 'water', 'sand', 'gold', name a scattered, extensively distributed, particular thing — the totality of water (sand or gold) that exists. If so, matter of a given kind is really an unusual kind of thing. On the other hand it might seem plausible that any lump, nugget or grain, pool, puddle or drop of a certain kind of matter is a collection of things. A lump of gold is after all a collection of gold atoms, and a puddle of water is a collection of water molecules. If these elemental things are not themselves made of matter of some kind, then, it may seem, matter consists of things, and discourse about matter should be eliminable in favor of discourse about things.

Similar questions can be raised concerning identifiability-dependence or independence of things and matter, as well as about conceptual and epistemic priority.

So far we have mentioned a range of categorial questions concerning the relations between substances and substance. But there are many important questions about the general category of matter itself. Water and milk, sand and soil are different kinds of stuff. Is water a particular thing (a scattered individual) or is it a universal, a general characteristic or feature? If milk is a general kind, what are instances of it? Fido is an instance of the sortal 'dog'; is the bottle of milk an instance of the general concept "milk"? Are instances of general kinds not of logical necessity particulars? So must not instances of concepts of kinds of matter be particulars picked out by referring expressions formed from a partitive prefixed to a stuff-noun, for example, puddle, glass, bottle, of milk?

Permanence and change of things is the source of endless metaphysical debate. But the permanence and change of matter is hardly less problematic. Things change, yet stay the same things throughout diverse changes. So too matter changes, from solid to liquid, from raw to cooked, from cheap to expensive, and yet remains the same matter. How is this possible? What determines the identity of matter through transformation? Things come into being and pass away, but it has seemed plausible to many thinkers that there can be no creation out of nothing. So when a thing is created, it is created out of something, and when it passes away, it leaves remains behind. The matter of the thing, we might be inclined to think, survives: the cup ceases to exist, the china (now in pieces) remains, the chair is smashed to pieces, the wood (now in splinters) remains. But matter too comes into existence and passes away. Transubstantiation of bread and wine into the body and blood of Christ is an unfathomable mystery. But transubstantiation of wine into vinegar, of wood into ashes, of petroleum into plastic are well understood processes. Yet what, if anything, remains throughout the transubstantiation? If wine changes to vinegar, there must, one might think, be something that is first wine and then vinegar. If mass is conserved throughout such transubstantiational processes, then there must be some-thing constant whose mass it is that is conserved. Or so it seems.

The problems are manifold. In the sequel we shall try to resolve some of them, dissolve others, and at least suggest lines of further reflection for the remain-ing ones. But our access to a pathway through this metaphysical morass is by way of grammar. For the conceptual structure with which we are concerned is embodied in the use, the conditions of application, of a certain class of nouns.[1]

2. THE GRAMMAR OF STUFF

Grammarians distinguish between *count* nouns and *non-count* nouns.[2] The numer-ous grammatical distinctions between the two classes will be elaborated in detail, but as a preliminary point the salient distinction is that count nouns have both sin-gular and plural forms, take numerals as adjectives, and the plural form takes the quantifiers 'many', '(a) few', 'several', and phrasal quantifiers 'a great number of', 'a large number of'. Non-count nouns cannot have a genuine plural form, except when used generically to refer to general kinds ('the wines of France', 'the metals of the earth'). They must be distinguished from anomalous plural invariable nouns (for example, 'oats', 'grounds') as well as unmarked plural invariable nouns (for example, 'cattle') and zero-plural nouns (for example, 'sheep'). There are other exceptions to be noted below. Non-count nouns are sometimes referred to as "mass nouns." We shall reserve this expression for a subclass of non-count nouns.

Count nouns may, of course, be abstract ('proposition', 'number', 'law') or concrete ('desk', 'house', 'room'), sortal ('cat', 'dog', 'man') or non-sortal ('tailor', 'player', 'victim'). Our interest in count nouns for present purposes is only by way of constrast to non-count nouns. Non-count nouns may be abstract or concrete. Abstract non-count nouns include expressions such as 'leisure', 'progress', 'success', 'ill-luck', 'knowledge', and also verbal nouns such as 'admiration', 'satisfaction', 're-finement', and adjectival nouns such as 'restlessness', 'clearness', 'safety'. Concrete non-count nouns include expressions such as 'water', 'sand', 'milk', 'furniture', 'sun-light', 'money', 'cake', 'glass'. The distinction between abstract and concrete non-count nouns turns *inter alia* on spatio-temporality. Success is nice to have, but one cannot pocket it. Water is nice to drink, but unpleasant to pocket. One can bask both in sunlight and in admiration, but not in the same sense. Instantiations of ab-stract non-count nouns are identifiability-dependent upon the substance whose property is designated by the abstract non-count noun, for example, Napoleon's success, Chesterfield's refinement, Richard's restlessness. Closely related to iden-tifiability-dependence is a difference in the nature of transferability. A teacher can impart his knowledge to his pupils without losing it, but not his money; a child may inherit both his father's wit and his luck, but not in the sense in which he inherits his wealth and his wine. If 'N' is an abstract non-count noun, the "transference" of N from A to B does not entail that A no longer has N.[3] Instantiations of concrete non-count nouns are not thus identifiability-dependent. Instances of concrete non-count nouns occupy space and can be spatially located ('The snow over there', 'The furniture in the room'). In some cases, especially, for example, liquids and gases, their identity has a kind of dependence upon substances, but the mode of dependence is quite different from that of logical ownership, for it is transferable. The water that was in the jug is the same water as the water now in the glass. To identify that specific (quantity of) water we may refer to a form specified by a partitive (for example, glass of, jug of, puddle of), but the same water may continue to exist in other forms. To the extent that there is an identifiability-dependence it is morphological, as when we speak of the air in the balloon, or constitutive, as when we speak of the bronze of which the statue consists, or nonlogical ownership, as when we speak of the gold of Montezuma, or, in more complex cases, derivative, as when we speak of the copper in the bronze of which the statue is made, or the sugar in the coffee that is in the cup. Non-count nouns that are not stuff nouns yet are genuine mass nouns, for example, sunlight, light, shade, fire, etc., have different kinds of identifiability-dependence, for example, upon sources, causes, areas, etc. We shall discuss this curious subcategory in the sequel. The transferability of instances of concrete non-count nouns is "genuine," that is, if (some) N is "transferred" from A to B, then what B gains has been lost by A.

Our concern is with concrete non-count nouns, but not with the whole category of them. 'Iron', 'rubber', 'bread', 'sand', are, we would intuitively claim, names of kinds of matter; or perhaps since 'bread', 'mutton', 'cabbage' would not ordinarily be termed kinds of matter, which term is reserved for more elementary constituents of reality than roast beef and Yorkshire pudding, kinds of *stuff*. The expression is ugly, but will have to do service. 'Light', 'sunshine', 'fire' and 'rain' are non-count nouns, but not names of kinds of stuff (rainwater is a kind of stuff, rain is not; burning coal is a kind of stuff, fire is not). But there are some non-count nouns that are neither mass nouns (in the sense in which both 'sand' and 'sunshine' are) nor stuff nouns (in the sense in which 'sand' is and 'sunshine' is not). Examples of what we might call "pseudo-mass nouns" are nouns such as 'furniture', 'cutlery', 'money', 'machinery', 'clothing', 'footwear'. Here, for reasons which will become clear in a moment, one is inclined to view the non-count noun as conceptually derivative from antecedently given count nouns (for example, 'chair', 'fork', 'shilling', 'drill', 'shirt', 'shoe') which have independent application to particulars that can also be picked out by prefixing a partitive (for example, 'piece of', 'item of') to the corresponding non-count (for example, 'piece of clothing', 'piece of cutlery').

To distinguish such pseudo-mass nouns from those that are our concern we must invoke the following characteristics: First, *consistency*, in the sense in which an item consists of something (stuff) or other. Second, *dissectivity*, in the sense in which a feature is dissective to the extent that if a thing has that feature, every part of the thing has that feature. We should distinguish absolute dissectivity from relative dissectivity. A feature is *absolutely dissective* if no matter how far one proceeds in dividing the featured item into parts, the resultant elements of division possess the feature. A feature is *relatively dissective* if it is dissective down to a certain level of division, but not further. Dissectivity clearly characterizes properties, relations, and stuff. The properties of being extended or being red are dissective, as is the spatial relation of being between two points, and of an instance of stuff, for example, in the case of the water in the pool or the gold of the crown, one may say that any division will yield parts that are water or are gold. Hence the use of the term "feature" to encompass properties, relations, constitutive properties (being made of, consisting of), and stuff. Absolute dissectivity is less common than might be supposed, and applies paradigmatically to spatio-temporal properties and relations, for example, being extended, being between two points. Relative dissectivity is common, for example, being of a certain color or consisting of a certain stuff. The third characteristic to invoke for present purposes is *form independence* and *specific quantity retention*. This will be explained below.

Countability is imposed upon non-count nouns by means of partitives. Partitives, for example, 'a bit of', 'a piece of', etc. can therefore be considered as count-noun-forming operators upon non-count nouns. One cannot count water or gold (but only kinds of water or gold), but one can count glasses and puddles of water, grains and nuggets of gold. One must, however, distinguish quantity designating partitives, 'a pound of', 'a pint of', etc., from particular designating partitives, 'a piece of', 'a fragment of'. Both types impose countability, but if one has five pounds of gold it does not follow that there are five things (particulars) in one's possession, whereas if one has five nuggets of gold there are five things that one owns. Quantity designating partitives impose countability in the sense of measurability or quantifiability according to the dimension of commensurability specified. Particular designating partitives may very crudely be divided into general and typical ones. Expressions such as 'a piece of', 'a bit of', 'an item of', are general, 'a slice of', 'a roast of', 'a loaf of' are typical. Of course, this distinction is vague: 'a bottle of' applies to any liquid, just as 'a piece of' to any solid. Is it general or typical? (To be sure, *greater* generality is displayed by 'piece of' for it applies to abstract non-count nouns such as 'news', 'advice', 'wisdom'). When stuff is commonly packaged in a typical way, the requisite partitive is frequently dropped and the non-count noun treated as a count noun in its own right in the context. Thus we can buy a couple of [bottles of] beers [beer] or a [wheel or ball of] cheese, and a waiter may bring three [cups of] coffees [coffee] and two [bottles of] lemonades [lemonade].

Given any individualization of a non-count noun of the type with which we are concerned (which we shall call, with due apology, 'stuff nouns') by means of a partitive 'P', the following holds true:

(1) Every P of S (where 'S' is a variable holding a place for stuff nouns) consists of S. Thus every pool, cup, drop, puddle of water consists of water, down to the level of nondissective elements of S (a molecule of water does not consist of water).

(2) Every *arbitrary division* of a P of S yields Ps of S (although not necessarily the same partitive parceling for each resultant P, nor the same parceling as manifest by the parent parcel) down to the level of nondissective elements of S. Thus an ar-

bitrary division of a nugget of gold will yield parcels—grains, nuggets, shavings, etc. of gold, down to the atomic level (water ceases to be dissective at the molecular level, blood at the molar level).

(3) The specific quantity of S of which a given P of S consists (the water of which the pool consists) as well as the specific quantity of S of which a given object O is *made* (the gold of which the golden ring is made) can retain its identity *qua* specific quantity despite change of form specified by the partitive P, or destruction of the object made of S. The puddle of water on the floor may be the same water as the water that was in the glass, the gold of which the brooch is made may be the same gold as the gold of which the ring (now melted down) was made, and the china of which the fragments consist is the same china as that of which the bowl was made.

It is consequently clear that nouns such as 'furniture', 'money', 'machinery', 'clothing', 'cutlery', etc. are not, in the preferred sense, stuff nouns. For it is not the case that every piece of furniture (that is, chair, table, stool) consists of furniture (but of wood), nor that every piece of money[4] consists of money (but rather of paper, copper, or nickel). Similarly, an arbitrary division of a piece of furniture will not yield a piece of furniture—at least not in the desired sense. If I chop a chair in half, I shall have two pieces of a piece of furniture—the pieces are not pieces of furniture but fragments of a piece of furniture. Likewise, an arbitrary division of a piece of money, bag of money or walletfull of money need not be a piece, bag, walletfull, or anything else of money, but merely pieces of paper or metal that are not pieces of money. So too with clothing, machinery, cutlery, and footwear. Finally, furniture, money, cutlery, etc., are not form indifferent or specific quantity retaining. The bronze of the brazen statue crushed beneath a steamroller is the same bronze, but if a tornado hits a furniture shop the owner cannot console himself with the thought that he still has the same amount of furniture. Nor is it the case that if a piece of furniture is thus crushed, the furniture of which it consists remains, for a piece of furniture does not consist of furniture.

The behavior of non-count nouns in partitive context will also enable us to separate mass nouns such as 'light', 'sunlight' (and names of other kinds of light), 'shade', 'fire', and 'rain' from genuine stuff nouns. Though nouns such as these seem very different from the anomalous categories just considered, which we have called "pseudo-mass nouns," they nevertheless strike one as intuitively quite different from stuff nouns. Light and shade are not kinds of stuff, and rain, though very different from shade or sunshine, is not a kind of stuff either (although rainwater is —it is water from a certain source). Fire, though it was conceived of by the Greeks as one of the elements, and although attempts were still being made in the mid-eighteenth century to weigh it, is not a kind of stuff but a kind of process. In what ways are these intuitions reflections of grammar?

It is striking that 'light' and its derivatives 'sunlight', 'moonlight', 'candlelight', etc., and 'shade' likewise do not lend themselves to general partitives. 'Light' and its derivatives take highly typical partitives such as 'ray of', 'flash of', 'glimmer of', or metaphorical ones such as 'pool of', 'shaft of', but not 'a piece of', 'a bit of', presumably because we do not think of light as space occupying. One can, to be sure, have a room 'full of light', as one can have a room full of air or smoke. But a room full of light is simply a well-lit room (whereas a room is normally 'full of' air, even if it is not well aired) and an area flooded with light, unlike an area flooded with water, is an area *illuminated* by powerful light, not *covered* with light. Similarly, 'light' takes intensity modifiers, not quantitative ones. 'More light' means 'stronger light', and if there is too much light, the light is too strong. 'More', 'much', 'little', 'less', etc. may signify when annexed to 'light' not only intensity but also, derivatively, quantity — not quantity of light, but rather quantity of illuminated area.

If quantities of light are intensities, then it is not surprising that one's intuitions are hesitant with respect to consistency. Are rays, shafts, pools, glimmers of candlelight, or moonlight particulars that are made of, or consist of candlelight or moonlight? One hesitates — perhaps because one does not think of light particulars as space-occupying things consisting of stuff, but as space illuminations. Certainly the feature of specific quantity retention appears not to apply. One cannot extinguish the ray of light and retain the light of the ray, nor can one blot out the pool of light and keep the light of the pool (as opposed to the light of the torch that cast the pool of light upon the floor). Similarly, dissectivity is anomalous: the "parts" of a pool of light (shaft of, ray of, halo of) are not "light particulars," but areas or volumes of space that are illuminated by the pool or ray of light.

Likewise shade possesses a kind of identity dependence on its source and a partitive dependence on the surface upon which *a* shadow is cast or which is *in* shade. Instances of shade, like light, are specified by their source — the shade of the tree (the light of the moon), not by partitives that designate particulars consisting of light or shade, or made of light and shade. If two moving discs cast two circles of shade upon a screen which merge and diverge, the continued identity of each circle is wholly dependent upon the identity of the disc that produces it. The anomalous dissectivity is area dependent, and there is no specific quantity retention through change of form.

Fire, though very different from light and shade, is no stuff noun. Of course, 'fire' has a more common use as a count noun, but in the sense in which a hero goes through fire and water, a cruel conqueror ravages the conquered lands with fire and sword, and an arsonist sets fire to combustibles, it is a mass noun. It is in this sense that the proverb claims there to be no smoke without fire, and it is from this usage that the adjective 'fiery' is formed. It serves as a prefix to a large number of compound expressions such as 'fire-bridge' (-ship, -brick, -escape, -insurance, etc.). Though a mass noun, like 'light', 'fire' is not the name of a kind of stuff. Does the fire of the furnace consist of fire? One is inclined to say rather that it consists of, or more naturally is produced by, the burning of the coals. A wooden statue consists (analytically) of wood, but a fiery furnace does not obviously consist of fire. Nor is it easy to find partitives so that one can say that every arbitrary division of a pool, ball, or pillar of fire is a something or other of fire. Divisons of fire, barring expressions such as the three just cited, are commonly generated by reference to fiery things, not by means of partitives. But fiery things, unlike wooden or brazen things, are not things made of fire, but burning things. In this respect 'fiery' is akin to a state of stuff (like 'liquid' or 'solid') rather than a kind of stuff. Nor do quantity modifiers apply to 'fire' as to genuine stuff nouns. 'More fire' may, of course, be used, but it would normally indicate more burning stuff. It makes little sense to speak of maintaining the same amount of fire, unless one refers to intensity of heat.

The examples of light, shade, and fire have been dwelt on not only for their intrinsic interest, but also because it is noteworthy that it is no coincidence that the pictures invoked in the mythology of the soul, in philosophy as elsewhere, so frequently draw upon such "unsubstantial stuff" as light, shade, and fire in depicting the immaterial substance that the soul has so often been conceived to be.

'Rain', though very unlike the previous examples, is yet puzzling. It behaves very much like a genuine stuff noun (for example, 'snow') but is nevertheless anomalous. The being of rain, one might claim, is to fall—hence it bears affinities to event names. For instances of rain are identified by reference to the events that consist of rain falling here, there, or elsewhere, that is, storms, showers, downpours. Since, unlike snow, rain cannot outlast the event of which the *raindrops* (which the rain consists of) are the substantial elements, nothing can be said to be made of, or consist of, rain. (No *thing*, not no *event*, for rainstorms consist of rain). Since the count-noun-forming partitives ('shower of', 'flurry of', etc.) are event-name-forming operators, and since events have no parts *strictu sensu* (but phases), it is not the case that an arbitrary division of a P of rain is a P of rain. Nor do we think of the rain of a rainstorm as form indifferent and specific quantity preserving, just because a rainstorm is an event, not a substance. The general point might be put thus: the mass noun 'rain', despite its grammatical similarity to 'snow', and despite the similarity of the physical phenomena of rain and snow, is not the name of a stuff, just because there can be snow here, there, and elsewhere, even though it is not snowing, but there can only be rain here, there, or elsewhere if it is raining.

So much for isolating the broad category that is our main concern. The division sketched in can be represented in the following diagram:

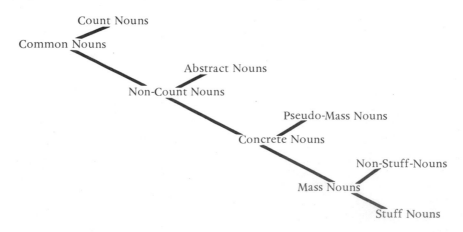

Stuff nouns thus include names of natural elements (gold, uranium, chlorine), chemical compounds, physical admixtures, natural kinds of material, foodstuffs (wheat, barley), edible flesh (mutton, beef, venison), manufactured materials (rope, plastic), etc. This huge class of nouns displays great diversity, and generalization will have to be very tentative and wary. When we think of natural elements and some compounds, we are inclined to think that, for example, solid, liquid, gaseous are the three states of matter, but this would hardly apply to stuff nouns of innumerable other types, for example, cotton and wool, veal and chicken, horse hair and leather. Nevertheless, a certain range of common features is discernible.

A few final anomalies should be pointed out. First, regular stuff nouns do not take a plural form, except for type designation ('the wines of France', 'ten different plastics') without change of sense ('the waters of the Thames', 'the sands of Tripoli'). Second, there are many terms with occurrence both as count and non-count noun forms, for example, 'cake', 'stone', 'glass', 'lamb', 'chicken', etc. It is noteworthy that the count-noun occurrence occasionally displays a marked change of meaning, for example, 'iron', 'ice', 'paper', 'wood'. Third, there are plural invariable nouns that need a partitive to be countable, but are nevertheless not mass nouns. These are *summation plurals*, tools and types of dress that consist of two symmetrical parts, for example, 'scissors', 'trousers', 'spectacles', and hence take the partitive 'pair of' to generate a count noun.

Having thus roughly isolated our category of stuff nouns, let us briefly provide a grammatical contrast with both singular and plural count nouns. It is perspicuously displayed in Table 1.[5] The differences and similarities are striking, and turn (as one would expect) on countability and singularity on the one hand, and quantity predication on the other.

3. STUFF

Stuff nouns differ from count nouns, and so *a fortiori* from sortal nouns. They designate stuff, not things, or properties of things ('made of iron' designates a property of a thing, but 'iron' does not). To be sure, to understand a given stuff noun, to grasp the concept of stuff of a given kind, one must know the criteria of identification or application—the defining features that identify that kind of stuff (however flexible, open textured, or porous the concept may be). Equally, these criteria must determine the limits of change consistent with precluding transubstantiation. Here, as with things, there is much flexibility. With certain kinds of particular one may begin with a sortal (for example, 'caterpillar') and then discover that things of that kind naturally undergo transformation (into chrysalis and later butterfly). It is then open to one to introduce a change in concepts so that what was a sortal term becomes a phase sortal, and a new sortal is introduced to cover the life span of the particular. A similar flexibility is evident with respect to stuff concepts. Liquid, solid, and gaseous states of those stuffs that can be liquid, solid, or gaseous (roast beef cannot, nor can scrambled eggs) may not be known to a given linguistic community, and it may be an empirical discovery that ice or snow are states of one kind of

Table 1

	Count Nouns Singular	Count Nouns Plural	Non-Count Nouns
1. The; possessive (my, our), whose, which, what; some (stressed), any, no.	√	√	√
2. Zero article, some (unstressed) any (unstressed) enough.	x	√	√
3. This, that.	√	x	√
4. These, those.	x	√	x
5. A(n), every, each, either, neither.	√	x	x
6. Much.	x	x	√
7. One.	√	x	x
8. Cardinal numbers greater than one.	x	√	x
9. Ordinals.	√	√	x
10. Many, (a) few, several.	x	√	x
11. Much, (a) little.[6]	x	x	√
12. Enough.	x	√	√
13. Plenty of, lots of, a lot of.	x	√	√
14. A great (good) deal of, a large (small) amount of.	x	x	√
15. A great (large, good) number of.	x	√	x

Rows 7–9 are bracketed as **Quantifiers**.
Rows 10–12 are bracketed as **Quantifiers**.
Rows 13–15 are bracketed as **Phrasal Quantifiers**.

familiar stuff. It is then open to one to treat 'water' as the name of the liquid state (as hitherto) or to treat it as the name of the stuff that can exist in the various states of liquid, solid, or gaseous, or to allow a degree of ambiguity (as we commonly do— "liquid water" would ordinarily be thought to be pleonastic).

There is, however, considerable difference between stuff and things with respect to identity which affects persistence and reidentification. It is part of the sense of a sortal noun that it determines what counts as one and the same object at a given time. A stuff noun, however, does not individuate a particular at all, but a specific quantity. But the specific quantity is not circumscribed by the sense of the stuff noun—the sense merely identifies the type of circumscribable stuff. The specific quantity may be circumscribed by the definite article and specification of a particular or set of particulars constituted of the stuff—for example, *the* water *of the lake*, *the* gold *of the rings*, or in some other way, for example, *the* gold *of Montezuma*. Where one type of stuff is a constituent of another kind of stuff (as copper is of brass) the specification may be indirect. Where stuff is scattered, the specification may be volumetric or by area. Specification may, of course, be ostensive; what the ostension picks out is a quantity of stuff of which a particular or set of particulars consist, or are made. Nevertheless, there are exceptions—where specification is of a nonparticularized distribution of stuff. Since no particular is picked out by the referential use of a stuff noun, the question of whether this S is the same S as . . . concerns only identity over time. There is no sense to the question whether this S here is the same as that S there, where reference is to a specific quantity rather than to a type.

Form indifference, a feature already encountered, marks a further distinction between stuff and things. To be sure, the physical shape of a material thing may change dramatically (sapling to oak, caterpillar to butterfly), and some things retain their identity through "reversible disintegration"—watches and motor cars, and even buildings can be taken to pieces and later reassembled to constitute the same watch, car, or building. But not *any* partitioning is consistent with persistence of a thing—if a car is taken to pieces, which pieces are duly melted down, reprocessed into new pieces, and assembled, the resultant car is not the same car at all, but a new car made of the same materials. Stuff, however, can undergo any amount or kind of partitioning consistent with its relative dissectivity, and remain the same stuff (not only the same kind of stuff, but the same specific quantity). The water in the glass can be frozen, evaporated, spilled on the floor, poured down the drain, and still remain the same water. It is, to that extent, form-indifferent. Moreover, where stuffs are fusible (particularly liquid, gaseous, granular, or powdered stuffs), we can speak of the stuff prior to fusion as subsequently contained in the greater quantity of stuff, even though we can no longer identify the specific quantity referred to, except in terms of its antecedent condition. Thus we may say that the water that was in the glass is now in the jug (having been poured back into the half-full jug), although we have no way of distinguishing between the water from the glass and the water that was not.

Form indifference and fusibility, as well as dispersability, affect reidentification. The persistence of a given quantity of stuff is indifferent to dispersion or fusion. Judgments of persistence are possible even though reidentification is impossible. Of course, reidentification requires persistence of the subset of quantities that the specific quantity contained. The brooch made from the gold of a ring consists of the same gold as did the ring, neither more nor less, as long as none (that is, no quantity) was lost or added. The gold of the ring, melted down with that of five other rings to make a bracelet, persists, but can no longer be identified.

Persistence of a thing through time does not require the persistence of its constituent matter; but for the stuff of which a thing consists to persist it must, tautologically, be the same stuff. It need not, of course, constitute the same thing. The distinction between two material particulars of a given kind at a given time rests upon their different spatial location as determined by the space-occupying matter of which they consist. The sense of a sortal noun, it is often said, provides criteria of distinctness for the things designated. Understanding a sortal noun involves understanding what constitutes the difference between two individuals of the same kind at the same time. Stuff nouns, however, contain no criteria of distinctness in this sense. We distinguish only kinds of stuff, or "parcels" (designata of particular partitives) of stuff, but not stuff particulars. Instances of stuff, as we shall elaborate in the sequel, are specific quantities, not particulars. There may be water in this glass, and *more* water in that glass—but not *another* water in that glass. The water in the two glasses is not two distinct things, for water is not a thing at all. If a criterion of distinctness is what differentiates one thing of a kind from another, then stuff nouns contain no criteria of distinctness as part of their sense. There are two glasses of water, that is, the partitive 'glass of' confers criteria of distinctness on the resultant count noun. There are also two measures of water—two glasseful, whether together in a jug, or separate in the glasses, that is, the quantity (amount) designating partitive 'glassful' confers dimensive commensurability on the non-count noun. Yet although there are no "two waters," there are two specific, distinguishable, quantities of water—the water in this glass and the water in that one. As sortal nouns individuate things of a kind, stuff nouns individuate specific quantities of a kind.

Where it makes no sense to talk of criteria of distinctness—that which distinguishes one *thing* of a kind from another—the question of countability cannot arise. A grasp of the sense of a count-noun involves an understanding of the question "How many . . . are there . . . ?"[7] This question cannot arise for stuff nouns; or rather, the only way in which it can arise is when the question concerns counting kinds. But there corresponds to countability the question of quantifiability. A grasp of the sense of a stuff noun involves an understanding of the question "How much . . . is there?" We shall revert to this in the sequel.

Like things designated by sortals, stuffs lend themselves to genus/species classification. Iron, brass, and copper are species of metal, mutton, lamb, and beef are kinds of meat, cotton, wool, and nylon types of fabric. As with things, so too with stuffs, systems of classification vary according to our interests, needs, and concerns. Is there a *summa genera*? The term 'stuff' or the more commonly used term 'matter' names the ultimate genus to which all kinds of stuff or material belong. The subcategory of non-count nouns that we have isolated consists of names of kinds of stuff. The other subcategories of non-count nouns that were eliminated by various criteria are not such names. Things that are made of, or constituted of, or consist of something or other (as opposed to being made *up* of, or consisting of some things or others) are made of, constituted of, or consist of some stuff or other. All genuine stuff is, in a broad sense, material stuff.

If this is correct, then 'stuff' or 'matter' is arguably not itself the name of a kind of stuff or substance, but in effect a variable of which the various names of kinds of stuff are substitution instances, and the various stuffs of the world are values. Classification of "what exists" into things (substances) and stuff (substance) is, therefore, not a classification of different kinds of items that themselves belong to some higher genus ("existents" perhaps). This is precisely parallel to the contention that ontological classification into substances and properties is not a classification of things, nor is it made into such a classification by philosophical circumlocutions such as 'that which exists'. 'Thing' or 'object' or 'substance' (in the singular) expresses a formal concept, defined by formal properties.

Two distinctive parallelisms obtain between the concepts of individual substances (things)—generally acknowledged to be a formal concept, and the concept of substance (stuff) with respect to being formal categories. Horses, cows, or sheep are kinds of animals, and animals are kinds of substances. That an animal is a horse is something that might be discovered, that an animal is an individual substance is not. If we ask in virtue of what features a horse is an animal, the answer will specify a list of material properties definitive of horses, properties that an animal might conceivably lack, yet be some animal or other for all that. But if we ask in virtue of what features an animal is an individual substance, the answer will not list a range of features animals have been discovered to possess. It is rather that the features by which animals are characterized are themselves of the form of properties of individual substances, that is, they are themselves substitution instances of the formal properties definitive of individual substancehood. This is paralleled by the concept of substance (stuff). Iron, copper, gold are kinds of metal, and metals are kinds of stuff. That a given quantity of metal is gold is something that might be discovered, but that it is stuff is not. That in virtue of which gold is a metal consists of a range of material properties definitive of gold, properties that a metal might lack, yet not cease to be a metal. But that in virtue of which metal is a kind of stuff is not a range of properties metals have been discovered to possess. Rather the material features that characterize metal have the general form of properties of stuff. The formal properties of stuff include such features, already elaborated, as non-particularity, non-countability, form-indifference and quantity-retention, quantifiability, dissectivity, etc.

A second parallel between the concepts of substances and substance concerns countability and quantification. The concept of an object, thing, or individual substance provides no criterion of distinctness for objects, things, or substances. What is necessary is that a sortal noun designating an object, thing, or individual substance must contain such a criterion. Consequently, the question "How many things are there in the room?" is unanswerable (unless the context makes clear what kind of thing is intended). It is noteworthy, however, that the non-countability of things does not preclude an (uncountable) characterization of a totality, for example, the request "Bring *all the things* in the suitcase" is a compliable (whereas "Count all the things in the suitcase" is not). The parallel with stuff is noteworthy. 'Stuff' or 'matter' contains no criteria of quantification (no criteria for specifying quantities) in the following sense. Stuffs not only constitute things made of them, but also stuffs that consist of them, as bronze consists of copper and zinc, or pastry of flour and butter. Just as one cannot count things, because some things consist of things (a book of pages, a library of books), so one cannot univocally quantify stuff because some stuffs consist of other stuffs. Yet as one can characterize an uncountable totality of things, so one can characterize a totality of stuff. Moreover, unlike things with respect to countability, one can measure the totality of a circumscribed amount of unspecified stuff—in terms of weight, or mass, or volume. But despite this one must note that such a measure of, for example, all the stuff in the room, will not add up to the sum of amounts of different stuffs (for example, the water, hydrogen, and oxygen, the brass, copper, and zinc, etc.).

Terms such as 'substances', 'substance', 'property' are therefore classificatory terms only in an attenuated sense. There is no range of items of which these terms are classifications—rather, they specify ranges and to that extent are arguably ultimate metaphysical categories. The appearance of constituting classificatory terms stems from the fact that the corresponding grammatical categories of count nouns (or the subclass of sortal nouns), non-count nouns (or the subclass of stuff nouns), adjectives (or some appropriately restricted subclass of them) are classifications of logico-syntactical categories of expressions. We then project our grammatical classification of different logical types of expression onto reality and misguidedly think that these variables are classifications of items in the world.

These contentions, if correct, will have serious consequences for much of traditional European metaphysics of the post-Cartesian period. For the thought that there are two ultimate types of substance, matter and mind, errs in two distinct but important ways. First, in conceiving of the concept of mind as that of a kind of substance of which individual minds are constituted. Second, in conceiving of the concept of matter as that of a kind of substance rather than as a formal concept.

Stuff nouns are names of types of stuff. Where we distinguish types we also distinguish instances. What are the instances of water, iron, sand, bread, etc.? The answer is clear from the foregoing discussion—but let us first examine other alternatives. One tempting answer will be that pools of water, sheets of iron, grains of sand, and loaves of bread are instances of the respective stuffs of which they consist. But this is erroneous, stemming from the preconception that every instance of a general concept must be a particular thing. The partitives 'pools of', 'sheets of', 'grains of', 'loaves of', and other general or typical partitives (other than quantity designating partitives such as 'a pound of', 'a litre of', etc.) are, as we have seen, count-noun-forming operators on non-count nouns. A pool of water, therefore, is an instance of the general concept pool of water, as a grain of sand is of the concept grain of sand, and a nugget of gold of the concept nugget of gold. 'Parcels' or 'packages' of stuff are not instances of stuff, for they are things not stuff. Another suggestion might be that things made of a given stuff are instances of the stuff of which they are made. Accordingly, a wood table is an instance of wood, and a steel chair an instance of steel. But this too is erroneous, and for the same reason. Chairs and tables are things, not stuffs, things made *of* wood or steel, not themselves wood (but wooden) or steel. It is rather *the* wood or steel of which a thing is made, or of which it consists, which instantiates the general concept of wood or steel.

Yet another suggestion might be that stuff nouns do not have instances at all, because they are not general but singular terms. Thus 'gold', 'water', or 'sand' might be thought to name particulars, as 'Agnes' might name a lamb. Clearly, the alleged particular named will be most singular—it will in effect be 'all the gold (water, sand) there is', and it will be a *scattered* particular, like the frieze of the Parthenon. Moreover, the various parcels, grains, nuggets, pools, drops, etc. of a given stuff will be considered as *parts* of the scattered particular conceived to be named by the stuff noun. This is surely misguided. It is true that the various substances of the world are distributed or scattered over the world. But what is thus distributed is not a thing, but a substance (stuff) of one kind or other. Things have parts, but water or gold do not; the only sense we give to 'a part of S' is in discourse of ratios of quantities of S (for chemical or culinary purposes). Parts of a thing, in the most elementary sense of 'part', are smaller than the whole of which they are parts. But a P of S (where 'P' holds a place for some partitive applicable to a stuff noun) is neither smaller nor larger than S. A pool of water is not smaller than water — it is rather that the water of the pool (the amount) is less than the water of the world (than all the water there is, that is, the total amount of water in the world). But even if the pool contained all the water in the world, the pool of water would be neither a part of water, nor the particular (now fully fused) named by 'water' — for 'water' names no particular. The pool, like any other pool of water, would consist of water, would contain all the water there is, but it would not be identical with water — for a pool is a thing and water is not. Some things wax and wane, but stuff does not — quantities of stuff increase or diminish. As the natural resources of the earth are used up, oil, nickel, and coal do not grow smaller, rather the quantities of these stuffs diminish. Parts of a thing (the Parthenon frieze) may be destroyed, but consumption of half the world's oil resources is not "destruction" or consumption of half of oil, but consumption of half the (quantity of) oil.

Stuffs, therefore, are not things but kinds, and instances of stuff are not things but quantities. The general concept of water is instantiated by the waters of the earth, the innumerable quantities of water that are contained in the seas, lakes, rivers, pools, and puddles throughout the world. All the water there is (on earth) consists of the total amount distributed over our planet. Its mode of distribution is various, for stuff, as we shall see, does not always constitute things. Specific quantities, however, are not to be equated with amounts. Two cups of coffee may contain the same amount of coffee, but they are two distinct quantities, distinguishable by their "parceling." Each specific quantity consists of, or contains, an amount (for example, 200 millilitres) — if the two quantities are poured into a jug there will be only one distinguishable quantity containing the previous two quantities and double the amount.

Stuff nouns stand to quantification as count nouns to enumeration. The concept of a so-and-so provides a means of counting so-and-sos, at least to the extent that it contains usable criteria of distinctness and identity. The concept of such-and-such stuff provides a measure, rendering intelligible the question "How much?" If there are some so-and-sos here, then there is a certain number of so-and-sos. If there is some such-and-such here, then there is a certain amount of such-and-such. The quantifiers 'some', 'plenty of', 'lots of', 'a lot of' are prefixed uniformly to both count nouns and non-count nouns. But while plenty of Ps are many Ps, plenty of S is much S; while a few Ps are a small number of Ps, a little S is a small amount of S ('little' in 'a little P', that is, a small-sized P, is a homonymous adjective, a homonymity not present in many other languages).

Specific quantities that instantiate stuff nouns are picked out by the use of the definite article together with some circumscribing description or ostension — 'the water of the pond', 'the air in the balloon', 'this bronze'. Amounts are specified by reference to some method of measurement. It is noteworthy that variations in results of measurement in some dimension or other (for example, weight or volume) because of factors such as pressure, temperature, or altitude do not affect the identity of a specific quantity over time. Thus the same oxygen in a balloon may increase or decrease in volume or weight, but yet remain the same specific quantity of oxygen over time.

Stuff concepts have quantities of stuff as their instances, and quantities of stuff are, at least frequently, "packaged" in the form of things that are made of the stuff, or "parcels," designated by partitives, which consist of the stuff. Is it, however, necessary that all stuff be the stuff of some thing or other? Is there stuff of which no thing is made or consists? Or must matter be "informed" by things? The question may be sharpened thus: If it is true that there is S here, does it logically follow that there is (or are) a P (or Ps) of S here? The answer seems to be that it does not so follow. Two kinds of case militate against the suggested entailment. The first turns on the fact that stuff is constitutive not only of things, but also of complex stuffs. From the fact that there is copper here, it does not follow that there are lumps, grains, or veins of copper here, for the copper may be here not in the form of a thing (designated by a syntactically simple count noun) which is made of copper, nor in the form of a "parceling" of copper (designated by a partitive — 'P of copper') but as a copper compound — a complex stuff that consists *inter alia* of copper, but is not a thing. A mountain may be rich in copper, although there are no objects in the mountain that are made of copper, nor are there any "parcels" of copper. Rather, there may be things, nuggets, veins, deposits of copper sulphate. These "parcels" consist of copper sulphate, and the copper sulphate in turn consists of copper, sulphur, and oxygen. But the copper sulphate that thus consists of copper, etc., is stuff, not a thing. A molecule of copper sulphate is, to be sure, a thing. And a vein of copper sulphate can be said to consist of molecules of copper sulphate (as a crowd consists of people). But such a molecule does not consist of copper (the stuff) — it consists of a copper and a sulphate ion — two particulars, not stuffs. And the copper ion does not consist of copper. So here we have at least a *prima facie* case of stuff that is not "parcelled" but constitutive of more complex stuff that is.

One need not go to chemistry, nor know any, for such examples. There is egg in good sponge cake, and milk in *café au lait* — but there are no pieces or fragments of egg in good cake, nor drops of milk in coffee. It is, rather, that egg is an ingredient of the sponge, and the coffee contains milk. But it is noteworthy that although cheese is made from milk, milk is not an ingredient of cheese, nor does it follow from the fact that there is cheese here that there is milk here. More puzzlingly, although coffee is made from coffee grain (or powder) and water, coffee contains no water unless it has been watered down, just as Chateau Lafitte '59 at a reputable table would not be expected to contain water.

It is a moot question what the assertion conditions are for "There is S here," where S is in a compound or solution. Neither the necessity for S in the production of S′ (water is needed to make coffee, milk to make cheese) nor the extractability of S from S′ (the milk cannot be extracted from the coffee),[8] nor even retention of antecedent S-characteristics (cake containing egg has a distinctive taste and texture, but not of raw or even cooked egg) is necessary or sufficient for the truth of "There is S here" said with reference to a compound or mixture. But be the answer what it may, we have here clear cases of unpackaged stuff.

The second kind of case concerns "free" gases. One can, of course, "partition" gas by means of containers, natural or artificial—balloons, cylinders, or bubbles. But the air of the atmosphere, consisting as it does of a multitude of gases, appears to be stuff that is not informed. We can, of course, refer to quantities of it—as in "the air on the hilltop was bracing"; however, the quantity is not circumscribed by a partitive, but merely by rough location. The only candidate for a thing that consists of the air of the atmosphere is, of course, the atmosphere. But the atmosphere is not a thing—merely the distributed totality of the earth's air. 'Half an atmosphere' is a measure of pressure, not half of a thing—and though we may talk of half of *the* atmosphere (as in 'half of the atmosphere is polluted'), we refer thereby to half the total amount—as we would in 'Half the water (or waters) of the earth are polluted'. We could, no doubt, refer to the waters of the earth (the sum of quantities of water) as 'the aquasphere', but it is not so easy to package the totality of water—naming a totality of stuff does not wrap it up.

If this is correct, it has a further interesting consequence. The first case of compounds suggested that stuff can exist "in the form" of a compound, so that the quantity of ingredient stuff was unpackaged, although the compound was packaged *qua* thing or things of some kind or kinds. It might have seemed therefrom that stuff must always be, at least indirectly, particularized. But if the example of air is correct, even this weaker thesis is false. For if there is carbon dioxide in the air in gaseous solution, then both the carbon dioxide and the air that consists, *inter alia* of it, are unpackaged. Moreover, it also suggests that the thesis that stuff nouns are in principle eliminable from language in favor of the verb phrase 'is-made-of' is false. For 'The air on the hilltop was bracing' cannot be rephrased in terms of a particular designating expression prefixed to such a verb phrase. There are, of course, many other reasons for rejecting such reduction, in particular the fact that the properties of things made of a given stuff are not always the same as, and sometimes cannot be intelligibly predicated of, the stuff of which they are made, and vice versa. (This point will be discussed later.)

It seems, then, that although 'There is S here' entails 'There is a certain amount of S (the amount contained in the specific quantity) here', it does not entail 'There is a P of S here'. Yet, it may well appear that if there is S here, there, or elsewhere, then there must be things of some sort *of which that stuff consists*—elements of stuff. Stuff, we have seen, is dissective—this is an *a priori* feature of stuff.

As a matter of fact, stuff is relatively dissective, but not absolutely dissective. We discover that blood is made up of corpuscles in a lymphatic solution, and that arbitrary divisions of a quantity of blood below the macroscopic level yields things (corpuscles) and stuff (lymphatic liquids) that are not blood. Equally the atomic theory of matter has revealed that a quantity of, say, gold is dissective down to the atomic level, but beyond that point it is not, for an atom of gold consists of things — subatomic particles, not stuff — and those things do not consist of gold. So might one not think that just as material things consist of stuff, so too a quantity of stuff consists of things?

The suggestion can be supported by a quite different consideration. A brief glance at the comparative table of singular and plural count nouns and non-count nouns reveals a degree of similarity between plural count nouns and non-count nouns. Neither type of noun takes any term implying singularity, for example, 'a', 'every', 'each', 'either', 'neither', 'one'. Both take 'neutral' quantifiers such as 'some', 'any', 'enough', 'plenty of', 'lots of', 'a lot of'. Just as partitives can be affixed to non-count nouns to yield count nouns, so a kind of partitive can be affixed to plural count nouns to yield countable pluralities or sets, for example, 'a box of', 'a heap of', 'a bus load of', 'a team of'. And just as statements of identity of specific quantities may be made without invoking partitives, 'This S is the same as the S which . . . ', so too statements of identity of sets may be made without invoking terms such as 'box', 'team', 'litter', for example, 'These Ps are the same Ps as . . . '. The limited affinities may, therefore, be exploited to yield a metaphysical picture of the constitution of stuff.

We might think of stuff of a given kind as consisting of a plurality of things, each of the same kind for a given kind of stuff. These things we might conceive of as the stuff elements. So a given kind of stuff S will be thought to consist of S-elements, and a given specific quantity of S is a *collection* of S-elements. Parallel to this it is suggested that stuff nouns be construed as plural sortal nouns of the form 'S-elements'. An S-element is, of course, a thing, but not a thing *of* S — it does not consist of, nor is made of, S — for an S-element does not consist of S-elements. So although 'There is S here' does not, as we have seen, entail 'There is (are) a P (Ps) of S here' (since an S-element is not 'of' S), it does entail 'There are S-elements here'. So it emerges that things do indeed underlie stuff, and that the notion of S-elements is ontologically more basic than that of stuff (although not epistemologically or conceptually so). Partitives affixed to stuff nouns, therefore, specify modes of collection of S-elements — into lumps, nuggets, drops, or pools.

This interesting proposal amounts to the exciting idea that our grammar, and hence our metaphysics, incorporates an *a priori* atomic theory of matter. The chemical atomic theory, triumphantly vindicated in the last century and a half (although not in respect of indivisibility of atoms), can thus be seen as an elaboration of a picture of the constitution of reality embedded tacitly in grammar.

Unfortunately, the proposal has its flaws and must, I think, be rejected. The two lines of argument that led to it, the argument from dissectivity and the argument from grammar (the construal of stuff nouns as plural sortals of the form 'S-elements') already contain signs of stress that are disregarded at peril. Dissectivity is an *a priori* feature of stuff, but that stuff is only relatively dissective is an empirical discovery. Nothing in grammar suggests that there must be Ps of S which, if further divided, will no longer yield Ps of S. For all grammar is concerned, stuff might be continuous rather than discrete. Indeed, Descartes, whose assimilation of matter to space is of great grammatical and metaphysical interest, thought it was. Equally the grammatical assimilation of stuff nouns to plural sortals is suspect. It is one thing to describe our grammar as it is, another to replace it by an allegedly spruced-up version. There are similarities between plural count nouns and non-count nouns, but also differences. 'This' and 'that' may be affixed to non-count nouns, but not to count nouns, 'these' and 'those' to count nouns, but not to non-count nouns. Count nouns take cardinal numerals greater than one, and ordinals, as well as such quantifiers as 'many', 'few', 'several', 'a large number of', that non-count nouns do not. They, by contrast, take 'much', 'a little', 'a large amount of', 'a great deal of', that count nouns do not. Any suggestion of assimilation or reconstrual of grammatical categories must be treated with care and distrust. For if metaphysics is a reflection of grammar, a controversial thesis to be sure, then it is a reflection of the grammar we have, not of some alternative that we might have had.

Is there any way of sharpening our suspicions to the point of providing counterarguments to the metaphysical atomism suggested? I think there is. Let us consider first such foodstuffs as fruit cake or minestrone soup, drinks such as milk-coffee, or alloys such as steel. In order for the notion of an S-element to be well defined for such cases, there must be applicable criteria of identity for such elements. The atomistic suggestion confronting us is that the notion of an S-element is defined as the smallest *object* yielded by dissection of S which is such that collections of such objects will constitute Ps of S. The element is an *S*-element, but does not consist of S or S-elements. Its character as an *S*-element derives from its being the final point of dissectivity of any quantity of S. The difficulty derives from the fact that with respect to the kinds of relatively dissective stuffs under consideration there is no determinate final point at which one can say that any further division will no longer yield "parcels" of S, just as in removing grains of sand from a heap there is no point at which one can say that one grain less will reduce a heap of sand to something less than a heap. All that one can say with confidence regarding the relative dissectivity of a "parcel" of stuff is that if one continues dividing the parcel, one will cease to generate "parcels" of stuff, but not that one will reach a *point* at which further divisions will not yield that stuff. But the notion of an S-element was introduced as the smallest object such that collections of uniform objects of that type will yield "parcels" of S, which itself does not consist of S. Yet just as there is no smallest heap, so too there is no such object determinable *a priori*.

The case thus far seems clear enough. We have no means, *a priori* or empirical, of determining the notions of a milk-coffee element, or fruit cake element, or steel element. Dissectivity in such cases will merely run into an indeterminate interval, beyond which we no longer obtain the stuff in question. It may seem, however, that the atomic theory of matter resolves the issue for stuffs that are chemical elements or compounds. Dissection of a piece of gold will yield pieces of gold until we arrive at gold atoms that are not made of, or consist of, gold. Further division of these will not yield gold. This is correct. However, the atomic theory of matter is an empirical theory, confirmed by experimental methods. It is an empirical, not an *a priori*, grammatical truth that any parceling of gold consists of a collection of gold atoms. The scientific conception of an atom is not defined by reference to the dissectivity of stuff, but in terms of scientific theory. If so, it cannot be claimed that it is a metaphysical truth that any "parcel" of stuff of a given kind is a collection of stuff-elements of that kind. Nor can it be legitimately argued that stuff nouns be construed as plural count nouns of the form 'S-elements', for this notion of an element is ill-defined.

We have already remarked that while the distinctness of things of a kind at a given time is dependent on the distinct spatial locations of their constitutive matter, the identity of a thing of a kind throughout its existence is not dependent upon the continued identity of the stuff of which it is made. Theseus' ship remained the same ship although the wood of which it was originally made was replaced by new wood. Conversely, the stuff of which a thing is made may continue to exist even though the thing ceases to exist. If a wooden ship is dismantled, and the wood used to build a house, the ship no longer exists, but one and the same quantity of wood was first constitutive of a ship, and subsequently of a house.

Just as things—individual substances—come into being and pass away, so too quantities of stuff come into being and pass away. Thus the wine in the bottle may turn into vinegar, the milk in the churner into cheese or butter, and wood (after a great deal of time) into coal. In the case of things, there is some stuff or stuffs that was first constitutive of such and such a thing, and later of another thing—as a quantity of fabric may be first a shirt, and later a washing rag. But transubstantiation is distinctively different. Wine turns into vinegar, but there is nothing (neither thing nor stuff) that was first wine and later vinegar. Midas's touch may transform a copper goblet into a golden one. One and the same goblet is first copper and then gold. But there is no stuff that was first copper and then gold—the copper became gold. One might argue that the same matter is first one chemical substance, later another. Chemical experiments are conducted in schoolrooms to show that, for example, despite transubstantiation the matter in a sealed vessel is conserved. Yet, if the foregoing arguments are correct, then this is incorrect, for matter is not a kind of stuff. The stuff prior to transubstantiation has the same mass as the quite different stuff after transubstantiation—but that does not make it the same stuff, anymore than conservation of momentum through impact between two billiard balls suggests that there is one moving object. Of course, in the case of a quantity of stuff that is an ingredient of a compound stuff, we may say that this specific stuff was first constitutive of the compound—which now no longer exists—and is now, after extraction, to be used as an ingredient in the generation of a different compound.[9] It is noteworthy that "parcels" of stuff, which are individual things, are identity-dependent upon the stuff of which they are parcels. A lump of coal, transformed into coke, is not the same lump that was first coal and then coke, a nugget of copper, transformed by Midas's touch into gold, is not the same nugget, and a bottle of wine that turns into vinegar is the same bottle only in the container sense, not the partitive sense of 'bottle'.

Individual substances and the substance of which they are made or constituted are categorially distinct. A thing is never identical with the stuff that, at a given time, is constitutive of it. The relationship between the properties of a thing and the properties of what it is made of is subtle and complex. One might, at the cost of considerable unclarity, distinguish between the material and formal properties of things. The material properties are generally derived from the matter of which the thing is made, the formal properties characterize the specific thing that consists of, or informs, that stuff. The weight, volume, density, and spatial location of a thing is the weight, volume, density, and location of the stuff of which it consists at a given time. But the weight of a thing may increase or diminish, without the specific quantity of stuff of which it consists increasing or diminishing in weight.[10] Rather, the loss or increase in the weight of the thing results from loss or addition of quantities of constitutive stuff. A growing apple increases in weight, but the specific stuffs of which it consisted do not increase in weight, but rather the amount of stuffs increases, and the apple consists of a greater quantity of those stuffs. The smell, taste, and texture of a thing is the smell, taste, and texture of its constitutive stuff, or at least of some ingredient or compound of its complex constitution. Color is a characteristic of stuff as of things. But although the color of a thing is frequently the color of the stuff of which it is made, this is not always so. For a thing made of, for example, wood need not have the color of wood—it may be painted blue, yet it is made of wood, not of wood and paint.

Shape or form, however, as is suggested by the ancient notion of concrete particulars as a "combination" of form and matter, is not primarily a property of stuff, but of things. A quantity of stuff has the form of whatever thing, designated by sortal noun or partitive, which is made or consists of that stuff. A gold ball is spherical, but the gold of which the ball is made is not. A gold ring is circular, but the gold of which the ring is made is not.

Conversely, atomic structure—or Locke's "real essence"—is primarily attributable to stuff, not to things from which it is made. The nominal essence of a ball is given by its sphericity—but it has no real essence given by the particulate constitution (if any) of its constitutive stuff—for the particulate constitution, be it what it may, does not differentiate a ball from a ring (or any other object) made of that stuff.

However, our general conception of a material object is indeed that of form imposed upon matter. To the extent that Locke was right in his contention that primary qualities are definitive of material objecthood, it is clear that the properties of extension, spatial occupancy, density and relative solidity are features of the matter constitutive of a material object. Shape or form, however, characterizes the thing made of that matter, and not, or not primarily, the matter of which the object is made. Indeed, it is evident that what was primarily missing from the Cartesian list of primary (definitive) qualities of material objecthood was the property of consisting of some stuff or other. Hume objected to Locke on the grounds that solidity is a relative property, and, hence, cannot define material objecthood by being added to the Cartesian list of geometrical properties. This is correct. But solidity is a (relative) property of the stuff (or its surface) of which a thing is made, and the property of being made of some stuff or other is not a relative property. Not surprisingly, what defines a material object is, *inter alia*, being made of some material or other!

We have already noted that the reduction of sentences containing stuff nouns to sentences containing the primitive verb phrase 'is-made-of x' is suspect in the context of unpackaged stuff. The non-transferability of diverse predicates of things and predicates of the stuff of which it is made are a further anti-reductionist consideration. This is particularly evident where the stuff of which a thing is made is a compound whose properties differ from the properties of its ingredients. Brief reflection upon the culinary arts make this evident. If this is correct, then ousiology is not a branch of mereology — ousiology, we may claim, is here to stay.

Notes

1. In order to render the argument smoother and reduce notes to a minimum, I have avoided explicit citation of the contemporary discussions of this topic. My indebtedness to other philosophers is evident from the appended list of sources at the end, but my greatest debt is to the illuminating work of Professor H. Cartwright.

2. It is noteworthy that there is occasionally a shift from one category to another. 'Pease' as in 'pease-pudding' was originally a non-count noun like 'wheat' or 'corn', but happened to have what sounded like a plural ending. Hence, we have 'pea' (singular count noun) and 'peas' (plural count noun), and similarly with 'cherris' ('cherry' and 'cherries'). Occasionally, there is a lag in the adjustment of countability, for example, 'richesse' (a non-count noun) was transformed into 'riches', taking the plural, but with unclarity over 'much' or 'many'.

3. 'Luck' and 'ill-luck' are curious. I may wish that I had your luck without wishing you to lose it. But just as the Israelites thought they could rid themselves of sin and guilt by transferring them to a goat, which they then drove out into the desert, so too the superstitious think of ill-luck as something that one may rid oneself of by giving it to another. This is to conceive of 'ill-luck' on the model of a concrete non-count noun rather than an abstract one. The connection between philosophical and grammatical misconception and myth, superstition and ritual is not coincidental.

4. 'Money' here is employed in the numismatists' sense, that is, the concrete means of exchange consisting of coins and notes, not in the abstract sense of measure of value, which is infinitely divisible (as in talking of the exchange rate as being $1.77895 to the £).

5. Derived from R. Quirk and S. Greenbaum, *A University Grammar of English*. (London, 1973).

6. 'A little' *qua* quantifier must be distinguished from the homonymous 'a little' *qua* adjective.

7. Subject to the qualification previously mentioned.

8. One might, of course, indulge in complicated technical procedures of extraction, but this does not vitiate the argument. One could evaporate the coffee, separate the coffee residue from the milk residue, and add the same amount of water to the milk residue to produce the same amount of milk. Same *amount* — but not same specific quantity, for the water from which the coffee was made is not distinguishable from the remaining water. No doubt the elements of that specific quantity of water (the molecules) could be "marked" and, if marked, would in principle be distinguishable and separable. But if they are not marked (and they are not normally so marked), then they are not, even in principle, distinguishable.

9. But it would, of course, be wrong to say of the ingredient that it *was* first the initial compound and afterward the other compound. It was, rather, first an ingredient of the one, later of the other.

10. Excluding such changes in weight attributable, for example, to variations in gravitational force, which are compatible with the continued identity of the specific quantity.

References

Anscombe, G. E. M., and Geach, P. T., *Three Philosophers* (Oxford, 1967).

Burge, T., "Truth and Mass Terms," in *Journal of Philosophy* 69 (1972):263-82.

Cartwright, H., "Heraclitus and the Bath Water," in *Philosophical Review* 74 (1965):466-85.

——, "Quantities," in *Philosophical Review* 79 (1970):25-42.

——, "Chappell on Stuff and Things," in *Nous* 6 (1972):369-77.

Chappell, V. C., "Stuff and Things," in *PAS* 71 (1970-71):61-76.

——, "Aristotle's Conception of Matter," in *Journal of Philosophy* 70 (1973):679-96.

Geach, P. T., *Reference and Generality* (Ithaca, 1962).

Goodman, N., *The Structure of Appearance* (New York, 1951).

Laycock, H., "Some Questions of Ontology," in *Philosophical Review* 81 (1972):3-42.

Parsons, T., "An Analysis of Mass Terms and Amount Terms," in *Foundations of Language* 6 (1970):362-88.

Prior, A., "Things and Stuff," in *Papers in Logic and Ethics* (London, 1976), 181-86.

Quine, W. O., *Word and Object* (Cambridge, 1960).

Strawson, P. F., *Individuals* (London, 1959).

Was Leibniz a Relationist?

JOHN EARMAN

The great debate between Newton and Leibniz on the nature of space and time
is widely billed as a clash between absolutist and relationalist theories. While
not entirely false advertising, this billing is seriously misleading. In the first place, the
billing tends to drag in extraneous issues, for there are a number of senses in which
Newtonian space and time are "absolute" and some are simply irrelevant to the real
guts of the debate.[1] Leibniz's main target was Newton's substantivalist conception
of space, and his main argument against this conception need not be interpreted as
using or entailing relationism proper (that is, the reduction of space to relations
among bodies). For, as I will argue, Leibniz's attack on Newton is consistent with a
position intermediate between absolutist-substantivalism on one hand and relationist-
reductionism on the other. And I believe that the textual evidence suggests that this
intermediate position provides a better explication of what Leibniz actually intended
than does relationism proper.

In a recent paper, Ian Hacking[2] says that Leibniz uses the principle of the
identity of indiscernibles (PII) as a "nutcracker to crush Newton's absolute space."
It is unseemly to quibble with such a beautiful metaphor, but quibble I must. Leibniz's Nutcracker has two handles: one is the principle of sufficient reason (PSR); the
other is not the pure PII but an adulterated verificationist version of it (see Sec. 2
below). But my main quibble is no mere quibble: Hacking does not convey just how
powerful this Nutcracker is. If it does indeed succeed in crushing Newton's absolute
space, then it also crushes space in anything like the ordinary sense and it also crushes
physical bodies. This naturally raises the question of whether the crushing operation
leaves only broken shells or whether a nut emerges. I will argue for the nut—a rather
abstract and non-relationist one—and I will try to show how this nut is the meat on
which Leibniz's phenomenalism feeds and how it helps to explain Leibniz's insistence
that both bodies and space are well-founded phenomena.

In sum, I believe that a proper reading of the implications of the Newton-Leibniz debate is important not only for an understanding of Leibniz's views on space and time but also for his central metaphysical doctrines.

1. BEFORE THE CRUNCH: SUBSTANTIVALISM.[3]

The application of classical tests for substance leads to a long list of substantivalist doctrines of space. I will consider the five of these doctrines that help to make clear just what is and what is not at issue in the Newton-Leibniz debate.

(1) Space is a kind of "stuff" of which matter is composed.

(2) Space is active or the source of activity.

(3) Space is real.

(4) Space is self-subsistent.

(5) Space is an object of predication.

(1) is not a bone of contention; both Leibniz and Newton reject the Cartesian version of (1), and no other version was in the offing. It is interesting to note, however, that Leibniz's initial criticism of (1) was based on a highly realist and not-relationist conception of space. In 1669 he writes:

It must be proved that there are no entities in the world except mind, space, matter and motion . . . matter is a being which is in space . . . motion is change of space. . . . (L. 100-102)

and two years later:

space and body are distinct . . . we can think of space without a body which is in it. Now two things are diverse if one can be thought of without the other. Therefore space and body are distinct. (L. 143)

Nor is (2) a source of disagreement. In *De gravitatione* Newton asserts that space

does not stand under those characteristic affections that denominate a substance, namely actions, such as are thoughts in a mind and motions in a body. . . .[4]

Except for the phrasing, this is a passage that might well have come from Leibniz's later writings.

(3) does lead to some real disagreements between Newton and Leibniz, but there is no neat way to pose them. As we have seen above, Leibniz began as an unabashed realist about space; but his struggle with the labyrinth of the continuum produced a major shift though not a complete turnaround. In the important essay "Primary Truths," written in the mid 1680s, Leibniz stated part of his negative solution to the problem of the composition of the continuum:

the continuum is not divided into points, nor is it divided in all possible ways. (P. 91)

From this he concludes that

> There is no actual determinate shape in things. . . . Extension and motion and bodies, in so far as they consist of these alone, are not substances but true appearances, like rainbows and mock suns. (P. 92)

A similar line of reasoning is to be found in the correspondence with Arnauld which dates from the same period (see, for example, L. 343).

I will argue below that Leibniz's phenomenalism is also the outcome of applying sufficient pressure to the handles of the Nutcracker. But at this juncture what I want to call attention to is the fact that Leibniz refers to space and extension not as mere appearances but as "true appearances." This attitude is confirmed in his correspondence with Arnauld where he affirms that space and time are "well-founded appearances" (see L. 343). So on the phenomenal level, Leibniz seems to be in agreement with Newton over (3), at least to this extent: both believe that space and time are real in that they are part of the lawful structure of the physical world.

However, this apparent accord makes Jonathan Bennett's puzzle all the more puzzling. Bennet notes that in the correspondence with Clarke, Leibniz tends to say that space is "imaginary" or "ideal" rather than "real."

> This is said not just about Newtonian absolute space, but about *space* . . . and that is puzzling . . . since the doctrine that the extended world is a relational appearance . . . is not part of the relational theory and is not deployed against Clarke.[5]

The solution to Bennett's puzzle is to be found in a careful attention to what Leibniz actually says in those passages which allegedly express a relational theory of space. In the third letter to Clarke, he writes:

> . . . space denotes, *in terms of possibility*, an order of things which exist at the same time . . . (A. 26; my italics)

and

> . . . space is nothing at all without bodies, but *the possibility of placing them* . . . (A. 26; my italics)

The same view is expressed in other sources. For instance, to de Volder he says:

> Space is the order of *possible* coexistents. (L. 531; my italics)

And this view is expanded in his reply to Foucher's objections to the *New System*:

> Extension and space . . . are nothing but relations of order or of orders of coexistence, both as regards to that which actually exists and as regards *possible* things that might be put in place of that which exists. (La. 329; my italics).

It is now clear how to derive Leibniz's conclusion. Space is not a substance in the sense of a subject of predication (see the discussion of (5) below). Nor is it an attribute or a collection of attributes inhering in subjects—it is out of subjects since it concerns not just actual subjects but possible ones. But being neither substance nor attribute it is therefore "ideal."

Substantivalism (4) has two subtheses of relevance here: (4i) the existence of space is not dependent upon the existence of anything else (especially bodies), and (4ii) space is not reducible to relations among bodies. In *De gravitatione* Newton rejects one form of (4i). Space, he says,

> does not subsist absolutely in itself, but as it were an an emanative effect of God and a certain affection of everything.[6]

Of course, if the only reason space lacks self-subsistence is that it depends upon God, then Newton's denial of (4i) is not very exciting. But the final phrase in the quotation indicates that Newton intends something more; this is confirmed by later passages:

> Space is an affection of a *thing qua* thing. . . . Nothing exists or can exist which is not in some way referred to space . . . space is an emanative effect of the first existing thing; because if anything is posited, space is posited.[7]

How to interpret this fascinating passage is an important though largely neglected problem. Sadly, it will remain neglected here since it is Leibniz, not Newton, who is the focus of attention.

Let us then turn to (4ii), for this doctrine does finally seem to give rise to a substantive disagreement; Newton, being an absolutist, affirms (4ii) while Leibniz, being a relationist, denies (4ii). But in what form does Leibniz deny (4ii)? The above quotations in which Leibniz characterizes space as the possibility of placing bodies show that he did not intend any crude form of relationism, according to which space is reduced to relations among actual bodies. But then what is the difference between an absolutist—especially one of the stripe who sees space as an "emanative effect" of bodies—and a sophisticated relationist—especially one who sees space as the possibility of placing bodies? In particular, is the relationist who sees space points as possible locations for bodies saying anything that conflicts with Newton's conception?

I believe that substantivalism (5) is the crux of the Newton-Leibniz debate. It is primarily to this doctrine that Leibniz directs his Nutcracker, and any further illumination on the issues concerning the reality (3) and the self-subsistence (4) of space must be shed by an understanding of how the Nutcracker works and what it produces.

Substantivalism (5) is the logical core of the so-called container view of space. To assert that bodies are literally in space is to assert (at least) that it is legitimate to analyze the logical form of some statements about the behavior of bodies as Q(S), where 'S' designates a region of space and 'Q' designates a property of S, and that Q(S) is not shorthand for a set of assertions of the form $R(b_1, b_2, \ldots)$, where the 'b_i' designate bodies and 'R' designates a relation among these bodies. What else is contained in the container view is a question that will not be broached here, for the notion that space is an object of predication is sufficient to set Leibniz's Nutcracker into operation. Before turning to an analysis of this operation, it is worth noting that the field theories of modern physics seem, *prima facie*, to endorse an extreme version of substantivalism (5); namely, the view that space (or to be more precise, spacetime) is not just *an* object of predication but *the* one and only such object. Some of the mathematical apparatus of these theories will be used below to sharpen the crux of the Newton-Leibniz dispute.

2. THE NUTCRACKER

Let us remind ourselves of Leibniz's own description of the Nutcracker as it appears in the third letter to Clarke:

> I have many demonstrations, to confute the fancy of those who take space to be a substance, or at least an absolute being. But I shall only use, at the present, one demonstration; which the author gives me occasion to insist upon. I say then that if space was an absolute being, there would something happen for which it would be impossible there should be sufficient reason. . . . Space is something absolutely uniform; and without the things placed in it, one point of space does not absolutely differ in any respect whatsoever from another point of space. Now from hence it follows, (supposing space to be something in itself, besides the order of bodies among themselves) that 'tis impossible there should be sufficient reason, why God, preserving the same situation of bodies among themselves, should have placed them in space after one certain particular manner, and not otherwise. . . . But . . . if space is nothing at all without bodies, but the possibility of placing them; then those two states, the one such as now is, the other supposed to be the quite contrary way, would not at all differ from one another. Their difference therefore is only to be found in our chimerical supposition of the reality of space in itself. But in truth the one would exactly be the same thing as the other, they being absolutely indiscernible. . . . (A. 26)[8]

In this formulation, the Nutcracker is being used to squeeze substantival space in sense (5). But in order to take account of the motion of bodies through time, as Leibniz must, the Nutcracker has to be applied to space-time. It is not an entirely trivial exercise to construct just the right space-time for these purposes: to accord with Leibniz's theory of motion, the space-time must have just enough structure that its automorphisms (the mappings of the space-time onto itself which preserve all of the space-time structure) preserve relative particle motions, that is, the automorphisms must preserve relative particle distances, relative particle velocities, relative particle accelerations, etc. Elsewhere I have tried to show how the requirements of this exercise can be fulfilled by what I call *enriched Leibnizian space-time*.[9] The details are irrelevant here, and only some general features will be used.

In the language of modern differential geometry, a *substantivalist world model* has the form (M, G, P), where M is a differentiable manifold to be interpreted as the space-time manifold, G is the set of geometric object fields on M that characterize the structure of the space-time, and P is another set of geometric object fields on M that characterize the physical content of space-time. To keep the discussion simple while staying close to Leibniz's plenum theory, let us suppose that P contains just one field, a vector field V which is interpreted as the velocity field of a system of unit mass dust particles which entirely fill space; thus, through each point of M there passes one and only one integral curve of V, the curve being the worldline of one of the dust particles. Both Newton and Leibniz assume that the geometry of space-time is absolute in the sense that "without relation to anything external, it always remains similar and immovable";[10] so any two physically possible substantivalist world models have the forms (M, G, V) and (M, G, V′), the M and G being the same in both cases since they are not influenced by the behavior of the dust.[11] Suppose now that we are given two such models that are related by an automorphism of the space-time geometry; that is, suppose that there is a mapping $\Phi : M \to M$ which is onto, which preserves G, and which carries V to V′ (in the notation of differential geometry, $\Phi*G = G$ and $\Phi*V = V′$ where $\Phi*$ denotes the "dragging along" by the mapping Φ). If G is the structure of the enriched Leibnizian space-time I mentioned above, then let us say that such models are *Leibniz equivalent* (it is easy to see that this is in fact an equivalence relation). In equivalent models the relative motions of the Φ-related dust particles will be exactly the same. Hence, Leibniz will hold that, on pain of contradicting PSR and PII, Leibniz-equivalent models must not be taken as describing different possible worlds but rather as giving different descriptions of the same world.

Much philosophical ink has been spilled in attempts to assess the force of Leibniz's argument. It seems to me, however, that most of these attempts have been premature, and many strike me as attempts to try the case on the basis of pretrial publicity, without any clear sense of what the charges and countercharges amount to. Before the trial can get under way, we need to have information about the prospects of completing the following threefold program:

(P1)   An entire Leibniz-equivalence class of substantival world models is supposed to correspond to a single physical reality. Show how to give a direct characterization of this reality (call it a *Leibniz world model*) without using the Newtonian descriptive devices that seem to embody substantivalism (5).

(P2)   Show how the laws of physics can be expressed directly in terms of the Leibniz world models.

(P3)   Explain how the equivalent substantivalist models arise as different but equivalent representations of the same Leibniz model

If it could be shown that there is no acceptable way to implement this Program, then I think it must be concluded that Leibniz's Nutcracker fails to crush absolute-substantivalist space. If, on the other hand, there is an acceptable implementation, then I would say that Leibniz's argument carries a certain conviction. To be sure, one handle of the Nutcracker, the PSR, loses much of its force when stripped of its theological associations. However, the other handle, the PII, seems to me to lead to a plausible methodological rule for scientific theorizing: in choosing between two theories, where one theory employs a descriptive apparatus that implies the existence of distinct possible states between which we cannot distinguish by means of any observation, while the other theory has no such implication, then, all other things being equal, the latter theory is to be preferred to the former.

The prospects for implementing parts (P1) and (P2) of the Program are examined in Sec. 3, and the consequences for part (P3) are taken up in Sec. 4.

3. AFTER THE CRUNCH:
PRE-SPACE, PRE-GEOMETRY, AND PRE-MATTER

Consider the vector field V of some one of the substantival models (M, G, V) of Sec. 2. In the terminology of differential geometry, V is a derivation on the smooth real valued functions F(M) on the manifold M; that is, V is a map $V : F(M) \to F(M)$ which is linear, that is,

$$V(\lambda f + \mu g) = \lambda V(f) + \mu V(g)$$

for all f, g, ϵ F(M) and all $\lambda, \mu \epsilon$ R, and which obeys the Leibniz rule

$$V(fg) = V(f)g + fV(g)$$

As is implicit in this notation, F(M) has the structure of a ring since the functions can be (pointwise) added and multiplied, and the scalar factors $\lambda, \mu \epsilon$ R can be thought of as the subring of constant functions. Thus, we can drop out the underlying substantivalist manifold M while retaining the structural features that define the vector field; in particular, we can focus on the algebraic object $((\Re, \Re_0), \mathfrak{D})$ where $\Re$ is a ring of elements, $\Re_0$ is a distinguished subring isomorphic to the reals, and $\mathfrak{D}$ is a derivation on $(\Re, \Re_0)$.[12] Taking this object as basic, we can now reverse the above process and look upon the substantivalist model (M, V) as a way of realizing or representing the algebraic object $((\Re, \Re_0), \mathfrak{D})$ — the elements of $\Re$ are realized as smooth functions on M in such a way that (a) the $\Re_0$ are realized as constant functions and (b) the derivation operation is realized as a vector field on M. (More formally, (M, V) represents or realizes $((\Re, \Re_0, \mathfrak{D})$ iff there is a map $\chi : \Re \to F(M)$ such that (i) χ is a ring isomorphism (ii) $\chi(\Re_0)$ are the constant functions, and (iii) for all $r \epsilon \Re$

$$\chi(\mathfrak{D}(r)) = V(\chi(r)).)$$

Robert Geroch[13] has shown how this procedure can be extended to cover more complicated types of geometric object fields, for example, tensor fields, and how differential equations formed from these objects can be expressed in terms of the resulting algebras. Thus, there is reason to be confident that the substantival models (M, G, P) can be replaced by algebraic models $((\Re, \Re_0), \mathcal{G}, \mathcal{P})$, where $\mathcal{G}$ and $\mathcal{P}$ are now sets of algebraic operations on $(\Re, \Re_0)$, and that the laws of physics which were originally expressed in terms of the (M, G, P) can be reexpressed in terms of the $((\Re, \Re_0), \mathcal{G}, \mathcal{P})$ structures.

It would seem, then, that algebraic structures of this kind are natural candidates for the Leibniz models that are needed to implement parts (P1) and (P2) of the Program. They certainly satisfy the obvious condition of adequacy: since they do not contain or appeal to the notion of a set of space (or space-time) points which are the locations for bodies, they avoid the difficulty confronting the substantivalist models, namely, that distinct but isomorphic models can be produced by shifting bodies around in space (or, more precisely, by shifting the world lines of bodies around in space-time). And they avoid the difficulty in a manner that explains the status of the different substantivalist models that are generated in this fashion—the substantivalist models are simply different but equivalent representations of the same algebra. Finally, since the algebras do not use any notion of continuity, they are quite congenial to Leibniz's attitude toward the continuum.

Alas, all is not light. For although the algebraic models shed the worst trappings of the substantivalist models, they still run afoul of PII and PSR. Just as there were distinct but isomorphic substantivalist models, so there will be distinct but isomorphic algebraic models. The Nutcracker then forces us to group the algebraic models into equivalence classes and maintain that all the members of one such class are simply different representations of the same underlying reality. And this raises the fear that we are now in the position of the Sorcerer's Apprentice; once we have set the Nutcracker into operation it is out of our control and it forces us into a never-ending descent of ever deeper levels of reality.

There are essentially three ways in which the Sorcerer can try to rescue the Program from the mess his would-be Apprentice has made of it. Taking a cue from Leibniz's dictum that there are worlds within worlds *ad infinitum*, the Sorcerer could admit that the infinite regress takes place, but he could maintain that the infinite sequence of levels converges to a limiting level. Any discussion of this strategy must await an explanation of what convergence of levels means. Since I do not have one to offer, I will pass to the next strategy.

Second, the Sorcerer could hold that although the regress gets under way, it terminates after a finite number of steps in an uhr level which does not admit distinct but isomorphic world models. And it might be thought that the monads are just the magic ingredient needed to construct the uhr level. However, on what I find to be the most plausible interpretation of Leibniz's mature monadology, it is hard to see how the upper levels can be representations of the monadic uhr level. The monadic uhr level is monadic in both senses: it is constituted by monads and their monadic (that is, nonrelational) properties.[14] If then, as Leibniz insists, representation is a structure-preserving relation, it is quite mysterious how the upper level relational structures can, in any interesting sense, be said to represent the non-relational uhr structures. Many commentators have puzzled over this problem[15] and a few have tried to solve it. I think that it is a problem to be avoided rather than solved.

The third strategy is to stop the threatened regress before it starts. The problem of distinct but isomorphic algebras can be avoided if one takes the algebraic models not to be concrete particulars but to be abstract types of which the substantival models are concrete realizations. This is the strategy I endorse.

Now it cannot be claimed that these algebras considered as abstract types are what Leibniz actually had in mind as the outcome of applying his Nutcracker to substantivalist space (-time). Nor is it profitable to speculate about what Leibniz would have said if he had known about the mathematical apparatus used to construct the algebras—for one thing, Leibniz was all too ready to seize upon any apparatus that might be turned to his advantage. What I do claim is that, irrespective of the rest of Leibniz's philosophy, this third strategy is an interesting and plausible way to construe the operation of the Nutcracker. Further, I claim that this strategy is congenial to Leibniz's notion that space is "ideal" in that it amounts to the possibility of placing bodies; and, as I will argue in Sec. 4, this strategy suggests a way of implementing part (P3) of the Program which is compossible with Leibniz's treatment of perception and relations in the mature monadology and which makes Leibniz's attempt at phenomenalistic reduction of the physical world much more believable than it would otherwise be. But in the remainder of this section, I will concentrate on the implications for the nature of space, time, and matter.

To summarize the argument to this point, when the handles of Leibniz's Nutcracker—the PII and the PSR—are squeezed hard enough, what emerges are three abstract types: *the pre-space* $(\mathfrak{R}, \mathfrak{R}_0)$, the *pre-geometry* $\mathcal{G}$, and the *pre-matter* $\mathcal{P}$, which are realized or represented in many different ways respectively by the substantivalist's space(-time) manifold M, the geometry G of space(-time), and the matter fields P contained in space(-time). One immediate upshot is that while Hacking's characterization of the Nutcracker as crushing absolute space is vindicated, it is shown to be incomplete since the Nutcracker also squeezes the "stuff" out of matter and leaves only an abstract skeleton. This result appears at first glance to be incompatible with the stance Leibniz takes in the very correspondence in which the Nutcracker is introduced. It must be remembered, however, that treating bodies as if they were a basic given is a polemical move which Leibniz made in order to engage Newton on his own ground, and when not polemicizing against Newton, Leibniz is careful to say that both space and bodies are (well-founded) phenomena.[16]

Another important result is that the argument against the substantivalist goes through without entailing relationism proper (or the reduction of space to bodies). Of course, there *might* be a way to reduce the pre-space and pre-geometry to pre-matter; but when Leibniz's argument is construed in terms of space-time—as it must be in order to take account of motion through time—and when it is seen what structure must be included in the geometry G of space-time and encoded in the pre-geometry $\mathcal{G}$ in order to achieve a viable theory of motion,[17] then such a reduction becomes implausible. Again, there *might* be a different way of constructing the Leibniz models so that a relationist reduction is plausible, but I do not see how this is to be done while preserving the important feature of the present construal of the Leibniz models—namely, that there is an interesting and precise sense in which the familiar substantivalist models are realizations or representations of the Leibniz models. In any case, the crucial point is that the Nutcracker operates perfectly well without such a reduction, so we have the promised example of a half-way house that is not crushed by the Nutcracker and that lies between the extremes of absolutist-substantivalism and relationist-reductionism.

Finally, it is worth noting what my explication takes as essential to the operation of the Nutcracker and what it takes as incidental. As it was set up in the correspondence with Clarke, Leibniz's argument relies on the symmetries of Euclidean three space. Recall that one of his premises is that "Space is something absolutely uniform," that is, (Euclidean) space is homogeneous and isotropic in that rigid translations and rotations preserve all of the geometric structure of the space. So by analogy, the generalization of Leibniz's argument to space-time would seem to rely on the symmetries of space-time. This has led some commentators (including myself[18]) to believe that a sufficiently non-uniform substantivalist space or space-time — one that did not admit any nontrivial automorphisms — would be immune to Leibniz's Nutcracker. We can now see that this belief is false. Consider again a substantivalist model (M, G, P), and let Φ be *any* diffeomorphism of M onto itself. By dragging along the objects in G and P by Φ we get a new substantivalist model (M, Φ^*G, Φ^*P). Now *if* Φ is a symmetry of the space-time geometry G, that is, Φ^*G = G, then the new model is equal to (M, G, Φ^*P), and the PII and PSR can be brought to bear in the way described above. But even if Φ is *not* symmetry of G, we still get models that, though not Leibniz-equivalent in the original sense, are still isomorphic enough to give the Nutcracker purchase.

In sum, the Nutcracker is much more powerful in some respects than has generally been realized, but much less powerful than has been generally claimed. It is powerful enough to work on substantivalist spaces (and space-times) that are non-uniform, and it crushes matter as well as space. But it does not by itself crush space into the mold of the relationist-reductionist.

4. AFTER THE CRUNCH: PHENOMENALISM

Any reconstruction of Leibniz's mature monadology must take as the central theoretical notion that of perception in the monads. But two main interpretations of "perception" are available. Some commentators take as the basic notion that of one monad perceiving another monad (or an aggregate of other monads). Others, including myself, prefer to take as basic the notion of a monad perceiving a state of the physical world.[19] That monad *m perceives* the state ψ means that m "mirrors" or "represents" or "expresses" ψ in that m's internal perceptual (as opposed to its apperceptual) state is structurally isomorphic to ψ. The *clarity* of m's perception is a function of its conscious awareness or apperception of its perceptual state, but just how this function is evaluated need not be considered here. If two monads, m_1 and m_2, both perceive the same state, then *ipso facto* they will mirror or perceive each other; but on the present proposal, this latter sense of perception is derivative, and it is conditioned on the assumption of the harmony of the basic perceptions of the monads. In keeping with Leibniz's assertion that the reality of phenomena consists in the agreement among the percipients,[20] we can postulate in his behalf: the state ψ is *actual* (or *obtains*) iff each monad perceives ψ.

Before an assessment of this sketch can be undertaken, more has to be said about the nature of the states ψ and the monads representation of them. My own proposal has three components. First, the states ψ should not be thought of as instantaneous time slices of possible worlds but as entire possible worlds. While not true to Leibniz's actual intentions, this move does rescue him from the potentially embarrassing problem of having to postulate a relation of co-existence or simultaneity on the set of instantaneous states of the monads.[21] Thus, an "at time t" clause does not have to be understood as flanking each side of the 'iff' in the above condition for actuality. The drawback for Leibniz, who relied heavily on analogies in explaining and defending his system, is that the theoretical concept of perception is no longer very analogous to ordinary perception. But in view of the benefits, I think this is a price well worth paying. Second, I propose that the ψ's should be seen as akin to the Leibniz algebras considered as abstract types. And third, I propose that space and time are the modes of perception in the monads so that the perceptual representations of the monads are akin to spatio-temporal realizations of the algebras.

Leibniz's mature monadology, viewed as offering a phenomenalistic reduction of the physical world,[22] faces a problem common to all forms of phenomenalism — Furth's no residue problem.[23] Grant for the sake of argument that the phenomenalist has succeeded in producing necessary and sufficient conditions C_ψ for the obtaining of the state ψ, where the C_ψ are couched in terms of the perceptions of human observers, or of monads, or whatever. It still remains to be seen whether a full reduction has taken place; that is, whether the C_ψ can be explained independently of the sense of ψ in such a way that the full content of ψ is captured, leaving no residue.[24] Furth has suggested that what makes Leibniz's brand of phenomenalism plausible is that he has an infinity of percipients, one for each possible "point of view." While there is some force to this suggestion, it seems to me to fall into the trap that has snared many phenomenalists. Most phenomenalists tend to concentrate on only one side of the reduction relation. By packing more and more into the notion of perception, or by using more and more actual or hypothetical percipients, they hope to cement the reduction relation. All this leads to a neglect of the other side of the reduction relation. My proposal is that the no-residue problem is solved not by the infinity of the monadic percipients but by this *plus* the PII and PSR. These principles form the handles of the Nutcracker which forces ψ to be viewed as an abstract structure. And because each possible realization of this structure is found in some monad, it is clear that the full content of ψ is captured, leaving no residue. To turn the point around, in a harmonious universe where all the monads are perceiving the same ψ, ψ is just the structure common to all the monadic representations.

Furthermore, the important but elusive notion of point of view now becomes an explained notion rather than an unexplained explainer;[25] that is, rather than taking point of view as a basic notion that explains the difference in the perceptions of monads all of whom are mirroring the same state, difference in point of view can be taken as a result of the difference in the representations of this state.[26] Other attempts have been made to explain point of view, but they all seem to me to founder on various problems. For instance, trying to use different degrees of apperception to explicate point of view leaves the "bare monads," who have no conscious awareness, without any point of view or else with the same point of view, neither of which Leibniz wanted.[27]

Finally, the assumption that in his mature philosophy Leibniz was tending to a course parallel to the one I have been describing helps to explain an otherwise puzzling move. When Leibniz gave up his early naive monadology according to which monads are point objects located in substantivalist space, he could have retreated to a position in which the monads, though not literally in space, enjoy relative spatial relations. But this position, which would seem to be the natural way to combine a relational theory of space with the metaphysical themes, is explicitly rejected. As he puts it to de Bosses:

there is no spatial or absolute nearness or distance between the monads. (L. 604)

5. CONCLUSION

I have urged that the Newton-Leibniz debate is more accurately billed as a clash of substantivalist and non-substantivalist theories of space rather than as a contest between absolute and relational theories. The centerpiece of my account is a non-orthodox interpretation of Leibniz's Nutcracker in which nonstandard answers are given to each of the following questions: What are the objects to which Leibniz's Nutcracker is applied? How does the Nutcracker operate? What emerges from its operation? My answer to the final question is that the nut that emerges is both non-substantivalist and non-relational. This answer is interesting in its own right because it shows that, contrary to what has been widely if not universally assumed, there is a coherent middle ground between absolutist-substantivalism and relationist-reductionism, so that by leaving one of these camps you are not forced into the other. This is a welcome result since many philosophers have felt uncomfortable with both camps, but, for lack of clear alternative, have felt compelled to sleep in one or the other.

I also claimed that this nonorthodox reading does at least as much justice to Leibniz's views on the nature of space and time as the more standard readings; and further, I claimed that it fits well with one attractive way of reconstructing the mature monadology. Whether or not these claims are correct is a matter that can only be settled by more detailed studies. I am, of course, hopeful that my claims will stand the scrutiny, but as for the ultimate resolution, I care little. For I am confident that these claims focus attention on issues that have remained neglected but that must be addressed before we can make real progress in charting the inner core of that alluring and exasperating labyrinth called Leibniz's philosophy.[28]

Notes

1. For an example of this point, see the discussion in Sec. 2 below; see also my paper "Who's Afraid of Absolute Space," *Australasian Journal of Philosophy* 48 (1970): 278-319; hereafter referred to as "WAAS."

2. "The Identity of Indiscernables," *Journal of Philosophy* 22 (1975): 249-56.

3. The following abbreviations will be used in giving citations to Leibniz's works: A: *The Leibniz-Clarke Correspondence*, ed. H. G. Alexander (Manchester, 1965); L: *Leibniz, Philosophical Papers and Letters*, ed. L. E. Loemaker (2nd ed.; Dordrecht, 1969); La: *Leibniz, The Mona-*

dology and Other Philosophical Writings, ed. D. Latta (Oxford, 1971); P: *Leibniz, Philosophical Writings*, ed. G. H. R. Parkinson (London, 1973).

4. *The Unpublished Scientific Papers of Isaac Newton*, eds. A. R. Hall and M. B. Hall (Cambridge, 1962), p. 99. The translations of this and the other passages cited from *De gravitatione* are due to Howard Stein.

5. *Kant's Dialectic* (Cambridge, 1974), pp. 150-51.

6. *The Unpublished Scientific Papers of Isaac Newton*, p. 99.

7. *The Unpublished Scientific Papers of Isaac Newton*, p. 103.

8. Note that Leibniz initially puts pressure on only one handle of the Nutcracker—namely, the PSR. At the end of the passage, he also puts weight on the other handle—the PII. But the "indiscernibility" of x and y is not taken to mean that $(\forall Q)(Q(x) \leftrightarrow Q(y))$, where the quantification ranges over all nonformal first-order properties. In order that PII have the polemical force Leibniz wants it to have, "indiscernibility" must mean something like: we (humans) cannot, by means of any possible observation, distinguish between x and y. This reading is confirmed by the fifth letter to Clarke, where Leibniz says: ". . . motion does not indeed depend upon being observed; but it does depend upon being possible to be observed." (A. 74). See also the discussion at the end of this section.

9. See my paper "Leibnizian Space-Times and Leibnizian Algebras," in *Proceedings of the Fifth International Congress for Logic Methodology and the Philosophy of Science*, ed. J. Hintikka; hereafter referred to as "LSTLA" (forthcoming).

10. From the Scholium of Newton's *Mathematical Principles of Natural Philosophy*.

11. There is room for some doubt on this point. Depending upon how one reads Leibniz's doctrine that God's miracles are built into the "general order" of things, one might take Leibniz as allowing changes in G in some physically possible worlds.

12. See R. Geroch, "Einstein Algebras," *Communications in Mathematical Physics* 26 (1972): 271-75.

13. *Ibid*.

14. See my paper "Perceptions and Relations in the Monadology," manuscript (1977); hereafter referred to as "PRM."

15. See, for example, *Kant's Dialectic*, p. 48.

16. See Leibniz's letters to de Volder (L. 515-39) and to de Bosses (L. 596-616).

17. See "LSTLA."

18. *Mea Culpa*! See "WAAS."

19. For some cogent arguments in favor of this reading, see M. Furth, "Monadology," *Leibniz*, ed. H. Frankfurt (New York, 1972).

20. "Matter and motion, however, are not so much substances or things as they are phenomena of percipient beings, whose reality is located in the harmony of the percipient himself (at different times) and with other percipient beings." (L. 537).

21. Leibniz apparently recognizes the problem; to de Volder he writes: "To coexist and to exist before or after are something real. . . ." (L. 519). De Volder later questions the resultant asymmetric status of space and time in the monadology, and Leibniz writes: "I had said that extension is the order of possible coexistents and that time is the order of possible inconsistents. If this is so, you say you wonder how time enters into all things, spiritual as well as corporeal, while extension enters only into corporeal things." For Leibniz's answer, see L. 531.

22. It must be admitted that Leibniz never entirely abandoned his earlier aggregate theory according to which physical bodies are aggregates of monads; for some discussion of this point, see *Leibniz* and "PRM."

23. "Monadology."

24. Leibniz's own comments on this problem are apt to strike one as rather feeble; to de Bosses he writes: ". . . we mean nothing else when we say that Socrates is sitting down than that what we understand by 'Socrates' and by 'sitting down' is appearing to us and to others who are concerned. . . ." (L. 605).

25. In his book *Leibniz, An Introduction* (Cambridge, 1975) C. D. Broad takes point of view as a primitive quality of monads. It is hard to see how to reconcile this move with Leibniz's insistence that there is nothing in the monads but perception, apperception, and appetition.

26. The substantivalist gets into trouble with the PSR because he holds that God has to choose to actualize one and only one of these representations; but on the present proposal, God realizes them all in the infinity of monads. This still leaves the PII to worry about. On my reconconstruction, Leibniz must hold that while these different representations correspond to the same physical state, they give rise to different appearances or perceptual states.

27. In addition, Leibniz's illustrations—for example, the representation of a circle by an ellipse and by another circle—strongly suggest that different perceptual states are involved in different points of view.

28. I wish to thank Professor J. L. Mackie and the members of the Department of Philosophy of the University of Minnesota at Morris for a helpful discussion of these topics.

Two Conceptions of Surfaces

AVRUM STROLL

I n this paper I shall raise and try to answer some questions about surfaces: What are they? Are they things? Can they be parts of things? Do they have depth? Can one scratch the surface of an object without scratching the object? Does everything have a surface? There are some related questions, concerned with the *seeing* of surfaces, that I shall not discuss. For example, can one see an object without seeing its surface? Can one see its surface without seeing the object? What exactly is it that one is seeing in such cases? In what follows I shall argue that the answers to all such questions depend on which of two quite different conceptions of surfaces one has in mind, or presupposes, in discussing them.

I

What are the two conceptions? An elegant expression of one of them is to be found in the writings of Leonardo da Vinci; for this reason I shall call it "The Leonardo Conception." In Part II I shall describe the second conception which I shall call "The Somorjai Conception," naming it after a contemporary scientist. Let us begin with Leonardo. I quote the passage dealing with surfaces in its entirety:

> The contact of the liquid with the solid is a surface common to the liquid and to the solid, and the lighter liquids with the heavier have the same.
>
> All the points are equal to one and one to all.
>
> Nothingness has a surface in common with a thing, and the thing has a surface in common with nothingness, and the surface of a thing is not part of this thing. It follows that the surface of nothingness is not part of this nothingness; it must needs be therefore that a mere surface is the common boundary of two things that are in contact; thus the surface of water does not form part of the water nor consequently does it form part of the atmosphere, nor are any of the bodies interposed between them. What is it, therefore, that divides the atmosphere from the water? It is necessary that there should be

a common boundary which is neither air nor water but is without substance, because a body interposed between two bodies prevents their contact, and this does not happen in water with air because they are in contact without the interposition of any medium.

Therefore they are joined together and you cannot raise up or move the air without the water, nor will you be able to raise up the flat thing from the other without drawing it back through the air. Therefore a surface is the common boundary of two bodies which are not continuous, and does not form part of either one or the other, for if the surface formed part of it, it would have divisible bulk, whereas, however, it is not divisible and nothingness divides these bodies the one from the other.[1]

The main (though not all) the points being made by Leonardo may be summarized as follows:

(i) When a liquid and a solid (no doubt Leonardo would say "any two media") come in contact, the point where they meet is a surface. An example: The interface of air and water.

(ii) Clearly, water and air are juxtaposed—you cannot raise up or move the air without the water; and conversely—and yet they are divided or separated from one another.

(iii) What, then, divides the atmosphere from the water? Answer: it must be a common boundary which is neither air nor water.

(iv) Such a boundary is not part of either medium. The surface of the water is not part of the water, the surface of the air is not part of the air.

(v) Such a common boundary must be without substance. For if it had substance or divisible bulk, it would be a body interposed between the two media, and thus would prevent their contact. But they are in contact; therefore what separates them cannot have divisible bulk.

(vi) Therefore the surface is not a thing.

The notion that surfaces are not things, that they lack divisible bulk, is the essence of the Leonardo conception. The same notion can be expressed in a number of different idioms. It has been said of surfaces, for example, that they are "conceptual entities only" or "logical abstractions," or "mere outsides," or "the outermost boundary of a thing," or "an outermost aspect." Of course, these same phrases may be given, as we shall see, other interpretations as well; but they are often used to express just the conception that Leonardo has in mind. When they are, it is implied that surfaces, being nothing at all, cannot be parts of objects either. If, for instance, one were to list the parts of an apple (and on the assumption, perhaps incorrect, that apples can be truly said to have surfaces), then the surface of an apple, according to this view, would not be part of it in the way that its skin and core are. This conception tends, furthermore, to assimilate surfaces to boundaries: A surface is not unlike the equatorial boundary that separates the northern and southern hemispheres of the earth. The equator is not a thing, has no bulk, cannot be seen, even in good light, by the weary traveler who crosses it; and it is not part of either hemisphere. Just so with the common surface that separates water from air: It is not a thing, has no bulk, and is not a part of either medium.

The Leonardo conception has a solid foothold in both science and common sense; in this respect it is like the Somorjai conception. But it also has implications which though acceptable to science may not be to common sense. Its common basis derives from a process of reflection about the nature of surfaces; there is thus a sense in which this conception is not part and parcel of the ordinary man's pre-analytical or unreflective acceptance of the world, but rather the outcome of some conscious thinking about it. As such it could, in principle, be reconstructed as a formal argument, having premises and a conclusion. But to do so is not necessary for our purposes here. The intuitive idea is that of a progressive thinning out of a surface, and this can be illustrated by examples. Consider the following. Suppose a person believes that a particular surface is a thing having some physical bulk: Say a certain depth. One might believe this of a road that had just been resurfaced with macadam, or of the uppermost stratum of the water of a large lake. In the latter case, one might think that the surface of the lake has a specific depth on the ground that, as a surface, it has properties that the mass of water beneath it does not have: For example, being rough, being of a light green color, and so forth. It might be possible if one scrutinizes the lake to see just how deep this layer goes: Suppose such properties hold of the water to a depth of one foot. One might thus say of the surface that it is a foot deep.

But, so the process of thinking runs, suppose now that one sees a fish swimming in the lake six inches below the point where the uppermost layer of water meets the air. Could we say that the fish is swimming below the surface? Obviously not if the surface is a foot deep. Yet it clearly makes sense to say that the fish is swimming just below the surface, even that it is swimming *six inches* below the surface. Yet how could this make sense if the surface is a foot deep? Well, then, shall we say it is six inches deep? Clearly if the fish were swimming three inches below the interface of water and air, we could still sensibly say it is swimming below the surface. Take any supposed depth and we obtain exactly the same result. If that is so, it follows that the surface cannot have *any* depth; it cannot be identified with a discernibly different layer of water that is a foot deep. In Leonardo's phrase, it cannot have bulk or "divisible substance." Moreover, as he says, it cannot be a part of the water; since any part of water will have *some* depth. The surface thus ultimately turns out to be no thing at all, but is a mere boundary between water and air. This process of "thinning out x," where x is the surface of y, will always result in the kind of progressive emasculation of x that turns it into a mere limit, an abstraction or logical entity, lacking physical properties and dimensions.

The Leonardo conception is employed both in ordinary discourse and in scientific talk about surfaces. Both scientists and ordinary persons arrive at the conception via the "thinning out process" I have characterized. One can say it is a concept both of common sense and of science. Yet when it is unpacked, it has implications that common sense, but not science, would find paradoxical. For while both common sense and science are in agreement that surfaces — on this interpretation — lack divisible bulk, they are not in agreement that wherever one has two media in contact the boundary separating them is a surface. This seems to be a view held only by science.

For science a cube-shaped, wooden tank of water, open at the top, has five (not six) interior surfaces. The water in the tank has six surfaces, five of them impinging against the wooden walls of the tank, the other against the open air. But ordinary speakers, left to their own devices and without special guidance, would be hesitant to say that the water in the tank has six surfaces. They would probably be equally hesitant to say that the tank itself, even if filled with water, has five interior surfaces; they might be more willing to say this if the tank were empty. If later the tank were carefully filled with water to the top, and then enclosed, thus forming a perfect wooden cube, filled with water, and with no interior air bubbles, science would say that both the tank and the water have six surfaces, while common sense would be likely to say that neither the interior of the tank nor the water in it has any surfaces. If the tank were then opened, so that one dimension were exposed to the air, a scientist might not find it odd to say that a heavy object inserted into the tank is sinking to a surface. Common sense would find this way of speaking confusing. It, instead, would say of the object that it is sinking to the bottom of the tank and would deny that insofar as it is doing so it is sinking to a surface. This is in part because it would presuppose that there is just one surface involved, and it is located where the water and the air intersect (that is, at the open end of the tank, and not at its bottom). It would find it bizarre, without some special instructions, to say for example that a swimmer is sinking to the surface or a surface. Again this would be in part a function of the logic of 'to sink'[2], and in part a function of holding that there exists only one surface in this particular case, and it is to be found where the water and the air come in contact.

Without relinquishing the Leonardo conception, common sense and science disagree about what the conception entails. Science feels no special tension in accepting the notion that surfaces can be thought of as boundaries that divide contiguous media. Insofar as it does, it accepts the Leonardo position that it is a *façon de parler* to speak as if each medium itself has a surface; no such attribution is to be taken literally. Thus, if one juxtaposes two solid billiard balls, what separates or divides them is a common boundary without substance or bulk. But such a boundary does not belong to either medium.

Common sense, however, would find Leonardo's question "What separates the two media when they are in direct contact?" puzzling. It would say that if they are in direct contact, nothing separates them. To be sure this is also explicitly what Leonardo says, but he adds, nevertheless, that what separates them is a surface belonging to neither medium. Common sense, unlike science, would be reluctant to add Leonardo's tag. Instead, it believes that each of the billiard balls has its own surface, a surface that exists before they are brought together, which they are not thought to lose while they are in contact. Common sense would be hesitant to assert that there is anything they have in common while in contact though of course not denying that their surfaces are touching at some point. Common sense might agree that this "point" represents a "common boundary," but if it made this concession, it would not go on to agree that this entails that either ball has lost the surface it originally had. Accordingly, common sense would seem to say that there is a sense, consistent with the Leonardo conception but not otherwise specified, in which each surface is "part of" the billiard ball of which it is the surface. This sense of 'part' would not, of course, entail that the surface *per se* had any divisible bulk; but it would entail that it somehow belonged to the particular billiard ball whose surface it is.

Science and common sense would differ in other ways, especially in terms of what each would partake of the Leonardo conception. Unlike science, which might be inclined to attribute surfaces indiscriminately to any sort of physical object or phenomenon, common sense would withhold such an attribution from whole classes of "entities." With respect to some of them, it would agree that they have boundaries which serve to mark them off from other items in their environments, but it would deny that such boundaries are surfaces. In yet other cases, it would maintain that though such entities are full-fledged physical objects, it would deny that surface talk was applicable to them, thus, in effect, denying that they have surfaces. In an earlier paper,[3] I described some of these cases in detail and the supporting arguments for these inferences. Rather than repeating the arguments here, I shall simply summarize the main findings.

One might begin by drawing a distinction between physical phenomena and physical objects. Shadows, rainbows, lightning (the list is, of course, much larger) fall into the former category, and in ordinary discourse such entities are not thought to have surfaces. Take shadows, for example. One can draw an outline around a shadow; in that sense it might be said that the shadow has a boundary. Yet it would seem odd to say that the shadow has a surface. No properties or features are attributable to the *surface itself* of a shadow. It cannot be said to be dark or light, thick or thin, smooth or rough, wet or damp; nor does it have depth or mass. It cannot be removed from the shadow, polished, washed, or sanded down. Though the locution "the surface area of a shadow" is sometimes used in ordinary speech, this expression would normally be taken to be referring to the surface area of the ground, earth, or water that is covered by the shadow, not to the surface of the shadow itself. And this is so because for common sense, as expressed in everyday speech, shadows do not have surfaces and are not the sorts of things that could have. Similar comments apply to the other items belonging to this category, such as flashes of lightning, rainbows, and so on.

Moreover, many things belonging to the class of full-fledged physical objects ("material things") are not normally said to have surfaces. Among these are included mountains, trees, persons, and animals. How do we speak about clouds, for example? Unlike a submarine, which may be described as coming to, floating upon, breaking through or just gliding beneath the surface of the sea, an airplane is not described in these ways with respect to clouds: It does not break through the surface, rest upon it, and so on. Why the difference? In my earlier paper I suggested that objects to which surfaces are ascribed must have a certain density or compactness, and reasonably determinate boundaries. As a medium, clouds stand intermediate between water (that is, a lake) which clearly satisfies these criteria and a medium such as air which does not; it is less dense than the former and more dense than the latter. But for ordinary speakers it is probably considered insufficiently dense and as lacking sufficiently determinate boundaries for surface talk to apply. It is for similar reasons that surface talk is held to be inapplicable to afro wigs, trees, deep grass. Why we withhold such talk from living persons (though not from statues of them) and from animals is more complicated; and in my previous article I suggested some reasons why this might be so. Whether those reasons are good ones or not I do not wish to debate here; my main point is that in ordinary speech surface talk is withheld from a variety of physical phenomena and objects.

I have, however, chosen to talk specifically about clouds because the considerations that apply to them enable us to identify another respect in which the Leonardo model would not be acceptable *in toto* by ordinary speakers. For, to take his specific example, we find that ordinary speakers would not describe both *the air* and the water as having a surface, but only the water. And even in such a case surface talk would apply to water only when it is in a fairly stable configuration, where the qualities of determinateness of outline, density, and compactness are apparent. So though surface talk is applicable to water in a lake (in fact, actually to the lake taken as a body of a certain density), it probably would not be applicable to water rapidly running out of a faucet. In accordance with this principle, ordinary speakers do not describe the interface of lake and air as the *surface of the air*. This may be because it is difficult to see air, and thus to ascribe to it the determinate boundaries that surface talk requires. It may also be that surface talk requires that an object be relatively localizable, and thus have a discernible autonomy, characteristics that air discernibly lacks. But in the end this may be simply another way of saying that unless something has reasonably determinate boundaries, surface talk will not be applicable to it.

So though common sense may, in some of its postures, accept the Leonardo model, it does not accept all of its consequences.

II

The Somorjai Conception of surfaces is also to be found in scientific talk and in ordinary discourse; yet it seems not only different from but actually incompatible with the Leonardo Conception. Since science and common sense make use of both concepts, are they each internally inconsistent? Let us defer consideration of this question until we have a clearer picture of this second notion.

A typical statement of it is to be found in a recent paper by the scientist G. A. Somorjai.[4] Like many scientists who talk about surfaces, Somorjai sometimes seems to have the Leonardo model in mind; for example, he speaks about the difficulties involved in studying "solid-liquid, and solid-solid *interfaces*." But the substance of the paper is concerned with examples of surfaces where surfaces are taken to be "things" (or in his parlance "systems"). He speaks, for example, about the coral reef, the leaf, and other photosynthetic "systems" with a high surface area, or as having a high surface-to-volume ration (A/V) (P. 489). In one place he writes:

Defining the surface to be studied as the topmost layer of atoms, one must obtain detectible signals from 10^{15} atoms or molecules in the background of 10^{22} atoms or molecules to obtain surface information. (p. 489)

A layer of atoms—perhaps the uppermost layer of atoms—is not so different from a last layer of water; this conception seems similar to that which common sense and science rejected in espousing the Leonardo Conception. There it thinned the latter out to the point where it became an abstraction or mere limit. But there is no doubt that Dr. Somorjai does not think of surfaces in this way. In his paper there are schematic representations, that is, actual drawings of what a surface looks like on the atomic scale. With his kind permission, I reproduce such a drawing from his article in *Science*.

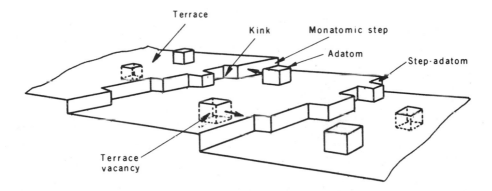

Fig. 1. Schematic representation of the heterogeneous surface on the atomic scale. Terrace, step, and kink atoms as well as point defects (adatoms and vacancies) have been identified by experiments. From G. A. Somorjai, "Surface Science," *Science*, vol. 201, No. 4355 (11 Aug. 1978, pp. 489-97). Reproduced with permission of author and publisher. Copyright 1978 by the American Association for the Advancement of Science.

The surface depicted in Figure 1 looks surprisingly familiar; it contains various topological features analogous to those one might find in a well-tended garden or orchard. Some of these he calls "terraces," "steps," "kinks," "vacancies," and so on. He states further that these features have been identified by experiments. Some of the features "Adatoms," look like ivory cubes, say like six-sided dice, except, of course, that they are writ much smaller. One committed to the Leonardo model might be tempted to ask of such features whether they themselves do not have surfaces, and where their surfaces begin. The thinning out process seems almost irresistible; yet Dr. Somorjai does resist it. The surface is the whole system which includes these features.

To a great extent his paper is a description of the physical and chemical properties of the kind of surface we see in Figure 1; for example, he holds that the surface of an ordinary solid is heterogeneous on the atomic scale (having just such different features as "steps" and "terraces") and that different types of surface features ("sites") have different chemistries (p. 490).

It seems clear that Somorjai takes surfaces to be things of a complex sort, having specific physical and chemical properties. It is also obvious that this is how common sense, as exhibited in ordinary ways of talking, sometimes conceives of surfaces. Indeed, depending on what one is speaking about, common sense holds not only that surfaces are things but even that they are physical objects. The Somorjai Conception is thus grounded in both science and common sense. But what is this conception that they both accept?

It begins from what it takes to be a fact, namely that surfaces have properties and are subject to various kinds of operations. Marbles are the kinds of things that have surfaces. Their surfaces can be described as rough, smooth, slippery, chipped, sticky, blemished, pitted, or damaged; one can speak about sanding, polishing, painting, wiping, or waxing their surfaces. In Somarjai's parlance, a marble is a "solid." It will indeed have a surface, which Somorjai will identify with its outermost layer of atoms. Corresponding to ordinary predicates such as "rough" or "pitted," Somorjai's vocabulary will speak about the surface as having "steps" or "kinks," or being "heterogeneous." Thus with respect to conceiving of surfaces as kinds of things, the views of common sense and Somorjai do not substantially differ.

But both views differ from the Leonardo Conception. For if, as Leonardo contends, a surface is a "mere common boundary," having no substance or divisible bulk, how is it possible that some surfaces can be correctly depicted as being rough or slippery, or as requiring painting or wiping? Surely if a surface were like the equator, a mere conceptual entity, none of the predicates would be applicable. The difference comes out most strikingly when we speak, as we did earlier, of a surface's having depth (or divisible bulk in Leonardo's phrase). For Leonardo, a surface being nothing cannot have depth; the surface boundary that separates water from air has no thickness or density or depth, and is not made up of layers. But according to Somorjai it would at least be one atomic layer thick. Or to vary the example, common sense would aver that when a road is resurfaced with a macadam covering, one could say either that the macadam is three inches thick or that its surface is three inches thick. Moreover, if the job were performed ineptly, one could remove the surface by removing the macadam. To do the one is to do the other. For common sense surfaces are often identified with such covering material as paint, lacquers, glosses; and it is these that are scratched or pitted or removed when the surface is said to be scratched or pitted or removed. But even when the surface is not taken to be a covering material —as, for example, the surface of a solid steel marble—its surface can still be said to be pitted or scratched. And this would only be possible if surfaces were things having depth or divisible bulk. According to this conception none of these ascriptions would be possible if surfaces were, as Leonardo states, "mere common boundaries," having no substance.

III

It does appear, on the basis of the preceding discussion, as if the two conceptions are different from each other. Yet the matter is not as simple as it looks. In the following two sections I wish to investigate the question of whether they are different from one another; in the end I shall decide that they are.

We have seen that the Somorjai Conception holds surfaces to be things and that the Leonardo Conception denies this. Put in this simple way the two views seem incompatible. Yet there are some complications arising from how the notion of being a "thing" is unpacked.

One of the grounds that both common sense and science have for holding that surfaces are things is that surfaces can truly be said to have properties and be subject to certain sorts of operations or procedures. But though Leonardo denies that surfaces are things, it is consistent with his conception of them as common boundaries that they can have properties and are subject to certain operations. If so, the mere possession of properties and susceptibility to operations may not be a sufficient condition for distinguishing the two conceptions from each other.

To illustrate the point, let us return to the equator analogy. Though the equator is, to be sure, nothing that one can scratch or pick up, and is not the kind of thing that reflects light, nevertheless it is true to say that it is equidistant from the north and south poles. A surface considered as a common boundary may well be equidistant from two arbitrarily selected points in the media that it divides. So the analogy seems close. Most such properties, such as that of being equidistant from x and y, would be relational properties rather than what might be called intrinsic properties. It thus might be argued that one can distinguish surfaces as boundaries from surfaces as things on the ground that the former have only relational properties and lack such intrinsic properties as length, mass, color, etc. But promising though this line seems, it probably will not do. It can be said of the equator, for example, that it is curved or that it has a measurable length at any given time, and, if so, one would be attributing some intrinsic properties to it. Generally speaking, there is nothing paradoxical about attributing intrinsic properties to boundaries; we do it all the time. The French-Spanish border, for example, belongs neither to France nor to Spain, yet it has a definite length. Clearly, we can measure the surface area of one face of a die, and so on. One can generalize beyond surfaces to see that the point is not decisive. Even nonexistent entities can have intrinsic properties; Pegasus, for example. Thus it is not the case that all things lacking substance or divisible bulk lack intrinsic properties. Tempting though this route may be, I do not think it will lead us to a distinction between the two conceptions of surfaces.

A second approach might take the following line. According to Leonardo, a common boundary is not only not a thing but it is not a part of anything either. So a surface for him is not a property either of the water or of the air that it divides. On the other hand, the Somorjai Conception allows the surfaces to be properties of things. An ivory die can be said to have the property of having six surfaces. Thus the difference between the two conceptions would be that one of them, the Somorjai, would allow surfaces to be properties themselves, while the other would not.

Unfortunately, this suggestion will not do either. For though Leonardo speaks as if surfaces cannot be parts of the media that ordinarily might be said "to have" them, they still might be regarded as being properties of those media. In particular, a given surface might be regarded as a common property that two media jointly have. This response would hold that "not being a part of x" does not entail "not being a property of x." There is a sense in which "the French border" and "the Spanish border" are different borders, even when one is speaking about points where they coincide. For example, the French border is manned by French police while the Spanish border is not. But there is a sense in which the two terms denote exactly the same border. In such a case, one might say that the two countries have a common property, that of having the same border.

Even more to the point, the border that France shares with Spain exactly defines a property that France has, that is, of being a certain width, for example. There is thus a kind of isomorphism between common boundaries and properties possessed by their associated media. The surface shared by air and water, even on the Leonardo conception, may exactly define the surface area of a given lake. Though even if one granted that the "surface" in Leonardo's sense was not made of water and hence was not part of the lake, it gives rise to certain derivative properties that are.

Yet despite these difficulties, I still believe that there is a fundamental difference between the two conceptions. So let us make another effort to see where it may be found. The key clearly will lie in how the Somorjai Conception unpacks the notion that surfaces are things. As we have seen, it will not be sufficient to maintain that surfaces have properties and are subject to various kinds of operations: What is at stake must turn on what kinds of properties and operations are involved.

These properties and operations cannot be what I called in my earlier paper "intensional" properties and operations. These are concerned with imagining, believing, thinking, intending, and so forth. One can imagine, for example, a given surface to be larger than it is, to be detached from the object that has it, to be bent in space when it is in fact not, and so forth. What is characteristic of such intensional properties and operations is that they may apply both to actual things and to nonactual ones; to things having divisible bulk and to things lacking substance. One can imagine Secretariat and Pegasus as being the same color; Bresnev with snakes in his hair and Medusa as bald; one can imagine the equator as a kind of elastic band, brown in color, tightly wound around the earth, itself conceived of as a golden ball set in an orrery. So one could imagine Leonardo's surfaces, those "mere boundaries," as having thickness and depth, as being of a certain color, or as made of fine-spun gossamer. Since both things having divisible bulk and things not having divisible bulk are capable of "possessing" such intensional properties and of being subject to such conceptual operations, we cannot distinguish surfaces in Leonardo's sense from surfaces in Somorjai's by saying that one type will have such properties while the other will not.

But there are sets of properties and operations that differ from the preceding, and can be used to distinguish between the two conceptions. I shall call them "physical" properties and operations. Examples of the first sort are being sticky, damp, pitted, rough; examples of the second kind are sanding, polishing, painting, wiping, waxing.

It is these kinds of properties and operations that do not apply to surfaces as characterized by Leonardo, but that do apply to surfaces as characterized by Somorjai. For if, as Leonardo claims, surfaces have no substance or divisible bulk, then how would it be possible to paint, wax or wipe them, or sand them down and refinish them; and how would it be possible for a "mere boundary" to be rough, smooth, slippery, damp, sticky, and pitted? Surely, if a surface were, as Leonardo suggests, like the equator, a mere conceptual entity, none of these operations or predicates would apply to it. But since they do have application, then what they apply to cannot merely be a boundary in Leonardo's sense.

Though it is difficult to specify in general the criteria that properties and operations must satisfy to be members of the class of "physical" properties and operations, the examples we have cited seem (and I stress the word 'seem') sufficient to enable us to distinguish the Leonardo and Somorjai Conceptions from each other.

IV

Why do I say "seem" sufficient, rather than "are" sufficient? As I mentioned earlier, there remains one major difficulty that must be overcome before we can conclude that there are two irreducibly different conceptions here. The reason for this is that the Somorjai Conception may in some important sense not be about *surfaces* after all, but rather about the objects that have such surfaces.

Let me quickly summarize the situation as it now appears from the preceding discussion. We have seen that Leonardo tends to "thin" out surfaces so that they become mere abstractions, having neither substance nor bulk. But we have also seen that Somorjai tends to assimilate surfaces to physical objects; and the question we must now ask is: Has this assimilation been carried so far that so-called surface talk is just talk about objects or parts of objects?

Somorjai produces representations of surfaces in which they look like landscapes. They have terraces, steps, kinks, holes, and various irregular protrusions. One could say that it is the object that has such terraces, steps, kinks. So, for example, to say that the surface of a mirror is chipped or pitted, or that the surface of the mirror has been wiped, or needs cleaning, is just to say that the mirror itself is chipped and has been wiped. One can say both that the road is rough and that its surface is rough; one can say that it is the table that needs refinishing and that its surface does. In applying these terms and predicates both to surfaces and to the objects that have them, are we not simply saying the same thing twice over; is it not the case that the terms are being applied to exactly the same thing in both cases? Is surface talk merely talk about the object, so that on the Somorjai Conception the distinction between a surface and the object that has it is a distinction without a difference, or at least without an ontological difference? The question at stake is: Are surfaces, considered as things, entities in their own right, somehow autonomous and different from the objects that have them? By this question I do not merely mean that a surface differs from the object that has it in the way that a scratch differs from the object that is scratched. What I do mean is: Is the surface of a road really identical with the macadam that covers it; is the surface of a refinished table really identical with the new paint that has been applied to it? And how are we to characterize how surfaces differ from their corresponding objects when we are talking about the surfaces of solid steel marbles or ball-bearings, for example? What is the surface identical with in such cases, since they possess no "covering materials" such as macadam or paint, but are homogeneous throughout?

It may be possible to distinguish surfaces from their corresponding objects in two ways: First, by showing that objects have properties their surfaces do not have; and then by showing that surfaces have properties their objects do not have. The kinds of properties (and operations) involved will have to be "physical" properties and operations, of the kind depicted above.

There are obviously some properties (and operations) that are applicable only to the objects and not to their surfaces. We can say of a particular table that it weighs 200 pounds, that it has four legs, and that it folds down the middle. None of these things can sensibly be said of its surface. But, of course, to show this is not yet to show that surfaces are autonomous things, or that they exist in their own right. For object-talk could simply be about the same object as surface-talk, but richer: Objects may simply have some properties that their surfaces do not have; and indeed the existence of such properties is consistent with surfaces having no physical properties at all. So in order to show that the Somorjai Conception really does differ from the Leonardo Conception, one would have to show that surfaces themselves have properties their objects do not have. If one can find the right properties, this should show that surfaces are, in some important sense, independent entities.

This sort of model we want could be described as follows: A leg of a table is part of the table. Yet it is an autonomous thing in its own right. It can have properties the table does not have, and is subject to some operations that the table is not. We can say of the leg that it is round or cylindrical, while saying of the table that it is rectangular or square. It is not clear that we could say that we can sand down the leg while denying that we are sanding down the table, but surely we can say that we have removed the leg without saying that we have removed the table.

Now, using this example as a guide, can we say of the surface of the table that it has properties and operations that are not applicable to the table itself?

It looks as if we can find some such properties and operations. We can, for example, remove the (old) surface of a table without removing the table; this seems a direct analogue of what we could do with the leg. If someone were asked to paint the surface of a table, he would understand this request to mean that he paint the top of the table. If that were so, he could not paint the surface without painting the table; and he could not scratch the surface without scratching the table. But one could measure the surface of the table without measuring the table, and one could cover the surface with a well-fitting plastic cover without covering the table. In such a case, one would be treating the surface as a part of the table in just the sense that the leg was. For one could fit it with a plastic cover and measure its dimensions, without fitting the table with a plastic cover or measuring its dimensions. Moreover, when one removes the leg of a table, say by unscrewing it, so that the leg remains intact and undamaged, one will have a recognizable entity, something that has not lost its identity as a table leg (this remark is subject to qualification, of course). When one scrapes the paint off a table in the process of resurfacing it, one might end up with an irregular pile of chips. In such a case, it is doubtful that a person would refer to the pile as the surface even if he knew that it had been removed from a particular table and could have been described as the surface before removal. If the paint had been taken off the table in such a way that it remained intact, then one seeing it off the table might well refer to it as "the old surface." This sort of case is not unfamiliar in the art world. In Florence at the present time, some scientists suspect that underneath a Vasari painting that covers a wall there is a Leonardo da Vinci "lost masterpiece," and there is evidence, based on sonar research, to this effect. These scientists plan to strip the surface of the wall containing the Vasari in order to expose the Leonardo. They will do it by an intricate masking process that takes off the surface of the wall in one long roll. This they can then transfer to a new wall. This will amount to transferring the Vasari intact to a new wall. In effect, then, they will be removing the surface of the wall by removing the paint (the Vasari); one might properly describe the result by saying that the Vasari was the old surface.

Of course, such examples are very context dependent; one can remove the surface of a wall without removing the wall, but one cannot remove the surface of an onion (if it has one) without peeling the onion.

Other examples might be the following: If we identify the surface of a table as "the top" of the table, then it is possible for the top to have a property not possessed by the whole table. For instance, it could be red, but the table could be multicolored; its surface could be dull, but the table might not be describable as either dull or not dull; its surface could be described as "flat" when this epithet would not apply to the table as a whole.

With respect to such "mantel covering" examples, therefore, it does appear as if surfaces have passed the two tests that certify them as autonomous entities: The objects that have them possess properties that the surfaces do not, and the surfaces possess properties that the objects do not.

But it may be queried whether objects without mantels — that is, lacking coverings, such as finishes, layers of material, and so on — could pass such tests. Take a solid steel ball, for example. It has no covering that is of a different material from the ball. It makes no sense to speak about removing its surface, though it does make sense to speak of sanding it down, for there is nothing to remove. Do objects of this sort provide an exception to the claim that their surfaces are autonomous entities?

I do not think so. Let us look again at the schematic representation in Figure 1. Suppose that what Dr. Somorjai has depicted is the surface of a homogeneous solid steel marble. Then it is clear that we can ascribe properties to it that we cannot ascribe to the ball. We can say of the surface that it has kinks, terraces, steps, is not smooth, and so on. But none of these ascriptions would be true if applied to the ball, taken as a macroscopic object. It follows that the surface has properties that the ball does not possess and, accordingly, that it is an autonomous object. And if so, it follows that the difference between objects having mantels and objects lacking them is not a significant difference with respect to the question of the autonomy of surfaces.

On the basis of such considerations, I conclude that the Leonardo and Somorjai Conceptions are irreducibly different from each other. The former regards surfaces as non-things, incapable of having physical properties; the latter regards them as things, capable of possessing such properties. Leonardo denies that surfaces can be parts of things, while Somorjai affirms the opposite. The conceptions are thus different from each other.

V

Let me conclude with two brief comments about the need for future research in this domain.

1. I had hoped to address the question of whether both common sense and science are internally inconsistent insofar as they embody both the Leonardo and Somorjai conceptions. The answer clearly depends on whether the two conceptions are not merely different but are in some strong sense logically inconsistent with one another. Obviously, logical incompatibility in this sense does not follow from mere difference. From the fact that 'statement' may be used on some occasions to denote the first presentation of a musical theme, and on others a written summary by a bank of one's financial standing, it does not follow that these uses of 'statement' are logically inconsistent. It can be held that words like 'statement' and 'bank' are homonyms, expressing different but not incompatible concepts.

One major issue here, then, is whether 'surface' is a homonym having differing uses (two of which we have described) that are not necessarily incompatible. I have not pursued the subject in this paper because of the complexities in deciding what a homonym is. One of the most difficult aspects of this question is whether 'surface' expresses a "paronymous concept" (to use Austin's term); that is, whether there is some common meaning strain that all uses of 'surface' embody—such as "being an outer aspect"—though the application of the term may be to different things. In such a case, we might find differing uses of 'surface' but no inconsistency among them.

My own intuition—I offer it without having done the necessary research for a positive answer—is that 'surface' is not homonymous in the way that 'bank' and 'statement' are. This intuition is partly based upon the fact that we cannot find the Somorjai and Leonardo Conceptions expressed as distinct entries in dictionaries in the way in which the various homonyms of 'bank' are, and partly on the observed fact that both in common sense and in science users of the term 'surface' seem to wobble between the two uses in a way in which they never do for real homonyms. But the matter is tricky and requires further study. Nevertheless, suppose that it does turn out that the two conceptions are logically incompatible; does it then follow that both science and common sense which employ, and which vacillate between these conceptions, can each of them be convicted of inconsistency?

2. As I mentioned at the beginning, these "ontological" investigations into the nature of surfaces have their inevitable "epistemological" counterparts, including, I believe, important consequences for the theory of perception. I indicated that I would not in this paper follow up these leads; but I should like to mention one that I think is worth pursuing.

Earlier in the paper I distinguished "intensional" properties and operations from "physical" ones. The question worth investigating is whether *seeing* is an intensional operation, a physical one, or neither.

On the basis of what has already been discovered, there is some reason for thinking that it is neither an intensional nor a physical operation. Let us take the example of seeing a solid steel marble to illustrate why.

I have already pointed out that intensional operations—believing, imagining, etc.—apply to surfaces on either the Leonardo or the Somorjai Conception, but that physical operations apply only to the latter. With respect to the marble, for instance, we can wash or wipe its surface; we cannot wash or wipe a "mere boundary." What is interesting about some of the physical operations that apply to certain objects is that there is no way of performing an operation on the surface without performing it on the object that has the surface, and conversely. There is thus no way of wiping or waxing the surface of a solid steel marble (intact of course) without wiping or waxing the marble - and most important, conversely.

In my earlier paper, I produced some compelling examples to show that it is possible to see a physical object without seeing its surface. I also believe, though the matter is very tricky, that there may be some cases where we could properly say that we see the surface but deny that we see the object that has it. The mere fact that we can say we see the object without seeing its surface shows that the logic of 'see' must be different from the logic of 'wipe', 'wash', and 'scratch', which are cases *par excellence*, of physical operations. It would be very interesting if it could be shown that we could see the surface without seeing the object that has it. If we could, this would show that *seeing* is not a physical operation in the sense previously defined; and that would have interesting and important consequences for epistemology.

Notes

1. *The Notebooks of Leonardo da Vinci*, 1, ed. Edward MacCurdy, (New York, 1958), 75-76.

2. The point is especially perspicuous in Italian. "Affondare" shows its sense in a way in which "to sink" does not; it means "to sink to the bottom" (fondo).

3. "Talk about Talk about Surfaces," (co-authored with Robert Foelber), *Dialectica* 31, Fasc. 3-4 (1977) especially 426-28.

4. G. A. Somorjai, "Surface Science," *Science* 201 (1978):489-97.

Indiscernibility Principles

RICHARD CARTWRIGHT

If a and a' are distinct variables and ϕ and ϕ' are open sentences alike save that ϕ' has a' free at one or more places at which ϕ has a free, then a universal closure of $\ulcorner (a)(a')(a=a' \rightarrow (\phi \rightarrow \phi'))\urcorner$ is an *indiscernibility principle*.[1] In certain recent discussions[2] of identity and substitutivity, and of such related matters as essentialism, special attention is given to a particular indiscernibility principle, namely,

(1) $(z)(x)(y)(x=y \rightarrow (z$ is a property of $x \rightarrow z$ is a property of $y))$.

Others tend to be ignored. It is of some interest, I think, to ask why (1) is thus singled out. Why not instead

(2) $(z)(x)(y)(x=y \rightarrow (z$ is a friend of $x \rightarrow z$ is a friend of $y))$,

or for that matter any number of other indiscernibility principles that are like (1) not only in point of a certain logical form but also in truth value and degree of certitude? According to (1), nothing is identical with a given thing unless it shares all the properties of that thing; according to (2), nothing is identical with a given thing unless it shares all the friends of that thing. Why the stress on properties rather than friends?

I

The idea that (1) has a special position among indiscernibility principles may sometimes originate in confusion over

(3) $(x)(y)(x=y \rightarrow (Fx \rightarrow Fy))$.

If this is not a closed sentence of some first-order language, it is naturally understood to be a schema, one that might have been used in characterizing indiscernibility principles: a sentence is an indiscernibility principle just in case it or some alpha-

293

betic variant of it is a universal closure of an instance of (3). But (3) may also be viewed as an open sentence in which 'F', in spite of its typography, is a variable on all fours with 'x' and 'y' and in which concatenation of a with β abbreviates $\ulcorner a$ is a property of $\beta \urcorner$. The result of prefixing '(F)' to (3), so understood, is simply a notational variant of (1). If these distinct construals of (3) are not kept apart, it can seem that (1) stands to other indiscernibility principles as axiom to theorems. To see the confusion, notice that prefixing '(F)' to (3) can as well be viewed as resulting in a notational variant of (2).[3]

The thought is, nevertheless, apt to persist that (1) stands in some asymmetric deductive relation to other indiscernibility principles. Thus we are inclined to say that if every property of x is a property of y, then every friend of x is a friend of y and hence that if (1) is true, so is (2). But there is no inclination to turn the thing around: we are not inclined to say that x and y share all their friends only if they share all their properties. Now, it is true that (2) is quantificationally implied by the conjunction of (1) with

(4) $(x)(y)((z)(z$ is a property of $x \rightarrow z$ is a property of $y) \rightarrow$
     $(z)(z$ is a friend of $x \rightarrow z$ is a friend of $y))$;

and although, similarly, (1) is quantificationally implied by the conjunction of (2) with

(5) $(x)(y)((z)(z$ is a friend of $x \rightarrow z$ is a friend of $y) \rightarrow$
     $(z)(z$ is a property of $x \rightarrow z$ is a property of $y))$,

(5) will no doubt be thought false. But why is (4) thought to be true? Presumably, there is thought to be some property, or collection of properties, possession of which by x and y guarantees that every friend of x is a friend of y. The guarantee must, of course, be independent of (2). It would not do to appeal, say, to

(6) $(x)(\exists z)(y)(z$ is a property of $y \leftrightarrow y=x)$,

for this provides such properties only via (2). What is wanted is, rather,

(7) $(w)(\exists z)(x)(z$ is a property of $x \leftrightarrow w$ is a friend of $x)$,

which affirms, for any given thing w, the existence of a property present in precisely those things of which w is a friend. And if (7) is at hand, (4) may be skipped: (7) quantificationally implies (4), and hence the conjunction of (1) with (7) quantificationally implies (2). Of course, it is also true that (1) is quantificationally implied by the conjunction of (2) with

(8) $(w)(\exists z)(x)(z$ is a friend of $x \leftrightarrow w$ is a property of $x)$.

But it will be said that whereas (8) is false, (7) is true. Indeed, (7) is apt to seem sufficiently trivial or obvious or otherwise incontestable that it may go unmentioned, allowing one to say simply that (2) follows from (1).

If a, a', ϕ, and ϕ' are as above, if ψ is like ϕ save for having free occurrences of a variable β at precisely those positions of a in ϕ at which ϕ' has a', and if γ is a variable other than β and not free in ψ, then a universal closure of $\ulcorner(\exists\gamma)(\beta)(\gamma$ is a property of $\beta \leftrightarrow \psi)\urcorner$ is a *comprehension principle corresponding to* indiscernibility principles that are universal closures of $\ulcorner(\alpha)(\alpha')(\alpha=\alpha' \rightarrow(\phi \rightarrow \phi'))\urcorner$; and since comprehension principles corresponding to an indiscernibility principle differ only in choice of variables or in order of initial universal quantifiers, there is no harm in speaking of *the* comprehension principle corresponding to a given indiscernibility principle. Thus (7) is the comprehension principle corresponding to (2), and (6) is the comprehension principle corresponding to

(9) $(x)(y)(x=y \rightarrow (x=x \rightarrow y=x))$.

Just as the conjunction of (1) with (7) quantificationally implies (2), so the conjunction of (1) with (6) quantificationally implies (9). In general, an indiscernibility principle is quantificationally implied by the conjunction of its corresponding comprehension principle with (1). And since the truth of the comprehension principle tends to be taken for granted, the indiscernibility principle tends to be thought of as following simply from (1). Thus (1) comes to be seen as the general truth of which other indiscernibility principles are special cases.

Some will propose an amendment: *true* indiscernibility principles one and all follow from (1). Anyone who accepts (1), and who thinks all other indiscernibility principles are special cases of it, will accept the amendment, seeing it as having no effect. But the view is abroad that some indiscernibility principles are false, and those who hold it do not see it as detracting from the importance of (1); on the contrary, they are apt to see in it further indication of the fundamental position of (1) among indiscernibility principles.

The view that some indiscernibility principles are false originates in reflection on certain counterexamples to the principle of substitutivity, the principle that the terms of a true identity sentence may be substituted one for another in any true sentence *salva veritate*. To have at hand a typical instance, let 'astro' abbreviate 'it is a truth of astronomy that' and consider

(10) astro Hesperus=Phosphorus

(11) Hesperus=Phosphorus

and

(12) astro Phosphorus=Phosphorus

Here (12) results from (10) by substitution on the basis of the true identity (11). Yet (10) is true and (12) is false. It is tempting to infer that

(13) $(x)(y)(x=y \rightarrow (\text{astro } x=\text{Phosphorus} \rightarrow \text{astro } y=\text{Phosphorus}))$

is a false indiscernibility principle; for it appears to conform to the above definition and yet to have the false substitution-instance obtained by putting 'Hesperus' for 'x' and 'Phosphorus' for 'y' in '$x=y \rightarrow (\text{astro } x=\text{Phosphorus} \rightarrow \text{astro } y=\text{Phosphorus})$'.

The example is not seen as threatening (1). We can put 'Hesperus' for 'x' and 'Phosphorus' for 'y' in the open sentence that follows the quantifiers of (1), but what is to be put for 'z'? An answer would be forthcoming if we could discern a property rightly attributed to Hesperus in (10) and then wrongly attributed to Phosphorus in (12). But (1) is sufficiently compelling that we are apt, rather, to see the failure of substitutivity as ground for denying that there is any such property. It would, in any case, be incoherent to suppose there to be a property z which, by virtue of the truth of (10), is present in Hesperus but which, by virtue of the falsity of (12), is not present in Phosphorus. Both

(14) $(y)(y=\text{Hesperus} \leftrightarrow y=\text{Hesperus})$. z is a property of Hesperus

and

(15) $(y)(y=\text{Hesperus} \leftrightarrow y=\text{Phosphorus})$. ~z is a property of Phosphorus

would have to be judged true. Hence also

(16) $(\exists x)((y)(y=\text{Hesperus} \leftrightarrow y=x)$. z is a property of x)

and

(17) $(\exists x)((y)(y=\text{Hesperus} \leftrightarrow y=x)$. -z is a property of x).

What, then, of the thing that is Hesperus? Would *it* have z? Evidently there would be no saying.[4]

There can seem to be here not only a defense of (1) but also an explanation of what is wrong with (13): it is false, and false precisely because of what we just now appear to have shown, namely, the falsity of

(18) $(\exists z)(x)(z$ is a property of $x \leftrightarrow$ astro $x=\text{Phosphorus})$.

Now, if (13) is an indiscernibility principle, (18) is its corresponding comprehension principle. So the defect in (13), on this view of the matter, is its failure to satisfy a condition necessary for the truth of any indiscernibility principle, namely, that the corresponding comprehension principle be true. True indiscernibility principles are those that are special cases of (1); but an indiscernibility principle qualifies as such only if its corresponding comprehension principle is true.

II

If the views I have been describing are nowhere explicitly affirmed, there are, nevertheless, signs of them here and there. A paper of my own[5] defended (1) against critics[6] who argued to its falsity from failures of substitutivity. I would have done as much for (2) had there been the occasion. Still, my reference to (1) as "the principle of identity," and my concern to distinguish it from the principle of substitutivity, suggest that I took (1) to be somehow fundamental among indiscernibility principles. I would not have called (2) "the principle of identity," nor would I have cautioned against confusing it with the principle of substitutivity. There is an echo of this in Wiggins. "It is not true," he writes, "the designations of the same thing are *everywhere* intersubstitutable. . . . What really is true is that *if x = y, then every property of x is a property of y*."[7] In a similar vein, Linsky[8] and Plantinga[9] call (1) "the principle of the indiscernibility of identicals" and contrast it in point of truth value with the principle of substitutivity. There is a hint, too, in Linsky's explanation of certain failures of substitutivity, of the view that an indiscernibility principle is true only if its corresponding comprehension principle is true: not every open sentence, he says, "expresses a property." And perhaps that view lies behind Plantinga's insistence that essentialist claims involve property attributions. He wants it understood, for example, that 9 is essentially composite only if anything identical with 9 is essentially composite; and he sees a guarantee in (1) together with the alleged equivalence of '9 is essentially composite' and '9 has the property of being essentially composite'.

That (1) has some distinguished position among indiscernibility principles is implied also in some recent discussions of the doctrine that if x is identical with y, then necessarily x is identical with y. A standard argument for the doctrine proceeds simply from the premises

(19) $(x)(y)(x=y \to (\Box x=x \to \Box x=y))$

and

(20) $(x)\Box(x=x)$

to the conclusion

(21) $(x)(y)(x=y \to \Box x=y)$.

Here (19) is looked upon as an indiscernibility principle, in need of no special defense. But in Kripke's presentation[10] (19) appears as second line of a derivation having (3) as first line. Now, as already noticed, (3) is subject to more than one interpretation: if, as we may safely assume in the present context, it is not intended as a closed sentence of some first-order language, it may be understood either as a schema or as tantamount to (1). Kripke seems to intend the latter. True, he calls (19) a "substitution instance" of (3), a phrase some will think better suited for the relation of instance to schema than for any relation (19) bears to (1); and he calls (3) "the law of substitutivity of identity," a description that can perhaps be taken to reflect confidence that (3) is a valid schema but that seems inappropriate to an instance of the schema: '2+3=5 or 2+3≠5' is not the law of excluded middle. Still, there is the fact that (3) appears as a line in the argument, seemingly on a par with (19), (20), and (21). And if this does not settle the matter, there is Kripke's comment that (3) "says that, for any objects x and y, if x is identical to y, then if x has a certain property F, so does y."

But if (3) is to be understood as a notational variant of (1), its presence in the argument might seem hard to explain. Evidently it is not designed to enhance the power of (19) and (20), so far at least as concerns the deduction of (21). And if intended as a premise to (19), it can seem insufficient: there is in (19) no talk of properties. What, then, is its function? Perhaps the following passage gives an answer: "Where [F] is any property at all, including a property involving modal operators, and if x and y are the same object and x [has] F, then y has to have the same property F. And this is so even if the property F is itself of the form of necessarily having some other property G, in particular that of necessarily being identical to a certain object."[11] Here we seem invited to regard (19) as a particular case of (1), as following from (1) in the sense of being a consequence of (1) in conjunction with

(22) $(x)(\exists z)(y)(z$ is a property of $y \leftrightarrow \square x=y)$,

which is the comprehension principle corresponding to (19) and the truth of which is taken for granted.

I have no desire to press too hard a few sentences from a transcription of a tape of a lecture delivered without a written text. And even if Kripke's remarks about (19) suggest the view that (1) stands to other indiscernibility principles as general truth to particular instances, there is no indication in anything he says of the doctrine that some indiscernibility principles are false. This doctrine is strongly suggested, however, in Wiggins's commentaries[12] on Kripke's argument.

Wiggins reads Kripke's argument much as I do: he takes Kripke's (3) to be a formulation of the principle that if x is identical with y then every property of x is a property of y, and he sees the argument as involving a "transition" from (3), so understood, to (19). It is, in fact, doubt about the legitimacy of this transition that makes him suspect the argument fails as convincing proof of (21). Specifically, Wiggins has doubts about (22), the comprehension principle that mediates the transition to (19). What reason, he asks, is there to think it true? His question is not intended to voice some general skepticism of comprehension principles. On the contrary, Wiggins thinks that if '$\square x=y$' could be shown to be an "extensional" open sentence, an open sentence substitution, instances of which do not generate failures of substitutivity, (22) would be in good standing. But he thinks there is a "real *prima facie* possibility" that '$\square x=y$' is a non-extensional open sentence, like 'Philip believes that x denounced y' or 'probably x denounced y', and that therefore (22) may be no better off than (18).[13]

It would be somewhat tangential to our main concerns to try to do justice to the subtle considerations that lead Wiggins thus to suspect '$\square x=y$'. Suffice it to say that, finding "possible worlds . . . an algebraic device . . . or nothing,"[14] he sees no explanation of '$\square$' that will accommodate its use as a sentence operator and at the same time enable us to see (21), for example, as thoroughly *de re*—"as simply saying of anything x and anything y, however described, that if x is y then x necessarily is y."[15] What must be noticed, however, is that Wiggins's doubts about the transition from (1) to (19) must carry over to (19) itself. Otherwise he would see a sound argument for (21) based simply on the premises (19) and (20). Indeed, if '$\square x=y$' *is* an open sentence that is not extensional, (19) is surely false. Non-extensionality of '$\square x=y$' would mean the existence of names a, β, and β' such that $\ulcorner \beta=\beta' \urcorner$ and $\ulcorner \square a=\beta \urcorner$ are true and yet $\ulcorner \square a=\beta' \urcorner$ is false. But then $\ulcorner \beta=\beta' \to (\square a=\beta \to \square a=\beta') \urcorner$ would falsify (19).

My account of Wiggins takes certain liberties with his text—partly for the sake of brevity and uniformity in approach, partly because I have not hesitated to resolve without argument questions of interpretation that are disputable. Wiggins does not, for example, separate as sharply as I have the schematic and nonschematic readings of (3). Neither does he explicitly formulate (22), and it would in fact be closer to his own way to represent him as questioning rather

(23) $(x)(\exists z)(z=(\lambda y)(\Box x=y))$.

I would say this is his way were it not for uncertainty on my part as to how to understand his use of lambda-notation. In (23) it must be understood as a device whereby singular terms (open or closed) are formed from open sentences. Although much that Wiggins says points in this direction,[16] there is more that points, rather, to taking his lambda-expressions as complex predicates,[17] so that $\ulcorner(\lambda a)\phi\urcorner$ has roughly the sense of $\ulcorner$is something such that $\phi\urcorner$. Thus understood, he should be represented as questioning

(24) $(x)(\exists z)(y)(z$ is a property of $y \leftrightarrow (\lambda w)(\Box x=w)y)$.

Notice that (23) implies (22) but goes further in purporting actually to mention, for a given thing x, the property of being something with which it is necessary that x is identical. On the other hand, (24) is equivalent to (22), since '$(\lambda w)(\Box x=w)y$' amounts simply to '$\Box x=y$'.

My account also omits mention of Wiggins's attempt to refurbish Kripke's argument. Very roughly, the idea is to use '$\Box$'—or 'nec', for purposes of distinguishing—as a modifier of lambda-expressions rather than a sentential connective. The advantage claimed is that essentialist doctrines—in particular, the doctrine that x is necessarily identical with anything with which it is identical at all—can thereby be more accurately represented. Thus '$(\lambda w)(\text{nec}(\lambda r)(\lambda s)(r=s)xw)$' is alleged to be superior to '$(\lambda w)(\Box x=w)$' in point of being constructible without suspicion of recourse to non-extensional open sentences, so that

(25) $(x)(\exists z)(y)(z$ is a property of $y \leftrightarrow ((\lambda w)(\text{nec}(\lambda r)(\lambda s)(r=s)xw)y)$

is free from the alleged defect of (24). But discussion of the refurbishing is best left to another occasion. Our present concern is with the views about indiscernibility principles that seem to Wiggins to make them desirable.

III

These views, as some will have long since anticipated, run afoul of Russell's paradox.[18] Surely

(26) $(x)(y)(x=y \rightarrow (\sim x$ is a property of $x \rightarrow \sim y$ is a property of $y)$

is a true indiscernibility principle. But its corresponding comprehension principle is

(27) $(\exists z)(x)(z$ is a property of $x \leftrightarrow \sim x$ is a property of $x)$,

which is demonstrably false. In order for an indiscernibility principle to be true, it is therefore not necessary that its corresponding comprehension principle be true. Of course, (26) is quantificationally implied by the conjunction of (1) with (27). But that is hardly ground for seeing (26) as standing to (1) in the manner of special case to general principle: recall the deductive powers of (2) when conjoined with false principles of friendship.

The instance is not, in Hume's phrase, "particular and singular." Another is

(28) $(x)(y)(x=y \rightarrow ((w) \sim(x$ is a property of w . w is a property of $x) \rightarrow$

$(w)\sim(y$ is a property of w . w is a property of $y)))$.

Moreover, (26) and (28) are only first and second in an infinite sequence of like cases.[19] And there are infinitely many others. One such is

(29) $(x)(y)(x=y \rightarrow (x=x$. $\sim x$ is a property of $x \rightarrow$

$y=y$. $\sim y$ is a property of $y))$;

for its corresponding comprehension principle is

(30) $(\exists z)(x)(z$ is a property of $x \leftrightarrow x=x$. $\sim x$ is a property of $x)$,

which has the false consequence

(31) $\sim(x)(x=x)$.

Others can be obtained by altering (29) only to the extent of replacing '$x=x$' with open sentences like it in having just 'x' free and in having true universal closures. We may, in fact, simply replace '$x=x$' with one or another arbitrarily chosen true sentence; for an instance of the schema

(32) $(\exists z)(x)(z$ is a property of $x \leftrightarrow p$. $\sim x$ is a property of $x)$

is true or false according as the sentence put for 'p' is false or true (assuming, as I suppose is fair in the present context, that there is at least one unexemplified property). This shows, by the way, that judgment as to the truth value of a comprehension principle may have to await the outcome of extensive scientific inquiry—or, for that matter, the outcome of next year's World Series.

If these examples seem to diminish the importance of (1), that is as it should be. Once they are recognized, it becomes difficult to see the point of singling out (1) as "the principle of the indiscernibility of identicals" or, as I unfortunately called it, "the principle of identity." It is a true indiscernibility principle, one among others; but it is not a general truth of which the rest are special cases. And to claim that it is a general truth of which *some* of the rest are special cases strikes me as at best a not very happy way of asserting that some indiscernibility principles are quantificationally implied by the conjunction of (1) with true comprehension principles. If we are to say that

(33) $(x)(y)(x=y \rightarrow$ (Boston will win next year's World Series .

$\sim x$ is a property of $x \rightarrow$ Boston will win next year's World Series .

$\sim y$ is a property of $y)$

is or is not a special case of (1) depending upon the course of next year's season, then we might as well say that

(34) $(x)(y)(x=y \rightarrow (x$ is a resident of Darrtown $\rightarrow$
y is a resident of Darrtown))

is or is not a special case of (2) depending upon whether

(35) $(\exists z)(x)(z$ is a friend of $x \leftrightarrow x$ is a resident of Darrtown)

happens to be true. There are, after all, *some* true friendship principles.

It should not be thought that the incapacity of (1) to serve as an all-purpose indiscernibility principle results from peculiarities of 'is a property of'. So far at least as the considerations just now adduced are concerned, no other predicate fares any better. No doubt 'is a member of' is clearer: sets are superior to properties with respect to individuation[20] and perhaps also with respect to conditions of existence.[21] But as a candidate for the principle of the indiscernibility of identicals

(36) $(z)(x)(y)(x=y \rightarrow (x \in z \rightarrow y \in z))$

exhibits deficiencies like those of (1). And we may say, if we choose, that x is identical with y only if everything true of x is true of y. But if this is taken as equivalent to a universal closure of an instance of the schema (3), it serves no better than (1) or (36). There is no indiscernibility principle that stands to the others, or to the others that are true, as general truth to particular cases. It should not be thought, either, that this circumstance is peculiar to indiscernibility principles. It is ubiquitous. Thus, among universal closures of instances of the schema

(37) $(x)(Fx \lor \sim Fx)$,

there is no one that generalizes on the rest. In particular,

(38) $(z)(x)(z$ is a property $x \lor \sim z$ is a property of $x)$

does not—and for reasons like those brought to bear in the case of indiscernibility principles.

IV

If the comprehension principle corresponding to a given indiscernibility principle is true, then certainly the indiscernibility principle itself is true: it is quantificationally implied by (1) together with the comprehension principle. Hence, if an indiscernibility principle is false, so is its corresponding comprehension principle. There may thus seem to be a point after all in emphasizing the truth of (1). It may seem that (1) is a peg on which to hang explanations of such anomalous cases as (13).

Now there is a step here that might well be questioned. It is indeed true that an indiscernibility principle is false only if its corresponding comprehension principle is false. But it is also true that an indiscernibility principle is false only if its corresponding friendship principle is false: the indiscernibility principle is quantificationally implied by (2) together with that friendship principle. So why not emphasize the truth of (2) and use *it* as a peg on which to hang explanations of cases like (13)? Whatever perplexity this question occasions would be serious were it not that the project of explaining the *falsity* of one or another indiscernibility principle is in any case wrongheaded. The reason is that there are no false indiscernibility principles.

This is not to say that there is nothing to be explained: (13) has the look of an indiscernibility principle and yet

(39)   Hesperus=Phosphorus → (astro Hesperus=Phosphorus →
astro Phosphorus=Phosphorus)

is false. The explanation has, in effect, been given by Quine. The defect in (13) is not falsity but unintelligibility. Falsity of (39) demonstrates the opacity of the 'astro'-construction, the function that assigns ⌜astro φ⌝ to a given sentence φ. That construction transforms a referential position, one subject to the substitutivity of identity, into a non-referential one. Thus (13) violates Quine's law that *"no variable inside an opaque construction is bound by an operator outside."*[22] The point is, of course, not that 'astro x=Phosphorus' is an open sentence whose free variable mysteriously resists binding from outside. Rather, it is not properly an open sentence at all.

Quine's own way has been to use his law in direct support of the validity of the schema (3):

... one feels that any interpretation of '*Fx*' violating (3) would be simply a distortion of the manifest intent of '*Fx*' and '*Fy*'. Anyway I hope one feels this, for there is good reason to. Since there is no quantifying into an opaque construction, the positions of '*x*' and '*y*' in '*Fx*' and '*Fy*' must be referential if '*x*' and '*y*' in those positions are to be bound by the initial '(*x*)' and '(*y*)' of (3) at all. Since the notation of (3) manifestly intends the quantifiers to bind '*x*' and '*y*' in all four shown places, any interpretation of '*Fx*' violating (3) would be a distortion.[23]

Briefly, the validity of (3) "rests on the incoherence of bound variables in any but referential position."[24] Although it is not my intention to disagree, I think it worthwhile to inquire into the credentials of the law. Why is there no quantifying into an opaque construction?

Quine has more than once argued substantially as follows.[25] Let us try to apply existential generalization to (10), thereby obtaining the apparent consequence

(40)   (∃x)(astro x=Phosphorus).

What is this object which, according to (40), is such that it is a truth of astronomy that it is identical with Phosphorus? According to (10), from which (40) was inferred, it is Hesperus, that is, Phosphorus; but to suppose this would conflict with the fact that (12) is false. Now, it is not altogether clear, I think, what the conflict alluded to is supposed to be. Quine has sometimes been understood as arguing simply that a double application of existential generalization to the conjunction of (10), (11), and (12) would result in

(41) $(\exists x)(\exists y)(x=y \,.\, \text{astro } x=y \,.\, \text{-astro } y=y)$,

which would conflict with the validity of (3); that, in general, quantification into opaque constructions would yield results incompatible with the validity of that schema.[26] For anyone already prepared to accept the validity of the schema, this is good enough. But validity of the schema was just now made to rest on the incoherence of quantification into an opaque construction. There appears to be a circle.

Perhaps Quine is to be understood, rather, as follows. It would be counter to astronomy to deny

(42) $(y)(y=\text{Phosphorus} \leftrightarrow y=\text{Hesperus})$,

and an application of existential generalization to the conjunction of (42) with (10) would yield

(43) $(\exists x)((y)(y=\text{Phosphorus} \leftrightarrow y=x) \,.\, \text{astro } x=\text{Phosphorus})$.

Again, no one could reasonably deny

(44) $(y)(y=\text{Phosphorus} \leftrightarrow y=\text{Phosphorus})$,

and an application of existential generalization to the conjunction of (44) with (12) would yield

(45) $(\exists x)((y)(y=\text{Phosphorus} \leftrightarrow y=x) \,.\, \text{-astro } x=\text{Phosphorus})$.

Consider, then, the thing identical with Phosphorus. Is *it* a thing such that it is a truth of astronomy that *it* is identical with Phosphorus? In view of (43) and (45), no answer could be given. There is some one thing identical with Phosphorus. But there is no settling the question whether it satisfies 'astro $x=\text{Phosphorus}$'. To permit quantification into opaque constructions is thus at odds with the fundamental intent of objectual quantification.

Whether or not this reasoning is Quine's, it does provide a way out of the circle. It can be put to use in direct support of any indiscernibility principle. Consider just one example. If it is suggested that, although x is identical with y, something z is a friend of x but not of y, then x, y, and z will be such that

(46) $(w)(w=y \leftrightarrow w=x) \,.\, z$ is a friend of x

and

(47) $(w)(w=y \leftrightarrow w=y) \,.\, \text{-}z$ is a friend of y.

Hence y and z will be such that

(48) $(\exists u)((w)(w=y \leftrightarrow w=u) \,.\, z$ is a friend of $u)$

and

(49) $(\exists u)((w)(w=y \leftrightarrow w=u) \,.\, \text{-}z$ is a friend of $u)$.

But then consider the thing that is y. Is z a friend of *it?* There will be no saying.

It is no accident that this reasoning parallels that given early on in defense of there being no property of Hesperus that is not also a property of Phosphorus. There the names 'Hesperus' and 'Phosphorus' occurred vacuously, of course; so, we now see, did 'is a property of'. Indeed, any indiscernibility principle can be defended in the same manner. Here, then, is added reason for refusing (1) a special place among indiscernibility principles.

V

I have come down firmly on the side of opacity of the 'astro'-construction. There is no alternative if the only available rule is that $\ulcorner$astro $\phi\urcorner$ counts as true if and only if ϕ itself is a truth of astronmy. It might be suggested, however, that a sentence such as (10) can be taken another way: as saying that Hesperus is a thing x and Phosphorus a thing y such that it is a truth of astronomy that x is identical with y. If (12) were read similarly, (10) and (12) would not diverge in truth value. This is not to say that their truth value would thereby be fixed. The task would remain of settling, somehow, which pairs of things satisfy 'astro $x=y$'. Here a fundamental constraint, consequent upon the intended interpretation of '=' and of devices of quantification, would be that

$$(50) \quad (x)(y)(x=y \to (\text{astro } x=y \to \text{astro } y=y))$$

come out true. But the question of the truth value of

$$(51) \quad (y)(\exists z)(x)(z \text{ is a property of } x \leftrightarrow \text{astro } x=y)$$

need not arise.

These remarks carry over to '□'. That symbol is sometimes so used that $\ulcorner\Box\phi\urcorner$ counts as true if and only if ϕ itself is necessary. If that is all there is to go on, we have no option but to count the '□'-construction opaque and hence (19) unintelligible. But (19), (20), and (21) are witnesses to a contemplated transparent '□'-construction. Now, the intelligibility of such a construction is not guaranteed simply by an antecedent understanding of quantification and of the opaque '□'-construction.[27] The problem remains of settling, somehow, which sequences of objects satisfy $\ulcorner\Box\phi\urcorner$ where ϕ is an open sentence. And a fundamental constraint on a solution to the problem is that indiscernibility principles involving '□' come out true. That their corresponding comprehension principles come out true is neither here nor there.

Notes

1. Strictly speaking, it is only with respect to one or another interpretation that a sentence is, or is not, an indiscernibility principle. I follow the common practice of suppressing reference to the intended interpretation where there seems no risk of confusion. But to guard against certain misunderstandings it must be said at once that I count a sentence an indiscernibility principle only if its variables are objectual and unrestricted in range. The second of these requirements could be relaxed in various ways, but I have not seen the point of doing so: variables unrestricted in range are unavoidable if justice is to be done to the views I intend to discuss, and

restricted variables serve no theoretical purpose once unrestricted variables are at hand. I am aware of the view that unrestricted quantification is somehow illegitimate; but the arguments given in support of it, insofar as I understand them, are unpersuasive, resting as they do on the gratuitous assumption that the various objects over which a variable ranges must belong to or comprise or be in some one object, the domain of values of the variable.

I take for granted throughout the (total) reflexivity, symmetry, and transitivity of '='. Given just symmetry, $\ulcorner(a)(a')(a=a' \to (\phi \to \phi'))\urcorner$ is equivalent to $\ulcorner(a)(a')(a=a' \to (\phi \leftrightarrow \phi'))\urcorner$.

2. See, for example, my "Identity and Substitutivity," in *Identity and Individuation,* ed. Milton K. Munitz (New York, 1971) 119-33; Saul Kripke, "Identity and Necessity," same volume, 135-64; Leonard Linsky, "Substitutivity and Descriptions," *Journal of Philosophy* 63 (1966):673-83, and *Referring* (New York, 1967), especially Chapter V; Alvin Plantinga, "De Re et De Dicto," *Noûs* 3 (1969):235-58, and *The Nature of Necessity,* (Oxford, 1974), especially Chapter II and Appendix; David Wiggins, "Essentialism, Continuity, and Identity," *Synthese* 23 (1974):321-59, "Identity, Necessity, and Physicalism," in *Philosophy of Logic,* ed. Stephan Körner (Berkeley and Los Angeles, 1976) 96-132, and "Reply to Comments," same volume, 159-82.

3. The interpretation of

$$(F)(x)(y)(x=y \to (Fx \to Fy))$$

according to which it is a rather curious notational variant of (1), is *not* any of its various second-order interpretations—if for no other reason than that on such interpretations the so-called individual variables must be restricted in range. (See George Boolos, "On Second-Order Logic," *Journal of Philosophy* 72 (1975).509-26.) No sentence, on a second-order interpretation, says that, whatever x and y may be, x is identical with y only if every property of x is a property of y.

4. This reasoning is set forth more fully, but with respect to another example, in my "Identity and Substitutivity," pp. 129-31.

5. "Identity and Substitutivity."

6. Such as E. J. Lemmon. See his "A Theory of Attributes Based on Modal Logic," *Acta Philosophica Fennica* (1963):95-122.

7. "Essentialism, Continuity, and Identity," p. 343, and "Identity, Necessity, and Physicalism," p. 109.

8. "Substitutivity and Descriptions," p. 681, and *Referring,* p. 79.

9. "De Re et De Dicto," p. 239, and *The Nature of Necessity,* p. 15. In the former the principle is put thus: "Where P is any property and x and y any individuals, x is identical with y only if x has P if and only if y has P." In the latter 'individuals' is replaced by 'objects'.

10. "Identity and Necessity," p. 136.

11. "Identity and Necessity," p. 137.

12. For which see "Essentialism, Continuity, and Identity"; "Identity, Necessity, and Physicalism"; and "The *De Re* 'Must': a Note on the Logical Form of Essentialist Claims," in *Truth and Meaning,* eds. Gareth Evans and John McDowell (Oxford, 1976) 285-312.

13. See especially "Reply to Comments," pp. 169-70 and 174.

14. "Identity, Necessity, and Physicalism," p. 105.

15. "Essentialism, Continuity, and Identity," p. 329, and "Identity, Necessity, and Physicalism," p. 103.

16. Thus Wiggins does not hesitate to use lambda-expressions as objects of the verb 'to have': "Identity, Necessity, and Physicalism," p. 112; "Essentialism, Continuity, and Identity," pp. 346 and 348; "The *De Re* 'Must'," p. 293. And $(\lambda x)(\lambda y)(x=y)$ is said to be "the relation of identity"; similarly $nec(\lambda x)(\lambda y)(x=y)$ is said to be "that relation which any r and s have iff they are necessarily identical" ("The *De Re* 'Must'," p. 293).

17. We are told repeatedly that 'nec' is a modifier of *predicates,* or a predicate (as opposed to a sentential) operator. See "Essentialism, Continuity, and Identity," p. 345; "Identity, Necessity, and Physicalism," p. 112; "Reply to Comments," p. 174. That lambda-expressions are complex predicates seems virtually required by their treatment in "The *De Re* 'Must.," See also

Christopher Peacocke, "An Appendix to David Wiggins' 'Note'," in the Evans-McDowell anthology, pp. 313-24.

18. This is pointed out, though not altogether satisfactorily, in my "Substitutivity" (Abstract), *Journal of Philosophy* 63 (1966):684-85. It is also noticed by W. V. Quine, Review of Munitz (ed.), *Identity and Individuation, Journal of Philosophy* 69 (1972):488-497, see especially p. 490.

19. To see how to construct the sequence, consult W. V. Quine, *Mathematical Logic,* revised edition (New York and Evanston, 1951), p. 130.

20. As Quine has repeatedly pointed out. See, for example, *Word and Object* (Cambridge, Mass., 1960), pp. 209ff, and *Set Theory and Its Logic,* revised edition (Cambridge, Mass., 1969), p. 2.

21. I have in mind those who see in the cumulative type structure an articulation of the intuitive concept of set.

22. *Word and Object*, p. 166.

23. *Word and Object*, pp. 167-68. Notation and numbering have been altered to conform with this paper.

24. Review of Munitz, p. 490.

25. See, for example, *From a Logical Point of View,* Second Edition, revised (New York, 1963), p. 148.

26. See Robert C. Sleigh, Jr., "On Quantifying into Epistemic Contexts," *Noûs* I (1967): 23-31, especially pp. 25-26.

27. Cf. Quine, *From a Logical Point of View,* p. 150.

Kripke is likely prepared to admit that ⌜α=α⌝ and ⌜α=β⌝ are different propositions, but this seems to have little effect on his position.

M. tries to force   Kripke [to] acknowledges a scope distinction for proper names. (This Dummett denies, as do we) M. tries to employ 'Socratizer caper'

Rigid Designation and Informative Identity Sentences

RICHARD L. MENDELSOHN

Frege's term in Geach & Black

In "On Sense and Reference,"[1] Frege observed that ⌜a=a⌝ and true ⌜a=β⌝ can differ in "cognitive value" even when a and $β$ are both proper names. To account for this difference, he distinguished the reference of the name, that is, the object for which it stands, from its sense, that is, the particular way in which the name picks out, presents, or determines its reference: a and $β$ can differ in sense despite having the same reference, and when this happens, Frege said, ⌜a=a⌝ and ⌜a=β⌝ will express different propositions. Recently, Saul Kripke[2] has criticized Frege's "description theory of names" and advanced instead a variant of Mill's rival view on which proper names are said to lack connotation. However, in this essay, I would like to call into question the extent of Kripke's disagreement with Frege. For Kripke, unlike other advocates of Mill's theory of names, apparently believes, like Frege, that ⌜a=a⌝ and true ⌜a=β⌝ *can* express different propositions when a and $β$ are both proper names. So Kripke must, like Frege, identify some difference between the names a and $β$ that will account for the fact that ⌜a=a⌝ and ⌜a=β⌝ express different propositions. It might be supposed that Kripke's view that proper names are rigid designators precludes their differing in this manner. But this, I will argue, is wrong. In fact, if my understanding of Kripke is correct, then the difference he locates between the two names turns out to look very much like what Frege said the difference was.

The puzzle about informative identity sentences poses a formidable challenge to one, like Kripke, who favors Mill's theory of names. For it is widely believed that the fact that ⌜a=a⌝ and true ⌜a=β⌝ can differ in cognitive value when a and $β$ are both proper names *demands* that a and $β$ differ in meaning; and so long as Kripke is unable to show otherwise, there remains the feeling that, despite Kripke's damaging criticism, Frege's description theory—or something very much like it—*must* be the right one. The reasoning is straightforward. If

(1)   Hesperus=Phosphorus,

and

(2)   Phosphorus=Phosphorus,

differ in cognitive value, that is, if they express different thoughts or propositions, then the information conveyed by 'Hesperus' would have to be different from that conveyed by 'Phosphorus'. Where is this difference in information to be located? Not, certainly, in the objects denoted, for 'Hesperus' and 'Phosphorus' denote the very same object. Nor, it is commonly argued, in the words themselves, for although the names differ, there is good reason to deny that the proposition expressed by (1), say, presupposes (or entails) the existence of a language. It would seem, then, that 'Hesperus' and 'Phosphorus' would have to differ in meaning. Conversely, if the sole significance of a proper name is to stand for the object to which it has been assigned, then it is difficult to see how (1) and (2) could express different propositions. Indeed, many of those who hold that proper names lack meaning would deny that ⌜a=a⌝ and true ⌜a=β⌝ express different propositions when a and $β$ are proper names.

Russell,[3] for example, maintained that if a were a logically proper name, the object a stands for—not a concept—would be a constituent of the proposition expressed by a sentence containing a. On Russell's view, then, ⌜a=a⌝ and true ⌜a=β⌝ would have to express the very same proposition when a and $β$ are both logically proper names—if, that is, any proposition at all is expressed by either sentence. For, an identity sentence would seem to be on a par with an existential sentence, and Russell explicitly held that ⌜a exists⌝ expresses no proposition when a is a logically proper name. More recently, Donnellan[4] has argued that much of what Russell claimed about logically proper names actually holds for ordinary proper names. In particular, he believes that (ordinary) proper names lack descriptive content so that substitution of codenotational proper names preserves truth value *and* proposition expressed.[5] So, for Donnellan, (1) and (2) must express the same proposition. And, in *The Nature of Necessity*,[6] Alvin Plantinga, another critic of Frege, held that proper names do express properties, but that different proper names of the same object all express the same property, so, again, when a and $β$ are both proper names, Plantinga holds that ⌜a=a⌝ and true ⌜a=β⌝ express the same proposition.

The view one holds, then, about whether proper names have or lack meaning is intimately connected with the view one holds about whether ⌜a=a⌝ and true ⌜a=β⌝ express the same proposition or not when a and $β$ are both proper names. Frege's theory of names appears to go hand-in-hand with the view that, for example, (1) and (2) express different propositions; Mill's theory of names, on the other hand, appears to go hand-in-hand with the view that (1) and (2) express the same proposition. And the preeminence of Frege's theory is a consequence of the widely held belief that sentences like (1) and (2) do express different propositions.

What reason is there for supposing that (1) and (2) express different propositions? One reason is this: it is widely believed that it is a necessary truth that Phosphorus = Phosphorus, and only a contingent truth that Hesperus = Phosphorus.

Kripke, however, denies this: he holds that $\ulcorner a=\beta \urcorner$ is necessarily true, if true at all, whenever a and β are proper names. His defense of this view relies heavily on his distinguishing the metaphysical issue of whether a given proposition is necessary or contingent from the epistemological issue of whether the proposition is known *a priori* or *a posteriori*. For, another reason for supposing that (1) and (2) express different propositions is that, while it is reasonable to suppose that it is known *a priori* that Phosphorus = Phosphorus (if it is reasonable to suppose that any proposition is known *a priori*), it would seem to be an *a posteriori* truth that Hesperus = Phosphorus. Now, it is on this issue, if I understand him correctly, that Kripke differs from other followers of Mill.

If the proposition that Hesperus = Phosphorus is the very same as the proposition that Phosphorus = Phosphorus, then if it is necessary that Phosphorus = Phosphorus, it is necessary that Hesperus = Phosphorus; and, more important, if it is known *a priori* that Phosphorus = Phosphorus, it is known *a priori* that Hesperus = Phosphorus. Mill's defender, then, is faced with the problem of explaining what it is that constitutes the great astronomical discovery: it could not be that the Babylonians discovered that Hesperus = Phosphorus, for this, as we have just seen, is something the Babylonians knew *a priori*. Nevertheless, the Babylonians, prior to their great discovery, had evinced different attitudes toward (1) and (2). Now, Plantinga has attempted to explain this difference in terms of the Babylonians' not having realized that (1) and (2) express the same proposition: they did not really know, he said, which proposition was expressed by (1). But Plantinga's explanation, I have argued elsewhere, fails[7]; in fact, Plantinga has himself come to this conclusion and he has abandoned the position he held in *The Nature of Necessity*.[8] This is the only attempt I have seen to explain how (1) and (2) could express the same proposition while differing in cognitive value, and I do not see the possibility of a more successful attempt along these lines.

Kripke's view, however, seems to be different. For, if I understand him correctly, Kripke holds that although (2) expresses a proposition that is necessary and *a priori,* (1) expresses a proposition that is necessary and *a posteriori*. Supposing, as is only reasonable, that no proposition can be both *a priori* and *a posteriori*, Kripke would appear to be committed to holding that (1) and (2) express different propositions even though 'Hesperus' and 'Phosphorus' are both proper names. I quote at length his statement of the distinction between the metaphysical and the epistemological notions:

> What do we mean by calling a statement *necessary?* We simply mean that the statement in question, first, is true, and, second, that it could not have been otherwise. When we say that something is *contingently* true, we mean that, though it is in fact the case, it could have been the case that things would have been otherwise. If we wish to assign this distinction to a branch of philosophy, we should assign it to metaphysics. To the contrary, there is the notion of an *a priori truth*. An a priori truth is supposed to be one which can be *known* to be true independently of all experience. . . . I will not have time to

explore these notions in full detail here, but one thing we can see from the
outset is that these two notions are by no means trivially the same. If they are
coextensive, it takes some philosophical argument to establish it. As stated,
they belong to different domains of philosophy. One of them has something
to do with *knowledge,* of what can be known in certain ways about the *actual* world. The other one has to do with *metaphysics,* how the world *could*
have been; given that it is the way it is, could it have been otherwise, in certain ways? Now I hold, as a matter of fact, that neither class of statements is
contained in the other.[9]

That is, the notions of necessary truth and *a priori* truth are not merely different
notions, but the predicates 'ʃ is necessarily true' and 'ʃ is *a priori* true' are not even
coextensive: the class of necessarily true propositions perhaps overlaps the class of
a priori true propositions, but neither class is contained in the other.

There are, then, for Kripke, four possibilities: a proposition might be (i)
necessary and *a priori,* (ii) necessary and *a posteriori,* (iii) contingent and *a priori,*
or (iv) contingent and *a posteriori.* Cases (i) and (iv) are relatively uncontroversial;
it is Kripke's claim that there are propositions of types (ii) and (iii) that is of significance. Kripke argues that sentence (1) expresses a proposition of type (ii), that is,
necessary and *a posteriori,* but he intends the result to hold good for the general
case: "We have concluded," he says, "that an identity statement between names,
when true at all, is necessarily true, even though one may not know it *a priori.*"[10]

If Michael Dummett's criticism of Kripke is correct, however, it would seem
that, on Kripke's view, 'ʃ is necessarily true' and 'ʃ is *a priori* true' would have to
apply to different things.[11] Dummett believes that statements of the form ⌜It is
necessary (contingent) that *a* is F⌝ are ambiguous, whether *a* is a proper name or a
definite description, and he also believes that this ambiguity is adequately diag-
nosed as an ambiguity in the scope of the necessity operator; furthermore, he believes this distinction in the scope of the necessity operator to correspond to the
distinction between a proposition's being necessary and an object's having a property necessarily. Dummett argues that, instead of drawing the scope distinction for
proper names, Kripke employed the metaphysical/epistemological distinction to
disambiguate modal sentences containing proper names. According to Dummett,
Kripke took the *de re* reading to be metaphysical necessity and the *de dicto* reading
to be epistemological necessity. So, as Dummett sees it, Kripke has applied these
notions to two different things: he has epistemic necessity applied to a proposition,
and he has metaphysical necessity applied, not to a proposition, but rather to the
object's having of a given property. What Kripke has shown, then, if anything, is
that the proposition that Hesperus = Phosphorus is *a posteriori* and that Hesperus
has the property of being necessarily identical with Phosphorus.

What makes this interpretation plausible is that Kripke, in explicating the
notion of metaphysical necessity, employs a possible world semantics in which individuals can exist in more than one possible world, while for the epistemological
notion of necessity, insofar as Kripke employs anything like a possible world se-

mantics, it is not the possible world semantics for necessity but something that, as Kripke describes it, is somewhat closer to Lewis's counterpart theory.[12] Consider, for example, this passage in which he defends his claim that 'This lectern is made of ice' expresses a necessary *a posteriori* truth:

> If someone protests, regarding the lectern, that it *could* after all have *turned out* to have been made of ice, and therefore could have been made of ice, I would reply that what he really means is that *a lectern* could have looked just like this one, and have been placed in the same position as this one, and yet have been made of ice. In short, I could have been in the *same epistemological situation* in relation to *a lectern made of ice* as I actually am in relation to *this* lectern. In the main text, I have argued that the same reply should be given to protests that Hesperus could have turned out to be other than Phosphorus, or Cicero other than Tully. Here, then, the notion of 'counterpart' comes into its own. For it is not this table, but an epistemic 'counterpart', which was hewn from ice; not Hesperus-Phosphorus-Venus, but two distinct counterparts thereof, in two of the roles Venus actually plays (that of Evening Star and Morning Star), which are different. Precisely because of this fact, it is not *this table* which could have been made of ice. Statements about the modal properties of *this table* never refer to counterparts. However, if someone confuses the epistemological and the metaphysical problems, he will be well on the way to the counterpart theory Lewis and others have advocated.[13]

[margin note: Note 15 p 93 Id & Nec.]

It seems to me to be reasonable for Kripke to distinguish *what might be the case* from *what might have been the case;* it does seem to me to capture a distinction we make in ordinary language between expressing some notion of epistemological possibility and some other notion of, following Kripke's terminology, metaphysical possibility. That is, to say that such-and-such *could be the case* or *might be the case* seems to mean something like: for all we know, such-and-such is the case. On the other hand, to say that such-and-such *could have been the case* or *might have been the case* is to mean something different (except where what we are talking about occurred in the past, in which case *it could have been the case* could be taken either way). 'The number of planets might be 7' would seem to mean something like, 'For all we know, there are 7 planets'; but 'The number of planets might have been 7', on the other hand, would seem to mean 'It is only contingently true that there are not 7 planets'. It might appear, however, from the way Kripke explains these notions, that *what might be* is one thing and *what might have been* another. What seems to be necessary is that Hesperus = Phosphorus; what seems *a posteriori*, however, is that the heavenly body in such-and-such position in the sky in the evening is identical with the heavenly body in such-and-such position in the sky in the morning. I do not see, however, that we are forced to suppose that Kripke was assigning different interpretations to (1). Rather, he seems to be arguing for distinct interpretations for

[margin notes: Go back to K. who talks about 'could have turned out.' / 'might be' is epistemic / 'might have been' is metaphys]

(3) It is metaphysically necessary that Hesperus = Phosphorus,

[margin notes: evers D., their ifies, for K. not consider □Fa, α = β / Dummett discusses external applic of □ to a proposition, and disavows the irrelevant ontic necessity]

and

(4)   It is epistemically necessary that Hesperus =
        Phosphorus;

for, what Kripke is seeking to distinguish are the metaphysical and epistemic notions, not the things to which the notions apply.

But Dummett's basic charge, namely, that Kripke acknowledges no scope distinction for proper names, seems to me to be inaccurate. To see this, however, we must turn to the scope distinction and Kripke's notion of a rigid designator.

It is widely believed that among true identities, some are necessary and others contingent. It would seem, for example, that

(5)   9 = 9

expresses a necessary truth: it simply could not have been the case that 9 be anything other than 9. On the other hand,

(6)   The number of planets = 9

would appear to express a contingent truth. It is true that there are exactly 9 planets, but, one is inclined to say, it is only contingently true; the facts could certainly have been otherwise. Yet there is a well-known argument that threatens the viability of this distinction, for it purports to show that if x is identical with y, then x is necessarily identical with y.[14] For, if we assume both

(7) $(x)(y)(x=y \supset (Fx \supset Fy))$,   *fails for accidental properties.*

and

(8) $(x) \square (x=x)$,

then, substituting '$\square (x=\zeta)$' for '$F\zeta$' in (7), we obtain,

(9) $(x)(y)(x=y \supset (\square(x=x) \supset \square (x=y))$;

and since (8) has been assumed true, we can delete '$\square (x=x)$' from (9) to obtain,

(10) $(x)(y)(x=y \supset \square (x=y))$.

Once we have derived (10), the rest is trivial. Suppose that we have a true identity,

(11) $a=b$.

Applying Universal Instantiation twice to (10), we obtain

(12) $a=b \supset \square (a=b)$;

and, by *Modus Ponens,* finally, we derive

(13) $\square (a=b)$.

Of the two assumptions made in the argument, (7) cannot plausibly be denied. One's suspicions, therefore, turn to (8). In considering (8), one must be careful to distinguish it from

(14) $\Box\,(x)(x=x)$.

One might be inclined to suppose that (8) is true because '$(x)(x=x)$' is a logical truth (of First-Order Logic with Identity), and all logical truths are necessary truths. Certainly, on the traditional view of necessity, all logical truths are necessary truths; and this is embodied in one of the rules of inference said to characterize *normal* modal systems, namely,

(15) If $\vdash p$, then $\vdash \Box p$.

But, from the logical truth '$(x)(x=x)$', (15) allows us to infer (14); it does not allow us to derive (8). In order to obtain (8) from (14), we require a principle that allows us to move the modal operator inside the quantifier, for example, the converse Barcan formula; this principle, however, is notoriously controversial.

What reason is there for accepting (8)? The difference between (8) and (14) corresponds to the distinction drawn by the Medievals between necessity *de re* and necessity *de dicto*. What is said to be necessary in (14) is the *proposition (dictum)* that each thing is identical with itself. In (8), on the other hand, it is the property of being identical with itself that is said to be necessarily true of each thing (*res*). With *de re* necessity, one is not speaking of a proposition's being necessarily true or contingently true, but of an object's having a property necessarily (*essentially*) or contingently (*accidentally*). Now, this distinction between essential and accidental properties is not particularly clear, but I would think that if there are any essential properties, *being identical with itself* would certainly be one. And so, it is this commitment to there being essential properties that leads one to believe (8) is true.

Anyone who rejects the notion of *de re* necessity will not be affected by the argument. So long as one restricts one's ascriptions of necessity to propositions, the argument poses no threat to the intuition that (6) expresses a proposition that is contingently true and that (5) expresses a proposition that is necessarily true. It is the Essentialist who is directly affected by the argument.

The Essentialist can gain some relief from the paradoxical conclusion by adopting Arthur Smullyan's extension of Russell's scope distinction to modal contexts.[15] According to Russell, when a sentence containing a definite description is itself embedded in a sentence, an ambiguity arises about the scope of the description. Smullyan shows that this holds true as well when we have a sentence containing a definite description embedded in a sentence containing a modal operator. In

(16) It is necessary that the number of planets = 9,

'the number of planets' might be taken as having large scope, in which case (16) would be symbolized as

(17) $(\exists x)(y)(x=y \equiv Py)\,.\,\Box x=9)$,

with '$P\varsigma$' abbreviating the predicate 'ς is a planet', or, 'the number of planets' might be given small scope, in which case (16) would be symbolized as

(18) $\Box\,(\exists x)((y)(x=y \equiv Py)\,.\,x=9)$.

When (16) is taken to have the logical structure of (17), it has the *de re* reading: *Smull* (16) expresses that that number, which in fact numbers the planets, is such that it is *de re* necessarily identical with 9. When, on the other hand, (16) is taken to have the logical structure of (18), it has the *de dicto* reading: (16) then expresses that the proposition that the number of planets is identical with 9 is necessarily true. Clearly, when (16) is given the *de dicto* reading, it expresses something false, for the proposition that the number of planets is identical with 9 is only contingently true. When (16), however, is given the *de re* interpretation, it is plausible to suppose that it expresses something true: that number, which, in fact, numbers the planets, is 9, and surely that number could not have been anything other than 9. Smullyan shows how, consonant with Russell's *Principia Mathematica* rules governing the iota operator, (17), that is, the true reading, can be validly derived from (6) and (10), while (18), that is, the false reading, cannot be validly derived. In this way, the paradoxical conclusion is somewhat disarmed: (6) expresses a contingent proposition, as we intuitively believe to be the case, and the *de re* reading does not controvert this, for on the *de re* reading of (6), it expresses that a particular number has an essential property, namely, that of being identical with 9.

Smullyan's proposal, however, works only for those identity sentences in *Smull* which we find definite descriptions. What happens when we have an identity sen- *& pr* tence $\ulcorner a=\beta \urcorner$ where a and β are both proper names? Here, Cartwright's comments *num* are pertinent:

> The ambiguity in question has been noticed by others, but some who have ✓
> seen it have gone on to characterize it inadequately. Arthur Smullyan saw it
> as having to do with the scope of definite descriptions, and he accordingly
> proposed to treat it by means of an extended version of Russell's theory. But
> though this may serve the purposes of disambiguation in some cases, it does
> not in all. For '9 is necessarily greater than 7' would appear to admit of both
> *de dicto* and *de re* readings. Of course, it is open to Smullyan to argue that '9'
> is in reality a disguised definite description; but he countenances names that
> are not, and with these sentences exhibiting the ambiguity will surely be con-
> structible.[16]

I agree with Cartwright that sentences of the form $\ulcorner \Box Fa \urcorner$ exhibit a *de dicto/de re* ambiguity, even when a is a proper name. Indeed, it seems to me that the sentence,

(19) It is necessary that Hesperus = Phosphorus,

exhibits this ambiguity: it might be read *de dicto*, expressing that the proposition *Socr* that Hesperus = Phosphorus is necessarily true, or, on the other hand, it might be read *de re*, expressing (say) that Hesperus is such that it, that is, that object, is necessarily identical with Phosphorus. However, I think that Cartwright has overlooked a relatively uncontroversial way in which Smullyan's proposal can be extended to handle cases like (19). Quine has, on numerous occasions, proposed eliminating proper names entirely by replacing 'Socrates', for example, by the description 'the Socratizer'.[17] Quine's trick does not appear to beg any of the important questions

M.'s idea is that using Q's "Socratizer" device, Kripke can

about proper names, and, what is more important, it does not appear to beg any of the important questions about proper names on Kripke's view either: *K. will disagree!*

> When I speak of the Frege-Russell view and its variants, I include only those versions which give a substantive theory of the reference of names. In particular, Quine's proposal that in a 'canonical notation' a name such as 'Socrates' should be replaced by a description 'the Socratizer' (where 'Socratizes' is an invented predicate), and that the description should then be eliminated by Russell's method, was not intended as a theory of reference for names but as a proposed reform of language with certain advantages. The problems discussed here will all apply, *mutatis mutandis*, to the reformed language; in particular, the question, 'How is the reference of 'Socrates' determined?' yields to the question, 'How is the extension of 'Socratizes' determined?' Of course I do not suggest that Quine has claimed the contrary.[18] *But K. doesn't buy this himself!*

If one takes proper names as definite descriptions in this way, then, Smullyan's scope distinction will be applicable to sentences like (19); and to this extent, then, contrary to Cartwright's remarks above, it would seem that Smullyan's scope distinction does characterize the *de dicto/de re* distinction adequately.

If what I have said so far is correct, then there is, for Kripke, a scope distinction to be drawn for sentences involving proper names, and, therefore, there is a *de dicto/de re* distinction to be drawn for such sentences as well. Actually, however, I would like to argue something stronger, namely, that Kripke requires these distinctions in order to make out his notion of a rigid designator. Let us now turn to this notion.

arg reversed? scope

A *rigid designator*, according to Kripke, is a term that designates the same object in every possible world in which the object exists. (If the object referred to exists in every possible world, that is, if it is a necessary existent, then the term is *strongly rigid*.) Kripke holds that 'Hesperus', for example, is a rigid designator, for it denotes the same object, namely, the planet Venus, in every possible world in which the planet Venus exists. 'Hesperus', then, contrasts with a uniquely specifying description of the planet like 'the most luminous body seen over the horizon at dusk' in that, although, as a matter of fact, Hesperus is the most luminous body seen over the horizon at dusk, it might not have been: there is a possible world in which some celestial body other than Hesperus is the most luminous body seen over the horizon at dusk. The description does not denote the same object in every possible world, and so it is a *nonrigid* or *accidental* designator.

Kripke provides the following test for determining whether a given expression is rigid or not:

> . . . we can perfectly well talk about rigid and nonrigid designators. Moreover, we have a simple, intuitive test for them. We can say, for example, that the number of planets might have been a different number from the number it in fact is. For example, there might have been only seven planets. We can say that the inventor of bifocals might have been someone other than the man

who *in fact* invented bifocals. We cannot say, though, that the square root of 81 might have been a different number from the number it in fact is, for that number just has to be 9. If we apply this intuitive test to proper names, such as for example 'Richard Nixon', they would seem intuitively to come out to be rigid designators. First, when we talk even about the counterfactual situation in which we suppose Nixon to have done different things, we assume we are still talking about Nixon himself. We say, "If Nixon had bribed a certain Senator, he would have gotten Carswell through," and we assume that by 'Nixon' and 'Carswell' we are still referring to the very same people as in the actual world. And it seems that we cannot say "Nixon might have been a different man from the man he in fact was," unless, of course, we mean it metaphorically: He might have been a different *sort* of person (if you believe in free will and that people are not inherently corrupt). You might think the statement true in that sense, but Nixon could not have been in the other literal sense a different person from the person he, in fact, is, even though the thirty-seventh President of the United States might have been Humphrey. So the phrase "the thirty-seventh President" is nonrigid, but 'Nixon', it would seem, is rigid.[19]

Let us see how this test works. Kripke says that the description 'the number of planets' is not a rigid designator because

> (20)   The number of planets might have been a different number from the number it in fact is

expresses a truth. Clearly, what Kripke has in mind here is not

> (21)   It is possible that (the number of planets ≠ the number of planets),

for this is trivially false; rather, he must mean

> (22)   The number of planets is such that it is possible that that number ≠ the number of planets.

It is (22) Kripke claims to be true, not (21); and the truth of (22) shows that 'the number of planets' is not a rigid designator. Obviously, then, in order to determine whether 'the number of planets' is a rigid designator, we have to distinguish the *de re* reading of (20) from the *de dicto* reading: it is the truth or falsity of the *de re* reading that determines whether the designator is rigid or nonrigid. And this must be true whether our designator is a definite description or a proper name. For, consider Kripke's claim that 'Nixon' is a rigid designator. 'Nixon', he argues, is a rigid designator because the following is false:

> (23)   Nixon might not have been Nixon.

What Kripke has in mind here, clearly, is not

> (24)   It is possible that (Nixon ≠ Nixon),

for, although (24) is false, it is trivially false, just as (21) is: the falsity of (24) does not distinguish 'Nixon' from any other singular term in an interesting manner. Hence, Kripke must mean that

(25) Nixon is such that it is possible that he $\neq$ Nixon

— in what way?

is false, and this, of course, is the *de re* interpretation of (23).

Kripke does, therefore, seem to be committed to the *de dicto/de re* distinction for modal sentences containing proper names as well as for modal sentences containing definite descriptions. It is clear that Kripke believes that Smullyan's scope distinction provides the basis for an adequate response to the modal paradox when the identity sentence contains definite descriptions. Why, then, does he claim that the appeal to the scope distinction constitutes an inadequate response to the paradox when the identity sentence contains proper names? The reason is not that Kripke denies that the scope distinction can be drawn for proper names, for he does no such thing. The reason is that, for Kripke, the identities *are* necessary if true, whatever scope is given: invoking the scope distinction for proper names is incorrect if it is attempted thus to show how there can be contingent identities when the expressions used in the identity sentence are proper names. A rigid designator, then, will be one, roughly, for which scope makes no difference.[20] Note that the claim that 'Hesperus' is a rigid designator does not require that Kripke regard

since proper names not subj. to analys.

(24) makes sense

(26) Hesperus is such that is is necessarily identical
      with Phosphorus

and

Two Scopes: Dere: (i) Scope of □ (ii) Scope of a desc. Does M. confuse?

(27) It is necessary that Hesperus is identical with
      Phosphorus

as expressing the same proposition. In fact, as we have argued, Kripke would seem to be committed to their expressing different propositions, the former, that Hesperus has an essential property, and the latter, that a given proposition is necessary. That 'Hesperus' is a rigid designator only requires that (26) and (27) have the same truth value.

No since they are self dual

Insofar, then, as Kripke champions Mill's theory of names, it has been thought that, for Kripke, (1) and (2) must express the very same proposition. But this is not so. To be sure, Kripke holds that 'Hesperus' and 'Phosphorus' are both rigid designators of the planet Venus. But this means only that one can substitute one name for the other inside the scope of the necessity operator and preserve truth value. That is, given that they are rigid designators,

K. (2)

(28) □ (if Phosphorus exists) Phosphorus = Phosphorus

and

(29) □ (if Phosphorus exists) Hesperus = Phosphorus

must have the same truth value. Suppose, however, that

318   RICHARD L. MENDELSOHN

(30) It is known *a priori* that Phosphorus = Phosphorus

is true. Does the fact that 'Hesperus' and 'Phosphorus' are both rigid designators allow us to infer that $(30) \Rightarrow (31)$

(31) It is known *a priori* that Hesperus = Phosphorus

is also true? I think not. To say that they are rigid designators is to say that they designate the same object in every possible world. But this notion of possible world has to do with metaphysical necessity, not the epistemological notion of necessity. *a prior* To say that 'Hesperus' and 'Phosphorus' are rigid designators is to allow us to substitute one for the other within the context 'It is necessary that'; it does not thereby license substitution within the context 'It is known *a priori* that'.

Important question

Indeed, it is not at all clear to me what the connection is between the claim, on the one hand, that proper names are rigid designators, and the claim, on the other hand, that proper names lack meaning or descriptive content. It is reasonable, I suppose, that if a term lacked meaning or descriptive content, it would be a rigid designator. But the converse does not hold: if a term is a rigid designator, it need *R.D* not be that it lacks meaning or descriptive content. First, since proper names can be *no sen* considered a species of description, in the sense that 'Socrates' can be replaced by *① Socra* 'the Socratizer', then there is no essential difference between proper names and definite descriptions that could be accounted for by the latter's containing a "predicative element" (as Donnellan puts it) that the former does not. Second, insofar *② scop* as Kripke acknowledges a scope distinction for proper names as well as for definite *distinc* descriptions, then the well-known picture Russell painted of a proposition expressed *for pro* by a sentence containing a logically proper name, with the object itself trapped in- *numes* side the proposition, could not be the picture Kripke has in mind. And, finally, *③ idea* some definite descriptions are rigid designators: for example, 'the ratio of the cir- *elemen* cumference of a circle to its diameter', which designates the number π in every possible world (in which the number π exists).

he doesn't

Apparently, Kripke believes that the description that constitutes the sense of *Fixing* the name for Frege serves to *fix the reference* of the name, not to give its meaning. *Referen* That is, the description serves to determine what the reference of the name is in the actual world, without its being the case that the description need pick out the same object in every possible world. The description, in other words, does not express an *essential* property of the object. For example, although Hesperus is, as a matter of fact, the most luminous body seen over the horizon at dusk, it might not have been: that very object, namely, Hesperus, might not have been the most luminous body seen over the horizon at dusk, and so it is not necessarily true that Hesperus is the most luminous body seen over the horizon at dusk. But this does not show that the name lacks descriptive content. For the description that is used to fix the reference of the name comes into its own when we shift our attention to the epistemological question of whether the proposition expressed by

(32) Hesperus = the most luminous body seen over the
        horizon at dusk

is known *a priori* or not. Although, on Kripke's view, (32) expresses a contingent truth, insofar as the reference of 'Hesperus' is fixed by the description 'the most luminous body seen over the horizon at dusk', he holds that (32) is known *a priori*. But this is extremely puzzling: How can the description be part of the content of the name if it does not constitute its meaning?

The only way out of this puzzle for Kripke I can see is one Plantinga has recently suggested.[21] Perhaps 'Hesperus' is a rigid designator and 'the most luminous body seen over the horizon at dusk' is not; but 'the most luminous body seen over the horizon at dusk in world W_1', where world W_1 is the possible world we, in fact, inhabit, is a rigid designator, and insofar as Frege had been unaware of the niceties of modal logic, we can charitably regard him as intending the latter description to give the sense of the name. Similarly, the sense of 'Phosphorus' would be 'the most luminous body seen over the horizon at dawn in world W_1'. The difference in the content of 'Hesperus' and 'Phosphorus' is precisely the difference both Frege and Kripke allude to to account for the fact that (1) expresses a proposition that is known *a posteriori* while (2) expresses a proposition that is known *a priori*. But since 'the most luminous body seen over the horizon at dusk in world W_1' and 'the most luminous body seen over the horizon at dawn in world W_1' are rigid designators of the same object, we are able to substitute 'Hesperus' for 'Phosphorus' within the scope of the necessity operator, so since (2) expresses a proposition that is necessarily true, (1) does also.[22]

Notes

1. Gottlob Frege, "On Sense and Reference," trans. Max Black, in *Translations from the Philosophical Writings of Gottlob Frege*, eds. Peter Geach and Max Black (Oxford, 1960), pp. 56-78.

2. Saul A. Kripke, "Naming and Necessity," in *Semantics of Natural Language*, eds. Gilbert Harman and Donald Davidson (Dordrecht, 1972), pp. 253-355, 763-69, and "Identity and Necessity," in *Identity and Individuation*, ed. Milton K. Munitz (New York, 1971), pp. 135-64.

3. See, for example, Bertrand Russell, "The Philosophy of Logical Atomism," rpt. *Logic and Knowledge*, ed. Robert Charles Marsh (London, 1956), pp. 175-282.

4. See, for example, Keith S. Donnellan, "Speaking of Nothing," *The Philosophical Review* 83 (1974):3-31.

5. He says, p. 28:

... our theory of reference denies that referring expressions such as "Socrates" conceal descriptions or introduce predicate elements. If we keep the predicative element the same and substitute a different referring expression—say, "Plato" for "Socrates"—then whether or not we have the same proposition depends upon whether or not the same thing is referred to.

6. (Oxford, 1974). Plantinga, The Nature of Necessity (posn abandoned in 8/)

7. See my "Plantinga on Proper Names and Propositions," forthcoming in *Philosophical Studies;* also Diana F. Ackerman, "Plantinga, Proper Names and Propositions," *Philosophical Studies* 30 (1976):409-12.

8. Alvin Plantinga, "The Boethian Compromise," *American Philosophical Quarterly* 15 (1978):129-38.

9. "Identity and Necessity," p. 150.

10. "Naming and Necessity," p. 310. Despite the awkward phrasing, that which is both necessary and *a posteriori* will be the proposition expressed by the sentence, not the sentence itself, for this would trvialize the claim that there are necessary *a posteriori* truths.

11. Michael Dummett, *Frege, Philosophy of Language* (London, 1973).

12. David K. Lewis, "Counterpart Theory and Quantified Modal Logic," *The Journal of Philosophy* 65 (1968):113-26.

13. "Identity and Necessity," p. 157.

14. This argument is found in W. V. O. Quine, *From a Logical Point of View,* 2nd ed. rev. (Cambridge, 1961), pp. 155-56.

15. Arthur F. Smullyan, "Modality and Description," *Journal of Symbolic Logic* 13 (1948): 31-37.

16. Richard L. Cartwright, "Some Remarks on Essentialism," *The Journal of Philosophy* 65 (1968):617-18.

17. See, for example, W. V. O. Quine, "On What There Is," rpt. *From a Logical Point of View,* pp. 1-19.

18. "Naming and Necessity," p. 343.

19. "Identity and Necessity," pp. 148-49.

20. Stating this precisely is problematic because it is not clear on Kripke's view (a) whether, for example, "Pegasus = Pegasus" expresses a necessary truth (let alone a truth) and (b) whether, for example, "Phosphorus = Phosphorus" expresses a truth in a possible world in which Phosphorous does not exist. So, we are prevented from saying: $\ulcorner (\iota x)Fx \urcorner$ is a rigid designator iff every substitution instance of

$$\Box \, [(\iota x)Fx] \, G(\iota x)Fx \equiv [(\iota x)Fx] \, \Box \, G(\iota x)Fx,$$

where "G" is a schematic predicate letter, is true.

21. "The Boethian Compromise," pp. 135-36.

22. The research for this paper was supported in part by The Research Foundation of the City University of New York, grant #11768, for which I am grateful. I would also like to express my thinks to Richard L. Cartwright for his criticism of earlier drafts. I alone, of course, am responsible for any remaining errors.

Identity, Properties,
and Causality

SYDNEY SHOEMAKER

I

I want to discuss in this paper a view about identity that goes back at least to Hume, namely that identity through time, or at any rate what we count as identity through time, consists at least in part in the holding of causal relations of certain kinds between momentary entities—events, or momentary thing-stages (phases, slices)—existing or occurring at different times. The idea is that what links these entities into the history of a single persisting object, or at least what makes us regard them as belonging to the history of a single object, is their being causally related in certain ways. The causal relation is, of course, not itself held to be the relation of identity. Rather, it is, in the terminology of John Perry, the "unity relation" for objects of the sort in question; that is, it is the relation such that its holding between numerically different entities constitutes their being stages of, or somehow belonging to (the history of), a single object of a certain kind.[1] Reichenbach seems to have been giving expression to such a view when he wrote that "A physical thing is . . . a series of events; any two events belonging to this series are called genidentical," and that "We apply the relation of genidentity only to events connected by a causal chain."[2] As Reichenbach uses the term, "genidentity" seems to be another word for Perry's unity relationship. An earlier expression of such a view occurs in W. E. Johnson's *Logic*: "The unity which I ascribe to the continuant is a causal unity of connection between its temporally or spatially separated manifestations; an observed or assumed causal formula, under which the character of these manifestations may be subsumed, is the sole ground for regarding them as manifestations of one and the same continuant."[3]

I shall discuss this idea in connection with another idea with which it may seem to be naturally linked. Crudely put, the second idea is that what we regard as persisting objects are logical fictions, or at any rate logical constructions, whose supposed identity is reducible to the holding of relations of various sorts between non-identical entities. The identity through time of these entities is thought of as being either wholly fictitious (which was Hume's view) or at least something somehow imposed on reality by human thought, human language, or human conventions. On such a view, one could in principle describe the world completely, or as completely as it can be described, without asserting any "cross-temporal identities" (as I shall call propositions asserting that something existing at one time is identical to something existing at a different time).

This formulation is, as I say, crudely put; it tars with the same brush a number of different views. To see what a range of views I mean to lump together for my purposes here, consider the variety of views compatible with the claim that a material object is "nothing over and above" a set, series, or mereological sum of temporary thing-stages. There are, of course, many sets, series, or sums of temporary thing-stages that we do not ordinarily think of as persisting objects—for example, the set or sum consisting of the stages of my knife on the even-numbered days of the month and the stages of my cat on the odd-numbered days. Now there are two *prima facie* very different views that agree in holding that the ontological status of what we ordinarily think of as persisting objects, that is, as "continuants," is on a par with that of such entities. On the one hand, there is the view that the identity of continuants is fictitious just because it is on a par with the identity of such spatiotemporally scattered objects. On the other hand, there is the view that the ontological status of such scattered objects, in being on a par with that of ordinary continuants, is much more robust than would ordinarily be supposed. What these views have in common is the idea that it is not a difference in ontological status, but only pragmatic considerations of various kinds, that accounts for the favored treatment which ordinary continuants receive in our language and "conceptual scheme"—for example, the fact that we have names for some of them, have common nouns and other sortal predicates that can be used to classify them, and so on. What the identity conditions are for a given kind of object will be a matter of linguistic convention, and only pragmatic considerations will limit what conventions are adopted, that is, what sorts of sets, series, or sums of thing-stages will be singled out for recognition in our language. On the one view, continuants are in a sense the creation of our conventions, and so are fictions. On the other view, what the conventions do is select rather than create; the various entities are all there, most of them scattered objects which we can afford to ignore, and our conventions provide rules for picking certain of them out. Both views can, I think, be described as conventionalist and reductionist views of the identity of material objects. On either view, what is asserted by a statement of cross-temporal identity can be expressed by a statement that does not invoke the notion of identity through time at all, and talks merely of momentary things and their interrelations.

I think it is natural to assume that anyone who proposes a causal analysis of cross-temporal identity, and says that the identity of material objects and persons over time consists in the holding of certain sorts of causal relations between momentary thing-stages, will be putting forward a conventionalist and reductionist view of this sort. And it has been common for philosophers who reject such views to reject any suggestion that the cross-temporal identity of genuine continuants can be said to consist in the holding of any relations other than the relation of identity itself. Thus Bishop Butler and Thomas Reid held that genuine identity is indefinable. And whenever, as in the case of organisms and artifacts, it seems plausible to say that identity over time does "consist in" the holding of certain relationships (spatiotemporal continuity, causal relationships, etc.) holding between entities existing or occurring at different times, they took this as showing that what we have in these cases is not identity in the "strict and philosophical sense" at all, but is, rather, what Butler called identity in a "loose and popular sense" and what Reid contrasted with "perfect identity" by calling it "something which, for conveniency of speech, we call identity." [4] This point of view is vigorously represented in our own time by Roderick Chisholm. Like Butler and Reid, Chisholm regards persisting tables and ships, and presumably trees and dogs as well, as "*entia successiva*," logical constructions out of more short-lived entities, and contrasts them with the "*entia per se*" to which alone identity through time in the "strict and philosophical sense" can be ascribed. [5] And he thinks, again like Butler and Reid, that the identity of persons, unlike the identity of tables and the like, is identity in the strict and philosophical sense—in other words, that persons are *entia per se*. One source of this view which I shall not discuss here is the allegiance of these philosophers to the doctrine Chisholm calls "mereological essentialism," which says that whatever parts a thing has are essential to it and so must belong to it throughout its history. But I suspect that where this view does not rest on confusion, it rests on the idea that only arbitrary or pragmatically based conventions could account for the fact that certain changes in the composition of a thing and not others are counted as compatible with its continued existence, and on the idea that the truth conditions for assertions of identity in the strict and philosophical sense cannot be determined by such conventions.

Despite my disagreement with much of what Butler, Reid, and Chisholm say about identity, including their mereological essentialism, I am sympathetic with their rejection of reductivism and conventionalism about the identity of continuants over time. I believe that there is a difference between the ontological status of what we ordinarily regard as continuants, on the one hand, and that of sets, series, or sums of thing-stages, on the other, which makes it appropriate to regard the former and not the latter as genuine continuants having an identity, or unity, across time which is something over and above the unity which any two arbitrarily selected things partake of in virtue of their joint membership in indefinitely many different sets or mereological sums—and that this is a unity, moreover, that is not conferred by linguistic conventions, or by the pragmatic consideratons that lead us to cut up the world in the way we do. But, and this will be my main point in this paper, I think that this is not only compatible with the view that identity through time "consists in" causal relations of a certain kind, but is actually implied by a causal account which I think is plausible on other grounds. The causal account I shall give, in fact, combines causal accounts of two different things—the nature of identity through time and the nature of the properties things have at the different times in their existence.

II

I shall begin with considerations that seem to me to show that it is a requirement for the cross-temporal identity of ordinary sorts of continuants that successive stages or phases in their histories stand in appropriate causal relationships, and that there is a good sense in which the holding of these relationships may be said to be constitutive of the identity. One route to this conclusion is through a consideration of memory theories of personal identity. Beginning with Locke, many philosophers have held that, as Hume put it, in the case of persons "memory not only discovers the identity, but also contributes to its production,"[6] and various examples have been produced that seem to support the claim that facts about memory are at least partially constitutive of personal identity.[7] But recent discussion has convincingly shown that the concept of memory is itself a causal concept—that a present belief or impression counts as a memory of a past action or experience only if it stands to it in an appropriate causal relationship.[8] If you put the memory theory of personal identity together with the causal theory of memory, and then generalize the result in a suitable way, what you get is a causal theory of the identity through time of continuants.

A second route to our conclusion is through a consideration of the role of similarity as evidence of identity. Similarity is not always good evidence of identity, so we need to ask under what circumstances it is good evidence. And while it is obvious that resemblance with respect to a certain property will be poor evidence of identity if the possession of that property is known to be common among things of the sort in question, it is not so often noticed that resemblance with respect to a property can be no evidence, or poor evidence, of identity even if the having of that property is rare. Suppose that the chairs in a certain building are all of the same shape and size, but rarely of the same color. Suppose further that once a year, on January 1st, all of the chairs in the building are repainted, and that the color a given chair is painted is chosen at random, so that only by coincidence will a chair have the same color before and after the repainting. And suppose I know all of this. If in December I am asked whether a given chair is the one I saw in February of the same year, the fact that it has the same color as that chair had then will be very good evidence for an affirmative answer. But if in December I am asked whether a given chair is the same as one I saw the previous December, the fact that it has the same color as that chair will be no evidence at all of identity. What this brings out is the following principle: if the way object B is at one time resembles the way object A was at an earlier time, it is reasonable to conclude from this that A is identical to B *only if* it is reasonable in the circumstances to conclude that B is the way it is at the later time *because*, among other things, A was the way it was at the earlier time. If we take the resemblance as evidence of identity, we are committed to thinking that if A had possessed different properties at the earlier time, B would have had correspondingly different properties at the later time—other things being equal, of course. This condition is satisfied in the first case involving the chairs. If the chair I saw in February was canary yellow, and the one I see now is canary yellow, then it is reasonable for me to conclude that this one is canary yellow because that one was, and that if that one had not been canary yellow, this one would not be canary yellow now; and in being entitled to believe this I am entitled to believe that they are one and the same chair. But in the second case, the condition is not satisfied. Supposing the chair I see now is sky blue, and the one I saw last December was sky blue, I am not entitled to suppose that this chair is sky blue because that one was then, or that if that one had not been sky blue then, this one would not be now. And just for this reason, I am not entitled to take the similarity as evidence of identity. It is worth observing that a similar principle governs our entitlement to take a correspondence between seeming memories and preceding actions or experiences as evidence of personal identity; if person S manifests at time t_2 an ostensible memory of doing an action of sort X at time t_1, and such an action was in fact done at time t_1 by person S', we are entitled to conclude on this basis that S is identical to S' only if it is reasonable in the circumstances to conclude that S has the seeming memory he does at t_2 because of what S' did at t_1, and that if S' had acted differently at t_1, S would have different memories at t_2.

What this strongly suggests is that those series of thing-stages that are histories of persisting things, genuine continuants, are distinguished from series that are not, that is, series made up of stages from histories of different things, by the fact that what properties are instantiated in later stages of a genuine history is a function of, among other things, what properties were instantiated in earlier stages of it. In the simplest case, where the thing has had minimal interaction with other things and has minimal internal complexity, the causal connections linking the stages will be what I shall call "property preserving" ones, and will result in similarity between successive stages. Such similarity is often used as evidence of identity; but as I have just argued, it is evidence of identity only insofar as it is evidence of counterfactual dependence, which in turn I take to indicate a causal relationship. And when things change, their new properties are normally a function of their old; how something is affected by interaction with other things will depend on what properties it had prior to the onset of the interaction, and in processes such as biological growth later stages are causally generated out of earlier ones in a way that yields a fixed pattern of change. If I squeeze a lump of clay, the shape of the resulting piece will depend on the shape and composition of the original piece as well as on how much force was applied and where. The mighty oak will have different properties than the sapling from which it grew; but the properties of the sapling provide a basis for predicting what the properties of the mature tree will be.

Returning briefly to personal identity, I think we can now see the relation of this to memory in a better light. That someone existing at a later time has the interests, values, and personality traits of someone existing at an earlier time can be just as good evidence of his identity with that person as the fact that he has seeming memories that correspond to things that person did at the earlier time. But mere cross-temporal similarity, whether it be physical or psychological, seems ill-suited for being constitutive of cross-temporal identity. It is probably because of this that philosophers who believe that personal identity consists in mental or pyschological facts have concentrated their attention on facts involving memory—the other relevant mental facts have been seen as reducing to cross-temporal similarities or chains of such similarities (as when there is gradual change over time). But we have seen that cross-temporal similarity is evidence of cross-temporal identity only insofar as it is evidence of a causal dependence of later stages on earlier ones, and that memory involves a similar sort of causal dependence. Seen in this light, the fact that someone's personality traits, etc., stand in appropriate relations of causal dependence to those of someone in the past has as good a claim to be constitutive of a fact of personal identity as does the fact that his mental states include memories (or, to avoid a possible circularity, "quasi-memories"[9]) of that person's past actions or experiences. Remembering is best seen as just a special, albeit very important, case of the retention of acquired mental states, which in turn is a special case of the sort of causal dependence that is central to the unity relation for continuants in general.

III

The suggestion most frequently made about the cross-temporal identity of material things is that this consists in spatiotemporal continuity—that what links different table-stages into the history of a single table is their belonging to a spatiotemporally continuous series of table-stages. But it is not difficult to show that the spatiotemporal continuity account is inadequate and has to be replaced or supplemented by an account in terms of causality. I shall begin with some fanciful examples.

Suppose, contrary to fact, that the following remarkable machines are possible. The first is a table canceller; if you have set its controls so as to pick out a certain location, then pushing a button on the machine will cause any table at that location to vanish into thin air. The second is a table producer; if you have set its controls so as to pick out a certain location, then pushing a button on the machine will cause a table to materialize out of thin air at that location, and the properties of that table will depend on the setting of the machine and on nothing else. I shall suppose that we have tried out both of these machines separately on many occasions and that they have always performed as described. We have rid the world of many hideous tables and created many handsome new ones. But now we set the controls of the machines so that the location picked out on both is that of my dining room table, and we push both buttons simultaneously. Assuming that the controls of the table producer are set to produce tables of the shape, size, and color of my present dining room table, it will look as if nothing has happened. There will be a spatiotemporally continuous series of table-stages, and it will appear to the casual observer as if the same table has persisted throughout. But knowing the powers of the machines, we know that this is not so. If t is the time at which the buttons were pushed, then the nature of the table-stages that occurred after t is due to the pushing of the button on the table producer at t, and not at all due to the properties of the table that was there before t; given that the button was pushed, we would have had such a table there after t even if there had been no table, or a very different table, there before. It seems plain that in this case one table has been replaced by another.

If you prefer a theological example, imagine an absent-minded deity who decides to arrange some miracles. He decrees that at a certain time a certain object—let it be a stone tablet—will disappear into thin air. Then, having forgotten all about this decree, and all about the existence of that stone tablet, he issues another decree, this one to the effect that at that time there will come into existence at a certain place a stone tablet of a certain description—and by coincidence the place and description are precisely those of the existing tablet at the time of its decreed annihilation. The time comes and the decreed events both occur. But the multitudes are unimpressed, for what they observe is simply a spatiotemporally continuous series of tablet-stages which they reasonably, although mistakenly, take to be the continued existence of a single tablet. What our deity has inadvertently done is to replace one tablet with another just like it, and in such a way as to preserve spatiotemporal continuity.[10]

Both of these stories are unlikely, to put it mildly; but they do not seem to me to be incoherent. And the claim that they are coherent fits with a causal theory, but not with the view that the identity of material things consists in spatiotemporal continuity. I do not know whether material persistence requires spatiotemporal continuity; but I suspect that if it does, this is because the relevant sorts of causality require it.

IV

Another objection to spatiotemporal continuity and continuity of properties accounts of cross-temporal identity has been made, independently, by Saul Kripke[11] and D. M. Armstrong.[12] This is based on the close connection there is between the notion of persistence, or cross-temporal identity, and the notion of motion. Among the properties that can be ascribed to a thing at a time are what might be called states of motion—for example, moving relative to some other thing at a certain velocity, accelerating at a certain rate, rotating with a certain angular velocity, and so on. But it seems obvious that it is impossible to give a noncircular analysis of cross-temporal identity in terms of relations between momentary thing-stages if we include states of motion among the properties that characterize or define our momentary thing-stages. At any rate, this is so on the usual understanding of the notion of motion; for on that understanding, the notion of motion must be explained in terms of the notion of cross-temporal identity—something that existed only for (or at) a durationless instant could not move, and could not have an instantaneous velocity. Now on a continuity analysis of cross-temporal identity, the truth values of all cross-temporal identity propositions that hold in a world should follow from a description of the history of that world as a series of what Kripke calls "holographic states" (think of a three-dimensional moving picture, each "frame" of which is a hologram), each of which is given by a maximal description of the world as it was at a particular temporal instant, where the description is not such as to imply the existence at any other moment of time of any of the things referred to or quantified over in it. Thus while such a state could include the fact that a red cube of a certain size is at a certain distance from a blue sphere of a certain size, it could not include the fact that these objects are moving toward each other, or the fact that the sphere was rotating at a certain rate; states of motion, since they imply facts of cross-temporal identity, cannot be included in holographic states. But Kripke points out that if the world described includes a perfectly uniform disk made of homogeneous material, the description of the series of holographic states will be the same whether the disk is stationary or rotating, and will be the same no matter at what rate it is rotating. So there will be identity questions, for example, whether the portion of the disk occupying a certain portion of space at one time (for simplicity we shall assume an absolute Newtonian space-time) is the same as one occupying that portion of space at another time, which will not be answerable on the basis of a spatiotemporal continuity or continuity of properties criterion of cross-temporal identity. Armstrong's example is the same, except that the homogeneous object is a sphere rather than a disk.[13]

Despite the similarity of their examples, Kripke and Armstrong have different purposes. Kripke's argument is part of a general attack on the idea that there are constitutive "criteria" for the identity through time of material objects, one version of which is the view that such identity consists in the holding of certain relations (specifiable without the use of the notion of cross-temporal identity) between momentary thing-stages. But Armstrong is a supporter of the latter view, which he calls the "Relational View," and introduces the example of the sphere in order to show that a causal version of the Relational View avoids the difficulty this example poses for other versions of the view. If the sphere is stationary, he says, then the phases of the eastern portion from t_1 to t_2 will bear to each other that special causal relationship which must hold between different phases of the same thing; in particular, the existence of the earlier phases will be "nomically required" in a distinctive way for the existence of the later phases. The causal relations will be different if the sphere is rotating.

Armstrong's suggestion would seem to be supported by the fact that different counterfactuals will be true of the successive phases of the rotating sphere than will be true of the successive phases of the stationary sphere. Suppose that between t_1 and t_2 the sphere rotates $180°$. Then it will be true (assuming that the sphere is made of scratch retentive material) that if at t_1 the eastern portion of the sphere had had a scratch of a certain shape on it, and the sphere had been otherwise unscratched, then at t_2 the western portion of the sphere would have had such a scratch on it, and the sphere would have been otherwise unscratched. Whereas if the sphere had been stationary between t_1 and t_2, a different counterfactual would hold, namely that if at t_1 the sole scratch on the sphere had been on the eastern portion, then at t_2 it would also be the case that the sole scratch on the sphere is on the eastern portion. It would seem that this difference in what counterfactuals are true in the two cases must be due to a difference in the causal relationships that hold between the different "sphere-phases" in the two cases, and that if we incorporate such causal relationships into our unity relationship, we avoid the difficulty raised by the Kripke-Armstrong examples.

It is natural to object that it seems very unlikely that we can specify the relevant causal relationships without invoking the notion of motion and with it the notion of cross-temporal identity, or of a persisting thing, which we are trying to analyze.[14] Let E_1 be the eastern portion of our sphere at t_1, E_2 the eastern portion of our sphere at t_2, and W_2 the western portion of our sphere at t_2. In the case where the sphere is stationary, the state of E_2 at t_2 is counterfactually dependent on the state of E_1 at t_1, and it seems reasonable to assume that this counterfactual dependence is grounded in causal relationships. Here, of course, E_1 and E_2 are identical. Likewise, in the case in which the sphere is rotating, and rotates $180°$ between t_1 and t_2, the state of W_2 at t_2 is counterfactually dependent on the state of E_1 at t_1, and again it seems reasonable to assume that this relation is grounded in a causal relationship. Here E_1 and W_2 are identical. But the causally relevant state of E_1 at t_1 cannot consist simply in its having a certain shape, size, and composition, for such properties are ones that E_1 has in both cases (that is, both when the sphere is stationary and when it is rotating) and so cannot account for the difference between the counterfactuals that hold in the one case and those that hold in the other. It would seem that the causally relevant state of E_1 at t_1 will crucially involve in the one case the fact that E_1 was stationary and in the other the fact that E_1 had a certain angular velocity. If the causally relevant properties include states of motion, then it seems that the attempt to analyse cross-temporal identity in terms of causality will be circular.

What we would have to do in order to answer this objection is to give an analysis of the notion of motion, and of such notions as the velocity of a thing at an instant, which does not invoke or presuppose the notion of cross temporal identity. If the analysis is in terms of the notion of causality, then so much the better. Let us see how an attempt at such an analysis might go.

I shall assume that we have available to us the notion of a spatiotemporally continuous series of thing-stages. The case of the rotating sphere shows that not every such series is the history of a persisting thing; there will be infinitely many continuous series of hemisphere stages that are not histories of single persisting hemispheres—for example, the series of eastern hemisphere-stages in the case in which the sphere is rotating around its north-south axis. It should be possible to define the notion of the spatial length of the segment of such a series that occurs during a given temporal interval.[15] (Roughly, this will be the distance something would have traveled during that interval if the members of that series had been stages of its history —but, of course, we cannot use this as a definition if our object is to define the notion of a persisting object.) We can also speak of the temporal length of such a segment, which will be just the length of the interval. Using these notions, and the notion of a limit, we can define the notion of the "velocity" of such a series at an instant; if S is the class of segments of the series that occur during intervals containing instant i, then the "velocity" of the series at i will be the limit of the ratio of spatial length to temporal length of the segments in S as their temporal length approaches zero. In a similar way we can define other "states of motion" for spatiotemporally continuous series—for example, "rate of acceleration," "angular velocity," and so on. To illustrate the notion of the "velocity" of a series which is not necessarily the velocity of any persisting object, consider a case in which a light-source is revolving around a sphere, illuminating one-half of it at any given moment. If the sphere is stationary, or rotating on an axis other than that on which the light source is revolving, the series of illuminated hemisphere-stages will not be the history of any particular part of the sphere. Nevertheless, it will have an "angular velocity" which depends on the angular velocity of the revolving light source.[16]

Let us now consider the subclass of spatiotemporally continuous series of stages which are such that for each stage S of the series, and for each segment of the series that includes S, that segment includes an earlier stage that stands to S in the appropriate sort of causal relationship. I shall speak of such a series as "causally connected." A thing-stage will include a certain state of motion, for example, a certain velocity, just in case the stage belongs to a causally connected continuous series of thing-stages, for short a CCCS, having the corresponding "state of motion," for example, a "velocity" of a certain value, at the time in question. In the case of the series of illuminated hemisphere-stages, the "velocities" are not velocities, because the series is not causally connected. This way of defining states of motion does not in any direct way invoke the notion of a persisting thing. (It remains to be considered whether it does so surreptitiously in its reliance on the notion of an "appropriate" sort of causal relation. I return to this in Section VIII.) And there is no obvious reason why states of motion, as thus defined, should not have the required sort of causal efficacy.

V

It is obvious that not just any relation of causal dependence between successive thing-stages is sufficient to make the states belong to the history of a single persisting object; otherwise forgeries of paintings would be identical to the originals from which they are copied, with all the absurdities that entails. I shall not attempt here the probably impossible task of giving a general and nontrivial characterization of a kind of causal dependence, the holding of which between successive thing-stages is always necessary and sufficient for their belonging to the same continuant. Instead, I shall content myself with a supervenience claim. Consider a world that is just like the actual world with respect to what properties are instantiated at each space-time point, and also just like the actual world with respect to what causal relations hold between these different property instantiations. I claim that if in the actual world a set of property instantiations all belong to the history of a single persisting object, then their counterparts in that other possible world likewise belong to the history of a single persisting object. More generally, if in any possible world a set S of property instantiations make up the history of a single persisting thing, then in any world that is qualitatively identical to that world, in the sense that the same properties are instantiated at the same space-time points, and also identical to it with respect to the sorts of causal connections that hold between the various property instantiations, the set of property instantiations in that world which is the counterpart of S will likewise make up the history of a single persisting thing. This gives expression to the idea that the persistence through time of continuants is *nothing over and above* the holding of certain causal and spatiotemporal relations between different property instantiations—and since momentary thing-stages can be thought of as sets of simultaneous property instantiations that are related in certain ways, this can also be put by saying that the persistence through time of continuants is nothing over and above the holding of certain causal and spatiotemporal relations between momentary thing-stages.

The view I have just expressed must surely sound like extreme reductivism about identity through time—that is, it must sound just like the view I said at the outset I was going to oppose. But I think that it can be understood in such a way that it is not. In order to show this I must first put forward a view about the nature of properties.

VI

There is a broad sense of the word "property" in which there is a property corresponding to any grammatical predicate. Properties in the broad sense will include relational properties, like being fifty miles south of a burning barn (to use Jaegwon Kim's example), and historical properties, like being two hundred years old and having been slept in by George Washington, as well as such ordinary properties as being spherical, weighing fifty pounds, and being blue. They will also include what only a philosopher would think to count as properties, for example, being such that Jimmy Carter is President of the United States (a property that belongs to absolutely everything right now), and being grue in Goodman's sense.

Now I think that it will be agreed that usually we use the word "property" in a narrower sense than this. Suppose that someone claims that two pennies are exactly alike, that is, share all of their properties. We would doubtless think that this claim is unlikely to be true—surely when we get down to the microscopic and submicroscopic levels, there will be some difference in their size and shape (in the number and arrangement of the particles of which they are composed). But we would not count it against the truth of this claim that the two pennies have had different histories and stand in different relations to other things—that is, that their historical and relational properties are different. Again, when my pencil loses the property of being fifty miles south of a burning barn (because the fire is extinguished, say), or when it loses the property of being such that Gerald Ford is President of the United States (because Jimmy Carter is inaugurated), we do not suppose that it thereby undergoes any genuine change. In other words, we seem to have a narrow sense of "property," which is correlative with our usual sense of "change," which excludes, as not genuine properites, relational and historical properties and the like. In the narrow sense, being spherical will be a property, but being such that Carter is President will not be. How are we to elucidate this sense? We could, of course, say that something is a property in the narrow sense if and only if its acquisition or loss constitutes a genuine change. But then we would be faced with the job of elucidating the required sense of "change," and distinguishing it from the broad sense in which everything in the universe underwent a change when Carter was inaugurated, or in which Socrates underwent a change when he became shorter than Theaetetus, in virtue of the latter's growth. We shall be going in a circle if we explain the latter by saying that a genuine change is one that involves the acquisition or loss of a genuine property. In the end, I am afraid, we shall have to settle for a circular account anyhow; but it is possible to make the circle a bit bigger than this.

My suggestion is that in order to elucidate these distinctions we must bring in the concept of causality. Consider a bed slept in by George Washington, and another bed, made by the same craftsman from the same design and the same stock of wood, that lacks this historical property. Our narrow sense of "property" should be such that it is possible for these beds to share all of their properties. Now it is plain that the beds could be so much alike that it would be impossible to *observe* any difference between them. But, of course, even if observation could detect no difference between them, one would allow that there was a genuine difference if they registered a different effect on some instrument. Suppose, however, that all of their causal powers and potentialities, all of their dispositions to influence other things or be influenced by other things, were exactly the same. Then, I suggest, they would share all of their properties in the narrow sense, all of their "intrinsic" properties. Likewise, when I say that the loss by my pencil of the property of being fifty miles south of a burning barn, or the property of being such that Gerald Ford is President, is not a real change, the cash value of this is that the acquisition or loss of these so-called properties does not in itself make any difference to the causal powers of a thing. This suggests a view about what intrinsic properties, properties in the narrow sense, are. According to this view, what constitutes the identity of such a property, what makes it the particular property it is, is its potential for contributing to the causal powers of the things that have it. Each of the potentialities that makes up a property can be specified by saying that in combination with such and such other properties that property gives rise to a certain causal power. Thus, for example, the property of having the shape of an ordinary kitchen knife—for short, the property of being knife-shaped—is partially specified by saying that if anything has this property together with the property of being made of steel, it thereby has the power of being able to cut wood if applied to it with suitable pressure. If we could indicate all of the ways in which the having of this property could contribute to the causal powers of things, we would have said all there is to say about the intrinsic nature of this property. Such, at any rate, is my suggestion.

It should be remembered, in considering this view, that we know what properties things have, and know what we know about these properties, from their effects, that is, from the effects of the activation of causal powers which things have in virtue of having the properties. This happens in a variety of ways. Observing something is being causally influenced by it in certain ways. If the causal potentialities involved in the possession of a property are such that there is a fairly direct causal relationship between the possession of it by an object and the sensory states of an observer related to that object in certain ways, for example, looking at it in good light, we say that the property itself is observable. If the relationship is less direct, for example, if the property can affect the sensory states of an observer only by affecting something else, a scientific instrument, say, we speak of inferring that the thing has the property from what we take to be effects of its possession. In other cases we conclude that something has a property because we know that it has other properties which we know from other cases to be correlated with the one in question. But the latter way of knowing about the properties of things is parasitic on the earlier ways; for unless the possession of a property had, under some circumstances, effects from which its presence could be concluded, we could never discover laws or correlations that would enable us to infer its existence from things other than its effects. This means that if, *per impossibile*, there were properties whose possession made no difference whatever to the causal powers of the things that have them, there would be no way at all in which we could know of their existence, or have any reason whatever to believe in it. It is likewise true, I think, that if the identity of properties consisted in something other than and independent of their potential for contributing to the causal powers of the things that have them, then we would have no way of knowing things which in fact we are clearly capable of knowing; we would have no way of knowing whether two things possessed the same property, whether the properties possessed by something had changed, and so on. For it is only on the assumption that sameness of property goes with sameness of causal potentialities that our observations and instruments indicate what we take them to indicate.

I hasten to point out that this account of properties is circular. It tells us, in brief, that properties (intrinsic properties) are identical just in case it is true in all possible circumstances that their coinstantiation with the same properties gives rise to the same powers. This makes use of the notion of sameness of property, which is the very notion being elucidated. It also makes use of the notion of sameness of causal power, the elucidation of which would doubtless require the use of the notion of sameness of property. Despite this, the account has substantive content—it links the concept of an intrinsic property with that of causality in a way that is not customarily done, and it has some surprising consequences which I cannot go into here. And as will emerge later in this paper, if this account is right, then my earlier account of identity through time in terms of causality appears to be circular in much the same way.[17]

VII

I want now to apply this theory of properties to the problem of identity. Earlier I put the causal theory of cross-temporal identity by saying that the identity of persisting things consists in the holding of a certain sort of causal relation between momentary thing-stages, this causal relation being the "unity relation" for continuants. But we can achieve greater generality if we take the terms of the unity relation to be momentary property instantiations rather than momentary thing-stages. This enables us to ask, not merely how property instantiations occurring at different times must be related in order to have the same subject, but also how simultaneous property instantiations must be related in order to have the same subject—where the "subject" of a property instantiation is the thing in which the property is instantiated. In fact, we might as well take a momentary thing-stage to be just a set of simultaneous property instantiations that is closed under the unity relation, that is, a set that contains all and only the simultaneous property instantiations that stand in the unity relation to any of its members. We can then divide the problem of identity into two parts. There is the problem of specifying the relationship that unites simultaneous property instantiations into thing-stages (for short, the relationship of "synchronic unity"), and there is the problem of specifying the relationship that unites different thing-stages (and their constituent property instantiations) into histories of persisting things (this will be the relationship of "diachronic unity").

The first of these problems (if it can be called a problem) is seldom discussed.[18] And it has seldom been given the sort of reductivist and conventionalist answer that is so often given to the second question. But it is worth showing that such an answer could not be correct; this will prepare the ground for an argument against reductivist and conventionalist answers to the question about cross-temporal identity, that is, about the diachronic unity of property instantiations and thing-stages. What I shall argue is that such reductivist views are ruled out by the account of properties sketched earlier.

Consider the property of being knife-shaped and the property of being made of steel. Each of these properties, according to my account, has an essential nature which consists in its potential for contributing to the causal powers of the things that have it. The essential nature of the property of being knife-shaped includes the feature, I call it a "conditional power," of giving rise to the power of cutting wood if combined with, that is, coinstantiated with, the property of being made of steel; and the essential nature of the property of being made of steel includes the conditional power of giving rise to the power of cutting wood if combined with the property of being knife-shaped. In other words, it belongs to the essential natures of these two properties that if they are coinstantiated, that is, instantiated in the same subject at the same time, this gives rise to a certain causal power. This rules out a reductivist account of the synchronic unity of property instantiations. For if one cannot say what a property is without saying what happens when it is coinstantiated with other properties, that is, what happens when instantiations of it *stand in the unity relation to* instantiations of other properties, then it cannot be the case that the synchronic unity of property instantiations is an optional logical construction out of property instantiations and some relationship between them (that relationship being specifiable without the use of the notion of synchronic unity). Moreover, it is clear that on my account the nature of properties imposes severe constraints on what the synchronic unity relationship can be. Nothing could be the unity relation between simultaneous instantiations of the property of being made of steel and the property of being knife-shaped unless its holding between these instantiations guaranteed that they jointly give rise to the appropriate power, namely the power to cut wood if subjected to suitable pressure. Similar constraints will be imposed by the essential natures of any set of properties that can be instantiated together. These constraints leave little scope, if any, for conventional decision in determining the unity conditions for simultaneous property instantiations.

To illustrate this with an example of a different kind, suppose that the following mental properties are instantiated at the same time: a desire expressible by "I want to survive," a belief expressible by "To survive, I must do A," and a belief expressible by "I can do A." If these are all states of a single person, then, *ceteris paribus*, they had better give rise to an attempt to do A. There are circumstances in which this could serve as a criterion of mental unity; if in the case of a split-brain patient we have reason to ascribe certain desires to the possessor of the right brain hemisphere, and certain beliefs to the possessor of the left brain hemisphere, then whether it is correct to say that these are states of one and the same person, or of one and the same "mind," may depend on whether they jointly give rise to the effects, behavioral and otherwise, that ought to result from the coinstantiation of these mental properties. If, as seems conceivable, a set of mental property instantiations associated with a single human body could fail to pass this test for synchronic unity, then the essential nature of mental properties rules out any such relation as *occurring in the same body as* as the unity relation for simultaneous instantiations of mental properties. ·

Now let us turn to the problem of identity through time—or, what comes to the same thing, the problem of specifying the unity relation for nonsimultaneous property instantiations and thing-stages. The essence of a property, I have argued, consists in its potential for contributing to the causal powers of the things that have it. A power, in turn, is specified by saying what will happen if the thing that has it is placed in various circumstances, or interacts in certain ways with other things. And usually this will involve saying what will happen if the thing remains in those circumstances over some interval of time, or is involved in an interaction lasting some period of time. For example, if a thing is malleable, then if subjected to sufficient force it will gradually undergo a change in shape, and will retain its new shape once the deforming force is removed; while if a thing is elastic, it will change shape when subjected to certain forces, but will resume its former shape when the forces are removed. Since a specification of the essential nature of a property will involve a specification of the powers to which it has the potential for contributing, and since a specification of the powers will say what happens to their subject *over time* given certain conditions, the essential nature of a property incorporates the persistence conditions, that is, the cross-temporal identity conditions, of the things to which it can belong. The attribution of a particular property will not have a determinate truth value unless the identity conditions for things having that property are already fixed; for the attribution of a property to a thing will imply propositions about what will happen to *that thing* under certain circumstances, and these propositions will have determinate truth value only if it is already settled under what circumstances a future happening is to count as an episode in the history of *that thing*. But if this is so, the unity conditions for nonsimultaneous property instantiations can be no more a matter for conventional decision than the unity conditions for simultaneous property instantiations.

One thing this brings out is that the laws that specify the contribution of particular properties to causal powers, and so (on my account) describe the essential nature of these properties, cannot be separated from the laws that say what happens over time to something having certain properties, including those that specify the conditions under which a property is retained or lost. In order to be able to specify the effects on a thing of various sorts of external influences, we need to be able to specify, as our baseline, the sort of history the thing would have if not subjected to those influences. And just as it is built into the nature of particular properties that a thing having those properties will undergo a certain change if subjected to a certain influence, so it is typically built into the nature of a property that in the absence of external influences (or of a change in external influences) a thing having that property will continue to have it. One might put this by saying that property instantiations have an inherent tendency to perpetuate themselves—although this would have to be qualified to allow for phenomena like biological growth and radioactive decay. The causality that works within a thing, and in general (although not invariably) works to preserve its properties, is what W. E. Johnson called "immanent causality" and contrasted with the "transeunt causality" by which one thing influences another.[19] While the nature of properties consists, or so I maintain, in their potential for contributing to both sorts of causality, it is the connection with immanent causality that is of special interest here. For it follows from this that any series of thing-stages that constitutes the history of a persisting thing must be "causally connected" in a sense akin to that of Section IV, not because talk of persistence is reducible to talk of causally connected series, but because of the very nature of the properties that are instantiated in these stages.

Let us say that a series of thing-stages is "immanently connected" if its later stages develop from its earlier ones in accordance with the laws of immanent causality that are, as it were, built into the nature of the properties instantiated in the states of the series (and in the stages of other series with which it interacts). What immediately follows from my account of properties is that it is a necessary condition of a series of thing-stages being the history of a persisting thing that it be immanently connected. The supervenience claim of Section V can now be put by saying that this necessary condition is also sufficient—that if a series of thing-stages is such that each stage influences subsequent stages in precisely the ways it would have to, given the properties invovled, if the series were the history of a single persisting thing, then the series will, in fact, be the history of a single persisting thing. This is not, as far as I can see, a consequence of my account of properties. But it is compatible with it and seems to me to be true. It something more than this is required for cross-temporal identity, for a series of thing-stages to be the history of a single persisting thing, then it is not clear what this "something more" could be, or how we could know whether it was present in particular cases.

VIII

It will be recalled that in Section IV the notion of a causally connected continuous series of thing-stages, or for short a CCCS, was introduced in order to provide a way of defining the notion of motion that did not employ the notion of a persisting thing. Such a definition was suggested as a way of defending causal analyses of cross-temporal identity against a charge of circularity; more specifically, the charge was that only if such analyses are so construed as to be circular can they handle the Kripke-Armstrong examples. The apparent circularity stemmed from the fact that the different momentary states of continuants will not be causally connected in the ways claimed by the causal theory unless they are construed as including states of motion, and the fact (or apparent fact) that the notion of motion has to be explained in terms of the notion of cross-temporal identity. If the notion of a CCCS can be explained without the use of the notion of cross-temporal identity, then the possibility of defining states of motion in terms of the "states of motion" of CCCS's would show that this circularity is only apparent.

But the definition of a CCCS invoked the notion of an "appropriate" causal connection between thing-stages, and this notion obviously cries out for clarification. We now have *a* way of clarifying it; we can say that the causal connection between thing-stages is appropriate just in case they belong to a series of thing-stages that is immanently connected. But as I have explained the notion of being immanently connected, this will reintroduce the circularity we were out to avoid; the notion of being immanently connected was explained in terms of the notion of immanent causality, which in turn was explained in terms of the notion of persistence, or cross-temporal identity.

Is there any hope of defining the notion of immanent causality, or the required notion of an "appropriate" causal connection between thing-stages, without the use of the notion of persistence? I do not think so. To do this we would have to be able to characterize the causal potentialities of properties without making use of the notion of persistence. We might be able to do this if we *already* had available a notion of a CCCS which was not explained in terms of the notion of persistence. If we had this, then instead of specifying the causal potentialities of a property by saying what will happen over time under various conditions to something having that property, we might try to specify them by saying what sorts of CCCS's would occur under various conditions when that property is instantiated. But it is precisely in order to define the notion of CCCS that we are trying to define the notion of an "appropriate" causal connection. So it now appears that in order to give a noncircular analysis of this notion, we would already have to have one; which is to say that it is not possible to give one.

The objection considered in Section IV suggested that states of motion will be the Achilles heel of any attempt to give a reductive analysis of cross-temporal identity in terms of relations between thing-stages. But these cause a problem only because of the difficulty, or impossibility, of giving a noncircular account of the notion of an "appropriate" causal connection, or of the notion of immanent causality. And this stems from the fact that what counts as an appropriate causal relation in a particular case depends on the nature of the particular properties involved in that case, and the fact that it seems impossible to characterize the relevant class of causal potentialities of properties, those relating to "immanent causality," without making use of the notion of persistence and cross-temporal identity.

IX

Now let us compare the status of those series of thing-stages (or property instantiations) that are histories of ordinary continuants (material objects of persons) with those—I shall call them "gerrymandered series"—that are made up of stages (or property instantiations) taken from the histories of different ordinary continuants, for example, the series consisting of the stages of my knife on the even-numbered days of the month and the stages of my cat on the odd-numbered days. We can agree that these series are ontologically on a par *qua* series; likewise the mereological sums of the members of the series are ontologically on a par *qua* mereological sums. One series or mereological sum is just as real as any other. Some philosophers would conclude from this that ordinary constituents are ontologically on a par with entities whose existence is not ordinarily acknowledged—entities that correspond to, or simply are, the gerrymandered series (or mereological sums of the members thereof). This seems to me clearly wrong. First of all, from the fact that the histories of continuants are, *qua* series or sums of thing-stages, on a par with the gerrymandered series, it does not follow that the continuants themselves are on a par with the gerrymandered series; for continuants are not identical with the series or sums of stages that are their histories. And if it is said that ordinary continuants are ontologically on a par with entities of which the gerrymandered series are histories, I would reply that there simply are no such entities for them to be ontologically on a par with. At any rate, it follows from the account of properties I have given, and seems to me intuitively correct, that there is no entity corresponding to a gerrymandered series that relates to it in the way ordinary continuants relate to the series of thing-stages that are their histories.

An ordinary continuant has certain properties at a given time if and only if its history contains a stage occurring at that time which includes instantiations of those properties. So if a gerrymandered series is likewise the history of a persisting entity, then at any moment of time that entity should have, should be the subject of, whatever properties are instantiated in a member of the series occurring at that time.[20] So any entity whose history includes the stage of my knife's history that occurred at Noon today has to have been knife-shaped and made of steel at Noon today. But if what I have said about the essential nature of properties is right, any entity that has those properties must have the causal powers that my knife had at Noon today. I have pointed out, moreover, that something's having such powers involves various conditionals being true of it, these saying what will happen to it over time under various conditions. But for any gerrymandered series, the existence of an entity having at each moment of time the properties instantiated in the series at that moment would falsify the conditionals that would have to be true of an entity having those properties. For example, if there were an entity having as its history the series consisting of the stages of my knife occurring on the even-numbered days of the month and the stages of my cat occurring on the odd-numbered days, then what happened to that entity at midnight on any given day (except on the thirty-first of the month) would violate the laws that spell out the essential natures of the properties that entity would have to have, and would falsify the conditionals that would have to be true of it. So there could not be such an entity. Here, then, is the (or at any rate, a) difference in ontological status between those series of thing-stages that are histories of ordinary continuants, on the one hand, and gerrymandered series, on the other: the former are, while the latter are not, histories of entities that are subjects of the properties instantiated in the stages.

It may still seem to some that for any series of thing-stages, including gerrymandered series, we can introduce the notion of an object having that series as its history, and can do so in such a way as to guarantee that the object exists if the series does. If a household has exactly one table in the kitchen and exactly one in the living room, let us say that there exists a "klable" having as its history the series of stages consisting of the stages of the kitchen table from midnight to Noon and those of the living room table from Noon to midnight (call this the "klable series," and call table-stages that belong to such series "klable-stages"). We shall stipulate, as one of the rules defining the meaning of "klable," that at any given time the klable in a household has those properties that are instantiated in the klable-stage occurring at that time in that household. Given that there are households of the appropriate sort, it might seem that our rules guarantee (or would if we spelled them out fully enough) that there are entities that share the properties of tables at particular moments but have klable series as their histories. But this is an illusion. Such rules for the use of "klable" could not give it the status of a sortal predicate, and could not give to such expressions as "my klable" the status of being singular terms; at best they could assign to these expressions certain roles in a code for talking about tables. They might guarantee that sentences like "My klable is made of oak now, but was made of maple an hour ago" are sometimes true. But the truth of such a sentence will no more imply that something was first made of maple and then of oak than the truth of "The average man as 2.3 children" implies that there is someone who has 2.3 children. What superficially appear to be the grammatical subjects of these sentences are not genuine terms, and are not accessible to existential quantification. If our rules, together with the facts, assign the truth-value "true" to the sentence "Klables exist," then in this use of the word "exist" it will be part of the code for talking about tables and will not have its ordinary meaning.

Of course, instead of introducing "klable" as part of a code (that is, by a set of rules assigning truth conditions to certain sentences or quasi-sentences containing it) we might introduce it by the following explicit definition: "x is a klable = df. x is an entity of a kind such that, necessarily, entities of that kind are paired one-one with households having exactly one kitchen table and exactly one living room table, and each such entity shares from midnight till noon the properties of its associated kitchen table and from noon to midnight the properties of its associated living room table." Now "klable" will be, syntactically at least, a genuine sortal term. But it will be false, and I think necessarily false, that there are any klables. Only if we confuse such an explicit definition with a set of rules assigning a word like "klable" a role in a code will it seem that entities with bizarre identity conditions can be defined into existence (or that they are there all along, awaiting linguistic recognition).

If indeed the term "table" had the same status as "klable" (on the code construal of it), then it would be appropriate to say that tables are logical fictions—or, to put this more appropriately in the formal mode, that the term "table" does not refer, despite the fact that it occurs as a quasi-noun in sentences that mimic existential and subject-predicate sentences and are so defined as to be true. But there is no reason whatever to suppose that this is true; to put this in the material mode (where it cannot really be said), there is no reason whatever to suppose that tables are ontologically on a par with klables.

X

I shall end by commenting briefly on the implications of what I have been saying for the topic of personal identity. People often do philosophy of mind in a way that implies that the nature of personal identity and the nature of mental states are pretty much unrelated topics. If the thesis of this paper is right, this is a mistake. The most important properties of persons are mental or psychological ones. And an understanding of what particular mental or psychological properties are will intimately involve an understanding of both the unity conditions for simultaneous instantiations of such properties and the unity conditions for nonsimultaneous properties of them—in other words, it will intimately involve an understanding of the identity conditions for the subjects of such properties.

Interestingly enough, this is just what functionalist accounts of mental states imply. On such accounts, one says what it is for a person to have a certain mental state, for example, a certain belief, by saying how the possesssion of that mental state combines with the possession of various combinations of other mental states (in particular, desires and other beliefs) to influence the person's behavior and his subsequent mental states. But to speak of the possession of a mental state "combining" with the possession of others is to invoke the unity relation between simultaneous mental states, while to speak of the influence of a mental state on subsequent mental states of the same person is to invoke the unity relation between nonsimultaneous mental states.

This is not to claim, however, that the notion of personal identity is logically or conceptually prior to that of particular sorts of mental states. Such claims of conceptual priority are to be avoided. To claim the conceptual priority of the notion of personal identity vis-à-vis other mental notions would be to move in the direction of the sort of account of identity favored by Butler, Reid, and Chisholm, according to which personal identity (and "strict" identity generally) is "indefinable" and propositions of personal identity have no nontrivial truth conditions. To claim the conceptual priority of notions of momentary mental states or property instantiations, or of momentary "person-stages," vis-à-vis the notion of personal identity would be to move in the direction of a fictionalist, or at any rate reductivist, account of personal identity. Both views seem to me mistaken. On the view I would urge, the notion of personal identity and the notions of particular mental states are internally related, but neither can be said to be conceptually prior to the other. If we want philosophical illumination here, we have no choice but to move in a circle. In elucidating particular mental concepts, we shall have to help ourselves to the notion of personal identity, while in elucidating the concept of personal identity, we shall have to help ourselves to various mental concepts. And so it is in general with the concept of a persisting substance or continuant, the concept of an intrinsic property, and the concept of causality; any elucidation of any of these concepts will have to make use of at least one of the others, and none of them can be eliminated in favor of the others.[21]

Notes

1. See John Perry, "The Problem of Personal Identity," in his anthology *Personal Identity* (Berkeley and Los Angeles, 1975), pp. 3-30.

2. Hans Reichenbach, *The Direction of Time* (Berkeley and Los Angeles, 1956), p. 38. See also section 26 of that book, "The Genidentity of Quantum Particles," and Reichenbach's earlier book, *The Philosophy of Space and Time* (New York, 1958), pp. 270-71.

3. W. E. Johnson, *Logic, Part III: The Logical Foundations of Science* (New York, 1964), p. 99.

4. See Joseph Butler, "Of Personal Identity," *The Works of Bishop Butler*, ed. J. H. Bernard (London, 1900), II, 281, and Thomas Reid, *Essays on the Intellectual Powers of Man* (Cambridge, 1969), p. 344. Butler's essay and the relevant chapters from Reid are reprinted in Perry's *Personal Identity*.

5. See Roderick Chisholm, *Person and Object* (La Salle, Illinois, 1976), Chapter III, "Identity Through Time."

6. David Hume, *Treatise of Human Nature*, ed. L. A. Selby-Bigge (Oxford, 1888), p. 261.

7. See, for example, Anthony Quinton, "The Soul," *The Journal of Philosophy* 59 (1962): 393-409, reprinted in Perry, *Personal Identity*, and my *Self-Knowledge and Self-Identity* (Ithaca, 1963), especially pp. 23-25. A classic statement of a memory theory of personal identity is H. P. Grice, "Personal Identity," *Mind* 50 (1941):330-50, reprinted in Perry, *Personal Identity*.

8. See C. B. Martin and M. Deutscher, "Remembering," *The Philosophical Review* 75 (1966): 161-96. See also David Wiggins, *Identity and Spatiotemporal Continuity* (Oxford, 1967) and my "Persons and Their Pasts," *American Philosophical Quarterly* 7 (1970):269-85.

9. For this notion, see my "Persons and Their Pasts."

10. In a paper entitled "Identity Through Time," which I saw in manuscript after this section was written, David Armstrong uses a very similar example to make essentially the same point. Armstrong's paper is to be published in *Time and Cause, Essays Presented to Richard Taylor*, edited by Peter van Inwagen.

11. In lectures on "Time and Identity" given at Cornell in the Spring of 1978. In response to these lectures, I have added the present section and Section VIII to this paper, and made minor changes elsewhere; but I cannot pretend to have done justice to Kripke's extremely rich, provocative, and illuminating treatment of the topic of identity through time.

12. In "Identity Through Time."

13. It might be suggested that the momentary states of a rotating disk or sphere will differ from those of a stationary one with respect to the forces that exist at each moment of time; the parts of the rotating object will be subjected to centrifugal forces, which must be balanced by centripetal ones. If reference to forces can be included in descriptions of "holographic states," then indeed the series of holographic states will be different depending on whether the object is rotating. But the notion of force is closely tied to the notion of acceleration, and so with the notion of motion. It would seem arbitrary, at best, to allow reference to forces in descriptions of holographic states while refusing to allow reference to instantaneous velocities and accelerations.

14. Something like this objection was made to me in conversation by Saul Kripke; but my formulation of it may not capture all that he had in mind.

15. This notion, and the notion of (linear) velocity defined in terms of it, should, of course, be defined so as to make the values of the lengths and velocities relative to frames of reference; but for present purposes this complication can be ignored.

16. It is worth noticing that there will be series of thing-stages that lack velocities at certain times because the distance-time ratios of the segments of the series around those times do not converge on limiting values. For example, suppose we have a sphere that is rotating at a certain uniform rate around its north-south axis. Let S_1 be the series of hemisphere-stages that is the history of the hemisphere that at time t is the eastern side of the sphere. Let S_2 be the series of eastern hemisphere stages of the sphere. At any time, S_1 has an "angular velocity" equal to the angular velocity of the sphere and S_2 has an "angular velocity" of zero. Now let S_3 be the series that includes the members of S_1 up to and including time t, and the members of S_2 at all times subsequent to t. S_3 will be a spatiotemporally continuous series. But at time t, the "angular velocity" of S_3 is undefined (at other times it has the "angular velocity" either of S_1 or S_2).

17. The account of properties sketched in this section is developed and defended at greater length in my paper "Causality and Properties," to appear in *Time and Cause, Essays Presented to Richard Taylor*, edited by Peter van Inwagen.

18. Except in connection with the problem of personal identity, where philosophers sometimes ask what makes simultaneous experience "co-personal," i.e., what makes them belong to the same "consciousness," or to the same "total temporary state." See Bertrand Russell, "On the Nature of Acquaintance," *Logic and Knowledge: Essays, 1901–1950*, ed. by R. C. Marsh (London, 1956); C. D. Broad, *Mind and Its Place in Nature* (London, 1925), Chapter XIII, "The Unity of the Mind"; H. P. Grice, "Personal Identity"; and my *Self-Knowledge and Self-Identity*, Chapter 3. Where I speak in the text of "synchronic" and "diachronic" unity, Broad speaks of "transverse" and "longitudinal" unity.

19. See Chapter VI, "The Continuant," in his *Logic*.

20. Anyone who thinks that stages of ordinary continuants are also stages of entities having gerrymandered series as their histories will want to put some restriction on what sort of property instantiations are to be taken as constituting these promiscuous thing-stages. Obviously such historical properties as "is something that a year earlier was in Paris" and "is something that will explode three minutes hence" will have to be excluded. And insofar as sortal concepts, like *table*, are thought of as encompassing criteria of cross-temporal identity for the entities that satisfy them, instantiations of sortal properties will have to be excluded as well. But as I argue in the text, these exclusions are not enough to protect this view from incoherence. To exclude instantiations of all properties whose natures constrain the identity conditions of the things that have them would be to exclude all property instantiations, or at least all instantiations of "intrinsic" properties.

21. Earlier versions of this paper were read at Cornell in December of 1976 and March of 1978, and parts of it were incorporated into my contribution to a symposium at the meetings of the Western Division of the APA in Atlanta in April 1977. I am grateful to a number of people for helpful discussion and criticism of the ideas in the paper.

This paper follows the line of the Encyclopedia of Philosophy by Rorty, which treats the two extreme cases of (1) All relations internal and (2) All relations external.

This paper considers bare particular anti essentialism: No property of an individual is essential

Anti-Essentialism

ROBERT STALNAKER

Log. Pt. of View p 155
An object... must be seen as having some of its traits necessarily and others contingently despite the fact that the latter traits follow just as analytically from some ways of specifying the object as ..

Aristotelian essentialism, according to Quine, is the doctrine that *things* may have some of their properties necessarily, not relative to how the things are described, but absolutely. To accept some form of this metaphysical doctrine is to adopt an "invidious attitude toward certain ways of uniquely specifying x . . . as somehow better revealing the essence of the object."[1] Further, Quine has argued, one is forced to accept this doctrine if one quantifies into modal contexts; "so much the worse for quantified modal logic," he concludes. "By implication, so much the worse for unquantified modal logic as well."[2]

Most contemporary modal logicians have responded to Quine's arguments by accepting the tie between quantified modal logic and essentialism, and by embracing essentialism. Rather than "so much the worse for quantified modal logic," they conclude "so much the better for essentialism." This reversion to metaphysics is supported first by a semantics that gives an explanation of essential attribution and shows it to be formally coherent, and second by intuitive examples that show that the invidious distinction lamented by Quine is well entrenched in our ordinary ways of regarding things. But although this is the majority reaction, there are those who wish to reconcile quantified modal logic with Quine's rejection of essentialism—the rejection of a discriminatory distinction between two ways that a thing may be related to its properties. It is a program of this kind that I want to discuss.

If the anti-essentialist accepts an explanation of necessity in terms of possible worlds, then he has an account of essential properties whether he wants one or not. An essential property is a property that a thing has in all possible worlds in which it exists. An accidental property is a property that a thing has in the actual world, but lacks in some other possible world. But the anti-essentialist can still try to remove the discriminatory feature of essentialism to which Quine objects: he can do this in either of two ways: first by arranging to have *all* properties be essential properties in the sense defined; second, by trying to set up his theory so that none of them are.

This hits the nail on the head. But what of the case where poss= log. poss ?

343

In both cases, essential attributions are *meaningful* (and thus the conclusion of Quine's arguments is not contradicted). But the problem of distinguishing true essential attributions from false ones is avoided in the first case by making them all true, and in the second by making them all false.   *via a ...?*

A philosopher who responded to Quine in the first way was Leibniz. According to him, every property of every individual is constitutive of its essence, and hence only existence is contingent. A modern descendant of this kind of anti-essentialism is David Lewis's counterpart theory. According to Lewis's theory, individuals have counterparts—things that resemble them more than anything else—in other possible worlds, but each individual itself exists in only one possible world. Hence no individual can have accidental properties in the sense defined above: properties that it lacks in some other possible world.[3]   *This he does not discuss*

The second kind of anti-essentialism I shall call *bare particular anti-essentialism*. This theory holds, roughly, that for every individual and every property, there are possible worlds in which the individual has the property and possible worlds in which it does not. For the sake of consistency, this generalization needs some qualification —for example, tautological properties like *being self-identical* will be exceptions—but this is the rough idea. The main problem in the development of this idea is to make clear and precise just what qualifications are necessary.   *a purely technical question*

The first thing I want to argue is that even after the relevant qualifications are   *Goa* made, one cannot make semantical sense out of bare particular anti-essentialism within the framework of the standard semantics for modal logic. In this respect, the bare particular theory contrasts with the Leibnizian version of anti-essentialism. The latter doctrine has a formal semantics which can be seen as a special case of the standard possible worlds theory. The second thing I want to do is to suggest an alternative to the standard semantics that can make sense out of the bare particular theory. The alternative semantics will not *require* that the anti-essentialist doctrine be true, but that doctrine will be embodied in a simple formal condition which is very naturally imposed on the models definable within the alternative semantics.

Do these people think that PW theories are or can be ?? true? Obviously they do!

My primary aim in pursuing this project is not to defend the bare particular thesis, which seems to me most of the time to be implausible. But while I doubt that this metaphysical doctrine is true, I think the fact that it does not even make sense within the framework of extensional semantics is a symptom of a limitation of that semantics. My real aim is not to argue against essentialism, but rather, by giving a formally coherent account of a contrasting doctrine, to raise some new questions about essentialism and to make clearer what the essentialist is committed to.

I shall begin on an intuitive level with the qualifications that are required in the thesis that all properties of all objects are accidental properties. There are three kinds of qualifications—three kinds of unobjectionable essential attributes. Each of these kinds of properties has been discussed by Ruth Marcus or Terry Parsons in articles on essentialism and modal logic.[4]

First, any property that is necessarily an essential property of everything is an unobjectionable essential property from the point of view of the bare particular doctrine. Such properties as *being self-identical, being either a kangaroo or not a kanga-*

roo, *being colored if purple* in no way limit the logical potential of any individual, or distinguish among different kinds of individuals. Hence they do not conflict with the spirit of the anti-essentialist thesis.

Second, certain relational properties that are defined in terms of specific individuals may be essential properties without conflicting with the intuitive idea behind anti-essentialism. Ruth Marcus has called these *referential properties*. For example, the following are attributes that everyone should admit are essential to Babe Ruth: *being identical to Babe Ruth*, *being either identical to Babe Ruth or fat*, *being fat if Babe Ruth is*, *being the same weight as Babe Ruth*. Even if there are possible worlds in which Ruth is a kangaroo, a tricycle, or a billiard ball, even if he has no essential nature which constrains the qualitative characteristics that he might have had, still, in all possible worlds he will have the properties mentioned above, since these properties are defined so that Babe Ruth could not lack them without lacking his own identity.

It might, of course, be controversial whether or not a given property was a referential property in this sense. According to an operationalist, for example, the property *being one meter long* would be one, since the operationalist believes it is defined as the property of being the same length as x, where x is a particular object. The standard meter bar is *essentially* one meter long, if the operationalist is right, but this does not prevent it from being, in other possible worlds, very very long or very very short.

Third, the so-called world-indexed properties invented by Alvin Plantinga are unobjectionable examples of essential properties.[5] Call the actual world *Kronos*. Then *being snub-nosed-in-Kronos* is defined as the property that something has in *any* world if and only if it has, in Kronos, the ordinary accidental property of being snubnosed. All snub-nosed people are essentially snub-nosed-in-Kronos, but being saddled with such an essential property puts no constraints on the qualitative characteristics that an individual might have had.

The problem is, now, to reconcile the bare particular thesis, qualified in these ways, with quantified modal logic. To carry out this job, we must incorporate the qualifications and the intuitive distinctions on which they rest into a formal theory. This problem has been attacked from a proof-theoretic point of view by Terence Parsons. He asked in his paper, "Essentialism and Quantified Modal Logic,"[6] what axioms are necessary to a sound and complete anti-essentialist theory—a theory that has as a consequence the denial of each objectionable essential attribution? But the axiom set that Parsons provides in answer to this question has the following unusual feature: there are sentences (for example, $(\exists x) \Box Fx \supset (x) \Box Fx$) which are theorems even though some substitution instances of them (for example, $(\exists x) \Box Rxy \supset (x) \Box Rxy$) are not theorems. What this means is that the atomic predicate 'F' does not represent an arbitrary property as is usually the case, but only an arbitrary property of a certain sort. Since the second sentence is a non-theorem, there must be some legitimate interpretations in which it is false. But then if we could interpret the predicate 'F' in the first sentence to mean what 'R-y' means in the interpretation which falsifies the second, then we could have an interpretation in which the theorem is false. But since theorems must be true in every legitimate interpretation, that interpretation of the predicate 'F' will have to be ruled out. Thus the predicate 'F' does not stand for an arbitrary property.

This consequence is not in itself objectionable, but it puts an additional burden on the semantics for the theory. If all and only the theorems are to be valid—true in every legitimate interpretation—then the rules for interpreting the sentences of the language must make a distinction between those properties that are appropriate to be values for the atomic predicates and those properties that are not. The required distinction, of course, is the distinction between intrinsic, qualitative characteristics on the one hand, and referential and world-indexed properties on the other; it must be assumed, at least, that all the atomic predicates express properties of the first sort. But this distinction is presupposed and not explained in Parson's account. The notion of an *atomic predicate* cannot contribute to such an explanation since it is a purely syntactical notion and cannot by itself do a semantical job. To complete the task of reconciling anti-essentialism with quantified modal logic, we need a distinction on the semantical level between those propositional functions that can be values for atomic predicates and those propositional functions that cannot.

In the now standard formal semantics for first-order modal logic, truth values for the sentences are defined relative to possible worlds. Each possible world has a domain of individuals—the individuals that exist in that world. Possible worlds and their individuals are the only primitive semantical elements of the theory—the only elements necessary to define the models that serve as the subject matter for the sentences of the language being interpreted. Other semantical notions such as properties and relations, individual concepts and propositions are identified with functions defined in terms of individuals and possible worlds. For example, a proposition is defined as a function from possible worlds into truth values, or equivalently, as a subclass of the class of all possible worlds. Properties are represented as singulary propositional functions—functions that take an individual as argument and a proposition as value, or, equivalently, functions that take a possible world as argument and a set of individuals as value. Intuitively, on this account, a property is a rule—any rule—for determining a class of individuals, given the facts. Any procedure for selecting individuals, whatever its basis, is a property of the individual selected.

In terms of this extensional account of properties (extensional in the sense that properties are defined by their extensions in different possible worlds), what corresponds to the intuitive distinctions between referential and purely qualitative properties, and between world-indexed and world-independent properties? Nothing. All properties are referential in the sense that they are defined in terms of the specific individuals that have them. All properties are world-indexed in the sense that they are defined in terms of the specific possible worlds in which things have them. While one can, of course, make a distinction between essential and accidental attributes in terms of the standard semantical framework, one cannot find any independent distinctions corresponding to the intuitive ones needed to state a coherent version of the anti-essentialist thesis. Thus there is no satisfactory way, without adding to the primitive basis of the semantical theory, to state the thesis as a further semantical constraint on legitimate interpretations of the language of modal logic.

There is one unsatisfactory way that should be mentioned just to be put aside. One could simply stipulate that in legitimate interpretations of anti-essentialist modal logic, atomic predicates always must express purely accidental properties (properties that no individual has essentially). In terms of propositional functions, this stipulation comes out as the requirement that the interpretation given to any one-place predicate be a propositional function that takes a contingent proposition as value for every argument. But even if a constraint of this kind were formally adequate,[7] it would be subject to the following objection. This requirement does not prevent objectionable essential attributions from being true; it just prevents them from being expressed in the language that is being interpreted. No limitation is placed on the model structures for the language—on the allowable subject matter for its statements. The limitation placed by the constraint is a limitation solely on what can be said about the structures in the language. This is a theory, not for an anti-essentialist, but for an embarrassed essentialist. It is no more an account of anti-essentialism than the traditional Victorian response to venereal disease—don't talk about it—was a cure.

What the standard semantics lacks is an account of properties that defines them independently of possible worlds and of individuals. If we are to make sense of the bare particular theory, a property must be not just a rule for grouping individuals, but a feature of individuals in virtue of which they may be grouped: not just a propositional function, but something that determines a propositional function. This independent specification of properties and relations is what I shall add to the semantics. It will give us a formal representation of the intuitive distinctions on which the doctrine depends.

The account of properties and relations that I shall borrow and incorporate into the possible worlds theory was developed by Bas van Fraassen.[8] He regarded it as an alternative account of modality to the possible worlds account. In contrast, I shall treat it as a supplement to the standard theory. He considered the main virtue of his theory to be that it avoided metaphysical commitments and questions. In contrast, I shall use it to raise metaphysical questions that cannot be raised within the standard theory.

Properties, on van Fraassen's account, are represented by regions of a logical space, or quality space. For example, the color spectrum might be a dimension of such a space; the color red would then be identified with a region defined by a segment of the color dimension. The temperature scale might be another dimension. The relation *warmer than* would be identified with a set of ordered pairs of points of the space defined by this dimension.

The basic semantic elements of the models for the languages interpreted by van Fraassen's theory are two independently specified sets—an arbitrary set representing the points in logical space, and a domain of individuals. The individuals are assigned properties by a *location function*—a function that maps the individuals into the logical space. Each individual is thus located at a specific point in logical space, and in this way gets a specific color, shape, temperature, mass, and so forth.

The language is interpreted by assigning to each one-place predicate a subset of the points in logical space. Such a predicate is satisfied by an individual just in case the location function locates the individual at one of the points included in the value assigned to the predicate. If the predicate is to mean *is red*, then its value will be the region of logical space defined by the relevant segment of the color dimension. The open sentence "*x* is red" will be satisfied by an individual just in case the individual is located somewhere in that region—just in case the location function colors it some shade of red. This account generalizes to cover n-place predicates and n-ary relations in the obvious way.

There are no possible worlds in van Fraassen's semantics, but there is a semantical construct that looks a lot like one: the location function—the function that determines all the properties of all the individuals, and all the relations that hold between them. There is only one such semantical construct in each of the models defined in van Fraassen's theory, but there is no reason not to consider many location functions at the same time—alternative ways that individuals might have been located in logical space. To do so, we need introduce no new semantical primitives into the theory.

Besides considering many location functions at once defined on the same logical space, the only other change I shall make in van Fraassen's theory is to substitute a domain of *possible* individuals for the ordinary domain. This change allows the domains of the different possible worlds—the sets of individuals located by the different location functions—to be different from each other.[9]

This is all we need for a semantic analysis of anti-essentialist modal logic. A model structure for the language will consist of just two elements: first, a set H representing the points in logical space, and, second, a domain D representing the possible individuals. The set of all possible worlds is *not* a primitive element of the model; it is defined in terms of the others. The set of possible worlds is the set I of all functions mapping some subset of D into H. The formal representation of a possible world, then, is a function that selects a subset of the set of all possible individuals to be actual, or to exist relative to that possible world, and that determines all the properties that the members of that subset are to have, and all the relations that are to hold among them.

Let me now show how this very simple semantical framework meets the specific problem that we encountered in trying to make sense of the bare particular doctrine within the standard semantics. That is, let me show how this framework yields a distinction between those propositional functions that express intrinsic properties and those that do not.

Since the models in our semantics contain both possible worlds and possible individuals, we can define, relative to any model, the class of all singular propositional functions—the class of all functions from possible worlds into sets of individuals. It should be clear that every *property* (every region of logical space) determines a unique propositional function in the following way: given any property, the value of the corresponding propositional function, relative to a given possible world, will be the class of individuals that have the property in that possible world—the individuals that are located in that region of logical space by the location function that represents the possible world. Thus every property determines a unique propositional function, and the correspondence is one-one: distinct properties never determine the same propositional function. But it is not the case that every propositional function corresponds to an intrinsic property, for the classes of individuals selected by a propositional function in the different possible worlds need not all come from the same region of logical space. Among the propositional functions, or properties in the broad sense, that do not correspond to regions of logical space are, of course, just those that the anti-essentialist wants to distinguish from full-fledged intrinsic properties. For example, referential properties such as *being the same weight as Babe Ruth* will clearly not correspond to regions of logical space. As the Babe waxes and wanes, moving up and down the weight scale from world to world, the class of people weighing the same as he will likewise move about in logical space. World-indexed properties like *being snub-nosed-in-Kronos* will also correspond to no particular region, since the noses that are, in fact, snub may grow to be aquiline, or Roman, or disappear altogether in alternative possible worlds. And if we consider a tensed version of logical space theory in which things may change their location in logical space over time as well as across possible worlds, then we can distinguish time-indexed properties, as well as world-indexed properties, from intrinsic properties. *Being grue*, for example, would not correspond to a single region of logical space (at least assuming that *being green* does), but to different regions at different times.

Thus the logical space possible worlds semantics yields a representation of the distinctions needed to make sense of bare particular anti-essentialism. With a relatively straightforward interpretation of the formal language in terms of this kind of semantical structure, we can validate all the axioms proposed in Parson's version of anti-essentialist modal logic. Since one-place atomic predicates must express properties in the narrow sense (regions of logical space), while open sentences with one free variable in general may sometimes express propositional functions that do not correspond to properties in the narrow sense, we have a semantic explanation for the failure of the substitution principle.

Now we can ask, should *any* subset of possible individuals located *anywhere* in logical space be said to determine a possible world? One might want to rule out some of these formal constructs as not representing genuinely possible counterfactual situations. But if one does rule some of them out, one will need a philosophical justification; and if one rules none of them out, one has a real bare particular theory. Thus, while the formal machinery I have sketched does not by itself commit one to anti-essentialism, it does make the doctrine clear, relative to the semantical primitives of the theory, and it does put the burden on the essentialist to justify his opposition.

From a pre-systematic, intuitive point of view, there is strong motivation for taking on this burden. If one does not, one is forced to admit that some pretty bizarre propositions about particular individuals are possibly true. I am not thinking just of such alleged possibilities as that Babe Ruth be a prime number or a social class. Even if we take the relevant domain of possible individuals to include just possible persons and physical objects, there is something implausible about the assumption that any of them might have had the properties of any other. But it is not easy to see why this is implausible.

Just to see how the philosophical debate might go, I shall look at just one kind of property, and at some arguments that might be advanced for the claim that properties of this kind are essential to the things that have them. Saul Kripke has suggested that the common names of natural kinds express essential properties.[10] The paradigm examples are the names of animal species. Kripke argues that the names of such kinds, unlike ordinary property expressions, are referential terms—terms whose denotations are determined by the causal connections holding between our uses of the term and the actual individuals that are members of the kind. 'Human being', then, is like a proper name of the natural class to which we all belong.

There is a way to interpret this claim so that it is not incompatible with the bare particular doctrine. It may be taken as a purely linguistic claim that certain commonplace predicates are in fact world-indexed properties (indexed to the actual world) rather than properties in the narrow sense—properties that correspond to regions of logical space. On this interpretation, Babe Ruth would be essentially human, but this would not prevent him from looking just like a billiard ball, or, in fact, from *being* just like a billiard ball all the way through. This purely linguistic essentialism is surely not the view of the natural kind theorists. They want to hold that natural kind predicates are essentially tied *both* to their actual denotations *and* at the same time to the structural and qualitative features that determine the real basis for the natural classification. This double tie is not just a linguistic thesis, but serves to constrain the movement of individuals in logical space. What is its justification? Why not be more liberal and let the Babe roam freely through the lower reaches of logical space? I cannot think of any point in making the counterfactual supposition that Babe Ruth is a billiard ball; there is nothing I can say about him in that imagined state that I could not just as well say about billiard balls that are not him, and if he does have the logical potential to be a billiard ball, it is of no interest that he does since on the bare particular theory this does not distinguish him from anything else. But that this alleged possibility is uninteresting is not sufficient reason to judge it impossible.

Before Kripke himself exposed the fallacy in such arguments, one might have reasoned as follows: the supposition that Babe Ruth is a billiard ball implies a denial of the common presuppositions that make reference to him possible. Hence such a supposition is self-defeating. This argument confuses the limits on conjectures about what might, in fact, be with limits on suppositions about what might, contrary-to-fact, have been. It is perhaps true that if someone proposed that maybe Babe Ruth *really was* a billiard ball, then I could reasonably conclude that that person could not possibly be talking about the thing that I refer to with that name. But this is beside the point. The conditions that make the expression of a proposition possible need to hold in the world in which the proposition is expressed, but not necessarily in the world about which the proposition is said to be true. With assertions and conjectures, these worlds coincide, but with contrary-to-fact suppositions they are explicitly distinguished. Hence there is no incoherence when the content of such a supposition implicitly denies the possibility of its own expression.

The causal theory of reference for natural kind terms might be thought to provide an argument for the conclusion that such terms express essential properties. Kripke and others have argued—persuasively, I think—that the configuration of traits that is necessary to being, say, a kangaroo, is not determined by the meaning of the word 'kangaroo', but must be discovered by a theoretical and empirical investigation into the nature of the actual creatures. The meaning of the word determines, roughly, its extension, and the facts about the members of the extension then determine the features that are essential to the kind. Actual kangaroos thus play a necessary part in fixing the nature of their kind. This is not, however, by itself a sufficient reason for concluding that being a kangaroo, with all that entails, is essential to the individuals that are in fact kangaroos. Kripke has shown how we might use a particular individual (like a standard meter bar) to fix the reference of a property expression (like *being one meter long*) without connecting the property necessarily to the object. Even though the standard in a sense defines the measure, it still can be true that that object might have been longer or shorter than one meter. In the same way, actual kangaroos might fix the reference of the kind without being essentially members of it.

The case for essentialism, I suspect, rests not on such general arguments, but on case-by-case intuitions about which descriptions seem to capture genuine possibilities and which do not. This is, however, a shaky basis since it is hard to separate the intuition that a proposed possible situation is too bizarre to be interesting from the intuition that it is too bizarre to be possible. And it is hard to separate intuitions about different kinds of possibility: epistemic, causal or temporal, metaphysical. It may be that the theory that best accounts for our intuitions and practices is one that explains away some of the judgments that we are all inclined to make about particular cases. I do not have such a theory. I do not even know which side I am on in the dispute over essentialism. Perhaps someone with stronger metaphysical convictions than I can develop an argument within the framework that I am recommending.

Instead of arguing about essentialism, I shall conclude by making some general remarks about possible developments and applications of this account of properties and relations.

First remark: the distinction between properties narrowly conceived and propositional functions in general is roughly analogous to the distinction between possible individuals (thought of as existing in many possible worlds) and individual concepts in general (functions from possible worlds into individuals). Just as some singular terms, such as 'the fattest man in America', are non-rigid designators—terms that express variable individual concepts, or pick out different individuals in different possible worlds, so some predicates may be non-rigid property designators—predicates that correspond to different intrinsic properties in different possible worlds. There was a tendency in some of the early explorations into the semantics for modality to conflate individuals with individual concepts, and some clarification resulted when the distinction was appreciated. But the mere drawing of a distinction between individuals and individual concepts did not by itself solve the metaphysical problems about the nature of individuals, or answer the linguistic questions about which singular terms were rigid designators and which were not. All it did was to give clear expression to some of these questions, and to their alternative answers. In the same way, the semantics I have sketched does not claim to solve metaphysical problems about the nature of intrinsic properties, or answer linguistic questions about which ordinary predicates express them. It does not lay out the structure of a particular logical space, or give criteria for making the distinctions in application that the theory allows for. So, for example, although the account provides for a representation of the distinction between properties like *being grue* and those like *being green*, it does not claim to give an answer to Goodman's riddle on its own terms. There is no formal reason why one could not construct a logical space with *grue* as a region of it. It would obviously not be *our* logical space, but the semantics offers no criterion or argument to justify this claim. The account I have proposed does change the focus of Goodman's puzzle: it takes the emphasis off the predicates—items of language—and puts it on a larger conceptual structure which lies behind them and in terms of which they are understood. It suggests that it is this non-linguistic conceptual structure that is entrenched and projected. But as to exactly how this happens, the abstract semantical framework is silent. It is at best the form of a philosophical theory, and not the theory itself.

I should add, however, that the theory is less abstract than the simple possible worlds theory since it gives at least some structure to the possible worlds. And there is, I think, considerable potential for further development—for saying more about the structure of logical space, and thus more about the relationships among properties and among possible worlds. We have called logical space a space, but have not yet exploited the spatial metaphor. So far, logical space is just a set of points. One may want to say more about the relationships among the points—about the topological and metric properties of the space. One property (region) may be adjacent to another, or separated from it (as *red* is next to *orange*, but separated from *green*). Disjoint regions may be comparable with respect to their area (*non-red* is a much bigger region than *red*). The appropriateness of adding such structure will depend on two things: first, whether there is direct intuitive support for the distinctions required; second, whether the structure can be used to explain facts about our cognitive behavior such as the inductive inferences that we judge to be reasonable and the way we evaluate counterfactuals. Since we do, sometimes at least, think of properties in terms of a spatial metaphor, the imposition of spatial structure on the properties will, I think, find intuitive support. And it seems to me likely that such structure could help to explain some of the semantic determinants that have been postulated in the semantics for counterfactual conditonals, and in inductive logic: on the one hand, comparative similarity of possible worlds; on the other, measures of the "logical width" of properties and the grouping of properties into "families." The application to Carnapian inductive logic seems particularly appropriate. For just as the notion of a possible world is the semantical child of the syntactical notion of a state description, so the notion of a point in logical space is the semantical child of Carnap's syntactical notion of a Q-predicate, or maximal predicate, which played an important part in the development of his inductive logic. In both cases, the move to the semantical notion frees the theory from a dependence on language.

Second remark: although the logical space account of properties and relations is a very abstract and flexible one which by itself says very little about the nature of properties, there is one substantive consequence of the formal theory—a consequence which some might want to deny. The following principle must hold in any application of the framework as it stands: all relations are grounded in intrinsic properties in the following sense: if one specifies all the intrinsic properties of a set of individuals, one *thereby* specifies all the relations that hold among them. To give all the intrinsic properties of some object is just to say what point in logical space it occupies, and the relations holding among a set of objects are determined by their locations in logical space. Might one deny this principle? Some who hold a relational theory of space will want to deny it. Such a theory says that spatial location is itself relational. That is, to give the location of an object in physical space is just to say something about its relations to other objects. According to some versions of this theory, there may be *no* properties that the objects have independently of other objects in virtue of which they stand in the spatial relations they stand in.

To represent such a theory in terms of the logical space account of possible worlds, we must assume that logical space is itself in part conventional. That is, we must assume that sometimes distinct location functions differ only conventionally, and thus represent the same possible world. For example, let the three diagrams shown below represent three distinct location functions locating the same three objects in a two-dimensional Euclidean space.

Now one might say that because the distance relations among the objects are the same in these three representations, they all represent the same situation. The point of saying this is *not* just that the co-ordinates are conventional — that it is conventional which point in the space is called the origin and what direction the x-axis is drawn. That would be true even if an absolute theory of space were correct. The point would be that there is no non-conventional identification of points in the space across possible worlds. To say that the origin of the co-ordinate system in one world is the *same* point as the origin in another is to make a purely conventional stipulation.

To put this possibility into the formal theory, we add to the model structure an equivalence relation defined on the location functions. To say that i is equivalent to j is to say that the location functions i and j represent the same possible world. A *real* intrinsic property (as opposed to a merely conventional intrinsic property) can then be defined as a region of logical space that is invariant with respect to this equivalence relation. That is, region F represents a real property if and only if for every member d of the domain of individuals and every pair of equivalent location functions i and j, i locates d in F if and only if j locates d in F. Real as opposed to conventional relations could be defined in the same way. In the relational theory of space, spelled out in this way, no intrinsic spatial properties would be real (except the property of being located *somewhere* in space), but some spatial relations would be real. There are, of course, more and less extreme versions of such a theory, depending on how the equivalence relation is defined.

The principle that all relations are grounded in intrinsic properties does not by itself commit one to an absolute theory of physical space. Leibniz seems to be someone who accepted this principle while at the same time denying that spatial location is an intrinsic property. But I think that to reconcile these two doctrines one would be forced to the conclusion that physical space as a whole is some kind of merely ideal construction out of the non-spatial properties of things. That is, I suspect that to reconcile the two Leibnizian doctrines, one must adopt an extreme version of a relational theory of space—the kind of theory that it seems Leibniz, in fact, held.

Final remark: Since the apparatus I have deployed here is shamelessly metaphysical, which goes against all my more positivistic instincts and training, I shall close with an anti-metaphysical comment. Sometimes I am tempted to believe that there is only an actual world. But we do represent to ourselves pictures of ways that things might be, or might have been, and this practice is not just the idle exercise of our imaginations; it is central to some of our more serious activities such as giving scientific explanations of how and why the *actual* world works the way it does. The semantical account that I have sketched is intended as *one* of the ways that we construct such representations of how things might have been. We do it, the account suggests, by making a conceptual separation between the things that inhabit our world and the properties that things have there, and then imagining the individuals with different properties, and the properties instantiated by different individuals. But, of course, it is all grounded in the actual world—in what we know and how things appear to us. Logical space is not given independently of the individuals that occupy it, but is abstracted from the world as we find it. Posed from this point of view, questions about essentialism, and about the identification of properties across possible worlds, are questions about how far it is useful, or possible, to carry this process of abstraction. How different can we imagine the facts being before we lose our grip on the structure of properties and relations, and on the individuals, that were abstracted from the facts? This is not, I think, a question that is metaphysical in any sense that is either objectionable or honorific, but is a question about how we understand and find our way about in the world.[11]

Notes

1. W. V. Quine, *From a Logical Point of View* (Cambridge, Mass., 1953), p. 155.

2. *Ibid.*, p. 156.

3. I do not want to suggest that David Lewis's theory is motivated by anti-essentialism. His counterpart relation, together with a different analysis of essential and accidental properties, reintroduces the invidious distinction.

4. See Ruth Marcus, "Essentialism in Quantified Modal Logic," *Nous* 1 (1967), Terence Parsons, "Grades of Essentialism in Quantified Modal Logic," *Nous* 1 (1967), and Parsons, "Essentialism and Quantified Modal Logic," *Philosophical Review* 78 (1969).

5. Alvin Plantinga, "World and Essence," *Philosophical Review* 79 (1970).

6. Parsons, "Essentialism and Quantified Modal Logic."

7. The constraint suggested would be necessary, but not sufficient. It does not rule out the possibility that some defined monadic predicates such as $(Fx \vee Gx)$ be non-universal, but essential to some things.

8. Bas van Fraassen, "Meaning Relations Among Predicates," *Nous* 1 (1967). In a later paper, "Meaning Relations, Possible Objects and Worlds," in *Philosophical Problems in Logic*, ed. Karel Lambert (Dordrecht-Holland, 1970), van Fraassen and Lambert generalize the logical space theory in a way different from the way I shall suggest.

9. The move from actual to possible individuals is a significant additional commitment. A motivation of van Fraassen's original theory was to give a non-metaphysical interpretation to the picturesque but objectionable notion of a possible individual; in his theory, possible individuals were replaced by points in logical space. I am here re-introducing the metaphysical commitment, which I agree is objectionable. A further development of the theory might reduce possible but non-actual individuals to some sort of construct out of the other elements of the model structure.

10. Saul Kripke, "Naming and Necessity," *Semantics for Natural Language*, ed. Gilbert Harman and Donald Davidson (Dordrecht-Holland, 1972).

11. Versions of this paper were presented to the University of North Carolina Philosophy Colloquium at Chapel Hill in 1972, and at Princeton University in 1973. It has been aging, in roughly the present form, for the past five years. The paper began as a response to Terence Parson's paper, "Essentialism and Quantified Modal Logic," and I have benefited from his useful comments at Chapel Hill.

Contingent Truths
and Possible Worlds

HIDÉ ISHIGURO

In recent discussions of modal concepts, philosophers have followed Hume and Kant in thinking that the main source of the philosophical problem of modality is a special conceptual difficulty about necessity or necessary truths. Various possible world models are thought to make clear the nature of different kinds of necessity and their comparative strength. Naturally any clarification of the nature of necessary truths must imply something about the nature of contingent truths with which they are contrasted, but what Kant and Hume were specially concerned about were the grounds for the universal validity, or necessity of some truths. Even if there were epistemological problems, they did not think there were metaphysical difficulties about contingent truths.

We probably derive our talk of possible worlds from Leibniz, but for Leibniz it was the metaphysical status of contingent truths which was puzzling. He thought that in a system like Spinoza's, or in the fatalism inherent in Pierre Bayle's doctrines, one would not be able to distinguish contingent truths from necessary truths. It was not the epistemological question how one can know that a truth is a contingent or a necessary one which troubled him, but the status or metaphysical foundations of contingency. And here I think we can follow him in being puzzled. What is it for a truth to be contingent? If it is contingently the case that S is P or aRb we have to be able to give content to our belief that it could have been otherwise. We have to do more than just express our intuitions. In what sense, if any, is it a necessary truth that the number two is even but not a necessary truth that Caesar crossed the Rubicon?

Without first trying to resort to the familiar distinction of *de dicto* and *de re* modalities, which contains much more difficulty than one might suspect, let us try to see what lay behind Leibniz's introduction of the notion of possible worlds in his attempt to make sense of contingency. For contrary to the views recently aired by some distinguished philosophers of logic working on Leibniz's thought,[1] it seems clear that Leibniz's talk about possible worlds was very closely linked with the problem of modality. In an early critical commentary on Spinoza's *Ethics*, for example, Leibniz severely attacks Spinoza's claim that there is nothing contingent in the nature of things. Leibniz holds that such a view is only possible because 'contingent' is used by Spinoza in an idiosyncratic sense, that is, to mean "without reason." Leibniz uses contingency, as he claims, to mean "that whose essence does not involve existence."[2]

The failure to give a place to contingency comes from confusing a metaphysical quest with an epistemological one: what is necessary and what is known with certainty.[3] From the fact that one can understand and come to know more and more truths about the universe, someone may mistakenly infer that all these truths are necessary. Leibniz claims that he too was tempted to make the confusion but was "pulled back from this precipice" by considering those possible things that neither are nor will be nor have been. For, if some possible things never exist, then existing things cannot always be necessary. It is here that Leibniz introduces descriptions of possible worlds that do not exist. "For it cannot be denied that many stories, especially those we call novels, may be regarded as possible even if they actually do not take place in this particular sequence of the universe which God has chosen."[4] Thus the description of possible worlds that do not exist, or worlds that God could have chosen but did not, shows the contingency of this world, and of the truth about things in them.

Leibniz also expressed the difference between contingency and necessity by saying that the former depends not only on God's understanding but also on his volition or free choice, in contrast to the latter which depends only on his understanding. In less theistic language, this is equivalent to the claim that contingent truths depend on how our world actually is, and would not always obtain had some state of affairs in it been different; and that necessary truths hold in all possible worlds—since such truths do not depend on how our world is—that is, they do not depend on which possible world is the actual one.

Thus if the proposition "Spinoza died in The Hague" expresses a contingent truth (as Leibniz believed it did), this is because, had the world been different, Spinoza could have died in another place than The Hague. Since "Spinoza" is the name of the philosopher who, among other things, died in The Hague, no one who died elsewhere would be identical with Spinoza. Does this not mean that it is necessary of Spinoza that he died in The Hague, and would this make it true of Spinoza that he could not have died anywhere else? No, this would be to confuse, as Leibniz says, (metaphysical) necessity with the certitude of our knowledge. The fact that we know for sure that Spinoza died in The Hague, and that therefore no one who died in, say, Leyden or London is Spinoza, is perfectly compatible with the fact that Spinoza could have died elsewhere. The fact that a good alibi exempts a man A from a criminal charge does not mean that it was *necessary* for the criminal B to have committed his crime at the time and place he did do so. We merely use our *knowledge* of a contingent fact—that is, that A was in a different place at the time of the crime—to conclude the non-identity of A and B. We grasp that someone who does not have all the properties of B could not be identified with him. The same follows for our knowledge about past and future events. Our ability to have certain knowledge of what will happen does not by itself remove the contingency of the fact.[5] Our inability to alter past events does not make the truths about them any less contingent.

Are there both necessary and contingent truths about one and the same individual? If we take the view that nothing can be individuated except as an individual of a certain kind, as Leibniz did,[6] and also think, as he did, that there are necessary truths about species, such that it is necessary that every individual which falls under that species has that property,[7] then it seems that there are necessary truths about individuals. For example, both "Caesar is a man" and "Caesar is an animal capable of thinking" seem to state necessary truths about Caesar. Contrast this with "Caesar crossed the Rubicon." It pertains to the nature of the individual which we name 'Caesar' that he is an individual man. Whereas the fact that Caesar crossed the Rubicon cannot be deduced from Caesar's nature alone.

Although Caesar had a good reason for crossing the Rubicon, which reflected his judgment, audacity, his belief about the state of affairs at the time, etc., yet his crossing of that stream depends on what the world was like—for example, on the fact that the Rubicon marked the boundary between Gaul and Italy. It is thus that Leibniz defends himself from those who accused him of making everything which happens to individuals necessary after all.

> To answer it squarely, I say that there are two kinds of connection or sequence. One is absolutely necessary for its contrary implies a contradiction, and this deductive connection occurs in external truths like those of geometry. The other is necessary only *ex hypothesi* and by accident, so to speak, and this connection is contingent in itself when its contrary implies no contradiction. A connection of this kind is not based on pure ideas and on the simple understanding of God but also on his free decrees and on the sequence of events in the universe.[8]

"Spinoza died in The Hague" expresses a contingent truth, not so much (as Bertrand Russell suggested[9]) because it is actually made up of two propositions one of which is analytic, that is, "whoever is Spinoza died in The Hague" and another proposition "Spinoza existed," which is contingent (as it indeed is) and which is not true in all possible worlds. Even given that he existed, his death in The Hague does not follow from his nature alone, but from the connection of other things in the world. Thus the proposition "whoever is Spinoza dies in The Hague," though true, is not a necessary truth according to Leibniz. That he died in The Hague is included in the individual concept of Spinoza, but this does not make the proposition analytic or necessary. If we try to derive the contingency from the fact that there are possible worlds in which Spinoza does not exist, then every singular proposition of the type "Spinoza is a man" also becomes contingent, which is not merely problematic for us but also goes against Leibniz's own intention.[10] We would also utterly fail to see why Leibniz has to invoke the two different kinds of connection between subject and predicate in his defense of contingency.

The predicate's being included in the subject (and both are concepts for Leibniz) does not mean that there is a logical connection between subject and predicate; it means merely that the predicate holds of the thing that instantiates the subject concept. And this is said to be an obvious (meta-linguistic) fact about any true proposition—not only about necessary propositions. "The required link between subject and predicate, he says, is that which exists only *a parte rei*, or from the side of the thing. It is only in this sense that he claims that *praedicatum inest subjecto*; otherwise I do not know what truth is."[11] In other words, the truth of subject-predicate propositions is understood in terms of satisfaction. The connection between the property of "dying in The Hague" and the man Spinoza, then, is quite different from the property of, say, having successive twos in its expansion and π. We do not know if the property is true of π and, as the expansion of π is infinite, we may never know. But if we come across the property, it is only because we have deduced it mathematically and we know that π necessarily has the property. In contrast to this, the place of Spinoza's death is not something that follows from his nature alone even if we were to know all about it. (Omniscient God is said to know about this property only because he knows everything about the other things in the world that are contingently there by his choice and their connections.)

What then is the point of Leibniz's analogy of contingent truth with infinite analysis? Can we make any philosophical sense of his claim that for a long time he was puzzled by the question "how the predicate concept could be in the subject (concept) without the proposition thereby becoming necessary"[12] and yet "the knowledge of infinite analysis showed me light, so that I came to understand what it is for concepts to be resolvable in infinity"?[13] For even if the concept of a differential of a function involves infinite analysis, it can be deduced from the nature of the function alone by logical means. Thus the relation between the two is a *necessary* one, which is precisely what the relation between the subject and predicate in a contingent proposition is said not to be. The fact of its involving infinite analysis does not throw light on the peculiar feature of contingent truths. A contingent truth cannot by any means be reduced to a necessary truth (some form of identity) by the analysis of the nature of the subject of the proposition alone.

The analogy throws light on the problem rather because we can obtain a differential of a function and without going through an infinite number of steps in an analysis—which is impossible even for God—by understanding *the rule* that gets the result of an infinite analysis. We can know exactly the limit of an infinite series even if, however long we enumerate the terms of the series, we never get to the limit. We also have a method of deciding for any number, whether it is a member of the series or not. Similarly with individual concepts and the contingent predicates that are contained in them. God has an *a priori* method of proving that the predicate is contained in the individual concept, because it is as a result of an *a priori* calculus (about, for example, the number of essences actualized in a world) which was involved in his choice of the best world that he has instantiated the individual concept anyway. Unlike God, we do not and cannot know the contents of a complete individual concept — that is, the concept which includes all true predicates of the individual (since there is an infinity of such predicates and since knowing them involves knowing everything about the universe). But we know what it is to be a complete concept of an individual and the rule that gives the contents of it. We understand what it is to have a concept *of* a particular individual. We grasp what it is to refer to a particular individual, and then understand that the complete concept of that individual should include everything that is true of him, her, or it. We therefore see that there is a method of deciding whether the predicate is included in the complete concept. The method is an empirical one for us. We refer to the individual by empirical means and establish whether it satisfies the predicate or not. And how *do* we refer to a particular and think *of* an individual? Not normally by having a set of predicates that uniquely distinguish it. Leibniz suggests that we do it by some demonstrative action like pointing, or picking features that characterize it in the given context.[14]

Our ability to grasp contingent truths, whether they are about individual things in the world, or about kinds of things, or about abstract objects, seems to depend on our being able to think *about* things without knowing many of their properties, and even without knowing any property that uniquely identifies the thing. We cannot deduce their yet unknown contingent properties from their other known properties. For these unknown properties also depend on how the other things in the world happen to be. For example, I can think of Caesar without any thought of whether he crossed or did not cross the Rubicon. And, as we have seen, the fact that he did cross the Rubicon cannot be deduced from Caesar's nature alone. Because we understand what it is to refer to individual things that have many predicates which we do not know, we understand that every individual has a corresponding concept *of* it which contains all predicates that are true of it, even if we do not know many of them, and have no way of proving *why* any predicate is included in it. In other words, we understand that an individual concept is a decidable set, whose members are predicates. For any predicate, there is in principle a way of deciding whether it is a member of the individual or not. It is by judging whether the particular individual of whom it is a concept satisfies or does not satisfy the predicate. If it does, it is a member of the individual concept.

The analogy then with the infinite analysis seems to be the following. We have a way of deciding whether a contingent predicate is included in an individual concept —even if the examination of the latter by enumeration would involve infinite steps and hence be impossible for God as well as for ourselves. This is because we have a method—which is not the *a priori* one only available to God—but a method that involves referring by empirical means to the individual, and of determining in principle whether the individual satisfies the predicate or not.

A complete concept or a full concept means a concept that includes all the predicates that are true of the entities that fall under the concept. This is contrasted with a partial concept. Concepts of species, or kinds of things, are only incomplete concepts. Leibniz did not think that kinds of things existed apart from the individuals that fall under them, and thus the concept of species did not include every predicate that was true of the individuals that fall under it. All things of which there are complete concepts are particulars *of* which we can have thoughts and to which we can refer.[15]

And since nothing in the world happens at random, someone who knew about all the other things in the world would know why, given the relation of the particular thing to the rest of the universe, any predicate would be true of it—that is, in Leibnizian meta-jargon, why the predicate would be included in the subject [concept]. The distinction between necessary truths and contingent truths about individuals, then, is the distinction between what is true of an individual, *given* the world he is in, and what would be true even if the other things in the world had been different.

Spinoza would have been a man even if the history of the world had been different, but he might not have died in the place he did if other things were not the same. This is to say that the nature of individuals does not determine all the truths about them. Each individual embodies the laws of nature of the world. But it is only *given* the state of other things that these laws determine each of his particular states through his history.[16] If the state of other things could not have been different, then, as Leibniz says, there would not be any distinction between necessary and contingent truths. This makes us realize how the concept of law of nature or regularity is intricately linked with the concept of contingency. Individuals embodying the *same* set of natural laws, would behave differently had the initial condition that determined the relation between each been different, or had there been more or fewer individuals (or different individuals) in the world in which they find themselves. It is only because of this that we can think that many truths about individuals could have been other than they are. Even in a world which was entirely deterministic (Leibniz was slightly ambivalent about this) there would be many contingent truths about individuals. Even if we were to agree with Leibniz that when a man acts with a reason, there are dispositions and desires in him that incline him to act in a certain way without necessitating him to act in that way, we would be able to conceive that the same man would have been inclined to behave differently had the condition of the world been very different.

Two points that have often been raised have now to be discussed. The first is this. Can the existence of contingent truths about individuals—that is, that certain properties of individuals could have been otherwise—be compatible with the notion that an actual individual is only a member of the actual world and no other possible world? Many modern logicians have indeed claimed that talk about what happens in other possible worlds cannot throw any light on contingent or necessary properties of a person in our world, unless the same person occurs in other possible worlds too. For example, they say we can understand that Caesar need not have crossed the Rubicon only because we can imagine a world in which the very same Caesar did not cross the Rubicon and followed the laws of Rome.

Let us examine two aspects of the question in turn, the first historical and the second conceptual. First a historical clarification. Leibniz was very concerned to defend contingency and to give a content to the concept of contingency—and, as we have seen, his talk of possible worlds was very closely linked with this concern. He thought this was compatible with his view that an individual concept includes not only the nature of the individual but also all that is contingently true of the individual given the sequence and states of other things in the world. And this view about individual concepts entails that no instantiation of an individual concept—that is, no individual—could be a member of more than one possible world. Leibniz makes this point rather vividly in the *Theodicy*, where there is a description of a palace where different rooms correspond to a different possible future of Sextus, each different from that which Sextus will actually have.

The worlds are all here, namely in thought. I will show you where one can find, not exactly the same Sextus whom you have seen (this is not possible, he contains always within himself what he will be)—but future Sextuses who will have all that you already know of the real Sextus, but not all which, without our perceiving it, is already within him, nor consequently all that will happen to the real Sextus.[17]

Now someone may say that Leibniz is obviously mistaken. We are thinking of the many possible futures of one and the same person—that is, the real Sextus—and not of someone very like him. One may say, as Kripke has done, that we do not discover that another possible world contains or does not contain an actual person—we stipulate that it does. "There is no reason why we cannot stipulate that in talking about what would have happened to Nixon in a certain counterfactual situation, we are talking about what would have happened to him."

Now, of course, if we think what could have become of Nixon had the Watergate burglary not been found out, we are thinking about Nixon himself. Neither would Leibniz nor recent defenders of counterpart theories deny that we make meaningful counterfactual suppositions about actual men. Leibniz writes: "what contradiction could there be had Spinoza died in Leiden and not in The Hague? There is nothing more possible than that. Thus either event was equally within the power of God."[18] To imagine a person to have a property that he does not have is to think about *him*; in doing so, however, one describes an imaginary person, that is, a person who does not actually exist in the manner we are imagining him to exist in. It thus corresponds to a description of a possible world (or possible worlds) and a possible individual (or possible individuals), that is, a world different (in any way) from how our world is, and an individual different in some way from how any actual individual is. Whether we should use the proper name of the actual individual or not is a quibble about the language with which we describe such possible worlds.

If I say "Had it stopped raining a day earlier, the landslide would not have happened," I am talking about a counterfactual situation of *this* world. I am not talking about another world. Yet the counterfactual description gives a possible world that is slightly different from the actual world. And just because I was thinking about what might have happened in our world, we would not object to calling it a different possible world. A possible world is not another world that exists side by side with the actual world. (The claim that the concept of "actuality" is indexical might mislead us into thinking in this way.)[19] All possible worlds apart from this actual one exist only as ideas, Leibniz claims. Possible worlds are individuated by the successive states of all the individuals they contain. This entails that any coherent description of a different sequence of states of a different set of individuals gives a different possible world. And to understand Leibniz's notion of individuals and their complete concepts, one should think of individuals precisely as modal logicians think of worlds. An actual individual has its own history and all its own properties, those that are contingently true of it as well as those necessarily true of it, both the relational and the non-relational. Any individual that has different properties is not the actual individual in question.

We now come to the second point, which concerns the relation between the

Leibnizian possible world analysis of counterfactual truths and recent counterpart theories. Although Leibniz explains the contingency of Spinoza's dying in The Hague by the possibility of God's making a world in which someone (very like Spinoza) dies in Leiden instead of The Hague, Leibniz does not suggest that there is a metaphysically demarcated set of possible individuals (demarcated in terms of, for example, closest similarity) which could be called "counterparts," consisting at most of one from each of those possible worlds that are compatible with the counterfactual situation. When Leibniz talks about the nature of an individual, he is referring to the dispositions and properties it has that determine its successive states and that make the individual what it is, given the state of the rest of the world. What is this nature? He states (in the *Theodicy* among other works) that many properties are essential to any individual belonging to the species to which it belongs. For example, a man thinks. And all individual substances by definition act and perceive. But none of these is a property that essentially distinguishes one thing from other things. Of course, each individual has a unique point of view in the universe. No other thing can have the same relation to the rest of the universe and represent the universe in the same way. But this is a contingent feature of God's having situated it in the world in a certain way. In Leibniz's sense of "individual nature," it is not the case that everything that happens to the thing can be deduced from its nature by reference to the laws of logic alone or by reference to logic and the laws of nature of the world that the individual embodies. As Leibniz repeatedly says: the nature of an individual determines what happens to it only given the sequence status of other things in the universe. Thus ". . . so that if one had enough insight into the inner parts of things *and also enough memory and understanding to take in all the circumstances and calculate them*, he would be a prophet."[20]

The kind of possible entities implicitly posited by counterfactual suppositions about actual individuals are varied and depend on the context (of our counterfactual thoughts). For example, in the case of the counterfactual futures of Sextus, described above, each possible world contains a person who has, so far as can be seen, a history and environment identical with that of the actual Sextus up to a certain time. However, without its having been apparent in the past, their characters were already different or some of their dispositions were different, and at a certain point this becomes manifest by virtue of what each decides to do in the same circumstance. The various Sextuses react differently to one and the same counsel of the Gods. One obeys, goes to a city, buys a small garden; another also obeys, goes to Thrace, and marries the daughter of the king . . . whereas the real Sextus defies the Gods, goes to Rome, and violates Lucretia. Since each does what he does with a reason, each has a different character which inclines him to react differently in the same situation. But parents, place of birth, etc., etc., are all similar.

When we think what would have happened had Adam not encountered Eve, or had not taken the apple, or had not fathered Cain, Leibniz suggests that we are thinking about quite different sets of possible individuals. In each of the possible worlds that correspond to our thought, Adam is the first man, who is put in a pleasure garden which he leaves through sin. This means that in physique or character he may be different from our Adam. There is no point in talking either in terms of an absolute scale of similarities or in terms of some essence common to all counterparts. That there are infinite numbers of possible worlds, some of them with individuals very much like actual individuals, is a metaphysical truth. Each counterfactual supposition about actual individuals carries implicitly a reference to some possible world and to certain individuals in it. This criterion of selection comes from our imagination and from the contexts to which our imaginings relate. It belongs to the pragmatics and not to the metaphysics or even semantics of counterfactuals. But the very possibility of such a selection reveals the contingency of the truth about the individual which is the contrary of the counterfactual we are imagining. This is a metaphysical matter. If no such selection is possible, we have not, within a Leibnizian model, given any content to contingency.

To conclude: we would all agree that individuals *do* have all the properties they do have and no other properties. No one would think that this makes all truths about individuals and their properties necessary. Leibniz's way of talking about possible individuals was such that from the uncontroversial fact just referred to, it followed that no possible individual having properties different from an actual individual could be said to be identical with the actual individual. It is important to realize that this claim does not on its own make all truths about actual individuals and their properties necessary. The (meta-)language that one uses to talk about possible worlds and possible individuals is a technical one. Possible worlds and possible individuals are intentional objects, and their principle of individuation reflects the opacity common to all intentional objects (and all the complexities and difficulties that opacity entails).

The actual world is not *merely* one of infinitely many possible worlds, and actual individuals are not merely a subset of possible entities. They are not mere objects of thought. They are actualized within a world, but since it was possible for individuals with the *same* initial constitution and nature to have been a part of a different world and to have acted, perceived, and developed in different ways, many truths about them are contingent. Indeed, possible worlds were introduced to give metaphysical content to contingent truth.

The identity conditions of Leibniz's possible individuals are such that it is misguided to ask of any possible individuals conceived to be in other possible worlds whether they are identical with any actual individual—just as it is misguided to ask of other possible worlds whether they are identical with the actual world or not. To deduce from this position that every property of an individual is necessary for it, and to ascribe to Leibniz a "super-essentialism" is surely perverse. I have tried to show that the way in which Leibniz talks of possible worlds need not lead to the denial of the distinction between necessary truths and contingent truths about actual individuals. But if someone believes that this is so, then the right thing to say is that Leibniz's talk about possible worlds does not do the meta-logical job he wanted it to do. It is a strange interpretation that assimilates Leibniz's view about individuals and their properties to the view of Spinoza, with which he so explicitly and repeatedly disagreed.

The interpretation I oppose seems to be based on a failure to distinguish between two separate questions. One is whether one can have a meta-language in which one can meaningfully talk about individual concepts and say of a predicate that an individual contingently satisfies that it is a constituent of the individual concept—that is, the concept of the individual. I have tried to show that the answer is yes. The second question is whether a model theory of the kind Leibniz tried to devise will preserve the distinction between necessary and contingent. This is a technical question and even a negative answer to this would not imply a negative answer to the first.[21]

Notes

1. For example, Rauli Kauppi, *Uber die Leibnizsche Logik, mit besondere Besüchsichtung der Intension und Extension*, Acta Philosophica Fennica 16; Robert Adams, "Leibniz's Theories of Contingency," forthcoming.

2. "On the *Ethics* of Benedict Spinoza," (1678). In G. W. Leibniz, *Philosophische Schriften*, ed. C. J. Gerhardt (7 vols; Berlin, 1875–90), I, 148. Also in G. W. Leibniz, *Philosophical Papers and Letters*, 2nd edition, ed. and trans. Leroy E. Loemker (Dordrecht, 1969), p. 203.

3. *Theodicy* (1710), Sec. 36, Sec. 37, Sec. 282. Gerhardt, VI, 123 and 284.

4. "On Freedom," (ca. 1679). Loemker, p. 263.

5. *Theodicy, ibid*.

6. For example, *New Essays*, Book III, Ch. 3, Sec. 6.

7. "Letter to Arnauld" (July 14, 1686). Gerhardt, II, 48. Loemker, p. 332.

8. *Discourse on Metaphysics* (1686), Sec. 13. Gerhardt, IV, 437. Loemker, p. 310.

9. And also more recently by Benson Mates and Fabrizio Mondadori.

10. This point was made by Jonathan Adler and John Earman.

11. "Letter to Arnauld" (July 14, 1686), Loemker, p. 337. In "Remarks on Letter of Arnauld" (1686. Gerhardt, II, 43), Leibniz writes about the subsistence of individuals that make different contingent propositions be about the same subject: for example, if "I who have been in Paris am now in Germany," then "my attributes of the earlier time and state as well as the attributes of the latter time and state, are predicates of the same subject." Leibniz says this is what is meant by the claim that the notion of each predicate is contained in the notion of the subject.

12. L. Couturat, *Opuscules et fragments inédits de Leibniz, extraits des Manuscripts de la Bibliothèque Royale de Hanovre* (Paris, 1903), p. 18.

13. *Ibid*.

14. "A certain individual is *this* one, whom I designate either by pointing or by adding distinguishing features. For although those cannot be features which distinguish it perfectly from every other possible individual, there are, however, features which distinguish it from other individuals which we meet." See *Leibniz: Philosophical Writings*, ed. G. H. R. Parkinson, trans. Mary Morris and G. H. R. Parkinson (London, 1973), p. 5, and Couturat, *Opuscules*, p. 360.

15. Leibniz sometimes writes that having a complete concept is a distinguishing feature of individual substances but often writes as if having a complete concept is a feature of any particular thing—whether it is an aggregate or a complex. Individual substances do have corresponding complete concepts—but other particulars have complete concepts too. For example, in a marginal note to a letter to Arnauld (July 14, 1686; Loemker, p. 348, note 2), Leibniz explains, "A *full* concept includes all the predicates of the thing; for example, of heat. A complete concept includes all the predicates of a subject; for example, of this heat. In individual substances they coincide." "Ignis calidi" is Genevieve Lewis's reading in *Lettres de Leibniz a Arnauld* (Presses Universitaires de France), p. 35. Gerhardt reads this as "hujus calidi" or "this hot thing." Whichever reading one adopts, that is, whether one takes the subject to be fire, or some physical thing like a hot pan, it is not an individual substance in the strict metaphysical sense. Fire is probably a process or a mode of a physical thing—an aggregate—and similarly a hot object like a pan is an

extended physical thing—a phenomenon, based on a plurality of individual substances. Mr. Roger Woolhouse drew my attention to Genevieve Lewis's reading.

16. For similar reasons, Leibniz distinguished what he called "Primitive Force" and "Derivative Force" in his works on dynamics. Primitive Force pertains to the nature of the physical object which can be examined by a law that tells how the thing would react dynamically, depending on the status of other things. Derivative force is the momentum of the object at any instant, which is how primitive force expresses itself, *given* the condition of other things.

17. *Theodicy*, Sec. 414. Gerhardt, VI, 363.

18. *Theodicy*, Sec. 174. Gerhardt, V, 218.

19. David Lewis, *Counterfactuals* (Cambridge, Mass., 1972), p. 85.

20. "On Destiny or Mutual Dependence," in *Leibniz: Selections*, ed. Philip P. Wiener (New York, 1951), p. 571. My italics. Also see *Discourse on Metaphysics*, Sec. 8. Loemker, pp. 307–8.

21. I profited from discussions on an earlier version of this paper at the Department of Philosophy, University of Minnesota, and at Brooklyn College, in autumn 1975.

The Causal Relation

PETER ACHINSTEIN

1. THE BASIC ARGUMENT

Is causation genuinely relational? If it is, then singular causal statements that purport to relate events, facts, or whatever, are referentially transparent in cause- and effect-positions. In "Causation, Transparency, and Emphasis"[1] (hereafter CTE), I have argued that the consequent of this conditional is false. Since claims of opacity in causal contexts bring rage to the hearts of extensionalists, I shall briefly restate my argument and then consider the responses of its opponents. I believe that they are not sufficient to restore legitimacy to causation as a relation.

Socrates, we are told, drank hemlock at dusk and died. Many of us are willing to make the stronger claim that

(1) Socrates' *drinking hemlock* at dusk caused his death

is true. The emphasis in (1) indicates that some feature of the situation—the hemlock drinking—was causally efficacious. Let us assume that 'Socrates' drinking hemlock at dusk' is an expression referring to a particular event (or fact),[2] and that it refers to the same event no matter which words, if any, are emphasized within it; that is,

(2) Socrates' drinking hemlock at dusk = Socrates' *drinking hemlock* at dusk = Socrates' drinking hemlock *at dusk*.

If singular causal statements are referentially transparent in cause-positions, then from (1) and (2) we may infer

(3) Socrates' drinking hemlock *at dusk* caused his death.

But (3) is false, since it falsely selects the time of the drinking as causally efficacious; it states that the event's being at dusk is what caused Socrates to die. Since we can infer a false causal statement from a true one by substituting expressions referring to the same event, I conclude that singular causal statements are opaque in the cause-

369

position. A similar argument shows that they are opaque in the effect-position as well.[3]

Now for the objections.

2. "CAUSATION IS NOT MIND-DEPENDENT"

The argument above cannot be right, it will be said, since if it were it would prove that causation is intentional—that causal contexts are like belief-contexts. The latter are intentional because they are mind-dependent. But surely causal contexts are not mind-dependent. Whether *a* caused *b* does not depend upon what anyone believes or intends. The movement of the moon would cause the tides even if there existed no minds at all.

I agree that (many) causal statements are not mind-dependent. However, "mentalistic" terms are not the only ones that can produce opaque contexts. Modal operators have a similar effect; so do quotation marks. And neither of these contexts need be mentalistic. How, then, does emphasis yield opacity in causal contexts? It does so via the phenomenon of *semantical aspect-selectivity*. An emphasized word or phrase in a nominalized cause term of a causal statement is selected as expressing an aspect of the situation that is causally operative. A shift in emphasis shifts the causally operative aspect and thus changes the meaning, and hence possibly the truth-value, of the resulting claim.

Two broad uses of emphasis can be distinguished: semantical and non-semantical. If I say that

(4) Socrates' drinking hemlock at dusk occurred in prison

and you, who are hard of hearing, think I said that his drinking hemlock at dawn occurred in prison, I might reply that

(5) Socrates' drinking hemlock *at dusk* occurred in prison.

This is what I have called the denial use of emphasis. I utter (5) and emphasize 'at dusk' because I believe that some related statement has been made or assumed which is false; and the aspect responsible for its falsity has been replaced by the emphasized expression. Or, suppose that you know that Socrates' drinking hemlock occurred in prison, but you do not know at what time of day this happened. I might utter (5) and emphasize 'at dusk' because I believe that you are unfamiliar with that aspect of the situation but familiar with the rest. The emphasized words provide the new information for you. Or, I might utter (5) and emphasize 'at dusk' simply to call attention to something I regard as particularly interesting, important, or surprising. In uttering (5) and employing a "denial," "new information," or "interest" use of emphasis, I am not uttering a statement whose meaning is different from that of (4); I am making the same statement, though in a different way, by the use of emphasis. These are non-semantical uses of emphasis. The meanings, and hence the truth-values, of (4) and (5) are identical.

The same is not so with (1) and (3) above, even though (1) and (3) differ only in emphasis. This difference in emphasis makes a difference in the meanings and also the truth-values of these statements. The reason is that the emphasized words become selected or captured by the word 'caused', indicating that a particular aspect is causally operative. This is a semantical use of emphasis; its use affects the meaning and the truth-value of what is asserted. In non-semantical uses, the speaker selects a word to emphasize because of certain beliefs he has about the statement, or aspects of it, or related statements, for example, the belief that a contrasting statement has been made that is false, or that some aspect of the situation reported in the statement is important. A shift in emphasis will not alter the meaning or the truth-value of what is asserted by the statement, though it may not adequately reflect the accompanying belief of the speaker. By contrast, in semantical uses such as (1) and (3), the emphasized word or phrase becomes captured by the emphasis-selective word 'caused', indicating the causal operativeness of the aspect selected by these words. A shift in emphasis will select a different aspect as causally operative. In both the semantical and non-semantical cases, use of emphasis can focus upon some aspect of the situation; in both cases we can have aspect-selectivity. But in semantical cases, because of an emphasis-selecting term in the statement, the statement itself makes a claim about that aspect.[4]

The term 'cause' is one of a number of emphasis-selecting words that generate opaque contexts. Others include 'explain', 'reason', 'advise', and 'know'. Each of these, to be sure, might be claimed to be "mentalistic," and so it should not be surprising that each generates opaque contexts. But there are non-mentalistic words in addition to 'cause' that produce such contexts as well, for example, 'dangerous', 'important', 'mistake', and 'illegal'. Thus,

    (6) Alice's *turning* suddenly was dangerous (important, a mistake, illegal)

might be true, while

    (7) Alice's turning *suddenly* was dangerous (etc.)

is false, even though

    (8) Alice's *turning* suddenly = Alice's turning *suddenly*.

The emphasized word is selected by 'was dangerous', indicating the danger of a particular aspect of the situation. (7) asserts that it was the suddenness of her turning that was dangerous, while (6) asserts that what was dangerous was her turning, which was done suddenly. There should be little temptation to trace the opacity here to mind-dependence. The truth-values of (6) and (7) are unaffected by anyone's beliefs or intentions.

Although emphasis selects an aspect of the situation as being causally operative, dangerous, important, etc., this does not mean that it also *excludes* other aspects. Both (6) and (7) might be true. The emphasis in (6) selects the turning as being dangerous without excluding the possibility that the suddenness of the turning is also dangerous. My claim is not that if (6) is true then (7) must be false, but only that this is possible.

An opaque context is one in which the substitution of co-referring terms does not always preserve truth-value. Opacity can have its roots in other than mentalistic soil. In the cases with which we are concerned, semantical aspect-selectivity is responsible.

3. "EMPHASIZED EVENT-EXPRESSIONS ARE NOT REFERRING EXPRESSIONS"

Next I will be said to have falsely supposed that event-expressions containing emphasized words are referring expressions. This charge is leveled by Kim, who claims that the sentence

(9) Susan's *stealing* the bike occurred at 3 p.m.

does not seem to make any sense; the reason, he suggests, is that the expression 'Susan's *stealing* the bike' is not referential.[5] I agree that if no context is supplied, I will be puzzled by (9). My puzzlement, however, will not be over what it means, but over why the word 'stealing' is being emphasized. (I would have the same kind of puzzlement if 'stealing' had been written in extra large or extra small letters or with pink ink.) The use of emphasis in (9) is non-semantical, and to understand the particular non-semantical use to which it is being put, a context will need to be provided. Thus suppose you claim that

Susan's borrowing the bike occurred at 3 p.m.

In response to your innocence, or lack of morality, or whatever, I utter (9)—thus employing a denial use of emphasis. Does what I have said make no sense? Is the sentence I have used meaningless? This seems too strong a claim to make.

An analogous point holds for referring expressions themselves. Suppose I am referring to Susan's stealing the bike, and you mistake me to be referring to her borrowing the bike. I reply that I am referring to

(10) Susan's *stealing* the bike.

When I use the emphasized expression (10) in saying what I am referring to, have I suddenly ceased to refer to anything? Again, this seems unwarranted. When I use the expression (10), I have indeed referred, though I have done so using emphasis in a non-semantical way. In using the emphasized expression (10) in the context imagined, I have performed two feats: I have referred to something, namely Susan's stealing the bike; and, by using emphasis, I have corrected a mistake you have made about the event I am referring to.

4. "EMPHASIZED EVENT-EXPRESSIONS ARE REFERRING EXPRESSIONS, BUT THEY DO NOT REFER TO EVENTS"

This claim is made by Fred Dretske, whose work on emphasis has been of seminal importance.[6] According to Dretske, a proposition such as

(11) Socrates drank hemlock at dusk

can be given different "embodiments," which he calls *propositional allomorphs*, depending on differences in emphasis. Thus,

> Socrates *drank hemlock* at dusk

and

> Socrates drank hemlock *at dusk*

are different propositional allomorphs of (11). When we nominalize a proposition such as (11), we obtain a noun phrase referring to an event. But, Dretske asks, what happens when we nominalize a propositional allomorph? To what does that refer? We should, he claims, be referring to something different when we refer to

> (12) Socrates' *drinking hemlock* at dusk

than when we refer to

> (13) Socrates' drinking hemlock *at dusk*.

Dretske's answer is that what these expressions refer to are not events but what he calls "event allomorphs"—aspects or features of events. Moreover, they refer to different aspects—the former to the hemlock-drinking aspect, the latter to the temporal aspect. This allows Dretske to agree that (1) is true and (3) false without having to abandon the doctrine that causal contexts are referential. He can do this because, he maintains, although the cause-terms in (1) and (3) denote entities, they do not denote the same entities; they denote different allomorphic events or event-aspects. Hence (2) is false, and (3) cannot be inferred from (1).

How does Dretske argue for his claim that expressions such as (12) and (13) denote different things? He does so by assuming that the *a*- and *b*-positions in statements of the form "*a* caused *b*" are transparent, that is, that causal contexts are extensional. Then, since a statement such as (1) is true, but (3) false, the emphasized expressions (12) and (13) cannot denote the same thing—otherwise both (1) and (3) would be true. Thus, Dretske argues, the transparency of causal contexts shows that different emphasized event-expressions (different nominalized propositional allomorphs) are not co-referential. He writes:

> When we nominalize different propositional allomorphs we obtain noun phrases that refer to quite different things, allomorphic events, and the difference in what is being referred to manifests itself when we begin to talk about the causal relatedness of these items.[7]

Dretske's argument that expressions such as (12) and (13) do not denote the same things should carry no weight for our purposes, since whether causal contexts are extensional is just what is being questioned. My claims in Section 1 are not refuted by an argument that depends crucially on the assumption that causal contexts are extensional. Nor does Dretske offer any argument in favor of this assumption beyond noting that it is a "prevalent view."[8] I would certainly agree with him that if causal contexts are extensional, and if the cause-terms in (1) and (3) are referential, then these cause-terms denote different things, since (1) and (3) have different truth-values. But the question is whether the first clause of this conditional is true. Until it is established, Dretske's argument that expressions (12) and (13) denote different entities is not decisive.

Putting aside Dretske's argument, let us ask, independently, whether it is reasonable to suppose that (12) and (13) denote different entities. Suppose I refer to

(14)   Socrates' drinking hemlock at dusk,

and you mistake me to be referring to Socrates' eating dinner at dusk, while someone else mistakes me to be referring to Socrates' drinking hemlock at dawn. To you I reply that I am referring to

(12)   Socrates' *drinking hemlock* at dusk;

to the other person, that I am referring to

(13)   Socrates' drinking hemlock *at dusk*.

Am I therefore referring to different things in (12), (13), and (14)? If so, this would preclude the denial use of emphasis as a means of correcting a mistake about which entity is being referred to. I could not use expressions (12) and (13) to correct the mistakes in question and to indicate what it is that I am referring to, because in each case I would be referring to something else.

Or suppose I am referring to Socrates' drinking hemlock at dusk, and you know that I am referring to Socrates' doing something or other at dusk, but you do not know what, while the second person knows that I am referring to Socrates' drinking hemlock at some time of the day, though he does not know what time. To you I reply that I am referring to

(12)   S crates' *drinking hemlock* at dusk,

and to the other person that I am referring to

(13)   Socrates' drinking hemlock at *dusk*,

where the emphasized words provide the new information for you and the other person about what I am referring to. If the introduction and shifting of emphasis in my referring expression entails a shift in reference, then emphasis is precluded as a means of providing new information about what is being referred to. A similar story could be told about the interest use of emphasis. In general, Dretske's position here commits him to what strikes me as an unwarranted abandonment of non-semantical uses of emphasis in referring expressions.

A more reasonable approach would seem to be that when I use expressions (12) and (13), I am referring to the same thing, and I am employing emphasis (on the above occasions) to correct mistakes of others about what I am referring to, or to fill in their informational lacunae about this, or to focus upon some interesting aspect of the referent. I do not change the referent in these cases simply by adding or changing emphasis. Interestingly, in his first paper on emphasis, "Contrastive Statements," Dretske himself accepts this very conclusion. He argues that there is no difference in meaning, and hence reference, between expressions such as (12) and (13).

5. "IF EVENT-ASPECTS ARE CAUSALLY OPERATIVE, THEN CAUSAL STATEMENTS MUST RELATE EVENT-ASPECTS"

Since I claim that

(1) Socrates' *drinking hemlock* at dusk caused his death

is true in virtue of the fact that the hemlock drinking aspect was causally operative, am I not committed to the claim that (1) reports a causal relationship between an event-aspect of Socrates' drinking hemlock at dusk and his death? Am I not saying that event-aspects are causal entities? (This claim is essentially Dretske's, though his argument for it depends crucially on the assumption that causal contexts are referential.) The answer to the question is no. To say that (1) is true in virtue of the causal efficacy of the hemlock drinking aspect of the event is not necessarily to say that the cause-term in (1) denotes an event-aspect. By analogy to say that

Socrates' *drinking hemlock* at dusk explains his death,

or that

Socrates' *drinking hemlock* at dusk is evidence for the fact that he died,

or that

Socrates' *drinking hemlock* at dusk was dangerous (important, required by law)

is true in virtue of the explanatory or evidential efficacy, or of the danger, importance, or legal requirement, of the hemlock-drinking aspect of the event is not necessarily to be committed to the claim that the expression 'Socrates' *drinking hemlock* at dusk' in these sentences denotes an event-aspect. The position taken by this expression in each of these sentences is referentially opaque. One need not postulate the existence of event-aspects as a new ontological species in order to make any of the claims above. Each of them can be true even though there exists no *entity* that caused, explains, or is evidence for Socrates' death, or which was dangerous, important, or required by law.

There is, however, a related objection. I have been speaking of focusing upon, or selecting, event-aspects. But how can one do this without assuming that they are entities (that is, without *referring* to them as entities)? Consider the event consisting of

Socrates' drinking hemlock at dusk in prison.

A number of questions about this event can be answered simply by examining the event-description itself, namely

When was Socrates drinking hemlock in prison?
Where was Socrates drinking hemlock at dusk?
Who was drinking hemlock at dusk in prison?
What was Socrates doing at dusk in prison?

To provide answers to these and other questions is to focus upon (and provide information about) aspects of the event. When we answer the last question by saying

> drinking hemlock
> it was drinking hemlock that Socrates was doing at dusk
> Socrates was *drinking hemlock* at dusk in prison

we are focusing upon a particular aspect of the event. But we need not be referring to any *entity* in so doing. One can use the expression 'drinking hemlock' by itself, or in a prominent position in the sentence, or with emphasis, to focus upon a particular aspect of the event without thereby referring to an entity, which is that aspect; by analogy, the term 'bald' can be used by itself or in

> It was bald that Socrates was
> Socrates was *bald*

to focus upon a particular aspect of Socrates, without thereby referring to an entity denoted by 'bald'.

Granted that we can focus upon aspects of events without assuming that they are entities, but how can we make claims about them without supposing that they are? In the *de re* sense of 'about', we cannot say anything about aspects of events if these are not entities. But we can in the *de dicto* sense. Just as we say that the non-extensional

> What Jones fears is terrifying

makes a claim about what Jones fears, without supposing that 'what Jones fears' denotes some entity, so we can say that

> (1)   Socrates' *drinking hemlock* at dusk caused his death

makes a (causal) claim about an aspect of an event without supposing that 'Socrates' *drinking hemlock* at dusk' in (1) denotes an entity.

6. "EMPHASIZED CAUSAL STATEMENTS ARE ELLIPTICAL"

A number of extensionalists have urged this thesis. The claim is that when an event-expression with emphasized words appears in a causal statement it does not refer. Instead the causal statement is to be understood as elliptical for something else. Let me mention four possibilities.

a. *The conjunction paraphrase*. This is proposed by Kim and Levin. The idea is that the emphasized cause-term in

> (3)   Socrates' drinking hemlock *at dusk* caused his death

does not refer to anything; instead (3) is to be understood as elliptical for a conjunction whose first member is the *unemphasized* (3)—in which the unemphasized cause-term is referential—and whose second member is a counterfactual, or a statement invoking a law, or another causal statement. For example, it might be claimed that (3) is elliptical for the conjunction

> Socrates' drinking hemlock at dusk caused his death, and if he had drunk hemlock at some other time he would not have died.

Levin claims that it is elliptical for

Socrates' drinking hemlock at dusk caused his death, and there is a law in which 'drinks at dusk' appears and which subsumes Socrates' death.[9]

Kim suggests

Socrates' drinking hemlock at dusk caused his death, but Socrates' drinking hemlock did not cause his death.[10]

In all these cases, the conjuncts contain only unemphasized causal statements whose cause-terms are referential and refer to the event of Socrates' drinking hemlock at dusk.

b. *The operator paraphrase*. There is another possibility, which I mentioned in CTE and which Kim also notes (without exploring it for the causal case). It asserts that in

(3) Socrates' drinking hemlock *at dusk* caused his death

the cause-term does not refer, and the emphasis is to be understood as an operator that operates on the entire causal statement without emphasis. We are to understand (3) as

(15) $E_{at\ dusk}$ (Socrates' drinking hemlock at dusk caused his death),

in which '$E_{at\ dusk}$' is an emphasis-operator that operates on the statement inside the parentheses to produce a statement in which 'at dusk' is emphasized, that is, (3). The cause-position in (15) is referentially transparent.

c. *The "fact that an event has a feature" paraphrase*. A third possiblilty is to say that the cause-term in (3) is non-referential and to paraphrase (3) into the unemphasized

(16) The fact that Socrates' drinking hemlock occurred at dusk caused his death.

In (16) the cause-term is of the form

The fact that (event) *e* had (feature) *f*,

which is to be understood as referential in the *e*- and *f*-positions.

d. *The "causally explains" paraphrase*. Finally, it might be said that the cause-term in (3) does not refer to an event and that (3) is elliptical for

Socrates' drinking hemlock *at dusk* causally explains his death.

Since 'causally explains' (on this view) relates sentences, not events, the above sentence is, in turn, elliptical for

The sentence "Socrates drank hemlock *at dusk*" causally explains the sentence "Socrates died,"

in which the cause-position is transparent, taking sentences as explainers.[11] Such a view might be suggested by Donald Davidson, who holds that causal statements like

> The collapse was caused by the fact that the bolt gave away so suddenly and unexpectedly.

are to be understood as saying not that one event caused another, but that one sentence causally explains another.[12] The causal sentences to which Davidson gives this paraphrase are importantly like the emphasized causal sentences I am considering: they involve selecting some features from the cause term as causally operative.

All four of these views suppose that emphasized event-expressions in causal statements do not refer to events; and the first three views suppose that in causal statements they do not refer at all. Now, of course, I am in agreement with these suppositions. But my reason is quite different from theirs. My reason is that causal contexts are referentially opaque—an assumption which all of those defending these paraphrases do not accept. What is *their* reason for claiming that emphasized event-expressions in causal statements do not refer (or do not refer to events)? It can only be that emphasized event-expressions *never* refer (or never refer to events) in any linguistic contexts. And these two claims I have already criticized in Sections 3 and 4.

Even so, one might wonder whether these paraphrase views are successful. Are the paraphrases trouble-free? Is the problem of emphasis really avoided? I think not.

Let me consider all the conjunctive paraphrases together. On the conjunctive proposals, a sentence such as

(1) Socrates' *drinking hemlock* at dusk caused his death

is supposed to be elliptical for a conjunction, one of whose conjuncts is

(17) Socrates' drinking hemlock at dusk caused his death.

(17) contains no emphasis at all. If so, then, I suggest, there are two possible claims we might make about it. One is that it is ambiguous and therefore without unique truth-value. Depending upon where emphasis is placed (or understood) in the cause-term, (17) becomes true or false, as the case may be. If 'drinking hemlock' is emphasized it is true; if 'at dusk' is emphasized it is false; as is, it is neither true nor false. The second possible claim is that (17) without emphasis is not ambiguous but is to be understood as if *all* the words in the cause-term are emphasized; it is to be understood as implying that all aspects of the event (implicit in its description) were causally operative. Emphasizing one word or phrase, for example, 'drinking hemlock', would indicate that it was the hemlock drinking that caused Socrates' death, but would make no claim about the causal efficacy of other aspects. But where all aspects are being claimed to be causally operative no emphasis is needed.[13]

In either of these cases the conjunctive view is in trouble. On this view, if (1) is true, then (17) must be true also. But this is not the case if (17) is ambiguous and therefore lacking in truth-value. Nor is it the case if (17) is construed as implying that all aspects of the event were causally operative; for this would imply that the time of the drinking was causally operative, which is false. It is the essence of the conjunctive paraphrase view to paraphrase a causal statement such as (1) into a conjunction whose members lack emphasis. But without emphasis a conjunct such as (17) either lacks a truth-value or else has one that is not necessarily the same as that of the statement being paraphrased.

The "operator" and "fact that an event has a feature" paraphrases of empha-sized causal statements lead to similar difficulties, and I refer the reader to CTE (Sec-tions 5 and 6) for the details. On both views, emphasized causal statements generate unemphasized ones which should, but may not, have the same truth-values as the originals.

The problem is a general one. When an event-expression of the form

x's A-ing y B-ly,

in which 'x' and 'y' are nouns or noun phrases, 'A' is a verb, and 'B-ly' is an adverb or prepositional phrase (or several such), is embedded in certain larger contexts, in-cluding

—— caused e

—— was dangerous (important, evidence that h),

the terms following the blank become aspect-selective. The meaning, and truth-value, of the resulting statement depend on which aspect(s) of x's A-ing y B-ly they select. Emphasis provides a key to selectivity. An emphasized phrase is captured by the em-phasis-selecting word and is understood as expressing the causally operative (danger-ous, etc.) feature. A shift of emphasis will shift the feature selected, and thus the meaning, and possibly the truth-value, of the claim. Without emphasis, either explicit or understood, statements of the form

x's A-ing y B-ly caused e (was dangerous, important, etc.)

will be ambiguous or (possibly) construed as asserting that all aspects are operative. The first three paraphrase views recommend paraphrasing an emphasized causal claim of the above form into a statement containing an unemphasized one. But without emphasis—without an indication of which aspect is being claimed to be causally ef-ficacious—we get ambiguity or the implication that all are. A causal claim is thus generated which either lacks a unique truth-value or has one that need not be the same as the original's.

Nor, finally, will the "causally explains" paraphrase be any more successful. On this view,

(1) Socrates' *drinking hemlock* at dusk caused his death

is elliptical for

(18) The sentence "Socrates *drank hemlock* at dusk" causally explains the sentence "Socrates died"

in which cause- and effect-positions are referential. Serious objections can be raised against taking sentences (or propositions) as explainers and as objects of explana-tion.[14] Also, Davidson provides no criterion for deciding whether a given causal state-ment is to be construed as relating events or sentences. But even ignoring these diffi-culties, the present proposal is not trouble-free. The introduction and the shifting of emphasis in the expression

The sentence "Socrates drank hemlock at dusk"

should not change the sentence being referred to. That is,

(19)   The sentence "Socrates drank hemlock at dusk" = the sentence "Socrates drank hemlock *at dusk*" = the sentence "Socrates *drank hemlock* at dusk."

But if the cause-position in (18) is referentially transparent with respect to expressions denoting sentences, then from (18) and (19) we obtain

The sentence "Socrates drank hemlock *at dusk*" causally explains the sentence "Socrates died."

But the latter is what

Socrates' drinking hemlock *at dusk* caused his death

is supposed to express, and this statement is false. In short, the shift from "cause" as a relation between events to "causally explains" as a relation between sentences will not prevent inferences from truth to falsehoods owing to shifts in emphasis.[15]

One final question about the "causally explains" view. How are we to construe *unemphasized* causal statements whose cause-terms are verb nominalizations? Presumably at least some of them are to be construed as relating events, not statements. This is Davidson's view. Thus he tells us that

(20)   Flora's drying herself with a towel on the beach at noon caused her splotches

relates events, not sentences. But (20) *unemphasized* generates the very same difficulties as the unemphasized hemlock statement (17). Either it is ambiguous, or else (possibly, though not plausibly in this case) it is to be understood as implying the causal efficacy of all aspects of the event. Use of such causal statements, then, will be severely restricted. If we want to avoid ambiguity, we will be able to use them only when we are prepared to make unusually strong causal claims. I am not saying that when someone asserts (20) he is making such a claim. (When someone utters (20) usually emphasis on some words in the cause-term is understood, at least implicitly.) I am saying only that if no emphasis is to be understood at all, and if ambiguity is to be avoided, then an unusually strong causal claim will have to be intended.

7. "EMPHASIZED CAUSAL STATEMENTS MUST BE UNDERSTOOD IN CONJUNCTION WITH A PARTICULAR ANALYSIS OF CAUSATION"

This idea, which is an extension of the paraphrase view, has been suggested to me by Kim, especially in connection with his own theory of causation.[16] Kim's theory asserts that singular causal statements relate events, where the latter are construed as things having properties at times. The event of Socrates' drinking hemlock would thus be rendered as

Socrates' having the property of drinking hemlock at time T,

which Kim symbolizes as '[Socrates, drinking hemlock, T]'. The causal statement

Socrates' drinking hemlock caused his death

is rendered by Kim as

(21) [Socrates, drinking hemlock, T] caused [Socrates, dying, T$'$] .

More generally, singular causal statements involving reference to one individual and one property (though not necessarily the same ones) in both cause- and effect-positions have the form

(22) [a, P, T] caused [b, Q, T$'$],

in which a and b denote individuals, P and Q properties, and T and T$'$ times. Now Kim proposes to give a Humean analysis of statements of form (22), the most important feature of which involves a constant conjunction requirement for the properties P and Q. Kim considers three such analyses, of which he seems to favor two. However, I will mention only one of those favored, since what I will say will be applicable to the other as well.

Using 'loc (a,T)' for 'the location of a at time T', one of Kim's analyses can be expressed as follows:

(23) [a, P, T] is a (direct contiguous) cause of [b, Q, T$'$] provided that
    (i) [a, P, T] and [b, Q, T$'$] both exist;
    (ii) loc (a,T) is contiguous with loc (b,T');
    (iii) If $a = b$:
        $(x)(t)(t')([x,\text{P},t]$ exists and loc (x,t) is contiguous with loc $(x,t') \rightarrow$
        $[x,\text{Q},t']$ exists)
        if $a \neq b$:
        $(x)(y)(t)(t')([x,\text{P},t]$ exists and loc (x,t) is continuous with
        loc $(y,t') \rightarrow [y,\text{Q},t']$ exists).

Kim then defines 'contiguous cause' in terms of the ancestral of direct contiguous causation. In what follows, however, I will focus on "direct contiguous causation," which I will simply call "causation." Kim's condition (i) requires the occurrence (existence) of both cause- and effect-events. ([a,P,T] exists, according to Kim, if and only if a has P at T.) Condition (ii) is a spatial contiguity requirement. Condition (iii) expresses a constant conjunction requirement involving the constitutive properties P and Q of the cause- and effect-events.[17] Kim does not specify any precise meaning for the arrow in (iii) except to say that it is to "denote whatever type of implication the reader deems appropriate for stating laws."[18] It is to convey the idea of "causal or nomological implication."[19]

We are now in a position to consider the present proposal. The emphasized statement

(3) Socrates' drinking hemlock *at dusk* caused his death

is to be rendered as a conjunction, namely,

(24) [Socrates, drinking hemlock at dusk, T] caused [Socrates, dying, T$'$], and
      [Socrates, drinking hemlock, T] did not cause [Socrates, dying, T$'$],

where T denotes the particular time at which Socrates drank the hemlock, and T' the particular time at which he died. How is (24) to be understood? It is to be understood in terms of the analysis provided by (23). Thus the first conjunct of (24) would be analyzed as:

(a) [Socrates, drinking hemlock at dusk, T] and [Socrates, dying, T'] both exist; and

(b) loc (Socrates, T) is contiguous with loc (Socrates, T'); and

(c) $(x)(t)(t')$ ([x, drinking hemlock at dusk, t] exists, and loc (x,t) is contiguous with loc (x,t') → [x, dying, t'] exists).

Kim's strategy for handling the emphasis in (3) thus amounts to this: capture the emphasis (that is, the semantical aspect-selectivity) in (3) by formulating the conjunction (24); but construe the latter as a Humean causal claim involving the idea of constant conjunction. The Humean translation once obtained, Kim would claim, contains no ambiguities and is not subject to semantical uses of emphasis. In Section 6, when I considered the conjunctive paraphrase view, (3) was formulated as

Socrates' drinking hemlock at dusk caused his death, but Socrates' drinking hemlock did not cause his death.

The complaint was that the first conjunct here is subject to various semantical interpretations depending on where emphasis is to be understood. The present proposal avoids this embarrassment, since the first conjunct of (24) is to be understood as the conjunction of sentences (a), (b), and (c), which are not subject to various semantical interpretations depending on emphasis. The truth-value of any member of this conjunction is not affected by the introduction and shifting of emphasis. The present proposal, then, purports to capture the semantical aspect-selectivity introduced by emphasis while retaining the extensionality of causal statements.

Does this invocation of Humean causation save the day? I am not convinced that it does. To begin with, it saddles us with a theory of causation subject to well-known difficulties (of which Kim is aware). If the arrow in the constant conjunction condition is construed quite broadly, then, as Kim himself notes (p. 235), there are counterexamples to the analysis which involve properties exhibiting a lawlike, but not causal, connection. Kim's analysis also seems overly restrictive, since it requires a nomological connection between the constitutive properties of (Kim's) events. Many causal statements that we ordinarily accept as true would thus be rendered false, including

(25) Socrates' drinking hemlock caused his death,

or Kim's (21), since there is no true law relating the properties of drinking hemlock and dying *in the way (iii) specifies*. (Whether one dies from drinking hemlock depends upon how much one drinks, whether one's stomach is pumped immediately, etc.)

Most important, is Kim correct in assuming that a Humean translation of the sort he advocates is not subject to semantical uses of emphasis? That depends on the interpretation to be given to the arrow in Kim's laws of constant conjunction. Let us focus on such laws and simplify them by omitting the contiguity clause. Kim's present solution commits him to the view that such sentences are not subject to semantical uses of emphasis, that the introduction and shifting of emphasis will not alter truth-values. Now I believe that such a view is correct for general sentences such as

(26) Voters in Maine are conservatives,

which carry no particular causal force. But there are other general sentences that do; and when they do, it is not so clear that they are (semantically) emphasis-insensitive.

Gazing at the awesome north face of the Eiger, I say

(27) Anyone who climbs *that wall* in the morning will die,

while you say

(28) Anyone who climbs that wall *in the morning* will die.

I believe that both of our claims have causal implications. Neither of us is claiming merely that climbing will be followed by death; we are saying, in addition, that death will result from, will be caused by, will occur because of, the climbing. Moreover, I suggest that our claims have different causal implications. My claim might be formulated more fully as being, or at least implying, (something like)

(29) Anyone who climbs that wall in the morning will die because it is that wall that he will be climbing.

Your claim might be expressed as

(30) Anyone who climbs that wall in the morning will die because it will be in the morning that he climbs it.

And these claims need not have the same truth-values. Sentences such as (27) and (28), by contrast with (26), would normally be understood as carrying causal implications. And the emphases here have different semantical consequences, since they focus upon different aspects of the event-type "climbing that wall in the morning" as being causally operative.

Accordingly, I suggest, Kim's position is faced with the following dilemma: Either the arrow in his laws of constant conjunction carries causal implications or it does not. (Either it permits inferences of sentences like (29) and (30) from (27) and (28), or it does not.) If not—if, for example, it expresses a material conditional or some nomological relation which is noncausal—then there are well-known counterexamples to the resulting Humean analysis. (Many false causal claims will be generated.) On the other hand, if the arrow, whether analyzed or primitive, carries causal implications, then the laws are semantically emphasis-sensitive, and emphasis is not eliminated from the final analysis of causal statements, as Kim requires.

8. "EMPHASIS DOES NOT AFFECT THE MEANING OR THE TRUTH-VALUE OF CAUSAL STATEMENTS"

So far all of my real and imagined extensionalist critics agree with me on at least one point, namely, that emphasis does affect the meaning and truth-value of causal statements. Dretske obviously holds this view; so do the paraphrase theorists, since differently emphasized causal statements, like (1) and (3), will have different paraphrases and truth-values. However, there are other critics who would deny the truth of this common assumption. Peter Unger, for example, argues that "emphasis never affects the meaning or truth-value of what is asserted in any type of statement."[20] Suppose I say

(1) Socrates' *drinking hemlock* at dusk caused his death,

and you mishear 'dawn' for 'dusk'. I reply:

(31) I didn't say anything about dawn, I said that Socrates' drinking hemlock *at dusk* caused his death.

According to Unger, in (31) I would be making the same causal claim as in (1), although the emphasis has shifted. Unger concludes

> So, emphasis does not alter the content of what is said. The reason for this is that it doesn't alter the meaning of the (unemphasized) sentence which standardly serves to express what is said. . . . Unsurprisingly, then, what emphasis does is just to emphasize. It helps get us to focus on what might be thought important to think about.[21]

I would have no quarrel with Unger here if his claim were only that there are uses of emphasis that do not affect the meaning or truth-value of what is asserted. These I have called non-semantical uses of emphasis, and Unger's "focusing on what is thought important" is an example of what I have called the interest use. What Unger is denying, and what other extensionalists are accepting, is that emphasis has semantical uses as well.[22] No doubt when one person asserts

(1) Socrates' *drinking hemlock* at dusk caused his death

and another asserts that

(3) Socrates' drinking hemlock *at dusk* caused his death

they are focusing on different things. But in a causal context this difference of focus has different semantical implications. The speakers here are not simply focusing on something of particular importance to them; they are focusing on something in such a way as to be making different causal claims. This is why the earlier extensionalists and I agree that (1) and (3) have different meanings. Where we disagree is over what this semantical focusing amounts to. Dretske wants to claim that it involves making a reference to entities, namely, event-allomorphs; some other extensionalists that it involves making an unemphasized conjunctive claim one of whose conjuncts is a causal statement referring to events and the other conjunct a counterfactual, lawlike, or causal statement; Davidson (perhaps) that it involves making a claim about causal explanation and a reference to sentences, not events, as relata; and I, that this focusing in causal and other emphasis-selecting contexts is a semantical phenomenon that does not involve reference to any entity focused upon.

Turning, then, to Unger's particular argument, am I making different causal claims when I utter (1) and (31)? I am prepared to agree with him that I am not. But this is because the linguistic context—in particular the first clause of (31)—makes it clear that emphasis is being employed here solely in its denial use, which is non-semantical. Although I have said that emphasized words in a causal statement such as (1) are selected as expressing a causally operative aspect, it is possible to cancel this type of selectivity in favor of a non-semantical one, if a suitable preamble or context is made explicit. But without this linguistic context—in the absence of the first clause of (31) or something akin to it—the most natural construal of emphasis in (31) is semantical. In the absence of such contextual semantical canceling, it seems most natural to take people who assert (1) and (3) to be making different claims.[23]

Notes

1. *Canadian Journal of Philosophy* 5 (1975):1–23.

2. In what follows I will speak of events; but everything I say will be applicable, as well, to facts, which are sometimes said to be causes.

3. See CTE, Section 9.

4. This is not the only semantical use of emphasis. Emphasis can also be used to disambiguate phrases and references and to give words special meanings; for examples see CTE.

5. Jaegwon Kim, "Causation, Emphasis, and Events," *Midwest Studies in Philosophy* 2 (1977): 100–3.

6. Fred I. Dretske, "Referring to Events," *Midwest Studies in Philosophy* 2 (1977):90–99. For an earlier study of emphasis, see his "Contrastive Statements," *Philosophical Review* 82 (1973):411–37.

7. "Referring to Events," p. 97.

8. *Ibid.*, p. 94.

9. Michael Levin, "Extensionality of Causation," *Philosophy of Science* 43 (1976):266–77.

10. "Causation, Emphasis, and Events." Kim offers this paraphrase in the context of his own particular theory of causation, according to which events are construed as things having properties at times, and causation is analyzed in Humean terms. In Section 7 Kim's paraphrase will be examined in the light of his theory of causation.

11. It will make no difference in what follows whether explanations are taken to relate sentences or propositions expressed by them.

12. Donald Davidson, "Causal Relations," *Journal of Philosophy* 64 (1967):691–703.

13. This second interpretation seems to me more dubious in the present case, if only because it is difficult to imagine someone who knows anything about the situation uttering (17) with the intention. But other examples provide somewhat more believable alternatives. Thus, someone might utter "Kennedy's suddenly dying caused great grief," without emphasis, intending to make the claim that the dying, the suddenness of it, and the fact that it was Kennedy were all causally operative.

14. See my "What is an Explanation?," *American Philosophical Quarterly* 14 (1977):1–15; and "The Object of Explanation," in *Explanation*, ed. S. Körner (Oxford, 1975), pp. 1-45.

15. It is, of course, open to the present paraphrase theorist to say that the cause- and effect-positions in "causally explains" statements are not referential. Conceivably, this is Davidson's view, although it does not seem to be, since he explicitly says that "explanations typically relate statements"; if causal-explanatory statements are genuinely relational, then the cause- and effect-positions must be referential.

16. See Jaegwon Kim, "Causation, Nomic Subsumption, and the Concept of Event," *Journal of Philosophy* 70 (1973):217–36.

PETER ACHINSTEIN

17. There is a problem with (iii) which suggests that 't is contiguous with t'' should be substituted for 'loc (x,t) is contiguous with loc (x,t')'. Kim informs me that he concurs; but in what follows I will leave (iii) as Kim does in his paper.

18. *Ibid*., p. 229, n. 19.

19. *Ibid*.

20. *Ignorance* (Oxford, 1975), pp. 78–79.

21. *Ibid*., p. 79.

22. It might be noted that while Unger refuses to countenance semantical uses of emphasis, Dretske's position, by contrast, commits *him* to abandoning non-semantical uses.

23. My thanks are due to Jaegwon Kim for fruitful discussions of these issues.

Causality and
the Concept of a "Thing"

MICHAEL A. SLOTE

What kind of causality is involved in the existence of objective physical "things"? What relations must exist between physical things and their parts? These two questions are not obviously interrelated. But sometimes the solution of one problem is tied to the solution of another, and insight into the solution of either requires us to see that both problems can be solved together. Exactly this is the case with the two questions with which we began, and the major part of this essay will be devoted to explaining why. Later on, I shall also attempt to show how the joint solution of our original problems provides the raw materials for a *causal definition* of what it is to be a physical thing. The definition of thinghood to be offered will, however, differ somewhat from other causal theories and analyses that have been proposed in recent years through its reliance on the technique I have elsewhere called "definition by essence and accident."

I

Since the appearance of Kant's *Critique of Pure Reason*, a great many philosophers have thought there were important relations between the concept of an objective physical "thing" and the concept of causality or of causal (or natural) law.[1] Kant himself, it seems, believed the notions to be very strictly related: objective things, and physical entities generally, had to stand in fully deterministic relations to the world around them and to their own parts. But even philosophers who have rejected this strong claim—in the light, say, of recent developments in quantum physics—have, in the main, believed that Kant was on the right track: they have thought that at least some important elements of causality or lawfulness were intrinsic to thinghood and/or objective existence generally. Nonetheless, it has remained difficult to specify just what causal or nomic relations were intrinsically involved in thinghood, and to do so in such a way as to convince those few skeptics—for example, J. L. Mackie in *The*

Cement of the Universe—who have expressed doubt about whether causality has any necessary role in the existence, persistence, or interrelation of physical entities or things.[2]

There are two possible forms of skepticism here. There is doubt about whether every possible physical world—every conceivable world containing physical entities —must be subject to some sort of causality or lawfulness; and, more specifically, there is doubt about whether causality is necessary to the existence of physical "things" or "objects" in some narrow but colloquial sense of those terms that does not apply to all physical entities and that may lack application altogether in *some* possible worlds where there are physical *entities*. That there is such a narrower, colloquial sense of (physical) 'thing' or 'object' should be fairly obvious.[3] There exists a sense of those terms that clearly applies to tomatoes, rocks, and chairs, and that clearly does not apply to magnetic fields, shadows, bodies of gas, or piles of leaves. And we shall be concerned here only with that more specific form of skepticism that wonders why causality should be thought necessary to the existence of physical things, or objects, in the colloquial, but fairly narrow sense just mentioned.

Before I propose my own answer to such skepticism, however, let us first examine some other ways in which one might attempt to relate causality and thinghood. The failures we meet with will be instructive and may serve to motivate the answer I shall eventually offer.

Why, for example, should we not hold, with Kant, that total determinism is necessary to thinghood? Kant based this claim on his transcendental deduction(s) and on his "analogies of experience," and though it is dangerous to take too short a way with Kant, it seems to me that his arguments, though deep and suggestive, have never been spelled out in such a way as to be both clear and convincing.[4] Of course, it would be impossible for me to justify this assumption within the present space; so perhaps it would be best simply to note the assumption, and pass on to other (to my mind) more promising, views.

There have, for example, been other attempts to prove the necessity of universal physical determinism based on one or another form of verificationism. It has been held that we cannot in principle verify or confirm the existence of an uncaused event or state of affairs, since any claim of causelessness is infinitistic in content. But compelling criticisms of verifiability principles abound in the recent philosophical literature.[5] And in any event, it is by no means clear that physics has not given us *actual* confirmation of the existence of uncaused events. In addition, it seems easy to imagine uncaused events or states of affairs, and the idea of such events or states of affairs seems intuitively understandable. So unless verificationistic arguments for universal determinism can somehow be reinforced, I think we have reason to assume that such determinism is not built into concept of a physical thing. Moreover, even if universal determinism were necessary to thinghood, that condition would, presumably, not serve to distinguish "things" or "objects" from other physical entities. But if, as I shall claim below, only some weaker causal condition is involved in thinghood, we may also be able to make use of that very condition in order to distinguish physical things from other physical entities.

If we are convinced, by the above considerations, that determinism is not nec-essary to the existence of physical things, then a number of other theories about the causality involved in thinghood will also have to be rejected. If the idea of an un-caused event is logically impeccable, so too is the idea of an uncaused movement on the part of a thing. Modern physics accustoms us to the causal unpredictability in principle of some of the movements of subatomic particles, so why should it not be metaphysically possible for the movements of a macroscopic thing to be uncaused?[6] It looks, then, as if the causality governing thinghood cannot, at least within certain limits,[7] be a causality governing where or how a thing moves. And for similar reasons, the causality involved in physical thinghood does not appear to be a causality of per-sistence. There seems to be nothing metaphysically, or logically, objectionable in the supposition that a thing (and its matter) might suddenly and causelessly cease to exist.

Perhaps, then, we should look to conditions of origin, rather than to conditions of persistence, in order to find causal conditions metaphysically necessary to thing-hood. After all, certain forms of Essentialism claim that a thing's origins are necessary to it in a way that its (mode of) persistence or continuation is not, and the necessity here is thought to be a strict or metaphysical one.[8] Thus it has been held that if a thing derives from certain matter in a certain way, it is metaphysically necessary that it exist only if derived from that matter in something like that way. If, for example, my body came from certain matter via orderly processes, it will, on this view, be (metaphysically) essential to it that it came about in something like that way, and so there will be a necessary connection between my body, a physical thing, and (some of) the causality of its origination.

All this may be true, but it is of little help to us. It establishes only that cer-tain physical objects require causality for their existence, but it does nothing to prove a necessary connection between causality and thinghood generally. To accomplish the latter, we would need to show that it was necessary that *every* physical object have (essential) causal origins. But there seems to be no greater inconceivability in the idea of a thing's coming into existence in an undetermined, acausal way, complete with all its matter, than in the parallel idea of a thing's acausal perishing. Putative facts about the essential causal origination of certain physical things are of no help to us in our attempt to show that it is not *possible* that a physical thing should exist in the absence of all causality.

A further argument may, however, suggest itself at this point. When a thing persists through the (total) replacement of its matter, the fact of its persistence as the same thing seems to depend on the fact that the thing itself has organized that replacement. Thus it is clear that our bodies persist through the (total) replacement of their matter (and cells), because it is our bodies themselves that organize this pro-cess in a lawful and orderly way. There is, on the other hand, real doubt as to wheth-er a sock that is darned and redarned until none of its original material remains, ex-ists at the end of that process. And one reason, I think, why such cases are at best only borderline cases of persistence is that the replacement of the sock's material is (arbitrarily) imposed on the sock from without and not internally organized and ordered. Consider further a case where there is persistence despite change of *form*.

We think of the metamorphosis of a caterpillar into a butterfly as the persistence of a single animal (insect), and our willingness to do so again appears to depend on our assumption that metamorphosis takes place in an orderly and internally organized way.

These cases suggest that it may be a necessary truth that *if* and *while* a physical thing persists, its mode of persistence must be (to some degree) lawful—even if its coming into being and ceasing to be can themselves occur without cause. This idea may stand in need of further elaboration, but it is clearly very forceful with regard to cases where an object changes form or matter or both. Unfortunately, it does not solve our particular problem. We are looking for causal conditions involved in the notion of a thing in general, and the cases of the human body and of the butterfly do nothing, I think, to show that causality is necessary in those conceivable cases where a thing persists *without* changing in form or in matter. Perhaps things made of the sort of matter that actually exists have to change in form or matter at least at the microscopic level. But we can conceive of unchanging physical objects not made of such matter, and our problem is to show that even such things require causality or lawfulness for their existence.

Perhaps the following thought can help us on our way: It is part of our common intuitive notion of a physical "thing" that in order to be a physical thing—even an unchanging physical thing—something must have a degree of organization that mere piles lack or can lack. But organization in a thing (with parts) is, presumably, organization *of* its parts, so it seems natural to suppose that thinghood may require a special relationship between any thing and its parts. In that case, if we can now show that this relationship involves causal factors, we shall have simultaneously clarified the relationship of parthood in a thing and put ourselves in a position to show that causality is necessary to thinghood. For if some form of causality is necessary for something to be *part of a thing*, it will be necessary in order for something to be a *thing with parts*. Let us first consider why parthood in a thing cannot be understood in purely spatial terms. What we have to say in this connection will not only suggest that causality is necessary to parthood in a thing, but will, in fact, lay the groundwork for our subsequent positive argument for that conclusion.

II

Consider, to begin with, a book inside a house. The book is within the spatial boundaries of the house, but is not part of it. And this is not because of the book's failure to meet some further spatial condition that is met, say, by the walls of the house. The book's failure to be part of the house is not, for example, due to its insufficient contact with other parts of the house, since clearly the air in the house could have sufficient contact of this sort and still fail to be part of the house in any ordinary sense of the term.

A recent example of Davidson's further illustrates the inadequacy of spatial notions for capturing the notion of parthood in a thing.[9] Davidson asks us to imagine a situation in which (congruent) chairs can be "stacked" not on top of one another, but in the very same place. After the second chair is stacked into the first, what results weighs twice as much as a single chair, but takes up no more room than a single chair; and the process can be continued in the same way for further stackings. Since in the imagined situation there is also a technique for getting chairs out after they have been stacked in, there is reason to describe the case as one in which chairs can conveniently be stacked in exactly the same place. (Of course, the stacked chairs cannot be thought of as having subatomic parts in different places, if the example is to serve our purposes. So perhaps we should not think of these possible chairs as composed of atoms and the like.)

If Davidson's example has any force, then the prospects for defining what it is to be a part of a thing in purely spatial terms seem dim. For we presumably do not want to say that the seat of one of the chairs becomes part of one of the other chairs stacked with it, even though it bears the same actual spatial relations to that other chair as that chair's seat bears to it.[10] Several results would seem to follow. The chairs in the above example overlap each other spatially, even if they have no common parts. But, in *The Structure of Appearance*, Nelson Goodman understands the notion of overlapping as involving the possession of a common part.[11] So if we allow Goodman's usage and Davidson's example is admitted as a logical possiblilty, there must be another sense of 'overlaps' that does not apply to the chairs of Davidson's example, a sense with more than spatial force. And so it would seem that the term 'overlaps' is ambiguous. The ambiguity is one that philosophers have, I believe, overlooked. Nor does it appear to have been recognized that Goodman's enterprise in *The Structure of Appearance* can successfully proceed only if the primitive 'overlaps' does not have its purely spatial sense.

For our purposes, however, the most important result of the Davidson example is the (further) reason it gives us to think that the relation between a thing and its parts cannot be merely spatial, in the way it is perhaps initially tempting to suppose. Some further element is needed, and that further element, I shall now argue, is causal or nomic.

Consider, then, some actual physical thing with parts—your own body will do— and abstract from all the changes that may occur within it. Some of those parts are attached to others: your liver, for example, is attached to others of your bodily organs or tissues. Now this attachment seems to involve some form of causality, and not to be merely a matter of spatial proximity or contact. If your liver really is attached to your hepatic artery, or some other organ, then as a matter of causal fact, it cannot be separated from that artery or organ, or from your body generally, without something being torn or otherwise affected. If one's liver really is attached to other things in one's body, it cannot simply pop out of one's body by itself and without cause. Something has to cause it to leave; it must be *extruded*. So when a body or any other thing has parts attached to one another in certain ways, it may follow that a certain kind of causality exists, and, in particular, that those parts cannot separate without cause and (other things being equal) without tearing or otherwise *affecting* each other.[12]

On the other hand, what reason is there to think that physical things—even unchanging physical things—have to have parts that are literally *attached* to one another?

A solid gold brick is a physical thing, and yet it seems to have no parts that are mutually attached in the way the liver is attached to other organs or parts of the body. There are, to be sure, forces of cohesion within gold bricks. But cohesion is a fact of our particular chemistry, not of every possible chemistry. And can we not imagine an unchanging physical thing composed of parts that are neither attached to one another nor kept together by chemical forces of cohesion?

It seems we cannot use the notions of attachment and chemical cohesion by themselves to prove that parthood in a physical thing requires causal or nomic factors. I nonetheless believe that causality is necessary to parthood in a physical thing—and I even think that there is a weak (somewhat technical) sense of 'attachment' in which a thing's parts have to be mutually attached. In order to show this, we shall have to make use of a *Gedankenexperiment*. I propose that we try to imagine a physical thing with parts purified of all those "accidental" elements of causality that obtain in the actual world, but not in all possible worlds. I shall argue that however distant we make the thing imagined from ordinary physical things, however much we purify it of causal elements in other respects, there will remain an element of causality in the thing imagined that we cannot eliminate without depriving if of its status as a *thing* with parts. The purity of our example should ensure that whatever causality is necessary to keep *it* a case of an abstractly imagined thing with parts is necessary *in general* to being a thing with parts. Thereafter, we shall argue from the claim that physical things with parts have to be governed by some causality to the general conclusion that all possible physical things stand under conditions of causality.

III

Consider the physical thing *a* depicted below.

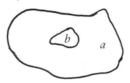

I hope that *a* is as amorphous as one could wish, and although part *b* of *a* is small in relation to *a*, nothing I shall say depends on that assumption. Nor need anything be said about the homogeneity of *a*'s stuff, about the change or lack of change in *a*, or about *a*'s origin or length of existence. Nothing particular will be assumed about how the parts of *a* are attached to it or to each other, and it will be left open that *a* (together with its parts) might causelessly cease to exist, move about, or alter. Have we, then, succeeded in picturing a physical thing with parts that exists in the absence of all causality? I do not think so.

Clearly *b*, which is now in *a*, could move or be moved outside *a*'s current boundaries. At least, we have said nothing to exclude this.[13] But could *b* move from *a*'s current boundaries without there being any causal explanation of this happening? We can certainly imagine a situation where a thing *y* within the boundaries of another thing x at a time t inexplicably left the t-boundaries of x. But will y have been part of x, and not merely within x's spatial boundaries? Our earlier examples of books in houses and chairs stacked in chairs indicated that existence within a thing's boundaries was not sufficient for parthood in that thing; and I want to say that the difference between mere spatial presence in a thing and parthood in a thing is a causal one. In particular, when I imagine the above-pictured part b of thing a in such a way that there is no causal explanation of why it stays in a (if it stays in a) or of why it does not stay in a (if it does not), then my feeling that b is part of a weakens to the vanishing point. I think that if we are to create an example, however abstract, where b is *part* of physical thing a at some time t, we must suppose that b's remaining within the boundaries a has at t, or its leaving those boundaries after t, will not be a matter of pure chance, without causal explanation.[14] Furthermore, if none (or few) of the physical entities within a's boundaries meets this sort of causal condition, it is impossible to think of a as a physical *thing*; it is merely an aggregation, pile, or what-have-you of the entities within it.

If that is so—and we have certainly relied on fallible intuitions about delicate matters of linguistic usage in reaching this point—then we have found a joint answer to the two questions with which this essay began. By relating causality and physical thinghood via the concept of a part, we have simultaneously discovered an element of causality in the concept of a thing (*with parts*—but we shall soon be in a position to drop the qualification) and clarified the difference between spatial presence and parthood in a thing. Moreover, the causal condition we have claimed to be necessary to being a physical thing (with parts) represents a kind of weak analog of the earlier suggestion that things have to have mutually attached parts. Attachment of part to part, we saw, entails, among other things, that the parts will stay together unless some force or thing causes their separation. And this, in turn, seems to entail our causal condition of physical thinghood, namely, that a thing's parts do not remain within it, or leave its bounds, without cause. So the causality required for things with parts, and for parthood in things, appears to be a weak part-attachment condition; there is thus at least *something* to the idea that thinghood requires mutual attachment of parts.

It is interesting to note, further, just how we have found causality to be necessary to the existence of physical things (with parts). Earlier, we allowed that a thing, together with its parts, might inexplicably come to be, cease to be, move, or alter (in certain ways).[15] But we have seen reason to think that thinghood at least involves a certain causal interrelation between a thing and its parts. And pehaps our results can be oversimply, but significantly, summarized in the claim that causality need not so much govern *how* a thing and its parts march together, as *whether* they do so.

In order further to clarify the argument we have given, however, I would like now to consider an objection to it that arises from a possible, and very natural, misunderstanding of the nature of the causal condition we have claimed to be necessary to partite thinghood. We have allowed the possibility that part b of thing a should be caused to leave the erstwhile boundaries of a; something c, inside or outside of a, could act, by contact or at a distance, to extrude b from a. And it seems possible in principle that b should be part of a at all times before some time t, but that some action or state of c, itself totally uncaused and inexplicable, should at t instantaneously dislodge b from the boundaries a had before t. Our description here involves instantaneous action by c on b, but we have said nothing to rule this out. More significant, it might be thought that our earlier argument sought to establish that in such a case as we have just described, b would not have been part of a to begin with. This would indeed be a problem for us, for there seems to be no inappropriateness in describing the above case as one in which part b of a is extruded by an uncaused state or event in another object c (that may or may not be part of a).

The causal condition we argued for does not, however, preclude such cases from involving genuine parthood. We never claimed that part b of a could not be caused to leave a by an event that was itself inexplicable; we said only that part b of a could leave a only if *that leaving* had a cause and explanation. Even if c's state (or what-have-you) at t is totally causally inexplicable, we may be able to explain b's removal in terms of c's state at t and various (causal) laws that obtain. After all, if an electron causes the death of a cat by moving down a grid, we can explain the cat's death even if the electron's movement down the grid is itself without cause and inexplicable. There is no incoherence, then, in supposing that c's uncaused state at t may cause part b of thing a to leave a's erstwhile boundaries. But this case is significantly different from the one imagined earlier in which b leaves a's boundaries for no reason at all, inexplicably. If an uncaused event or state in something c causes b to leave a, it may still be natural to think of b as having been part of the thing a;[16] but if b leaves the boundaries of thing a for no reason at all, it is extremely difficult to think of b as having been part of a. The case is too much like that of a book in a house.[17]

So far, we have, of course, argued our point about causality only for physical objects or things with parts. It is time to generalize the argument. Our task would be simplified if we could show that thinghood required the having of parts. And indeed there are reasons for thinking this to be so. To begin with, even though there can be physical bodies that we would not call physical things or objects—bodies of gas, for instance—it does seem to be a necessary truth that every physical object or thing is a physical body. Since it also seems necessary that bodies be extended in space, we could perhaps make a convincing case that things have to have parts, if we could reasonably hold that *extended* physical things have to have parts.[18]

But consider the physicist's search for fundamental particles, for quarks. It is not assumed that quarks are dimensionless or unextended, but in conceiving of them as the ultimate building blocks of the material universe, the physicist often thinks of them as not containing, or being composed of, parts. Now it is not entirely clear to me that such a conception is completely coherent. Surely, if—to simplify to one dimension—quark q extends from point r to point t, and point s is between r and t, it makes sense to talk of something like q-from-r-to-s, and is not this entity, however rebarbatively specified, a part of q? But if q is an ultimate particle, then it cannot be split apart, and q-from-r-to-s cannot exist apart from q in the actual physical world. And that may be sufficient reason to deny that q-from-r-to-s is part of q. But even if extended partless things are possible, there is no reason to think physical things can exist acausally. If quarks are extended but partless physical things, they nonetheless count as such only because they are indivisible extended things; and indivisibility itself appears to be a nomic or causal property of physical things (bodies) extended in space.[19] So even if partless things are possible, such things cannot exist in the absence of all causality and law, and given our earlier arguments, we can conclude that causality and/or law are logically necessary to physical thinghood generally.

IV

Let us now make use of our previous discussion to say something about the difference between physical things and such other physical entities as piles of leaves, bodies of gas, and fogs. There is something odd about speaking of the leaves in a pile of leaves as parts of the pile, but if we ignore the oddness, it seems possible in principle that there should be a pile of leaves whose parts, the leaves in it, could leave the boundaries of the pile without cause. A pile could be made up of leaves whose remaining in or leaving of the pile whichever, in fact, happened in each particular case—was totally inexplicable. The "parts" of such a pile would fail our earlier specified causal condition of parthood in a thing, so such a pile would not be a physical *thing*, and if the leaves in it are to be thought of as parts of it, then that earlier causal condition is necessary to parthood in a thing, but not to parthood in a physical entity generally. For similar reasons, there could be a body of gas, some or many of whose parts remained within (or left) its boundaries without cause. There is no impossiblity in the idea of a body of gas that contains parts or elements that only randomly remain within it. Such a body of gas would, again, fail to be a thing; and its parts, if they are parts, would fail our causal condition on parthood in a thing. Similar things could be said about fogs, clouds, and many other possible physical entities.

Unfortunately, it is not immediately obvious how to turn these facts to advantage and use them to define the notion of a physical thing. The causal condition we have stressed is necessary to thinghood—apart from complications due to the possibility of partless things, which we shall ignore, for brevity's sake, in much of what follows. But that causal condition is not sufficient: even if there can be piles of leaves failing that condition, there can be piles of leaves that meet it and that are nonetheless non-things. In a deterministic universe, for example, piles of leaves would meet our condition, but still not be physical objects or things. (After all, we think of piles of leaves as not being things—in the narrow colloquial sense of the term—independently of having views on determinism.) The same problems arise for bodies of gas and fogs, as well, since they too can be governed by deterministic laws without counting as physical *things*.

All is not lost. It may be possible to distinguish things from piles, bodies of gas, and the like—however deterministically governed—by use of the technique called definition by essence and accident. Roughly speaking, the basic idea behind this technique is that if it is necessary that all and only *f* entities have a certain (possibly complex) property *e* essential to them—but it is not necessary that all and only *f* entities have e simpliciter—then we may be able to define 'is an f' as 'is an entity that has e essentially'. The notion of essence—in many cases together with the notion of accident as well—can thus be used in the *definientia* of various concepts.[20] (Note, however, that definitions by essence and accident need not reify properties in the above manner, as our subsequent definition of physical thinghood should make clear.)

Our previous discussion may give us a clue about what properties are, of necessity, essential to all and only physical things, and in that case we can perhaps define physical thinghood by essence and accident, in terms of the concept of being a physical body that has those properties essentially.[21] What seems to be true of piles of leaves, bodies of gas, etc., but not of physical things or objects is that they are at most (logically) accidentally governed by the causal condition specified earlier.[22] Consider a pile p of leaves whose leaves have, up to now, remained in it or left it only in deterministic ways. It seems distinctly imaginable, with respect of p, that it should continue to exist (as a pile of leaves) even if it somehow started to be the case that the leaves in it remained in it or left it in totally random ways. We have already seen that it is possible for a pile of leaves (always) to fail our causal condition, so if p ceased to meet that condition, a pile of leaves would presumably still be there. And surely that pile would not be numerically different from the pile that was originally there. Thus the continued existence of p seems logically independent of whether its containment of particular leaves continues to be causally explicable. Even a pile of leaves in a deterministic universe that, *a fortiori*, meets our causal condition seems only accidentally to meet, or continue meeting, it. And the same, I believe, can be said for bodies of gas, fogs, and the like.

Physical things, on the other hand, seem different. In order to count as a physical thing, we have seen, a body must either have parts that meet our causal condition or lack parts by virtue of being indivisible. And I wish to claim that every (possible) physical thing that fulfills this disjunction of conditions essentially does so. I believe, in other words, that we have a deep-seated tendency to think of things as being essentially things. If, for example, we imagine a wooden table being planed away into (a pile of) shavings, we automatically think of the table as ceasing to exist; and we do so, I believe, because we conceive the case as one in which a partite physical thing "gives way" to a mere pile or aggregation of "parts." It seems similarly natural to hold that a partite physical thing that remains divisible but ceases to meet our causal condition —so that its parts begin to remain within or leave its boundaries for purely random reasons—has thereby ceased to be; for if what we have been saying is correct, this case too involves the replacement of a physical thing by a mere aggregation. On the other hand, it may be possible for a thing with parts meeting our causal condition to become indivisible without ceasing to exist; and it may even be possible for such a process to occur in reverse. If, for example, we have a divisible physical thing with parts governed by our causal condition and try to imagine it gradually "coalescing" into a state of partless, but extended, indivisibility, we do not seem to be imagining its destruction or ceasing to be; and I think at least part of the reason for this is that the imagined alteration—assuming it really *is* imaginable—involves no loss of physical thinghood.

I am inclined to believe, then, that thinghood, is and has to be an essential property of the entities that have it.[23] And what seems, as a result, to be true, of necessity, of all and only physical things is that they *essentially* meet one or the other of the two causal/nomic conditions we have been discussing. It seems necessary, in other words, that all and only physical things *essentially* either contain physical entities whose staying within them, or leaving of them, is causally explicable or are indivisible (physically impossible to divide or break into). On the other hand, the possibility of deterministically governed piles of leaves shows that it is not simply necessary that all and only physical things either contain physical entities whose staying in them, or leaving of them, is causally explicable or else are indivisible. So the word 'essentially' is crucial to our above specification of logically necessary and sufficient conditions for physical thinghood, and this suggests that we explicitly define the concept of a physical thing by essence and accident as follows:

⌜*a* is a physical thing (object)⌝ means the same as ⌜*a* is a physical body that essentially either contains physical entities whose staying within it, or leaving of it, is causally explicable or else is physically indivisible⌝.[24]

If the main arguments of this essay are correct, then we have stated a necessary condition of parthood in a thing and of partite thinghood, and have used that condition, together with the concept of a body and the nomic notion of indivisibility, to give a causal definition, by essence and accident, of the notion of a physical thing *simpliciter*.[25] We have, in the process, also said something about the nature of the individual physical things we encounter every day. For definition by essence and accident specifies what is essential (or accidental) to various entities at the same time that it analyzes certain concepts under which those entities fall. And, in particular, the above definition of physical thinghood tells us something about the essential nature of physical things by specifying a disjunctive causal/nomic property that physical things have essentially, but that such non-things as bodies of gas and fogs either lack or have accidentally.

There may, of course, be other causal conditions (properties) essential to (partite) things and necessary to (partite) thinghood. We have claimed, for example, that partite thinghood requires certain causal relations to exist between things and their parts; but perhaps certain causal relations between some of the parts and others are also necessary and can be shown to be so on the basis of the assumptions we have been making. Such additional causal conditions might also force us to revise the definition of thinghood we have given, but there is no time at present to pursue the matter further. In any event, it is worth pointing out that I have nowhere in this essay assumed that any form of causality was necessary to the existence of (a world of) physical *entities*. If a world of physical entities *could* exist in the absence of all causality and law, then our previous arguments do tell us that it is at most a world of physical *phenomena*, not physical things.[26] But, on the other hand, it may be possible to show (for example) that there cannot be physical entities without there being physical things (or causally governed physical monads) and thus, given what we have argued here, that causality is logically necessary to physical existence in general. I have taken no sides on this question, and for the moment it must remain an unresolved issue and, I hope, a challenge.

Let me point out, in conclusion, that our inclusion of causal factors in our definition of physical thinghood can help to bolster some common-sense intuitions about thinghood that we briefly alluded to earlier. To be indivisible or to have parts subject to our earlier causal condition on parthood in a thing is to possess a form of organizedness lacking, say, in a pile of leaves whose "parts" stay or leave for purely random reasons, that is, without cause. Of course, in a deterministic universe even piles of leaves will be subject to the aforementioned causal condition; but they will not be *essentially* subject to that condition (or to the disjunction of that condition with indivisibility). And I would venture to say that it is the essential possession of this causal/nomic disjunction that is adumbrated in the intuitive thought that things have to be organized, or unified, in a way that piles of leaves and the like are not and that represents the higher degree of organization that even deterministically governed piles of leaves lack.

None of this is intended, however, to suggest that we could just as easily have defined the notion of physical thinghood by speaking directly of the organized unity, or organization, that physical things possess. For on the one hand, the notion of organized or organic unity has, I think, become deservedly suspect through its frequent use (by Idealists) as a catch-all in places where argument and/or analysis is needed. And on the other hand—though this is really another side of the same coin—terms like 'organized unity' are inherently too vague to be of any use to us in defining a notion like physical thinghood. There are simply too many kinds of organizedness, or organized unity, for such terms to serve the purposes of definition. Philosophers of art, for example, often characterize works of art as possessed of a distinctive kind of organized unity; and if there is anything at all to this thought of theirs, then we, for our part, cannot define physical thinghood in terms of organization unless we are clear about the difference between the organization physical things have and that possessed by works of art. But then we presumably need to be able to *say* something about that difference, about that particular form of organization that is possessed by all and only physical things; and once we can do so, surely we should incorporate that information into our definition of physical thinghood, rather than making it rely on vague terms like 'organization' or 'organized unity'.[27]

The definition of thinghood offered above takes this advice seriously. For it is natural to view that definition as breaking down into philosophically better understood, or more familiar, components, the particular concept of organizedness or organized unity that we associate with physical thinghood, but not, say, with the concept of a work of art. Our definition thus avoids the numbing vagueness inherent in terms like 'organizedness', and also clarifies the concept of organizedness that we intuitively associate with thinghood but are typically unable to say much about.[28]

Notes

1. I can find no distinctions between causality and causal (or natural) law that seem relevant to the present essay. I take it that the concept physical object is pretty much the same as the con-

cept physical thing, and shall also be using the terms 'metaphysically necessary' and 'logically necessary' interchangeably.

2. See *The Cement of the Universe: a Study of Causation* (Oxford, 1974), pp. 110ff.

3. For just one example of such usage of 'thing', see N. Chomsky, *Problems of Freedom and Knowledge* (New York, 1972), p. 14.

4. Kant invented the notion of transcendental illusion, but I wonder whether that notion is not somehow applicable to many of his own arguments. For despite the inability of philosophers to develop versions of his transcendental arguments that are at one and the same time sound and perspicuous and my own tendency to "give up" on ever finding such an argument "in" Kant, I inevitably find Kant's arguments forceful and deep when I am actually following them in the *Critique of Pure Reason*. Borrowing from Austin, we might say that it takes one sort of philosophical genius to produce arguments that retain a hold on us even after we have persistently failed to produce clear and sound versions of them and have come to despair of ever being able to do so.

5. See, for example, A. Plantinga's *God and Other Minds* (Ithaca, 1967), p. 227 and ch. 7 *passim*.

6. It will not be important for us to consider whether subatomic particles count as physical *things*.

7. There may be limits to how (far) a thing may causelessly move, but I have yet to find any fruitful way to pursue this issue.

8. See, for example, Saul Kripke's "Naming and Necessity," in *Semantics of Natural Language*, ed. Davidson and Harman (Dordrecht, 1972); and my *Metaphysics and Essence* (Oxford, 1975), ch. 2.

9. See his "The Individuation of Events," in *Essays in Honor of Carl G. Hempel*, ed. N. Rescher (Dordrecht, 1969), pp. 230 ff.

10. The chairs may have different dispositions for spatial relations; but to bring in such dispositions would precisely be to bring in causality, rather than pure spatiality, at the very moment when we are trying to see whether we can avoid it.

11. See *The Structure of Appearance*, first edition (Cambridge, 1951), p. 44.

12. The inclusion of a *ceteris paribus* clause here does not affect the fact that causality is involved. It abbreviates certain further, perhaps unknown, causal factors.

13. Whether *b* could still be a part of *a*, or within *a*'s *later* boundaries, if this happened is not easy to decide. We sometimes think of a watch some of whose pieces have been removed from its casing as broken, dismantled, and in disrepair—but not as ceasing to exist altogether. And perhaps some of the removed pieces remain part of, and inside the boundaries of, the still existent but dismantled watch. (After all, the Temple of Dendur is not thought of as ceasing to exist when it is dismantled for shipping and when it is in transit, say, to New York.) Similar reasoning may apply to the relation between *b* and *a* when *b* is taken from *a*'s current boundaries.

14. That is not to say that *b*'s precise location inside, or outside, *a* must be able to be explained. Furthermore, if the surface of a thing is in motion relative to its insides, the question whether something is inside previous boundaries may sometimes not admit of an answer, but this vagueness in the concept of boundaries does not substantially affect our main point.

15. We earlier saw some reasons why *some* kinds of alterations in things might require orderliness and/or causality.

16. I leave open the question whether, in order for *b* to be part of a thing *a*, the causal explanation of *b*'s leaving (remaining in) *a* in terms of some state of action of *c* has to be fully deterministic or, on the other hand, can make use of statistical lawfulness.

17. However, on an appropriate *de re* reading, it is possible for a part of a physical thing to leave that thing without cause. For this entails only that something that in fact will not randomly leave a certain physical thing might have been in a position to do so (if things had been otherwise) and so might not have been a part of that thing. The claim in the main text is unaffected.

I am assuming, in addition, what may well not even need mentioning: that if something leaves a thing's boundaries for no reason at all, then there was no reason why it should not have causelessly *stayed* within those boundaries. Note, however, the further complication involved in supposing that a given part *b* of *a* first meets our causal condition, later fails to meet it, and still later meets it again, all while remaining within *a*'s boundaries. Do we want to say that *b* ceases to be part of *a* and then becomes part of it again later? Our present position commits us to saying this, but we may be able to avoid the commitment by specifying our causal condition on parthood in a thing in a way that is less relative to particular times.

18. In reasoning thus, I am assuming that dimensionless physical monads, if possible at all, would be neither physical bodies nor physical things in the colloquial sense. At the very least, I think such monads are "don't care's" from the standpoint of establishing an analysis of physical thinghood.

19. It cannot, I think, be a merely logical or conceptual fact about something physical that it is both extended and cannot be broken into or divided up. Note, too, how fastening on the concept of parthood enables us to show that causality is necessary to thinghood in a way that our discussion of the origins of things, or the conditions of their alteration, did not. Even if, for example, the alteration of things can be seen to require causal lawfulness, it still is hard to see why *things that do not alter* require causality. But once we see that a thing with parts cannot exist without causality, it is easy to show that causality is necessary to thinghood generally: because *partless (extended) thinghood* clearly requires the causal/nomic condition of indivisibility.

20. See *Metaphysics and Essence*, introduction and ch. 1, for a fuller and technically less sloppy discussion of this sort of definition.

21. In *Metaphysics and Essence*, the notions physical entity and physical body were defined by essence and accident via other primitives. See chs. 4 and 7. For brevity and perspicuity, however, I shall leave those terms undefined within the definition of physical thinghood to be offered below. The definition of physical bodyhood in *Metaphysics and Essence* assumed that piles and heaps count as physical bodies, but our definition of physical thinghood is easily freed from this particular assumption.

22. The earth is supposed originally to have condensed out of a gas-and-dust cloud. Does this mean that the earth, a physical thing, originally *was* a body of gas and dust? I shall leave it to the reader to consider what effect (if any) this question, and the correct answer to it, has on the enterprise and assumptions of this essay.

23. I assume here that an extended physical thing cannot come to *exist as* a dimensionless monad and thereby come to be a non-thing.

24. The definition is, for the sake of simplicity, deliberately vague about the times of leaving or remaining and about the proportion of the entities contained in *a* that must meet our causal condition. For discussion of a closely related issue, however, see *Metaphysics and Essence*, pp. 117ff.

25. Incidentally, the fact that it is not immediately obvious whether our definition of thinghood is correct or open to counterexample is not a valid objection to it. Definitions are always in some sense defeasible hypotheses "about" linguistic usage and dispositions, and even the supposedly innocuous definition of "brother" as "male sibling" is open to question because of the difficulty of deciding whether a brother who has a sex-change operation remains someone's brother.

26. It is interesting that the totally natural use of the English term "phenomena" in this context stands radically opposed to Kant's use of the term, according to which it is precisely phenomena that have to stand in completely deterministic relations to one another.

27. For an explication of the concept of a *material object* (partly) in terms of the idea of unity, see W. D. Joske, *Material Objects* (London, 1967), ch. 2. Joske's full characterization of material objecthood is unduly specific, and he seems oblivious to the specificity that *is* involved in the notion of a physical *thing*; but there is no space here to pursue these criticisms further.

28. I want to thank Edward Erwin, Carroll Hardwick, Frederick Schmitt, Peter Unger, and Andrzej Zabludowski for helpful criticisms and suggestions.

The Extensionality
of Causal Contexts

ALEXANDER ROSENBERG and ROBERT M. MARTIN

Writing about the question whether causal statements were extensional, Ans combe once exclaimed that

> the question here is not whether one can defend a thesis through thick and thin (we know that already), but really whether there was originally any good reason for this thesis at all. Here I am in a bit of difficulty. For I have no sure insight into the source of the conviction that causal statements are extensional.[1]

Whether or not this passage was written tongue in cheek, it is worthwhile setting down an answer to this question, if only to show how powerful is the motive for finding an extensional account of sentences that report causal relations. In the present paper we attempt to provide an answer to Anscombe's question and to offer a defense of the thesis so motivated.

I

Among sentential contexts that are clearly intensional are those that report psychological attitudes such as knowing that . . ., fearing that . . ., and descriptions of other characteristically human activities such as explaining. The truth of propositions of these sorts is, in an old-fashioned way of talking, "mind-dependent," and it is upon this "mind-dependence" that their intensionality rests. That is, the explanation of why substitution of co-referring terms and co-extensive predicates does not preserve truth-value in these sentential contexts usually makes mention of human logical lapses, or ignorance that some item satisfies different descriptions, or some other feature of the mental states of persons who assert intensional sentences or about whom they are asserted. For present purposes, it is worth illustrating this point with reference to the intensionality of *explanation* and its source. Consider the following examples of the sentential context ". . . explains . . .":

1. Oedipus's marrying his mother explains his subsequent madness.

2. Oedipus's marrying Laius's widow explains his subsequent madness.

Intuitively 1 is true while 2 is false, yet 2 varies from 1 only in respect of the way Jocasta is described. Since this variation in truth-value results from a change in description that preserves reference, explanatory contexts are intensional. And this intensionality consists in the "mind-dependence" of explanatory contexts: that is, the truth value of a sentence reporting an explanatory relation between two items rests on the existence of particular beliefs about the items, the terms by which they are described, and the connection between items of the kind under which their descriptions bring the items. Accordingly, if reference-preserving descriptions are varied without compensating variations in beliefs about whether the *relata* of an explanatory relation answer to the changed descriptions, an explanatory statement can change from true to false. It is the crucial role of beliefs that make explanations mind-dependent and thus explains their intensionality.

But, causal relations between events are not supposed to be mind-dependent. The course of nature is supposed to be objective, and independent of the beliefs and descriptions of mortal minds. If we were all swept away, desires, fears, hopes, and explanations would all disappear with us and our artifacts. Nature, however, is no artifact. The relations between natural events would continue unimpaired; and paramount among those relations is that of cause and effect. That is why the truth of statements about causes and their effects is assumed to be independent of human beliefs, desires, and linguistic descriptions.[2] If mind-dependency makes for intensionality, and causal statements are not mind-dependent, then it might be supposed to follow that they are extensional. But this conclusion does not, in fact, follow *simply* from the mind-dependence of causal statements.

To reach this conclusion validly, we need to introduce at least one of the two following claims: (1) Mind dependency is not only a generally sufficient condition for intensionality, it is also a universally necessary one; (2) the only reason to suspect that causal statements are intensional is their similarity in form and employment to statements, like explanatory ones, whose intensionality does consist wholly in their mind-dependence. Without the establishment of at least one of these two claims, it is open to someone to argue that there are other sorts of intensional contexts that are not mind-dependent, and that causal contexts are members of this further class of intensional contexts. Can (1) and/or (2) be demonstrated, or at least convincingly defended? Demonstrating (1) is, of course, tantamount to a substantial analysis of intensionality and well beyond the scope of the present paper. Therefore, we shall attempt to sustain (2).

In the literature on causation, there is a tradition of attempting to analyze the causal relation into explanatory ones or even to assimilate causation to explanation. Hanson expressed such a view in *Patterns of Discovery*, asserting that "there are as many causes of x as there are explanations of x. . . . The fact that x has been stretched can explain some event y. Or, x's having been stretched can be the *cause* of y." More explicitly, Scriven has written, "a cause is an explanatory factory (of a particular kind). Causation is the relation between explanatory facts (of this kind) and what they explain." According to Beardsley, "to specify the causes of an event is to give a causal explanation of it, and if explanatory contexts are non-extensional, as many would hold, then I don't see how causal contexts could fail to be non-extensional as well. They stand or fall together." In "Causal Relations," when faced with apparently non-extensional causal statements, Davidson "suggest[s] . . . that the 'caused' of [such statements] is not the 'caused' of straightforward singular causal statements, but is best expressed by the words 'causally explains'. The affinities between causation and explanation are manifest.[3] Both causal contexts and explanatory ones seem capable of taking either fact-like or event-describing expressions as arguments. Many features of causal language are distinguished by reference to intuitions about explanations: for example, the distinction between causes and conditions is often said to turn on whether one of an effect's necessary conditions provides its explanation, or merely one of its conditions.[4] Appeals to explanatory intuitions have also been brought to bear in attempts to refute the so-called regularity view of causation. It seems obvious that if causal contexts do turn out to be intensional, then it must be because they are of a piece with explanatory contexts. Clearly, the logical form of causal statements is very different from that of other intensional statements. For example, they are very different from the modal operators, such as 'Necessarily (. . .)', and from quotational contexts. Both of these intensional contexts involve features of human language (with the possible exception of *de re* expressions, should they prove to be intelligible, and independent of *de dicto* ones). This involvement may well make such expressions mind-dependent in the sense that psychological attitude contexts and explanatory ones are (if it does, then the suggestion that mind-dependence is necessary as well as sufficient for intensionality will have been strongly confirmed). But many of the complex of syntactical and semantical issues that surround modality, and quotation, are quite foreign to concerns about the form and meaning of causal statements. So, even if such contexts turn out to be intensional for reasons that have nothing to do with mind-dependence, this will have very little effect on the hypothetical claim that *if* causal statements are intensional, *then* this intensionality is due to their being, like explanations, mind-dependent. Moreover, even if those who assimilate causation to explanation are wrong about the intensionality of the former notion (as we shall argue), they are certainly warranted in finding a close relation between the concepts. Explanations typically appeal to causes, and it is mainly to satisfy explanatory demands that events and facts are cited as causes. It is just this similarity of function and form between causal and explanatory contexts that encourages philosophers to incautiously treat causal statements as intensional, and which is, paradoxically, an essential component of the motivation for arguing that, in fact, they are extensional. For, the similarities philosophers have detected underwrite the very qualification that our argument for extensionality requires: namely, (2) the only reason to suspect that causal statements are intensional is their similarity in form and employment to statements, like explanatory ones, whose intensionality does consist wholly in their mind-dependence. With this claim in hand, it follows directly from the mind-independence of causal statements, that they are extensional.

Here at any rate, we have an answer to Anscombe's question. For now we see that the source of the conviction that causal sentences are extensional is the even stronger conviction that causal relations are "in the objects," so to speak, and are not "mind-dependent." More precisely, the conviction behind the claim that causal contexts are extensional is the view that the truth of intensional statements rests on the truth of other statements that assert or deny the existence of mental states, while the truth of at least some causal statements does not rest on any such assertions or denials of the existence of mental states. (The only reason that the qualification "at least some" is introduced is, of course, that some causal statements describe causal relations between mental events. Even in these cases, the relation that a causal statement asserts to obtain between mental events is not of the sort or kind of relation that is mind-dependent in the sense described above. Thus, the statement that "belief *b* caused action *a*" expresses a relation between *b* and *a* that also obtains between non-mental events, like a short circuit and fire.)

There can be no more compelling foundation for a philosophical conviction than the fundamental commitment to the existence of a world of events independent of our thoughts about those events. As a motive for the conclusion that causal sentences which report relations in this world are extensional, the strength of this conviction is obvious. The difficult question here is not Anscombe's wonder about the source of this conviction, but whether we can convert this conviction into something approximating demonstration. Thus, in the remainder of this paper we turn from an explanation of why a view is held to an argument that it is a correct one to hold.

II

Causal sentences can be analyzed into sentential contexts and their arguments, where these arguments may be either singular terms or sentences themselves. Typically, when the sentential context is ". . . causes . . .," the arguments that it takes are singular terms that refer to events, states, or conditions. When the context is ". . . because . . .," the arguments are sentences in their own right. An example of the first sort, which takes terms as arguments, is

3. The Titanic's striking an iceberg . . . *caused* the sinking of the Titanic.

An example of the second sort, which takes sentences as argument, is

4. The Titanic sank *because* it struck an iceberg on 14 April 1912.

Now, to say that sentences like these are extensional is to say that any substitution of co-referring terms or co-extensive predicates in the arguments that leaves the argument's references unchanged in the case of a term-type argument, and leaves the argument's truth-value unchanged in the case of a sentence-type argument, will also leave the whole sentence unchanged in truth-value.

The singular terms of 3 and 4 seem to pass this test without difficulty. After all, we could substitute identicals from any of the following statements into 3 or 4 and preserve their truth-values:

The Titanic = the largest passenger liner afloat before 1930 = the newest ship in the White line in 1912 = the sistership of the Olympic = the ship that struck an iceberg on the night of April 14, 1912, and consequently sank.

The sinking of the Titanic = the event that Walter Lord wrote his first best-seller about = the event that cost Lloyd's of London more money than any other in 1912 = the event that resulted in the only mass grave in the Halifax cemeteries.

Some of these substitutions would be unusual, and might never find their way into versions of 3 or 4 uttered in order to explain the sinking or state the effect of the Titanic's striking the iceberg. But this has no bearing on the truth of 3 and 4 when they embody such substitutions. Therefore, we may conclude that causal contexts are extensional, in the sense of referentially transparent.

But what of the substitution of co-extensive predicates into sentences like: since "x struck an iceberg on April 14, 1912" is co-extensive with "x carried Lady Astor among its passengers for the last time," substitution of co-extensive predicates into 4 yields the patently false

5. The Titanic sank because it carried Lady Astor among its passengers for the last time.

Must we infer from this failure of truth preserving substitution that the causal relation is intensional?[5] One way to circumvent this sort of counterexample is simply to argue that the apparent failure of extensionality in 5 results from misconstrual of the real logical form of such sentences. On this view, the real logical form of 4 is identical to that of sentences in which causation is a relation between events, and is thus represented by

6. There is an event x in the sinking of the Titanic, and an event y, the striking of an iceberg by the Titanic on the night of April 14, 1912, and x caused y.

This thesis leaves no scope for counterexamples like the inference from 4 to 5 by making all sentence-taking causal contexts implicitly term-taking ones. Such a tactic is parallel to Frege's suggestion about the logical form of ". . . after . . ." Although this operator takes sentences as arguments, and may change truth-value when its contained sentences are substituted for, without change of truth-value, Frege argues that its actual logical form involves the existence of events and a claim that one follows the other in time.[6] Although attractive and plausible, the trouble with this approach is that it ties the thesis of extensionality for causal contexts to issues in metaphysics of the broadest kind, and provides sentence-taking causal contexts with nothing like the direct and more formal test of extensionality that term-taking causal contexts pass. Its plausibility as an argument for the extensionality of sentence-taking causal contexts rests entirely on the strength of arguments claiming that their logical form differs from their apparent form, for considerations that transcend issues in the philosophy of language alone. A more convincing argument for the extensionality of such causal contexts would show that, without appeal to underlying logical form, these sentences pass a test for extensionality that paradigm cases of intensional sentence-taking contexts do not pass. It is to a sketch of such an approach that we turn.

The admission that causal statements fail the test of extensionality in the case of substitutivity of co-extensive predicates into sentence-arguments is not very damaging, since it is tantamount to the admission that causal statements are not truth functional, and this something that we know already.[7] More important, we may make a revision in or qualification on our criterion of extensionality under which such causal statements will qualify as permitting the substitution of co-extensive predicates in their contained sentences where other sorts of statements, such as those expressing beliefs, modalities, or explanatory relations, will not. The original criterion required an extensional statement to permit the substitution of co-extensive predicates in contained sentences without changing the whole statement's truth-value. But suppose, instead, the criterion demanded not that the whole sentences' truth-value remain unchanged, but that a sentence-taking context is extensional if *the references of the gerundive nominalization of the contained sentences remain the same*. Every sentence has a number of nominalizations, among which there is its gerundive nominalization. For example, the gerundive nominalization of "the Titanic sank" is "the sinking of the Titanic." Such nominalizations have the logical form of singular terms—that is why causal contexts that take them instead of sentences as arguments pass our original test of extensionality without difficulty. If we require for substitutivity with respect to co-extensive predicates that these nominalizations retain the same reference, then we can take advantage of the fact that term-taking causal contexts pass our test to formulate a new test of extensionality that sentence-taking causal context pass, but that intensional contexts do not pass.

Thus, using our revised criterion, it turns out that the substitution that took us from a truth like 4 to a falsity like 5 provided no fair test of extensionality, since the nominalizations of the respective antecedent contained sentences of 4 and 5, "The Titanic's sinking" and "The Titanic's carrying Lady Astor among its passengers for the last time," clearly are not co-referential. By contrast, while substitution of co-extensive predicates that does preserve the reference of gerundive nominalizations preserves the truth-value of causal statements, it fails to do so for explanatory or psychological attitude statements. For example, the true statement

7. The fact that Oedipus went mad is explained by the fact that he married his mother.

is made false when we substitute "married Lauis's widow" for "married his mother," even though this substitution preserves the reference of the gerundive nominalization. Similarly, the true statement

8. Steve believes that Larry is his brother.

may be turned into a false one by the substitution of the co-extensive predicate "male sibling" for brother, even though such a substitution would preserve the reference of the nominalization. And again, the presumably true statement

9. Necessarily $(9 > 5)$.

is made false, when "the number of the planets" is substituted for '9', even though "9's being greater than 5" and "the number of the planets being greater than 5" have the same reference, although what their reference is may be difficult to say.

Thus, in terms of our revision or qualification of the criterion of extensionality for substitutions of co-extensive predicates, we may conclude that causal contexts pass this test, while, of course, intensional ones do not.

But, it may be objected to all this that our revision is simply a wholesale change, which bears no interesting connection to the traditional criterion and so bears no significant consequences for the question whether causal contexts are extensional. In effect, it may simply be suggested that our criterion is tailor-made to beg the question at issue. In reply to this change, it should be noted that our new criterion does isolate some real difference between causal contexts on the one hand and indubitably intensional contexts on the other. It seems equally obvious that this difference reflects the permissibility of substitutions that preserve reference. Whether the difference should go under the name extensionality vs. intensionality may be a terminolgoical issue. Perhaps we should coin a new term to describe the property in question: *Nominal Extensionality* seems appropriate, both because it involves appeal to nominalizations and because there may be doubts about whether it really is a kind of extensionality. In favor of describing nominal extensionality as a form of extensionality, there are the following considerations. Marcus has argued that "we cannot talk of *the* thesis of extensionality, but only of stronger and weaker extensionality principles." Marcus shows that the strength of a principle of extensionality varies with the sense of the "equivalence" that is required to obtain between intersubstitutable arguments of a context under examination.[8] If we adapt this thought of Marcus's, we may reply to doubters that denying our criterion the title of a principle of extensionality involves denying that equivalence of reference under transformation to gerundive nominalization is any sort of equivalence at all. And such a denial will be difficult to accept, if, as Chomsky has suggested, "Gerundive nominalizations can be formed freely from propositions of subject-predicate form, and the relation of meaning between the nominal and the proposition is quite regular." He writes further, "Gerundive nominalization involves a grammatical transformation from an underlying sentence structure. . . . The semantic interpretation of a gerundive nominalization is straightforward in terms of the grammatical relations of the underlying propositions in deep structure."[9]

Naturally, our quotations of Marcus and Chomsky represent something of an argument from authority, but we cannot hope in this context to summarize their findings, nor need we do so in order to render nominal extensionality plausible, and to show obstacles in the way of its denial.

A final consideration in favor of adopting our criterion of nominal extensionality as a test for extensionality is that it answers to our need for a criterion that will show that causal statements are not mind-dependent on the ground that they are not intensional. But, unless this consideration is successfully buttressed by the facts adduced above, it will have little force for those not already convinced of the extensionality of causal contexts. On the other hand, if this conviction can be suitably buttressed, we shall have an answer to Anscombe's original question. For we shall have not only a strong motive for the thesis of the extenionality of causal contexts, but a *good reason* as well.[10]

Notes

1. G. E. M. Anscombe, "Causality and Extensionality," *Journal of Philosophy* 66 (1969):155.

2. There is a powerful statement of this view in Hume's *Treatise* (Oxford, 1888), pp. 167–68: ". . . causes operate entirely independent of the mind, and would . . . continue their operation, even though there were no mind existent to contemplate them, or reason concerning them. Thought may well depend on causes for its operation, but not causes on thought. This is to reverse the order of nature, and make that secondary which is really primary . . . the operations of nature are independent of our thought and reasoning. . . ."

3. See N. R. Hanson, *Patterns of Discovery* (Cambridge, 1958), pp. 54, 58. This section is reprinted in *Philosophical Problems of Causation*, ed. T. L. Beauchamp (Encino, California, 1974), which also contains a critical examination of Hanson's views, "Vincula Revindicata," by Alexander Rosenberg and David Raybrooke; M. Scriven, "Causation as Explanation," *Nous* 9 (1975): 11; M. Beardsley, "Actions and Events: The Problem of Individuation," *American Philosophical Quarterly* 12 (1975):272; D. Davidson, "Causal Relations," *Journal of Philosophy* 64 (1967): 703.

4. See, for example, J. L. Mackie, "Causes and Conditions," *American Philosophical Quarterly* 2 (1965):327–36; S. Gorovitz, "Causal Judgments and Causal Explanations," *Journal of Philosophy* 62 (1965):695–711; A. Collins, "Explanation and Causality," *Mind* 75 (1966):482–500.

5. Føllesdaal seems committed to this conclusion on the strength of a similar argument in "Quantifying into Causal Context," *Boston Studies in the Philosophy of Science*, ed. Wartofsky and Cohen (New York, 1965), p. 264.

6. Gottlob Frege, *Philosophical Writings*, trans. Black and Geach, (Oxford, 1952), p. 77.

7. There is, of course, a well-known and very controversial argument to the effect that if a context is extensional, then it is truth-functional. This set-theoretical argument has its origins in the work of Frege, but its contemporary locus is W. V. O. Quine's "Three Grades of Modal Involvement," reprinted in *The Ways of Paradox* (New York, 1966). Quine employs the argument in advancing objections to modal logic, but its force has also been assessed with respect to causal statements by Anscombe, *Causality*, note 1, Føllesdaal, "Quantifying," note 6, and Davidson "Causal Relations," note 5. In this connection, the argument has been employed to show that since causal contexts are acknowledged to be non-truth-functional, it follows that they are not extensional for substitution of either predicates or terms. The argument has been criticized as invalid by Arthur Simullian, "Modality and Description," *Journal of Symbolic Logic* 13 (1948): 31–37, R. Cummins and D. Gottleib, "On an Argument for Truth-Functionality," *American Philosophical Quarterly* 9 (1972):256–59, and by J. L. Mackie, *Cement of the Universe* (Oxford, 1974), chapter 10. These authors have, in Mackie's words, "drawn the claws of an argument to which excessive deference has been shown" (p. 254).

8. Ruth Barcan Marcus, "Extensionality," *Mind* 69 (1969):55–62, reprinted in *Reference and Modality*, ed. L. Linsky (Oxford, 1971), p. 46.

9. N. Chomsky, "Remarks on Nominalization," *Studies on Semantics in Generative Grammar* (Hague, 1972), p. 16.

10. The authors wish to acknowledge special debts for comments on previous versions of this paper to Jaegwon Kim, Terence Tomkow, and Lawrence Lombard. However, no agreement with any of these views should be attributed to them.

The Extensionality of
Causal Contexts:
Comments on Rosenberg and Martin

LAWRENCE BRIAN LOMBARD

I

It is a very good thing to ask why we, if we do, continue to believe that causal contexts are extensional. This question needs asking and answering, but not because we might entertain doubts about the extensionality of causal contexts; for we know, as Quine and Anscombe point out, and Rosenberg and Martin remind us,[1] that we can defend that thesis come what potential counterexample may. The turning away of putative counterexamples comes *after* we see a motive for turning them away, a motive which shows why the thesis itself is worthy of being defended against such examples. So the answering of the original question will show us just what that motive is. And, further, it will undoubtedly, as can be seen from Rosenberg's and Martin's discussion, teach us a great deal about the thesis being defended.

Another reason for asking and answering this question stems from the very way Professors Rosenberg and Martin have chosen to deal with the issue. Their strategy is most interesting; it forces the issue and it is the right strategy. Their strategy consists, in part, of pressing the similarities between causal contexts and explanatory contexts, almost to the point where one begins to wonder, as others have, why anyone would believe what is clearly true, namely, that explanatory contexts are *not* extensional, and yet also believe causal contexts *are* extensional. It is pointed out that, in an important sense, explanatory contexts are the "closest" of all non-extensional contexts to causal contexts. That is, causal contexts are more like explanatory ones than they are like epistemic, psychological, modal, and quotational contexts—largely, I take it, because of the sorts of entities spoken of in such contexts. Thus, it is conjectured, if causal contexts fail to be extensional, they will fail to be so for the *same* reason that explanatory ones fail to be so. But then it is argued that the feature of explanatory contexts that makes them non-extensional is a feature which is lacking in causal contexts. If so, and if no other intensionality-producing feature is seen in causal contexts, then a powerful reason will have been given for thinking that causal contexts are extensional, and there will be a strong motive for defending that claim against potential counterexamples, however persuasive or recherché.

409

This strategy seems to me to be just the one we needed. And Rosenberg and Martin are owed a debt by all of us who worry about this problem for making us see the problem in this light. I think, however, that they have lighted upon the wrong differential feature.

II

Rosenberg's and Martin's claims are that explanatory contexts are "mind-dependent" and that that fact accounts for their intensionality. Explanatory contexts are mind-dependent, they suggest, in the sense that "the truth value of a sentence reporting an explanatory relation between two items rests on the existence of particular beliefs about the items, the terms by which they are described, and the connection between items of the kind under which their descriptions bring the items." (p. 402). Their example is this:

(1) Oedipus's marrying his mother explains his subsequent madness.

(1), they claim, is true and is mind-dependent, presumably because its truth rests, at least in part, on there being a belief (whose?) that marrying one's mother is the sort of occurrence that does (at least sometimes) lead to deleterious psychological consequences. The result, however, of replacing the phrase 'his mother' by the name 'Jocasta' or the term 'Laius's widow' turns (1) into a falsehood, for there is no (widespread?) belief that such events as marrying Jocasta or Laius's widow (by Oedipus?), so described, lead to madness. On the other hand, the truth value of causal sentences, such as 'Oedipus's marrying his mother caused his subsequent madness', does not depend on belief in this or in any other way (see p. 402). So, it is argued, in this way, that the differential feature is mind-dependence; explanatory contexts have it, causal ones do not, and since there is apparently no other relevant feature that would account for the non-extensionality of causal contexts, causal contexts are extensional.

But this account of the intensionality of explanatory contexts seems to me to be wrong. In the first place, (1) seems to be false. What explains Oedipus's madness is not his marrying his mother, but *his coming to believe* that that is what he did in marrying Jocasta. Had he not come to have that belief, he would not have gone mad. He would not have gone mad, unless, for example, the gods saw that that is what he did, got annoyed, and made him mad—but in that case (1) would be false anyway. Still, *ceterus parabus*, he would not have gone mad if he had not acquired the belief that he had married his mother. And that is so, because, say, there is some psychological theory connecting one's belief that one has married incestuously, feelings of guilt, and madness as a result of failure to cope with such guilt. If people did not feel something like guilt (either consciously or unconsciously) when they discovered that they had married incestuously, they would not go mad, at least not for having so married. We cannot be asked to believe that one will go mad simply as a result of marrying one's mother. So the correct explanation of Oedipus's madness is *not* his marrying his mother.

So what? So we replace (1) by (1'):

(1') Oedipus's coming to believe that he had married his mother explains his subsequent madness.

(1') is still intensional; for replacement of 'his mother' by 'Jocasta' or by 'Laius's widow' turns (1') from a truth to a falsehood. But is (1') mind-dependent in the way Rosenberg and Martin suggest? Does the truth of (1') rest on anyone's belief in a psychological theory connecting awareness of incestuous marriage and madness (so described)? No, I think it does not! It is true that one's *acceptance* of (1') as a truth may rest on one's belief that there is such a theory. But there merely being such a true theory is enough for the truth of (1'), acceptance or rejection notwithstanding. The truth of "the failure to seal the pipe's pieces together securely explains the seeping of the oil" does not depend in any way on anyone's belief in a connection between faulty pipe seals and oil leaks; it depends on their being such a connection. To be a correct explanation is not necessarily to be an explanation that, in fact, quells doubts or satisfies one's desire to know why.

I am inclined to conjecture that the claim that explanatory contexts are mind-dependent is motivated by examples like (1), where the case seems plausible. And it seems plausible because it is easy to believe that one cannot marry one's mother without coming to believe that that is what one has done, and because it is natural to think that one has not explained anything to an audience unless it comes to believe that it has understood something. But both of these inclinations are wrong. Of course, one cannot explain, say, why Oedipus went mad, unless one has some theory, however rudimentary, in mind. But that cannot make explanatory contexts mind-dependent; for, similarly, one cannot assert that grass is green unless one has a belief about colors; but that does not make color contexts mind-dependent. If all this is right, then explanatory contexts are not intensional because mind-dependent. But then what does explain the intensionality of explanatory contexts and the extensionality of causal ones?

III

This question is made especially difficult because, as Rosenberg and Martin suggest, we do ordinarily speak of events and facts explaining other events and facts, and that too is the way we sometimes, in everyday speech, speak of the causal relation. That is, so far as the surface appearance of explanatory and causal statements is concerned, they may sometimes look virtually indistinguishable. The same sorts of grammatical constructions can flank both the verb 'explains' and 'causes' (see (1) above, for example); and 'because' often replaces both these verbs (when the flanking constructions are sentential), though, perhaps, not in the same cases. So, the absence of a distinguishing surface feature drives one to look for something hidden—for example, mind-dependence. But, here, reliance on similarity of surface appearance leads to trouble. Let me illustrate with another, but related, aspect of Rosenberg's and Martin's paper.

Rosenberg and Martin attempt (p. 404) to save the extensionality of a *causal* reading of a statement such as:

(2) The Titanic sank because it struck an iceberg on April 14, 1912,

from assault owing to the failure of (2) to retain its truth value when co-extensive predicates are substituted for 'struck an iceberg on April 14, 1912'. The salvaging is achieved by introducing an apparently suspicious revision of the usual principle of extensionality, and by going to some lengths to defend the legitimacy of revising such a principle. The revised principle, the Principle of Nominal Extensionality, says that a sentential context (such as that involved in (2)) is extensional if the references of the gerundive nominalizations of the contained sentences remain the same when substitutions of co-referential singular terms or co-extensive predicates are made for the singular terms or predicates that appear in the contained sentences. This revised principle is suspicious, first, because it looks *ad hoc*. It is suspicious, in the second place, because, despite whatever truth there is to the claim that there is no unique criterion of extensionality, its introduction seems to change the subject. After all, our original concern was over the extensionality of causal and explanatory contexts, where the notion of extensionality that occasioned the inquiry was the usual one, substitutability *salva veritate* of co-referential singular terms (and co-extensive predicates) in the sentence whose extensionality is in question. And, finally, it is suspicious simply, I think, because it is a revision of a principle that ought not to need revision. Still, in spite of these misgivings, the revised principle is an absolutely correct principle to employ in testing the extensionality of a sentence like (2). And it is instructive, I think, to ask why that is so.

I suggest that the reason why the criterion provided by the Principle of Nominal Extensionality, and not that provided by a more customary extensionality principle, is the right one to apply to sentences such as (2) (as it appears) is simply that to apply the test of nominal extensionality to (2) as it appears is just to apply the usual test of extensionality once one has properly understood (2)'s logical form. And the reason for that is that (2) is being understood by Rosenberg and Martin (see the first paragraph of section II of their paper) as *causal*. And the causal relation is one that holds between *events*. If so, then insofar as (2) asserts a causal relation to hold between two events, the "real" form of (2) must be something like this:

(2′) The sinking of the Titanic was caused by the striking of an iceberg by the Titanic on April 14, 1912.

But, then, the suspicious test of nominal extensionality applied to (2) just is the usual test of extensionality applied to (2′), because *the event-describing terms of (2′) are just the gerundive nominalizations of the sentential components of (2)*. The test of nominal extensionality is merely the test of regular extensionality applied to a sentence before one gets at its logical form. Nominal extensionality works here because it combines a test for regular extensionality with a covert transformation of the sentence tested to its true form.

In considering a proposal of the sort I have just made, Rosenberg and Martin say the following (p. 405):

Although attractive and plausible, the trouble with this approach is that it ties the thesis of extensionality . . . to issues in metaphysics of the broadest kind, and provides sentence-taking causal contexts with nothing like the direct and more formal test of extensionality that term-taking causal contexts pass. Its plausibility . . . rests entirely on the strength of arguments claiming that their [sentence-taking causal contexts] logical form differs from their apparent form, for considerations that transcend issues in the philosophy of language alone. A more convincing argument for the extensionality of such causal contexts would show that, without appeal to underlying logical form, these sentences pass a test for extensionality that paradigm cases of intensional sentence-taking contexts do not pass.

Frankly, I find this response unsatisfactory; and my reasons are these.

The question, Is the sentence

(3) Jones believes that the F is G

extensional or not?, is, in an important sense, ill-formed. We do not know how to begin to answer it without first inquiring as to whether (3) is to be understood with 'the F' as having large or small scope. Once that issue is settled, then we can answer our original question, (3) is extensional when 'the F' has large scope and intensional if 'the F' has small scope. But unless that issue is settled, we do not know what inference is in question; and that is what the question of extensionality was all about. Are we worrying about this inference:

(4) Jones believes that there is a unique F which is G
   the unique F = the unique H
   ∴ Jones believes that there is a unique H which is G.

or about this one:

(5) There is a unique F and Jones believes about it that it is G
   the unique F = the unique H
   ∴ There is a unique H and Jones believes about it that it is G?

Until that question is resolved, we do not know what to say about (3)'s extensionality. For (3) is not extensional or intensional except as interpreted as having some particular logical form. No sentence's extensionality is subject to a "direct" test, unless it wears its logical form on its sleeve; but whether or not that is the case is not a matter of "direct" inspection. Now up to this stage, the issue of the extensionality of sentences involves only considerations that are semantic or interpretive. But we are not far from matters metaphysical. For if (3), for example, is so taken that 'the F' has large scope, and if, in addition, (3) is, so interpreted, true, then one cannot escape concluding that there is such a thing as the F.

Similarly, the issue of the extensionality of (2) only arises, as Rosenberg and Martin raise the issue, because (2) is being construed as a sentence-taking *causal* sentence. After all, construed as explanatory, it is obviously not extensional. To construe (2) as causal is, I insist, to say that (2)'s apparent form is not its real form, since its apparent form reveals nothing of its causal subject matter. To construe (2) as causal is, I presume, to construe it as about events [thus (2′)]. If so, then no test of extensionality that relies on (2)'s apparent form is of any interest; and indeed, I tried to show that nominal extensionality does not so rely. But whether or not logical form is apparent or hidden is not the point. The point is that we cannot make serious sense at all of talk of extensionality apart from talk of logical form. For extensionality is a matter of the validity of certain inferences, and questions of validity involve questions of form. Validity, after all, is just truth due to form.

Again, I see no clear way to keep metaphysical issues entirely divorced from such semantical considerations. For once the question of form is settled, the truth of sentences with such a form may imply the existence of certain entities. This is particularly true when matters of extensionality are involved; one need only remind oneself of the lengths to which some philosophers, at work on the semantics of sentences about propositional attitudes, go to avoid so construing such sentences that their truth implies the existence of propositions. Indeed, it seems to me that only by bringing in metaphysical considerations can we begin to see how to sort out some of the issues concerning the extensionality of causal contexts and the intensionality of explanatory ones. It is with a brief sketch of what I have in mind by this last remark that I would like to conclude these remarks.

IV

Both causal and explanatory statements can employ, on their surfaces, both fact— and event-like expressions. That and the fact that we often explain by talking about causes account for the intuition that explanatory context the "closest" among the intensional ones to causal contexts. But the differences emerge at a deeper level, and the differences explain why explanatory contexts are intensional.

Whatever it is that explains why *Mary* (as opposed to Jane) stole the bicycle explains neither why Mary *stole* (as opposed to borrowed) the bicycle nor why Mary stole the *bicycle* (as opposed to the pogo stick).[2] And this is true despite the fact that the gerundive nominalizations of all three versions of "Mary stole the bicycle" are the same, namely, "The stealing of the bicycle by Mary." If she stole that bicycle only once, there is, I insist, only one event that was the stealing of the bicycle by Mary. Why then will not one explanans explain all three explananda? The reason, in this case, is that what gets explained is *not* the occurrence of an event that in fact has a certain feature, but rather the *fact* that that event has that feature. That it was *Mary* who performed that action, that that action was *stealing*, and that what was stolen was a *bicycle* are different facts about different features of Mary's stealing of the bicycle. This must be what lies behind the idea that "events explain other events *only under a description*"; though describing is an activity that is mind-dependent, explaining, in this case, is explaining that an event is describable in a certain way, and describability is not a mind-dependent idea. The point is that insofar as it makes sense to speak of explaining an event, by talking about another, the sense it makes is, perhaps, this: there is some law or generalization that says that events with certain features are correlated with events that have certain other features. So, to explain an event's occurrence or its having a certain feature is to show that the explanans-event has a feature which some generalization says is a feature of events that are correlated with events that have some other feature, a feature had, in fact, by the explanandum-event. [When we explain the occurrence of an event by saying that it occurred because this other event occurred, we only succeed in explaining because there is some generalization that deals with features of the cause and of the effect. But it should be noticed that 'e occurred because e' occurred' is straighforwardly extensional.] What explain and get explained are the facts about things, not things themselves. Thus, it is not surprising to find that substitution of co-referential event-denoting terms, or of co-extensive predicates of things that change, or of materially equivalent event-reporting sentences, does not necessarily preserve the truth-value of the explanatory sentences in which such expressions appear. For in preserving reference to the requisite entities, the features, the having of which by an event was to be explained and in terms of which the event is described, may no longer be the features in terms of which the event is described after the substitutions are made. What get explained are facts; and in redescribing an *event* we may describe it in terms of different *facts* about it. [Similar remarks apply to the explanans.]

But what causes events to occur causes them to occur with all of their features. To cause a ship to sink is to cause an ugly or a well-built ship to sink (if the ship is ugly or well-built) and to cause a ship to sink is to cause it to sink rapidly or fifty miles from the nearest restaurant (if that is how or where the ship sinks). Causation is a relation between events; explanation relates facts. That is why causal contexts are extensional and explanatory ones are not, in spite of the similarities in the ways in which we express causal and explanatory relations. It is just that it is hard to mention events without mentioning some facts about them and hard to mention facts about events without mentioning the events about which they are facts.

Notes

*A version of this paper was originally read as a comment on an earlier version of Rosenberg's and Martin's paper, "The Extensionality of Causal Contexts," which was presented at the Western Division Meetings of the APA, in April 1977.

1. Alexander Rosenberg and Robert M. Martin, "The Extensionality of Causal Contexts," pp. 000-00, this volume.

2. See F. Dretske's, "Referring to Events," *Midwest Studies in Philosophy* 2 (1977).

The Concern to Survive

DAVID WIGGINS

1. Under the influence of certain thought experiments[1] modern inheritors of Locke's conception of personhood have recently been led to draw a distinction between questions of identity of a person and questions about survival. "Certain important questions [about such matters as survival, memory, and responsibility] do presuppose a question about personal identity. But they can be freed of this presupposition. And when they are, the question about identity has no importance."[2] "We can, I think, describe cases in which, though we know how to answer every other question, we have no idea how to answer a question about personal identity. . . . Do they present a problem? It might be thought that they do not, because they could never occur. I suspect that some of them could. . . . But I shall claim that even if they did they would present no problem."[3]

2. I have attempted in another place[4] some reassessment of the thought experiments that prompted Derek Parfit to draw these strange and disturbing conclusions. I have also suspected sometimes that Parfit's conception of the identity relation rests on a rejection of the idea, which to me at least seems overwhelmingly plausible,[5] that the predicate 'is the same as' is as primitive and irreducible as any other predicate that one can think of. But my present question is neither the status of thought experiments involving the putative division of persons, nor the nature of identity (whether, as Parfit puts it, identity can be "a further fact" of some matter[6]). It is the separability that Parfit alleges of questions of survival from questions of identity—and not even the whole of that issue.

What I want principally to discuss is the separability of two *concerns*—the separability, for instance, of a man's 31st December 1978 concern to survive until 31st December 1990 at least and the concern that such a man has on 31st December 1978 that, at every moment between then and 31st December 1990 at least, there should exist something identical with him. I concede that, even as regards survival, this separability or inseparability is only one small part of what needs to be discussed; but nobody can judge my question irrelevant who undertakes, as Parfit did,[7] to reach out to our actual concern with death or to distinguish in theory between a legitimate apprehension that lurks in fear of death and something supposedly less rational therein, having to do with identity. Where this is what Parfit set out to do, it cannot be a question of simply no importance how faithful his conception of survival is to the actual phenomenology of the concern to survive. I shall contend that it is not faithful. But I shall not attempt to estimate here just how much damage this does to Parfit's main contentions—e.g., the contention that, if cases of division of persons are both conceivable and actual, then "that presents no problem." It will be obvious, however, that this last is a contention with which I think there is reason to disagree; and it will become almost equally obvious that I write from the general position of one who holds that, although experiential memory is one component in an inner nucleus of conceptual constituents of what it is for a person to continue to exist (to persist), there is no necessary or sufficient condition of identity through time that we can formulate in terms of experiential memory.

Insofar as there is some general disagreement between Parfit and myself then, it is about the importance of identity in the philosophy of persons, and about the relation between identity and mental connectedness, not about whether importance attaches to mental connectedness. The disagreement is a disagreement within the class of friends of mental connectedness who see much to applaud in Locke's definition of a person as "a thinking intelligent being that has reason and reflection, and can consider itself as itself, the same thinking thing in different times and places."[8] It must be that there are corrections that Parfit would urge Locke to make to this chapter. But the chief correction I myself should press upon Locke is only to stipulate that x is a person if and only if x belongs to an *animal kind* whose *normal* members have reason and reflection, and can each consider itself as itself, the same thinking thing. . . .

3. These convictions have been rehearsed only in order to set the general scene for the dispute. This is not the place to try to give the reasons I have for them, and I shall say no more of them now. What I want to argue here is much more briefly stated. Suppose I express the fervent and enduring wish to survive until 1990 at least. Then, so far from its being possible (as a pure mental connectedness account of survival would hold that it was possible) to separate my concern that there should exist something identical with me at every moment between now and 1990 from my concern that my mental life should flow on under the cognitive and affective influence of my present memories, beliefs, and character (even as these themselves evolve between now and 1990)—so far from this separation being possible—, I hold that absolutely any adequate description of the second concern will have to presuppose the validity and importance of the first one. According to me, this presupposition between the two things arises from something central to the phenomenology of these matters—something whose elimination or modification cannot be relied upon to leave undisturbed the desire itself to survive into the future. This last desire is not, I claim, a thing that we can treat as a brute datum. It comes with thoughts and conceptions that require philosophical attention and description; and some of

these thoughts and conceptions have a content that involves identity inextricably. That at least is the thesis to be defended here.

4. The first deficiency I find in the opposing pure mental connectedness account of survival and the concern for survival is that it ignores or redescribes the fact that consideration of who and what he is, or what value he puts upon himself, is sometimes crucial to a man in deliberations about life and death. If a man dislikes himself very much, that may diminish his desire to survive (or may diminish it subject only to the countervailing influence of fear of the alternative). Again, an unassuming man in a setting of domestic peace who finds himself faced with a choice between a dangerous act of heroism and living out his days in what he will conceive as dishonor may well come to value simple survival far less highly than he previously did. To describe what happens here we need to see the issue of survival as the issue of the survival of a *continuant* that can be assessed in certain relevant ways. We shall return to this probelm at the end of Section 8 below. But at least as I see it, the question is one of what substitution the mental connectedness theorist can make for this man's preoccupation with *what* would survive if he were to take the easy way out.

5. Next I think we must consider consciousness and survival, and the requirement that the mental connectedness theorist will make that the person who survives should know in 1990 that he has got what he wished for in 1978 and should remember his wishing to survive that long. There is something very plausible in this. But let us approach it by way of the question of desiring things in the future perfectly in general.

Men care about all sorts of future things that they know they will never know about. A grandparent of eighty may care now in 1978 about what his eight-year-old grandchild's life will be like in the 21st century. Normally when we care about something, we value highly the opportunity to know how matters turn out. But the concern to know is surely separable in principle from the concern for the thing itself. It is true that a grandparent who was offered by some magic the opportunity to live into the 21st century in order to witness the life and fortunes of his grandchild would have to see that there was *something* to value in this opportunity—that to the extent that he cared about his grandchild, he would have to regard it as at least in some respect a good thing to be able to know of his grandchild's fortunes. Nevertheless, before he made the choice whether to live that long or not, he would have to weigh in the balance the fact that he might lapse into the condition of a Struldbrug in the interim, or that by the year 2000 he might be blind, feeble-minded, and incontinent. In itself, the concern for the grandchild's future is not conditional on *knowing* anything at all about the actual outcome. *A fortiori* it is not conditional on any mental or cognitive connectedness between the wishing and the fulfillment of the wish.

6. This is the normal case, but no doubt there is something very special about knowing about the satisfaction of one's own wish to survive. That which is special about this is indeed one part of the foundation of the pure mental connectedness theory

of survival. What would it be to live up to 1990 and not know that in doing so one had got what one wished? Surely, it will be said, life without the experiential memory required to remember the wish of 1978 (or any similar and subsequent wishes to survive) is survival as a mere vegetable, not as a person. That is what will be said by most neo-Lockean philosophers, and it is well known where the thought leads. It leads to that which leads in the end to the pure mental connectedness theory. But there is an alternative answer to the question, and this explains no worse than the theory of mental connectedness the intuitions that underlie the Lockean position. The alternative answer is that this sort of survival would not be the survival of enough of what is presupposed to that which made one value onself and one's own continued life as dearly as one did. What made me dear to myself and fond of myself, what made me into something I thought it was *worth* caring about the survival of – surely this required and presupposed my still having my faculties at least.

7. At this point one may muster the courage to ask the question what is so good, either absolutely or for me, about my own mental life's flowing on from now into the future. Surely this depends on what kind of person I am or think I am, and what sort of mental life it is. Well, not quite. There is something instinctive here and as irreducible as the commitment (where it exists) to make prudent provision for the future. These are things that we need reasons to opt out of rather than things that we have to look for deep reasons to opt into. That is how human rationality is. It involves these things constitutively. The instinct for survival has played its part in the determination of what we mean by "rational." But what is the content of the said instinct? The content is surely that this animal that is *identical with me* should not cease to be, but should survive and flourish.

8. Of the two answers implied by Section 7 above to the question what (when uncertainty is left out of account) is bad about death, it may seem, nevertheless, that the more rational answer is the former answer, carrying with it my idea of myself as a continuant with certain moral or aesthetic qualities that command my allegiance. If so, then one is bound to wonder how a man who survives, and gets that which, in wanting to survive, he envisaged himself having, will actually conceive of that survival. One natural answer will be that he envisages this as the persistence of a certain bearer of a certain range of predicates that are irreducibly mental. Such is the answer that is suggested by Strawson's thesis of the primitiveness of the concept of a person. (A thesis that can be cited here without any commitment to the particular details of the account given in *Individuals*[9] of the principles of the distinction between M- and P-predicates, without commitment to the disjointness of these ranges, and without commitment to deny that the mental predicates are indirectly body-involving.) Indeed this will be *the* natural answer, provided that we are prepared to allow that Strawson's thesis either recapitulates or at the very least organizes our actual conception of what a person is. But I think that Strawson's thesis does effect some such recapitulation of that conception, and that it is susceptible also of a further development that will enable us to see the body-involving non-mental properties of a person as integral to the proper expression of his mental

properties. I readily concede that the full answer to Parfit (which will extend much more widely than I propose that this note should) will not be complete without this further development and will require its application to the content of this person's concern that this person should survive. But here I will add only that, on the theoretical (non-phenomenological) plane, the thesis of the primitiveness of the concept of *person* has another relevant virtue. It structures the dispute we find here in philosophy.

Abandoning Strawson's even-handed treatment of the two ranges of predicate and shifting the emphasis onto one or the other of the two classes of predicate, we arrive at two twin deviations. By relegating body-involving predicates, predicates of the whole organism as an organism, to secondary status and demoting some to unimportance, we arrive at Parfit's identity-free conception of survival. By promoting the predicates involving the whole organism as an organism to special prominence, we arrive at Bernard Williams's equally notorious and surprising suggestion[10] that one exists so long as one's whole body exists, and that whatever one is or does one's body is or does.[11]

9. The Strawsonian answer is the natural answer, I hold, to the question how the person who wants to survive envisages his survival. What does the theorist of mental connectedness who proposes that we dispense with identity want to substitute for this? Either he substitutes nothing, because he regards the desire to survive as a brute datum (but is is not); or else he substitutes for the Strawsonian conception of survival a conception of the continuation of a certain line of consciousness. But here we must ask: ought this new idea to command the same allegiance? *Would* it indeed command it — once it was appreciated that metaphysical reality was being held to require that we substitute for an ontology of persons an ontology of mental events, and once it was appreciated that within this new ontology there is no real room for the idea of an individual biography? Indeed so soon as we try to make room within it even for a *line* of consciousness linking mental events, and to reconstruct the evaluation of persons in terms of the evaluation of such lines, we restore identity itself to the content of the concern to survive, contrary to Parfit's intention.

Surely it was, in the first place, some allegiance to the idea of an individual biography that made Locke's conception of persons interesting to us. It was some chord that this struck in us that made mental connectedness seem important. But if so, any theorist of mental connectedness who has come to the point of desperation where he is preparing to sacrifice the notion of an articulated, indefinitely amplifiable, individual biography has cut off the very branch he was sitting on.

10. It is important not to confuse the considerations that I have just urged with the prediction that, if a man were told that tomorrow there would certainly be nobody who was him, then he would decline all offers to the effect that, if only he assented to this, it would be arranged that there would be people tomorrow who bore to him Parfit's relation of mental connectedness. The prediction that this would be refused is no doubt false in many cases. But it is irrelevant. For it is not obvious that a man's

acceptance of the offer would tell us anything at all about that which motivated the original desire to survive—the desire as that exists among actual human beings.

When the desire not to cease to exist comes to accept its own long-term futility, it can be commuted into all sorts of distinctively different sorts of desire to *leave traces*: to be remembered by one's pupils or to live on in one's works. "And now thou art lying, my dear old Carian guest, / A handful of grey ashes, long, long ago at rest, / Still are thy pleasant voices, thy nightingales awake; / For Death, he taketh all away, but them he cannot take." Callimachus (trans. Cory). Again the desire to leave traces can take the form of desiring that some little good one did be not instantly eroded or that someone somewhere learn something from what one learned oneself the hard way. These things can be desired for themselves, but they can also appear as sublimations of the desire not to cease to exist. They are typical accommodations to the certainty of death. To me at least it is not clear how much more there would be to the possession of mentally connected descendants than there is to these more etiolated forms of survival. Indeed I think that I myself prefer the more etiolated forms. What I am certain about is that I do not see how the offer of any of these things, Parfitian *or* etiolated, can be taken for a proper surrogate (equivalent on the level of imagination, conception, and desire) for the continued existence of the one and only person that is me. Unless, of course, I no longer want that continued existence—in which case the etiolated forms of survival are again not equal or tantamount, but simply better. They are no effort and, with care, it might be arranged that they were at least to some extent private.

11. I have already stressed that this note is not to be confused with the whole of a response to Parfit's article on personal identity. But I hope that I have said enough to suggest why it is not as easy as he has sometimes suggested it is to purify our actual concerns of every taint of the personal identity concept, and then persevere in —or "identify ourselves" with—the purified desires that emerge.

Notes

1. Sidney Shoemaker, *Self Knowledge and Self Identity* (Ithaca, 1963), p. 22; David Wiggins, *Identity and Spatiotemporal Continuity* (Oxford, 1967), p. 50; Derek Parfit, "Personal Identity," *Philosophical Review* 80 (1970):5.

2. *Identity and Spatiotemporal Continuity*, p. 4.

3. "Personal Identity," p. 3.

4. David Wiggins, *Sameness and Substance* (Oxford, 1979), Chapters 3 and 6.

5. *Ibid.*, Chapter 2, Section 1, and *Longer Notes* 2.30, 3.19, 4.02.

6. I doubt that we really know what it is to describe a case for which we know how to answer *every question*, or *every question except one*. Certainly no such case ever presents itself in concrete reality.

7. "Personal Identity," pp. 3 and 27.

8. John Locke, *An Essay Concerning Human Understanding*, Essay II, xxvii, 11.

9. P. F. Strawson, *Individuals* (London, 1956).

10. Bernard Williams, "Are Persons Bodies?" in *Problems of the Self* (Cambridge, 1973).

11. *Identity and Spatiotemporal Continuity*, p. 45, *Sameness and Substance*, Chapter 6, Section 6. I am now content to allow the second (predicability) point to settle the less important (and surely vague) question of how long a person continues to exist.

Analyticity and Apriority:
Beyond Wittgenstein and Quine

HILARY PUTNAM

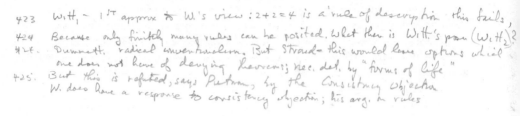
B oth Wittgenstein and Quine have had important insights in connection with the nature of mathematical and logical "necessity," and both have written things that have transformed the discussion of this topic. But it is the burden of this paper to show that the views of both are unacceptable as they stand. I hope that a short and sharp statement of why both sorts of views will not do may help take us to a new stage in the discussion.

PART I: WHY MATHEMATICAL NECESSITY IS NOT EXPLAINED BY HUMAN NATURE, "FORMS OF LIFE," ETC.

Wittgensteinian Views

Just *what* Wittgenstein's contention is, in connection with philosophers opinions, theories, and arguments on the topic of "mathematical necessity," has been a subject of considerable controversy. Clearly he thinks the whole discussion is nonsensical and confused; but *why* (in his view) it is nonsensical and confused, and whether he offers any explanation at all of why we *think* there is such a thing as mathematical necessity and of what the difference is between mathematical and empirical statements, is a subject on which there seems to be a great deal of disagreement among his interpreters.

I shall not attempt to do any textual exegesis here. I know what the (several) views of *Wittgensteinians* are, even if I do not know for sure which, if any, was Wittgenstein's; and what I shall try to show is that not even the most sophisticated of these "Wittgensteinian" views is tenable.

Here is a first approximation to Wittgenstein's view: when we make a mathematical assertion, say "2 + 2 = 4," the "necessity" of this assertion is accounted for by the fact that we would not *count* anything as a counterexample to the statement. The

W.'s view Capprox

423

statement is not a "description" of any fact, but a "rule of description"—that is, a directive to the effect that cases in which we *seem* to add two things to two things and get five, or whatever, are to be explained away (e.g., by saying that a fifth thing must have been produced by the interaction). In a terminology employed by other philosophers, the statement is *analytic*.

The problem with such views—a problem Wittgenstein himself clearly points out, which is why the above cannot be more than a *first approximation* to Wittgenstein's view—is that the set of theorems of mathematics is infinite (or appears to be infinite—I shall explain the reservation shortly). Only a finite number of mathematical truths, e.g., "2 + 2 = 4," "every number has a successor," can possibly be *primitive* rules of description (be what Carnap called "Meaning Postulates"); most mathematical truths are not *directly* meaning stipulations, or "rules of description," or whatever, but only *consequences* of "rules of description."

Now, the thesis that every theorem of mathematics is either true by convention (a Meaning Postulate, in Carnap's sense, or a "rule of description" in Wittgenstein's) or else a *consequence* of statements that are true by convention has often been advanced as an *epistemologically explanatory* thesis (e.g., by Ayer in *Language, Truth, and Logic* and Carnap in the *Foundations of Logic and Mathematics*), but it cannot really explain the truth of the theorems of mathematics (*other* than the ones in the finite set that are *directly* "true by convention") at all, for a reason pointed out by both Wittgenstein and Quine: namely, *it takes logic to derive the consequences from the conventions*. The "exciting" thesis that logic is true by convention reduces to the unexciting claim that *logic is true by conventions plus logic*. No real advance has been made. *one could claim a 'reduction' of math. to logic, from this position*

What then was Wittgenstein's view? Call the Wittgenstein who held (or seemed to hold) that "2 + 2 = 4" is true by convention (a "rule of description") "Wittgenstein₁." Call the Wittgenstein who pointed out the emptiness of the Ayer-Carnap position "Wittgenstein₂." What could Wittgenstein₂'s position have been? (Not to mention Wittgenstein₃, Wittgenstein₄, . . .)

Michael Dummet suggested a daring possibility: namely, that Wittgenstein was a *radical conventionalist*.[1] That is, Wittgenstein was a conventionalist who held not just that some finite set of Meaning Postulates is true by convention, but that whenever we accept what we call a "proof" in logic or mathematics, an *act of decision* is involved: a decision to *accept* the proof. This decision, on Dummett's reading, is never *forced* on us by some prior thing called the "concepts" or "the meaning of the words"; even given these *as they have previously been specified*, it is still *up to us* whether we shall accept the proof as a valid deployment of those concepts or not. The decision to accept the proof is a *further* meaning stipulation: the "theorems of mathematics and logic" that we actually prove and accept are not just *consequences* of conventions, but *individually* conventional. Such a "radical" conventionalism, Dummett pointed out, would be immune to the Quine-Wittgenstein objection to the Ayer-Carnap sort of conventionalism.

In response, Barry Stroud pointed out[2] that the position Dummett calls, "radical conventionalism" cannot possibly be Wittgenstein's. A convention, in the literal sense, is something we can legislate either way. Wittgenstein does not anywhere say or suggest that the mathematician proving a theorem is *legislating* that it shall be a theorem (and the mathematician would get into a lot of trouble, to put it mildly, if he tried to "legislate" it the opposite way).

Basing himself on a good deal of textual evidence, Stroud suggested that Wittgenstein's position was that it is not *convention* or *legislation* but our *forms of life* (i.e., our human nature as determined by our biology-plus-cultural-history) that cause us to accept certain proofs *as* proofs. And Stroud's reply to Dummett's interpretation appears to have been generally accepted by Wittgenstein scholars.

The Consistency Objection

It appears to me that Stroud's reply, while correct as a response to Dummett's interpretation, does not speak to the real philosophical point Dummett was making. The real point is that if *either* Dummett *or* Stroud is right, then Wittgenstein is claiming that mathematical truth and necessity *arise in us*, that it is human nature and forms of life that *explain* mathematical truth and necessity. If this is right, then it is the greatest philosophical discovery of all time. Even if it is wrong, it is an astounding philosophical claim. If Stroud does not dispute that Wittgenstein advanced this claim —and he does not seem to dispute it—then *his* interpretation of Wittgenstein is a revision of Dummett's rather than a total rejection of it.

Unfortunately, there seems to be a devastating objection to Wittgenstein's position (i.e., to "Wittgenstein₂") if Stroud has really got him right: consider number theory (Peano arithmetic) in any of its standard formalizations. Even if our acceptance of the Peano axioms is just the acceptance of a bunch of *meaning determinations* (whether these be *stipulations*, i.e., acts of legislation, as on the "conventionalist" interpretation, or fixed by our "forms of life," as on Stroud's interpretation), still they are not *logically arbitrary* determinations, for they are, after all, required to be *consistent*. Our nature, our forms of life, etc., may explain why we *accept* the Peano axioms *as opposed to some other consistent set*; but our nature cannot possibly make an *inconsistent* set of axioms *true*. And consistency is an *objective mathematical fact*, not an *empirical* fact. Thus, there is at least *one* mathematical fact—namely the consistency of the meaning determinations themselves, *whatever* these be produced by—which is *not* explained by our nature or "forms of life" in any intelligible sense.

Sometimes the reply to this is merely the textual point that Wittgenstein poohpoohed consistency ("Why this *one* bug-a-boo?"), pointed out that an inconsistent system could still be usable (if one avoids drawing the contradiction), etc. But these remarks do not speak to the objection. Wittgenstein had better have something *better* than this to say in response to the objection or he is done for (as a philosopher of logic and mathematics).

And he does have something better than this to say. His *real* response to the consistency objection goes to the very depths of his philosophy, and without drawing it out, one cannot begin to do justice to his thought.

But, everyone agrees, consistency is tied to entailment. Putnam is just appealing to the notion he is trying to explain

Putnam conflates Wn-rules with the unfeasibility of an infinite process. Does Wittgenstein do this also?

stated always in mentalese

Wittgenstein on "Following a Rule"

Suppose I have a certain concept in my mind. Whatever introspectible *signs* there may be that I have the concept, whatever mental presentations I am able to call up in connection with the concept, cannot specify the *content* of the concept, as Wittgenstein argued in the famous sections of *Philosophical Investigations* which concern "following a rule"—say the rule "add one." For, if two species in two possible worlds (I state the argument in *most* un-Wittgensteinian terminology!) have the same mental signs in connection with the expression "add one," it is still possible that their *practice* might diverge; and it is the practice, as Wittgenstein shows, that fixes the *interpretation*; signs do not interpret themselves—not even mental signs. (Or, one might add for the benefit of physicalists like Hartry Field or David Lewis, signs in the brain). To take a simple example—a variant of Wittgenstein's own "add one" example—even if someone *pictures* the relation "C is the ponential of A and B" (i.e., C follows from A and B by *modus ponens*) in his mind just as we do and has agreed with us on finitely many cases, (e.g., that q is the ponential of $(pvr) \supset q$ and (pvr)), still he may have a divergent interpretation of "ponential of" which will only reveal itself in some future cases. (Even if he agrees with us in his "theory"—i.e., what he *says* about "ponential of"; for he may have a divergent interpretation of the whole theory, as the Skolem-Löwenheim theorem shows.)

The relevance of this to philosophy of mathematics is immediate. First of all, there is the question of *finitism*: human practice, actual and potential, only extends finitely far. We cannot "go on counting forever"—even if we *say* we can, not really. If there are possible *divergent extensions of our practice*, then there are possible *divergent interpretations of even the natural member sequence*—our practice, our mental representations, etc., do not (in set theoretic terminology) single out a unique "standard model" of even the natural number sequence. We are tempted to think they do because we easily shift from "we could go on counting" to "an *ideal machine* could go on counting" (or "an *ideal mind* could go on counting"); but talk of ideal machines (or minds) is very different, Wittgenstein reminds us, from talk of *actual* machines and persons. Talk of what an ideal machine could do is talk *within* mathematics; it cannot fix the interpretation *of* mathematics.

Second, if Wittgenstein is right (and I am presently inclined to think that he is), then the statement "there are seven consecutive sevens in the decimal expansion of π" may have *no* truth value—speaking set theoretically, it may be true in some models that fit our practice and false in others. And similarly, and for the same reason, "Peano arithmetic is consistent" may have *no* truth value—for this statement too talks about an infinite sequence (the sequence of *all* theorems of Peano arithmetic), and the sequence may not really be determinate. *shaky. A finite seq. could show inconsistency, and a finite sentence express it.*

Still, assuming some number—say 10^{20}—is small enough so that we could collectively and over time (perhaps several generations) examine all proofs with fewer than that number of symbols, the question "Is Peano arithmetic 10^{20}-consistent?" should have a determinate answer even on Wittgenstein's view.

not plausible

Why Wittgenstein's View Does Not Work

To see why Wittgenstein's view does not work, it is necessary to resolve an ambiguity in the view. It is true (and, as we have conceded, it is also a profound observation) that even so simple an operation as *modus ponens* is not "fixed" once and for all by our mental representation of the operation; it is our actual "unpacking" of the mental representation in action, our *de facto* dispositions which determine what we *mean* by "ponential of." But there are two "scenarios" as to *how* our dispositions might determine the extension of "ponential of." *Scenario* (1): Given a putative proof (with less than 10^{20} symbols) one checks it by going down line by line, verifying that each line with *ax* next to it is an axiom, and that each line with two-numbers (n) (m) next to it is the ponential of the lines numbered (n), (m) respectively. If the last line is "$1 = 0$," one announces "Peano Arithmetic has turned out to be inconsistent." *Scenario* (2): Given a putative proof (with less than 10^{20} symbols) one proceeds as in scenario (1) *except that* if *any* line is "$1 = 0$" (or anything verifiably false by just elementary calculation and truth-functional logic), then one *modifies what counts as ponential* so that the line in question is said *not* to be the ponential of the relevant lines (n), (m).

Both scenarios are logically possible. And if our actual dispositions were as described in scenario (2), then Peano Arithmetic would certainly be consistent in the absolute sense, and this consistency would *arise from us*, be explained by our nature (our dispositions) in a clear sense. But the actual scenario, the scenario that describes the dispositions we actually *have*, is scenario (1). And *that* scenario does not "build in" absolute consistency. Perhaps "ponential of" is only defined "finitistically" in the way we described in the preceding section; perhaps the extension of "ponential of" is not *fixed* in the case of proofs and formulas that are beyond human and machine reach; certainly, in the cases where it *is* fixed, it is fixed only by our dispositions and not just by the thought-signs in our minds or the representations in our brains; *but the 10^{20}-consistency of Peano Arithmetic is still not an artifact of this dispositionally fixed interpretation.*

Note that I am *not* denying that mathematical truth is "perspectival" in the sense of depending for its very *content* on our actual existential natures and dispositions (think of how many different things could be *meant* by the words, thought-signs, etc., that we use to represent Peano Arithmetic to ourselves and each other; imagine different possible worlds in which the words, thought-signs, etc., are the same but the *practice* diverges from ours at various points). *All* truth is perspectival in this sense, and I agree with Wittgenstein that this makes nonsense of metaphysical talk of our representations "copying" reality. But perspectival facts are still facts. The content of the judgment that there is a large Mountain Ash on my property depends on our "forms of life," *granted*; the fact that there is a Mountain Ash on my property is in that sense, perspectival, *granted*; but it is *not an artifact of the way we use the words* that there is a large Mountain Ash on my property. And no more is it an *artifact of the way we use the words* that Peano Arithmetic is 10^{20}-consistent. The truth of the judgment that there is a Mountain Ash on my property depends on our nature, but also on more than our nature; it is not a truth that is *explained* by facts about human nature; it does not *arise from us*. And similarly, the fact that Peano Arithmetic is 10^{20}-consistent depends on our nature, but also on more than our nature; it similarly is not a truth that is *explained* by facts about human nature; it too does not *arise from us*. Only if our dispositions were described in scenario (2) would they *explain* the truth of the consistency-statement.

Another Wittgensteinian Move

There is a move that may also have been in Wittgenstein's mind which we shall briefly consider here. One might hold that it is a presupposition of, say, "2 + 2 = 4," that we shall never *meet* a situation we would *count* as a counterexample (this is an *empirical* fact); and one might claim that the appearance of a "factual" element in the statement "2 + 2 = 4" arises from *confusing* the mathematical assertion (which has *no* factual content, it is claimed) with the empirical assertion first mentioned.

This move, however, depends heavily on overlooking or denying the circumstance that an empirical fact can have a partly mathematical *explanation*. Thus, let T be an actual (physically instantiated) Turing Machine so programmed that if it is started scanning the input "111," it never halts. Suppose we start T scanning the input "111," let T run for two weeks, and then turn T off. In the course of the two-week run, T did not halt. Is it not the case that the *explanation* of the fact that T did not halt is simply the *mathematical* fact that a Turing machine with that program never halts on the input, *together with* the empirical fact that T instantiates that program (and continued to do so throughout the two weeks)?

Similarly, if human beings spend millions of years searching through all the proofs with less than 10^{20} symbols in Peano arithmetic and they never find a proof of "1 = 0," is not the *explanation* of this fact simply that, as a matter of *mathematical* fact, Peano Arithmetic is 10^{20}-consistent, *and* the human beings took sufficient care so that the putative proofs they examined during the long search really *were* proofs in Peano Arithmetic?

As for the case of the statement "2 + 2 = 4": suppose that on five thousand occasions two things are added to two other things (using some physical operation of combination) and the resulting group is counted. Suppose that 4,800 times the result of the count is "4"; that 198 times the result is "5"; and that 2 times the result is "3." Suppose a careful investigation is made, and it is found that in the 198 cases in which the result was "5," some interaction (e.g., sexual reproduction) added an individual to the group, and that in the 2 cases in which the result was "3," some interaction destroyed a member of the group. Is not the explanation of the fact that in the remaining 4,800 cases the result of the count was "4" just the fact that in *those* cases no individual involved in the combining process was destroyed or otherwise removed from the group counted at the end; that no individuals were added to the final group by any interactions; and that, as a matter of simple arithmetic fact, 2 + 2 = 4?

If this is merely something we *say*, then *granted* that that explains what we say about these 4,800 cases, how is it that we actually *found* (as opposed to just *positing*) an explanation of what went wrong in the deviant 200 cases? If one says that it is just a *surd* empirical fact that one *does* find such explanations in such cases, then is one not abandoning the whole world view of science since Newton for a very strange metaphysics? On the scientific view, *many* facts have partly mathematical explanations (and much of the business of science consists in giving them); on the alternative metaphysical picture, there are just all these surd empirical facts *and* a way we *talk* about them. We do not often come up with apparent counterexamples to "2 + 2 = 4," but it is not *because* two and two *do* make four that we do not. Rather, on the picture just suggested, it is *because* we do not often come up with apparent counterexamples that we *say* "2 + 2 = 4." Why should anyone believe *this*?

Perhaps if the world were such that we regularly came up with apparent counterexamples to "2 + 2 = 4" in some context (say, counting bosons), then the best language-cum-theory might be one that said that in some cases two and two make five. If such a case could be *coherently* described, this would be reason to think that *arithmetic is empirical*; but it *still* would not be reason to think that arithmetic is not *factual*.

The Conceivability of the Mathematically Impossible

What I have argued is that "Peano Arithmetic is 10^{20}-consistent" and "Turing machine T will not halt if run for so-and-so many operations on input '111'" are *mathematical facts*, and that these facts are not explained by our "natures" or "forms of life." It is not that these statements are true because we have a disposition to *protect* them from what would otherwise be falsifiers; we have no such disposition. What I want to consider in the present section is the nature of such mathematical facts.

Unlike "2 + 2 = 4," which certainly seems *a priori*, the two facts just mentioned have a quasi-empirical character. We can conceive of their being false, whereas we doubt we can conceive of "2 + 2 = 4" being false; it may be, in the case of the second fact, that there is no *proof* that Turing machine T won't halt on the given input in so-and-so-many steps which does not amount to *running* the machine, or a calculation which exactly simulates the operations of the machine, *through* so-and-so many steps (some combinatorial facts seem "brute"); both statements can be overthrown by a well-attested *calculation*.

But is there *really* a sense of "conceivable" (of any philosophical importance) in which the *falsity* of these *mathematically true* statements is *conceivable*? How can the *mathematically impossible* be conceivable?

The answer is that there is no part of our language in which it is more wrong to think of our understanding of the sentences as consisting in a sort of Cartesian "clear and distinct idea" of the *conditions under which they are true* than mathematics. We do not understand Fermat's Last Theorem by having a "clear and distinct idea" of the conditions under which it is true—how could we? Our mastery of mathematical language resides, at least in part, in our knowledge of *proof-conditions* as opposed to *truth conditions*, in our knowledge of the *conditions of verification* holistically associated with the sentences by mathematical practice. But part of the notion of a *verification condition* in both mathematical science and empirical science is this: Verification conditions are conditions that correspond to a certain *skill*: the skill of being able to tell when a sentence has been proved (or, in empirical science, confirmed). It is part of the notion of such a skill that one can have it without knowing in advance whether the sentence in question *will* be proved or disproved (confirmed or disconfirmed).

Understanding Fermat's Last Theorem, for example, consists at least in part of being able to recognize a proof or at least a counterexample; the *weird* view is the view of Ayer and Carnap according to which *all* true mathematical assertions have "the same meaning" and it requires a *psychological* explanation (allegedly) to say why we do not *recognize* that Fermat's Last Theorem has the same meaning (assuming it is true) as "2 + 2 = 4." *Only* the supposition that the meaning is the *truth-conditions* could have led to such a view (and then only on a view according to which grasp of the truth conditions is something like an eidetic image of all the worlds in which they obtain).

In short, we can understand "T will halt," although, in fact, it may be *mathematically impossible* for T to halt, because we are *not* mathematically omniscient, because our *understanding* of *most* mathematical sentences has to consist (in part) in a skill of recognizing whether they are proved or disproved, and because *this* kind of understanding *never* involves *knowing in advance* whether the statement *will be proved or disproved*. In this respect, "2 + 2 = 4" may be different; knowing that "2 + 2 = 4" may be involved in knowing the arithmetical language; but knowing whether Peano Arithmetic is 10^{20}-consistent or not is *not* presupposed by knowing the arithmetical language. I *understand* the statement "Peano Arithmetic is *not* 10^{20}-consistent," even though it is in fact *mathematically false*, because I have a skill (or participate in a society that has that skill)! I (we) could *tell* if we found a proof that Peano Arithmetic is inconsistent. The fact that the *specification* of that ability is possible *independently* of whether the proposition to be understood *can* be proved or not should not surprise us; if it were *not* the case we could *understand* only those mathematical statements that are already decided!

The "Revisability" of Mathematics

The remarks I have been making have a connection with a curious fact which I now wish to point out: although *all* mathematical truths are "metaphysically necessary," i.e., true in all possible worlds, simply because nothing that violates a truth of mathematics *counts* as a *description* of a "possible world," *some* mathematical truths are "epistemically contingent." What I have in mind is the following: there may be no way in which we can *know* that a certain abstract structure is consistent other than by seeing it instantiated either in mental images or in some physical representation. For example, the only way to convince myself that it is possible to make *n* triangles using *m* rigid bars of equal length (for certain values of *n* and *m*) may be to actually produce the figure; the only way to show that a certain Turing machine halts may be to run it (or simulate its running on paper) until it halts; the only way to know that a certain formal system is inconsistent may be to *derive* the contradiction in it.

Now the statement that *these m* matches (or whatever) are arranged so as to form *n* triangles is certainly an *a posteriori* statement. It is even an *empirical* statement. Yet my rational confidence in the mathematically necessary statement "it is possible to form *n* triangles with *m* rigid bars" is *no greater* than my confidence in the empirical statement. If I come to doubt the empirical statement, then, unless I have some *other* example that establishes the truth of the mathematical statement, I will come to doubt the mathematical statement too. Nor need there be any way in which I could "in principle" *know* the truth of the mathematical statement without depending on some such empirical statement about mental or physical objects, diagrams, calculations, etc.

If this point has not been very much appreciated in the past (although Descartes was clearly aware of this problem) it is because of the tendency, we remarked, to think that a fully rational ("ideally rational") being should be mathematically omniscient—should be able to "just know" all mathematical truths *without proof*. (Perhaps by surveying all the integers, all the real numbers, etc., in his head.) This is just forgetting, once again, that we *understand* mathematical language *through* being able to recognize *proofs* (plus, of course, certain empirical applications, e.g., *counting*). It is not irrational to need a *proof* before one believes, e.g., Fermat's Last Theorem —quite the contrary.

Of course, the status of "2 + 2 = 4" is quite different. We do not need a *proof* for this statement (barring epistemological catastrophe—e.g., coming to doubt *all* our past *counting*: but it is not clear what becomes of the concept of rationality itself when there is an epistemological catastrophe). Perhaps "2 + 2 = 4" is rationally unrevisable (or, at least, rationally unrevisable as long as "universal hallucination," all my past memories are a delusion," and the like are not in the field). But, considering that "2 + 2 = 4" can sometimes be part of an *explanation*, is the fact (if it is a fact) that a rational being could not believe the denial of "2 + 2 = 4" (barring epistemological catastrophe) an explanation of the *truth* of "2 + 2 = 4"? Or is it rather just a fact about *rationality*?

Putting this question aside, like the hot potato it is, let us briefly consider the status of such mathematical truths as "Peano Arithmetic is consistent" and the Principle of Mathematical Induction. These are not like the singular or purely existential combinatorial statements lately considered ("This formal system is inconsistent," "There exists a way of forming *m* triangles with *n* matches," "This Turing machine halts in less than *N* steps"). Certainly our beliefs in the consistency of Peano Arithmetic and in induction are not epistemically contingent in the way that my belief that one can form *m* triangles using *n* matches (imagine I have just convinced myself by finding the arrangement) is epistemically contingent. I believe that arithmetic is consistent because I believe the axioms are true, and I believe that from true premises one cannot derive a contradiction; I have also studied and taught the Gentzen consistency proof; and these are *a priori* reasons. Yet there are still circumstances under which I would abandon my belief that Peano Arithmetic is consistent; I would abandon that belief *if I discovered a contradiction*.

Many philosophers will feel that this remark is "cheating." "But you *could not* discover a contradiction." True, it is mathematically impossible (and even "metaphysically impossible," in the recently fashionable jargon) that there should be a contradiction in Peano Arithmetic. But, as I remarked above, it *is not epistemically impossible*. We can conceive of finding a contradiction in Peano Arithmetic, and we can make sense of the question "What would you do if you came across a contradiction in Peano Arithmetic"? ("Restrict the induction schema," would be my answer.)

As a matter of fact, there are circumstances in which it would be rational to believe that Peano Arithmetic was inconsistent *even though it was not*.

Thus suppose I am caused to hallucinate by some marvelous process (say, by making me a "brain in a vat" without my knowing it, and controlling all my sensory inputs superscientifically), and the content of the hallucination is that the whole logical community learns of a contradiction in Peano Arithmetic (Saul Kripke discovers it). The proof is checked by famous logicians and even by machine, and it holds up. Perhaps I do not have time to check the proof myself; but I would believe, and rationally so, I contend, that Peano Arithmetic *is* inconsistent on such evidence. And this shows that even "Peano Arithmetic is consistent" is not a fully rationally unrevisable statement. (Neither is full first-order induction, since an inconsistency in Peano Arithmetic would make it rational to suppose that unrestricted induction was contradictory.)

This is messy. Clearly, philosophy of mathematics is *hard*. But the Wittgensteinian views that (1) mathematical statements do not express objective facts; and (2) their truth and necessity (or appearance of necessity) arise from and are explained by *our* nature, cannot be right.

If *our* nature explains why we shall never come across a contradiction in Peano Arithmetic, then, in exactly the same sense and to the same degree, it explains why there is a Mountain Ash in my yard. Both facts are dependent on my conceptual lenses; but neither fact is an artifact of these lenses. I do not create the properties of individual proofs in Peano Arithmetic any *more* than I create the berries on the Mountain Ash.

PART 2: RE QUINE

Introduction

These criticisms of Wittgenstein are grist for Quine's mill. Quine, at least as early as Wittgenstein, criticized the moderate conventionalist position for emptiness. But, whereas Wittgenstein departed from moderate conventionalism in the direction of radical conventionalism (= the truth of the theorems as well as that of the axioms arises from us), Quine departed from moderate conventionalism in the direction of *empiricism*. In Quine's view, the unrevisability of mathematical statements is greater in degree than that of, say, the three-dimensionality of space or the Conservation of Energy, but not absolute. Truths of mathematics are partly empirical and partly "conventional" like *all* truths; mathematics is as factual as physics, only better "protected."

Everything I said against Wittgenstein's view is consonant with these views of Quine. But Quine's views, like Wittgenstein's, will not do as they stand.

The problem with Wittgenstein's views is that they exaggerate the unrevisability of mathematics and logic. The problem with Quine's views is that they underestimate it. The view I wish to defend is not that classical logic or mathematics are *a priori*; I myself have argued elsewhere that logic is revisable, and that a form of modular logic ("quantum logic") should be adopted for the purpose of formalizing physical theory, and not classical logic. What I think (I blush to confess) is that what *is a priori* is that *most* statements obey certain logical laws. This view will very likely offend both platonistically minded and constructively minded philosophers (and both Wittgensteinians and Quinians); nevertheless, I shall try to make it plausible.

Quine and the A Priori

Are there *a priori* truths? In other words, are there true statements which (1) it is rational to accept (at least if the right arguments occur to me), and (2) which it would never subsequently be rational to reject no matter how the world turns out (epistemically) to be? More simply, are there statements whose truth we would not be justified in denying in any *epistemically* possible world? Or is it rather the case that for *every* statement *s* there is an epistemically possible world in which it is fully rational to believe that not-*s*? *A PRIORI DEF'N.*

It is easy to see that this question depends crucially on the notion of a *statement*. *Statement* and not *sentence*: since for any *sentence* ϕ we can imagine a circumstance in which it would be rational to deny ϕ by just imagining a world in which it is rational to *change the meanings* of the words in ϕ in some suitable way (as those meanings are given by a standard translation manual connecting the language to which ϕ belongs at the two different times to some neutral language). So no one can possibly hold that there are unrevisable *sentences*. Accordingly, one response to the question for a philosopher who denies, as Quine does, that *synonymy* makes any sense— that is, a philosopher who denies that there is any clear sense to the question "does ϕ express the same statement at the two different times?"—is simply to say that a priority is a meaningless notion. The notion of a priority presupposes the notion of synonymy as much as the notion of analyticity does, and is meaningless for the same reason that the notion of synonymy is meaningless.

There is one trouble with this argument, and that is that it has not the slightest persuasive force for someone who is unconvinced, as I am unconvinced, that no sense can be made of the notion of *synonymy*. To my way of thinking, any philosophical claim that rests on the contention that no reasonable standard of synonymy exists at all, not even an interest-relative one, founders in absurdity. It may well be, of course, that Quine would not wish to deny the existence of an *interest-relative* standard of synonymy; however, if there is such a standard, then it makes sense to ask whether there are any sentences ϕ such that (1) *given the way we presently interpret them*, no fully rational being could deny them; and/or (2) if the world turns out to be such that a fully rational being *does* subsequently deny ϕ, then that will be because the *meaning* of ϕ, as specified by the way *we* translate ϕ into our present language, given *our* interests, will have changed. In short, if there is something—something useful and important, even if, in a sense, "relative"—to the notion of synonymy, then why should there not be *as much* to the notion of a priority?

As I have pointed out elsewhere, however, Quine has *another* argument against apriority, one that does not depend at all upon his attacks on synonymy and on a "linguistic" notion of analyticity. As Quine puts the argument, in the form of a rhetorical question,

> Any statement can be held true come what may if we make drastic enough adjustments elsewhere in the system. Even a statement very close to the periphery can be held true in the face of recalcitrant experience by pleading hallucination or by amending certain statements of the kind called logical laws. Conversely, by the same token, no statement is immune to revision. Revision even of the logical law of the excluded middle has been proposed as a means of simplifying quantum mechanics; and what difference is there in principle between such a shift and a shift whereby Keppler superceded Ptolemy, or Einstein Newton, or Darwin Aristotle?[3]

Quine's argument, in a nutshell, is that previous scientific revolutions have required us to give up principles that were once thought to be *a priori*. And in this trenchant paragraph he is suggesting that the proposal to use a nonstandard logic in quantum mechanics is not fundamentally different from the proposal to use non-Euclidean geometry in the theory of space-time, which has been accepted since Einstein's General Theory of Relativity.

In "Carnap and Logical Truth," where he employs a similar argument, Quine draws the moral explicitly: "We had been trying to make sense of the role of convention in *a priori* knowledge. Now the very distinction between *a priori* and empirical begins to waver and dissolve, at least as a distinction between sentences. (It could of course still hold as a distinction between factors in one's adoption of a sentence, but both factors might be operative everywhere.)"[4]

It is this *argument from the history of science* that I challenge.

Here is a simple counterexample:

Could a fully rational being deny that *not every statement is both true and false*? To fix our ideas, let us specify that by a statement we mean simply a *belief or possible belief*, either one's own or someone else's, and that the term "statement" is not intended to presuppose that beliefs are or are not "propositions" as distinct from "sentences" or even "inscriptions." Could someone, then, think all his own beliefs (and everyone elses) were both true and false? Let us also stipulate that we do not presuppose any particular account of "truth" (e.g., that truth is or is not distinct from maximum warranted assertibility). If you do not like "true," could someone believe that all his own beliefs (and everyone else's), and all possible beliefs, for that matter, are both fully warrantedly assertible and that their negations are fully warrantedly assertible as well?

At first blush, the answer is clearly "no." By *our* lights, to believe that all one's beliefs are both true and false (or whatever) is to give up *both* the notions of *belief* and *truth* (or warranted assertibility). In short, to believe *all* statements are correct (which is what we are talking about) would be to have no notion of rationality. At least *one* statement is *a priori*, because to deny that statement would be to forfeit rationality itself.

One a priori truth. It is, of course, possible to be skeptical about the existence of rationality itself. What I have in mind is not the possibility of total skepticism or relativism; what I am rather thinking of is the possiblity that "rational" or "rationally acceptable" or "warrantedly assertible" may not be the right notions for epistemology/ methodology. Perhaps one should not say that statements are warrantedly assertible, but that they have a certain numerical "degree of confirmation," as Carnap urged, or perhaps one should use some notion that is not thought of yet. But then the question, whether some statements (and some rules or inference) are such that it is always rational to accept (deny) them, will have an analog in terms of the new notion of degree of confirmation, or whatever. The question *"Are there any a priori truths?"* is a *question within* the theory of rationality; as long as we accept the theory, or the prospect of such a theory, we cannot justify rejecting or accepting any particular answer by the consideration that the theory of rationality itself may need recasting. What we are trying to answer by our lights (and by who else's lights should we try to answer it?—a question Quine is fond of asking) is whether an ideal theory of rationality would have certain features: we can speculate about this just as physicists speculate about whether an ideal physical theory would have certain features, while recognizing, just as they do, that our answer itself is a provisional one and that the true shape of future theory will be different in many unforeseen ways, from what we now envisage.

This being said, it does seem, as we remarked, that there is at least one *a priori* truth: that not every statement is both true (or fully correct to assert) and at the same time false (or fully correct to deny). But, of course, this statement itself admits of more than one interpretation. To bring out more clearly the interpretation I have in mind, let me speak of the rule: *infer every statement from every premise and from every set of premises, including the empty set*—as the Absolutely Inconsistent Rule (A.I.R.). It is clear from the notion of rationality itself that to accept the A.I.R. would be to abandon rationality. And the interpretation of "Not every statement is both true and false" (or, more simply, "not every statement is true") that I have in mind is simply the interpretation under which to affirm this statement is simply to *reject* the A.I.R. In particular, acceptance of this statement, like rejection of the A.I.R., does not commit one to any particular view of what truth and falsity are (or what correctness is, or what inference is). It assumes what we may call the *generic* notions of truth (or correctness) and falsity (or incorrectness), and not the particular philosophical notions (e.g., the realist notion of truth, or the notion of warranted assertibility) which arise when one *refines* or *philosophically* analyzes the generic notions. I take it that there is a clear enough sense to the notions of rejecting the A.I.R., and of denying that every statement is both true and false. What I suggest is that it cannot seriously be maintained that there is an epistemically possible world in which acceptance of the A.I.R. would be fully rational and warranted; and, further, I maintain that the point that acceptance of the A.I.R. would involve abandonment of rationality itself is one that a fully rational mind should be able to see in any world. In short, the A.I.R. is *a priori* rejectable.

The reader may wonder why I stated the Principle of Contradiction in such a weak form. Why did I not take "not both *p* and not-*p*" as my example of an *a priori* truth? The answer is that our intuitions about what is true of *every* statement are much hazier than our intuitions about typical or normal statements. Consider the Russell Antinomy: "There is a set ⴰ such that ⴰ has as members all and only those sets that do not have themselves as members." Suppose some future logical genius discovers a very elegant way of avoiding the antimony without paying the usual price of stratifying the universe into types by admitting that some statements—in particular the "paradoxical" ones, like the Russell Antimony—are *both true and false*. Is this *really* ruled out *a priori*?

The reader may reply that this would not work because it is well known that from even one instance of "$p\bar{p}$" one can derive every statement. But this assumes that certain rules of propositional calculus are retained; perhaps the new scheme would depend on Relevance Logic (in which *it is not* true that "every statement follows from a contradiction"). It seems to me that this is not something we can rule out *a priori*. Rather, this is just the sort of case in which we want to look at the whole proposal in the whole theoretical context before deciding. Perhaps there are epistemically possible worlds in which it is rational to believe that the Russell Antinomy is both true and false. But this does not affect our argument that it would be an abandonment of rationality to believe that *every* statement was both true and false (or to believe that *typically* statements are both true and false).

Again, it may be objected that "Normally statements are not both true and false" contains the vague term "normally." And also, even the statement "Not every statement is both true and false" involves rather vague (I called them "generic") notions of "statement," "truth," and "falsity." If all *a priori* truths contain such vague notions, then it may be that a priority is a phenomenon that affects only our ordinary language; that in the canonical, regimented, totally precise notation that Quine refers to in *Word and Object* as "our first class conceptual system," there are indeed no *a priori* truths.

But the fact is that most of science and metascience cannot even be expressed in a perfectly precise notation (and all the more so if one includes philosophy under the rubric "metascience" as Quine does). Words like "normally," "typically," etc., are indispensible in biology and economics, not to mention law, history, sociology, etc.; while "broad spectrum" notions such as "cause" and "factor" are indispensable for the introduction of new theoretical notions, even if they do not appear in "finished science," if there is such a thing. Philosophy cannot be limited to commentary upon a supposed "first class conceptual system" which scarcely exists and whose expressive resources cover only a tiny fragment of what we care about.

So far the picture that is emerging from our discussion looks like this: There are some *a priori* truths, truths certified by the theory of rationality itself; but they have the character of *maxims*—general principles that are not, or at least may not be, exceptionless, and they involve "generic," or somewhat pretheoretical, notions rather than the (supposedly) perfectly precise notions of an ideal theory in the exact sciences. That, barring a new treatment of very exceptional cases such as the Russell Antinomy, a statement is not both true and false (in the ordinary pretheoretic sense of "true" and "false") is an example.

A Priority and Analyticity

The argument I have given for the *a priority* of "not every statement is true" and "not every statment is both true and false" suggests another argument, an argument based on meaning theory rather than theory of rationality. This argument goes as follows: If someone accepts "All statements are true," then, by the principle of Universal Instantiation (which we may take to be involved in the *meaning* of the universal quantifier), he is committed to *"Snow is white" is true*, to *"Snow is not white" is true*, to *"My hand has five fingers" is true*, to *"My hand does not have five fingers" is true*, etc. In short, given the rule of Universal Instantiation, acceptance of "every statement is true" (and of one's various beliefs and candidate beliefs and their negations as "statements," in the relevant sense) commits one to acceptance of the A.I.R. And this is why the statement must be rejected.

Even if this argument is correct, it does not wholly avoid the theory of rationality, for the argument depends on the fact that one cannot accept the A.I.R., and this is based on considerations about rationality rather than upon considerations about meaning. It might be suggested, however, that if we agree that the *meaning* of the universal quantifier requires us to accept Universal Instantiation, then we can *immediately* give an example of an *a priori* (in fact, of an *analytic*) truth, *viz.* any suitable instance of "If for every x, Fx, then Fv"; we already committed ourselves to *a priori* truth (it might be contended) when we rejected Quine's contention that the theory of meaning is an unsalvageable wreck.

One answer to this contention might be Quine's answer, already alluded to in my discussion of Wittgenstein: to derive the individual statements "If for every x, Fx, then Fv" (where "v" is a name for some member of the domain the quantifier ranges over) from the Principle of Universal Instantiation (and the fact that implication is validity of the conditional) one needs *logic*; the argument does not show that the "U.I.-conditionals" just mentioned (the conditionals corresponding to individual applications of the Rule of Universal Instantiation) are true by meaning theory *alone*. This answer does not affect the argument I gave for rejecting "Every statement is both true and false"; for that argument did not purport to explain the *origin* of logical truth (whatever that might mean); we were concerned to determine something about the notion of rationality, assuming reasonable constraints and reasoning in a reasonable way (which, of course, means using logic). We were not showing *why* logic is true (whatever that might mean), but rather showing that if there is such a thing as rationality at all, then it seems that it could never be rational to reject one very weak logical principle. That we had to assume logical principles to argue this is not any kind of vicious circle.

Even if the meaning-theoretic argument is advanced in the same spirit as ours, as a defense of the claim that certain statements are unrevisable but not as an explanation of their truth, its conclusion cannot be as strong as the conclusion we reached above. For even if "for every x, Fx" implies "Fv" by virture (in part) of the *meaning* of the quantifier itself, this only shows that the inference (x)Fx/Fv must be a good one *in every language that contains the universal quantifier*. Whether an adequate language *must* have or can have quantifiers with such properties as this one is certainly not a question about *meaning*. Just as there are adequate languages that lack the *Eculidean* notion of a straight line, so, it might be claimed, there could be adequate languages that lack the classical quantifiers.

Our argument was that (1) the A.I.R. cannot be accepted by any rational being; (2) it seems reasonable that a fully rational being should see and be able to express the fact that the A.I.R. is incorrect; (3) any clear statement to the effect that the A.I.R. is incorrect can be translated into *our* language here-now by the words "Not every statement is true." Only (3) depends at all on meaning theory; (1) and (2) are premises from the theory of rationality. In particular, I only require that the *whole thought* "Not every statement is true" should somehow be expressible by a rational being; not that it be expressible in those words. In particular, some rational being might express that thought by a sentence no part of which corresponds to our universal quantifier.

Finally, I am not claiming that it is *analytic* that "A rational being cannot believe that every statement is true." Nothing said here commits me to the view that we can develop the theory of rationality by just reflecting on the meaning of the word "rational." And this is good, since the whole history of philosophy, methodology, and logic is strong evidence to the contrary.

Revision of Logic

Intuitionists propose to revise classical logic by giving up the *Law of the Excluded Middle*, $p \vee \bar{p}$, among others. Such a proposal is instructively different from the proposal to give up $p\bar{p}$, which no one has advanced, or to give up the even weaker principles of contradiction discussed above.

I have alluded a number of times to the existence of a family of truth-notions: being verified (proved, warrantedly assertable, justified, etc.) and being true in the full "realist" sense (which builds in bivalence and the notion that what is true is *made* true by a mind-independent reality, according to Michael Dummett) being the best-known members of the family. There are other members of the family as well; there are notions of truth like Peirce's which identify truth with some *idealization* of warranted assertibility rather than with (tensed) warranted assertibility itself; and there are notions of truth which I would consider "realist," but which are not realist in the very strong metaphysical sense Dummett has in mind. I agree with Dummett that the primitive notion of a correct statement does not yet distinguish between these "realist" and "non-realist" conceptions of truth; that it represents a generic conception from which the others arise by a process of philosophical reflection.

The Law of the Excluded Middle is not evident on the *generic* notion of truth, however, at least not for *undecidable* statements. If truth is given a "verificationist" interpretation, and disjunction is given the standard intuitionist semantics (to verify a disjunction one must verify one of the disjuncts—and also verify *that* a *particular* one of the disjuncts has been verified), then undecidable statements will give rise to instances of $p \vee \bar{p}$ which fail to be true (although their negations are not true either). My argument for the a priority of the Law of Contradiction (or of a suitably "hedged" version of the Law of Contradiction) did not depend on *choosing between* realist and non-realist views of truth; if a decision between these views of truth cannot be made on *a priori* grounds (or if it can, but it goes *against* the classical view, as Dummett thinks), then not all of classical propositional calculus will be included in the part of logic that is *a priori* correct. The debate about whether there is *a priori* truth is somewhat separate from the debate over "deviant logics," even if some logical principles are *a priori* (or "*a priori* in normal cases"—itself a significant weakening of classical claims).

The issues raised by proposals to use modular logic ("quantum logic") in the interpretation of quantum mechanics are still more complex. Quantum logic has been advocated under *both* "realist" and "verificationist" construals. The issues posed by the suggestion to adopt quantum logic plus a "verificationist" semantics are similar to those posed by the suggestion to adopt intuitionist logic; on the other hand, the suggestion to adopt quantum logic plus a "realist" semantics cannot be properly worked out and evaluated until one has further clarified the notion of "realism." If "realism" is simply the commitment to the empirical model of the cognitive subject as a system which constructs a representation of its environment, for example, then it would seem that realism, in that sense, is compatible with a "verificationist" account of how the cognitive subject *understands* his representation. Such issues, however, are far beyond the present paper.

Fallibilism

I do not see any reason to believe that the nature of rationality can be figured out *a priori*. Not only would it be Utopian to expect rationality itself to become theoretically transparent to us in the foreseeable future, but even the partial descriptions of rationality we are able to give have had to be revised again and again as our experience with the world, our experience in cooperating with and understanding each other, and our experience with theory construction and explanation have all increased. Even if we restrict ourselves to scientific rationality, the fact is that we construct, test, and evaluate theories today that are of *kinds* undreamed of in earlier centuries. Neither the objects we call "theories" today (e.g., quantum mechanics and relativity) nor the sorts of considerations involved in the testing and acceptance of these objects are of sorts an ancient Greek could have envisaged.

But is it consistent to say, on the one hand, that some things are *a priori*, i.e., rational to believe in all epistemically possible worlds, but on the other hand, that the metatheory of rationality on which we base this claim (or the considerations which I have advanced as to what such a theory should say if there really were one worthy of the name) is itself in the process of endless change and revision? To say, that is, that any sketch of a theory of rationality or of parts of a theory of rationality that we ever give are to be accepted in the open-minded and tentative spirit that Peirce called "fallibilism"? The answer is that it *is* consistent; but perhaps it does not seem so, and this may be the deep reason that Quine's appeal to fallibilism tend to convince some scientifically minded philosophers that there are no *a priori* truths at all.

Of course, if fallibilism requires us to be *sure* that for every statement *s* we accept *there is* an epistemically possible world in which it is rational to deny *s*, then fallibilism is *identical* with the rejection of *a priori* truth; but surely this is an unreasonable conception of fallibilism. If what fallibilism requires, on the other hand, is that we never be totally sure that *s* is true (even if we believe *s* is *a priori*), or, even more weakly, that we never be totally sure that the *reasons* we give for holding *s* true are final and contain no element of error or conceptual vagueness or confusion (even when *s* is "Not every statement is true"), then there is nothing in such a modest and sane fallibilism to prejudge the question we have been discussing.

Quine and Wittgenstein

The present discussion of Quine's view may not seem to connect directly with the problems discussed by Wittgenstein, but the relevance is, in fact, immediate. If there were *nothing* to the idea that logic and mathematics are *a priori*, then we would resolve the difficulties with Wittgenstein's view by concluding that all of mathematics and logic is empirical. To Kripke's (unpublished) objection that this is incoherent, because the notion of *testing* a statement makes no sense unless *something* is fixed (*Why should we accept the view that quantum mechanics requires us to change our logic?*, Kripke asks. *If nothing is a priori, why do we not instead conclude that we should revise the statement that quantum mechanics requires us to change our logic?*), we could answer, with Quine, that we are not denying the existence of an *a priori* factor in *all* judgment: we are simply denying that it is as *simple* as a rule that some statements are never to be revised. Answering Wittgenstein in this way would in no way require us to reject the insight contained in "use" accounts of meaning, or Wittgenstein's insights about the way our practice unfolds the very meaning of our terms. But if, in fact, some logical and/or mathematical truths (the principle of contradiction, "every number has a successor") *are a priori*, then this is blocked.

On the other hand, if large parts of logic and mathematics are revisable (and many of the parts that are not, as far as we know, revisable for *empirical* reasons are *a posteriori* in the way that I argued the statement that a proof exists of a certain theorem or that a particular Turing machine halts may be known *a posteriori*), then any philosophy that takes the *problem* to be: *given* that logic and mathematics consist of *a priori* knowledge, how do we account for it? is also blocked.

Actually, things are even worse. Even with respect to the part of logic and mathematics that is *a priori*, it seems to me that the a priority tells us something about the nature of *rationality*, not something about the nature of *logic*. There is a temptation to say, "the truth of the Minimal Principle of Contradiction (*Not every statement is true*) is explained by the fact that (insofar as we are rational) we hold it immune from revision." But I find this unintelligible.

The analogy people use is to a game like chess: assuming "chess" is a rigid designator for a game with certain rules, "in chess the rook moves in straight lines" is a necessary truth. Moreover, it was known *a priori* by the people who invented the game of chess. (Compare Kripke's famous discussion of "the meter stick in Paris is one meter long.") In the same way it is suggested, "Not every statement is true" can be known *a priori* because it is *we* who have made up the "language game" to which "statement," "not," and "true" belong.

The trouble is that if we are puzzled about whether there is a *possible* (consistent) game with certain rules, we appeal *not* to our stipulations but to an appropriate theorem of mathematics (which may be quite elementary if the game is simple). But if we are puzzled about why it is *possible* to have a language in which not every statement is true, this is (on the view I am criticizing) supposed to be answered *just* by an appeal to our stipulations or, alternatively, our "forms of life"). I frankly do not see the analogy. I do not see any explanation. If one gets *comfort* by saying "the principles of logic (some of them) are true *because* we hold them immune from revision," that is fine (some people enjoy chanting "Hare Krishna," too), but the "because" escapes me. Why should one not just as well say, "We are *able* to stipulate that *some* but not *all* statements should be true (or assertible) *because* the Minimal Principle of Contradiction is true?" My own guess is that the truths of logic we are speaking of are *so* basic that the notion of *explanation* collapses when we try to "explain" why they are true. I do not mean that there is something "unexplainable" here; there is simply no room for an explanation of what is presupposed by every explanatory activity—and that goes for philosophical as well as scientific explanations, including explanations that purport to be therapy.

So where does all of this leave us? Let us return for a moment to our earlier example: the statement that Peano arithmetic is consistent (or 10^{20}-consistent). This is hardly *a priori* in the strong sense: conceivable mathematical findings would lead us to change our minds. (It may, of course, be "*a priori*" in weaker senses than I have considered.) There is clearly a *factual* element—an element of *objective combinatorial fact*—in the consistency of Peano arithmetic. But nothing argued here goes against the view that if Peano arithmetic *is* consistent as far as human beings can tell (and has no *mathematical* consequences that would lead us to modify it, e.g., provable ω inconsistency), *then* it counts as *true* partly by convention, or something analogous to convention (though not, of course, in the sense of *arbitrary* convention). Quine's view that there may be an *element* of convention, or a priority, or whatever, in mathematical knowledge, as in all knowledge, even where there is some revisability, is unshaken. On the other hand, our notion of rationality cannot be quite as flexible as Quine suggests.

Notes

1. "Wittgenstein's Philosophy of Mathematics," (1959), reprinted in Dummett's *Truth and Other Enigmas* (ch. 11), (Cambridge, Mass., 1978).

2. "Wittgenstein and Logical Necessity," *Philosophical Review* 74 (1965):504–18. For a related discussion, see John V. Canfield "Anthropological Science Fiction and Logical Necessity," *Canadian Journal of Philosophy* 4 (1975):467–79.

3. "Two Dogmas of Empiricism" in W. V. Quine, *From a Logical Point of View*, second edition (New York, N.Y., 1961), p. 43.

4. In W. V. Quine, *The Ways of Paradox* (New York, N.Y., 1966), p. 115.

Notes on Contributors

Peter Achinstein is Professor of Philosophy at the Johns Hopkins University. He is the author of *Concepts of Science*, *Law and Explanation*, and numerous articles in the area of the philosophy of science.

Annette Baier is Professor of Philosophy at the University of Pittsburgh.

Tyler Burge is Associate Professor of Philosophy at the University of California at Los Angeles. He has published papers in the philosophy of language, philosophy of logic, metaphysics, and the history of philosophy.

Richard Cartwright is Professor of Philosophy at the Massachusetts Institute of Technology.

Roderick Chisholm is Andrew W. Mellon Professor of Humanities at Brown University. His publications include *Perceiving: A Philosophical Study*, *Realism and the Background of Phenomenology*, and *Theory of Knowledge*. He is editor of works by Brentano and Meinong, and has authored many journal articles. He is past president of the American Philosophical Association (1969) and the Metaphysical Association of America (1972-73).

John Earman is Professor of Philosophy at the University of Minnesota.

Richard E. Grandy is Associate Professor of Philosophy at the University of North Carolina at Chapel Hill. He is the editor of a volume on theory and observation, and the author of a logic book. He has contributed numerous articles to various journals.

P. M. S. Hacker is a Fellow of St. John's College, Oxford. He is author of *Insight and Illusion*, co-editor of *Law, Morality, and Society*, and co-author of *Wittgenstein: Understanding and Meaning*.

Hidé Ishiguro is Reader in Philosophy at University College, London. She has written on the philosophy of mind and the philosophy of logic. Professor Ishiguro is the author of *Leibniz: Philosophy of Logic and Language*.

Jaegwon Kim works in metaphysics, theory of knowledge, and philosophy of mind, and has taught at Swarthmore, Brown, Cornell, and Johns Hopkins. He is presently Professor of Philosophy at the University of Michigan.

Lawrence Brian Lombard is Assistant Professor of Philosophy at Wayne State University. He has presented papers at meetings of the American Philosophical Association and published articles on events, change, and the theory of action in *Philosophical Studies*, *Philosophia*, and the *Canadian Journal of Philosophy*.

J. L. Mackie is a Fellow of University College, Oxford. He is the author of *Truth, Probability, and Paradox*, *The Cement of the Universe*, *Problems from Locke*, and *Ethics: Inventing Right and Wrong*. He was recently the Hill Visiting Professor at the University of Minnesota, Morris. He has also written many articles that have appeared in the major philosophical journals.

Robert M. Martin is Chairman of the Philosophy Department at Dalhousie University. He has been a visiting professor at the University of Michigan and Simon Fraser University, and is the author of a number of papers on the philosophy of language and the philosophy of literature.

Richard L. Mendelsohn is Assistant Professor of Philosophy at Herbert H. Lehman College of The City University of New York. He has written in the areas of philosophy of logic and philosophy of language.

Christopher Peacocke is a Fellow of New College, Oxford. He is the author of *Holistic Explanation: Action, Space, Interpretation* and several articles in philosophical logic and the philosophy of language.

Hilary Putnam is Walter Beverly Pearson Professor of Modern Mathematics and Mathematical Logic at Harvard University. In addition to his many journal publications, Professor Putnam is also the author of *Philosophy of Logic* and *Meaning and the Moral Sciences*.

Alexander Rosenberg is Associate Professor of Philosophy at Syracuse University. He has been a visiting professor at the University of Minnesota, and the University of California at Santa Cruz. He is the author of papers on causation and the philosophies of biological and social science, as well as *Microeconomic Laws: A Philosophical Analysis*. He taught previously at Dalhousie University, where he collaborated on a number of papers with Robert M. Martin.

Sydney Shoemaker is Susan Linn Sage Professor of Philosophy at Cornell University. He is the author of *Self-Knowledge and Self-Identity*, and of numerous articles on metaphysics and philosophy of mind.

Michael A. Slote is Professor of Philosophy at Trinity College, Dublin. He has published numerous articles in journals and collections, and is the author of *Reason and Scepticism*, *Metaphysics and Essence*, and *Conditions on Morality*.

Robert Stalnaker is Professor of Philosophy at the Sage School of Philosophy at Cornell University.

Peter Strawson is a Fellow of Magdelen College, Oxford. He is the author of *Introduction to Logical Theory*, *Individuals*, and *The Bounds of Sense*, and has also written articles that have been published in major journals. Professor Strawson has been visiting professor at Duke and Princeton Universities.

Avrum Stroll is Professor of Philosophy at the University of California, San Diego. He is the author, co-author, or editor of seven books, and has published numerous articles, mainly in the areas of philosophy of language and epistemology.

Peter Unger is Professor of Philosophy at New York University. His primary interests are in the areas of metaphysics, epistemology, and philosophy of language. He is the author of *Ignorance: A Case for Skepticism* and of various articles in these areas.

David Wiggins was a Fellow of New College, Oxford, 1960-67, and is Professor of Philosophy at Bedford College, University of London, 1967 to the present. He is the author of *Identity and Spatiotemporal Continuity*, *Truth, Invention and the Meaning of Life*, and *Sameness and Substance*.

George Wilson is Assistant Professor of Philosophy at the Johns Hopkins University and has published a number of articles on philosophical topics. He has also written on film and the aesthetics of film. He recently completed a book on the theory of action.